# CAVALRY
## OF THE
# HEARTLAND

Also by the Author

*Lincoln's Cavalrymen: A History of the Mounted Forces of the
Army of the Potomac*

*Lee's Cavalrymen: A History of the Mounted Forces of the
Army of Northern Virginia*

*The Cavalry at Gettysburg: A Tactical Study of Mounted Operations
During the Civil War's Pivotal Campaign*

*Gentleman and Soldier: A Biography of Wade Hampton III*

*Worthy Opponents: William T. Sherman and Joseph E. Johnston,
Antagonists in War, Friends in Peace*

# EDWARD G. LONGACRE

# CAVALRY

## ⚜ OF THE ⚜

# HEARTLAND

### THE

# MOUNTED FORCES

#### — OF THE —

# ARMY OF TENNESSEE

WESTHOLME

Westholme Publishing, LLC
Eight Harvey Avenue
Yardley, Pennsylvania 19067
Visit our Web site at www.westholmepublishing.com

First Printing October 2009
10 9 8 7 6 5 4 3 2 1

ISBN: 978-1-59416-098-1

Printed in United States of America

In Memory of

MAJOR LELAND HEATH, USAFR

# CONTENTS

### List of Maps

# PREFACE

THE ARMY OF TENNESSEE HAS NEVER RECEIVED historical coverage commensurate with the importance of its efforts on behalf of its fledgling nation. For that matter, until relatively recently it received virtually no coverage at all, at least not as a corporate body. Until the 1960s, the only book-length treatment was Stanley F. Horn's *The Army of Tennessee*, which first appeared in 1941, was republished in 1953, and was reissued fifteen years later. Then, in 1967, appeared Thomas L. Connelly's *Army of the Heartland: The Army of Tennessee, 1861-1862*, followed four years later by *Autumn of Glory: The Army of Tennessee, 1862-65*. Connelly's works gave new attention to, and enhanced the significance of, the principal Confederate command in the western theater of operations. This area Connelly defined as encompassing Tennessee, northern Georgia, and northeast Mississippi, a "large, irregularly shaped region of some 150,000 square miles [that] was the physical heart of the Confederacy."[1]

Connelly's massive study (a combined 816 pages of text and references) set the stage for later, less voluminous works devoted to one aspect or another of the army, including Richard M. McMurry's *Two Great Rebel Armies: An Essay in Confederate Military History*, a comparative study of the Army of Tennessee and the Army of Northern Virginia, first published in 1989; two studies by Larry J. Daniel: *Cannoneers in Gray: The Field Artillery of the Army of Tennessee, 1861-1865*, and *Soldiering in the Army of Tennessee: A Portrait of Life in a Confederate Army*, which appeared in 1984 and 1991, respectively; and Andrew Haughton's *Training, Tactics and Leadership in the Confederate Army of Tennessee: Seeds of Failure*, published in 2000.

These works and a few others that have treated the Army of Tennessee in a more peripheral fashion pale in comparison to the scholarly attention long accorded Robert E. Lee's army in the East. This disparity is understandable for a number of reasons, not the least being that while the Army of Northern Virginia had a number of impressive victories to its credit, the Army of Tennessee had very few. Moreover, while the Army of Northern Virginia was blessed not only with Lee—arguably, America's most revered soldier—but also with a body of talented and admirable subordinate commanders, the Army of Tennessee was saddled with a collection of generals with long political experience but whose credentials as leaders and tacticians were few and meager. Although he overemphasizes their shortcomings, and fails to appreciate the organizational and morale-building talents of Joseph E. Johnston, McMurry is essentially correct in observing that "it was the misfortune of the Rebels' western army to have been burdened with a set of incompetent leaders" for the better part of its existence.[2]

Reasons beyond inadequate leadership hobbled the Army of Tennessee, including its consistent numerical inferiority to its enemy; an area of operations, stretching from the Mississippi River to the Appalachian Mountains, that was too vast to be properly defended; a government that alternately neglected the army's needs and interfered with its functioning; logistical problems that as the war went on grew from the severe to the nigh-impossible; inadequate and stagnant training programs; and a failure to formulate and adopt tactical innovations. Yet another handicap was the army's lack of a major objective to defend, such as Lee's troops had in the Confederate capital at Richmond. The Army of Tennessee thus found its movements more flexible, less constrained by the strategic predilections of the Confederate government. For this reason, Braxton Bragg could undertake his circuitous and ill-conceived campaign in Kentucky in the summer of 1862, and John Bell Hood could launch his disastrous invasion of Tennessee in the autumn of 1864.

Another factor in the army's lack of strategic and tactical success—one generally overlooked by scholars—was its consistently uninspired, shortsighted, and inappropriate use of its mounted arm. On many fields, the army's cavalry performed more effectively than its infantry and artillery comrades. Had the cavalry's contributions to scouting, intelligence-gathering, and combat support been properly exploited, victory might have come more frequently and more fully. Too often, the army's horsemen were allowed to operate apart from the main force or were not properly integrated into it for combat purposes, with predictable results. This was the case especially when battle neared. Time and again, Bragg and Hood detached their horsemen and sent them on missions of questionable value instead of keeping them in hand to support the rest of the army.

The army's failure to use its cavalry to greater effect is curious, given the advantages that arm enjoyed in material and personnel. Unlike the army as a whole, its horsemen consistently outnumbered their opponents, often by a wide margin—a marked contrast to the situation in Virginia, where Lee's army was fortunate to field three-quarters as many horsemen as its opponent, the Army of the Potomac, enjoyed. As Confederate historian John P. Dyer notes, "in the fall of 1862 Confederate cavalry in the Army of Tennessee outnumbered the opposition in a ratio of 7 to 3. In June, 1863, the proportion favored the Confederates 6 to 4. By November of the same year the proportion was 8 to 5. In 1864, at the beginning of the Atlanta campaign, the proportion of Confederate to Federal cavalry was 9 to 5, and during the height of the campaign was 11 to 7. At no time during the four years of war in the West did the Federal cavalry outnumber the Confederate except for very brief intervals."[3]

Another factor that handicapped the army as a whole but not its mounted arm was the quality of its leadership. While the cavalry's longest tenured commander, Major General Joseph Wheeler, was neither a strategic genius, an effective disciplinarian, nor an inspiring leader, he was responsible for notable successes in the field and generally enjoyed the confidence of his officers and troopers. Several of Wheeler's subordinates were more gifted militarily and made more substantial contributions to their army's fortunes. These included the redoubtable Nathan Bedford Forrest, who despite a rudimentary education and scant prewar military experience became the finest cavalry leader of the war; John Hunt Morgan, whose long-distance raids achieved dramatic benefits that outweighed his shortcomings as a strategist and disciplinarian; the tactically astute if sometimes confrontational John Austin Wharton; the callow but formidable John H. Kelly, about whom one of his men wrote, "nothing in man could be more inspiring than his presence on the field, with the enemy in front"; and such unheralded but capable and sometimes exceptional performers as Frank C. Armstrong, Abraham Buford, James Ronald Chalmers, William Y. C. Humes, William Hicks ("Red") Jackson, and Lawrence Sullivan ("Sul") Ross. This book details the major operations of these and other cavalry leaders when assigned to the Army of Tennessee and summarizes their more notable activities when they served apart from the command.[4]

Many of the supply problems that dogged and occasionally hobbled the main army appear not to have had as great an impact on the cavalry. Like all Confederate troopers, those of the Army of Tennessee furnished their own horses throughout the war. While this practice had obvious draw-backs—the most serious being that whenever a mount was rendered *hors de combat* his rider had to straggle, capture a remount, or return home to obtain one—it permitted the fielding of a ready-made force early in the conflict, one composed of sound, well-cared-for animals, in contrast to the broken-down plugs that unscrupulous contractors foisted on the Union cavalry.

Unlike the situation that prevailed in the picked-over area of operations in the East, an abundant supply of horseflesh was available to the Army of Tennessee in the wide-open expanse it called home. And although short-ages of weapons, equipment, and ammunition beset the cavalry to much the same extent it did the rest of the army, the mounted arm, given its inherent mobility and, it would seem, its innate resourcefulness, more eas-ily overcame these deficiencies through capture or confiscation.

The many long-distance raids conducted by the Confederate horsemen in the West ensured maximum access to enemy supply caches. As Dyer illustrates, in early December 1862, at the outset of its celebrated raid against Union communications in West Tennessee, Bedford Forrest's brigade had fewer than half the shoulder arms and a fraction of the ammu-nition it needed to contend successfully with its enemy. By the time the expedition ended, however, the command "was fully armed and equipped, well supplied with provisions, guns, ammunition, and blankets." Dyer adds: "Similar stories might be related of most of the other Confederate cavalry leaders in the West."[5]

Perhaps not surprisingly, given their advantages—or, more properly, their relative paucity of disadvantages—the horse soldiers of the Army of Tennessee achieved a record of consistent, if isolated and often temporary, success. The flaw in the design, however, was that this success rarely improved the fortunes of the main army. Too often, through ignorance or carelessness, the high command—a succession of celebrated but flawed leaders, including Leonidas Polk, Albert Sidney Johnston, P. G. T. Beauregard, Bragg, Joe Johnston, and Hood—failed miserably to tap the cavalry's peculiar strengths. They used their horsemen to guard the army's flanks and rear, to guide it through unknown territory, and to cover its many retreats, but when battle loomed, they seemed to forget they com-manded mobile as well as foot troops. Too often they detached their riders and sent them on missions of dubious value, instead of utilizing their fire support and ability to gather real-time intelligence. Moreover, until too late they failed to appreciate Forrest's genius, preferring to rely on the more limited capabilities of Wheeler and to indulge the reckless daring of Morgan and other Kentucky cavaliers.

Thus it can be argued, as Dyer does, that its innate gifts made the cavalry of the Army of Tennessee "the most spectacular fighting arm in the war." Yet given the shortsightedness of the army's leaders, "it was impossible for Bragg, Johnston, or Hood to exact the maximum from the cavalry." The result was that the troopers of the West were doomed to share fully in the fate of their army, a fate that virtually ensured historical neglect.[6]

An editorial note: Unless otherwise indicated, all regimental and battalion references are to cavalry units.

From left to right: General Nathan Bedford Forrest, CSA; General John Hunt Morgan, CSA; General Joseph Wheeler, CSA. (*Library of Congress*)

# ONE

# THREE WHO WOULD LEAD

A T TWENTY-FOUR, NATHAN BEDFORD FORREST had successfully con-tended with snakes, bears, panthers, and other beasts that roamed the Tennessee backwoods where he had been born in February 1821; he had also survived more than one life-threatening illness. Struggles with opponents external and internal had hardened him to the point that the gray-eyed, broad-shouldered, narrow-waisted young man—already a giant among his peers, towering nearly six feet two inches tall—feared no comer, whatever the species. Therefore, on the afternoon of May 10, 1845, when he tethered his horse in the town square in Hernando, Mississippi, his home for the past three years, Bedford Forrest, although expecting no trouble, was prepared for any that came his way.

On this particular day, trouble was brewing in the streets of Hernando, although, strictly speaking, it did not concern him. A local planter, T. J. Matlock, harbored a grudge—apparently the result of a mercantile trans-action gone bad—against Bedford's uncle and business partner, Jonathan Forrest. The aggrieved party, accompanied by two of his brothers as well as the family overseer, had come to town to settle affairs by any and all means necessary. Hernando, although a thriving commercial town, was also a part of the often-lawless frontier, and gunplay in its streets was a regrettable but common occurrence. As far as can be ascertained, however, the elder Forrest had never been a party to such activity, and his protective nephew, turning from the hitching post and taking position across the Matlocks' path, intended to keep it that way.

The Matlocks took his intervention as a mortal threat. Before the young man could say a word, two of them drew pistols. To the accompaniment of what a newspaper reporter called "some exciting language," they opened fire, striking Forrest in the arm. Another round flew past him to mortally wound Jonathan Forrest, who had emerged from his store in response to the confrontation.

Drawing his own handgun—a companion he was never without—Bedford Forrest responded with unusual calmness and precision. Aware that his weapon contained only two rounds, he chose his targets carefully. One bullet cut down T. J. Matlock; the other nearly took off the arm of one of his brothers. This stopped the assailants, but only briefly. Seeing that Forrest had exhausted his ammunition, the other two made to rush him. They halted when a bystander, his sense of fair play offended by the lopsided fight, tossed Forrest a knife. Brandishing the weapon and bellowing at the top of his lungs, the young man charged his opponents as he had once challenged the beasts of the forest. He was not quick enough: the unwounded brother and the overseer fled down a side street, content to escape with their lives.[1]

Forrest was already well-known locally for his prowess with gun, knife, and fists, and his encounter with the Matlocks did nothing to diminish his reputation as a man of action and fortitude. While decrying "the most bloody affray" that had upset the daily life of Hernando, the newsman who recorded the encounter spoke fondly of Jonathan Forrest, whom he described as a thrifty and honest businessman. Reflecting the view of the community, the reporter applauded the incarceration and pending trial of the surviving assailants. He devoted most of his reporting, however, to Bedford Forrest's coolheaded and courageous act of self-defense, which reflected manly qualities much admired by the good citizens of Hernando.[2]

These qualities defined a man of purpose and determination. Despite disadvantages of birth and breeding, and although sometimes ruled by a fiery temper and an inclination to violence, Nathan Bedford Forrest knew what he wanted from life and strove mightily to attain it. Born in a log cabin, the son of a farmer-blacksmith, eldest child in a family of eight boys and three girls, the recipient of no more than six months' formal schooling and thus functionally illiterate, he refused to allow his humble origins and lack of social polish to hinder his pursuit of happiness, prosperity, and respectability. One step in this process was the establishment of a family of his own. Short months after facing down the Matlocks, he engineered a whirlwind courtship that swept demure, well-educated Mary Ann Montgomery off her feet and into his arms. Their marriage at year's end, which would produce a son and a daughter, not only filled a void in Forrest's life but enabled him to climb a rung in the social ladder of his community.[3]

After Forrest became a husband and father, his tendency to impetuosity and violence eased, but only slightly. Although never fueled by strong drink—he had taken a temperance pledge in his youth, one he adhered to throughout his life—his temper too often continued to get the better of him, involving him in conflicts with kinsmen and later with business competitors. He also had run-ins with public officials, many of whom he rightly considered either corrupt or corruptible. The struggle to maintain self-control in his personal and professional dealings would consume him until the day he died.

In the decade and a half following his marriage, Forrest entered numerous occupations and took on myriad responsibilities—not only farmer and merchant but also horse trader, constable, militia officer, real estate broker, brick mason, stage-line operator, and, eventually, slave dealer. The last-named profession brought him the prosperity and social standing he craved. Although a white supremacist through and through, Forrest was no fanatic on the race issue: for him slavery was simply an economic necessity. Throughout his residence in Mississippi, he and Mary Ann owned few slaves, mainly a woman and her two children. They worked the fields alongside the Forrests and those members of Bedford's family who periodically shared their modest home in Hernando. It was in Forrest's interest to meet the physical needs of his workforce, but he betrayed no squeamishness in working his chattels long and hard. A lifelong believer in the benefits of discipline, he inculcated that quality in his slaves through shouted commands, threats of punishment, and, as a last resort, application of the lash.

Forrest began to traffic in human beings while living in Hernando, but his business dealings increasingly took him north to Tennessee. In 1851, he uprooted his family and the kinsmen who lived with him and relocated to Memphis. There he expanded his slave dealership, which quickly became the second largest such concern in that bustling river town. Just as quickly, Forrest established a reputation for dependability and honesty that earned the respect not only of his customers but of his competitors as well. By 1855, he and his partner, Josiah Maples, could advertise an inventory of more than three hundred chattels of both sexes, many imported from adjoining states, as well as from venues as distant as Missouri and Louisiana. They sold their own slaves as well as those on consignment from other dealers, boasting of "the highest market price always paid for good stock."[4]

Slave dealing was a uniquely profitable business. The closing of the trans-Atlantic trade almost fifty years earlier ensured that a mature, able-bodied slave was an ever-valuable commodity; demand for the product appeared relentless, and the market seemed unaffected by economic down-turn. Forrest's dearth of education and social grace had little effect on his commercial success, and his growing wealth helped compensate for any deficiency elsewhere in his makeup. By 1858, he was affluent enough to purchase a plantation in Coahoma County, Mississippi. Green Grove spanned almost two thousand acres and by some accounts was tended by almost as many field hands. Forrest strove to expand his property; over the next three years, the plantation nearly doubled in size. Although the manor house in its midst was modest in comparison to those of some of his neigh-bors, it testified clearly to the wealth and prominence of its owner.[5]

The social position of the slave dealer in the antebellum South remains a subject of dispute. Some historians contend that the occupation con-ferred merely a semblance of respectability on men who were regarded as dirtying their hands in the flesh trade. Other historians believe that, espe-cially in less settled, less civilized communities such as Memphis in the 1850s, slave trading, rather than carrying a stigma, was hailed as a pillar of the Southern economy. However his profession was viewed by the public, it is reasonable to conclude that Forrest, given his strong work ethic, his reputation for fair dealing, and his unwillingness to flaunt his recent pros-perity, made a generally favorable impression upon neighbors, customers, and business associates alike.

Even so, there is every reason to believe that a newly prosperous slave dealer would not be welcome in the company, and especially in the homes, of some of the older, more established families of Coahoma County. Failure to gain entree to the upper levels of local society, to be numbered among the elite of his community, may have intensified the restlessness that continued to gnaw at Forrest's mind and heart and the anger that seethed within him, at times to erupt in profanity-laden tirades that not even Mary Ann Forrest could quell.

Character flaws notwithstanding, he continued to advance in the esti-mation of his townsmen. Around the time he settled down at Green Grove, the voters of Memphis elected him to the local board of aldermen, upon which, as befit his business expertise, he won a seat on the finance committee. In this position, he was responsible for advancing measures affecting how the city disbursed public funds. At times his proposals incurred the stringent opposition of other members, but he advanced them with characteristic determination. Although some of his decisions and actions generated controversy and protest, when he quit his post a year later to devote his time to running Green Grove, it was to the accompaniment of resolutions of regret from fellow officials, including several with whom he had crossed swords.[6]

Sometimes those swords—more accurately, pistols—were real. Dueling being a time-honored means of settling personal disputes along the Tennessee-Mississippi border, Forrest was called to the field of honor more than once, usually by political adversaries or business competitors he had offended by his bluntness of speech and forcefulness of will. Some of their disputes were settled short of bloodletting, but at least once he opted out of a duel by absenting himself from Coahoma County on the appointed morning. His opponent was quick to brand Forrest a coward for thus violating the *code duello*, but, as one recent biographer has observed, "if Forrest 'ran off' to Memphis to avoid the duel, it was not from any fear for his own life; he had risked it too many times before and would do so too many times again, in the face of greater odds, for such a motive even to be considered. In fact, it conforms to a pattern that recurred consistently throughout his life: his anger was quick and impetuous, but when it had time to cool he tended to opt for the more prudent course." It may be, too, that he backed out because he had come to realize that he was in the wrong and the other man in the right, but for one reason or another was unwilling to apologize.[7]

Forrest's semiseclusion in Coahoma County following his resignation from the local board of aldermen lasted only a few months. Early in 1860, he returned to Memphis, where he regained his seat on the governing board. He served in a low-key manner, except for a single confrontation over a contract let to one John Loudon to build a new wood-and-stone wharf for the city. The work that Loudon performed met Forrest's approval, but not that of fellow aldermen, who complained that a section of the stonework had been loosened by an unexpected rise in the turbulent Mississippi. The contractor proposed to repair the damage, but the board members, hastily conferring among themselves, voted to condemn the work and to refuse to pay Loudon.

When an astonished Forrest demanded to know the basis for the refusal, he was confidentially informed that the other aldermen wished to "break up old man Loudon," who was not one of their cronies. They intended to reassign the contract to a close friend, who would pay a kickback for the privilege. The proposal infuriated Forrest, who, within earshot of Mayor R. D. Baugh and other leading citizens, heaped anger and scorn on the alderman who had disclosed the scheme, calling him an "infernal scoundrel," and worse. The object of his wrath paled and fell silent as Forrest added: "I have a big notion to pitch you into the Mississippi River. Now, I warn you if you ever presume to address such a damnable proposition to me in [the] future I will break your rascally neck!" No one said anything further about ousting Loudon. The contractor successfully repaired the wharf and received full compensation for his labor.[8]

Perhaps disillusioned by the tenor of local politics, Forrest considered quitting the board for good, as well as selling his slave dealership and leaving Memphis. But following another brief hiatus at Green Grove, he decided to resume his business dealings. He continued to reside in the area until the sectional divide that had gripped the country for at least four decades erupted into secession and war.

As a native Southerner, Forrest staunchly defended the right of any state to resist coercion at the hands of the government in Washington. And as a vocal advocate of slavery, one who had become rich beyond his wildest dreams as a direct result of the institution (at this period his personal wealth approached one and a half million dollars, a fantastic sum for the times), he would fight to uphold the right of Caucasians to traffic in and profit from the sale of African Americans.

In a sense, war came at the right time for Bedford Forrest. He had amassed as much material wealth as any man of undistinguished parentage and rudimentary learning could have hoped to accumulate in a lifetime. He had reached the pinnacle of power to which any local politician of his time could have aspired. And he had gained as much respectability as any Deep South slave dealer had a right to expect. He was ready to move on to a new profession, one in which he could seize the kind of power and authority that was currently beyond his reach.

His local prominence, coupled with his long experience with weapons, his inherent knowledge of horses and horsemanship, and his stint in command of a militia company, recommended Forrest for a position in one of the many military units that began forming in the wake of the April 1861

bombardment of Fort Sumter, the act that touched off the national powder keg. Even before the first shots were fired, Tennesseans, along with
other farsighted Southerners, had banded together to form volunteer militia units. Clad in variegated uniforms (or no uniforms at all), shouldering
antiquated weaponry, and practicing drill-plain maneuvers on cornfields
and in pastures, these would-be soldiers formed the nucleus of Confederate
war mobilization. However, Forrest, preoccupied with his municipal duties
and the demands of running a plantation, did not seek to enlist in these
early organizations. His military career began exactly two months after
Sumter's surrender to South Carolina troops led by Brigadier General P. G.
T. Beauregard. On June 14, Forrest enlisted as a private soldier in a company of mounted riflemen organizing in Memphis and the surrounding area
under Captain Josiah White. Following him into the unit were his youngest
brother, Jeffrey, and Forrest's fifteen-year-old son, William.[9]

Although Forrest's reasons for enlisting as a private soldier remain
obscure—his name alone should have guaranteed him a commission—it is
not difficult to understand why he chose White's unit, the first incarnation
of the soon-to-be-famous 7th Tennessee Cavalry. The mounted arm was
the preferred branch of service for the horse-loving Forrest. Yet cavalry
proper—whose members wielded traditional weaponry such as sabers, pistols, and short-barreled, lightweight shoulder arms known as carbines—
was something that only highly populated locales with access to sources of
military supply could support. A majority of the residents of towns such as
Memphis went to war toting their own weapons, removed from the family
gun cabinet, and these consisted almost exclusively of long-range rifles.
Rifles substituted for carbines in most of the mounted units organized in
the Deep South, although the long arm would prove cumbersome to use in
the saddle and difficult or impossible to reload.[10]

Forrest did not remain in the ranks for long. Within days of enlisting,
he learned that some of Memphis's most influential citizens had returned
from conferring in Nashville with Tennessee Governor Isham G. Harris
and the local Confederate commander, Major General Leonidas Polk. They
brought formal authority for Forrest to raise and command a unit of
mounted rangers—not merely a one-hundred-man company, but a several-
company battalion. At once he set to work, placing recruiting notices in the
local papers and dispatching agents throughout the countryside. These
men scoured not only northern Tennessee but also the upper counties of
Alabama and Mississippi for recruits.

Forrest himself made a covert trip to Kentucky—a self-proclaimed neutral state but with a large pro-Union population—where arms and equipment were reported to be stockpiled. Bypassing large population centers such as Lexington and Frankfort, he called on Confederate sympathizers of means—the kind of people he had brushed shoulders with in Memphis—and they furnished him with all manner of materiel. According to Forrest's best-known biographer, John Allan Wyeth, who served under not only Forrest but also John Hunt Morgan, "soon all the pistols, guns, saddles, blankets, and other cavalry equipment that could be procured without attracting attention and carried south in wagons by unfrequented highways were gathered up and sent away." Many of the items came gratis, the gift of diehard secessionists, but most were paid for out of Forrest's pocket. How much he disbursed to equip his battalion is unknown, but undoubtedly it amounted to a considerable sum.[11]

Returning to Tennessee, he labored to complete the organization of his command. Within weeks the battalion comprised a second company of horsemen raised in the Memphis area, as well as another Tennessee company, four companies from northern Alabama, and two companies recruited in Kentucky. So prominent was Forrest's reputation as a fighter, and so universally accepted his capacity for command, that a company raised in far-off Texas subsequently joined him in Tennessee. By the end of October, the battalion numbered 650 horsemen and was ready to begin active service. In the spirit of Southern democracy, the rank and file had elected their own officers. Their first choice was Forrest, who accepted the position of lieutenant colonel, the highest rank a unit of that size could support.

Its rolls complete, the battalion prepared to move to its first duty station, a garrison then being erected on the Cumberland River near Dover, Tennessee. As it moved out under Forrest's command, one of his old business associates, Samuel Tate, president of the Memphis & Charleston Railroad, wired General Albert Sidney Johnston, commander of Confederate forces west of the Allegheny Mountains: "Colonel Forrest's regiment [sic] of cavalry, as fine a body of men as ever went to the field, has gone to Fort Donelson. Give Forrest a chance and he will distinguish himself."[12]

Forrest would have that chance, and he would make the most of it.

BORN IN HUNTSVILLE, ALABAMA, IN JUNE 1825, John Hunt Morgan moved with his family to Lexington, Kentucky, the hometown of his mother, when he was five years old. John's father, Calvin Morgan, had inherited a coveted position in Cumberland Valley society through his marriage to Henrietta Hunt, daughter of one of the wealthiest men west of the Alleghenies. Calvin had also made a name in military circles: years earlier, at the callow age of twenty-one, he had been elected lieutenant colonel of a militia regiment formed in his native Tennessee. In attaining this lofty position, Calvin had followed in the steps of forebears, including General Daniel Morgan, hero of Cowpens and other battles of the American Revolution. Thus, John Morgan—the first of ten children born to Calvin and Henrietta—could gaze proudly on a family history seemingly awash in affluence, social position, and military distinction.

Even when a series of business reverses wrought havoc on his family's finances, forcing Calvin to seek employment with his father-in-law, John and his many siblings enjoyed a mainly carefree upbringing thanks to the "genteel and suitable support" of their grandfather John Wesley Hunt. Poverty may have gnawed from time to time at the edges of the family, but its firstborn, who grew to maturity on his grandfather's three-hundred-acre farm outside Lexington, an estate tended by a small army of slaves, always considered himself the scion of successful, well-to-do Kentuckians.[13]

Physically and athletically, John Hunt Morgan was archetypal Bluegrass elite. By his late teens he stood six feet tall and had developed, as a relative put it, "features [that] were eminently handsome and adapted to the most pleasing expressions. His eyes were small, of a grayish blue color, and their glances keen and thoughtful. His figure on foot or on horseback was superb." According to one of the young man's many female admirers, his most distinctive feature was a ready smile that disclosed gleaming teeth: "It comes over his face like the laugh over a child's countenance—having in it an innocence of humor which is very beautiful to me."[14]

Innocent humor was not, however, one of Morgan's most enduring qualities. By 1842, when he entered Lexington's Transylvania University, he had acquired a wild streak, a passion for pleasure, and a set of vices happily indulged, including a fondness for drink, gambling, and horseplay. He spent almost as much time frolicking with the other members of a fraternity-like organization known as the Adelphia Society as he did reciting Greek and dissecting algebraic equations. The Adelphians cultivated a reputation for "very disorderly conduct," in which Morgan joined early and often. More than once he was hauled before the university administration for having committed pranks and vandalism in Lexington, as well for harassing campus visitors with profane, alcohol-induced tirades.[15]

Such acts were considered minor violations of the school's conduct code, but during his sophomore year he committed a serious transgression by challenging to a duel a fellow Adelphian who by word or deed had offended Morgan's sensibilities. The circumstances of the encounter, including the weapons used, remain obscure, but neither party suffered bodily injury. The duel made an instant celebrity of John Morgan, who had achieved nothing else of distinction at Transylvania, but it came to the attention of university officials, who feared that the reckless act might tempt other students to copy it. More to the point, dueling, although a rite of passage for manly Southerners, was not sanctioned by the laws of Kentucky.

Morgan and his opponent were made to appear before the school's board of trustees and ordered to justify their actions. Apparently they failed, for both were found guilty of violating university regulations. Although the standard penalty for such an offense was expulsion, Morgan's antagonist got off with a reprimand. Morgan, who was judged to have played a more prominent role in the affair, was suspended for the remainder of the term.

Although it incurred punishment, his decision to seek satisfaction on the field of honor not only buttressed his sense of self-worth but, in the words of one biographer, constituted "an initiation rite into the world of adult men, his personal 'graduation' from the university; it rescued him from a frustrating life as a college student and established his honor." This was, in fact, the only form of graduation Morgan would experience. With the huzzahs of fellow students impressed by his boldness ringing in his ears, he left Transylvania, never to return.[16]

As his entrance into a duel and his reaction to its aftermath suggests, although no stranger to self-worth, John Hunt Morgan had a difficult time mastering the art of self-discipline. The concept was as deeply buried, as inaccessible, as the most arcane bit of textbook knowledge. He disciplined himself only enough to make his way successfully in the world. Initially, he failed in this effort. After leaving Transylvania, he made fitful attempts to start a business, but, unable to secure sufficient seed money from his grandfather, he failed to establish himself.

Given his family's military antecedents, his next move was a logical one. The year following his expulsion he applied for a commission in the United

States Marine Corps. This, too, proved a failure. Although his family connections secured the support of his local congressman and other influential officials, the War Department responded with less-than-desired urgency. For two years, during which he appears to have lived off the largesse of his family, he waited in vain for a reply. He finally was rescued from his enforced idleness by the Mexican-American War. Young America's first foreign conflict, an avowed war of conquest and territorial expansion, it attracted thousands of Kentuckians, along with the adventurous youth of nearly every state in the Union, and placed them in the ranks of a volunteer army poised to attack across the Rio Grande.

Morgan's long-indulged passion for riding and fine horseflesh meant that only cavalry service would do. In company with his brother Calvin and his uncle, Alexander Morgan, a prosperous local farmer, the twenty-one-year-old enlisted in one of two mounted companies organizing in Fayette County, commanded by a local worthy with a historic name, Oliver Hazard Perry Beard. On June 4, 1846, Beard's unit, including the three Morgans, left Lexington for points south, cheered on by townspeople in the throes of war fever.[17]

John Morgan may have regarded field service primarily as a means of quitting a life that had frustrated and disappointed him. Still, as a patriotic son of the Republic with aspirations of military distinction, he probably looked forward to combat. A capable performance in arms would not only uphold family tradition but would also validate his self-image as a defender of honor—his country's, his region's, and his own.

He got off to a good start. When Beard's company reached Louisville, it embarked on a one-year term of service as Company K of Colonel Humphrey Marshall's 1st Kentucky Mounted Volunteer Regiment, more than eight hundred strong. To Morgan's gratification—perhaps also to his surprise—when officer elections took place, he was chosen second lieutenant of his company. Soon afterward, he was promoted to first lieutenant. Apparently a combination of traits and qualities—many of which he shared with Nathan Bedford Forrest—fitted him for these positions, including a striking (and, in Morgan's case, a highly attractive) appearance, an evident mastery of horse and sword, and a recognized capacity for leadership. It can be surmised that his well-known descent from stalwarts of the militia and volunteer service also spurred his rise to commissioned rank. In time, these attributes would impress Captain Beard and Colonel Marshall as much as they had the electors of Company K.[18]

Regrettably, the realities of service en route to and in the war threatened to dash Morgan's dreams of military glory. While traveling south via steamboat to Memphis and then by overland march to San Antonio in the newly annexed state of Texas, Company K lost dozens of recruits to sickness, forcing them to lay over in distant venues until they could recover and overtake their outfits. These unfortunates included John and Calvin Morgan, who were forced to recuperate in Little Rock, Arkansas. By the time the stragglers reached their regiment's duty station at Camargo, Mexico, headquarters of General Zachary Taylor's Army of Occupation, it was mid-November—too late to take part in the fighting in that quarter, which had included Taylor's much-heralded victories at Palo Alto, Resaca de la Palma, and Monterrey. Instead of Mexican foot troops or lancers, the newcomers battled a second wave of illnesses—measles, yellow fever, diarrhea—most of them spawned by the unsanitary conditions prevailing in Taylor's camps.

Lieutenant Morgan and his comrades finally escaped the scene of squalor and disease when, shortly before year's end, they were transferred to Saltillo, then to a campsite just above Monterrey. However, not until February 1847, when Marshall's regiment joined Taylor's main army at Buena Vista, did the prospect of battle become reality. On the twenty-second, Taylor's little army clashed with the more numerous but less disciplined Mexicans under General Antonio Lopez de Santa Anna. The 1st Kentucky Mounted Rifles—reduced by sickness and detachments to fewer than three hundred effectives—saw only peripheral action; even so, a few of its members had the opportunity to distinguish themselves. At one point in the fighting, John, his brother, and a few comrades clambered up a mountainside to exchange rifle fire with an enemy detachment. For a time, they held the enemy at bay, but they were hastily recalled when enough Mexicans arrived to take the high ground by storm.

This proved to be the extent of John Morgan's experience under fire. The following day, Santa Anna attacked along the length of Taylor's line and met a signal repulse. Their defeat was the first in a long series of reverses the Mexicans suffered while falling back upon their capital. Mexico City would surrender to Taylor's successor, Brevet Lieutenant General Winfield Scott, the following September. But the 1st Kentucky would not be there to witness the denouement. Long before that day, the regiment, having completed its twelve-month enlistment, would be back in its home state.[19]

John Morgan returned to the Bluegrass feeling restless, dislocated, and unfulfilled. And yet, despite the hardships and dangers and evanescent glory he had experienced, he had enjoyed his year in arms. He had also proven to superiors and subordinates alike that he possessed the qualities of a leader. For this reason, as the war wound down, he petitioned the War Department for authorization to recruit a unit of his own. As he informed a high-ranking acquaintance, "I'll raise a Company to serve either as an independent Company or to be attached to some Regiment. I should like very much to get to raise a *Cavalry co.* But General I'll willingly take any situation they would give me. Please write and let me know my fate." He heard nothing; a month after he filed his petition, the Treaty of Guadalupe Hidalgo ended hostilities between the United States and Mexico.[20]

Denied a wartime assignment, he laid aside his martial ambitions and strove to resuscitate his hopes of a business career. After a few prospects fell through, he formed a partnership with a friend, Sanders Bruce, the son of one of Lexington's more prominent families who had established a china and glassware business. The firm of Morgan & Bruce prospered immediately, as did a side trade in leasing to local farmers, haulers, and steamboat captains the few slaves the partners had managed to acquire.

At the same time, Morgan's private life began to flourish. In November 1848, the young entrepreneur married Bruce's eighteen-year-old sister, Rebecca. The union was a happy one, but it suffered when, in the fifth year of their marriage, Becky gave birth to a stillborn son. Since returning from Mexico, her husband had suffered periodically from depression; after his child's death, the condition worsened. It was not ameliorated when Becky began to suffer from a baffling disease that infected one of her legs. Morgan accompanied his wife to physicians' offices in cities near and distant, but a cure proved elusive. In time Becky became bedridden, and the prospect of producing a child to take the place of the lost son became an unrealistic hope.[21]

In the late 1850s, using funds provided by his mother after his father's death, John dissolved his partnership with Bruce and went into business with his brother Cal, first in hemp production, then in woolen purchasing, and finally in woolen manufacturing. Like Forrest, Morgan became increasingly involved in the purchase, sale, and leasing of slaves, a profitable adjunct to the business that provided the Morgan brothers with the majority of their revenue and capital.

Morgan never repressed his hunger for military life. In 1852, he joined the state militia, organizing a company of light artillery of which he was elected captain. His return to arms lasted less than two years; it ended when the Kentucky legislature, seeking to economize, effectively disbanded the state forces. Morgan and other would-be soldiers responded by forming dozens of volunteer units to take the militia's place. In 1857, the clamor these warriors raised resulted in the reestablishment of the militia system. A triumphant Morgan promptly organized a new company—this one composed of foot soldiers—known as the Lexington Rifles. The shoulder arm wielded by Morgan's sixty men had largely supplanted the venerable musket of the Revolution, the War of 1812, and the Napoleonic Wars. In contrast to the smoothbore musket, which could be fired accurately at a range of up to two hundred yards, the rifle, which fired the bullet-shaped minie ball, was capable of hitting a target five hundred yards away and could kill at eight hundred yards. Captain Morgan dressed his troops in stylish green uniforms, trained them under the supervision of a drill instructor of long experience, and led them in complex tactical evolutions. The dexterity and precision they displayed on the drill field impressed not only local spectators but the crowds they attracted in neighboring counties to which the Rifles traveled in hopes of expanding their reputation and their membership.[22]

Morgan rode hard on his men, fining those who were late for practice, forcing absent members to resign. It is instructive that their captain was gigged for infractions of the rules he himself had established. His efforts to instill discipline in his unit paid dividends. Historian Howard Swiggett observes that within a few years, when the entire South went to war and "Morgan was . . . recruiting across Kentucky, it was in the Lexington Rifles, whose uniforms and bearing had caught many feminine eyes from Bowling Green to Cynthiana for years, that men enlisted."[23]

Morgan himself caught numerous feminine eyes. Although outwardly devoted to his invalid wife, he made little attempt to ward off the female admirers he attracted in the course of his business and military pursuits. Because he did not flaunt his dalliances, relatives considered him a loving and attentive husband. Friends, however, gossiped about his romantic entanglements and sexual conquests. Morgan was a regular patron of Lexington-area brothels, just as he was a habitué of gambling dens, billiard parlors, and racecourses. In the mold of red-blooded Southerners addicted to pleasure and risk, he wagered large sums on the turn of a card, the carom of a ball, and the fleetness of thoroughbred stock. Then, too, he continued to indulge—but never to quench—the thirst for alcohol he had acquired in young manhood. It is nowhere recorded, however, that he habitually drank to excess.

Morgan was no hypocrite. Although sufficiently discreet in his personal behavior to avoid a scandal that would mortify his wife, he did not attempt to excuse or downplay his more immoderate behavior; nor did he criticize those who shared his weaknesses. His future brother-in-law and ranking subordinate, Basil Duke of Scott County, Kentucky, admitted that "General Morgan was essentially no 'saint'—his friends may claim that he had no right to that title and not the slightest pretension to it. While he respected true piety in other men . . . he did not profess, nor did he regulate his life by religious convictions." Duke was quick to add that "Morgan's kindness and goodness of heart were proverbial. His manner . . . was gentle and kind, and no doubt greatly contributed to acquire him the singular popularity which he enjoyed long before he had made his military reputation."[24]

Saint or sinner, Morgan was politically astute. When the presidential election of 1860 drew near, raising the likelihood of a sectional rift, the inveterate gambler won five hundred dollars by betting that native Kentuckian Abraham Lincoln would gain the White House. At first Morgan gave Lincoln the benefit of the political doubt, denying that he would shove the South into secession. Thus he was dismayed by the president's determination to maintain U.S. Army garrisons on Southern soil, including Fort Sumter.

The South's reaction to Lincoln's policies was uneven, a reflection of differing regional influences. The Cotton States responded hotly and immediately, while much of the Upper South did so less precipitately, acting not with an outpouring of vitriol but with a sense of regretful resignation. The residents of border states such as Kentucky had to make the most difficult and emotionally charged decisions, in which economic considerations played a large role. Unlike the Deep South, Kentucky was less a planter society than a network of small, independent farms. The institution of slavery had been losing ground in the state for many years. In the end, a majority of Kentuckians rejected secession. In May 1861, the state legislature's small but vocal pro-Union majority compelled the secessionist-leaning governor, Beriah Magoffin, to declare the state neutral ground. Thousands of Kentucky's Confederate-sympathizing sons immediately headed south to enlist, convinced they could not maintain honor and dignity by remaining in a state that had made orphans of them.[25]

The sympathies of John Morgan, the erstwhile conditional Unionist, were with the brethren who left Kentucky vowing not to return till their state had redeemed its good name. Yet he did not officially join the fight until September 1861, almost five months after Fort Sumter's surrender and several weeks after the first large land battle of the war—a dramatic Confederate victory—was fought near a Virginia rail depot named Manassas Junction and a stream called Bull Run. Apparently he remained absorbed in his business activities and militia duties, and he may have hoped that coming state elections would turn the legislature into a pro-Confederate body (instead, they strengthened the Unionists' hold on the governmental apparatus). Another factor that kept him from enlisting in the wake of the firing on Sumter was the deteriorating health of his wife, who, following amputation of her ulcerated leg, died on July 21, the day of the fighting at Manassas.

Yet there seemed little doubt which way Morgan would lean when decision time arrived. Even before he cast his lot with the Confederacy, he displayed his sentiments by attaching the Lexington Rifles to the Kentucky State Guard, the pro-Southern militia command Governor Magoffin had formed before the legislature tied his hands. By August, Morgan appeared ready to fight. That month he commanded his company during a confrontation in the streets of Lexington with a Union militia unit being issued arms and ammunition. The tense standoff nearly erupted in bloodshed before prominent local officials, including John C. Breckinridge, Lincoln's recent opponent on the pro-slavery Democratic Party ticket and a future Confederate general and Cabinet member, mediated a peaceful end to the crisis.[26]

Morgan curbed the growing eagerness of his company to go to war until September 18, when, provoked by Confederate violations of the state's neutrality, the lawmakers in Frankfort declared their unambiguous support of the federal government. The following day, a Union regiment that had been formed at Camp Dick Robinson, just south of Lexington, entered the city and placed it under martial law. This was the final straw for Morgan and thousands of pro-Confederate Kentuckians. On the evening of the twentieth, he led a detachment of his company out of town under cover of darkness, hauling behind it two wagons filled with rifles filched from the local armory. The little band headed out the Versailles Road toward a Confederate rendezvous in Hart County. Word of its passage spread like a grass fire; by the time it reached the camp at Woodsonville, two hundred strangers had flocked to Morgan's standard.

The following month, while these men trained under the tutelage of Basil Duke and other experienced instructors, they were sworn into the service of the Provisional Army of the Confederate States of America. Unsurprisingly, Morgan was elected captain of the company thus formed. Higher rank, greater responsibility, and a much larger command—the 2nd Kentucky Cavalry, one of the war's premier mounted organizations— would follow in due course.[27]

In striking contrast to the robust Forrest and the athletic Morgan, Joseph Wheeler, Jr., stood five-foot-two in his stocking feet and weighed no more than 120 pounds. He was fifteen years younger than Forrest, and eleven years Morgan's junior. The difference encompassed more than age and stature. Unlike the Tennessean and the Kentuckian, Wheeler was a professionally trained soldier with Northern roots. Although born in Augusta, Georgia, in September 1836, he had spent his formative years in Connecticut, to which his merchant and miller father, a native New Englander, had returned following the death of Joseph's mother, Julia Knox Hull Wheeler.

Joseph received his formative schooling at an exclusive institution, the Episcopal Academy of Connecticut, before moving to New York City to live with a married sister and then to neighboring Brooklyn to board with a wealthy aunt. In May 1853, although not yet seventeen, he began applying to the United States Military Academy. His application was endorsed by the local congressman, a fellow graduate of the Episcopal Academy, but because of his age he was not accepted for more than a year. In July 1854, he left his aunt's house and took a steamboat up the Hudson River to what would be his home for the next five years. At that time West Point, in common with many European universities, was experimenting with an extended curriculum; thus Cadet Wheeler became a member of the Class of 1859.[28]

Like John Morgan, Wheeler's family had a military tradition, although not uniformly a distinguished one. While one of his uncles, a regular army officer with a Harvard degree, had died heroically at Lundy's Lane near the close of the War of 1812; earlier in that conflict, Joseph's paternal grandfather, General Isaac Hull, was forced to surrender the garrison of Detroit, Michigan Territory, to a besieging British force.[29]

Young Wheeler did not appear equipped to forge a record that would eradicate this stain on the family escutcheon. Not only did he lack the physical attributes characteristic of a successful warrior, but he failed to demonstrate intellect in the classroom, or athletic prowess on the embryonic competition fields of West Point. In fact, his academic record appeared a study in futility. At the close of his plebe year, he ranked twenty-fourth out of thirty-five cadets. The following year, when his class was pared down by resignations and academic deficiencies to twenty-nine, he finished eighteenth. During his third-class year, when subjects such as military drawing were added to the curriculum—till then top-heavy with mathematics and language courses—he sank almost to the bottom of the class. He fared even worse during the 1857-58 academic year, intimidated by those engineering courses that constituted the core of the academy's curriculum; at its close, he ranked next to last in the class.[30]

He improved only marginally in his first-class year, on July 1, 1859, graduating nineteenth out of twenty-two cadets. In that final year at the Point, tactical courses finally achieved academic primacy, but the change was no boon to Wheeler. He ended his cadet career ranking sixteenth in infantry tactics, eighteenth in ordnance and gunnery, and dead last in mounted tactics—an incomprehensible record considering the celebrity he was to achieve as a cavalry leader.

Although a cadet's class standing depended on personal deportment as well as academic performance, Wheeler could not excuse his poor showing on the ground that he had accumulated too many demerits. The penalties he incurred for violating the academy's lengthy and arcane compendium of regulations were far short of the number that would have cost him a place or two on the conduct roll. More alarming was the nature of those violations. He was gigged not only for such trivial offenses as reading, or visiting after lights-out, or smoking in the barracks, but for "neglect of duty," "allowing disorder in the ranks," and being "inattentive at cavalry drill." Such infractions suggested that, at least on occasion, Wheeler failed to take his military responsibilities as seriously as a future army officer should have. Apparently they combined with his low class posting to deny him cadet rank, for he held none throughout his tour in contrast to the dozens of cadet lieutenants and captains who would go on to win rank and distinction after graduation.[31]

If he was no scholar, neither was he an athlete. His slight build relegated him to fringe roles on the few intramural teams the academy fielded, including soccer. In fact, his stature (or lack of it) gained him a nickname popular among his fellow cadets: "Point." Wheeler's earliest biographer,

John Witherspoon Du Bose, explained the moniker in geometric terms: its bearer displayed "neither length, breadth, nor thickness."[32]

Throughout his years at the academy, Wheeler maintained a reserved and serious demeanor—"an inordinate dignity," as a later biographer puts it, "which, as the years went on, caused him to be somewhat pompous and pedantic." One of his classmates recalled him as "earnest and quiet . . . a true gentleman always," but one who "rarely spoke when he had nothing to say" and who never showed a sense of humor. Another contemporary theorized, probably correctly, that "had the corps of cadets been called upon to predict who of the class would be the last to emerge from obscurity, the chances are that the choice would have fallen upon Wheeler."[33]

Despite his introverted personality, he made a number of friends among the corps, including Robert F. Beckham of Virginia and Charles R. Collins, a Northern-born resident of the Old Dominion. In fact, Wheeler appears to have preferred the company of Southerners, of whom he considered himself one. He may have spent most of his life in New England and New York, but he was a native Georgian, a fact that gave him a social and political identity, one he would cling to throughout his life. His core beliefs were those he shared with other Southern-born cadets: a sense of honor and decorum, an attunement to family pedigree, and a fondness for the agrarian lifestyle. He longed for the life of a gentleman farmer, which he hoped to become after completing the eight-year hitch in the regular service to which he had pledged himself upon entering West Point. Therefore, when the rising tide of sectionalism and war began to penetrate the cloistered walls of the academy, spawning confrontations, verbal and physical, between cadets from different parts of the country, Wheeler let it be known that his sympathies were with his Southern brethren.

His unfortunate class standing denied him an assignment to the elite branches of the service, the topographical and construction engineers, which went to the most astute cadets. And yet the position that was offered him was much to his liking: a brevet second lieutenancy in the mounted service. His initial assignment was to the 1st United States Dragoons, a hybrid organization formed in 1833 by a retrenchment-minded Congress. The officers and men of this regiment were armed, equipped, and trained to fight on horseback and afoot as conditions dictated. The brevet rank was a temporary posting that offered the bearer the pay and authority of a position that would officially be his only when a vacancy opened in the commissioned ranks of the tiny peacetime army. A brevet officer often went several months—in some cases, a year or longer—before securing permanent rank. This undesirable situation owed to the lack of an adequate pension system that forced aged and unwell officers to remain on the rolls, even when unable to perform their assigned duties, because they could not afford to retire. In Wheeler's case, his brevet status would outlast his first unit assignment.[34]

When the three-month leave granted to every West Point graduate ended, Wheeler was ordered to report to the Cavalry School for Practice at Carlisle, Pennsylvania. His posting seems to have had a dual purpose. Even as he tutored raw recruits in the nuances of mounted service, he would strive to strengthen his own apparently shaky grasp of cavalry tactics.

Regardless of whether he had to learn almost as much as the would-be cavaliers assigned to his charge, his stint at Carlisle paid dividends. He had time to study the characteristics that differentiated the various units stationed there, which included a detachment of the Regiment of Mounted Rifles. Congress had organized that outfit in 1846 as a complement to the two dragoon regiments then in service. To an even greater degree than a dragoon, a mounted rifleman was a foot soldier temporarily on horseback. His steed was only a mode of transportation to the field of battle, where he dismounted to fight with the long-range rifle, rather than with the short-barreled carbine of the cavalryman or the already antiquated musketoon issued to the dragoon.

Perhaps because he lacked a solid grounding in cavalry tactics, the life of a mounted rifleman had greater appeal to Brevet Second Lieutenant Wheeler. In the late spring of 1860, when his tour at Carlisle ended, he took leave in Washington, D.C. Stopping in at the War Department, he applied for a commission in the outfit that had caught his attention. Perhaps he knew of a pending vacancy, or perhaps his application was expedited by professional contacts—one of his West Point instructors, for instance—for his transfer came through with unusual speed, as of June 26. Six weeks later, he was informed that he finally held the full rank of second lieutenant.[35]

Upon his joining the Mounted Rifles, Wheeler's military career took flight. Most of his new comrades were serving on the southwestern frontier; regimental headquarters was at Fort Craig, New Mexico Territory, on the Rio Grande 150 miles south of Santa Fe. The fort was situated in the midst of a bleak, forbidding country that was home to Apaches, Comanches, and other warlike tribes. Serving in those parts would be an adventure. Getting there in one piece from the point of embarkation, Hannibal, Missouri, would be a challenge in itself.[36]

In fact, Wheeler found himself fighting Indians before halfway to his destination. Upon reaching Hannibal, he was assigned to a section of a supply train bound for New Mexico that included a pregnant woman, traveling to join her officer husband at Santa Fe. Three days into the journey, she went into labor, forcing the commander of the train to detach a mule-drawn ambulance to shelter her until she gave birth. Wheeler and a military surgeon were detailed to minister to the woman until she could resume travel. Their only companion was the mule skinner, whose skill with firearms was an unknown quantity. It was as dangerous a situation as travelers in that part of the country could have experienced—especially after the main column, to avoid endangering the entire train, resumed its journey, leaving the ambulance behind.

Only hours after the woman gave birth and received postpartum care, Wheeler directed the wagon to resume its trek toward regimental headquarters, he riding alongside on his own horse. Predictably enough, a band of hostiles—fortunately, a small hunting party—attacked before the ambulance was well on its way. Before a storm of arrows could break upon his head, Wheeler halted the ambulance, had the surgeon take the driver's seat, and placed the mule skinner on another horse that had been tied to the rear of the wagon. At his signal, the surgeon lashed the team into as much speed as habitually stubborn animals were capable of.

Describing the situation years later, Wheeler claimed that "we had gained the crest of a slight hill, the Indians closing in on us, when the driver swung directly toward an Indian, sprang from his horse, dropped to one knee, and fired. A redskin tumbled, and instantly the Indians were after the driver in a bunch. The air seemed filled with arrows. That was my chance. I charged the crowd, knocking down a horse with a shot from my musket. Then I threw away my gun and went at them with my Colt pistol. The driver came in with his Colt and the Indians were on the run."[37]

The attackers' swift departure ended the crisis, for they did not reappear. Before darkness came, Wheeler and his charges made contact with the balance of the supply train. The ambulance and its passengers spent the night inside the protective embrace of the other wagons.

No details are available to describe the rest of the journey, but the train made it through to Fort Craig. Soon afterward, mother and child were united with a much-relieved husband and father. Word of Wheeler's quick thinking under pressure and straight shooting quickly made the rounds of the post and nearby settlements. According to some accounts, the lieutenant's conduct gained him the sobriquet that would adhere to him for the rest of his life: "Fightin' Joe." Whether this is how the celebrated title originated is open to dispute. Whatever the circumstances, Wheeler would have welcomed it, if only because it supplanted the less-flattering nickname he had acquired at West Point.[38]

For all the potential adversaries that lurked atop the mountains and in the canyons surrounding Fort Craig, Lieutenant Wheeler found his duty tour in the New Mexico Territory quiet and routine. Patrols sent from headquarters clashed sporadically with hostiles, but the regiment suffered few casualties. The officers and men of the outfit were thus left with much time on their hands but few places outside the garrison in which to spend it. Inactivity took its toll, encouraging soldiers to find solace in hard drink, gambling, and wenching among the Mexican women to be found in the ramshackle cantinas outside the fort and among those laundresses informally attached to the army who doubled as prostitutes. As far as can be determined, the quiet, introverted Wheeler, for whom self-control was the basis of a productive life, engaged in none of these activities, at least not on a regular basis.

It can be presumed that he entered more fully into another garrison pastime: discussion and debate of national political issues. This activity became increasingly popular as the presidential election of 1860 drew near. Most of the officers at Fort Craig, including the commander and executive officer of the Mounted Rifles, were native Southerners who made no attempt to disguise their secessionist leanings. They would have counted Wheeler as a kindred spirit. And they were right to do so, for the lieutenant, notwithstanding his inclination to avoid heated debate on any divisive issue, shared their views and inclinations.

When news of Lincoln's election belatedly reached New Mexico, Wheeler confronted the implications of his allegiance to a region where he had lived only briefly as compared to the many years he had spent in the North. By now he was certain of the course he would take should Georgia and the rest of the South vote to quit the Union, a possibility that had been looming at least since the Nullification Crisis in South Carolina thirty years before. Wheeler's dilemma was that he felt an allegiance not only to his native region but to the institution that had educated and trained him, employed him, and paid his salary. But if he engaged in a battle with mind and heart, it was not a protracted one. Shortly before Georgia voted to secede, he wrote to his older brother, William, who continued to live in Augusta as did Joseph's sisters, Lucy and Sara: "Much as I love the Union, and much as I am attached to my profession, all will be given up when my state, by its action, shows that such a course [i.e., secession] is necessary and proper."[39]

He kept to his word. On January 19, 1861, Georgia joined not only South Carolina in secession but also Mississippi, Florida, and Alabama (over the next three and a half months, six other states would leave the Union to form the Confederate States of America). On February 27, apparently as soon as he received word of his state's action, the lieutenant submitted his resignation from the U.S. Army. Presumably he felt more than just a twinge of regret in thus violating his pledge to serve at least eight years in a blue uniform. By now, however, more than a few members of the Mounted Rifles, officers and enlisted alike, had made the same wrenching decision. When leaving Fort Craig, Wheeler probably headed east in the company of some of these men.

He could not have said what awaited him at the end of his journey, for he had no knowledge of the actions his brother had taken on his behalf. Even before Joseph petitioned for his release from the army, William Wheeler, a figure of some prominence in his community, had begun to organize a company of light artillerymen that he planned to offer to Georgia's governor, Joseph Emerson Brown. When writing of his intentions to Brown, the elder Wheeler put in a strong word for his brother, emphasizing Joseph's professional education, his service in the Mounted Rifles, his loyalty to Georgia, and his intention to offer his services to the state in any suitable capacity. Evidently William did an effective job of showcasing his sibling's qualifications, for by the time Joseph resigned his commission, Brown had appointed him a lieutenant in Georgia's state forces. On March 6, as Joseph began the long and arduous trip from Fort Craig to his family's home via Fort Smith, Arkansas, William accepted the governor's offer in his brother's behalf.[40]

The War Department did not accept Wheeler's resignation until April 22, eight days after the troops inside Fort Sumter surrendered to the Confederates who had been bombarding them for thirty-four hours straight. By then Joseph was either in Georgia or days away from arriving. By then, too, his appointment in Georgia's state forces had been superseded by a commission tendered him from Montgomery, Alabama, capital of the fledgling Confederate government.

Apparently the Confederate secretary of war, Leroy Pope Walker, had learned of William Wheeler's plans to raise an artillery unit. Connecting this information with word of Joseph's pending return from New Mexico and his desire to help his native region, Walker had appointed the returning Georgian a second lieutenant of artillery in the Confederate Regular Army, an organization designed to parallel the Provisional Army of the Confederate States. The former was conceived of as a wartime force that would remain in existence after the new nation had won its independence. The much larger Provisional Army would play the primary role in defeating any effort by the United States to coerce, overawe, or invade the South; it would disband as soon as peace had been secured.[41]

Why Walker did not offer Wheeler a position in the branch of the service in which he had been trained remains unknown. It may have been a symptom of the organizational changes Montgomery was undergoing. The Confederate government was under pressure to create, as quickly as possible, an army out of whole cloth. Its first job was to secure the manpower needed to defend its territory. When time permitted, it would devote attention to personnel matters, including the assignment process.

In fact, Wheeler's stint in the artillery was relatively brief. Within five months he gained a transfer—to the infantry. By then he was serving in the defenses of Pensacola, Florida, where his duties had included constructing artillery positions from which the local troops could oppose Union warships in Pensacola Bay and the U.S. Army garrison inside neighboring Fort Pickens. The energy and intelligence Wheeler demonstrated in this capacity had brought him to the attention not only of the local commander, Major General Braxton Bragg, but also to visiting officials from Alabama who were seeking an experienced soldier to take command of a leaderless regiment serving locally. With the endorsement of the junior officers of this outfit, Secretary Walker had been persuaded to promote Wheeler to regimental command in the Provisional Army.

Thus it was that on September 4, 1861, the ex-mounted rifleman found himself a colonel in charge of the 19th Alabama Infantry. Wheeler would earn distinction in his new position, but infantry service would not be his final posting. Another nine months would pass before he gained command of a cavalry force. Only then would he find his proper station in the profession of arms.[42]

# TWO

# TROOPERS IN THE MAKING

**T**HERE WAS A REASON WHY THE ARMY OF TENNESSEE—which drew its troops from the region between the Mississippi River and the Appalachians—took its name from a single state. It grew out of the Provisional Army of Tennessee, organized by that state's pro-secessionist governor, Isham Harris, beginning in May 1861, a month before the state voted to leave the Union. Ostensibly formed to defend a state independent of both Union and Confederacy, the provisional army was actually intended as a holding organization for soldiers who would eventually serve in the Confederate ranks. Short weeks after the command began recruiting—a process that continued through the year—the Tennessee legislature, at Harris's urging, offered it for Confederate service. Not until the close of July, however, did the long and cumbersome transition process begin.[1]

Harris's army became the primary source of manpower for Department No. 2, which had been created on July 13 by the new government sitting in Richmond, Virginia. Originally assigned to Major General Leonidas Polk, the department consisted of West Tennessee as well as slices of eastern Arkansas, northeastern Louisiana, northern Mississippi, and northern Alabama. This vast domain, headquartered at Memphis, was bordered on the northwest by the White River and on the northeast by the Tennessee River; its lower portion was split by the Father of Waters. As if it did not encompass enough territory, within two months of its formation the department was extended to embrace the entire states of Tennessee and

Arkansas, as well as the area of military operations inside the hotly contested border state of Missouri.[2]

When General Polk took charge of the Second Department, he effectively superseded Gideon J. Pillow, commander of Harris's provisional army. The transition resulted in Pillow's demotion from major general of Tennessee volunteers to brigadier general in the Confederate service, which dealt a blow to Pillow's pride. Relations between the two commanders immediately became strained, although the extent of Pillow's disgruntlement would not be fully evident for some time. Assigned a division of infantry under Polk, Pillow refused to subordinate himself to the department commander. In fact, he sometimes acted as if equal in rank and authority to Polk.[3]

One reason may have been the seeming incongruity of Polk's assignment to command a military organization of any kind. The fifty-five-year-old native of North Carolina had graduated from West Point in 1827, one class ahead of Confederate President Jefferson Davis, one of Polk's closest friends at the academy. Soon after joining the regular army, the deeply religious Polk resigned his commission to enter the Episcopal ministry. In his new calling, he rose to the position of missionary bishop of the Southwest. Although a committed secessionist, when war approached in 1861, Polk appears to have had no intention of doffing his vestments for a gray uniform. Two months after the fall of Fort Sumter, however, he traveled east from his clerical post in Louisiana to monitor the religious facilities available to the troops from that state then serving in Virginia.

En route to the eastern theater, the bishop stopped in Nashville to confer with Isham Harris. At Harris's request, he carried to Richmond the governor's entreaty that Confederate officials approve the strengthening of several unfinished or unmanned forts recently thrown up in Tennessee and elsewhere in the Mississippi Valley. While in Richmond, Polk visited the Confederate White House and had a cordial reunion with the old friend who inhabited it. The West Point classmates talked not only of religious matters but of military strategy and command personnel. With regard to the defense of the Mississippi, one of the most critical aspects of Confederate war planning, the bishop urged Davis to place in command of the theater which encompassed a long stretch of that river, a West Point comrade of both men, Albert Sidney Johnston.[4]

Johnston was one of the most celebrated Southern-born officers in the Old Army. Most recently commander of U.S. forces on the Pacific Coast,

General Leonidas Polk, CSA, left, and General Albert Sidney Johnston, CSA, right.

he was even better known for having commanded the armed forces of the Texas Republic from 1836, when that province won its independence from Mexico, until 1838, seven years before Texas attained American statehood. After resigning his military post, Johnston entered political life, for two years serving as the republic's secretary of war. The success he had gained in both capacities appeared to recommend him for the highest positions the government in Richmond had to offer.[5]

High station might await Sidney Johnston, but the man had only recently severed ties with the army of his new nation's enemy. Even as Davis and Polk conferred, he was making the same cross-country jaunt that Joe Wheeler had recently completed. Given his embarkation point, Johnston's journey would be even more protracted. Believing he must act quickly to assure Tennesseans and their southern neighbors that they would be protected, Davis surprised Polk by asking him to return to military service. He wished the bishop to fill the command void in the West until Johnston could arrive to supersede him. It took some persuading, but eventually Polk acceded to his friend's request. After running his pastoral mission, he returned to Tennessee, this time in the garb of a Confederate major general. Polk considered the change of raiment a temporary condition. He did not resign his clerical duties but put them on hold until Southern independence was secured.[6]

Clad in gray, the bishop-general arrived in Memphis and took command on July 13. He quickly gained an appreciation of the immense responsibilities that had been laid, however temporarily, at his feet. The front he had been asked to defend was vast. To hold this territory, which included some of the most fertile farming lands in the Confederacy as well as vital manufacturing centers and sources of raw materials critical to the war effort, Polk found at his disposal fewer than twenty thousand troops of all arms, primarily those Isham Harris had recruited.

"All arms" referred to the three combat branches of the nineteenth-century army, but while Harris claimed to have turned over to Confederate authorities twenty-four fully equipped regiments (as well as a few batteries of artillery), twenty-two of those outfits were composed wholly of infantry. This disparity violated a well-regarded axiom that to be truly effective, any army should comprise foot and mounted units at a ratio of seven- or eight-to-one. Given the theater that Polk had to defend, his need for a mobile arm seemed to be even greater than that of most commanders. Two regiments would hardly suffice.

Moreover, Polk found that when Harris's units were sworn into Confederate service, much of their paper strength seemed to vanish. To form outfits of proper size under standard tables of organization, consolidation became necessary. Cavalry as well as infantry units thereby shrank to unacceptable levels. Fortunately for Polk, with the help of Harris and the governors of the other states encompassed in Department No. 2, reinforcements were soon on the way, including a veritable surfeit of horsemen.[7]

They came forth for a variety of reasons. The Tennesseans did so largely because they feared their state would soon come under attack. A member of what would become the 8th Confederate Cavalry, an outfit in the Confederate Regular Army recruited largely in Tennessee, explained that he and his comrades donned battle array "with one common purpose, the defense of altar and fireside." One of those comrades insisted that "when a Southern home is threatened, the spirit of resistance is irrepressible. . . . A God fearing people will never be delivered over to their enemies."[8]

Especially after it became unlikely that Kentucky would provide the upper boundary of the western Confederacy, Governor Harris's constituents realized they were responsible for manning the front line in the struggle to come. Their homes, farms, and business establishments appeared vulnerable to occupation by forces from the Old Northwest—Illinois, Indiana, Ohio—and perhaps also from the Bluegrass State itself should its neutrality prove short-lived and its officials provide entry to blue-coated invaders. Many Kentuckians viewed their political leaders as collaborators and thus anticipated an alliance with the government in Washington. A future officer in the 5th Kentucky, a regiment that would serve under John Morgan, considered invasion inevitable. Thus, if "the Yanks were designed to molest me, my only place of refuge was in the ranks of the Confederate States Army."[9]

Many who flocked to Polk's banner, including those who intended to ride to war, were prompted by regional pride, a desire to protect local political and economic institutions, a hatred of the accursed Yankee, or—in a preponderance of cases—all of the above. Others, much like their Union counterparts, enlisted for entirely different reasons: a restless spirit, a yearning for adventure, a desire to quit the onerous routine of farming and clerking for a life that promised to be interesting, invigorating, and fulfilling. Few Southerners expected their time in uniform to end short of total victory, for most of them held to the cherished belief that their region produced men who were inherently more militaristic, more conversant with weaponry, more responsive to discipline, and more eager to fight for an honorable and just cause than the average Northerner, who was regarded contemptuously as materialistic, complacent, irreligious, and lacking in manly virtue.[10]

While many western recruits were self-motivated—"all afire for a chance to fight," in the words of a member of the 6th Texas Cavalry—others were swept into the ranks through the actions, and especially the oratory and lung power, of their community leaders. An enlisted member of the 4th Alabama, writing years after the war, described a spring 1861 gathering "of old and young" some twenty miles north of his home in Morgan County. The attendees were addressed by a chorus of war enthusiasts, including "a well educated old judge. . . . I can almost see him now giving us one of the hottest war speeches that ever fell from the lips of any man." The orator's harangue, especially his dire comments on "the Yanks and what they would do if we let them come down South," had the desired effect: "About every young man there was soon in line as volunteers. I was third in line." God-fearing youngsters were likewise motivated to enlist by clergymen who gave a religious tone to war fever by equating blue-coated invaders with the locusts that had plagued ancient Egypt.[11]

Family members exercised great influence on their sons' decision to enlist. A recruit in a Montgomery-area company that became part of the 7th Alabama recalled that nearly every comrade "was a boy whose father was a man of wealth and prominence, who wanted to have his son appear as well, if not a little bit better, than anybody else. Therefore the members of this company comprised the very cream of the boys of Montgomery and adjoining Counties."[12]

Yet another potent motivator was the local womenfolk. The most patriotic of these broke off courtships and ended engagements to swains who held back from enlisting. As a member of the 7th Tennessee recalled, the women of his community "threatened to put petticoats on the young fellows who did not enter the ranks promptly."[13]

Having determined to fight, aspiring Confederates had no trouble deciding which branch of the service to join. The color and drama of mounted warfare, which harked back to the days of knights-errant, lived forever in Arthurian legend and in the works of Walter Scott, with whose writings every impressionable son of the South was intimately familiar. Moreover, most Southerners thought of themselves as centaurs—half man, half steed. In part this self-impression was a byproduct of simple necessity. Given the general lack of public transportation throughout the South, especially west of the mountains, the average recruit had learned to ride almost as soon as he toddled. Not surprisingly, Westerners as a class were partial to mounted service. Historian Stephen B. Oates cites a "definite preference for cavalry service among the Texans"—not only those who joined the forces operating in the Trans-Mississippi theater, but also those east of the river: "Every man wanted to join the cavalry and make a lasting impression on young ladies and relatives by riding off to war on a powerful horse as an improvised band played 'The Girl I Left Behind Me' or 'The Yellow Rose of Texas.'"[14]

Besides its claims to chivalry and gentility, fighting on horseback seemed eminently preferable to pounding roads afoot, slogging through seas of mud, and choking on clouds of dust. Those who had gone to war in the infantry quickly appreciated the difference. The Alabama youngster who had been third in line to enlist originally joined a company of foot soldiers whose leader drilled the men to within an inch of their lives. Soon enough, "quite a number of us began to think that to be in the Cavalry service would be much better . . . so, as our Captain did not object, we all went home, mounted ourselves, and soon had a Battalion of well equipped cavalry."[15]

In some quarters, the cavalry was regarded as a haven for those who did not appreciate being shot at with any degree of frequency. A semiliterate foot soldier from Texas advised his brother, who intended to follow him into the ranks, "to go into the cavelry service; they are what we call life-insured companys. Never join the 'weeb foots' ['web-foot,' a derisive term for an infantryman] for . . . I have tried it surficencly to know it hasant paid me. About the time I become skilled in ditching, the Yankeys shot and disabled me, so I shall have to learn some other trade. This thing what they call chargin brest works is not the thing it is cracked up to be. It is very unhealthy. It has ruined our brigade."[16]

Claims made for the cavalry as a more survivable branch of the service had some validity. In battle, horsemen were likely to serve on the periphery of action, more often used to guard their army's flanks and rear rather than committed to headlong assaults alongside infantry comrades. Even when placed in the thick of battle, cavalrymen were less likely to suffer serious injury than their "web-foot" friends. Cavalry could be neutralized just as easily by downing the horse as by shooting the rider—more easily, in fact, since the animal made a much bigger target. Thus, cavalry historically suffered fewer combat losses than infantry units of comparable size.

On the other hand, due to its inherent mobility, cavalry saw more active and arduous service than the other branches. Foot soldiers and artillerists spent much more time in camp than they did on the march or in combat, but horsemen were active on a daily, often an hourly, basis, serving as scouts, pickets (mounted sentinels), couriers, orderlies, escorts for high-ranking officers, and skirmishers. The last-named was, in fact, a dangerous mission. Mounted skirmishers initiated contact with the enemy, advancing on his presumed location and drawing his fire so that foot units coming up from the rear could align their advance and direct their firepower. In performing this duty, horsemen were usually opposed by troops wielding long-range rifles. Cavalrymen traditionally were armed with carbines or rifles with short barrels, both of which lacked the range of infantry weapons. It was on these occasions when the fighting was especially uneven that mounted units suffered the heaviest casualties.

Another disadvantage Rebel cavalrymen faced was the almost constant dearth of remounts. Since Southerners furnished their own horses—in contrast to their adversaries, who were provided with a steady stream of remounts by their well-resourced government—they remained cavalrymen only as long as their mounts survived the rigors of service. If a Confederate trooper lost his horse through wounds, illness, or overwork and could not procure an immediate replacement, he was out of luck. Most troopers, unless personally wealthy, could not afford to purchase a remount, the price of which rose throughout the war even as the value of the Confederate dollar in which they were paid plummeted like a rock in deep water.[17]

To avoid the unenviable fate of the unhorsed trooper—enforced transfer to the infantry—the Confederate had to accompany his unit on campaign, carrying an empty saddle on his back, until able to capture a steed or confiscate one from some helpless farmer. Occasionally the unhorsed trooper could procure a furlough in order to return home and raid the family stable. Understandably, however, commanders were reluctant to permit a soldier fighting in Tennessee or Kentucky to go home to Texas or Louisiana in hopes of returning mounted, an errand that might consume weeks if not months.[18]

Then there was the problem of getting enough forage to keep a cavalry horse healthy. At war's outset, the typical cavalryman of the Confederate Heartland appeared to have greater access to farming lands rich in foodstuffs and horseflesh than his counterpart east of the Appalachians. But as the conflict progressed, the escalating needs of the Confederate armies and the depredations committed by the invading Federals steadily denuded the theater of crops, including oats, wheat, and corn that furnished provender for the cavalry's mounts.

Even when troopers served in areas not yet stripped of resources, inadequate supply and transportation facilities hampered their ability to gain suitable quantities of forage. Writing specifically of Forrest's cavalry, logistics historian Jac Weller observes that "supply was the basic problem of the Confederacy. Before the final defeat, Confederate armies were forced into ineffectiveness by starvation and exposure." He notes however, "that this took place in some parts of the South, whereas there was plenty of food, clothing, and tentage in other sections."[19]

This disparity—added to a general shortage of appropriate weaponry and equipment throughout the West—ensured that Rebel troopers in that theater faced an increasingly uneven fight. The situation was reminiscent of that prevailing in the East. Yet, given the greater scarcity of transportation facilities in the West, including highways, rail lines, and navigable rivers not controlled by the enemy, the disadvantages that plagued Confederates in that region—and especially those assigned to such a resource-dependent arm as the cavalry—were proportionally greater and more difficult to overcome. Only in the wilder, more barren vistas beyond the Mississippi were the burdens shouldered by Confederate cavalrymen more onerous, more widespread, and more contributive to defeat.

THE YOUNGSTERS WHO JOINED THE CAVALRY of what eventually became known as the Army of Tennessee—whether the sons of the landed gentry, or sons of the soil—believed they knew what lay ahead: a life of color, camaraderie, and corporate endeavor with a decidedly masculine air. If by joining the ranks they expected to live in interesting times, they would not be disappointed. But if they envisioned an easy life and a fun-filled experience, they were sadly mistaken and faced severe disillusionment.

One of the first misconceptions to be exploded was that the cavalryman was the master and the horse his humble servant. Would-be troopers used to treating horses as a means of transportation to be cared for only when maintenance was imperative quickly learned that their mounts were the focal point of their existence. Everything that went into the composition of a trooper, to say nothing of his identity as an elite warrior, depended on the well-being of the animal that bore him from camp to duty station and back again.

Recruits learned, often from painful necessity, that before they could attend to their own needs they must first water, feed, groom, and, if conditions permitted, stable their mounts. At all times they must be attuned to their horses' health and fitness; in the absence of such specialists in their units, they must assume the duties of farrier, saddler, and horse doctor. A member of the 4th Tennessee observed that "a good Confederate cavalryman would go hungry himself before he would permit his mount to suffer for necessary food. I have seen him time and again carry in a sack behind his saddle rations of corn hundreds of miles to meet an emergency rather than let his horse go hungry. I have seen him give a hundred dollars [Confederate] for six horseshoe nails and tack on the shoe himself rather than permit his horse to go lame. He and his horse consequently were always ready for active service, and it was this that made him more effective as a soldier than his enemy."[20]

This last comment was a thinly veiled and often voiced criticism of the typical Union trooper. In contrast to the care that most Confederates lavished on their animals, Yankees were suspected of neglecting and abusing the seemingly inexhaustible supply of horses at their disposal. This charge was more often accurate when applied to the bluecoats in the eastern theater, who served in proximity to the remount depots managed by the War Department and, after spring 1863, by its subsidiary organization, the Cavalry Bureau. It is likely that the Union cavalrymen who fought in the West were more conscientious in caring for their mounts. Many served at

Typical western Confederate cavalrymen.

greater distances from their army's remount corrals, and a much larger number furnished their own horses, for whose care and handling they were held personally responsible.

In those few Confederate units whose horses were provided by wealthy benefactors, the men not only had to learn to care for their mounts but to break them to the saddle and train them for service in the field. This could prove a dangerous, even deadly, business. One of the companies in the 8th Texas, a regiment known throughout the army as Terry's Texas Rangers, was furnished with mounts, many of which, as one Ranger recalled, "had never been haltered before. . . . [S]ome of the older ones had been handled some but spoiled in attempting to break them and turned out on the range to go free." Soon after enlisting, this man attempted to procure for a comrade an unbroken mount from a pasture near the company corral. He had no recollection of the events that followed until waking to find his buddy pouring cold water on his head. In answer to a befogged question, the comrade explained that "I had early in the morning gone out in the pasture and had driven up a bunch of horses . . . made a dash at them and had lassoed one of them and being unable to manage the animal I was riding, the lassoed animal made a quick circuit around me, jerked me off on the ground upon my head," knocking him unconscious. Lashed together by the man's lariat, both horses had raced across the pasture, eventually running "on each side of the same tree, bringing on a collision resulting in the death of the one and the fatal wounding of the other."[21]

Some men had the infinitely more difficult task of breaking mules to a saddle. Mules were almost as plentiful in the farming regions of the Heartland as horses, and they constituted a passable substitute when the latter were in short supply. Making a mule behave in a way that facilitated soldiering was never a simple matter, especially when the long-eared critter was unused to being ridden. In addition to being notoriously stubborn, a mule could not be expected to keep up a pace consistent with that of a horse. Yet even in Bedford Forrest's hard-riding command, mules were a popular means of transportation. One teenage mule rider in Forrest's 5th Alabama, who stood well below six feet tall and weighed barely one hundred pounds, was luckier than most of his comrades similarly mounted. He recalled his animal as "a large gentle one, a good traveler." He admitted that "neither the boy nor his equipment would make a formidable looking soldier or inspire terror," but "the mule could travel and the boy could shoot, and either could very nearly find their own rations. These three formed the chief requisites for a soldier in Forrest's Cavalry."[22]

Becoming conversant with the needs and wants of his animal was only one of the demands made of a cavalry recruit. He also had to learn how to manage the limitations of the equipment and weaponry at his disposal. In sharp contrast to his opponent, whose equipage was the finest that government dollars could buy, the average Confederate—again, especially he who served in the West—was more likely to provide his own saddle, harness, and other equipment. More often than not, these articles were homemade. The Alabama muleteer spoke for hundreds of his comrades, whichever beast bore them, when he recalled that "my bridle was made of home tanned fox or coon hides. The bit was made in a shop near by. . . . The saddle, home made also, consisted of two pieces of poplar-shaped [leather] . . . to fit the mule's back as they lay length-ways on her. These were fastened together in fron[t] by a piece of tough oak with rivets made of iron in the shops nearby, the back part was fastened the same way. . . . The saddle had holes mortised, through which a leather strap fastened with a ring and this made the girth. . . . When this was covered with a heavy woolen blanket spun and woven at home by my mother and sister and colored with bark, the soldier, dressed in clothes made the same way by the same loving hands, was ready to mount and be off to war."[23]

Most of the western cavalryman's weaponry also came from home. When the first wave of volunteers reported for service under General Polk, they came armed with every imaginable type of firearm, including antiquated flintlocks, squirrel rifles, and sawed-off shotguns—obsolete or inappropriate arms that could not be considered fully effective in any combat situation. A private in the 4th Tennessee, a regiment he recalled as "the finest fighting machine I ever saw on horseback," nevertheless lamented its original complement of arms, which he called "something pitiful to behold. Nearly the entire command were provided with muzzle-loading, double-barreled shotguns. There were scarcely thirty long-range rifles in the regiment. The shotguns were . . . loaded with buckshot and at short range constituted a most effective weapon, but at a distance of two hundred yards they were worse than useless."[24]

Although many of the early weapons were replaced at the first opportunity, usually through capture, there was rarely any consistency as to types and models of shoulder arms within a regiment or battalion. When the Texas Rangers reported to Polk, the outfit boasted twenty varieties and calibers of rifles. Neither Polk nor any of his successors, nor their chiefs of cavalry, succeeded in standardizing arms or ammunition (just as they failed to standardize the variegated uniforms of the western army beyond persuading the typical soldier to wear at least one item of outer clothing distinctively gray).[25]

Perhaps the most effective effort at standardizing cavalry weaponry was made in late 1863 and early 1864 by Joseph Wheeler, then the major general commanding the cavalry of the Army of Tennessee. Although unable to rearm anything close to his entire command, Wheeler managed to procure enough short-barreled versions of the British-made Enfield rifle, one of the most accurate and reliable shoulder arms of the war, to outfit numerous regiments and battalions. The "Short Enfield," though a single-shot muzzleloader in contrast to the breech-loading arms of the enemy, some of which could fire six or seven rounds at a clip, thus became the closest competitor to the standard-issue carbine of the Union cavalry.[26]

Very few western Confederate units were armed and equipped in such a way as to meet the nineteenth-century definition of cavalry. In the strictest sense, a cavalryman was defined by his weapons: usually a saber, a breech-loading carbine, and a pistol. Cavalry fought cavalry at close range using the saber, while assigning second priority to sidearms—usually .44 or .36 revolvers, the standard caliber of the Colt's Army and Navy model, respectively. The carbine was used in various tactical situations, especially when skirmishing or defending the flanks and rear of the main army. True cavalryman, in other words, fought solely or mainly in the saddle, although as the war progressed, troopers in all theaters showed an increasing tendency to fight afoot when conditions called for it, in the manner of the prewar dragoon.

A preference for cavalry fighting in the classical tradition was mainly limited to the eastern theater. There Union troopers, many of whom had been instructed by veterans of European armies with Old World notions of combat, clashed with the horsemen of Major General James Ewell Brown Stuart, an aspirant to the cavalier tradition and a devotee of the old-fashioned saber charge. In the West, both Union and Confederate horsemen were more properly characterized as dragoons or mounted riflemen. They rode only as far as the scene of battle, where they dismounted to fight behind cover with shoulder arms accurate at greater range than most carbines. While some Rebels eschewed the pistol, others carried two or three holstered or tied to their cartridge belts or saddles. Thus, especially compared to his well-supplied antagonist, the typical Confederate trooper traveled light. Those who were more fully equipped sometimes suffered for it. A member of the Noxubee Troop, a well-heeled militia unit that became a part of the 1st Mississippi, recalled that when he and his comrades first "buckled on our navies and cartridge box and sabres and swung our carbines around our shoulders, sabres to the left and carbines to the right, we kind of felt as though we were weighed down, and it was somewhat difficult to mount into our saddles."[27]

Since they rarely fought at close range, most troopers did not carry sabers. A typical horseman recalled that in his regiment, the 3rd Alabama, swords were "abandoned as useless weapons." In some instances they were replaced with long-bladed Bowie knives, much less frequently with pikes or lances. Edged weapons, especially when used on horseback, could be as dangerous to the cavalryman as to his opponent. Brigadier General Lawrence Sullivan ("Sul") Ross, a well-respected Texan who fought under Forrest and Wheeler, reminded his veterans after the war about one recruit who had whetted his homemade knife, which he intended to use in the mode of a saber, until razor sharp, "and then went out in the woods to practice, and in an attempt to make a grand right and left cut against an imaginary foe, the first whack he made he cut off his horse's right ear, and the next stroke he clipped a chunk out of his left knee, when he immediately dismounted and poked the dangerous thing up a hollow log."[28]

WHETHER MOUNTED ON BLOODED STOCK or plow horses, lightly accou-
tered or borne down by excess equipment, the fledgling troopers of the
Confederate army of the West began their military service in training camp.
In its truest sense, "camp" applied mainly to the better organized companies,
battalions, and regiments, whose leaders had the wherewithal to establish a
well-appointed rendezvous complete with shade trees, an accessible source
of water, well-aligned rows of canvas tents, and a carefully laid-out drill plain
lined with stables or paddocks. Many another unit—perhaps the majority—received their training upon a forlorn expanse of sun-baked earth
pocked with rocks and overgrown with weeds, where the men bivouacked in
the open and hobbled their mounts or tethered them to picket lines.

The time the men could devote to learning the basics of their new profession varied widely. The more fortunate lolled in camp for two months or
longer; those whose presence in the field was deemed an immediate necessity were lucky to get several days or a couple of weeks of intensive training.
However much or little instruction they received, few recruits ever forgot
the experience, their initiation into the life of the lordly cavalier.

The aspect of training that spawned the most vivid memories was the
drill the men underwent on a daily basis. The evolutions of mounted service were many, complicated, and difficult to master, even for experienced
equestrians. One military text published on the eve of the war described
the objective of cavalry instruction thus: "The man should be brought to
manage his horse with ease and address over all kinds of ground and at all
gaits, to swim rivers, to go through certain gymnastic exercises . . . to fire
very frequently at a mark, and to handle his weapon with accuracy and
effect at all gaits, and in all situations."[29]

This was a tall order, but the tactics were designed to enable rider and
horse to act and react as one, perhaps for the first time in the lives of either.
"Tedious and severe" was how one young Georgian described the training
regimen, but there was a purpose to it. Eventually, unstinting repetition
yielded results. Riders and horses learned to form lines and columns, and
to maneuver so as to create appropriate subformations. Initially, the basic
combat formation comprised two lines of horsemen, usually separated by a
few hundred yards, as called for by the tactics manuals of the era. Over
time, however, the single line—which saved manpower, helped reduce the
disorder a two-rank assault could produce, and supposedly generated a
more powerful shock to the opposing force—became the norm in the
Confederate cavalry in all theaters.[30]

The would-be trooper had to master numerous other tactics. He learned to transition from marching column to battle line, to recall and reform lines, to advance as flankers and as skirmishers, to form columns of twos and fours and of platoons, and to wheel right and left in response to given orders, uneven terrain, and obstacles such as fences and plowed fields. And while they learned the drill, the recruits also learned to cue their mounts to advance, halt, back, and perform numerous other evolutions as responsively and precisely as possible.

The men were also taught to handle their weapons from the saddle. A Mississippi bugler described his regiment's weapons drill: "It was first, 'Present Carbines,' shoulder carbines, then drop carbines, draw sabres; present sabres; sheath sabres; draw navies, present navies, belt navies, and so on. . . . We would be drilled in all the forms of drill, mounting and dismounting, maneuvres on horseback, dismount, maneuvre on foot, remount and divide off and fight sham battles, skirmish, charge and receive a charge." Troopers armed with rifles and carbines took as much target practice as their camp's supply of ammunition permitted, while those wielding sabers hacked away at a line of dummies dressed to resemble enemy infantry.[31]

Most of the trainee's time was taken up with mounted gyrations and saber exercise, but a portion of each drill period was devoted to infantry-style operations—i.e., fighting afoot. Although it was much easier to wield weapons, especially shoulder arms, on solid ground than when bobbing about on horseback, dismounted tactics were never popular with the typical Southerner, who, as one of J. E. B. Stuart's troopers famously remarked, "felt he was only half a man when separated from his horse." The centaur mentality was even more firmly embedded in the western army, where dismounted fighting was often regarded as an esoteric art not worth mastering. An adage that became popular as the war went on held that when ordered to fight dismounted, the only happy Confederate was the one in every four detailed to go to the rear with his own horse and those of three comrades. The aphorism exaggerates, but it contains a nugget of truth.[32]

Some units left camp well-versed in the maneuvers and tactics of their arm. Others received relatively little training and suffered for it when going into action. Much depended on the commander's commitment to formal instruction. When he organized the battalion that became his first command, Bedford Forrest was notoriously lax in seeing that his men trained thoroughly and properly, especially on foot. His attitude changed when field campaigning began. Jac Weller points out that early in the war, Forrest "knew little of the proper orders for close maneuvers and didn't realize their value. He was a natural fighter. He learned about drill somewhat slowly, but when finally convinced of its value, he characteristically did more of it than other commanders."[33]

John Hunt Morgan was another who initially overlooked the value of persistent and careful practice. A typical son of the Bluegrass, Morgan believed a trooper needed only to know how to ride and shoot, and how to look after his horse—book learning, especially when the book was a drill manual, had little to offer natural-born horsemen. Added to the general lack of discipline and order that characterized the "alligator riders" who followed Morgan into battle, this lack of formal instruction, while it may not have kept the Kentuckians from being good fighters, prevented them from being highly efficient soldiers.

The same could not be said of the men who served under Wheeler after Fightin' Joe gained his first cavalry command in the summer of 1862. Wheeler, a stickler for drill, not only ensured that his regiments spent hours on the practice field even when in bivouac in the war zone, but also compiled his own instructional manual. He made certain that copies of this text, which adapted long-accepted cavalry tactics to the peculiar needs of mounted riflemen, were issued to and studied by the leaders of every brigade, regiment, and battalion within his command.[34]

While the majority of recruits received their training at the hands of well-versed drillmasters, others were taught by officers whose knowledge of tactics was scarcely more extensive than their own. Lieutenants and captains—and in many cases, majors and colonels—pored over tactics books long into the night to keep one or two lessons ahead of the recruits assigned to them. To some extent this was the result of the practice popular among Confederate forces (and many Union regiments) whereby enlisted men elected their own officers, many of whom were wholly ignorant of the duties and responsibilities thrust upon them.

Sometimes the election process was a foregone conclusion: men of standing in the local community, especially those who had recruited the unit or had furnished it with uniforms, equipment, and tack, gravitated naturally to high rank and position. Many of these men, however, proved too old, too infirm or, more often, too untalented to fulfill their acquired obligations. Historians point out that, given the highly stratified society that defined the South, a greater proportion of those voted into office—

men of education and social standing to whom lesser mortals deferred—
were more deserving of the honor than their Union counterparts, a preponderance of whom were politically connected but militarily inept.

In the western armies, class structure was less rigidly defined than in
those commands east of the mountains. This fact, coupled with a leveling
influence more in evidence in the West, often resulted in the election of
officers marginally better educated and more experienced in military affairs
than those who had voted them into their positions. Even so, a high per-
centage of those who gained commissions were eminently deserving of
their promotions, having acquired a reputation for clarity of thought, firmness of purpose, fair-mindedness, and, most important, leadership.[35]

The election of company-level officers, even highly competent ones,
could serve as an impediment to good order and discipline. Many captains
and lieutenants (some companies had as many as three of the latter)
attained their positions through old-fashioned electioneering, making
stump speeches in camp, pumping hands and slapping backs, passing out
cigars and on occasion the whiskey jug, and making promises that might
prevent them from showing a firm hand toward those who had elected
them. In many cases only passing time—and the replacement of elected
officers with those who had gained promotion on merit—solved this problem bred of mid-nineteenth-century political egalitarianism.

BEING FORCED TO REMAIN IN CAMP AND HAVING tactics drummed into
their heads was an unhappy experience for young men used to the freedom
they had known in civilian life. Tireless repetition on the drill plain bred
fatigue and frustration, and boredom affected every man to some degree. "It
is terribly irksome," wrote an officer in the 8th Texas from the training station at Bowling Green, Kentucky, "to stay in camps day after day with nothing for the men to do but stand guard duty," even though the Rangers were
at least "20 or 25 miles from the Yankees."[36]

Ennui overtook the men even when they were off the practice field. "No
drill today," observed Private Thomas Jefferson Jobe of the 1st Arkansas
Mounted Rifles, writing from his unit's rendezvous near Fort Smith in July
1861. "Everything gets to looking dull when there is nothing to do in camp.
Some of the boys are asleep . . . others are busily engaged [in] doing nothing generally." William Barry of the 2nd Mississippi Battalion complained

that "we have nothing to do but . . . report ourselves night & morning to Hdquarters so they can know that we are about."[37]

Boredom intensified feelings of loneliness and homesickness, natural afflictions for those far from loved ones for the first time in their lives. Family members sometimes saw their sons and brothers off to camp, and the parting often produced what one Texan called "some right affecting scenes . . . in the way of weeping and the wetting of handkerchiefs, etc." Teenage boys suddenly apart from their mothers cried themselves to sleep, although they were careful not to allow comrades to hear their sobs.[38]

Enforced estrangement was especially hard on family men who yearned for the company of wives and children. Passes and furloughs were hard to come by in camp, leaving troopers to pine for the loved ones they had left behind. A Texas trooper informed his wife that "it is not fear that causes me to wish to be at home again; but I would give all I have on earth, but liberty, to hold my darling in my arms once more." When men could not procure a furlough, some asked their wives to visit them, even urging them to find accommodations close to the regimental camp. Typical of the latter was David Purvine of the 1st Mississippi, who begged his wife to visit him at Union City, Tennessee, "and board in the country some where so that I could see you once or twice a week. . . . [I]t would be worth a fortune to be where I could get to see you." Evidently Jane Purvine found this impossible, for less than a month later her husband wrote: "To think that we are only one days travel apart and not get to see each other. I can't stand it."[39]

Boredom and loneliness could not always be avoided, but not every experience in training camp was disagreeable. Some men found they enjoyed roughing it in the field, where they had to fend for themselves for the first time in their lives. They gained gratification from learning new skills, such as preparing rations, and washing and mending clothing. An enlisted man in the 8th Confederate Cavalry informed the folks at home that "camp life agrees with me finely. I never enjoyed better health or endured so many hardships." He explained that "our cook has been sick, and I was installed chief of the culinary department. I had never cooked before except occasionally on a camp hunt. All hands predicted evil of my present assignment but . . . you ought to see what nice biscuit[s] I make, how finely I smother a steak or cook an egg! And when it comes to batter cakes, I find my forte."[40]

Instruction was not continuous, so the men had time to improvise amusements and diversions. Trooper Purvine was able to leave camp almost every evening to hunt for squirrels and birds. Competitive games in camp, including town ball (forerunner of modern-day baseball), generated "some fine fun ... there is a game going on all the time," Purvine recorded. William Barry wrote his sister that his brookside camp afforded good fishing. Almost every day he would "catch a great many very fine ones, wish I could send you some." Games of chance—chiefly poker, but also euchre, keno, bird cage, and brag—were popular diversions, as was the consumption of liquor, whenever it could be surreptitiously procured (regulations prohibited the sale of alcohol to enlisted men, but these were inconsistently enforced, and sometimes unenforced).[41]

Not every recruit indulged in recreational vices. Seventeen-year-old Isaac Dunbar Affleck of Company B, 8th Texas, scion of a strong Christian family, assured his parents that "there is a great deal of gambling in camp, and I have sworn never to touch a card again while I live. . . . As to whiskey or any other kind of drinks they can not be bought not even for medicine." But Affleck did not deny that comrades managed to obtain liquor with some regularity, as a result of which they were not always fit for duty.[42]

Alcohol was more readily available to soldiers in a fixed location such as training camp than it was in the field, thanks to those civilian merchants known as sutlers, who set up shop outside camp grounds and whose most profitable ware was whiskey. Some vendors made no pretense of selling anything except spirituous drink; often their establishments were twenty-four-hour saloons. After elections were held in the 1st Arkansas, Private Jobe noted in his diary that his entire company "went to the bar and drank to our hearts content. Several got too much, I think I was one of them." Given the greater accessibility of liquor, units of all arms experienced a greater incidence of alcoholic consumption and its corollary, drunkenness, during their first weeks in service than they did at any later period of their existence.[43]

Though not always ignited by drunkenness, disciplinary problems plagued many units during their stint in camp. Historians seem to agree that discipline was much weaker in the Army of Tennessee than in Robert E. Lee's Army of Northern Virginia; only the troops who fought beyond the Mississippi displayed less discipline. Larry J. Daniel, chronicler of the common soldier of the Army of Tennessee, observes that "in their various attitudes toward soldiering, the differences in the character of the westerners were more subtle. . . . The western boys, however, had more rough edges, less self-discipline, and fewer of the gentler refinements." Outside observers noticed this difference from an early date. In the spring of 1862, a reporter for the *Richmond Dispatch* visited Corinth, Mississippi, and described the soldiers he met there, especially the cavalrymen, as lacking the discipline and soldierly bearing of the troops he had observed in Virginia. The rank and file of the Army of Tennessee were, in the main, sturdier, coarser, and "less cosmopolized" than those of the newly christened Army of Northern Virginia; the reporter characterized their prevailing attitude as "don't-care-a-damativeness."[44]

That attitude had repercussions for many newly formed units camped in Tennessee, Mississippi, Georgia, and elsewhere in the West. Unless firmly under the control of commanders such as Forrest, they could run amok. Unhappy with their dreary existence, many deserted at the first opportunity, an action facilitated by the mobility afforded by their mounts. Other disgruntled recruits, determined to make visible their grievances, rioted. They overturned tents, vandalized equipment, broke into stables and stampeded the horses, set fire to camp buildings (especially cook shacks, where the fare was scanty, tasteless, or indigestible), and assaulted their officers.

Disciplinary breakdowns could have extreme consequences. During the early days of the regiment's service, enraged enlisted men in the 9th Texas attacked the regimental adjutant, whom they accused of bigamy and an even graver offense: abolitionism. A member of the regiment noted that the latter charge "being pretty strongly proven upon him, the boys en masse took him out & hung him and gave his outfit to a poor boy" in the regiment. It is not known whether the crime was suitably punished, but if it was it provided little deterrence. Only two weeks later, a member of Company D, accused of trying to rape a woman who lived near the unit's camp, suffered the same fate as the adjutant.[45]

Such behavior was the exception, not the norm, but it cannot be denied that training camps were breeding grounds of discontent and insubordination. And yet, looking back, more than a few recruits came to view their instructional period as a precious moment of rest and respite, a pleasant contrast to the arduous and peripatetic existence the regiment led after it began active service. One who viewed things this way was W. F. Mims of the Prattville Dragoons, later Company H of the 3rd Alabama. The Dragoons spent an unusually long period in training camp—ten months on the beach at Pensacola, Florida, a region that in 1861 and early 1862 constituted a backwater of the conflict. Mims, who would rise to captain of his company, fondly recalled his first campsite: "A more beautiful spot could not have been assigned us, in a grove fronting the bay, fanned and tanned by balmy gulf breezes." He had pleasant memories, too, of the life spent there. His unit's "seasoning process, physically and morally developed wonderful surprises. Sickness and even death visited our camp, furloughs and discharges were granted. New members came in to keep up the roll of the company," and life, in general, moved at an acceptable pace.[46]

Not all of Mims's comrades, fed up with the endless routine of training, initially agreed with his assessment. But when the Prattville Dragoons broke camp in February 1862 to report for duty at Corinth, where the service required of them was as harsh and unremitting as the local weather, many of them realized that at Pensacola "we had been living a sweet dream," one they would never recapture.[47]

# THREE

# THE OPENING
# MOVES

S PORADIC, SMALL-SCALE ENGAGEMENTS MARKED Leonidas Polk's tenure as provisional commander of the Second Department, a period characterized by uncertainty and apprehension, plans drawn up but never implemented, operations set in motion and then canceled, and much internal wrangling. Although it is doubtful he would have admitted it, either to himself or anyone else, as a departmental administrator, the good bishop was out of his depth. As Thomas Connelly points out, Polk failed to devote sufficient attention to the most vulnerable section of his realm, the one-hundred-mile stretch between the Mississippi and Tennessee Rivers. Instead he concentrated his manpower inside the forts that guarded the Mississippi, treating his landward defense line as an afterthought. Moreover, he appeared to spend as much time arguing with disgruntled subordinates—especially Gideon Pillow, former commander of Governor Harris's provisional army and now leader of Polk's 1st Division—as he did striving to defend his extended realm with the meager resources at his disposal.[1]

General Pillow was more politician than soldier, but he had led an infantry division in the Mexican-American War (thanks to the patronage of President James K. Polk, Pillow's former law partner), and his modest accomplishments below the Rio Grande had produced delusions of martial prowess. He considered himself a better strategist and tactician than Polk, who had even less experience in active field command, and he believed he had a clearer perception of the military situation in Tennessee and adjoining states. With the backing of Harris and other civilian officials, Pillow managed to talk Polk into approving two campaigns outside the boundaries of Department No. 2. One eventually was aborted; the second was implemented, with potentially disastrous consequences for Confederate strategy in the West.[2]

The first campaign, designed to take place in the summer of 1861, involved an invasion of Missouri, from which the state's pro-Confederate governor, Claiborne Jackson, had been driven after a small but spirited engagement at Boonville. Intensive planning followed, and in late July, Polk sent Pillow's six thousand Tennesseans across the Mississippi to New Madrid, Missouri, there to be reinforced by a small army from Arkansas for an advance against St. Louis. At the eleventh hour, however, Polk suspended the movement and ordered Pillow to remain at New Madrid. The bishop had learned that Governor Jackson had exaggerated the size of the forces available to support Pillow; furthermore, Polk belatedly realized he lacked the authority to campaign in Missouri. Not until September 2 would the government in Richmond expand Department No. 2 to include Arkansas in its entirety and "all military operations in the State of Missouri."[3]

By then the southwestern corner of Missouri had hosted the second-largest land battle of the war to date, one that did not include any of Polk's forces. This engagement, fought near Springfield on August 10, featured dramatic charges by Confederate cavalry and mounted rifle regiments, some of which had a major influence on the outcome. On the west side of Wilson's Creek, forces under Sterling Price, commander of the Missouri State Guard, and Confederate Brigadier General Ben McCulloch defeated a much smaller Union command under Brigadier General Nathaniel Lyon that had taken the offensive to preempt any attack on St. Louis.[4]

The battle, which turned on Lyon's death early in the day, temporarily placed a large swath of Missouri in Confederate hands. At first it appeared that the victory would lead to additional gains elsewhere in the state. David Purvine of the 1st Mississippi, still in training camp in his home state, rejoiced in the news that Lyon's opponents had "cut his army to pieces. If it is so . . . and it is believed to be true, I see a better prospect of peace than has ever been yet." In time, however, Wilson's Creek came to be regarded as a Pyrrhic victory: the Confederates had suffered more than their routed opponents, and neither St. Louis nor the state capital, Jefferson City, fell to Price and McCulloch. Although represented by a star on the Confederate flag, Missouri, the scene of bitter strife for the remainder of the war, much of it in the form of irregular warfare, would never officially sever its ties with the Union.[5]

The campaign that Polk did mount, which took place less than a fortnight before Albert Sidney Johnston arrived at Memphis to assume departmental command, was intended to bring Kentucky into the Confederate fold. Johnston as well as Polk believed an invasion of the Bluegrass would diminish the power and stature of the state legislature by demonstrating its inability to protect residents who supported unionism or neutrality. Despite outward appearances to the contrary, Confederate authorities believed the state contained a sizable pro-secessionist population, the young male portion of which would flock to the Stars and Bars should Rebel troops suddenly appear in its midst. This notion was reinforced by thousands of "orphan" Kentuckians within the Second Department, including John Hunt Morgan and Basil Duke. Nathan Bedford Forrest, who several times had slipped into Kentucky to arm and equip his battalion with the assistance of Confederate sympathizers, also believed that the state could become a permanent source of military, political, and moral support. If an invasion was the best way to ensure this, Forrest believed, then let it be done as expeditiously as possible.

There appeared to be important strategic reasons for occupying Kentucky. Polk had long had his eye on the Mississippi River village of Columbus, thirty miles above the Tennessee border, where a major railroad that could facilitate Confederate movements, the Mobile & Ohio, terminated. He was persistently urged to seize the place by Pillow, who warned that if the Confederacy did not claim Columbus, then Union troops gathering around Cairo, Illinois, at the confluence of the Mississippi and Ohio Rivers, would surely do so.

Kentucky Governor Beriah Magoffin, although widely suspected of pro-Confederate sympathies, warned Polk against any action that would violate his state's neutrality. Pillow, however, kept insisting that a move be made. He persuaded his superior that the forts being erected on the bluffs of the Mississippi (one of which bore Pillow's name) were too lightly defended to withstand attack should Federal forces push south from Columbus to challenge them.[6]

Polk finally acted after learning of the presence of a Union force at Belmont, Missouri, on the river opposite Columbus. Without informing Richmond of his intentions, on September 2 he sent Pillow's division across the border to occupy the railhead. The move produced a political firestorm. While it prompted many Kentuckians to join Pillow's ranks, it tipped the scales against the Confederates. Even citizens who had long supported their state's neutrality applauded the legislature's subsequent move to declare Kentucky's unambiguous support of the Union cause. The invasion also established a new, more precarious Confederate defense line in the West, one that expanded north one day after Columbus's occupation when Union forces under a recently appointed brigadier named Ulysses Grant retaliated by occupying Paducah, thirty-some miles to the northeast.

General Gideon J. Pillow, CSA.

Having invited a counterinvasion, Polk had to worry about enemy troops concentrating along his flanks and possibly in his rear as well, something he had not been concerned about when occupying staunchly pro-Confederate West Tennessee. All in all, the invasion proved a major blunder, the first of many that Confederate commanders in the West would be guilty of over the next four years. In the words of Thomas Connelly, "Leonidas Polk left few achievements as evidence of his summer's work, but did bequeath many problems to his successor."[7]

IN MID-SEPTEMBER, WHEN GENERAL JOHNSTON took charge of the Second Department (which was becoming known, semiofficially, as the "Western Department"), he found his defense force no larger than in previous weeks, but its territorial responsibilities much increased. His domain now comprised all of Tennessee and Arkansas, as well as western Mississippi and the area of military operations inside Kentucky, Missouri, Kansas, and a portion of the Indian Territory (latter-day Oklahoma).

By including the Bluegrass State in Johnston's department, the government in Richmond gave tacit approval to Polk's invasion of Kentucky. Johnston indicated his determination to operate actively in Kentucky by ordering troops into the countryside around Bowling Green and Cumberland Gap. The Bowling Green concentration, which involved some four thousand troops, he initially assigned to Brigadier General Simon Bolivar Buckner, native Kentuckian, West Point graduate, and Mexican War hero, who had demonstrated his Southern loyalties by vehemently rejecting a generalcy in the Union ranks. Soon after Buckner moved to his duty station, he was joined by a contingent from northeastern Arkansas under William J. Hardee, another highly regarded brigadier, author of a manual of infantry tactics favored by drillmasters in both armies. The combined force at Bowling Green, eventually numbering about twenty-five thousand, was styled the Army of Central Kentucky. The older and more experienced Hardee was promoted to major general to command it.

Johnston then turned his attention to Cumberland Gap, the vast gorge athwart the borders of Tennessee, Kentucky, and Virginia that formed the chief passageway through the Central Appalachians. To command the four thousand troops assigned to that sector, he appointed Brigadier General Felix Kirk Zollicoffer, a veteran of the Seminole Wars. Zollicoffer, a newspaper editor who had held several state administrative offices in Tennessee, as well as a seat in the U.S. House of Representatives, was believed to have enough political ability to hold in check the pro-Unionists of East Tennessee. From Cumberland Gap, Zollicoffer's force would protect the right flank of Johnston's defense line, while Hardee and Buckner held its center, and Polk and Pillow anchored its left.[8]

Having made personnel assignments, Johnston set about to obtain additional manpower. He boldly called on Isham Harris, Governor Henry M. Rector of Arkansas, and Governor John J. Pettus of Mississippi to provide his department with fifty thousand reinforcements. Nothing came of Johnston's levy. Pettus, with backing from Richmond, refused to comply, while the troops Rector raised were detailed to local defense. Only the energetic and patriotic Harris worked long and hard to supply Johnston; by year's end he had sent the department commander fifteen thousand more troops. The additions gave Johnston about fifty regiments with which to defend his domain. The commander at New Orleans, in answer to a subsequent call, forwarded a couple of regiments to Polk at Columbus, and in January 1862, the government at Richmond sent Johnston two small infantry brigades from Virginia.

More than this Jefferson Davis was unwilling to give. Preoccupied with a more immediate threat—a massive army training around Washington under the Union's "Young Napoleon," Major General George B. McClellan—Davis and his chief military adviser, Robert E. Lee, viewed

Johnston's operations as a sideshow that merited a finite supply of resources. When Johnston sent an emissary to the Confederate White House in January 1862, to plead for more troops, the president petulantly instructed the officer to "tell my friend, General Johnston, that I can do nothing for him, that he must rely on his own resources."[9]

Those resources may have appeared inadequate in light of what the government expected of Johnston. Still, increasingly they began to resemble a true army, one whose composition included a more equitable distribution of combat arms. The forces of Polk, Hardee, and Zollicoffer each contained cavalry units as well as infantry regiments and artillery batteries, as did the inchoate garrisons on the Mississippi. In the last days of September, John Hunt Morgan's recently enlarged company, the nucleus of the 2nd Kentucky Cavalry, had joined Buckner's forces at Bowling Green, and the following month Bedford Forrest's battalion, which would expand to become the 3rd Tennessee Cavalry, moved northeast of its initial station on the Cumberland River. It took position at Hopkinsville, Kentucky, headquarters of the area commander, Brigadier General Lloyd Tilghman, ready for more active service.[10]

General William J. Hardee, CSA.

Upon their arrival in the war zone, Morgan's and Forrest's troopers were placed on outpost duty. They spent their days scouting toward the positions of those Union forces now flooding into the Kentucky theater of operations. When opportunity arose, they cut off and captured isolated detachments, interrogated prisoners, waylaid supply columns, and wrecked communication lines that facilitated the enemy's advance or withdrawal.

The Kentuckians and Tennesseans quickly discovered that this brand of warfare was to their liking. Ambushing wagon trains, burning bridges, and ripping up railroad track involved risk taking, hard riding, quick thinking, and grace under fire, qualities that appealed to adventurous youth who fancied themselves heroes in the Walter Scott tradition. And by operating well in advance of their nearest supports, dashing through the no-man's land between the armies, they gained a degree of autonomy that their infantry and artillery comrades never knew.

Though attractive, this service had its drawbacks. Although not until April 1862 did the Confederate Congress pass legislation authorizing such units, the troopers under Morgan and Forrest increasingly fit the definition of partisan rangers, engaged in irregular warfare. They remained attached to a conventional military organization and thus were not guerrillas—quasi-soldiers; in reality, freebooters—who fought their own war independent of government sanction and army control. Still, in the eyes of some of their superiors, they were unconventional soldiers. In time, that identity would limit their usefulness to the army of Sidney Johnston and his successors.[11]

Not every superior considered a willingness to operate on the ragged edge of the war a bad thing. Morgan's company was initially attached to the brigade of Colonel Roger W. Hanson, with headquarters on the south bank of the Green River a few miles above Bowling Green. Hanson, a close personal friend of Morgan's, indulged the captain's preference for self-governance and gave him latitude in his choice of missions. Basil Duke recalled that when Morgan's expanded troop reached Green River—the de facto dividing line between Union and Confederate Kentucky—Morgan learned that previous to his coming, Hanson's cavalry had pretty much limited itself to picket duty. This mission, while an important one, was too tame for Morgan: "Altogether devoid of excitement," wrote Duke, it "did not accord with his nature, which demanded the stimulus of adventure."[12]

The daredevil from Lexington continually pushed closer and closer to Federal positions near Elizabethtown. Four or five times a week, he led detachments of his company—sometimes joined by other mounted units under Hanson's command—across the river and into the enemy's rear. Duke noted that most of these excursions consumed twenty-four hours or more. On a few such occasions, Morgan and his men clothed themselves in Union blue, thus adding an aura of espionage to the operation and, by raising the stakes (capture in enemy garb was a hanging offense), heightening the excitement level.[13]

At intervals throughout the summer and autumn, Morgan, sometimes by himself, more often accompanied by a small escort, conducted a variety of operations helpful to his superior. Most were long-distance reconnaissances. Some were designed to capture or kill the leaders of pro-Union guerrilla bands or home-guard units. A few were aimed at seizing supply trains, blocking roads, and burning bridges to stymie movements out of Louisville.

When Morgan rode forth at the head of a detachment large enough to defend itself against most opponents, he would challenge enemy bodies, even those that outnumbered him, head-on. One autumn morning, he and Duke, accompanied by fifteen members of their command as well as some forty Tennesseans who had volunteered for the expedition, left Green River to reconnoiter toward Nolin Creek, halfway between Bowling Green and Louisville. Twelve miles out, Morgan's outriders spied the bayonets of infantrymen topping a rise squarely in their path. Thus far undetected, Morgan, Duke, and the others took to the thickets that lined the sides of the road and began counting muskets. To get a better view, Morgan rode alone to a farmhouse less than two hundred yards from the road. His vantage point enabled him to estimate the enemy force as at least seventy men. He also spied a second column, this of unknown size, advancing some distance behind the first.

Forced to relinquish his perch before the first column came abreast of it, the captain remounted and galloped back to his command. The foot soldiers advanced to within fifty yards of the Rebels' hiding place, when, having detected their enemy's presence, they shuddered to a halt. According to Duke, "Captain Morgan immediately stepped out into the road, fired at and shot the officer riding at the head of the column." The Yankees hastily deployed and unleashed a volley, but it was pitched too high to inflict damage. Morgan's pea-green troopers returned fire just as unsteadily. Duke made light of the result: "The fight was much like a camp-meeting, or an election row."[14]

After ten minutes of ineffective blasting, Morgan, fearing his more numerous foe intended to outflank him, called retreat. Hauling his men out of harm's way, he returned in good order to Green River, his only loss being "one man slightly wounded and several shot through the clothes." The fight may have been, as Duke admitted, "a very insignificant and bloodless" affair, but Morgan's conspicuous daring gained favorable publicity at Hanson's headquarters, helping add to his reputation as a cavalier worthy of the jaunty plume he had begun to wear in his hat.[15]

While Morgan indulged his passion for drama, Forrest, from his station farther west, performed similar feats, but without the props and costumes. One of his first scouting missions, by order of General Tilghman, was a mid-November reconnaissance of the area northwest of Hopkinsville, where Union forces were believed to be operating. Forrest led his scouts as far north as Smithland, on the south bank of the Cumberland River near its confluence with the Ohio. At the local ferry landing, Forrest spied a Union steamer anchored in the river. At his order, his men boarded and seized the steamer, appropriated her cargo, loaded it aboard some captured wagons, and started for Tilghman's headquarters.

Although some vehicles got stuck in the mud of the river bottom and others overturned, strewing captured rations and equipment for miles along the road, enough spoils reached Hopkinsville to give local morale a tremendous boost. Basking in the applause of Tilghman's officers, Forrest's men were, as one of them wrote, "the proudest boys in the army." Morale rose even higher a few days later when a carefully laid ambush set by Forrest nearly resulted in the capture of a Union gunboat in the river outside Canton. Though tied to solid ground, Forrest's raiders had become, for a time at least, kings of the Cumberland.[16]

ALTHOUGH GENERALLY HAPPY WITH THEIR ROLE ON the periphery of regular operations, many of the troopers at Bowling Green and Hopkinsville yearned to see action on a larger scale. The reputation they wished their units to earn could only be won in large-scale, conventional combat that caught the attention of the entire country, especially the Yankee portion thereof. That opportunity eluded them through the first weeks of the fall, although at one point their enemy appeared poised to force a confrontation. In early October, General Buckner at Bowling Green messaged Johnston, who was then at Columbus overseeing the strengthening of Polk's defenses, that the Federals at Louisville under Brigadier Generals Robert Anderson (Fort Sumter's commander during the war's opening act) and William Tecumseh Sherman were advancing with the apparent intention of giving battle. Johnston hastened to Bowling Green and assumed command of Buckner's and Hardee's forces. He advanced them toward the Green River village of Munfordville as if to lash out at any Yankees who ventured within striking distance. Johnston's forces, however, remained committed to the defensive. Aided by skirmishers under Morgan and Forrest, he shifted Hardee's troops about so conspicuously as to persuade his opponents that he was too strong to be attacked, which had been his intention all along.[17]

He need not have worked so hard, for the Yankees entertained no thoughts of taking the offensive: reports of a move on Bowling Green had been erroneous. Sherman, who had taken over the Kentucky command from the aged and unwell Anderson, believed that he, not Johnston, was outnumbered. He felt so threatened by Hardee's and Buckner's presence that he informed the visiting secretary of war, Simon Cameron, that sixty thousand troops (more than three times as many as he had on hand) were required to hold Kentucky, and that two hundred thousand would be needed to drive out the Confederates. Unable to obtain anything close to these numbers, Sherman was verging on a nervous breakdown by mid-November. His shattered health led to his relief and his replacement by an officer of less ability but steadier nerves, Major General Don Carlos Buell.[18]

Soon after Buell assumed command of the so-called Department of the Ohio, his superiors in Washington, including George B. McClellan, the newly installed general-in-chief, began urging him to advance into East Tennessee. Such a move would have strategic value; it would also produce political benefits by giving aid and comfort to the region's large pro-Unionist population. Buell appeared to give serious consideration to the idea, but in fact he considered East Tennessee an objective of secondary importance. Thus he countered the War Department's proposal with a plan for a two-column invasion of Middle Tennessee, one column to move down the Tennessee and Cumberland Rivers by steamers, the other to advance overland against Nashville, the state capital. If his plan were accepted, Buell desired that diversionary operations be launched in Kentucky to threaten Columbus and Bowling Green.

In the end, nothing came of Buell's project. One reason was the commander's obsession with preserving secrecy. As one observer of the war in Kentucky writes, "until he was ready to move, he desired to do nothing to put the enemy on the alert. His brigades and regiments were allowed to remain in apparently objectless dispersion" until the day chosen for the start of his campaign—which he kept to himself. His elaborately concealed design was upset shortly before year's end, when Confederate cavalry began attacking his outposts and communication lines out of Louisville.[19]

One such blow was delivered early in December by a detachment of Colonel William Wirt Adams's Mississippi regiment, which slipped out of Bowling Green, attacked one of Buell's outposts near Russellville, Kentucky, evicted its garrison, and pursued the fugitives for several miles. A more highly publicized strike at the Louisville area was the work of John Morgan and his raiders. Concurrent with the attack on Russellville, Morgan led a scout toward Munfordville and Bacon Creek. En route he pursued a couple of "notorious" guerrilla leaders, though it is unclear from Morgan's report whether he caught them. He made a more dramatic contribution after midnight on December 5 upon reaching the Louisville & Nashville Railroad bridge over Bacon Creek, a few miles north of Munfordville. For some reason, the recently destroyed bridge, which Union fatigue parties were in the process of rebuilding, was guarded only by day. Encountering no opposition, Morgan had the span set afire; within a few hours it was reduced to kindling. Of this mission, Basil Duke writes: "The damage inflicted was trifling, and the delay occasioned [to Yankee supply trains] was of little consequence. The benefit derived from it by Morgan was two-fold—it increased the hardihood of his men in that species of service, and it gave himself still greater confidence in his own tactics."[20]

It accomplished something more. Perturbed by Morgan's depredations, Buell, hoping to deter future attacks, advanced one of his infantry divisions to Munfordville. The head of this force crossed the Green River and mixed with Confederate pickets on the south bank. As the encounter expanded, a detachment of an Indiana infantry regiment, deployed in skirmish lines, tangled with a mounted contingent from Hardee's command. This action has been cited as a rare example of a sustained encounter in open country between foot and mounted units.[21]

The Hoosiers had collided with the mobile element of a one-thousand-five-hundred-man column under Hardee's senior subordinate, Brigadier General Thomas C. Hindman. The Confederates had been moving into position to break the Louisville & Nashville in the vicinity of Woodsonville, John Morgan's old training rendezvous. A few miles south of his objective, Hindman had detached the 8th Texas, under the regiment's commander and co-founder, Colonel Benjamin Franklin Terry, to occupy high ground in advance of the main body. Meanwhile, the rest of Hindman's cavalry, an Arkansas battalion under Major C. W. Phifer, moved north to Green River to protect the Rebel left.

His dispositions complete, Hindman tried to lure the enemy into attacking his main body, which he kept concealed in woods nearly a mile from the river, near Rowlett's Station on the L&N. When the Indiana regiment took the bait and pressed forward, however, the only force in its path was a seventy-five-man detachment of Terry's regiment under Terry himself. Ignoring Hindman's order to remain on the defensive, the impetuous Texans piled into the head of the enemy force, some three hundred strong. The outcome should have been predictable: a mounted assault on a large, coherent body of infantry was sure to be repulsed under almost any imaginable scenario. In this case, however, Terry and his Rangers hit home before their enemy could form hollow squares, the preferred defense against charging horsemen, and the advantage passed to the attackers. One of them recalled proudly that "our Shot guns threw up a blaze of fire & shot almost into their faces—the distance between our lines did not exceed ten or fifteen feet & in some instances the boys did not fire until the muzzles of their guns were within a few inches of the Enemy's heads causing horrible mutilation. Shrieks of their wounded filled the air, still they stubbornly held their position till our guns & Six Shooters were nearly exhausted, and more than half their number were either killed or wounded."[22]

By now many Yankees had begun to run for cover, but they had taken a toll on their assailants. One Hoosier had knocked the forty-year-old Terry out of his saddle, a minie ball in his head. Undeterred, his men pursued their quarry across an open field until a rail fence and, behind it, a brace of cannons, persuaded them to desist. The Rangers re-formed on the flanks of Hindman's infantry, who came up to continue the battle. Within minutes, the Federals broke contact and scrambled across the river. They made a stand on the north side, but they "kept out of our range & the fighting ended after a fight at intervals of about two hours and a half, leaving about 100 Federal[s] killed & 8 prisoners. On our side 4 were killed, one mortally wounded & Eight who will probably recover."[23]

This casualty estimate is open to dispute. Hindman estimated that seventy-five Yankees had been killed and seven taken prisoner, while reporting his own loss as four killed, including Terry, and ten wounded. Yet the brigadier wildly overstated the size of his opposition, believing that several regiments had engaged him throughout the fight. For their part, the Federals reported a loss of eleven killed, twenty-two wounded, and five missing.

As was becoming the standard for after-action reporting, both sides claimed success in this fierce little engagement. Without doubt, the participants who gained the most from it in terms of favorable publicity and enhanced reputation were the officers and men of the 8th Texas, whose ill-conceived but dramatically successful charge became the talk not only of Hindman's brigade but of Hardee's entire division. The Rangers would proudly bear the distinction they had won this day—that of an elite fighting unit—through the rest of the war.[24]

Two weeks after John Morgan burned the bridge over Bacon Creek, Nathan Bedford Forrest and his battalion saw combat for the first time. Their baptism of fire offers the first glimpse of the intensity, the passion, and the ferocity that ever afterward characterized Forrest in battle—qualities that left an equally chilling impression on comrades and opponents.

Early on the morning after Christmas 1861, having spent a frigid but quiet holiday in camp near Hopkinsville, Forrest routed his men out of their bedrolls and ordered them to saddle up. Bidding farewell to his wife and son—Mary Ann and fifteen-year-old Willie were sharing with him the few comforts and many hardships of winter camp—Forrest started northeast at the head of a three-hundred-man scouting force. The mission was the brainchild of Forrest's superior at Hopkinsville, Brigadier General Charles Clark, who wished to fix the position of a Union infantry division under Brigadier General Thomas L. Crittenden, recently reported to be operating near the river villages of Calhoun and Greenville.[25]

Forrest's column, stretched out for a mile on the Greenville Road, maintained a brisk pace despite being drenched by a near-freezing rain. Four miles from base, Forrest split the command, personally leading one wing east toward Rochester while the other, under Major David Kelley, continued toward Greenville.

On the morning of the twenty-eighth, having found Rochester free of the enemy in contradiction of reports, Forrest reversed course. That night he rejoined Kelley's wing, which had been augmented by forty Tennesseans under Lieutenant Colonel James W. Starnes and Captain W. S. McLemore. Forrest learned that the previous day, Kelley had encountered a large force of Federal cavalry near Carrolton and, after a short skirmish that inflicted casualties on both sides, had broken contact and gone into camp outside Greenville. Although Kelley's men were bedding down for the night, Forrest refused to sleep with Yankees running loose in the area. He remounted everyone and started for Calhoun, the last known position of Kelley's opponents.

Thanks to the intelligence-gathering abilities of two of his most enterprising scouts, David Martin and Adam R. Johnson (the latter destined for promotion to brigadier general), the next morning Forrest caught up with the Union force, estimated at five hundred strong. Intending to take it by surprise, Forrest cautioned his men to move quietly into attack positions. They achieved only partial success, for as he later reported, he found it "impossible to suppress jubilant and defiant shouts" from his troopers, who, instead of advancing gingerly, covered the distance to the enemy at a full gallop. Their enthusiasm carried them across muddy fields into the farming village of Sacramento, recently occupied and pillaged by the Yankees.[26]

Numerous inhabitants, alerted by the sound of approaching horses, turned out to shout encouragement as the Tennesseans thundered through Sacramento's only street. One civilian, whom Forrest described as "a beautiful young lady, smiling, with untied tresses floating in the breeze," galloped up to warn him of the nearness of an enemy force larger than Forrest suspected. Impressed by her pluck and daring, in his report of the day's action he credited her with "infusing nerve into my arm and kindling knightly chivalry within my heart." (Of course, such fanciful prose could not have come from the pen of the functionally illiterate Forrest; his reports were composed by well-educated members of his staff, primarily Majors J. P. Strange and Charles W. Anderson.)[27]

A mile beyond Sacramento, the pursuers overtook their quarry. At first the Yankees were uncertain of the identity of the mud-spattered newcomers; believing they might be poorly attired comrades, they hesitated to fire on them. All doubt was dispelled when Forrest, at the head of the column, opened on them with a rifle borrowed from an enlisted man. Almost as one, the cavalry turned and galloped over a hill, at the base of which they tried to form a line of defense. They unleashed a ragged volley as Forrest's pursuers closed to within two hundred yards of their position. Though they inflicted few casualties, the volume of their fire persuaded Forrest that too few men had kept pace with him to make an equal fight of it. He reined in and fell back in company with as many Tennesseans as had heard his shouted order to withdraw.

While not intended as a stratagem, Forrest's pullback encouraged dozens of Yankees to remount and charge him. Before they could break into a gallop, however, the balance of Forrest's force, just now coming up, slammed into them. Many bluecoats were shot out of their saddles, some falling beneath the flailing hooves of their mounts. Those who remained seated shot and hacked away at their opponents.

Hoping to exploit the check given to his enemy, Forrest sent detachments to strike both of their flanks simultaneously. When the Federals began to give ground under the three-directional pounding, he reassembled his main body and had his bugler blow the charge. One trooper recalled that as soon as the spine-tingling notes rang out, "we raised the yell and away we went." They not only propelled the bluecoats into flight but also extricated their commander from a tight spot. Having charged in advance of the main body, Forrest was "about 50 yards ahead of us fighting for his life. I believe there was at least fifty shots fired at him in five minutes." By some miracle none found its target, although one wounded Forrest's mount. Before the Rebel leader broke free of this deadly embrace, he had downed several Yankees through expert use of pistol and saber.[28]

By now the enemy had been reduced to "a panic stricken mass of men and horses," in full flight. Forrest pursued for several miles; many were overtaken and captured. When the race temporarily halted, an animated Forrest joined Kelley, Starnes, and McLemore south of Sacramento. Kelley was amazed by the transformation his superior had undergone: "I could scarcely believe him to be the man I had known for several months. His face flushed till it bore a striking resemblance to a painted warrior's, and his eyes, usually mild in their expression, were blazing with the intense glare of a panther's springing upon its prey. In fact, he looked as little like the Forrest of our mess-table as the storm of December resembles the quiet of June." The change of mien and mood concerned Kelley, a clergyman by profession, who feared that Forrest's combat-inspired passion had left him "almost equally dangerous to friend or foe."[29]

Although the fight appeared over, Forrest was not done. Exchanging his disabled horse for a remount, he rallied his men and returned to the chase. Overtaking the fugitives yet again, he engaged a new band of opponents hand-to-hand, dispatching with pistol and sword all who could not, or would not, run. In the process, he lost a second horse to an enemy bullet— the first of almost thirty that would be shot from under him during the four years of war that lay ahead. By the time Forrest called a final halt, some sixty-five Federals had been killed and thirty-five taken prisoner, at a cost of five Confederate casualties.

Forrest's first battle was over, but his reputation as one of the most desperate fighters on either side of this war had only begun to take shape. General Clark paid official notice to his heroics, describing the fight outside Sacramento as "one of the most brilliant and successful cavalry engagements which the present war has witnessed," one that "gives a favorable omen of what that arm of our service will do in future on a more extended scale."[30]

For some time after the fighting this day, David Kelley and some of his colleagues questioned the psychological well-being of their commander, "as it seemed to some of us, he was too wildly excitable to be capable of judicious command. Later we became aware that excitement neither paralyzed nor misled his magnificent military genius."[31]

Sidney Johnston's forces had avoided a major confrontation in October, but beginning in the first week of November, sizable clashes with the enemy dominated the strategic landscape of the Heartland. These continued over the next three months as Union commanders who had come to view Johnston's static posture as a sign of weakness took the initiative in the theater. They struck first at his left flank, then his right, before hurling a one-two punch at the perimeter that stretched from the Tennessee River to the Cumberland. The cumulative effect was the collapse of the Confederate defense line in the West.

The first engagement took place too far to the west of Morgan's and Forrest's stations to involve them in the proceedings. Early in November, having gained the erroneous impression that Confederates out of Columbus were crossing the Mississippi for the purpose of joining Sterling Price's army in western Missouri, Ulysses Grant decided to move south from his headquarters at Cairo toward Belmont, Missouri. Near that ramshackle village and its adjacent steamboat landing, Leonidas Polk had established a camp of observation and a recruiting rendezvous. None of the soldiers there was going anywhere—certainly not to Price's bailiwick on the far side of the state—and Grant must have known it. His true intention was to threaten Polk's defensive line. He would personally lead the advance on Belmont, while a second column, out of Union-held Paducah under Grant's ranking subordinate, Brigadier General Charles F. Smith, would descend upon Columbus.[32]

Grant and his three-thousand-one-hundred-man force, carried downriver by six transports and escorted by a pair of gunboats, landed a few miles above Belmont on the morning of November 7. Once he detected Grant's coming, Polk ferried four infantry regiments under Pillow across the river to strengthen the camp there, while the Rebel batteries at Columbus fired on Grant's gunboats and, later, the head of Smith's column. Initial success went to Grant, whose troops routed the camp at Belmont and scattered their denizens. In his postaction report, Polk, who later joined Pillow on the Missouri side along with three regiments under Brigadier General Benjamin F. Cheatham, described the first phase of the six-hour battle as "alternations of successes and reverses," during which the fugitives from Belmont were nearly shoved into the river.[33]

Once Cheatham's troops reached the field of battle, Confederate fortunes improved. Absorbing their displaced comrades, the newcomers circled upriver to interpose between Grant's men—many of whom had halted to loot the abandoned camp—and their transports. The upshot was that Grant, after reassembling his untried, undisciplined recruits, was forced to run a gantlet of fire to reach the boats, losing men every step of the way. He managed to get his main body back upriver in time to avoid turning the once-victorious mission—his first combat effort as a general officer—into an unmitigated disaster.

Heartened by Grant's turn of tail, Polk, Pillow, and Cheatham claimed a lopsided victory. They crowed loudly in the congratulatory orders that were circulated throughout the army. The bishop-general did not fail to add his "profound acknowledgment of the overriding providence of Almighty God." Relieved that his army's defense line in the West appeared to remain intact, Jefferson Davis chimed in by tendering Polk his "sincere thanks for the glorious contribution that you have just made to our common cause. Our countrymen must long remember to reward the activity, the skill, the courage, and devotion of the army at Belmont."[34]

The battle had been mostly an infantry and artillery affair, although horsemen had been involved on both sides. Grant's column included two companies of Illinois troopers whose duties included screening the main force from its landing site to Belmont, and, at battle's end, covering their panic-stricken comrades as they scrambled to reembark. Although details remain unclear, one of these companies clashed with the only body of horsemen Polk committed to the fight, a two-company detachment of Lieutenant Colonel John H. Miller's 1st Mississippi Battalion.

By the account of Grant's ranking subordinate at Belmont, Brigadier General John A. McClernand, Miller's men fled pell-mell from the captured camp, only to be routed a second time at river's edge by the Illinoisans of Captain J. J. Dollins. The reports of Miller and his second-in-command, Captain A. J. Bowles, tell a completely different story. From the hour the fight commenced, the squadron at Belmont, under Bowles's command, "held the enemy in check most steadily until time was given to dispose our forces and form the line of battle." When finally pressed back to the river, the squadron retreated in good order: "No men ever fought more bravely or retired more steadily when forced from their position by overwhelming numbers than did many in our lines."[35]

Confederate accounts admit that Bowles's squadron was pummeled by enemy horsemen "outnumbering us two or three to one." Forced into a seam between the river and a dense patch of timber, the Mississippians appeared on the verge of extinction. "Seeing our desperate position," Miller wrote, ". . . I felt that a desperate move alone could extricate my noble little band. I knew they were equal to the emergency, and in desperation I ordered 'Charge,' and 'charge' rang from a hundred voices; the enemy fled in wild confusion, and we were safe."[36]

Obviously, Miller was no slouch when it came to fanciful, self-serving reporting, but his description of the disorderly retreat of Grant's soldiers was essentially accurate. As the war went on and grew ever more fierce, the fighting at Belmont would be remembered as little more than a glorified skirmish productive of only one thousand two hundred casualties evenly divided between attackers and defenders. Still, under the circumstances, the Confederates may be excused for playing up their victory for all its worth.[37]

JOHNSTON, POLK, AND THEIR SUBORDINATES FOUND IT more difficult to massage the results of the battles that involved their troops during the first six weeks of 1862. The string of tactical and strategic defeats had its origin in the efforts of Felix Zollicoffer to launch an offensive in East Tennessee. Only a few weeks after Belmont, the politician-general decided to abandon the line assigned him at Cumberland Gap, whose strategic value he misperceived. Without gaining Johnston's approval, he shifted his little army west in hopes of wresting the initiative from Union forces assembling in his bailiwick under a slow-moving but fiercely determined Virginian, Brigadier General George Henry Thomas.

Zollicoffer's move to Mill Springs, on the south side of the Cumberland between Somerset and Logan's Cross Roads, Kentucky, did not find favor with his superior. Johnston was even more upset when Zollicoffer led his four thousand men (only three-quarters of whom were armed) across the notoriously high-rising river to Beech Grove, within striking distance of Thomas's much larger force. Johnston quickly dispatched a second brigade to Zollicoffer's assistance and placed both under an experienced professional, Major General George B. Crittenden. Yet he could not supply Zollicoffer's command with the arms it desperately needed.[38]

Nor could he prevent Thomas, early in January, from advancing from Lebanon, Kentucky, toward the Rebel left flank in furtherance of the strategy of Don Carlos Buell. Heavy rains slowed Thomas's advance, but by the seventeenth he was in position at Logan's Cross Roads to attack. Forewarned of his advance and unwilling to maintain the defensive, Crittenden, just after midnight on January 19, vacated the earthworks Zollicoffer had built around Beech Grove, and in the murk of early dawn piled into the head of Thomas's column.

The four-hour battle that ensued was fought in a driving rainstorm that made it difficult and at times impossible to tell friend from foe and rendered the flintlock rifles shouldered by many of the Rebels unserviceable. The elements and the boggy terrain limited Crittenden's ability to use his artillery and his half-dozen companies of Tennessee cavalry, led by Lieutenant Colonels B. M. Branner and George McClellan (no relation to the Union's "Young Napoleon") and Captains Willis S. Bledsoe and T. C. Sanders. Crittenden's lengthy casualty list for the day included a depressing number of infantrymen but only a single wounded trooper.

Early in the confused fighting, Felix Zollicoffer strayed inside Union lines and was cut down at close range by an infantry volley. Panicked by his death, his brigade began to dissolve. The confusion spread rapidly to the rest of the army, and the day was lost. Shortly before noon, Crittenden broke contact and returned his serried ranks to the works at Beech Grove. Thomas pursued and the following morning lashed the defenses with artillery. The bombardment drew no response: although the Cumberland was at flood stage, during the night Crittenden had transferred what remained of his command across the river in flatboats attached to a sternwheeler. The evacuation had been as confused as the battle itself: scores of soldiers, afraid of being cut off and captured, drowned while trying to swim to the south bank.[39]

The debacle at Logan's Cross Roads had been preceded by a less highly publicized but equally strategic victory by Union forces operating astride the Kentucky-Virginia border. On January 10, four thousand troops of all arms led by Colonel (later major general and, twenty years hence, president of the United States) James A. Garfield attacked a Confederate force less than half as large under Brigadier General Humphrey Marshall (John Morgan's Mexican War superior) along the forks of Middle Creek near

Prestonburg, Kentucky. In the manner of Crittenden's command, Marshall's lacked a sufficient force of cavalry: four companies all told, two of which were armed with cumbersome and ineffective Belgian-made infantry rifles. Partially because of Marshall's lack of mobile reconnaissance, his right flank, which rested precariously on a ridge above Spurlock's Branch, was taken by surprise. Although the plucky defenders repulsed four Union assaults, the following day Marshall quit the field and withdrew into the mountains of Virginia.[40]

Combined with Garfield's success, Thomas's victory at Logan's Cross Roads appeared to render Union control of Kentucky a *fait accompli*. His right flank unhinged, Johnston feared that a full-scale invasion of East Tennessee was imminent. Such a move would not only force his withdrawal from every section of Kentucky but would give aid and comfort to local Tories who were already harassing Johnston's outposts, rail lines, and supply depots.

But no invasion took place. Thomas's and Garfield's forces had been disorganized by victory just as Crittenden's and Marshall's had been disorganized by defeat; moreover, as General Buell had surmised, the supplies needed to support such an incursion could not be procured in that part of Tennessee, enclosed by mountains, riven by watercourses, and sparse of arable land. But if Thomas and Garfield failed to follow up their success, in the end it did not matter, for Sidney Johnston soon found he had a problem on his hands that dwarfed the prospect of an occupied East Tennessee.[41]

# FOUR

# DEFEAT AND RETREAT

ALTHOUGH GENERAL BUELL DECLINED TO INVADE East Tennessee, the diversionary movements he had requested—barren of short-term success but productive in the long run—had gone forward. Early in the new year, in response to orders from Washington, Major General Henry W. Halleck, the St. Louis-based commander of the Department of the Missouri, set in motion an advance toward Columbus to make Johnston, Polk, and Pillow worry anew for the safety of the Confederate left. Command of the operation fell to Grant, who following the near-calamity at Belmont had returned to his old post at Cairo. On January 10, he commenced a two-column invasion of Kentucky.

The wing Grant accompanied, five thousand two hundred strong, although hampered by extreme weather, roads alternately frozen and swimming in mud, and rain-swollen streams, advanced to within striking distance of Columbus—a distance of nearly one hundred miles—before turning around and countermarching to Cairo. Once back at district headquarters, Grant wrote to a family member about "the great expedition into Kentucky." He explained that "my orders were such and the force with me also so small that no attack was allowable. I made good use of the time however, making a splendid reconnaissance of the country over which an army may have to move."[1]

Grant paid special attention to the experience of the more easterly column, two brigades led by Charles Smith, which had moved down the

Tennessee River from Paducah to Callaway, Tennessee, and back. The chief object of this reconnaissance-in-force, which was supported by a gunboat and a paddle-wheel steamer, was Fort Henry on the Tennessee. Smith described the work as "strongly built, and I believe well garrisoned," but not impregnable. Even more vulnerable was the subgarrison at Fort Heiman, on the west bank opposite Henry, which appeared to be half-complete. Smith personally accompanied the captain of the gunboat as the vessel reconnoitered and then shelled Fort Henry. Unhampered by return fire, Smith got a good look at the fort's exterior defenses. After careful study and calculation, the brigadier returned to his column and sent it on to Paducah. He himself repaired to Cairo, where he reported his findings to Grant.[2]

The commander of the district that included Fort Henry, General Tilghman, was not sure what to make of Smith's operation, especially since no ground attack had been launched. For much of the time that Smith was in the area, Tilghman was holed up at Fort Donelson on the Cumberland, twelve miles east of Henry; thus he had an imperfect understanding of what was transpiring on the Tennessee. He was left to wonder if the movement presaged a strike against the railroad that crossed the river twenty miles below Henry.

On the twenty-third, when Smith started back to Paducah, Tilghman, whose available force was clearly dwarfed by the Federals, followed at a prudent distance. Tilghman described the pursuit force as consisting of almost one thousand cavalrymen plus some infantry and artillery (he identified only one mounted unit, the Tennessee company of Captain Henry Milner). The Rebels got no closer than eleven miles from Paducah before returning to Fort Henry, leaving Tilghman in the dark as to Smith's intentions. For his part, when it was reported to him, Sidney Johnston saw nothing in the raid to cause alarm. Tilghman was not so sure.[3]

The brigadier's concern was not misplaced. After debriefing Smith, Grant decided that Fort Henry was vulnerable on both its land and river sides. He suspected that the larger, more heavily defended Fort Donelson was similarly vulnerable, and he determined to capture both works. With the grudging permission of his superior, Halleck, on February 2 Grant sailed up (i.e., south along) the Tennessee at the head of seventeen thousand troops, their transports convoyed by a fleet of gunboats under Flag Officer Andrew Hull Foote.

Tilghman's worst fears were realized when, on the third, he learned that Grant was at Smithland, Kentucky, and heading his way. The following day

Fort Henry, now inundated by the rain-swollen Tennessee, came under sporadic fire from Foote's heavily armed ships. Then Tilghman, who had assumed command of the garrison, witnessed the landing of five troopships. Hastily he concentrated all available troops, including the fatigue parties that had been laboring on Fort Heiman, while petitioning his superior, Polk, for reinforcements. But the bishop-general, preoccupied with the defense of his post at Columbus, had no troops to spare.[4]

The upshot was predictable enough, although the fatal blow to Tilghman's garrison was delivered not by Grant's forces but by Foote's gunboats. The fort's twelve cannons were no match for the more numerous and longer-range guns of the navy. Within two hours of opening fire, Foote's seamen had beaten down the fort's defenses, ripping apart its parapets and disabling two of its pieces.

Seeing the hopelessness of his situation, Tilghman ordered an evacuation to save as many of his two thousand six hundred men as possible. Screened by cavalry, including elements of the 1st Mississippi and 4th Alabama, the garrison made its way safely along the muddy road to Fort Donelson. Its commander remained behind through a sense of honor and was taken prisoner minutes after he raised a surrender flag. By now the water inside the fort was waist deep; one of Tilghman's aides claimed that "if the attack had been delayed forty-eight hours, there would hardly have been a hostile shot fired; the Tennessee would have accomplished the work by drowning the [powder] magazine."[5]

When Fort Henry's escapees reached the larger, better defended work on the Cumberland, they came under Gideon Pillow, whose division Johnston had dispatched there from Clarksville in hopes of holding the fort as long as possible. In common with virtually every Confederate in Middle Tennessee, Johnston doubted that Grant's offensive would cease after Henry's fall. Soon Pillow was augmented by the Kentuckians of Simon Buckner, hastily transferred from Bowling Green and Russellville.[6]

The concentration at Donelson swept up other forces as well, including miscellaneous mounted units. These did not include John Morgan and his raiders, who after burning the Bacon Creek bridge had been wintering at Bell's Tavern, twenty-five miles east of Bowling Green. The alligator riders had spent the past weeks, as they had their first three months in service, scouting, capturing pickets, running down guerrillas, and striking miscellaneous targets of opportunity. These were essential missions, but, as Basil Duke commented, they would appear "greatly inferior in dash and execution to the subsequent cavalry operations of the West." Still, they "served to educate Morgan's men and Morgan himself for the successful conduct of more daring and far more important enterprises."[7]

Morgan's men remained in winter quarters until February 14, when Johnston decided to evacuate the Bowling Green area to avoid being outflanked by his larger and better supplied enemy. The withdrawal was the outcome of a council of war involving Johnston, Hardee, and Johnston's newest subordinate, General Beauregard. Of the three, only Beauregard, a Louisiana Creole whom the Southern public regarded as the hero of Fort Sumter and Manassas, argued that a stand should be made not at Nashville but at Fort Donelson. As a recent transferee from the East, Beauregard, although egotistical, strongly opinionated, and sometimes overbearing, deferred to the shared opinion of his new colleagues. In the end they agreed on a more cautious course. Grant's invasion and the threat posed by Buell's army sparked a consensus that Hardee's force should be withdrawn to Nashville, while most of the troops at Columbus, whom Johnston had assigned to Beauregard, should be evacuated to Humboldt and Jackson, Tennessee, via the Mobile & Ohio Railroad. Donelson's garrison—less than half the size of the force moving to attack it—would thus be left on its own. It is difficult to determine whether Johnston truly believed the fort would hold out against Grant. Some of his statements appear to indicate that the garrison's fall was inevitable. Other comments suggest that Johnston would have been shocked to learn of its capture or surrender.[8]

Mounted units other than Morgan's could not avoid transfer to Fort Donelson. In the first week of February, General Clark ordered Forrest's battalion to bolster the garrison on the Cumberland. Forrest dutifully left Hopkinsville, heading southwest. On the tenth he crossed the river, and the following day entered the fort. Pillow welcomed him, but was not as hospitable toward a visitor who arrived on the evening of the twelfth. This was John B. Floyd, a more senior brigadier, to whom Pillow surrendered command of Donelson. Floyd and his brigade of Virginia infantry had been transferred from Cumberland City, almost twenty miles to the south.

Floyd may well have considered his posting a suicide mission. He was a politician, not a soldier, having served as governor of Virginia and later as James Buchanan's secretary of war. Johnston's choice of Floyd to command was hardly a statement that Donelson would resist Grant to the bitter end. In fact, Johnston, having studied reports of Fort Henry's precipitate demise, had begun to doubt Donelson's ability to survive an all-out assault, especially one mounted on land. A sprawling earthwork whose extended defenses enclosed the village of Dover, Donelson had been constructed primarily to withstand a naval assault; most of its heavy guns—thirteen in all—were aimed at the river. To the south and southeast, where a ground attack would come from, the garrison was undefended except for a semicircular line of entrenchments. If Johnston's initial idea was wrong and Donelson proved to be vulnerable, he expected Floyd, Pillow, and Buckner to make a token defense, upholding the garrison's morale, and then evacuate by forced marches to Nashville, there to join him for a decisive effort against Grant and/or Buell.[9]

The rains that had placed Henry under water had turned the road to Donelson into a lagoon. Not until the eleventh was the ground sufficiently dry to permit Grant to advance to the Cumberland. Thanks to Johnston's decision to forgo a confrontation short of his enemy's objective, the movement went uncontested. By the fourteenth, Grant was in position to attack or besiege Floyd's work.

The navy opened the ball early on the fourteenth, pounding the fort on its river side. But the success that Foote had enjoyed the previous week deserted him; Donelson's batteries struck several of his gunboats, disabling three, including his flagship. All had ventured too close to their target for comfort. Failing to make headway, the flag officer hauled his fleet out of range, giving Grant's troops the opportunity to force a surrender.[10]

When Grant withheld a general attack, his conservatism permitted Donelson's troops to attempt a breakout. On the morning of February 15, Floyd sent Pillow to attack the left and center of the siege lines. Initially the sortie appeared a success; it forced McClernand's division to recoil and fall back, momentarily opening a path to Nashville. Then, thanks largely to Pillow's ineptitude, the movement lost momentum. It guttered out when Grant shored up the unhinged flank and launched a vigorous assault against the other end of the line. By sundown, those Confederates who had not been shot down trying to carve out an escape route were back in their trenches, cold, hungry, and exhausted. Donelson's fate had been sealed.[11]

That night Floyd and Pillow, unable to determine how to proceed, called a series of war councils. At first both generals opted for a renewed breakout effort, but Simon Buckner, who although third in command was

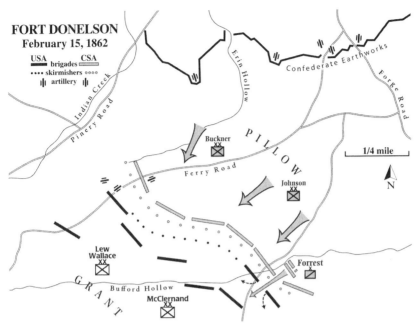

Fort Donelson, February 15, 1862.

the only real soldier in the group, argued persuasively that the men were in no shape to attack. Considering the situation hopeless, especially in light of reports that reinforcements had reached or were about to reach Grant, Floyd and Pillow decided to evacuate—themselves. As secretary of war, Floyd had been criticized throughout the North for transferring munitions to arsenals in states on the brink of seceding—an act of treason that he feared carried the death penalty. Now, to avoid capture and punishment, before dawn Floyd escaped by boat to the east side of the Cumberland. He was preceded by Pillow, who, deluded to the last, considered himself too valuable a resource to be lost to the Confederacy. The departing commanders left Buckner to surrender the garrison to Grant, whom the Kentuckian had known at West Point and with whom he had served in the prewar army.[12]

Like Floyd and Pillow, Buckner's cavalry could not abide the thought of surrendering. Unlike their infantry comrades, they had at their disposal the means to avoid it. Moreover, they had not been fought out, although they had seen spirited combat over the past several days.

One day after reporting to Pillow, Forrest had been ordered to reconnoiter toward Fort Henry with a three-hundred-man detachment of his battalion. About three miles west of Donelson, he encountered a body of cavalry that he estimated as twice the size of his own. Forrest nevertheless pitched into the enemy, inflicting numerous casualties. Soon he had the Yankees on the run. He chased them for six miles before returning to Donelson with prisoners in tow.[13]

That night, after hearing Forrest's report of operations, Pillow named him to command every trooper in and around the fort, including several battalions and companies from Kentucky and Tennessee. The next morning, Forrest led one of these battalions and three separate companies, in addition to his own command, on the road to Fort Henry. Two miles out, he met the head of an enemy force of all arms, which he initially propelled into retreat. Eventually, the Yankees halted, threw out skirmishers, and began maneuvering along a road parallel to Forrest's.

Forrest quickly blocked that route with two squadrons (four companies) of mounted riflemen. As he reported, when the cavalry in the Union vanguard neared his position, "I again attacked them vigorously." For a time the contest was an even fight, but soon the enemy's numbers began to tell, threatening part of Forrest's force on all sides. At Forrest's command, Major Kelley charged at the head of three squadrons, taking the Yankees in flank. Though Kelley drew shells as well as carbine and rifle fire, he managed to extricate the embattled detachment before it suffered major loss. Discovering that the force opposing him was even larger than he had estimated, Forrest by early afternoon was falling back slowly and in good order. En route, a courier from Buckner reached him with instructions to withdraw to the fort.[14]

Once they were back at Donelson, General Floyd ordered Forrest's troopers to dismount and join their infantry comrades in improving the trenches that constituted the only land defense of consequence. They were still laboring when, on the morning of the thirteenth, Foote's gunboats launched a preliminary attack on the river face. As Forrest (or, rather, Major Strange) wrote, "our intrenchments were vigorously attacked at all points, and for six hours there was scarcely a cessation of small-arms and artillery." But then the navy retreated, permitting Grant's artillery to continue the contest. Donelson's guns replied; the combined barrage did not cease until well after dark.

On the fourteenth, when Foote attacked in force only to be repulsed, Forrest's men saw limited action thanks to confusing orders. Ordered out of the trenches to probe Grant's lines, the troopers were mysteriously recalled soon afterward. By order of General Pillow, two of Forrest's companies spent the balance of the day dismounted, acting as sharpshooters. Their well-directed fire dislodged snipers from ridges and trees overlooking Donelson's rifle pits. Forrest himself joined in the countersniping; borrowing a rifle from an enlisted man, he sighted, squeezed the trigger, and brought down a Yankee who, from a treetop, had been "annoying" the entrenched infantry.[15]

General Simon Bolivar Buckner, CSA.

That night Floyd, Pillow, and Buckner thrashed out plans for a breakout. In tribute to Forrest's well-earned reputation as a fighter, he was chosen to spearhead the movement. He and his men gave a strong account of themselves even if, in the end, it went for naught.

The attack began in the predawn darkness of the fifteenth with Forrest guiding Pillow's troops against the Union right. At the start, the operation went well, driving a wedge through McClernand's lines. Forrest pressed ahead with such vigor that his men soon outdistanced their comrades afoot. Although isolated from support and increasingly vulnerable, he refused to withdraw as long as Yankees gave way before him.

When the fog and mist of that winter morning dissipated to reveal a battery of six guns in his path, Forrest did not hesitate. Tactics manuals cautioned cavalry against attacking any body of infantry unless it was demoralized, fragmented, or in retreat—Forrest had already violated that rubric. Artillery was considered a much more formidable target; a mounted charge against a well-manned battery was almost certain to fail bloodily. But not today, not for Forrest. Supported in rear by infantry comrades, he spurred forward, and his men followed at an extended gallop. They reached the battery before its guns could be wheeled into position to fire on them. With pistol and sword, the attackers killed every battery horse and almost every cannoneer. All six of the unit's pieces were soon in Forrest's hands. The Tennesseans paid a price for their improbable success: several men were felled by the battery's infantry supports, and both Bedford and his brother Jeffrey had their horses shot from beneath them. This was the first of three mounts the battalion commander would lose today.

Forrest, shaken but unhurt, wanted more spoils. In a sense, he got them. Over the next three hours, his command dispersed one body of Federals after another. Each tried gamely to make a stand but was ridden over by horsemen hell bent on annihilating their enemy. At one point Forrest dismounted dozens of his men, advanced on an occupied ravine, fired into it, and left two hundred infantrymen dead or wounded. Before Forrest could remount his skirmishers, he discovered that another artillery unit was going into position to rake his flank. "I now ordered a charge on this battery," he wrote, "from which we drove the enemy, capturing two guns. Following down the ravine [we] captured the third, which they were endeavoring to carry off, gunners and drivers retreating up the hill. In this charge I killed about 50 sharpshooters, who were supporting the guns."[16]

Forrest's furious, extended offensive ended in midafternoon, when he was ordered back to Donelson. Considering the inroads Pillow and Buckner had made on many parts of the field, the recall puzzled and troubled the cavalry commander. He was openly incredulous when he learned that Pillow had called off the attack and withdrawn the army to the entrenchments it had evacuated before dawn. Supposing that his superior intended to renew the fight come morning, Forrest bedded down his men, but only after they had removed their wounded and collected abandoned weapons.

Forrest turned in before midnight, but just short of two a.m. he was awakened by a staff officer requesting his presence at yet another war council. If Forrest had been confused by his recall from inside McClernand's lines, he was dumbfounded by the decisions reached at this conference. The thought of surrender made him almost physically ill, and when he learned that Floyd and Pillow intended to flee the trap their inept leadership had created, Forrest considered escaping with his entire force. He sent three of his best scouts upriver to determine if the enemy had reoccupied his original positions, as Floyd and Pillow feared, and to certify that the roads leading south, all of which were under water at some point, were passable. Presently, the scouts returned with good news. One of them, a trooper of the 4th Alabama, reported that upon hitting the water they had ridden "far enough into it to see that we could ford it." En route, they had passed few enemy campsites, all of them deserted.[17]

This was all Forrest needed to hear. Returning to garrison headquarters, he found Floyd and Pillow on the verge of decamping. With sparks flashing in his gray eyes, "I told them that I neither could nor would surrender my command." He added that if his men followed him, "I intended to go out if I saved but one man."[18]

Pillow, impressed with his subordinate's determination, urged him to go ahead; Floyd did not attempt to dissuade him. Minutes later, both generals got into the boats that would carry them to safety. The subordinate they left behind was likewise supportive of Forrest's decision, although he rejected the latter's suggestion that he evacuate the infantry and artillery under cover of the cavalry's breakout. Buckner was certain that such an attempt would result in the loss of three-quarters of the garrison.

While his superior commenced preparations for surrendering the post, Forrest got his slumbering troopers back on their feet and into the saddle. In the frigid darkness of morning, he led a long column—his own battalion plus two hundred troopers from other units, and some mounted artillerymen—down the rain-sodden road to Dover and, beyond, Clarksville. They moved as stealthily as possible, horse equipments muffled by blankets or handheld to minimize clanking and jingling.

Forrest's only hindrance was the river road, sections of which were under several feet of water. A mile out of Donelson, the column sloshed through a particularly deep slough formed by the Cumberland's overflow. The freezing water, which in places rose to the height of the men's saddle skirts, took a toll on legs and feet, and the bone-numbing weather left several lightly clad troopers frostbitten. Forrest later surmised that had Buckner followed him, "the infantry could not have passed through the water and have survived it."[19]

It took two hours to clear the estimated position of the closest Union camps. In the event his passage was detected, Forrest left Major Kelley and one of the battalion's staff officers, along with a single company, to guard the rear. The precaution proved unnecessary; by dawn of the sixteenth, shortly before Buckner relinquished his sword to his West Point comrade, five hundred cavalrymen and mounted riflemen had outflanked Ulysses Grant's siege lines. "More than two hours had been occupied in passing," wrote Forrest. "Not a gun had been fired at us. Not an enemy had been seen or heard."[20]

Once beyond danger, Forrest accelerated the southward jaunt, reaching Nashville on the morning of the eighteenth. In the Tennessee capital he met the fugitive General Floyd, to whom he reported. Forrest and his men, until then exhilarated by their daring escape under the noses of their enemy, were heartsick to find Nashville in the throes of evacuation. Reacting to Donelson's fall and the city's imminent occupation by Grant or Buell, General Johnston had determined to withdraw all under his authority out of harm's reach, even if it meant abandoning Tennessee.

Forrest had no time to question the propriety of the order, for Floyd had placed him in charge of overseeing Nashville's evacuation. Then the peripatetic Floyd fled the city. His habit of evading responsibility, however, would catch up with him. Within a month he would be relieved of duty, a casualty not so much of Donelson's loss as of the moral infirmity he had repeatedly displayed.[21]

THE DISASTER ON THE CUMBERLAND SHOCKED, angered, and demoralized soldiers and civilians throughout the Confederacy. As Basil Duke later observed, "no subsequent reverse, although fraught with far more real calamity, ever created the shame, sorrow, and wild consternation which swept over the South with the news of the surrender of Donelson." That news, which came hard on the heels of a well-publicized prediction of victory by Floyd (delivered only hours before he fled his post), struck the citizens of Nashville especially hard. Duke was astounded by "the gloom which hung over Nashville when the troops entered. It is impossible to describe the scene."[22]

Suspecting that the army was soon to depart and leave them to the mercy of the invader, Nashville's people verged on panic. Hundreds prepared to flee in the soldiers' wake, packing their belongings in conveyances in preparation for a new life as refugees. Lawlessness broke out in many sections of the city, forcing those engaged in policing the streets, including Forrest's and Morgan's troopers, to combat vandalism and arrest looters. While black residents prepared to welcome the Yankees as liberators, fearful and angry whites shook their fists at the passing troops and cursed their commander. They were reacting not only to the defeats Johnston's command had suffered over the past month and a half. They felt duped by the commander's many public pronouncements that Kentucky and Tennessee were too well protected to suffer invasion. It had become shockingly evident that

Johnston's troops were too few, too badly positioned, and too poorly led to protect anyone, including themselves.

The army's reaction to its recent reversal of fortune and its suddenly clouded future was mixed. Some soldiers remained optimistic, choosing to regard their current plight as aberrant and temporary. One of these, an officer in Terry's Texas Rangers, wrote to his wife from his newly assumed position in Middle Tennessee: "I am afraid we have lost Kentucky and this state for the present," although "God will help us" recover the lost territory. The majority of the rank and file, however, had been mired in gloom when they followed Johnston to Nashville and then farther south. Discontent seemed to grow with each passing mile. Soon it seemed as if everyone in gray was damning Albert Sidney Johnston as a fool and a coward, and cursing himself for having followed the man's banner.[23]

The censure directed at the once-stalwart Kentuckian spread far and wide quickly. Within days of Fort Donelson's fall, editors across the South were denouncing Johnston, while political officials were complaining that his reputation had been grossly inflated. The Tennessee legislature, furious at the prospect of being driven from its state, demanded Johnston's head, calling him "not a general" in the true sense. Influential citizens petitioned Jefferson Davis for his ouster, arguing that only a change of leaders could cure the army's demoralization and stem the flurry of desertions that had begun to deplete it. Some critics begged Davis, a hero of the Mexican War who considered himself more soldier than politician, to personally replace Johnston. Others pleaded that Johnston be removed in favor of commanders in whom the public had greater confidence, such as Beauregard and Hardee. Then came a wave of personal attacks, including the charge that when Donelson fell, Johnston was not only absent but also drunk.[24]

Morgan and Forrest reacted differently to their army's disgruntlement. Although Morgan did not share the prevailing opinion that his commander was solely to blame for the army's reverses, and though he considered complaining of this nature not only demoralizing but also unseemly, he closed his ears to the clamor around him. Morgan's refusal to curb his men's anger and bitterness was an example of his inability or unwillingness to enforce corporate discipline. It was as if he feared the loss of his men's favor should he try to muzzle them, especially when their discontent had a basis in fact.

Forrest, on the other hand, refused to allow his Tennesseans to carp and complain; he kept them so active and occupied both in Louisville and afterward that they had little time to voice their grievances. While at Nashville, he set the men to policing the streets, breaking up clots of unruly citizens, guarding property liable to be stolen or vandalized, and putting out fires wantonly set. He also had his troopers haul off the contents of military warehouses, too often the targets of pillagers. Commandeering every vehicle that would serve the purpose, he saw to it that tons of materiel, critical to the sustenance of Johnston's army, were carted to the rail depot and shipped in box and flat cars down the Nashville & Chattanooga Railroad toward Stevenson, Alabama, the retreat route of Johnston's main column. Any supplies that could not be carried off were either destroyed or judiciously distributed among the citizenry.[25]

On February 25, with Buell's appearance on the north bank of the Cumberland imminent, Forrest massed his battalion and led it south to Murfreesboro in the role of rear guard for the already departed main body. Other units had been assigned Forrest for this mission, including Morgan's Kentuckians. This marked the first time the two celebrated horsemen had served side by side, and the first time Morgan had been subordinated to his older colleague. The alliance lasted one day; on the twenty-sixth, Morgan was detached from Forrest and assigned to John C. Breckinridge, the former politician who had helped Morgan avert a shootout in Lexington the previous summer and who, although yet to don a uniform, was now a major general commanding an infantry division. To give Morgan's force staying power, Forrest detached a portion of his battalion and assigned it temporarily to the Kentuckian.[26]

When the army reached Murfreesboro, thirty miles south of Nashville, Johnston kept it in bivouac for a week. There he was joined by what remained of the command that had been routed at Logan's Cross Roads. The layover and the manpower addition raised hopes that the withdrawal was over. But Johnston departed Murfreesboro on the twenty-eighth, heading southwest.

The prospect of a longer retreat only deepened the truculent mood of the rank and file, but there was no help for it. Screened not only by Forrest but by a second battalion of Tennesseans under Lieutenant Colonel F. N. McNairy, as well as by Wirt Adams's Mississippians; the 8th Texas under Benjamin Terry's successor, John Austin Wharton; Colonel John S. Scott's 1st Louisiana; and Colonel Ben Hardin Helm's 1st Kentucky, Johnston guided his column to Shelbyville, Tennessee, then to Decatur, Alabama, across the Tennessee River, and, after turning west through Courtland and

Tuscumbia, into Mississippi. This route not only placed a major river between the army and any pursuers but enabled it to draw from a secure supply line that linked it to fertile regions of the Deep South.[27]

After fording the Tennessee, Forrest received permission to take his battalion to Huntsville on the Decatur & Charleston Railroad. Under orders to refit and reorganize, as soon as he reached Huntsville he gave his men a two-week furlough, confident they would be on hand when recalled March 10. His trust was not misplaced; John Allan Wyeth notes that "without exception the men reported back on the date given, newly clad and fitted out for the rough and trying campaign which they well knew was in store for them." Many returnees brought relatives and friends who hungered to fight under Forrest. Enough recruits reported at Huntsville to swell his command to eleven companies, the size of a full-fledged regiment. One of the new components had been formed by another of Forrest's brothers. In the elections that followed the transformation of the command, Jesse Forrest was voted captain of this unit, while Bedford, to no one's surprise, was promoted to colonel to command the regiment known as the 3rd Tennessee Cavalry.[28]

While Forrest enjoyed a timeout from active operations, Morgan set up shop at Murfreesboro and nearby La Vergne, where he served in various capacities for his new superior. The change of station not only provided Morgan with renewed opportunities to invade Yankee lines but gave a boost to his love life. During a visit to the home of Colonel Charles Ready, one of Murfreesboro's leading citizens, he met and was attracted to his host's vivacious elder daughter, Martha. Fifteen years younger than her father's guest, the twenty-one-year-old Mattie became infatuated with the dashing cavalry leader. With the speed of a raider on the attack, Morgan began an intense courtship that swept the young woman off her feet. They would wed before the year was out.[29]

Days after meeting Mattie, Morgan conducted his first mission under Breckinridge's supervision, a raid on occupied Nashville. The idea behind it was typical Morgan: a high-spirited escapade with military application. Conceived of as a night mission involving only the raiding leader and a dozen others, it appears to have been designed mainly to showcase Morgan's enterprise and scorn of danger. A daylight reconnaissance by a larger force, properly supported by infantry and cavalry, would have achieved as much if not more, but it would have lacked the degree of risk such a clandestine undertaking carried.

Like many of Morgan's adventures in enemy territory, the expedition began well and ended on a jarring note. Slipping inside the city via the Lebanon Turnpike, Morgan's band noted the location of camps and picket posts. Then they headed for the river, where a steamboat laden with supplies for Buell's army was tied up at the Front Street wharf. Morgan concocted a plan to set the steamer ablaze, cut it loose from its moorings, and send it drifting toward a fleet of gunboats and troopships anchored downriver. In his report he recalled that from the wharf he "could see the soldiers distinctly sitting upon the boats [transports], and they were full of them."[30]

The plan, while enterprising, was hastily conceived and poorly thought out. While Morgan and a few others remained behind as sentinels, the remaining raiders boarded the steamer, corralled her crew, and set it adrift in a yawl. Then they set fire to the boat and prepared to cut her loose. To Morgan's delight, the proceedings drew a large audience: "At least 2,000 citizens gathered around us while we were waiting for the boys to get back from the steamer. They begged us to leave; told us the Federal cavalry were scouring the city; that a large party of cavalry had just passed through the street we were on."[31]

Minutes later, a group of Yankee horsemen came on the scene, forcing Morgan and his men to decamp prematurely. The chains linking the burning steamer to the wharf had proven too strong to break, and thus no damage could be done to Morgan's most important target, the ships downriver. Before their opponents could overtake them, Morgan and his band rushed to their waiting horses, threw themselves into the saddle, and took off through the night. But they had lingered too long; although almost everyone got off unscathed, a shot rang out and one of the riders fell from his saddle, mortally wounded—the first of many who would lose their lives following Morgan's plume.[32]

JOHNSTON WAS WELL AWARE OF THE DAMAGE DONE to his reputation by his protracted flight. Once beyond pursuit, well rested, and fully resupplied, he intended to recoup prestige and restore his troops' morale by taking the offensive. Without warning, he would turn and smite his astonished enemy with overwhelming force. To accomplish this, however, he needed reinforcements—a great many of them, and not merely the survivors of that minor debacle in East Tennessee.

Jefferson Davis, belatedly attuned to the needs of his western army (for weeks his attention had been fixed on the mighty host with which George B. McClellan intended to attack Richmond), and conscious of the military and political ramifications of permitting that army to collapse, was agreeable to strengthening it substantially and rapidly. He approved the stripping of the defenses of Columbus and the addition of the troops there to Johnston's ranks. The abandoned garrison included four infantry regiments recently sent up from New Orleans. He also ordered to Johnston's side ten thousand of the troops under Bragg that had been stationed in and around Pensacola and Mobile. These forces included the regiment of Alabamians recently assigned to Joseph Wheeler, the artillery lieutenant-turned-infantry colonel. Since January, Johnston had been petitioning Richmond for authority to assimilate the Confederacy's coastal defenders, whom he perceived as unneeded in their present location. Only in the wake of Donelson's fall had his civilian superiors acceded to Johnston's requests, an action that, had it been taken weeks earlier, might have averted the disaster on the Cumberland.[33]

Outposts and garrisons whose position had become precarious as a result of the retreat from Kentucky also joined Johnston at Corinth, Mississippi. Beauregard, acting on Johnston's behalf and with Richmond's tacit approval, even urged Sterling Price and Earl Van Dorn (the latter commander of the Trans-Mississippi District, embracing Missouri, Arkansas, the Indian Territory, and a portion of Louisiana) to cross the river from Arkansas and add their support to the army assembling in Mississippi.[34]

The newcomers joined Johnston at Corinth, where the roundabout, two-hundred-mile retreat from Kentucky and Tennessee finally ended on March 22. Johnston immediately set to work organizing his enlarged command, which on the twenty-ninth he christened the Army of the Mississippi. One of his first moves in his new station—intended as a gesture of sacrifice for the good of his fledgling nation—was to offer field command of the army to Beauregard, who enjoyed public as well as government support. Should Beauregard accept, Johnston intended to confine himself to administrative control of the theater of operations. With equal magnanimity, the Creole rejected the proffer and expressed his willingness to accept the position of Johnston's senior subordinate.[35]

Johnston then gave full attention to tables of organization. He divided the army into three corps, commanded, in order of seniority, by Polk,

Bragg, and Hardee, with a reserve corps under Breckinridge. Polk's and Bragg's commands each comprised two divisions; Polk's were led by Generals Clark and Cheatham, Bragg's by Brigadier Generals Daniel Ruggles (who led the troops from New Orleans) and Jones M. Withers. Hardee's and Breckinridge's commands were basically large divisions, each consisting of three brigades.

As was too often the case, Johnston's army was top-heavy with infantry; only a few mounted units were attached to it. Polk was supported by a single regiment, the 1st Mississippi, under Colonel Andrew J. Lindsay, plus a small battalion of cavalry from the same state under Major Charles Baskerville and three companies of Alabamians, Louisianans, and Mississippians led by Lieutenant Colonel Richard H. Brewer, a distinguished prewar dragoon officer. Outside of a small escort force, the only cavalry assigned to Bragg consisted of Colonel James Holt Clanton's 1st Alabama and a five-company battalion of Alabamians under Captain Thomas F. Jenkins. Hardee's corps was served by Captain Isaac W. Avery's company of Georgia Dragoons. Forrest's battalion and Morgan's command (the latter recently enlarged to three companies) formed part of Breckinridge's corps; their only companion was a company of Kentuckians led by Captain Philip B. Thompson. Four units—two mounted regiments (Adams's and Wharton's) and two artillery batteries—remained unattached.[36]

As of March 29, Johnston's horsemen had a titular commander, Brigadier General James Morrison Hawes of Kentucky, a West Point graduate (Class of 1845); a veteran of the Mexican War, in which he had received a brevet for gallantry; and for two years a student at the prestigious cavalry school at Saumur, France. Despite these impressive credentials, Hawes had direct authority over only those forces "not hereinbefore assigned to divisions and brigades [and which] will be held in reserve." Thus, the highest-ranking cavalry officer in the Army of the Mississippi led no more than two regiments. The position was so inconsequential that a few weeks after assuming it, Hawes was relieved at his own request to take charge of an infantry brigade. Historians award Sidney Johnston high marks for his handling of cavalry, but he appears not to have appreciated the need for a cohesive organization and a proper command structure for his mounted arm.[37]

The reinforcements Johnston had received from Florida, Louisiana, and elsewhere had raised the effective strength of his army to almost forty thou-

sand officers and men, roughly twice the size of
the force that had abandoned Kentucky and
Tennessee. The enemy force that Johnston had
his sights on—Grant's so-called Army of the
Tennessee, which had assembled on the west
bank of its namesake river near Pittsburg
Landing, only a few miles above the
Mississippi line—was only slightly larger.
Despite the intelligence-gathering abilities of
his cavalry, Johnston had no firm idea of
Grant's strength, but he suspected that it was
not prohibitively superior to his own.

General Ulysses S. Grant, USA.

By mid-March, Johnston had determined
to attack Grant before the latter could strike
him, a plan approved by President Davis and his military adviser, Robert E.
Lee. The trick was to land a blow before Grant could join forces with Buell,
whose Army of the Ohio was reported on the march from Nashville to
Savannah, on the opposite side of the Tennessee north of Grant's camps. A
junction of the two armies had been ordered by the regional commander,
Halleck, now commander of the Department of the Mississippi, a position
that gave him control of Union operations west of the Alleghenies.[38]

Johnston believed he knew what to expect of Grant and Buell. Acting
on information gleaned by Forrest, Morgan, and other sources, including
spies and civilian informants in and around Louisville, the Confederate
leader had concluded that his opponents were sufficiently far apart that if
he moved swiftly he need not fear having to take on both at once. Moreover,
he believed that his enlarged and rejuvenated army had gained a new confidence in itself—high morale might make the difference in battle.

Not even the quickly fading hope that Van Dorn and Price would join
him in time to strike the Yankees deterred Johnston. In fact, Van Dorn had
rejected Beauregard's petition to cross the Mississippi, opting instead for an
offensive toward St. Louis. Then the mercurial Van Dorn—like
Beauregard, a self-styled master of grand strategy—veered into Arkansas
to oppose a smaller force under Brigadier General Samuel Ryan Curtis,
successor to Nathaniel Lyon. The result was a two-day battle (March 7-8)
known as Pea Ridge or Elkhorn Tavern, in which Van Dorn was soundly
defeated and his noted subordinate Ben McCulloch mortally wounded.
The denouement, which scotched Van Dorn's reputation as a great captain,

had a unique feature: the participation of three regiments of Native American horsemen fighting under the Confederate banner. The Indians—specimens of the finest light cavalry North America ever produced—conducted dramatic charges, inflicted numerous casualties (they were permitted to scalp their victims), but failed to turn the tide of battle. The defeat forced Van Dorn to retreat to Memphis, where he was in no position to add his weight to the offensive against Grant.[39]

Undaunted, Johnston moved north from Corinth on April 3. As always, cavalry led the way, hewing out a path of advance. Lindsay's and Brewer's men screened Polk's advance, Adams and Wharton did the same for Bragg's column, Avery's dragoons escorted Hardee, and Forrest and Morgan made smooth the way of Breckinridge. The backwoods Tennessean and the Kentucky cavalier now were of equal rank. Morgan's well-publicized missions behind Yankee lines had brought him the long-coveted commission of colonel. The promotion had come through even before his squadron expanded into the 2nd Kentucky regiment, his command for the next eight months.[40]

The twenty-mile march to Pittsburg Landing provided strenuous exercise for Johnston's recruits, many of whom, sore of foot and dry of throat, straggled every step of the way. The only troops not plagued by fatigue were those who led the way on horseback, covering the head and flanks of the moving columns. Vexing but insurmountable delays kept Johnston from getting into striking distance of his enemy till late on the fifth. The march had taken twice as long as he and his subordinates had estimated.

Beauregard, who feared that the movement must surely have been detected, costing Johnston the all-important advantage of surprise, made an eleventh-hour plea to withdraw rather than attack. His superior refused. For one thing, contact with the enemy had already taken place. On the fourth, horsemen in advance of Bragg's corps had sparred at middle distance with advanced pickets of the division that held the far Union right, William T. Sherman's. Although Sherman captured several members of Clanton's 1st Alabama, he failed to appreciate that a full-scale attack was coming his way. Neither did Grant, who at the time was miles away from his army at Savannah, where he expected to remain until the head of Buell's command reached the east side of the river. Beauregard's worst fears would not be realized.[41]

At about five a.m. on Sunday, April 6, Hardee's corps launched Johnston's initial attack, targeting Sherman's men in the area of a log church

known as Shiloh Meeting House. Apparently
Beauregard, perhaps in concert with other colleagues, was still urging Johnston to reconsider
attacking, for, as an Alabama-born member of
the headquarters cavalry escort recalled, when
"the roar of a gun broke upon his [Johnston's]
ears, he immediately faced the group and said,
'Gentlemen, the ball has opened. No time for
argument now,' or words to that effect."[42]

The ball began well for the Rebels, who, in
the words of another Alabama trooper, crashed
into the exposed Union flank "like an Alpine
avalanche." As they hurtled toward Sherman's

General Earl Van Dorn, CSA.

lines, the attackers unleashed a spine-tingling wail that grew louder and
louder as additional men picked it up—the first chorus of the Rebel Yell
heard in the West. Years later, recalling that moment, the escort member
exclaimed: "Oh! Who that has ever heard that peculiar yell, welling up from
thousands of throats, wild with the joy of combat and victory can ever forget [it]?"[43]

Taken wholly by surprise, the nearest Yankees unleashed a ragged volley, then ran, abandoning miles of campground that Hardee's troops quickly overran. The vast quantity of rations, equipment, and personal articles
thus yielded up was a glorious and beguiling sight. One of Brewer's
Mississippians rhapsodized over "the most beautiful camp I ever beheld—
every thing was neat and orderly—the tents, handsome in themselves, were
beautifully arranged and supplied with all the conveniences that one could
think of. Clothing of the finest quality, in abundance, in the quarter-mas-
ter's department, while the sutlers tents and cabins furnished almost every
luxury that an epicure might ask for. On these luxuries our soldiers feasted
highly."[44]

By halting to seize and partake, the Confederates allowed Sherman's
troops to regroup farther east. Their commander cobbled together a new
line and, although it gave ground again and again, it finally held. For three
hours, its defenders and those on their left fought desperately to stem the
advance of the more numerous enemy. Hardee's attack, at first gloriously
successful, was slowed to a crawl by Yankees who refused to abandon
ground pounded by artillery fire, including a salient that attracted so many
missiles it became known as the Hornet's Nest.

Almost three hours after the first shots were fired, Johnston committed Bragg's corps, supported by Polk's. Breckinridge's reserves would be sent in once the Union line gave way. The second wave made critical progress, driving Sherman and his comrades slowly but steadily toward the bluffs of the Tennessee. One of the units that helped force the Yankees east was Joseph Wheeler's 19th Alabama. Although not his service branch of preference, Fightin' Joe this day performed superbly in support of a roughly handled brigade under Brigadier General James Chalmers, another infantry leader who would find his niche in the cavalry service. After helping empty the Hornet's Nest, Wheeler gouged the survivors from their subsequent position along a sunken lane adjacent to the Pittsburg Landing road. The several charges the 19th delivered throughout the afternoon cost it heavily—more than 150 casualties during one forty-five-minute interval. But they earned its leader the kind of notice that would propel him to higher command and heavier responsibility. In his after-action report, Wheeler's division commander, General Withers, declared that this day, the colonel "proved himself worthy of all trust and confidence, a gallant commander and an accomplished soldier."[45]

Hardee's, Bragg's, and Polk's attacks were conducted almost solely by infantry, closely supported by artillery (sixty Confederate cannons were directed against the Hornet's Nest alone). The army's mounted units were widely dispersed and for the most part minimally engaged. Most were relegated to service as scouts, couriers, and escort units. As Basil Duke put it, "the cavalry was promiscuously disposed—indeed, no one in authority seemed to think it could win the battle."[46]

There were notable exceptions to this regrettable state of affairs. Clanton's Alabamians were heavily engaged guarding Chalmers's flanks before Wheeler's infantry joined the fray. Until driven off by a murderous blast of artillery at point-blank range, the 1st Mississippi provided close and effective support to the attacks that finally overran the Hornet's Nest. Late in the day, a battalion of the 1st, under Lieutenant Colonel John H. Miller, pursued a battery of Michigan artillery near the intersection of the roads from Corinth and Savannah. The dogged Mississippians overtook their quarry, capturing five cannons and almost sixty gunners.[47]

On the following morning, the second day of battle, Wharton's 8th Texas, accompanied by an Alabama battalion, swung around the Union left flank and menaced the enemy's rear, threatening to cut off escape routes, until ambushed by a well-hidden force of infantry and forced to withdraw.

Later that day, Wharton led his Rangers on a more dangerous mission, an assault on a Union battery. The effort failed, costing the regiment numerous casualties but winning plaudits from infantry comrades impressed by the Texans' grit and determination.[48]

Charging artillery was a dangerous business to be sure, but several mounted units were assigned the almost equally risky job of supporting their own artillery. Most shared the experience of Brewer's battalion, whose men, while guarding a bank of guns involved in the April 6 attack on Sherman, were "subjected to a perfect storm of grape, canister, bombs and winged shot." The description of incoming missiles might be inexact, but it gives a vivid impression of what Brewer's troopers faced during the opening phase of the battle.[49]

Improper positioning and the reluctance of division and brigade commanders to commit their horsemen combined to limit and complicate the cavalry's role in the fighting. The troopers of Morgan and Forrest, though anxious to see action in a critical situation, for a time were denied an opportunity to do anything of consequence. Until fully committed to the fighting of the sixth, General Breckinridge kept a tight hold on Morgan's squadron. A frustrated and sometimes exasperated Basil Duke noted that for hours on the first day, he and his comrades "listened to the hideous noise, and thought how much larger the affair was than the skirmishes on Green river and around Nashville. . . . We wondered if those before us would finish the business before we got in."[50]

Around noon on the sixth, with Grant's army apparently fleeing en masse to the banks of the Tennessee, Johnston called up Breckinridge and urged him to "sweep them into the river." Full of pent-up energy, Morgan's men accompanied their infantry friends into a sector where the head of Breckinridge's column had become mixed up with other Confederate commands. General Hardee suddenly appeared out of the battle smoke and informed Morgan that he intended to have him charge a battery whose fire was impeding the advance of his corps. The order, however, was never issued.[51]

Morgan's squadron was subsequently transferred to the far left of the army, where it spent the remainder of the day looking for lucrative targets. At length it came upon a regiment of infantry dressed in blue—a not-uncommon occurrence even one year after war's outbreak—which it nearly attacked before discovering it hailed from Louisiana. Later Morgan's people encountered skirmishers from an Illinois regiment that appeared to be in mid-retreat. Deciding to help it on its way, they chased it across an open field and into a woodlot. Among the trees the galloping troopers frantically pulled rein. They were face to face not only with the balance of the regiment, drawn up in line of battle, but also with a battery of light artillery, its guns pointing straight at them. For some reason the cannons did not fire, but the foot soldiers unleashed what Duke called "one stunning volley, the blaze almost reaching our faces, and the roar rang in our ears like thunder." Morgan pulled his men out of harm's way, although too late to avoid losing several men killed and wounded.[52]

The murderous denouement ended the alligator riders' involvement in the first day's fighting. By the account of one Kentucky infantryman, however, Morgan's men failed to learn the lesson taught them this day, charging another well-emplaced battery and taking another round of casualties on the seventh. If Morgan's men had hoped for an exciting and dramatic introduction to combat, they found it at Shiloh, but not in a way calculated to add luster to their reputation, or to their leader's.[53]

Bedford Forrest's command experienced many of the same difficulties that beset Morgan's. Throughout the morning of the sixth, the newly organized regiment idled three miles in the rear, guarding a position of no evident value along Lick Creek in cooperation with a couple of infantry regiments. When, shortly before noon, the foot soldiers departed to join in the battle, Forrest was left without orders. The sounds of distant combat were too much to bear, but he was unwilling to take action unless assured of the total support of his men. Able to endure inactivity no longer, he rode along the line of his regiment, shouting, "Boys, do you hear that rattle of musketry and the roar of artillery?" The men replied "yes" in anxious unison, and Forrest added: "Do you know what it means? It means our friends and brothers are falling by hundreds at the hands of the enemy and we are here guarding a damn creek. We did not enter the service for such work . . . we are needed elsewhere. Let's go and help them. What do you say?" [54]

The men responded with cheers and war hoops, and followed him to the front. They happened upon comrades who were hammering away at the Yankees who had been evicted from the Hornet's Nest. Here the regiment came under the control of General Cheatham, who refused Forrest's request to charge a battery that was showering his division with shot and shell. After Forrest strongly remonstrated, Cheatham finally agreed to the attack as long as Forrest accepted responsibility for the outcome.[55]

Cheatham had no worry on that score. Forrest hastily formed his men in column of fours, and, with flank support from an Alabama infantry regiment, charged the Yankees across an expanse of open ground. At the far end of the field, Forrest's column struck not the battery that had been shelling it but a regiment of Missouri infantry that had been defending the guns. Screaming Tennesseans chased the foot soldiers from the field and into a dense patch of underbrush. In the process, Forrest's men were struck by an incoming shell that emptied four saddles at once. Forrest feared having to attack the battery head on, but minutes later the Alabama regiment that had gone in on his flank seized and silenced the artillery unit. Then a second body of blue infantry rushed up to take the place of their fleeing comrades. This marked the end of Forrest's offensive, which had lost momentum to the underbrush through which his men had attempted to pursue the regiment they had uprooted. One of Forrest's officers offered the simple observation that "we were unable to go further and were ordered to fall back."[56]

Forrest's day of battle was over; so, too, was that of the Army of the Mississippi. By the close of the sixth, Grant's troops were holding on for dear life to the high ground overlooking the river—beaten, routed, hundreds of them demoralized beyond the ability to continue the fight. They were saved from annihilation by a phalanx of artillery that defied Rebel efforts to penetrate their final position on the bluffs, and by the murderously effective fire of naval gunboats in the Tennessee. Were it not for these, a Mississippi cavalryman informed his wife, "we would have killed drowned or taken every one of them. We run them smack to the edge of the river but the gunboats compelled us to give back."[57]

Two other events had turned the battle against the attackers. In the middle of the afternoon, Johnston, having ridden from the scene of the opening action to the center of his line, was struck below the right knee by a rifle ball. Although hours passed before it took effect, the wound proved mortal. Johnston's successor, Beauregard, never as fully committed to the offensive as his superior, failed to push the attack to its conclusion, permitting Grant's nearly vanquished army to live over another day. The second event of consequence occurred early that evening when, under a sudden but steady downpour, the leading division of Buell's army began to cross the Tennessee to reinforce Sherman and his colleagues.

Beauregard had not bargained on Buell's arrival, and he refused to believe it. He might have been forced to accept the fact but for the delinquency of a subordinate. Sometime after midnight, scouts in blue uniforms whom Forrest had sent to infiltrate the enemy's lines reported that Grant was being reinforced in considerable strength. Forrest at once conveyed the news to his nearest superior, Hardee, but the corps leader failed to relay it to Beauregard. The Creole began operations early on the seventh in ignorance of the situation facing him, which now included the opposition not only of Buell's entire army but also of an errant division of Grant's command that had failed to add its weight to the first day's fighting. The newcomers enabled Grant to counterattack with such power that Beauregard's deferred effort to finish the previous day's work could not be resumed. For hours the outcome hung in the balance, but by late in the afternoon, Beauregard's beaten and bemused troops were in full retreat to Corinth.

As during the march from Donelson, Forrest's and Morgan's men brought up the rear, shielding the army from further harm. It was a job they were getting good at, thanks to frequent practice.[58]

# FIVE

# RAIDING
# SEASON

THE DEFEATED, DEJECTED CONFEDERATES BEGAN the weary return to Corinth on the morning of April 8. Grant's army, having suffered a major setback on the first day of the battle and now preoccupied with integrating Buell's reinforcements, was in no shape to make a full-fledged pursuit. Beauregard was unaware of this; he feared being overtaken short of Mississippi and pummeled anew. If that happened, as General Bragg warned him, "we will lose all in the rear." Bragg, whose corps was in the middle of the retreat column, had observed enough chaos en route to assess the troops as "utterly demoralized" and the roads "almost impassable." The army and its horses had "no provisions and no forage; consequently everything is feeble."[1]

Bragg's dire view of things darkened the mood of his superior, who verged on despair. The next day, Beauregard importuned Richmond for as many reinforcements as could be sent to Corinth, as rapidly as possible. He advised Davis and Lee to strip the seaboard garrisons, predicting that unless these troops were sent to him promptly, "we lose the Mississippi Valley and probably our cause."[2]

Because Grant would mount some form of pursuit sooner or later, it was imperative that the rear of the army be well-protected. The job fell to John Breckinridge, who assigned the most critical work to the mobile forces available to him. These included Forrest's regiment and Morgan's squadron. Another, larger defense force was carved out of Hardee's corps: a provisional brigade of four hundred foot soldiers (most of them from the 19th

Alabama, with some Louisiana troops attached) and two hundred troopers. Breckinridge placed this organization under Joe Wheeler. The infantry colonel had seen hard fighting over the past two days, but although his regiment had suffered heavily it remained substantially intact, and its commander was willing to "take charge of any troops" assigned him for rear defense. Thus, on this occasion, for the first time, three colonels who would rise to higher rank and fame in the army's mounted arm—a fiery Tennessean, a dashing Kentuckian, and a highly competent young Georgian—served virtually side by side in pursuit of a common goal.[3]

Fightin' Joe's role in the proceedings proved to be minor. Once the Yankees finally stirred themselves to follow up their victory, their movement toward Corinth was so slow and half-hearted that they failed to overtake Wheeler's column. However, the most advanced pursuers—two brigades under Sherman, joined by the division of Brigadier General Thomas J. Wood of Buell's army—caught up with Forrest's troopers, covering the extreme rear of the army. Arriving at the junction of two south-leading roads on the morning of the eighth, Sherman led his troops down the more westerly Ridge Road, while Wood took the road to Monterey, the point at which Wheeler had assembled his column. A few miles past the fork, Wood suddenly struck a detachment of Wirt Adams's regiment, bringing up Wheeler's rear. Infantry and horsemen mixed it up for a few minutes before Adams fled the scene. As if having well-completed a task, Wood turned about and returned to his camps along the Tennessee.[4]

More intent than his colleague on accomplishing something of purpose, Sherman pressed ahead on Ridge Road. He moved with something less than desirable caution, for around noon he fell into an ambush set by Bedford Forrest amid a large expanse of fallen trees. From a heavily wooded section of a ridge parallel to Sherman's trail, Forrest's force—a provisional brigade consisting of forty men of his own regiment, a much larger detachment of the 8th Texas under Major Thomas Harrison, two of Morgan's companies under Morgan himself, and one of Adams's companies—sprang upon their enemy, whom they caught trying to clear the fallen timber as well as a nearby creek. The charge fell upon Sherman's skirmish force, two companies of the 77th Ohio, whose commander never forgot the "fierce yell" Forrest's men sent up as they spurred toward his flank and front.[5]

Armed mostly with revolvers and double-barreled shotguns effective only at close range, the Confederates held their fire until a few yards from their target. Once they began shooting, the skirmishers scrambled back to the woods from which they had come. They were soon replaced by the balance of the 77th, which came up slowly and cautiously. The regiment had been cut up and demoralized on the first day of the fighting around Shiloh Church and remained gun-shy. Forrest's attack had already unnerved an Illinois cavalry battalion that had been supporting the skirmishers; it, too, was now in rapid retreat. Sherman and his staff, who had ridden too far to the front and came within an ace of being captured, followed the cavalry to the rear. "The slaughter was great," wrote one Confederate, who described the fight, known as Fallen Timbers, as a confused melee, "cavalry and infantry, running in every direction, officers shouting and cursing and the hurt [soldiers] groaning."[6]

At Sherman's order, the rest of his command hustled up to join the 77th, forming a line of battle athwart the road and loosing a volley at the charging cavalry. Sherman was desperate to blunt Forrest's attack, which already had inflicted more than one hundred casualties, including forty Ohioans and Illinoisans taken prisoner. He succeeded: unwilling to test this new, more formidable obstacle, most of Sherman's attackers—including Morgan's detachment, which appears to have had little involvement in the fight—promptly withdrew.

Forrest could not join them. His horse, maddened by the furious rattle of small arms, carried his rider to within fifty yards of the blue battle line. Aiming to make the best of his precarious situation, Forrest snapped his pistol again and again, cutting down every antagonist who ventured near, while attempting to wheel his fractious mount about. Before he could extricate himself, a musket ball crashed into his left side just above the hip, lodging near his spine. Stunned, barely able to retain his seat, he sank spurs into his horse's flanks and galloped off. A blizzard of rifle balls somehow missed him but struck his mount in two places. Although mortally wounded, the animal carried his rider clear of the field. At the time, Sherman was content to see him disappear into the distance. Given the trouble that Forrest later caused his forces and their supply lines, Sherman, in his postwar memoirs, stressed his regret that the cavalryman's wound had not been fatal.

Having become the last casualty of the Shiloh campaign, Forrest was compelled to relinquish his command and leave the army to recuperate at home in Memphis. So eager was he to return to duty that he left his sickbed less than three weeks after the delicate surgery that removed the ball from his side. He paid the price for his impetuosity: a few days after rejoining his regiment, the wound reopened, forcing him to undergo a second operation. Another two weeks would pass before he was able to return.[7]

THE ARMY MADE BETTER TIME RETURNING TO Corinth than it had when leaving it for Pittsburg Landing. By the evening of the eighth, soldiers were trickling into the town, which Beauregard feared he could not hold should his pursuers recover their nerve and attack him there. He could not know that a further pursuit would be long in coming. Not until the close of April would Grant's command—by then part of an army group led by the departmental commander, Halleck—start from Tennessee for Mississippi. This force would comprise not only Buell's Army of the Ohio but also a smaller army under Major General John Pope, whose recent capture of Island No. 10—one of those poorly garrisoned defenses on the Mississippi—had placed virtually all of Tennessee in Union hands.[8]

By the time the cautious Halleck started for Corinth, Beauregard had assimilated reinforcements of his own: the twenty thousand survivors of Pea Ridge whom Van Dorn and Price had failed to add to Johnston's army in time to fight at Shiloh. Yet the additions failed to assuage Beauregard's concern that Corinth was fatally vulnerable. David Purvine of the 1st Mississippi shared the belief of many comrades that "Beauregard aims to make a general stand at this place," but on May 30—hours before the slow-moving Federals drew within artillery range of Corinth—Beauregard completed his evacuation. He guided his sixty-five thousand soldiers on a fifty-mile march along the Mobile & Ohio Railroad. The withdrawal, which went virtually uncontested, ended June 9 at Tupelo, a town blessed with more natural defenses than Corinth, as well as a more abundant water supply.[9]

By now the Army of the Mississippi had been considerably revamped. Beauregard's organizational efforts took in the cavalry, which he grouped into a cohesive force, a single large brigade, instead of leaving it attached, helter-skelter, to the army's several components. As originally constituted, Beauregard's mounted arm consisted of six regiments (including Forrest's), eleven battalions (including Morgan's, which, thanks to Beauregard's solicitude, had grown to four companies), two separate squadrons, and several independent companies. In later weeks, units came and went, and the table of organization underwent several revisions. One notable change was reflected in an order, published April 28, that fixed the brigade's composition at five regiments, five battalions, and sixteen companies, under the overall command of Brigadier General William N. R. Beall, a West Pointer from Kentucky and a veteran of the 1st United States Cavalry. The regiments assigned to Beall included the 3rd Tennessee under the still-absent Forrest, Clanton's 1st Alabama, Wharton's 8th Texas, Adams's unnumbered Mississippi outfit, and the 6th Confederate Cavalry of Colonel Thomas Claiborne (later superseded by Colonel John F. Lay). The separate battalions were commanded by Lieutenant Colonels Brewer, Thomas F. Jenkins, Jacob Biffle, and James Bennett, and a Major Barnett. On paper, at least, the command numbered six thousand four hundred officers and troopers.

Beall's term in command lasted only six weeks; early in June, following a less than satisfactory performance covering Beauregard's retreat to Tupelo, he was replaced by James Chalmers, now a brigadier general. By this time the composition of the brigade had changed again. Wharton's regiment had been detached to East Tennessee, and Forrest's had been reduced by transfers and detachments to a single battalion (commanded by now-Lieutenant Colonel David Kelley) and a separate squadron. The losses had been more than made up by the recent addition of three regiments—the 1st Mississippi of Colonel Richard A. Pinson, Colonel William Slemons's 2nd Arkansas, and Colonel Red Jackson's 7th Tennessee—as well as Lieutenant Colonel Clark R. Barteau's 2nd Tennessee Battalion. In later weeks, Chalmers's command would further expand with the addition of three newly organized regiments: the 6th Tennessee, the 3rd Alabama, and the 8th Confederate Cavalries led, respectively, by Colonels Biffle, James Hagan, and William B. Wade. When Biffle's outfit was subsequently transferred to Van Dorn's Army of the West, Chalmers was left with nine regiments, as well as the remnant of Forrest's original outfit. The brigade constituted the largest, most formidable body of Confederate cavalry west of the Alleghenies.

A second brigade of cavalry had been added to the army in May, the result of an incursion into northwest Alabama by one of Buell's divisions, that of Brigadier General Ormsby M. Mitchel. When Mitchel's troops pushed as far as Tuscumbia, only fifty miles from Corinth, Beauregard decided to augment the two regiments that had been detached to patrol that region, Scott's 1st Louisiana and the 1st Kentucky, now under Lieutenant Colonel T. G. Woodward, Ben Helm having been promoted to brigadier general. To this demibrigade Beauregard added Wharton's Texans and the 2nd Tennessee Battalion. To command the whole he selected

Colonel John Adams, a Tennessean who had graduated from West Point, served in the 1st Dragoons, and fought in Mexico. Beauregard directed Adams not only to keep tabs on the Yankees around Huntsville but to threaten their principal supply line, the railroad that connected Nashville and Decatur, Alabama.[10]

General Braxton Bragg, CSA.

Beauregard's contributions to army organization would be lasting, but his tenure in command would not. Never tired of lecturing his civilian and military superiors on matters of policy and strategy, the Louisianan had been at odds with the Davis administration since before Manassas. His decision to abort the first day's offensive at Shiloh with victory seemingly in his grasp, and his retreat to Tupelo (during which General Pope loudly but falsely claimed to have cut off and captured ten thousand prisoners and one hundred and fifty thousand stands of arms) had further lowered Beauregard's stock with government officials. When, in mid-June, he took sick leave in Mobile without clearing it with the War Department, a disgruntled Davis named Beauregard's temporary successor, Bragg, to permanent command of the army.[11]

Unlike Beauregard, Bragg enjoyed Davis's trust and confidence, which he would retain for many months despite his mediocre leadership skills. Bragg was neither an astute strategist nor an able tactician, and he could be irresolute and immobile in times of crisis. Unlike Beauregard, he had no delusions of brilliance, but he also lacked his predecessor's ability to plan on a grand scale, and he was incapable of striking the poses by which the Creole had dazzled governors, editors, and the soldiers under him.

A humorless ascetic, Bragg was burdened with a personality that can only be described as miserable. Although talented at organizing and training troops, he was incapable of inspiring them. His well-meaning efforts to convince his army that it could succeed in the face of daunting odds were never persuasive. His saving grace, so far as his career was concerned, was that he knew when and how often to salute, a quality that Jefferson Davis found indispensable in his field generals. That quality would serve to compensate for the many limitations Bragg would display over the next sixteen months.[12]

JOHN MORGAN AND HIS MEN HAD BEEN included in the table of organization of the army's first cavalry brigade. By the time General Beall assumed command of it, however, the Kentuckians had been detached to Burnsville, Mississippi, on the railroad southeast of Corinth, to prepare for a raid in rear of the enemy. Shortly before his relief, Beauregard had authorized strikes against Halleck's long and fragile lines of communications. One mission in West Tennessee had been entrusted to Claiborne's 6th Confederate Cavalry, which, in cooperation with Red Jackson's regiment, set out early in May to attack Grant's rear supply base at Paducah. The combined force of 1,250 moved to its objective by way of Dresden, near which town on the fifth it encountered a much smaller force of Iowa cavalry. Claiborne and Jackson made short work of the Iowans, killing, wounding, or capturing at least half of them and mortally wounding their leader. They chased the survivors toward Paducah. The raiders never reached that place, however, being forced into a roundabout withdrawal to evade a much larger cavalry force sent to track them down.[13]

Two other missions were entrusted to Joseph Wheeler, now a provisional brigade commander. On May 10, Wheeler led a detachment of his regiment, along with other units of Withers's division, in forcing a body of infantry to evacuate a strategic position near Farmington, east of Corinth. Three weeks later, he again moved north in the vanguard of a sizable column, 350 infantry and cavalry. This time he drove some of Sherman's men from the village of Monterey, preventing any disruption of Beauregard's evacuation of Corinth. The success these operations achieved would pay dividends for the man who conducted them. Although he remained short in height, Wheeler's stature was growing incrementally.[14]

Morgan's larger, more ambitious expedition was aimed at distant objectives: Middle Tennessee and, if accessible, Kentucky. He left Burnsville on April 26 astride his favorite war horse, the strikingly handsome Black Bess, followed by 325 of his more adventurous troopers. The picked force consisted of the better part of his own command (minus Basil Duke, then convalescing from a severe wound received at Shiloh) plus a detachment of Wirt Adams's regiment and most of McNairy's battalion. Bringing up the rear of the column was a cordon of pack mules lugging extra rations and ammunition.

The men rode recently reshod horses and carried newly issued weapons, including a number of short Enfield rifles, the fruit of a fifteen-thousand-dollar weapons stipend provided by Beauregard's headquarters. Numerous riders wore blue overcoats to confuse Unionist civilians and soldiers. The attire was heavy enough to ward off the early spring chill, but the ruse was quite thin. At one of their first stops, an elderly civilian informed the raiders: "You need not tell that tale to me. I've seen you before, you're Morgan's men!"[15]

Trotting southeast along the railroad, the column passed though Iuka, Mississippi, and camped at day's end six miles from the Tennessee River. The stream having been raised by recent rains, two days were required to pass everyone to the north bank using the single ferryboat available. Turning sharply north, Morgan reached Lawrenceburg, Tennessee, on the afternoon of the thirtieth and spent the night there. The next morning he neared Pulaski, which, according to reports, bulged with Yankee troops— mainly convalescents wounded at Shiloh. Morgan hastened to the village and made prisoners of them all. One captive was found to be the son of General Mitchel; Morgan paroled the young officer in hopes of exchanging him for the raiding leader's brother, Captain Charles Morgan, who himself had been wounded at Shiloh and, while recuperating at Huntsville, had been captured.

Riding alertly through country infested with Union cavalry, Morgan and his men neared Pulaski in midmorning May 1. Drawing near, they were warned by residents that a body of four hundred Federals had just passed by on the road to Columbia. Hoping to flush the game, Morgan galloped after them. Presently, he came up to a detachment that was stringing a telegraph line to connect with General Mitchel's headquarters at Huntsville. The Yankees tried to block the road with overturned wagons, but Morgan's advance guard surmounted the roadblock, surrounded the position, and rounded up 250 prisoners, including civilian telegraphers. The newest company to join Morgan's command pursued the few escapees toward Columbia, overtaking a few; they rejoined their comrades before they entered Pulaski.[16]

The local populous, Southern sympathizers all, welcomed the raiders with open arms and proffered goods, including all manner of edibles. Admirers of fine horseflesh clustered about Morgan's steed, stroking her glossy coat and feeding her sweet cakes. Morgan had Black Bess stabled before a group of ladies with scissors in hand so they could take souvenirs from her mane and tail. After seeing to his men's refreshment, paroling his gaggle of prisoners, and saying his good-byes, Morgan led the column north toward Murfreesboro. Bypassing that heavily occupied town, he continued north, crossing Stones River and reaching Lebanon on the sodden evening of May 4. Morgan intended to cross the Cumberland River, eight miles to the north, and a few miles farther on to enter his home state.[17]

As if an armed homecoming would not be sufficiently entertaining, on the outskirts of Murfreesboro, Morgan had one of his men, a nimble-fingered telegrapher from Canada known as "Lightning" Ellsworth, tap into the Yankees' telegraph lines using a pocket instrument (or "bug") that could cut into a circuit without breaking the current. Skilled at impersonating other telegraphers, whose personal techniques he expertly mimicked, Ellsworth engaged the operator at Louisville in conversation long enough to obtain information of great value to Morgan. Ellsworth then relayed bogus reports of Morgan's location and intentions, and even planted a story that Forrest's cavalry had captured Murfreesboro—as he soon would in fact. As the raiding leader's most recent biographer observes, Ellsworth's attempt at obfuscation "accomplished nothing—the Federals were not tricked—but it gave Morgan a great deal of pleasure."[18]

Although by now almost two hundred miles outside the lines of the Army of the Mississippi and only thirty miles west of the Union stronghold of Nashville, at Lebanon Morgan was again on safe ground. The townspeople were overjoyed to see him and his men; one raider recalled that they were permitted "to camp almost anywhere." Morgan and some of his officers availed themselves of the local hospitality, dining at the homes of prominent citizens and bedding down at the local hotel. Most of their men bivouacked in the fields surrounding the town; a few occupied the Giles County courthouse and the campus of Cumberland University.[19]

No incident during the war illustrates more clearly the lax discipline that plagued Morgan's command than his failure this night to establish and maintain sentinels. Guards were asleep or missing from their posts when, at dawn on May 5, six hundred Union cavalry under Brigadier General Ebenezer Dumont, who had been trailing Morgan the past two days, came charging through the streets of Lebanon, shooting and shouting.

One of the few conscientious pickets managed to dash into the center of town and sound the alarm. His valor cost him his life, but it permitted Morgan and his subordinates to rush to their posts—many of them half-dressed and sleep-befogged—and improvise a defense. Several of their men, alerted by the commotion, fled their bivouacs, galloped into town, and took up shooting positions inside private residences. Along with a number of shotgun-toting citizens, they poured a wicked crossfire into the leading Union outfit, Colonel Frank Wolford's 1st Kentucky Cavalry.

In the melee that ensued, Wolford, one of Kentucky's most formidable Unionists, suffered a disabling wound. Attempting to disengage from the fight, he rode inside Morgan's lines, mistaking blue-coated Confederates for his own men. In a typically chivalric gesture, Morgan paroled the colonel on the spot and offered to release him that he might be attended to by his outfit's surgeons. The antagonists would meet, and clash, again, under table-turned circumstances, fourteen months hence.

Reacting to Morgan's defense and Wolford's capture, the 1st Kentucky withdrew from the town square, but minutes later it returned at a gallop accompanied by the balance of Dumont's command. The Yankees came not only in overwhelming force but wielding repeating rifles with which the raiders' Enfields and shotguns could not compete. Eventually the Confederates were forced to remount and race through the town and out the turnpike toward Carthage and Rome. Dumont pursued furiously for almost twenty miles, overtaking dozens of raiders, capturing most of them, and cutting down many. The embarrassing retreat, ever afterward known as the "Lebanon Races," did not cease till those raiders who had eluded pursuit—no more than a dozen—crossed the Cumberland on the single available boat. The vessel was too small to accommodate their horses, which were left on the south bank. Morgan would never recover his beloved Black Bess, "the most perfect beauty I ever beheld," in the estimation of one of his men.[20]

Reportedly, Morgan was so humiliated by his ignominious flight that he broke down and wept. In time, however, he would find that his reputation remained untarnished. In fact, it grew as a result of his recent exploits, clearly aimed at liberating Tennesseans from Yankee occupation. A local physician's wife noted in her diary that prior to Morgan's unexpected presence in Giles County, "our spirits were low and our hearts faint for we felt that the iron chain of despotism was fastening upon us as time rolled on." However it ended, Morgan's visit had raised the corporate morale, persuading the oppressed to persevere.[21]

Making his way on foot and then on borrowed horse to Rome and Carthage, on May 6, Morgan and the others who had escaped pitched camp near Sparta, at the foot of the Cumberland plateau. Over the next three days, they were joined by perhaps fifty raiders who had ridden far and wide to cut their way out of Lebanon (sixty-five of Morgan's men had been taken prisoner in the town; forty-three others had been killed or wounded). Reunited with the nucleus of the unit he had trained at Woodsonville in the war's palmy days, Morgan allowed himself to believe he could still deal body blows to those who had defiled his region. His attention focused, as it always did, on Kentucky. Thus, instead of turning back to Mississippi, he gathered up the remnant that had followed him from Burnsville and started north. Three days later, all were passing unmolested through the familiar countryside around Glasgow and other Green River villages.[22]

Finding Glasgow crawling with soldiers, Morgan pushed on to the railroad he had intended to strike at expedition's start. On May 12, just outside Cave City, eighty-some miles south of Louisville, Morgan halted his little band and, accompanied by four of his men cloaked in blue uniforms, gingerly entered the Barren County village, which had recently been occupied in some force. Happily finding the place Yankee-free, he called in the rest of his command. They seized and burned the locomotive and cars of a freight train on the local siding, denying its contents to the troops in Glasgow.

Later that day they captured a unique prize, an incoming train filled with passengers, including several Union officers and their wives. As at Lawrenceburg, Morgan paroled his prisoners, releasing the married men to the custody of their spouses. Rifling the cars for valuables, he carried off a safe filled with Yankee greenbacks. For the sake of the ladies who could have sheltered nowhere else, he refrained from burning the train. Instead, after treating his men and some of the parolees to a meal at Cave City's only hotel, he allowed the engineer to reverse course and return the train to its point of origin, Louisville.

Before yet another train—this carrying troops seeking his scalp—could arrive, Morgan and his men left Cave City in a cloud of dust. He fled south via Burkesville and a crossing of the Cumberland. The trip back to his own lines was unimpeded, permitting spirits to rise. He and his followers had accomplished something of purpose even when it appeared that nothing could be salvaged from a botched expedition. Morgan could go home confident of his welcome. He could expect to be greeted with open arms instead of with smirks, shrugs, and *sotto voce* references to the Lebanon Races.[23]

BY THE SECOND WEEK IN JUNE, BEDFORD FORREST was sufficiently recovered from his wound at Fallen Timbers to rejoin his outfit. Soon after Forrest reported to army headquarters, Beauregard, in one of his last moves before relinquishing command, ordered him to proceed to Chattanooga, Tennessee, a stronghold of the District of East Tennessee. Forrest was to assume command of a brigade of cavalry assigned to the district commander, Major General Edmund Kirby Smith, and to complete its organization.

The prospect of higher station invigorated Forrest, but he learned to his regret that his old regiment would not be a part of his new command. The 3rd Tennessee would remain in Mississippi under Lieutenant Colonel Kelley. Forrest was permitted to take with him a few of the outfit's officers, along with twenty picked men as his personal escort. One who would accompany him was his brother, Captain Bill Forrest, Bedford's choice to command the escort unit.[24]

The little band reached Chattanooga on June 19. There Forrest learned that he would supersede Colonel Adams and that his new command would consist of the 8th Texas, the 1st Louisiana, the 1st Kentucky, and Colonel Winburn J. Lawton's 2nd Georgia. At this early date, however, only the Texans and Georgians were available for field service. Both regiments were understrength, making a combined force of little more than one thousand. Because Colonels Wharton and Scott were senior to Forrest by date of commission, Beauregard had requested of the War Department that Forrest be appointed a brigadier general. The promotion would come through July 21. By then, however, John Scott had obtained his release from the brigade for refusing to serve under a junior officer. Kirby Smith would replace Scott's outfit with Colonel James Morrison's 1st Georgia. Then the 1st Kentucky, whose one-year enlistment was up and whose officers had petitioned to be transferred to John Hunt Morgan's command, opted out of the brigade. Forrest was left with Wharton's, Lawton's and Morrison's regiments. Kirby Smith promised to add units as soon as they became available for service in his department.[25]

Forrest's superior wished to see his brigade in the field at the earliest opportunity; he needed a well-appointed, solidly led mounted force to help him out of what he considered, with some justification, a nearly impossible situation. The Florida-born, Virginia-bred Smith had become, along with Beauregard, one of the Confederacy's earliest heroes. At the First Battle of Manassas, where he had taken a painful wound, the well-timed appearance of his infantry brigade had helped bring victory. Smith felt poorly compen-

sated for that effort, which had won him the
nickname "Blucher of the Confederacy," after
the Prussian field marshal who opposed
Napoleon. His present command appeared a
minor one and his area of operations a backwater rather than a stage on which to play out his
outsize ambitions.[26]

Thus he was pleased when, a few weeks
after Forrest joined his command, the war
office in Richmond redefined it as a separate
department, presumably coequal with Bragg's.
For some reason, however, Secretary of War
George W. Randolph neglected to inform
Bragg of the change in Smith's status; Smith
enlightened him when Bragg, soon after

General Edmund Kirby Smith, CSA.

replacing Beauregard, wrote him in hopes of gaining a better understanding of the boundaries of his new department. The new situation placed
Forrest in a rather anomalous position. Although operating under the
direct command of Smith, the cavalryman was still technically assigned to
the Western Department. Bragg seemed to consider him on loan to East
Tennessee, liable to be recalled whenever his presence was deemed necessary with the Army of the Mississippi.

An even greater source of discontent than the second-tier status of
Smith's fiefdom was its attenuated area of operations—almost two hundred miles long, from Cumberland Gap south to Chattanooga—which
Smith had been attempting to defend with eight thousand troops. This
vast domain appeared to be under mortal threat. A little more than a week
before Forrest's arrival at Chattanooga, Buell's sixty-one thousand-man
Army of the Ohio had begun to advance from northern Alabama toward
East Tennessee. To slow this movement, Forrest's new superior wished him
to strike Buell's supply lines in Middle Tennessee. Any disruption of traffic
on the Nashville & Chattanooga Railroad promised to pay dividends.[27]

Before Forrest began this critical mission, he needed to group his units,
familiarize himself with their officers, and train the men to act in unison in
the field. For the first time in his war career, he threw himself into the business of tactical instruction. At the outset, the effort showed sparse results,
although Forrest's determination to create order from chaos impressed his

new soldiers. One trooper watched as the colonel ordered Lawton's Georgians to attack an imaginary target while firing their weapons at the extended gallop, the result being "about fifty of the Regiment tumbling over their horses heads." The deplorable exhibition provoked a torrent of oaths from Forrest, which put all involved on notice not to provoke him again.[28]

The training regimen may have made Forrest wonder just what kind of command he had inherited; nevertheless, he determined to start his thousand men for Middle Tennessee on the morning of July 9. By now his scouts had gathered valuable information about his prospective objectives. A sizable garrison, comprising forces of all arms, held Murfreesboro, seat of Rutherford County, the most critical outpost on the Nashville & Chattanooga. At that point the greatest damage to Buell's offensive could be done with a single stroke. Accordingly, the farming village thirty miles southeast of Nashville became Forrest's primary target.

Crossing the Tennessee River at Chattanooga, Forrest's compact force climbed Walden's Ridge, then crossed the broad and fertile Sequatchie Valley to Altamont, where it bivouacked for the night. The following day brought the raiders to the health resort of Beersheba Springs. They did not linger to take the waters but pushed on to McMinnville, the Warren County seat. There Forrest welcomed three units that Kirby Smith had assigned him, which expanded his brigade to one thousand four hundred officers and men: a portion of Morrison's 1st Georgia, and two squadrons, one of Tennesseans under Major Baxter Smith, the other detached from the Kentucky battalion of Lieutenant Colonel Thomas G. Walker.[29]

Forrest spent the early part of the twelfth conferring with his new subordinates and inspecting their men and horses. Satisfied with what he saw, that afternoon he started on the next-to-last leg of the journey to Murfreesboro, fifty miles away. If the long ride prompted grumbling in the ranks, it never reached Forrest's ears; his men were already familiar enough with his temperament that no one dared to test it by griping.

This arduous stretch of travel brought the two-mile-long column to the village of Woodbury after dark. In the manner of the reception given John Morgan at Pulaski, the local folk turned out to greet the troopers and cheerfully provide them with food and drink, and their horses with provender. They wore worried expressions, however, when informing Forrest that a dozen of their fellow citizens had been rounded up by a party of Union cavalry that had entered the village hours earlier. They had been carried off to

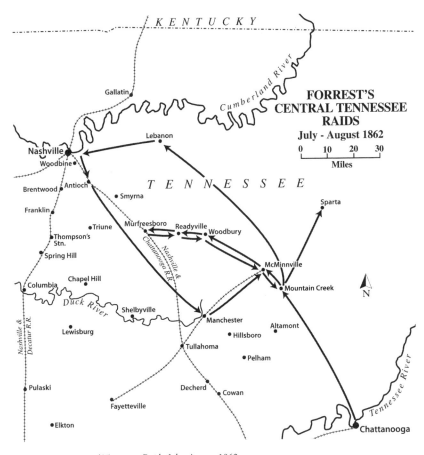

Forrest's Central Tennessee Raids, July–August 1862.

jail at Murfreesboro, their only offense being their strong pro-Confederate sympathies. One was a Baptist preacher, another a sixteen-year-old boy. Forrest promised to free them all when he called on their jailers.[30]

Cautiously approaching Murfreesboro from Readyville, twelve miles east of his objective, Forrest dispatched Colonel Wharton, with a select detachment, to capture a picket post along the turnpike from Woodbury. The Texans did their job stealthily and well; taken in the rear, the hapless sentinels surrendered without firing a shot. Forrest then called in his subordinates and mapped plans for taking the garrison by storm. Dividing the command into three columns, he sent them to strike as many targets. The occupiers were widely dispersed; most of them occupied camps on opposite ends of the town. The arrangement owed to bad blood among their commanders, each of whom desired to put distance between his unit and those of his disliked colleague.[31]

Forrest's multipronged attack began shortly after dawn on Sunday, the thirteenth, the raiding leader's forty-first birthday. He had informed his troopers of his desire to celebrate the occasion with a resounding victory. His men had shouted out their desire to make the day a memorable one, but now that they were in a position to do so, they faltered. The attack had been carefully designed, but it suffered because of the overeagerness of the raiders to engage the foe, as well as to the stubborn resistance they encountered.

Forrest, at the head of Morrison's battalion, galloped into the center of town, where he was unexpectedly joined by many of Wharton's men. The latter had failed to obey orders to attack a camp occupied by six companies of the 9th Michigan Infantry, three companies of the 7th Pennsylvania Cavalry, and four companies of the 4th Kentucky (Union) Cavalry, commanded by Colonel William Duffield and situated on the northeast edge of the town. The balance of Wharton's regiment—too few to overawe the opposition—failed to seize its objective outright. When Wharton went down with a severe wound, the fighting in that quarter degenerated into a confused melee, the result very much in doubt.

The column consisting of Lawton's Georgians, Smith's Tennesseans, and Walker's Kentuckians struck the other major encampment, on the Nashville Pike a mile and a half northwest of Murfreesboro. They found themselves engaging nine companies of a Minnesota infantry regiment, supported by two sections (four guns) of a Kentucky battery, all under Colonel Henry C. Lester. Here, too, resistance proved heavy and the fighting indecisive until Forrest reached the scene. Already he had helped Colonel Morrison rid the center of town of defenders. The prisoners taken there included the post commander, Brigadier General Thomas T. Crittenden, first cousin of the ranking Confederate at Logan's Cross Roads. Forrest had made a special mission of seizing the jail and liberating the captive Woodburians, some of whom had been under sentence of death. He had also seen to the occupation of the town's telegraph office and the severing of the local cable. Finally, he had exchanged shots with Federals up in the courthouse. The occupiers ran up a white flag only after Morrison's troopers smashed in the front door and set fire to a first-floor hallway.[32]

Forrest's presence northwest of Murfreesboro did not decide the issue, for a succession of charges on the infantry and artillery camp failed. Some of the officers involved in the unsuccessful effort advised their superior to break off the fight. Lester's men had barricaded themselves in their camp; by the time they were rooted out, reinforcements from Nashville might be on the scene. Forrest would not hear of it. "I did not come here to make half a job of it," he declared. "I mean to have them all."[33]

And he succeeded—not through continued fighting, but through persuasion. Leaving the barricaded camp, he galloped back into town, then out to Duffield's post, now commanded by Lieutenant Colonel John G. Parkhurst, Duffield having been seriously wounded. Forrest had Wharton's Texans cease firing and sent a surrender demand to the Union commander. In his note, the crafty Forrest stated that he had forced the surrender of Lester's troops, explained that he desired to avoid further bloodshed, and warned that should resistance continue, he would give no quarter. Taken in by Forrest's ruse and cowed by the tenor and implication of his threat, Parkhurst bowed to his opponent's demand shortly after noon.[34]

Forrest was not finished—he had one more enemy to conquer. Returning to the barricades northwest of Murfreesboro, he had his men stop shooting while he sent in a second surrender demand. This stratagem also succeeded. Granting Colonel Lester's request to consult with his wounded colleague Duffield before answering the demand, Forrest escorted the man through the town to the captured camp. As he did, he concocted a second ruse he thought might prove effective. Borrowing a page from John Morgan's book of military theatrics, he gave a covert order to one of his subordinates. The officer led his men in a single long column through the streets of Murfreesboro and past the Yankee colonel. Turning around in an area hidden to enemy view, he countermarched through the town to give the impression that Forrest handily outnumbered his opponents. Lester fell for the trick, surrendering what remained of the town's defenders. Now Forrest indeed had them all—more than one thousand two hundred prisoners. An additional two hundred Federals had been killed or wounded, as against nearly as many Confederate casualties. The equal numbers indicated the narrow margin of victory.[35]

As his troopers corralled their captives, the citizens of Murfreesboro, who had been hiding in cellars and garrets in hopes of eluding errant bullets, came forth to welcome and thank their liberators. Their hospitality exceeded anything Forrest's men had experienced at Woodbury. The townspeople believed the raiders had earned it, if only for reviving the local morale. "That day," a resident later recalled, "was the happiest day experienced by the citizens of Murfreesboro during the war."[36]

There was, however, a sinister aspect to Forrest's visit. At least one, and quite possibly two, of those taken captive in the camps outside town—African-American servants to Union officers—were personally killed by the raiding leader. The first was gunned down after grabbing a pistol, firing repeatedly at Forrest, and missing his mark. The likely second victim, a free mulatto from Pennsylvania, had not taken part in the fight. Seized and brought to Forrest's headquarters at day's end, he was questioned by Forrest, roundly cursed, and shot dead. Most of Forrest's biographers ignore the incident or dismiss it as hearsay or fabrication, but modern historians give it credence. Given Forrest's long-held antipathy toward blacks in general and his unbounded hatred of those who would ally themselves with the enemies of the South, the account does not strain credulity.[37]

Having subdued his enemy, Forrest paroled most of them, holding Crittenden and other high-ranking officers for exchange. He then set to work destroying Murfreesboro's ability to supply Buell's nascent offensive. By sundown the depot was in ashes; so, too, were four boxcars stocked with provisions Forrest could not carry off. He refused to leave behind the four artillery pieces he had captured; he hauled them off along with most of the fifty-some wagons his men had seized in the town. In all, he destroyed or confiscated more than a quarter million dollars' worth of enemy property.

Leaving town the following morning, Forrest marched back to Readyville, then headed for McMinnville before deciding to camp ten miles farther on, at Mountain Creek. There he gave his exhausted troopers four days' rest. On the eighteenth he started northwest to begin a reconnaissance in the neighborhood of Nashville. Having learned that seven hundred Yankee cavalry had been sent from that city to Lebanon, he determined to raid the town where John Morgan had been so rudely treated ten weeks earlier.

Before resuming the march, Forrest made one of his rare speeches to his assembled command. One man recalled that he "told us he was going all over Tennessee, and our next raid was on Lebanon which was a long and hard march all night." In his official report, Forrest remarked that "we dashed into the city in fine style," but found it empty of Yankees. Forewarned of his approach and aware of his death threat at Murfreesboro, the garrison had decamped for Nashville.[38]

Forrest remained in Lebanon for three days before resuming his journey to Nashville. He got to within sight of its steeples and spires before deciding that his real objective lay outside the city limits. "I moved then around the city," he wrote, "semicircling it and the Nashville and Chattanooga Railroad, passing within 3 miles of the city, and capturing on the way 2 additional pickets [i.e., picket posts]. I moved on the road for the purpose of destroying the bridges on the railroad near the city, and to my entire satisfaction accomplishing the purpose, destroying three important railroad bridges over Mill Creek and cutting the telegraph wires." At each bridge, as well as at Antioch Station, his men mixed with guard forces of various sizes. Forrest reported killing ten Federals and wounding twice as many, while making prisoners of ninety-four enlisted men and three officers.[39]

Rapid marching and hard fighting had taken a toll, so Forrest began the long return to the camp at Mountain Creek. Following a short rest there, he moved north to Sparta, Morgan's recent haven. At Sparta, Forrest and his men would spend the month of August, preparing to assist the future operations of Kirby Smith or Bragg.

Forrest took pleasure in informing Bragg that "my demonstration on Nashville, I am advised, created great excitement in that city." In fact, the alarms his approach set off in the state capital prompted Tennessee Provisional Governor (and future President) Andrew Johnson to appeal repeatedly for reinforcements and for volunteers to build up Nashville's defenses. Pursuit forces started out after the raiders, but the bridges Forrest had burned stymied them.

The damage inflicted on the Nashville & Chattanooga closed that critical supply conduit for two weeks. The unexpected interruption prevented Buell from advancing on Chattanooga, just as Kirby Smith had hoped. The Union commander plainly was displeased. Referring to the capture of Murfreesboro, he fumed that "few more disgraceful examples of neglect of duty and lack of good conduct can be found in the history of wars." He took out his anger on General Crittenden, whose career effectively ended when a court of inquiry convened by Buell demolished his reputation.[40]

Belatedly aware of the fragility of his communications, Buell detailed two divisions to protect the railroad in his rear. The move came too late to prevent the initiative in his theater from passing to the commander of the Department of East Tennessee and his counterpart at Tupelo. Urged on by the government in Richmond, Smith and Bragg would not hesitate to use the advantage Forrest had given them. In the words of one historian, Forrest's raid marked "the first decisive victory for Southern arms in

Tennessee, and coming at a time when repeated reverses had made much of the Southwest despondent, it had an enormous effect on the morale of both the civilian population and the army."[41]

WITHIN THREE WEEKS OF HIS RETURN FROM Cave City, Morgan not only reconstituted the command that had left Burnsville in the last days of April, he built the regiment that forever after would be linked to him, the 2nd Kentucky. Confederate sympathizers, stirred by his exploits and ignorant of his flight from Lebanon (Southern newspapers avoided mention of the aberrant setback), had flocked to his recruiting camp outside Chattanooga, where Morgan, prior to Forrest's arrival, had come under the command of Kirby Smith. Bragg had traded Morgan to his colleague in exchange for the 2nd Georgia Cavalry. The exchange benefited both armies, but the impetus behind it was Bragg's doubtful regard for Morgan. Rather than a team player who could be counted on to serve closely with the main army, Bragg considered him a raider—too free-spirited, too independent-minded to attach himself to a force larger than his own and become a useful adjunct to it.

Many enlistees in Morgan's regiment hailed from the Bluegrass, including a Lexington-area band under John B. Castleman and Thomas H. Hines, both of whom would number among Morgan's most enterprising subordinates. Other newcomers had arrived from Mississippi along with the now-recuperated Basil Duke (upon rejoining his brother-in-law, Duke was named lieutenant colonel of the new regiment). Former members of the recently disbanded 1st Kentucky Infantry had crossed the mountains from Virginia to learn the cavalry trade under Morgan. Two companies had come all the way from Texas, another from northern Alabama. The most distant acquisition had been the British adventurer George St. Leger Grenfell, a veteran of European armies whose proffered services as drillmaster and adjutant Morgan readily accepted.[42]

Early in June, Kirby Smith moved Morgan's spanking-new outfit to Knoxville, where the colonel spent another two months organizing and training. He clothed his men in natty uniforms, armed them with the short-barrel Enfield, and permitted Duke and Grenfell to drive them to the brink of exhaustion on the drill field. Once Morgan considered the regiment in shape to take the field, he conferred with his new superior on how best to utilize it. As he had done with the recently arrived Forrest, Kirby Smith directed Morgan to prepare himself to deliver a blow that might delay, if not halt, Buell's imminent advance through northern Alabama and into East Tennessee.

By the first week in July, Morgan was ready. On the fourth—the eighty-sixth anniversary of America's declared secession from the British Empire—he sallied forth from Knoxville in the van of his command, which consisted not only of his new regiment but also Colonel A. A. Hunt's regiment of partisan rangers and a battalion under Major R. M. Gano consisting of two companies of Texans and two of Tennesseans. Effectively a brigade, though a small one, this force would remain under Morgan's command for months to come. Morgan put its strength at nine hundred, but the figure seems low—his own regiment fielded that many. The addition of Hunt and Gano probably gave him at least one thousand five hundred officers and men. When spread out in marching formation, the command made an impressive spectacle, especially given the men's shiny coat and sleeve buttons and rifle barrels. The rear of this well-tailored column embraced not pack animals but two mountain howitzers (dubbed "Bull Pups" for their bark when fired) assigned to Lieutenant J. E. Harris. Riding beside Morgan and Duke in the forefront was Champ Ferguson, an accomplished guide who had accompanied Morgan on his raid to Cave City. The murderous Ferguson was also one of the war's most notorious guerrillas.[43]

By way of Sparta, Morgan's old stomping ground and Forrest's future summer encampment, Ferguson conducted the column north to the Cumberland River village of Celina. After a brief stopover in the town, the raiders forded the stream and, a few miles farther on, entered the Bluegrass State. As they passed the line, the hundreds of "orphans" riding with Morgan cheered loudly and long. The crossing constituted the opening act of a fateful drama to be played out on a stage intimately familiar to them all. They hungered for the happy denouement sure to follow.

The first opportunity to punish the occupiers of Kentucky and liberate their chattels occurred at Tompkinsville, eighteen miles northwest of Celina, in the small hours of July 9. Having learned that a camp holding a large detachment of the 9th Pennsylvania Cavalry lay just south of the village, Morgan surrounded the encampment in the darkness and, when dawn broke, hit it with a "dashing charge." Advancing on both sides of the Mill Creek Road, Hunt's Georgians on the left, Duke and the 2nd Kentucky on the right, the attackers sent the discombobulated Yankees scrambling to their horses, aboard which they galloped off in every direction. By desperate maneuvering they managed to elude Gano's battalion, which Morgan had positioned northeast of town in hopes of cutting off the anticipated retreat. Undaunted, Duke and Hunt mounted a dogged pursuit. The running fight, which covered several miles, resulted in the capture of thirty bluecoats, including their commander, Major Thomas Jordan; more than twenty other Pennsylvanians were killed, and upwards of forty went down with wounds. When the pursuit flagged, Morgan ransacked the 9th's camp, destroying its tents, stores, and miscellaneous equipage. When it resumed its march, the raiding column included a "valuable baggage train," pulled by thirty mules.[44]

Morgan conveyed his captives to Glasgow, the village he had avoided entering en route to Lebanon during his spring foray inside enemy lines. Then the town had been reported as occupied in force; this day it was free of the hated foe, who had scurried out of town hours before Morgan's arrival. The garrison had abandoned commissary, quartermaster's, and medical supplies, which Morgan destroyed, as well as a cache of rifles, which he distributed to the two hundred raiders who had departed Knoxville unarmed. Leaving Glasgow early on the eleventh, Morgan took the main road to Lexington, crossed the Barren River, and for the second time in two months entered Cave City. While Morgan chatted with the villagers, digesting news about other occupation forces, Lightning Ellsworth proceeded to the local telegraph office where he tapped into the cable to gain additional information from the mouths (or, rather, the fingers) of the Yankees themselves. His latest impersonation convinced local telegraphers that he could be trusted with sensitive intelligence. What Ellsworth learned would enable his boss to avoid clashes with enemy bodies throughout the balance of the expedition. From Cave City, Morgan also sent three companies to destroy the bridge over Salt River, "that the troops along the line of railroad might be prevented from returning to Louisville."[45]

From Cave City, the almost two-mile-long column wended its way through baking heat and choking dust to Lebanon, where Morgan's outriders surprised sixty Yankees and seized a well-stocked supply depot. Warehouses were put to the torch; huge quantities of clothing and equipment earmarked for delivery to the garrison inside Cumberland Gap went up in smoke. Here, too, Ellsworth used his bug to disseminate bogus reports of Morgan's whereabouts and irrational speculation about his intentions. Meanwhile, Gano's battalion demolished a railroad bridge on the Lebanon Branch.

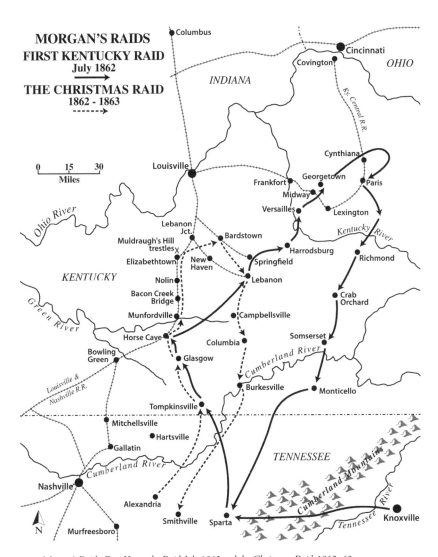

Morgan's Raids: First Kentucky Raid, July 1862 and the Christmas Raid, 1862–63.

On the twelfth, the raiding column moved on to Springfield and Mackville, where it had a sharp but successful encounter with a body of home guards. Then Morgan veered sharply east to Harrodsburg, whose citizens gave the visitors a "very encouraging" reception. Morgan was pleased that "the whole population appeared to turn out and vie with each other as to who should show us [the] most attention." Regretting his inability to linger, that evening he said his good-byes and moved on to Lawrenceburg, twenty miles to the north and only fifteen from the state capital at Frankfort. Morgan considered a raid on the city but changed his mind upon learning that it was held by two or three thousand regulars and home guards. Angling east, he headed to Shyrock's Ferry, where he crossed the Kentucky River aboard a ferry boat dredged up from the bottom where a Yankee demolition team had sent it. Then it was on to Versailles, where another lightly defended supply base yielded up three hundred horses and mules carrying United States Army markings.

On the fifteenth, Morgan paused between Midway and Georgetown to capture a troop train out of Frankfort. He reported that "I tore up the track and posted the howitzers to command it and formed my command along the line of the road, but the train was warned of our presence and returned to Frankfort." A second opportunity arose when Ellsworth intercepted a message that a train would be sent down from Lexington, twelve miles away, if the track was found to be clear. Send away, Ellsworth replied. Morgan made preparations to meet the train at Georgetown, but it, too, was warned off.[46]

The greeting Morgan and his people received at Georgetown was even warmer, and the hospitality provided even more abundant, than at Harrodsburg. The raiders laid over in the village for a day, reshoeing, reprovisioning, and fanning out to raze home-guard camps, demolish the railroad connecting Midway with Lexington and Frankfort, and destroy bridges and rolling stock. From Georgetown, Morgan sent Kirby Smith a report of his recent operations. He boasted that he had a force sufficient to hold the territory outside Lexington and Frankfort, which he described as defended mainly by home guards. He urged his superior to join him in this area, claiming that if he did so, as many as thirty thousand Kentuckians would join his command.

Meanwhile, Ellsworth continued to monitor the telegraph for reports of the progress of pursuit forces. There was no shortage of these. By now the state was swarming with pursuers dispatched in all directions from Louisville, headquarters of Brigadier General Jeremiah Boyle's District of Kentucky. Morgan had created such havoc in Boyle's bailiwick that the latter's reports to his superior, Buell, were fraught with biblical allusions ("Morgan is devastating with fire and sword"). Louisville was not the only prospective target alarmed by Morgan's depredations. Points as distant as Cumberland Gap and Cincinnati feared his coming. Even Washington, D.C., was aroused; a disturbed Lincoln asked General Halleck to look into the "stampede in Kentucky." But no one devised an effective means of combating the Rebel raider. Thanks to the confusion generated by Ellsworth's nimble brain and fingers, and to Morgan's ability to spread his presence so widely and promiscuously, no pursuit force large enough to give him trouble picked up his trail. The lack of opposition ensured that the balance of his expedition would proceed much in the manner it had thus far.[47]

Morgan had such a free and easy time of it that when near Versailles, he considered making a dash on Lexington. The temptation to return in glory to his old haunt was almost irresistible, but he had begun to worry that he could not forever elude the mob that was after his head. For once he gave way to caution, detouring well to the north of his city on a course that led to Cynthiana, on the south fork of the Licking River. Although careful to threaten the city as boldly as possible, he limited himself to dispatching John Castleman's company to wreck the railroad bridges between Lexington and points north. The daring Castleman, accompanied by a few equally adventurous souls disguised in Union blue, slipped into Lexington long enough to reunite with family members and to distribute recruiting posters that Morgan had had printed up in Georgetown. They departed the city just as stealthily and returned to the main column.[48]

On his homeward leg, Morgan collided with one force worthy of his opposition. On the seventeenth, the garrison at Cynthiana, consisting of infantry, horsemen, and cannoneers, almost all of them native Kentuckians, stoutly resisted the raiders' attempt to cross Licking River upon a covered bridge. After more than an hour of skirmishing with their blue-clad neighbors, Duke's men succeeded in fording the stream. Comrades scrambled over the bridge under heavy fire, while Gano's battalion, having circled around the enemy position, attacked from the rear. Assailed from so many angles, the Federals were gouged out of their defenses and compelled to surrender. The outcome gave Morgan, by his own count, 420 additional prisoners. The Yankees had lost more than fifty men killed or wounded, as against thirty-seven casualties in Morgan's ranks.[49]

Weary of marching, countermarching, and fighting, Morgan turned his back on the midsection of his state and, carting off his abundant spoils, headed for Tennessee. Content to evade rather than confront pursuers, he returned to home base along a route studded with villages with names fancy and plain: Paris, Winchester, Richmond, Crab Orchard, Somerset, and Monticello. By July 27, his men, their fancy uniforms covered with dust and spattered with grime, reached Confederate lines, stronger by three hundred recruits (from which four independent companies would be created) than when they had left Knoxville twenty-four days earlier. In his official report of the lengthy expedition, Morgan enumerated his accomplishments: more than one thousand miles traversed, seventeen enemy-held towns captured and occupied, thousands of Yankees bested in combat, one thousand two hundred regular troops captured and paroled, one thousand five hundred home guards dispersed, immense quantities of supplies burned or carried off, dozens of miles of rail line broken, countless bridges, storehouses, and railroad cars put to the torch, and miles of telegraph cable downed—after they had served to confuse and deceive those who had strung it. These achievements made Morgan's First Kentucky Raid—in terms of its impact on enemy manpower and resources—the most devastating of the conflict thus far.[50]

Bold in conception, nearly flawless in execution, the operation would encourage Morgan to mount additional incursions into occupied Kentucky. He found irresistible the prospect that he might outdo himself, accomplishing even more than he had this time out. Yet he must have considered the possibility, however remote it might seem, that future excursions might have a different outcome. Should he encounter enemy forces with the strength and courage to match him blow for blow and stratagem for stratagem, or with enough stamina and determination to pursue him to the death, future sojourns through his home state might not end as happily as this one had.

# SIX

# RETURN TO KENTUCKY

T HE COMBINED EFFECT OF FORREST'S AND Morgan's raids was to derail Buell's push toward East Tennessee. Other strikes at the Union leader's communications had also contributed to this, though their accomplishments were smaller in scale and less dramatic, and thus attracted less attention. These were outgrowths of Bragg's desire to interrupt service on the Memphis & Charleston Railroad in northern Mississippi and western Alabama.

Many of the less celebrated operations were the work of Captain Philip Dale Roddey, who commanded a regular company of Tennessee cavalry (he would later serve under Forrest) but waged war in the mode of a guerrilla. Roddey's exploits were not solely directed at railroads. Early in July, his band surprised a squadron of Ohio cavalry at Russellville, Alabama, and after an hour and a half of hard fighting drove his larger enemy back to Union-held Tuscumbia. A few weeks later, the Decatur branch of the Memphis & Charleston came under repeated attack by cavalry based in Mississippi, attached to Sterling Price's Army of the West. These troopers were commanded by Colonel Frank Armstrong, the darkly handsome scion of a distinguished military family (stepson of a general officer); a six-year veteran of the U.S. dragoons, with whom he had served at First Manassas; and a former member of Ben McCulloch's staff.[1]

Armstrong's operations, which included the July 28 rout of a garrison at Spangler's Mill, Alabama, consisting of several companies of Michigan cavalry, were a constant source of vexation to Buell. The Yankee leader lacked the manpower to keep safe the rail lines that connected his headquarters to points from which he could mount an offensive: the Memphis & Charleston, the Louisville & Nashville, the Nashville & Decatur, and the Nashville & Chattanooga.

The constant attacks on these fragile ribbons of supply—especially the critical and vulnerable stretch of the Nashville & Chattanooga between Louisville and Stevenson, Alabama—drove the Federal commander to exasperation. By the close of July he was writing to Major General William S. Rosecrans, the newly installed leader of a Union command known (to the confusion of some students of the war) as the Army of the Mississippi: "My communications . . . are swarming with an immense cavalry force of the enemy, regular and irregular, which renders it almost impossible to keep them open." In a later dispatch to Washington, Buell despaired of continuing his advance along the Memphis & Charleston, complaining that it had become "necessary both to accumulate from our extended lines a force sufficient to meet the force of the enemy threatening to advance on this city and to open our communications, now effectually closed."[2]

Buell's only hope of regaining momentum for his advance on Chattanooga was to mass his own horsemen and send them after his tormentors. Following Forrest's raid on Murfreesboro and his demonstration toward Union headquarters at Nashville, Buell organized an expeditionary force to run him to earth and render him incapable of further mischief. Buell entrusted the column to Brigadier General William Nelson, whose arrival at the head of an infantry division late on the first day at Shiloh had helped Grant stave off defeat. Nelson, who was considered rugged and determined enough to prove a match for his wily opponent, left Buell's lines at the head of a combined force of cavalry and infantry, promising to hunt down "Mr. Forrest, [who] shall have no rest."[3]

In the end, it was Nelson who was driven to exhaustion. Late in July, after three weeks of fruitless wandering across dusty trails in Middle Tennessee, always a step or two behind his quarry, the brigadier informed his superior that "to chase Morgan and Forrest, they mounted on race horses, with infantry [in] this hot weather is a hopeless task."[4]

While Nelson strained to catch Mr. Forrest, Buell sought a means of bagging Morgan. The force he sent out, unlike Nelson's, overtook its quarry, but the results were even more discouraging, the outcome less easy to abide.

Buell's choice to waylay Morgan was Brigadier General Richard W. Johnson, a native Kentuckian who, like Nelson, had experience leading both foot and horse. Also like Nelson, Johnson overflowed with confidence, bragging to Southern sympathizers that he would bring Morgan "back in a band-box." But he had to catch him first.[5]

By the time Johnson set out, late in August, Morgan had recently returned from yet another expedition aimed at the Louisville & Nashville. That operation had begun as the result of an order from Bragg, who was preparing to mount an offensive against Buell in concert with the forces of Kirby Smith. Both generals had been impressed by Morgan's foray through his home state, especially the fear and consternation it had spread from Louisville to Washington.

General Don Carlos Buell, USA.

Now they wanted Morgan to wreck Buell's rail connection with Gallatin, Tennessee. Morgan knew the place well, having raided it the previous March, capturing a railroad-repair train and wrecking the local depot. North of Gallatin the railroad passed through tunnels that, if blocked, would snarl military traffic for weeks if not months. A successful strike at that critical point on Buell's northernmost supply line might force the Army of the Ohio not only to abandon its base in Alabama, but to discard plans for operating anywhere in Tennessee and Kentucky.[6]

Thus it was that on August 11, the consummate raider broke camp at Sparta and guided his command—augmented by an influx of recruits inspired to enlist by the publicity given the First Kentucky Raid—along a route north by northwest. At dawn the next day, Morgan neared Gallatin, which he found occupied by four hundred Federals. As usual, he shrugged off the possibility that he might be biting off more than was digestible: he simply charged into the railroad village and took it by storm. He struck so swiftly that no one in blue fired a shot, even to sound an alarm. The garrison surrendered en masse, giving the raiders possession of everything they had been seeking.[7]

Morgan immediately headed for the point seven miles north of town where twin tunnels carried the tracks of the L&N through a rugged outcropping of the Cumberland Mountains. After brief deliberation he chose to block access to the larger of the two—"Big South," eight hundred feet in length—and assigned the task to a team headed by the ever-resourceful John Castleman. The wrecking crew, several of whose members had been railroad men in civilian life, heaped crossties in the center of the tunnel, then ran a captured locomotive, pulling flatcars filled with wood that had been set afire, into the pile at full throttle. The locomotive's boiler exploded upon contact; rock loosened by the flames fell from the roof onto the wreck; the timbers that braced the tunnel walls caught fire and collapsed; and the fires spread to a vein of coal that would burn for days and smolder for weeks. The devastation exquisitely rendered, Morgan led his riders east to Hartsville on the Cumberland River, where he went into camp.[8]

Morgan had scored a direct hit on his enemy's ability to wage war. It would take four months for work crews dispatched by officials of the L&N to unclog Big South, where debris was piled twelve feet deep in places. The crews also had to rebuild the trestle bridges north of Gallatin, which Morgan's men had destroyed, and replace hundreds of feet of track they had levered up on both sides of town before twisting them around trees to prevent their reuse. Buell's troops, denied the regular flow of rations and materiel from Louisville, would suffer greatly for Morgan's imagination and resourcefulness.

Enraged by the interruption to his supply lines, Buell expected General Johnson to make a finish of Morgan and his vandals. Johnson felt such pressure to move as early as possible that when he set out August 18 from his base at Murfreesboro, he led fewer than eight hundred cavalrymen. None of the foot soldiers that Buell had promised him had reached him in time to take part in the expedition.[9]

Johnson reached Hartsville on the twenty-first, only to learn that Morgan and his men had returned to Gallatin in response to reports that another Union force, this conveyed by train, had seized and pillaged the town. Angry that the inhabitants had greeted Morgan warmly when he entered the place on the twelfth, the Yankees carried several of its residents off to jail in Nashville.

By hard riding, Morgan overtook the enemy train, which had been halted some miles outside town by a burned trestle. Attacking furiously, he killed, wounded, or captured several passengers. Most of the bluecoats managed to escape aboard handcars, but their prisoners had been released. Galloping in the direction of Nashville, Morgan's men failed to overtake the fugitives but did capture a few of the stockades and blockhouses that Buell had built to protect the railroad. In so doing, Morgan bagged an additional one hundred prisoners.[10]

His prey having eluded him at Hartsville, Johnson proceeded toward Gallatin. He did not get far before he made contact with Morgan's outriders near the junction of the Hartsville and Scottsville Roads. When he learned the identity and size of Johnson's presence, Morgan was not cowed; turning to his second-in-command, he told Basil Duke: "We will have to whip these fellows, sure enough. Form your men, and as soon as you check them, attack."[11]

Duke complied by dismounting the lead squadron of the 2nd Kentucky and deploying it in woods to the left of the Hartsville Road. The unit immediately attracted the fire of Johnson's troopers, most of whom were also dismounted. The field of fire expanded as units on both sides arrived to add their weight to the contest. Morgan reported that "the fight . . . was maintained without much advantage on either side, the enemy having perhaps rather the best of it at first, until about 8.30 o'clock, when they began to fall back and my men to redouble their efforts." Within an hour, the Rebels had driven their adversaries almost four miles, and what was left of Johnson's line had become overextended. At this point the fighting suddenly died down. Johnson sent forward a white flag and sought a truce during which to bury his several dead. Morgan refused the request, demanding that his opponent surrender unconditionally.[12]

Morgan reacted sharply when he discovered that Johnson had used the respite to form a more compact line of battle. The raiding leader responded by dividing his force into three detachments: Gano's battalion, under Morgan's personal command; five companies of the 2nd Kentucky, which he placed on the left under his cousin, Major "Wash" Morgan; and three companies of the 2nd Kentucky, led by Duke and positioned on Morgan's right. When Johnson saw Morgan deploy as if to charge, he broke contact and raced off in the direction of Nashville. Morgan chased him down, his men screaming the Rebel Yell. Johnson was overtaken after a two-mile race, and, as Morgan wrote, "compelled to fight."[13]

At this point Morgan appeared to have the upper hand, but both he and his cousin had been carried afield by the excitement of the chase, overshooting their target and leaving Duke's detachment to take on Johnson's entire force. Morgan's brother-in-law may have seemed a prohibitive underdog, but he deployed and managed his force so expertly that after fifteen minutes of exchanging fire with him, Johnson—undoubtedly fearful of being cut off by the balance of Morgan's command—remounted his force and resumed his flight.

Presently Morgan's wings linked up and pursued as one. Blessed with faster and sturdier horses than their opponents rode, they cut off and captured large chunks of Johnson's command, making prisoners of Johnson himself and several of his officers. Morgan noted contemptuously that the remaining Yankees "escaped to the hills through the woods and high corn, making for the Cumberland River." Counting heads, he found that he had bagged two hundred prisoners. His men had killed or wounded dozens of other Yankees, at minimal cost to their own command.[14]

Morgan celebrated his most recent triumph by distributing among his men a proclamation lauding their "gallant bearing" throughout the day's action. While he was doubtful that their achievements, glorious though they were, would make the history books, he assured them that they would be "engraven deeply in my heart."[15]

If the depredations of Forrest, Morgan, Armstrong, Roddey, and other raiders had not forced Buell to defer his invasion of East Tennessee, Forrest's ability to elude Nelson, and Morgan's shellacking of Johnson, surely had. Realizing this, Bragg and Kirby Smith sought to cooperate on a plan to redeem Kentucky for the Confederacy. The ambitious Smith had been maneuvering toward an offensive in the Bluegrass since early July, seeking repeatedly to enlist the support and approval of Bragg and Jefferson Davis. Both had been initially uncooperative—Bragg because he wished to mount an offensive of his own in the rear of Buell's army, Davis because he was preoccupied with defending Richmond against attack or siege by McClellan's mammoth army, which in early May had advanced against the capital from Union-held Fort Monroe at the tip of the Virginia Peninsula.

After early July, when McClellan's thrust finally was repelled and the Army of the Potomac recalled to northern Virginia, Confederate officials focused on a Union army that was forming between the Rappahannock and Rapidan Rivers under John Pope, who on the basis of his success against Island No. 10 had been transferred to Virginia. In time, the Army of Northern Virginia, now under Davis's former military adviser, Lee, would neutralize Pope's threat and demolish his army, but until then the government would make no decision on western strategy; it merely expressed the hope that Bragg and Smith would team to thwart Buell.

Naturally enough, Davis, another native Kentuckian, looked with favor upon any incursion into his state, which he considered the heart of the Heartland. For months, other natives of the Bluegrass, including John Morgan, had been clamoring for an armed invasion while promising that as soon as Rebel forces set foot in the state, thousands of its sons, armed, mounted, and overflowing with patriotic zeal, would flock to their ranks. Davis believed this to be true and encouraged any planning that had a liberated Kentucky at its heart.[16]

Smith finally persuaded Bragg to move to East Tennessee, but Bragg acted mainly in response to Smith's repeated warnings that Buell was about to strike at Chattanooga. The Confederacy could ill afford to lose that city, the gateway to an area teeming with military-related resources. Not realizing that Smith was more intent on invading Kentucky than defending East Tennessee, on July 23, Bragg started his thirty-five-thousand-man army by rail from Tupelo to Chattanooga. His foot soldiers took the cars to Mobile, were ferried across Mobile Bay, then proceeded by rail and steamboat to Montgomery. From that first home of the Confederate government they took the train to West Point and Atlanta, Georgia, then across the Tennessee border to Smith's mountain stronghold. Bragg's cavalry, artillery, and supply trains avoided this circuitous route by marching overland via Tuscaloosa, Alabama, and Rome, Georgia. By any measurement, the operation was a mammoth undertaking, but the overburdened and much-maligned Confederate transportation system worked to near-perfection. On July 28, the day Bragg's rear echelon departed Tupelo, the head of his army entered Chattanooga.[17]

Bragg's horsemen, who had undergone a recent shakeup, did not make the journey as a single unit. Short days before leaving Tupelo, Bragg replaced the ill General Chalmers, who had commanded the army's cavalry since early June, with Colonel Joseph Wheeler. The diminutive Georgian had impressed Bragg on several occasions, dating to his conduct of the rear guard on the retreat from Shiloh and including his successful operations at Farmington and Monterey. More recently, during a flag-of-truce parlay with some well-placed Union officers, including the soon-to-be-famous Philip Henry Sheridan, Wheeler had carried off an effective ruse. In conversation with his opponents, he seemingly let slip the news that Bragg's army—whose size he greatly magnified—intended to remain in its present position until able to stock up on rations during the autumn harvest. Then, Wheeler intimated, Bragg intended to move not east but north toward the line of the Mississippi Central Railroad.[18]

Thus, Wheeler's enterprise and cunning had been suitably rewarded. How long Bragg expected him to remain in command of the army's mounted arm is uncertain; at this same time, Forrest, on the strength of his spectacular raid to Murfreesboro, was donning the wreathed stars of a general officer. Believing that he would need as much cavalry as possible for the coming campaign, Bragg planned to recall Forrest from Kirby Smith's command; at his new rank, Forrest would be Wheeler's superior.

On the eve of leaving Tupelo, Bragg gave Wheeler his first assignment, one intended to further the deception he had perpetrated when conversing with Sheridan. Wheeler was directed to mount a diversionary raid into West Tennessee, in the opposite direction from Bragg's intended route. Saluting smartly, Wheeler grouped his new command at Holly Springs, sixty miles above Tupelo. At the depot he made first contact with the four regiments and one additional unit that had been assigned to him: Clanton's 1st Alabama, Hagan's 3rd Alabama, Lay's 6th Confederate, Wade's 8th Confederate, and Major W. C. Bacot's Alabama battalion. The other five regiments Chalmers had commanded would not immediately go to Wheeler. When Bragg departed Tupelo, they would remain behind, attached to Price's and Van Dorn's commands. Concerned that he needed additional cavalry, Bragg would subsequently order them to join him on the march.[19]

What was left to Wheeler numbered on paper approximately four thousand five hundred officers and men. However, battle casualties, sickness, and detachments to venues beyond his reach had combined to reduce the force by almost three-fourths, which bothered the acting brigadier no end. New to the realities of cavalry service in the West, he was also dismayed to find that few of his troopers carried carbines or short Enfields—most toted shotguns and pistols—and only a few officers appeared to own sabers.

Properly armed or not, the expeditionary force set out for the Tennessee line on the sweltering morning of July 25. Wheeler's primary objective was the railroad garrison at Bolivar, where he intended to wreck track and trestles. He aimed to continue his work of destruction toward Jackson, the state capital, torching materiel stockpiled there, which reportedly included hundreds of bales of cotton seized from local farmers.

A small body of Mississippi infantry had been assigned Wheeler for the expedition; he planned to use the foot soldiers—who trudged in the rear of his column, choking on the cavalry's dust—to attack the garrison at Grand Junction, south of Bolivar. When the post was found abandoned, he left the infantry behind and rode on toward his more important objectives. The Mississippians lingered in the area to further the impression that Bragg was heading that way; they improved the time by burning two hundred cotton bales, thereby preventing their sale in the North for cash to fund the Union war effort.

Wheeler and his remaining force—barely five hundred horsemen—moved on to Middleburg, capturing three hundred more bales of contraband cotton, as well as numerous Federal soldiers, horses, arms, and ammunition. Then he entered Bolivar, seventy miles inside enemy lines. With unexpected ease, his advance guard chased off the local pickets and forced the rest of the garrison to batten down inside the town. On the outskirts and in adjacent towns, patrols dispatched from Bolivar seized and burned more cotton—upwards of three thousand bales, all told—while also confiscating a multitude of military supplies.

His work at Bolivar well done, Wheeler poised to advance on Jackson but was deterred by a recall message from Bragg, who by now had joined Kirby Smith at Chattanooga. Before he headed east, however, Wheeler added to his reputation as a grand deceiver by dispatching one of his most resourceful troopers into Bolivar, where, posing as a deserter, he persuaded the commander of the penned-up garrison that Wheeler was merely the advance element of a force of much greater size—presumably Bragg's main army—coming right behind. The officer rushed the news to the area commander, General McClernand, who hastened troops to Bolivar by train from Corinth and Jackson. The denuding of Jackson's defenses enabled one of Wheeler's parties to burn bridges outside the city and to sever telegraph lines.[20]

Calling in his outriders, Wheeler began his return march. He reached Holly Springs on August 1, and Tupelo a few days later. He could take pride in what he had accomplished on his first all-cavalry operation. As one modern-day historian observes, "without a doubt, Wheeler had conducted a brilliant raid and had accomplished all that Bragg had requested." A grateful Bragg would earmark the colonel for increased rank and expanded responsibility.[21]

WHEN BRAGG AND SMITH MET AT CHATTANOOGA on July 31, they came to an agreement on a combined offensive against Buell, who had left his base in northern Alabama for Tennessee. This, however, was about all they agreed upon. Neither commander was candid about what he intended to accomplish following their uniting. Although he promised to cooperate closely with Bragg, behind the scenes Smith was seeking Richmond's approval of an independent campaign in Kentucky, not only to return the Bluegrass State to the Confederate fold but to advance his own career at the expense of Bragg's.

For his part, Bragg was careful to give the impression that he intended to follow Jefferson Davis's advice to defeat Buell before entering Kentucky. In actuality, Bragg feared that even with Smith's close cooperation this would prove to be a tall order, especially if Buell fortified himself inside Nashville and refused to fight except on his own terms. A more prudent course would be to link with Smith inside Kentucky, perhaps in the Lexington area, once Smith tended to a long-deferred task, ridding strategic Cumberland Gap of the Yankee garrison commanded by the pesky Brigadier General George Washington Morgan. After linking with Smith at or near Lexington, Bragg would advance on the state capital, where he had been asked to install a Confederate government headed by Provisional Governor Richard C. Hawes. From Frankfort, assuming a slow pursuit by the cautious Buell, Bragg could move against population centers on either side of the Ohio River, striking terror in Yankee hearts and winning for himself the fame and glory that his colleague was seeking.[22]

The army leaders did agree on a division of forces, including mounted units. Previously, Bragg had augmented Smith's smaller command with an infantry division as well as with the horsemen of Forrest, Morgan, Scott, and other commanders. Now Bragg wanted some of these people back. As Smith's senior, he compelled the return of Forrest's brigade—Wharton's Texans, Lawton's Georgians, and Baxter Smith's Tennesseans—to the Army of the Mississippi. During the coming campaign, Forrest would support the right wing of the army, recently assigned to General Polk. The head, rear, and flanks of Bragg's left wing, under Hardee, would be protected by Wheeler's brigade, which would be expanded by the attachment of new units. In addition to the regiments he had led to Bolivar, in the weeks ahead, Wheeler would gain Colonel William W. Allen's 1st Alabama, Colonel J. Warren Grigsby's 1st Kentucky, the 9th Tennessee of Colonel J. D. Bennett, Colonel Martin J. Crawford's 3rd Tennessee, the 1st

Confederate Cavalry of Lieutenant Colonel C. S. Robertson, a Kentucky battalion led by Major J. W. Caldwell, and Captain Lemuel G. Mead's company of Alabama partisan rangers.[23]

Although forced to give up Forrest, Kirby Smith still had plenty of mobile assets. In advancing from Chattanooga toward Lexington through the Cumberland Gap, he could call upon not only Morgan's raiders but also the brigades of John Scott and Colonel Benjamin Allston, along with a number of unattached units. Considering that his army was smaller than Bragg's, Smith had long enjoyed a proportionally greater cavalry force. This fact suggested that the commander of the Department of East Tennessee had a better appreciation of the value of horse soldiers than Bragg, who neither understood cavalry's peculiar needs nor knew how to tap its potential.

Bragg was not ready to leave Chattanooga until the last days of August, by which time his elongated supply train had wended its ponderous way to East Tennessee. Well before then, Wheeler had ended his overland trek from Tupelo, and Forrest had completed preparations to join his well-rested brigade to Polk's column. In Smith's quarter, the campaign was well under way. Scott's brigade already had begun the first leg of what would prove to be a 160-mile climb across the Cumberland Mountains to cut the supply line of George Morgan's Yankees at London, Kentucky. The next day, Smith led his main body—four divisions of infantry—in an attempt to outflank Morgan and cut off his retreat from Cumberland Gap. The operation succeeded in forcing the Union commander to evacuate the position he had occupied for the past four months, but the attempt to bag his division failed. Despite the efforts of Scott and John Hunt Morgan to obstruct with rocks and felled trees the mountain defiles through which the Federals retreated ("he did his work gallantly and well," the Union Morgan admitted of his namesake), the Federals eluded capture with a hasty retreat through Boonville to the Ohio River. Morgan managed the retreat expertly, especially given the ruggedness of his escape route: he lost fewer than one hundred men, no guns or wagons.[24]

Bragg's army started from Chattanooga on August 28 by crossing the Tennessee River near Bridgeport, Alabama. Whether or not his army fully appreciated the fact, the movement constituted the middle component of a grand offensive that reached across the spectrum of operations East and West. On the sixteenth, Kirby Smith's cherished incursion into Kentucky had begun with his crossing of the Cumberland Mountains on roads converging toward Lexington. And on September 5, Robert E. Lee, having disposed of John Pope during the Second Manassas Campaign, would lead the Army of Northern Virginia across the Potomac River into Maryland, the first invasion of what was considered Union territory. Rebel hopes would never again rise as high as they did on the wings of this historic effort to wrest the advantage from an enemy that occupied so many quarters of the Confederate Heartland.

On the morning of the twenty-eighth, Wheeler forded the Tennessee in advance of Hardee's wing, riding at the head of the only regiments currently available to him, the 1st Alabama and 1st Kentucky, the latter only six companies strong. His abbreviated brigade crossed Walden's Ridge and moved through the Sequatchie Valley, a venue that Forrest had recently traversed and that Wheeler would revisit more than once over the next two years. Two days later, Wheeler's column passed through Beersheba Springs and reached the mountain hamlet of Altamont. Outside Altamont, Wheeler dismounted a large portion of his command and watched it scuffle with the infantrymen of Major General Alexander M. McCook's division. But the Yankees were not disposed to mix it up; their undersize opponents drove them off without working up much of a sweat. General Buell, mistaking Wheeler's dismounted action for an infantry attack, had withdrawn McCook to the Murfreesboro area. Thus began Buell's effort to group his scattered forces for a perhaps-imminent showdown with Bragg.[25]

Realizing that he had gotten too far in front of the foot soldiers in his charge, the next day Wheeler fell back across the Sequatchie and reestablished contact with Hardee's advance. Thereafter he stayed close to Hardee as he moved on to Carthage, less than thirty miles from the Kentucky line. On the way, he detached units of both regiments in his column. Scouts with these detachments took up positions from which to keep a sharper eye on Buell's troops. Others located and cut sections of the L&N that Forrest and Morgan had failed to sever, or that had been subsequently repaired.

One of Wheeler's new subordinates was impressed by the energy and attention to detail he observed in his commander: "He was throwing every obstacle possible to be conceived [of], in the way of the enemy's march to check and hinder his progress—Every bridge, however small or insignificant, on the road was destroyed and the track torn up" at numerous points.[26]

Having reestablished contact with Hardee, Wheeler did not shy from confrontation, even when the opposition included heavy ranks of foot soldiers. On September 12, having passed through a couple of John Morgan's old haunts, Hartsville and Gallatin, he crossed into Kentucky and reached the village of Woodburn. There he turned about in an attempt to ambush the head of a Yankee division that his scouts had discovered to be pursuing them, albeit slowly. This force was led by General Thomas L. Crittenden— not the officer whose career Forrest had ruined at Murfreesboro, but his first cousin, another Kentucky-born subordinate of Buell's. Wheeler's trap failed when the cautious cousin broke contact and withdrew after a mild skirmish.[27]

Minutes later, Wheeler nearly clashed with a more famous colleague. Forrest, now engaged in screening Bragg's right wing, approached Woodburn from the south just as the Wheeler-Crittenden fracas ended. Unable to gain a clear understanding of what was transpiring up ahead, and unaware that another body of Confederate cavalry was in the area, Forrest mistook Wheeler's troopers, some of whom wore pieces of blue clothing, for Yankees. Acting with unusual haste, Forrest ordered the 8th Texas to pile into Wheeler's rear, pistols blazing. Friendly fire was averted at the last minute when one of Colonel Wharton's subordinates correctly identified the troopers in his sights and called off the attack.

Then ensued the first face-to-face meeting between two of the major figures in Confederate cavalry history. Although accounts are sketchy, it would appear that the confab was not cordial. Forrest, who knew little or nothing about Wheeler, appears to have accused him of blundering into his path and failing to identify himself. Later, Forrest also criticized Wheeler's conduct of his fight with Crittenden, claiming that as he came on the scene, Wheeler's men were "falling back helter skelter and in much confusion," and that they scattered shamefully in the face of Wharton's abortive attack. Neither contention can be verified, but Forrest's claims appear symptomatic of the friction-laden relationship the officers were destined to forge.[28]

Forrest's view of Wheeler's conduct may have been colored by jealousy, the product of the favoritism shown Wheeler by their common superior. Only one month earlier, Forrest, meeting with Bragg in Chattanooga, had been assured that he would command every horseman in the Army of the Mississippi. Historians theorize that Bragg told Forrest this only because at the time Wheeler was still en route from Mississippi and Bragg wanted immediate cavalry support, hence his recall of Forrest from Smith's department. But Forrest's attachment to Bragg's army lasted only until the generals' next meeting, a fortnight after the incident at Woodburn. On that occasion, Forrest was told that he was being relieved from duty with the Army of the Mississippi. He was ordered to proceed to Middle Tennessee to recruit, organize, and command an independent brigade. Forrest was authorized to raise six regiments, two of cavalry and four of infantry—something his vast popularity in that region would accomplish in record time—with which to batter enemy communications in and around Nashville. On September 27, Forrest departed the army for his new area of operations.[29]

A number of considerations factored into Bragg's decision to divest himself of a soldier already gaining recognition as one of the finest mounted commanders in American history. For one thing, Bragg was an inconsistent evaluator of his subordinates' talents and a poor judge of their value. He had rid his army of John Morgan's Kentuckians because he believed they, and especially their leader, were too undisciplined, too independent-minded, to support a larger command closely and faithfully. His assessment may well have been correct, but in applying the same opinion to Forrest, he did the latter a disservice. It was true that Forrest sometimes chafed under higher authority. He did not suffer fools gladly, and he had already served under a host of incompetents such as Pillow, Floyd, and Polk. But, despite his independent bent, his casual disregard of military etiquette, and his volatile temper, Forrest was an able tactician, a fearless combatant, and a firm and fair leader who sometimes inspired fear in his men but unfailingly commanded their trust and respect.

In Bragg's eyes, Forrest's basic shortcoming was that he was not a West Point-educated professional soldier like Joe Wheeler (whom he inconveniently outranked), nor did he attempt to act like one. On at least one occasion, Forrest had substituted his own judgment for Bragg's by disregarding the latter's instructions for the disposition of his command. On balance, Forrest seemed more suited to serving in a secondary theater and in a rural setting where professionalism counted less than the ability to ride hard and fight no less hard against both irregular and regular troops. Bragg may have had Forrest all wrong, but he had enough rank and authority to make his error stick.[30]

AFTER DETERMINING TO JETTISON FORREST, Bragg considered transferring his brigade, which already had been depleted by a series of detachments, to Wheeler. The army commander seems to have decided that, with the army's cavalry scattered across such a wide arc, Wheeler could not be expected to group and integrate it in a desirable period. Thus he decided to keep what remained of Forrest's command a separate entity, assigned to Colonel Wharton. As one cavalry historian has observed, Bragg would have preferred to place someone with regular army experience in charge of the organization, but none was available. Bragg did not entertain a high opinion of Wharton, who had angered him by refusing to serve under officers junior to him, resulting in the 8th Texas's removal from John Adams's brigade. Still, Wharton, like Forrest, was mentally and physically tough, and his men regarded him as a worthy successor to their beloved founder, Benjamin F. Terry.[31]

By September 14, Bragg's army was closing up at Munfordville, a Green River village on the railroad between Bowling Green and Louisville. Three days later, following stubborn opposition, the local garrison surrendered. Meanwhile, Wheeler patrolled toward Bowling Green, then in the process of being occupied by Buell, who finally was moving with a full head of steam toward a showdown with the invaders of Kentucky.[32]

By all indications, Bragg would have to oppose the Yankee commander by himself. Kirby Smith's so-called Army of Kentucky, covered in front, flanks, and rear by its abundant cavalry, including John Morgan's men, was traveling far from its sister command. Smith had done a certain amount of heavy lifting—on August 30 he had surrounded and captured the four-thousand-man post of Richmond, Kentucky—and now he intended to treat himself to some light entertainment. He remained far more interested in frightening the cities along the Ohio than in teaming with the Army of the Mississippi to battle Buell. On the fifteenth, Smith attained one of his goals by occupying Covington, across the river from Cincinnati. Wholly inadequate forces defended the city and its environs, but Smith had no intention of doing more than threaten. The next day, having scared his target audience out of its wits, he fell back to Lexington.

As Bragg collected his spoils at Munfordville, Joe Wheeler reconnoitered toward Bowling Green by way of Oakland Station on the Louisville & Nashville. On his way south, his scouts detected northwestward marching columns of infantry, artillery, and wagons, suggesting that Buell was heading for Louisville, there to group his far-flung units prior to giving battle. When Wheeler passed his observations on to Bragg, the latter seemed strangely disinterested. He appeared to believe that Buell would not be able to strike before Bragg and Smith could link. With this in mind,

Bragg dispatched an aide to Lexington to ask Smith to meet him at Bardstown, almost fifty miles northeast of Munfordville.[33]

But Bragg's plans changed as a result of an unexpected setback suffered by Joe Wheeler on the seventeenth—a most fateful date on the Confederate calendar, the day Robert E. Lee met defeat along Antietam Creek, effectively ending the Army of Northern Virginia's sojourn in Maryland. The setback, which confirmed Wheeler's suspicion that his brigade remained too small to cover the army and at the same time defend itself, occurred when an enemy force of unknown size attacked him in front, driving in his pickets and threatening his main body. Closely pressed throughout the day, Fightin' Joe could not prevent another force from out-flanking him on the road to Louisville and overwhelming the rear guard he had positioned between Bowling Green and Glasgow. Wheeler, feeling sud-denly vulnerable, called in his outlying units and his supply wagons, and amidst a downpour marched to Bragg's headquarters at Munfordville. Wheeler's report of the day's activity persuaded his superior to call off his proposed move to Bardstown. Instead, Bragg hunkered down inside the works he had captured, while ordering Wheeler to return to his station of that morning and confirm his earlier sightings.

Wheeler marched back to his old position in heavier force than when he had abandoned it. A flurry of manpower additions had bulked up his brigade, which now comprised not only Allen's and Hagan's regiments but also the 3rd Georgia and a two-hundred-man body of Bennett's 9th Tennessee. The additions were not sufficient to enable Wheeler to main-tain contact with every bluecoat flooding into southern Kentucky, but he was happy to be accompanied by two pieces of horse artillery, light-weight cannon manned by artillerymen who rode horses capable of keeping pace with the cavalry units they supported.[34]

Reestablishing contact with the enemy around Cave City, Wheeler observed a buildup that could only mean Buell was prepared to strike with his entire army. At first Bragg did not seem unduly concerned; when Wheeler returned to Munfordville on the nineteenth, his superior expressed himself as confident of success in any engagement with Buell, whether or not he enjoyed Smith's assistance. But within a few hours the army leader grew nervous and agitated—as he frequently did when a crisis loomed—as well as doubtful of the situation facing him. As if disbelieving Wheeler, he dispatched Simon Buckner's infantry division to reconnoiter the same area the cavalry leader had scouted. The Kentuckian reported back that the nearest Yankees appeared content to maneuver and skirmish at long range. Somewhat relieved, Bragg returned to his plan to join Smith at Bardstown. On September 20, Wheeler's horsemen covered the army's rear as it departed Munfordville for that locale.[35]

Wheeler was assisted in this duty by Forrest's brigade, under its new commander. The move from Munfordville marked the first time Wheeler and Wharton had served together for an extended period. Wheeler sized up his colleague as a highly competent cavalryman, with a streak of independence comparable to Forrest's. Wharton, a college-educated attorney, gave Wheeler the impression of a military politician of the first rank—ambitious, a bit haughty and condescending, and acutely sensitive to matters of rank and seniority. Throughout the operation, Wharton visibly chafed at his enforced subordination to a fellow colonel who until recently had been a web-foot. The man's abrasive personality would embroil him in future conflicts, not only with Wheeler but with other superiors and subordinates, one of whom would shoot and kill him during a quarrel days before war's end.[36]

General John A. Wharton, CSA.

Wheeler's role in Bragg's withdrawal from Munfordville became more difficult on the twentieth, when some of the advancing Federals shoved his brigade to and across Green River. To ensure the safety of the fording operation, Allen's regiment pitched into the nearest pursuers, relieving pressure on Wheeler's main body but suffering several casualties, including the mortal wounding of Lieutenant Colonel T. B. Brown. The next day, as Wheeler pressed along the Bardstown Pike, he fought another delaying action against the ever-annoying people in his rear. When they finally drew off, he received orders to close up on Hardee at Hodgenville. The Federals did not pursue, enabling Wheeler to rest his men in the little town—the birthplace of Abraham Lincoln—until the twenty-seventh. That day he rejoined Wharton, whose brigade had pressed ahead to Bardstown, connecting there with the rest of the army.[37]

Bragg had asked Kirby Smith to meet him in that corner of the state, the heart of Kentucky's horse-breeding country, but Smith had not complied. He continued to loll in his comfortable camps around Lexington, almost fifty miles northeast of Bardstown, and showed no desire to leave. Having been denied the cooperation promised him at the start of the campaign, Bragg was properly furious. Nor had Smith been the only colleague to desert him. Ten days before entering Bardstown, Bragg had reissued orders for Earl Van Dorn and Sterling Price to support him by sweeping into East Tennessee. But Van Dorn had persuaded Price instead to attack Grant's lines along the Tennessee-Mississippi border. Anticipating such a strike, Grant sent his subordinate, Rosecrans, to oppose Price. The result was Price's defeat at Iuka, Mississippi, on September 19. Two weeks later, Van Dorn and Price would further anger Bragg by attacking Rosecrans in his new position at Corinth; the two-day battle would end in heavy loss and abject retreat. The Mississippi interlude may have assisted Bragg to some extent by preventing Grant from reinforcing Buell, but it fell far short of the long-term benefits Bragg had hoped to derive from Van Dorn's and Price's operations.[38]

ABSENCE OF COOPERATION HAVING DASHED HIS plans for a triumphal march through Kentucky, Bragg now abandoned any hope of planting the Stars and Bars on the banks of the Ohio. He decided to assume a defensive posture in the Bluegrass region and allow events to play out around him. It would prove to be a fatal miscalculation. Bragg's movement to Bardstown had opened the road to Louisville, which the head of Buell's army reached on the twenty-fifth. In the first days of October, having consolidated his army and supplied and provisioned it for the field, Buell was bearing down on Bragg, no longer content to probe his flank and rear but ready to strike him head-on.

On October 4, Wheeler's brigade was called to Bardstown to guard the left flank of the army, which was now under Polk's command, Bragg having gone to Frankfort to tend to the political element of his operation by overseeing the installation of Richard Hawes's government. Bragg's entrance with a portion of his army and Hawes's subsequent inaugural were both well received, but the response of the local population had a hollow ring, failing as it did to conform to observed realities. Confounding Confederate expectations, relatively few of the state's sons had come forward to swell Bragg's ranks, raising questions about the depth of Kentucky's desire to rid itself of the blue-uniformed conqueror.[39]

On the fifth, the stubborn Polk, instead of moving the army north toward Harrodsburg as Bragg wished, advanced to Danville, thirty-some miles east of Bardstown. The move, which Polk deemed imperative in the face of the fast-approaching enemy, was made despite the absence of an adequate screening force. Wharton's brigade had been moving hither and yon thanks to conflicting orders from Bragg and Polk, causing it to be near-ly surrounded near Bardstown by Buell's cavalry advance. An officer of the 8th Texas explained that "we were cut off . . . by 2500 cavalry and immedi-ately upon learning it Col Wharton ordered our Regt to move at a gallop over toward Bardstown and just at the Fair Ground we were met by a dead-ly volley of Sharp[shooters'] balls. We halted not but put the spurs deep into the sides of the horses. The gallant boys headed by Col Wharton raised the war whoop and ran over them outright. They broke and fled in every direction." Polk, who was partially responsible for the Texans' plight, publicly congratulated them on their "gallant action" and narrow escape. Polk failed to add that Wharton's roundabout route back to the main army kept his men out of action for days, forcing Wheeler not only to reconnoi-ter ahead of the army but to protect the rear in the direction of Perryville, a hamlet on the railroad between Bardstown and Danville. Both armies were moving toward that place, which lay near Doctor's Creek, a tributary of Chaplin's Fork of Salt River. The surrounding area had been in the grip of a severe drought, parching Rebels and Yankees alike, but pools of water were known to be standing in the bed of Doctor's Creek. It was at Perryville that Buell's advance made contact with Polk's command (soon again under Bragg) on the morning of October 8, inaugurating the engagement that decided the fate of the Kentucky campaign.[40]

As was too often the case, the cavalry saw only peripheral involvement in the battle and exerted relatively little influence on the result. On the sixth and seventh, however, Wheeler's brigade had been heavily involved in resisting Buell's push to Perryville, fighting and falling back from one posi-tion to another to delay a large force of all arms, including a brigade of foot soldiers. This tactic—one Wheeler would employ on so many future fields that he would become expert at it—proved quite effective. Frustrated by Wheeler's opposition, on the afternoon of the seventh, the commander of the troops in closest contact with him sent a mounted regiment to clear the road from Bardstown to Perryville. The Union horsemen spurred into a hell-for-leather charge—and right into a carefully laid trap. As Wheeler later noted, concealed sharpshooters, supported by their horse artillery comrades, opened on the charging Federals "with excellent effect, thoroughly stampeding their entire front." The ambush had one undesirable feature: "So effectual and unexpected was this stampede of so large a force of cavalry, artillery, and a portion of their infantry that our cavalry could not be placed in a position to charge them in time to accomplish all that could be desired."[41]

Only when a heavier force—part of Major General Charles C. Gilbert's corps—came up in rear of the skedaddling troopers did Wheeler fall back to the outskirts of Perryville. He stayed there for the balance of the seventh. Just before dark, however, he moved forward to exploit his army's repulse of a limited attack by Gilbert's leading division. Advancing with unaccustomed impetuosity, Wheeler fell into the same sort of trap he had set earlier in the day: Yankees hiding in "cornfields behind a staked and ridered fence" broke from cover and swarmed over the 1st and 3rd Alabama, which had charged down a ridge about a mile and a half from Perryville. Allen's and Hagan's men suffered few casualties, but Wheeler was forced to recall them to Peters Hill, perhaps a mile from Perryville.[42]

Although Wheeler's and Wharton's troopers played a secondary role during the fighting on the eighth—a day marked by Confederate attacks that fell just short of success—they enjoyed a few opportunities to distinguish themselves. Wheeler's most prominent involvement was another lengthy delaying action, this directed at the division of Thomas L. Crittenden, with whom he had tangled shortly after entering Kentucky. Mounting the fighting retreat they had begun to perfect, Wheeler's men, most of them fighting afoot, so slowed Crittenden's advance toward the Confederate left (south) flank that his division added little to the counterattacks Buell launched in that sector.[43]

The fighting this day was characterized not only by Confederate assaults parried and repulsed but by an acoustic shadow that prevented units on both sides from discovering battle had been joined only a short distance away. As a result, fewer than half the potential combatants saw action at any point during the eighth. By dark, when the bloodletting ceased, the advantage appeared to have swung to Bragg. On Buell's left flank, a full corps had been pushed back a mile from its original position. Buell's center had also been forced to give ground and, thanks largely to Wheeler, the Union forces on the right had made little progress south and west of Perryville.[44]

Undismayed, Buell intended to renew the fight come morning. That night, however, the Confederate high command called the latest in a series of demoralizing war councils dating back to Fort Donelson. Bragg, Polk, and Hardee agreed that their gains had come too late in the day to be exploited; furthermore, the men were in no shape to continue the struggle. The army was not only weak from blood loss—preliminary reports put its casualty rate at 30 percent—but also suffering from the continuing scarcity of potable water. Bragg had committed his only reserves, and his left flank, although well guarded by the cavalry, appeared vulnerable to infantry assault. He concluded that it would be folly to reengage the enemy until he could unite with Smith. Around midnight he sent a courier to importune his colleague to meet him at Harrodsburg. Soon afterward he issued orders that recalled the forwardmost troops to the strong defensive positions they had thrown up at battle's start.[45]

Then Bragg sent for Joe Wheeler, himself nearly exhausted from a difficult day's work under a brutal sun, and informed him that, once again, the cavalry was to cover a retreat—a retreat that ultimately would return the army to Middle Tennessee. Bragg's Kentucky campaign was effectively dead. It had succumbed to inadequate planning, to a general failure to cooperate and coordinate, and to a basic misconception on the part of military and political leaders across the South, who had believed that Kentuckians could be delivered from Union occupation, and desired to be.

# SEVEN

# AUTUMN OF HOPE

S OME MILITARY OBSERVERS CLAIM THAT BECAUSE he had driven the Union left flank well beyond its position of early October 8, Bragg emerged from the battle as the de facto victor. A typical postmortem on the battle comes from Joe Wheeler, writing years after the war: "During this sanguinary engagement, our line had advanced nearly a mile. Prisoners, guns, colors, and the field of battle were ours; not a step which had been gained was yielded. The enemy, though strongly reinforced, was still broken and disordered. . . . At every point of battle the Confederates had been victorious."[1]

Latter-day historians, including Bragg's most recent biographer, beg to disagree. Grady McWhiney contends that "the Confederates had gained only a limited tactical success at Perryville. It was not a victory because they achieved nothing and suffered almost as many casualties as they inflicted on the Federals: some 3,396 Confederates and 4,211 Federals were killed, wounded, or captured (or were missing)." McWhiney points out that Bragg's handling of his troops was clumsy and inconsistent. At times attempting to bull his way to victory, he recklessly attacked in waves, using up his reserve forces; at other times he committed his troops "in driblets." In sum, "the battle proved that Bragg was no better at commanding an army than he had been at leading a corps."[2]

McWhiney notes that Bragg could and did blame various subordinates for the outcome, mainly for giving him incorrect or insufficient intelligence on Buell's whereabouts. This deficiency, added to the effects of the acoustic shadow, led Bragg to stumble into battle without a clear picture of the situation. Not until late afternoon did he begin to comprehend the scope of the engagement and to sense its flow, permitting him to make accurate judgments about when, where, and how to commit his forces. Bragg's saving grace was that his opponent was equally ignorant of the true condition of affairs and the parameters of the fight.

Because information-gathering was by definition the responsibility of the cavalry, and because in the extended absence of Wharton's brigade that responsibility fell to Joe Wheeler, Bragg might have been expected to place much of the blame for fighting "blindly," as McWhiney puts it, on the little Georgian. Some historians assign him a large share of culpability. Perryville historian Kenneth Noe faults Wheeler for concentrating his energy throughout the fight on engaging the Federals in his front at long range. Noe believes that the Federals opposite Bragg's left were not fooled by Wheeler's maneuvers or paid them much notice. Noe also blames Wheeler for failing to inform Bragg until midafternoon of the extent of the Union buildup on his part of the field: the battle might have ended differently "had Bragg known that an unbloodied Federal corps [T. L. Crittenden's II Corps] waited to the southwest of Perryville. And Bragg should have known—it was Wheeler's job to tell him." Noe, however, fails to explain how the battle would have changed had Bragg possessed this information. Other historians condemn not Wheeler but Hardee, to whose command Wheeler's and Wharton's brigades were attached before and during the battle. Hardee had given Wheeler vague and incomplete orders, and there is no evidence that he urged Wheeler to gain more accurate or more timely intelligence about the Federals in front of him.[3]

As to claims that Wheeler provided little support to Bragg or Hardee throughout October 8, it is a fact that the Yankees facing Wheeler, who were strong enough to have overwhelmed the Rebel left had they gotten into action, remained largely quiescent in the face of active cavalry opposition. Moreover, Bragg appears to have leveled no criticism at Wheeler for failing to keep him informed of the enemy's movements. In fact, during the army's subsequent retreat to Middle Tennessee, on at least two occasions Bragg complimented Wheeler on his intelligence acquisition. On October 10, when the retreat got under way, he praised his cavalry leader for sending him a particular report "regarding the enemy's movements. The information you furnish is very important. It is just what I needed and I thank you for it. This information leaves no doubt as to the proper course for me to pursue." Later that day Bragg informed Wheeler, through his chief of staff, that "your report of your operations from the 14th to this date has been full and thoroughly satisfactory." In his official report of the campaign, Bragg claimed that although pursuers pressed the army at various points during the retreat from Perryville, its rear "was so successfully protected by the cavalry, under the admirable management of Colonels Wheeler and Wharton, that but little annoyance was felt."[1]

Little annoyance was felt because the pursuit was cautious, sluggish, and tentative. A military commission that delved into aspects of Buell's generalship during the campaign severely criticized his conduct in the days after the battle. A major result was Buell's relief from command and his replacement by William Rosecrans, who early in November established in Nashville the headquarters of the newly designated Army of the Cumberland.[5]

This is not to say that the job Wheeler did to protect Bragg's withdrawal from Kentucky was without difficulty. When the army pulled out of Perryville, heading for Harrodsburg and Bryantsville, Wheeler and Wharton, under overall command of the former, held the enemy—cavalry in front, foot soldiers close behind—in check, preventing Buell from detecting the extent of the withdrawal. Moving west to Danville behind Bragg's main body, early on the eleventh, Wheeler skirmished briskly with the pursuing cavalry, taking casualties but inflicting just as many. On the twelfth, the cavalry leader put a water barrier between Bragg and his pursuers, crossing Dick's River near the celebrated Union recruiting rendezvous known as Camp Dick Robinson and preventing the enemy from fording.[6]

Wheeler's conduct of the rear guard pleased not only Bragg but other observers as well. Major Baxter Smith, whose Tennessee battalion formed a part of Wharton's brigade, believed that Wheeler "particularly distinguished himself" by his "untiring and sleepless" efforts to complicate and delay Buell's pursuit. Smith appreciated Wheeler's determination to ensure that "nothing . . . necessary to check the enemy's advance" was omitted. The major was as impressed by the man as he was by the soldier: "[I] found him to be . . . as gentle as a woman, and as courteous as a cavalier of an older time. . . . [His] habits were strictly temperate, and he usually laid down to sleep at night, with his men in bivouac."[7]

On October 13, Wheeler received glad tidings: Bragg had conferred upon him the title of chief of cavalry of the army. Heretofore, Wheeler had commanded strictly by virtue of seniority, and he had given orders to Wharton only when their brigades served side by side. From now on, his authority encompassed the cavalry's entire area of operations.

South of Dick's River, Wheeler discovered that he had been assigned to cover not only Bragg's retreat route but also Kirby Smith's. The Army of Kentucky, which had studiously avoided cooperating with Bragg throughout the seminal portion of the campaign, had linked with the Army of the Mississippi at Harrodsburg, in time to join it in retreat. Leaving behind forces to block the most accessible fords, Wheeler led his main body back to the north side of Dick's River. There his brigade took the Lancaster Road, on which Smith's command was marching; Wharton guarded the southwestward-running road to Stanford, Bragg's route of retreat. As Wheeler wrote, "the enemy were pushing forward, but, by continually fighting them, they repeatedly deployed their lines for battle, and consequently progressed very slowly." Here was evidence of Wheeler's growing ability, through active maneuvering and ambush tactics, to make the enemy believe his force was much larger than it was, inducing caution. It was a tactic he had learned, and learned well, from those Indian parties his mounted rifle regiment had contended with in the Southwest in the months prior to Fort Sumter.[8]

Wheeler's proximity to Smith's column brought him into contact with potential reinforcements. Near Lancaster on the thirteenth, he was joined by half the cavalry assigned to the Army of Kentucky, the brigades of John Hunt Morgan and Colonel Henry M. Ashby. Because Buell's pursuit continued to be conspicuously timid, Wheeler felt confident in fending off the Yankees with his own command; for this reason, he courteously refused Morgan's and Ashby's offer of help. They moved on, joining the balance of Smith's command as it withdrew eastward by way of Richmond, Kentucky. Bragg's army, which Wheeler soon rejoined in order to augment Wharton's hard-pressed brigade, was taking a more westerly route toward Cumberland Gap via Crab Orchard.[9]

The combined weight of Bragg and Smith served as a further deterrent to Buell, who, uncertain of the strength of the force he was now facing, pursued with ever greater caution. It was well that he did, for Smith, upon their junction, had urged Bragg to throw both armies at their common opponent. Some historians agree with the opinion of several contemporary observers, including General Gilbert of Buell's army, that a joint blow, if delivered promptly and without restraint, might have wrecked the Army of the Ohio.[10]

After rejoining Wharton, Wheeler engaged Buell's mounted advance between Crab Orchard and Mount Vernon, fighting, as he later recalled, "behind stone fences and hastily erected rail breastworks, and when opportunity offered [we] charged the advancing enemy." On the sixteenth, he began to obstruct the roads with felled trees, rocks, fence rails, and anything else that would take time and sweat to remove. "These devices were continually resorted to," Wheeler noted, "until the 22d, when the enemy ceased his pursuit." For two days, Wheeler maintained his position near the village of London, venturing forth to stab at the winded pursuers. On the nineteenth, he struck at the nearest Yankees with a portion of an infantry brigade that had been sent to increase his ability to inflict pain. Wheeler noted pointedly that "this was the only occasion where any infantry engaged the enemy after the battle of Perryville."[11]

Fightin' Joe remained substantially in this same position until Bragg and Smith crossed back into Tennessee through the now-Yankee-free Cumberland Gap. His job done, Wheeler could take pardonable pride in the protection he had afforded his army throughout its journey from Perryville. He expressed that pride in prose typical of the reports he had composed ever since Shiloh. On October 23, he published an address in which he lauded his troopers' "gallantry in action" and "cheerful endurance of sufferings from hunger, fatigue, and exposure. . . ." He claimed victory in "twenty pitched fights, many of which lasted throughout the day" against "largely superior numbers of the enemy's troops of all arms," and no fewer than one hundred skirmishes: "In this continual series of combats and brilliant charges many gallant officers and brave men have fallen. We mourn their loss; we commend their valor. Let us emulate their soldierly virtues."[12]

Wheeler's superiors added generous dollops of praise. In his postaction report, Bragg thanked him for his "admirable management" of the rear guard throughout the retreat. Polk cited his indebtedness to both Wheeler and Wharton "for their vigilance and activity in protecting our flanks and for the vigorous assaults made by them upon the enemy's lines." The bishop-general singled out Wheeler and his brigade for special praise: in every phase of the campaign they displayed "the same dauntless energy and courage for which they have become distinguished." Hardee in his report referred to Wheeler as "that brave and able officer," and described his operations in the recent battle as "brilliantly managed." Tributes such as these fell sweetly on Wheeler's ears, for he was intensely ambitious, as his own self-congratulatory reports of the campaign clearly demonstrate. He dared hope that these encomiums would help gain him the brigadier general's rank his position called for.[13]

Bragg's army broke through the Cumberland Mountains at Morristown, Tennessee, on October 21. His foot soldiers were given less than a week's rest; on the twenty-seventh, they were put aboard the cars of the East Tennessee Railroad and shuttled to Chattanooga, then to Bridgeport, Alabama. Crossing the Tennessee River aboard ferries, they endured another rocking, jouncing train ride to Murfreesboro. There they would spend the next two months, waiting for an opportunity to engage Rosecrans so successfully as to wipe out the stigma that Perryville represented. Almost as soon as he established his headquarters in Middle Tennessee, Bragg was called to Richmond to explain to government officials just how he proposed to do that.[14]

While the infantry rode the rails and the water, Wheeler's horsemen, accompanied by most of the army's artillery, journeyed to Murfreesboro by means of an overland march through Winchester, Tullahoma, and Shelbyville, Tennessee. Even without the bone-jarring train ride, the trip was an ordeal. According to one Georgia trooper, "half the time [we were] without anything to eat but some walnuts that we . . . chance[d] to pick up marching along." A comrade in another Georgia outfit elaborated on the trials the cavalry endured: "For days and days we marched. Most of the horses had been killed mine among the others. I was barefooted, as were most of my companions. Our rations were exhausted and for three days we had not a thing to eat. We asked for bread at every house we came to, but all of the people declared that they themselves had not a thing. Some of them told the truth for the war had reduced the people to a pitiful condition."[15]

Meanwhile, Smith's command did not return to East Tennessee but followed Bragg to his new venue. There it underwent a major reorganization at Jefferson Davis's behest. After Bragg returned from Virginia, the president called Smith—who in recent days had severely criticized Bragg's conduct throughout the campaign—to Richmond for a clear-the-air session. At Davis's urging, Smith agreed to subordinate himself to Bragg. Davis was so appreciative of his willingness to serve as one of Bragg's corps commanders that he promoted Smith to lieutenant general, only one rank below Bragg's full generalship. As if in recognition of a campaign successfully concluded, he conferred the same promotion on Polk and Hardee.[16]

Because other organizational changes were in the wind, Smith spent only a month as Bragg's subordinate. In mid-December, one of his remaining divisions was sent to reinforce Vicksburg, Mississippi, the principal Confederate defensive work on the Mississippi River. The transferees thus became a part of Lieutenant General John C. Pemberton's Department of Mississippi and East Louisiana. And by then the three commands— Bragg's, Smith's, and Pemberton's—had become elements of the Department of the West. A geographical command not to be confused with one of its subsidiaries, the Western Department, the Department of the West encompassed not only the areas of operations of those armies but also northwestern Georgia and a section of northwestern South Carolina. Less than a week after its establishment, the department was expanded to include control of the military defenses of Atlanta, the great manufacturing and supply hub of the Deep South.[17]

Command of the Department of the West, which Davis had established in the hope of centralizing operations between the Alleghenies and the Mississippi, went to General Joseph E. Johnston, a fifty-five-year-old Virginian. A veteran of thirty-three years in the army, Johnston was widely regarded as a military genius on a par with his West Point classmate Robert E. Lee. Along with Beauregard, Johnston had been one of the South's earliest heroes, the senior leader of the victorious army at First Manassas. He had been on convalescent leave since being severely wounded on the Virginia Peninsula the previous May. Although he did not share Davis's belief that a single commander could coordinate the forces of Bragg, Smith, and Pemberton, Johnston saw departmental command as a means of retaking the field in a meaningful capacity. Upon being hospitalized he had relinquished command of the Army of Northern Virginia to Lee, whose subsequent string of highly publicized victories meant Johnston had no chance of regaining his old job.[18]

Soon after taking command, Johnston lost one of his lieutenants. After sending troops to Bragg and Pemberton, Smith was left with a force so small that he asked to be relieved. Early in 1863, Davis sent him west to head the Confederate Trans-Mississippi Department, while lowering the status of the command Smith left behind. Johnston tried to restore the perceived depletion of his realm by incorporating the small army operating in northern Arkansas under Lieutenant General Theophilus H. Holmes. Richmond vetoed the proposal, insisting that Holmes's troops remain a part of Smith's new fiefdom.[19]

Yet another administrative change announced at this time had a psychological impact on Bragg's army. It was made not only to avoid confusion with other newly established commands, especially Pemberton's at Vicksburg, but also to embrace the fact that Bragg's army was now ensconced in a state in which it could maneuver with some measure of flexibility and freedom. On November 20, Bragg announced to his troops that they were no longer members of the Army of the Mississippi. From now on, they would fight under the banner of the Army of Tennessee.[20]

EVEN BEFORE OFFERING SUPPORT TO Wheeler's cavalry at Lancaster, Morgan's men had seen extensive and difficult service during the Perryville campaign, aspects of which showed their commander in a new and unflattering light. Morgan's involvement in the invasion of Kentucky began with an August 28 order from General Smith to meet him in Lexington during the coming week. For some time Morgan, anticipating service under Smith or Bragg, had been outfitting and provisioning the 2nd Kentucky for the field. The day following his receipt of Smith's directive, he was leading his nine-hundred-man command—Duke's Kentuckians, Gano's Texans, and miscellaneous units attached for the campaign—out of Hartsville. Marching via Glasgow, Columbia, and Houstonville, Morgan orchestrated a gala homecoming in Lexington, one he delayed to give his men time to brush the dust from their uniforms, polish their weapons, and groom their horses.

At ten a.m. on September 4, Morgan and his raiders staged a triumphal entry. One of his biographers observes that "all [the] successful raids Morgan had led, all the newspaper stories written about him, indeed all the exploits combined could not top this moment, filled as it was with the most impressive pomp and circumstance he could muster." Hundreds of well-wishers—family members, long-time neighbors, and Lexingtonians who knew Morgan only by reputation—crowded the streets; church bells pealed joyfully; and bands thumped and tootled in welcome. When he dismounted to meet with General Smith, who had arrived in town two days before, Morgan was mobbed by adoring fans. They gave his regiment a welcome no less warm and demonstrative. The troopers were roundly cheered and plied with choice victuals, and their horses enjoyed provender aplenty.[21]

After conferring with Smith, Morgan rode out to Hopemont, his mother's Georgian-style mansion, where he established his headquarters. There he held court, greeting his closest relations and friends. Many came bearing gifts. Delegations of local officials bestowed on him a pair of silver spurs and a hand-sewn banner for his regiment, while an old friend named Richards presented him with a magnificent Thoroughbred gelding named Glencoe.[22]

One of Morgan's first items of official business was to print and circulate a recruiting broadside. The dramatic appeal paid quick dividends; within days it attracted enough enlistees to enlarge the 2nd Kentucky to thirteen companies, making a total of one thousand one hundred officers and men. Eager recruits kept coming, providing the basis for additional regiments, the foundation of a full brigade. Captain Gano received permission to detach his squadron from the 2nd and to make it the nucleus of the 7th Kentucky Cavalry. Morgan permitted three other subordinates to raise new outfits: Leroy S. Cluke (the 8th Kentucky), William C. P. Breckinridge (9th Kentucky), and David W. Chenault (11th Kentucky). The expansion of Morgan's command would ensure his promotion to brigadier general, while Basil Duke would succeed him as colonel of the 2nd.[23]

The raiding leader remained in and around Lexington until September 19, when he received orders to intercept the retreat of George Washington Morgan's Federals from Cumberland Gap. Bound for Richmond, whose garrison Kirby Smith had recently captured, John Hunt Morgan departed his hometown at the head of a small portion of his force: one company of the 2nd Kentucky (the rest of the regiment would remain in Lexington, assimilating recruits and training under Duke's instruction), and a body of recent enlistees that had been entrusted to Colonel Cluke. Upon reaching Richmond, Morgan was joined by now-Colonel Gano and Major Breckinridge, who had been recruiting in that area, as well as by the embryonic 7th and 9th Kentucky. Morgan led the combined force, approximately one thousand officers and troopers, to Cumberland Gap through the towns of Irvine, Proctor, and West Liberty.[24]

Morgan started his mountain campaign in high spirits, confident of cutting off his Yankee namesake and capturing his entire division. Instead, the fighting around Cumberland Gap proved to be difficult, frustrating, and largely unsuccessful. Not only did Morgan fail to bag his quarry despite blocking the roads and passes by which it retreated, he was repeatedly ambushed by Unionist guerrillas and home guards operating with impunity along the Kentucky-Tennessee border. On more than one occasion, he barely avoided falling victim to the bushwhackers he both despised and feared.

Morgan retaliated for this harassment in ways that belied the gentle-man-soldier reputation he had so carefully cultivated. On October 1, his failure to receive infantry support promised him by Kirby Smith foiled a carefully prepared trap by which he intended to ensnare his enemy near Grayson, Kentucky. The following day, already on the return leg of his march, Morgan himself was ambushed by home guards near Olive Hill. The citizen-soldiers caused several casualties before Morgan could deploy to engage them, whereupon they disappeared into the hills. Morgan took out his frustration on a civilian prisoner, a pro-Unionist state senator named Grier, whom he roundly cursed and threatened to kill, and whose home he put to the torch while Grier's family was still fleeing from it.[25]

Concerned that bushwhackers might strike again, Morgan told the captain who had captured Grier to shoot him down at the first hint of further opposition. The senator believed himself a dead man when gunshots rang out from atop the mountains surrounding Olive Hill. He survived only because the officer guarding him refused to commit cold-blooded murder. In the confusion that erupted during a subsequent ambush, Grier broke free and escaped.

Finally chasing his opponents away, Morgan headed south and west from Olive Hill along a route heavily populated by Unionist families. He had his men burn almost fifty of their dwellings while destroying all the crops in the fields they passed. By these acts, Morgan and his men displayed, in the words of one historian, "a ruthlessness that Union Major General William T. Sherman—the scourge of Georgia—might have admired." Among the homes destroyed was that of George Underwood, a pro-Union counterpart of Champ Ferguson, the ruthless guerrilla who had guided Morgan on two of his raids. Joined by vengeance-driven relatives, Underwood repaid Morgan by harassing his column throughout the rest of its journey, cutting off and capturing numerous raiders, and shooting down others without mercy. It is claimed that Underwood and other irregulars dispatched fifty of Morgan's men, while home-guard units accounted for thirty more. The losses so enraged Morgan that he returned to Olive Hill the evening after departing it and reduced to ashes what remained of the town.

Morgan's adversaries dogged his heels almost to the day he returned to Lexington. The last shots of the campaign were fired by a band of youthful partisans near West Liberty, one of whom, a fifteen-year-old sharpshooter, claimed credit for killing Colonel John Shawhan, a Mexican War comrade of Morgan's. All in all, the horsemen who straggled back into Lexington on October 4 looked nothing like the mighty phalanx that had entered the town to the huzzahs of the citizenry exactly one month earlier.[26]

REUNITING AT LEXINGTON WITH THE 2nd Kentucky, Morgan learned that in his absence the regiment, under Basil Duke, had attacked Yankee camps and ships on the Ohio River. Kirby Smith had ordered the portion of Duke's regiment that had not accompanied Morgan into the mountains to march to Covington, Kentucky. That town, which sat on the river opposite Cincinnati, hosted the field headquarters of Brigadier General Henry Heth, whose division lacked cavalry support. Soon after Duke joined him, however, Heth fell back to Georgetown in the face of a mounting presence at Cincinnati. The 2nd Kentucky remained on the river, hoping to delay the shipment of reinforcements from the Queen City to the Federals opposing Smith.

In the days that followed, Duke engaged the full spectrum of enemy troops: regulars, militia, home guards, and partisans. His operations began when he learned that a large contingent of citizen-soldiers was gathering at Augusta, Bracken County, forty miles upstream from Cincinnati. As Duke later recalled, "I wished to take the town, if possible, with little loss, and cross into Ohio, and marching toward Cincinnati, so threaten the city that the troops at Walton [about eighteen miles south of Cincinnati] would be hurried back to protect it."[27]

Marching through Brookville, eight miles southwest of Augusta, Duke on September 27 surprised the enemy rendezvous but found it defended by two stern-wheelers in the Ohio, each carrying riflemen and a 12-pounder cannon. Deploying his men dismounted, Duke attacked the ships at long range, opposing their guns with the 2nd Kentucky's howitzers. The Bull Pups fired only three rounds, but they were enough to scare off both boats, which weighed anchor and steamed upriver. Now able to attend to his primary objective, Duke led two of his companies through the streets of Augusta, making directly for home-guard headquarters. Manifestly outnumbered, the enemy commander surrendered on the spot, though some of his men, holed up in private dwellings, sprayed the Rebels with rifle fire. As Duke wrote, "I immediately ordered that every house from which shots came should be burned. A good many were soon in flames, and even then the fighting continued in some of them."[28]

Slowly but methodically, Duke's men rooted out their opponents. They were greatly aided by the Bull Pups, which, when fired at point-blank range, reduced houses to piles of rubble. Even so, the occupiers took a heavy toll. They killed more than twenty attackers and wounded almost as many others; the dead included John Morgan's cousin Sam.

General Basil W. Duke, CSA.

Despite leveling a part of the town, Duke was frustrated to find that resistance continued in some sectors. Late in the afternoon he called off the assault, gathered up his casualties, limbered up the howitzers, and withdrew. He returned to Brookville, where he paroled the nearly two hundred Federals he had seized in Augusta. The next day he returned to Cynthiana, whose Union garrison the 2nd Kentucky had helped capture on Morgan's first raid through the state. Duke remained in that town, now free of the hated enemy, for five days before heading for Lexington to connect with Morgan.[29]

Although the battle of Perryville was still days away, Morgan informed Duke upon their reunion that Smith was poised to evacuate Lexington. Duke expressed hope that the campaign in Kentucky was not over, but Morgan, ever the gambler, bet that Bragg would soon abandon the state and return to Tennessee. Within a fortnight, his prediction came to pass. Morgan and Duke followed Smith's infantry and artillery to Harrodsburg, where they linked with Bragg's army. Thereafter, Morgan covered the rear of Smith's army as it withdrew to Richmond.

On October 15, two days after offering his assistance to Joe Wheeler, Morgan, who hated the arduous and monotonous work of covering a retreat, won Smith's permission to select his own route out of Kentucky. He promptly relinquished the rear-guard mission to his colleague Henry Ashby, whose brigade Morgan augmented with the 8th and 11th Kentucky. At the head of the remainder of his brigade, almost two thousand strong, he rode back to Lexington. From his hometown he planned to circle into the rear of Buell's army. There he could take on the more appealing job of cutting off and capturing Yankees and fracturing their supply lines—especially the L&N near Gallatin, where repair crews, working feverishly, had nearly cleared the tunnel called Big South of the debris Morgan had piled there in August.

If General Bragg had had his way, Morgan would not have enjoyed as much latitude as Smith granted him. En route to Lexington, Basil Duke met a courier bearing Bragg's order that Morgan abandon his proposed operation, pass east through the Cumberland Mountains to Wytheville, Virginia—site of mineral deposits critical to the Confederate war effort—and patrol the area until further notice. Well aware that this was the last duty his brother-in-law wished to take on, Duke pocketed the communiqué before Morgan learned of its receipt.[30]

The confiscated order enabled Morgan to make the most of his opportunity to discomfit his enemy. On October 17, on the road to Lexington, his command clashed with a detachment of an Ohio cavalry regiment. Morgan encircled the Ohioans and cut off their rear guard, capturing one hundred men—almost one-third of their force—and persuading the rest to beat a hasty retreat. Two days later, he reentered Lexington to a slightly less effusive reception than he had received six weeks earlier. Dispatching two companies of the 2nd Kentucky to occupy the town, Morgan led the balance of the regiment to nearby Ashland, where he approached a woodside encampment occupied by the main body of the regiment he had routed on the seventeenth. He planned an elaborate attack from many directions at the same time, but he positioned his riflemen so poorly that they fired into one another, felling several comrades. One of those killed or mortally wounded in the mismanaged assault was Major Wash Morgan, the second of the raiding leader's cousins to be killed in action over the past three weeks. The carnage was avoidable; the heavily outnumbered garrison surrendered almost at once, giving Morgan's command 350 more captives.[31]

Morgan's stay in Lexington, where he paroled the POWs, was brief. That afternoon, with winterlike winds raking the Cumberland Plateau, he and his men departed, heading northwest toward Lawrenceburg. Passing through Versailles, they bivouacked for the night amid familiar surroundings at Shyrock's Ferry on the Kentucky River.

One of Morgan's chronic weaknesses, a lack of vigilance, hurt him that night. His failure to ensure that camp guards were posted properly was inexcusable given his proximity to roving bodies of Federals. One of these, under Morgan's old antagonist Ebenezer Dumont, called on him before sunup the next morning, pistols and rifles blazing. Taking casualties right and left, Morgan had all he could do to pass the body of his command over the river to safety. Since Dumont's force consisted largely of foot soldiers, once they reached the far bank the raiders easily outdistanced their pursuers. They galloped through Lawrenceburg a good half-hour before the footsore bluecoats straggled in.[32]

Morgan moved quickly to Bloomfield, where the secessionists who predominated in that locality gave him a hearty welcome. Wishing to put greater distance between himself and Dumont, he spent only an hour among friends before turning south and heading for Bardstown. Finding that town heavily occupied, he bypassed it and camped six miles beyond. This night, presumably, he took greater pains to guard the slumber of his men.

It was in this area that Morgan chalked up his most impressive accomplishment of the closing phase of the Perryville campaign: capturing, rifling, and then burning a 150-wagon supply train bound for Buell's army. Because the flames consumed a large quantity of medical supplies supposedly earmarked for soldiers who had been wounded on October 8, Morgan's action was roundly condemned by the state's Unionist editors. Lest his reputation be besmirched, he caused to be published in pro-Southern newspapers his claim that the medicines were actually bound for one of Buell's healthy and hearty divisions.[33]

On the twentieth, Morgan rode into Elizabethtown, a Louisville & Nashville depot. His men wrought havoc on tracks and culverts along both approaches to the station. Next morning, a troop train chugged unsuspectingly into Elizabethtown. From trackside cover, dismounted troopers sprayed the cars with rifle balls. The passengers scrambled out and returned fire; the result was a two-hour standoff that caused few casualties on either side.

At length tiring of the inconclusive fight, Morgan remounted his men and led them cross-country via Litchfield to Hopkinsville, scene of some of Forrest's earliest operations. The staunchly pro-Confederate citizenry gave him a welcome as enthusiastic as any he had received in much more populous venues. He and his weary men lay over for three days, soaking up the local hospitality. But the respite was no holiday. From Hopkinsville, Morgan dispatched Gano's regiment to mangle a section of the L&N that extended into Tennessee. The 7th Kentucky did a thorough job, demolishing bridges, levering up track, and consigning rolling stock to the flames.[34]

A few days earlier, while at Litchfield, Morgan had detached Company D of the 2nd Kentucky under the resourceful John Castleman and sent it north to divert a body of cavalry reported to be in the Hartford area. Once he located Colonel John Shanks's 12th Kentucky (Union) Cavalry, Castleman began to emulate Morgan, the actor. He maneuvered his little band in such a way as to give the impression of size and confidence. He reported that "this pretense of strength was always a protection, and we always moved on and out of danger before the enemy discovered our weakness." The bold front that Company D put up, coupled with the fearsome reputation Morgan had gained in more than a year of well-publicized operations, persuaded the Union leader to make for the Indiana border, burning bridges behind him to stymie pursuit. Thus Castleman could boast that "we scared Shanks out of Hartford"—out of Kentucky, in fact.[35]

On November 1, Morgan called in his detachments, including Castleman's, and led the way south, crossing the Tennessee line and camping at Springfield. In this stretch of secessionist country, a new influx of recruits added to the already formidable strength of his command. After a two-day respite, Morgan left Springfield for Gallatin, hoping to discover that his closure of Big South was still in effect. But at Gallatin, where he received another hero's welcome, he had little opportunity to inspect his handiwork. Soon after arriving he was ordered by John Breckinridge, commanding at Murfreesboro, to strike yet again at the L&N.

The new target was Edgefield, Tennessee, a suburb of Nashville, where dozens of boxcars filled with supplies for Buell had been collected. Morgan would be supported by Bedford Forrest, who would make a diversionary attack across the Cumberland from the town. The plan sounded promising, but the project proved a bust. Forrest failed to draw enough troops from his colleague's route of march, with the result that Morgan's November 6 attack was an embarrassing failure. Morgan had set fire to only a dozen cars before an aroused garrison drove him off. In the confused fighting, the raiding chieftain blundered inside enemy lines but talked his way out by impersonating a Union officer, something he had become expert at. Duke ascribed Morgan's escape to his uncanny ability "of subjecting every one to his will," the effect of which "was almost mesmeric." A suddenly chastened Morgan withdrew to a point near Lebanon, within riding distance of Breckinridge's headquarters.[36]

Morgan's latest venture behind enemy lines had achieved mixed results: a great deal of damage to Buell's communications but also failed attacks, heavy casualties, and the loss of nigh-irreplaceable subordinates such as Cousin Wash. Including as they did his misadventures in the mountains near Cumberland Gap, the past two months appeared to have sullied Morgan's reputation as the Confederacy's ablest raider. Even so, he had accomplished enough to win the public and official recognition he craved. In the aftermath of his jaunt from Lexington to Springfield, the Confederate Congress declared that Morgan and his troopers "were entitled to the love and gratitude of their countrymen for the magnificent feat accomplished by them in October, whereby Middle Tennessee was preserved to this Government."[37]

SOON AFTER REACHING THE MURFREESBORO AREA, the newly christened Army of Tennessee settled into winter quarters. Bragg, who had pitched his headquarters at Tullahoma, thirty-five miles farther south, felt he could suspend active operations for the season, believing that his current adversary, Rosecrans, was comfortably situated at Nashville. Surely Buell's successor, being new to command, would remain in garrison through the cold-weather season. He would need time to organize his forces, see to their provisioning, acquaint himself with a host of new subordinates, and tend to those administrative functions that seemed as numerous as stars in the sky. Come spring, when warm weather cleared muddy and ice-covered roads, giving his army a critical degree of mobility, he would sally forth to engage his foe. By then Bragg expected to have his own army—which he considered well on its way to recovering the strength and morale it had lost at Perryville—in the best possible condition, not only ready for a fight but eager to test Rosecrans's ability to manage an army in battle.

One of Bragg's first acts upon returning from his conference in Richmond was to re-form his cavalry, which now included some units that had been attached to the Army of Kentucky. He divided the arm into five brigades and placed all of them under Joe Wheeler, who would retain direct command of the brigade he had led through the recent campaign. Bragg considered Wheeler's brigade "regular cavalry," in that it was commanded by an officer experienced in close support of the main army. Two other brigades of what Bragg called "mounted gunmen" also fit this description: those under John Wharton and Brigadier General John Pegram. The latter, a Virginia-born West Pointer with dragoon experience, had been chief of

staff to Kirby Smith. His brigade, formerly John Scott's, currently consisted of the 1st Georgia and 1st Louisiana; in coming weeks it would be materially expanded.[38]

Bragg considered the other units that made up Wheeler's command to
be partisans. Naturally enough, they included Morgan's Kentucky brigade.
Not so logically, Bragg lumped in with Morgan the newly formed brigade
of Forrest's, consisting of the 4th, 8th, and 9th Tennessee, the 4th Alabama
Cavalry, and a battery of light artillery. Bragg could not be persuaded that
Forrest's men were more than raiders. He considered them able to operate
effectively only in the enemy's rear, where opponents were too few or too
dispersed to stop attacks on rail lines and supply depots. More than once in
the days to come, Bragg would pay for his strategic myopia.

The army leader assigned specific areas of operation to his "irregular"
cavalry. On November 24, he detailed his intentions to Jefferson Davis:
"Morgan [is] to operate with his cavalry brigade north of the Cumberland,
on the enemy's lines of communication, which, I am confident, will prevent
the enemy from using the Louisville Railroad, which is not yet in running
order, and their wagon trains will be in constant danger. Forrest, with his
cavalry brigade, is to work south of the Cumberland and west of Nashville.
With a fine battery of rifle guns, he will destroy their transports on both
rivers. He is instructed now to seek a crossing, which he is confident of
finding; throw his command rapidly over the Tennessee River, and precipitate it upon the enemy's lines, break up railroads, burn bridges, destroy
depots, capture hospitals and guards, and harass him generally. Thus we
may create a diversion in favor of Pemberton, and, if successful, force the
enemy to retire from Mississippi."[39]

The last sentence referred to the vulnerability of Vicksburg, one piece
of real estate the Confederacy could not afford to give up. Its loss would
mean Union control of the Mississippi, from source to mouth. The fall of
Vicksburg and the less heavily fortified garrison at Port Hudson, Louisiana,
would cut the Southern nation in two, while allowing the Federals to invade
any section of the South they wished to occupy and fortify.

Plans aimed at accomplishing all of this had long been under way at
Ulysses Grant's headquarters at La Grange, Tennessee, forty-five miles
east of Memphis. Grant was preparing to implement strategy drafted by
his superior, General Halleck, who was now ensconced in Washington as
the Union's general-in-chief. Halleck's plan, as revised and expanded by
Grant, called for an overland advance on Pemberton's city by parallel

columns. Unwilling to challenge the garrison
on its north side, where swamps and bayous
would hamstring an offensive, Grant determined to lead two divisions from his advanced
supply base at Holly Springs, Mississippi,
down the Mississippi Central Railroad to
Jackson. From the state capital, he and
Sherman, commanding three divisions operating along Grant's right flank, would turn west
in unison to assault the citadel over more hospitable terrain.

General John Pegram, CSA.

The concept appeared sound, but early in
December, military-political developments
persuaded Grant to rethink and revamp. He
still aimed to move down the tracks from Holly Springs to Jackson, but
now Sherman would load his command on transports convoyed by naval
gunboats and would descend the Mississippi to the mouth of the Yazoo
River. He would ride the Yazoo to Chickasaw Bluffs, north of Vicksburg.
Sherman would strike from that direction just as Grant moved in from the
east, pushing Pemberton's outnumbered forces before him and bottling
them up inside Vicksburg.[40]

Attuned to the threat taking shape on the Mississippi although not
privy to the particulars, Bragg and Pemberton reacted by dispatching cavalry to strike at Grant's communications in hopes of staying his hand.
Many of Pemberton's troopers were now led by Earl Van Dorn, whose dramatic defeats at Pea Ridge and Corinth had resulted in his demotion from
army command to a subordinate role under the officer who had superseded him. Not even his acquittal by a court of inquiry probing alleged dere-
liction of duty at Corinth had restored luster to Van Dorn's reputation. The
pending mission, aimed at sacking and burning the supply hub at Holly
Springs, represented his last, best hope of redemption.[41]

While Van Dorn raided the Mississippi Central—he left Grenada,
Mississippi, on the railroad seventy-five miles south of Holly Springs, on
December 12, accompanied by three thousand five hundred troopers—an
equally ambitious expedition targeting another enemy supply line got
under way in West Tennessee. This was the undertaking entrusted to
General Forrest, aimed at wrecking the Mobile & Ohio from Jackson,

Tennessee, north toward Columbus, Kentucky, Grant's principal supply base. Forrest, who had recently risen from a sickbed, was eager to begin the operation; he wished to demonstrate what his newly formed brigade of four regiments and a battery—temporarily augmented by the 51st Alabama of Colonel John T. Morgan—could do at the raiding game.[42]

Early indications were promising. In the first week of November, Forrest had received an order from John Breckinridge, the new commander in the Murfreesboro area, to push up the turnpike from Columbia to Nashville and test the strength of the Tennessee capital. At daylight on the fourth, Forrest, leading not only his own command but also two infantry brigades and four batteries, drove in "the Abolitionists' pickets" to a point about three and a half miles from Rosecrans's stronghold. At that point resistance stiffed, so Forrest sent forward Colonel A. A. Russell's 4th Alabama, which shoved a larger body of pickets another mile and a half closer to Nashville.[43]

Feeling out the enemy's strength and studying his positions, Forrest decided he could proceed even farther. Supported by their infantry and artillery comrades, Colonel James W. Starnes's 4th Tennessee, the 8th Tennessee of Colonel George G. Dibrell, and a battalion of the 51st Alabama led by Major De Witt Clinton Douglass joined Russell's Alabamians. The combined force advanced on three parallel roads, Forrest's troopers evicting the Yankees from one picket post after another.

Forrest kept up the pressure until midmorning, when, having gained the information he needed, he slowly withdrew. Accompanied by Starnes's and Dibrell's regiments and two batteries, he dug in along the Franklin Pike about five miles below Nashville. Some time afterward, he reported being attacked by a force of all arms including a dozen cannons under Brigadier General James Scott Negley, formerly the post commander at Nashville. Hastily deploying on the west side of the pike, Forrest held Negley at arm's reach with artillery and dismounted skirmishers until the Union commander tired of the standoff and began to pull back. Forrest hastened him on his way by charging the rear of the departing troops with the men of Starnes and Dibrell. Finally, Forrest called off the chase and redeployed. In his official report he claimed to have killed or wounded forty Yankees while making prisoners of twenty more.[44]

Gratified by this minor but solid performance, Forrest felt assured of the battleworthiness of his new command, with a single caveat. As John Allan Wyeth notes, approximately half of those who had joined Forrest's new brigade "had no other arms than shot-guns and squirrel rifles which they had brought with them from home. Many of the army weapons issued to them were of ancient pattern and not efficient as compared with those in the Union ranks. Dibrell's regiment alone had 400 flintlock muskets." Forrest was concerned about the deficiency, but he expected to rectify it through captures on the coming expedition. [45]

On December 11, he started on his mission, the importance of which he fully and deeply appreciated. Two days later, after an uneventful march, the two-thousand-one-hundred-man command—which had lost the 51st Alabama to transfer but had gained Major N. N. Cox's 2nd Tennessee Battalion and two companies of Kentuckians—reached the Tennessee River at Clifton. A cold rain that had been falling for some hours had turned to sleet, the winds were biting, and the fast-moving river, three-quarters of a mile across at this point, was a formidable obstacle. It took two days, "working night and day," to build enough flatboats to ferry everyone to the west bank. The boats were then sunk to evade enemy detection. At expedition's end, they would be dredged up, bailed out, and brought over, ready for crossing. [46]

The difficult, time-consuming crossing did not—could not—go undetected. By the fifteenth, Union patrols had begun to hunt for Forrest, and the several garrisons on the Mobile & Ohio had gone on high alert. Fortunately for Forrest, his opponents had gained an erroneous notion of the size and composition of his force. Rumors planted by raiding parties including the celebrated company of scouts led by Forrest's brother Bill, not only exaggerated the size of the expedition but portrayed it as composed mainly of infantry.

Still, the Yankees were eager to challenge the raiders. Leaving the river on a northwesterly heading, Forrest encountered a considerable body of cavalry near Lexington, Tennessee. Captain Frank Gurley, leading a thirty-man detachment of the 4th Alabama, made first contact with the enemy— the lead element of a force estimated at eight hundred officers and troopers, including a section of guns—near a dismantled bridge over Beech Creek. At first the bluecoats offered stiff resistance, but, as Gurley wrote, soon they "had to give way & they ran back to the bridge. . . . [T]hey put up a strong fight but I got the advantage & broke their line." [47]

Forrest was vastly pleased. In his report he exulted that "we routed them completely, capturing the two guns and 148 prisoners," including the commanding officer. The raiders also seized seventy horses, which Forrest added to the teams of Captain Samuel L. Freeman's battery. Here, as elsewhere when prisoners were taken, Forrest's men exchanged their antiquated arms for state-of-the art weaponry: breech-loading carbines and repeating rifles.[48]

From Lexington, Forrest veered sharply left toward the Mobile & Ohio, striking its tracks south of Jackson. After driving in the local pickets, he had Dibrell's Tennesseans tear up rails, burn ties, and chop down telegraph poles. Ranging north along the tracks, Dibrell then encountered a stockade crammed with infantry, one hundred of whom he forced to surrender after a brief skirmish. In the meantime, Colonel Russell's regiment cantered down the tracks to destroy bridges and culverts toward the Mississippi border.

The next morning, the nineteenth, Forrest moved against Jackson with a picked force that included two of Captain Freeman's guns. The detachment was strong enough to chase skirmishers inside the fortifications that ringed the strategically located village. It could not compete, however, with the reinforcements that Forrest discovered to be inundating the area by midday. Feigning an attack, he held the garrison in place, then pulled out. In the frigid darkness of early evening, he detoured around the town, continuing north toward Humboldt and Trenton. En route he made contact with Dibrell, whose regiment Forrest sent to destroy the bridge over Forked Deer Creek. Concurrently, he dispatched Starnes's regiment to attack Humboldt. With Biffle's 9th Tennessee, Cox's battalion, and Freeman's guns, Forrest planned to strike a third target, the garrison at Trenton.

Two of the three detachments accomplished their missions. Meeting strong opposition from a stockade that protected the bridge over Forked Deer Creek, Dibrell failed to reach his objective. After a sharp skirmish, he turned back to rejoin Forrest's main body, no doubt dreading to report a failure to his unforgiving superior. Meanwhile, Starnes occupied Humboldt, capturing one hundred garrison troops and destroying depot facilities and a trestlework. For their part, Forrest and Biffle took Trenton without much effort, thanks mainly to the moral effect of Freeman's accurate shelling ("on the third fire from the battery," Forrest reported, "they surrendered"). His already large haul of captives was thus swelled by seven hundred men and horses. The latter was usually of greater value to Forrest, but on this occasion the great majority was found to be too young, too old, or too broken down to be fit for service.[49]

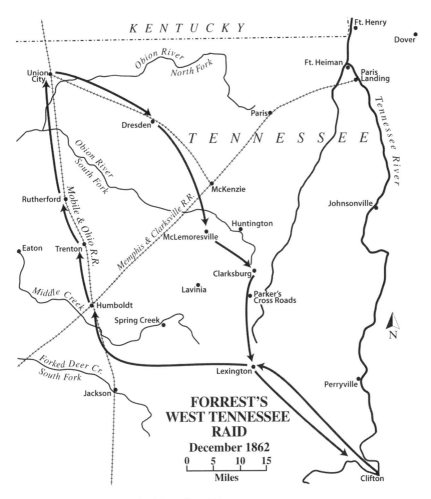

Forrest's West Tennessee Raid, December 1862.

Forrest remained in Trenton overnight, fighting not Yankees but the bitter cold. His men warmed themselves by setting fire to the local facilities, destroying not only the rail depot but also warehouses crammed with cotton, tobacco, and foodstuffs. Resuming the march on the twenty-first, the raiders destroyed bridges over both forks of the Obion River near Moscow, including "nearly 4 miles of trestling in the bottom between them." They also captured detachments of railroad guards, at one point surprising and making prisoners of more than one hundred Federals "without firing a gun." As always, they paroled the POWs to avoid being slowed by their unwieldy presence in the column.[50]

Forrest and his men spent Christmas Day resting at Union City, just below the Kentucky border and within thirty miles of the great depot at Columbus. While at Union City, he dispatched parties to destroy railroad trestles. They did their work thoroughly and efficiently, prompting their leader to boast that "we have made a clean sweep of the Federals and roads north of Jackson." One of Starnes's troopers agreed, although his claim of long-term effects was a bit exaggerated: "From Jackson to and including Union City [we] absolutely destroyed the rail road so that it was not used any more during the war." Amid the smoldering ruins, Forrest made contact with Lieutenant Colonel Thomas Alonzo Napier's recently organized 10th Tennessee Battalion, five companies strong, and added it to his command.[51]

Having wrought enough havoc on the Mobile & Ohio, and aware that by moving farther north he would pick up overwhelming numbers of pursuers, Forrest turned southeast and descended the railroad that linked Union City with McKenzie. Learning that reinforcements had reached many of the venues he had struck over the past week, including Trenton and Humboldt, the raiding leader abruptly left the railroad at Dresden, fifteen miles short of McKenzie, and marched by country roads toward one of his early ports of call, Lexington. As he rode he sent Biffle's regiment to engage a mounted force reported to be moving against the column from Humboldt.

On the night of December 27-28, Forrest's main body crossed the south fork of the Obion below McKenzie. Fearing that the local bridge would not support the passage of horses, guns, and wagons, Forrest organized fatigue parties and had them reinforce the span with beams cut from waterside trees. Early on the twenty-eighth, he got the entire command across the stream; reportedly, Forrest himself drove over the first wagon to prove that the bridge was now safe. Even so, he was forced to drag Freeman's guns through the creek bottoms, an exhausting task for men who had been riding and fighting for the past ten days.

On the last day of the year, Forrest's pursuers—a mixed force dispatched from Trenton by the district commander, Brigadier General Jeremiah C. Sullivan—managed to get ahead of the raiders near Parker's Cross Roads, a few miles north of Lexington. Establishing a blocking position across Forrest's path, the expeditionary commander, Colonel Cyrus L. Dunham, awaited his opponent's coming. As soon as Forrest arrived, he attacked head-on; the upshot was a battle that lasted into the evening.

Before darkness fell, Forrest—although hard-pressed for most of the fight and having suffered many casualties, including the mortal wounding of Colonel Napier—succeeded in driving Dunham's five regiments into a woodlot, where he pounded them relentlessly with shell and canister from Freeman's guns. While the artillery thundered away, Forrest devised a multidirectional attack by mounted and dismounted troopers. He sent Starnes's regiment against Dunham's left flank, and Russell's regiment and a supporting battalion toward the Union right.

Both forces gained ground, largely because Forrest's opponents, most of whom were foot soldiers, were worn down and famished from the long, forced marches they had made in hopes of overtaking their quarry. As one of Dunham's officers put it, "our Regiment has been so abused that with their sore feet and sickness one hundred & 30 remained behind this morning" at Trenton. As for those who had kept up, "it is difficult to tell if they are most in want of sleep or food." [52]

The multipronged assault was so powerful that Dunham's men were chased from three successive positions and forced to abandon their artillery and wagon train. But just as Forrest assumed the upper hand, a second pack of pursuers—the brigade of Colonel John W. Fuller, led personally by General Sullivan—swept down from the north and slammed into the rear of his column. Forrest had known of Fuller's proximity, but he had expected advance warning of the man's arrival. To provide it, he had stationed two squadrons in the direction of Clarksburg, whence Fuller had come. The Yankees, however, had taken a road other than the one Forrest's detachment had guarded.

Thus Forrest found himself fighting an enemy in front and rear at the same time. As he would later admit, it was the tightest corner he had ever been in, but he was nevertheless confident of fighting his way out. Nothing seemed to faze him this day. When an excited staff officer needlessly informed him that they were being pressed on two sides, Forrest shouted: "We'll charge them both ways!"[53]

Though aware that his men were exhausted from hours of combat and that their ammunition was running low, Forrest counterattacked with characteristic power and decisiveness. Eventually he pushed Dunham's force toward the rear, capturing three pieces of artillery. At some points he observed "Federals scattering in every direction." Still, he could not say how long his advantage would endure: new bodies of Yankees were continually arriving to blast his front and rear with small arms and artillery fire.[54]

Forrest realized that eventually he must give ground, but he was unwilling to do so until able to break contact cleanly and without incurring heavy loss. When darkness came, he withdrew in reasonably good order. Because Dunham and Sullivan had not linked, he was able to escape through the gap between them, in the direction of Lexington. His getaway was assisted by a masterful diversionary attack by Starnes's 4th Tennessee. Even so, Forrest had to leave behind the guns he had captured, as well as three hundred or more dismounted troopers of Cox's battalion, whose horses had stampeded upon Fuller's coming, stranding their riders. Forrest believed the casualties he had inflicted compensated for these losses. His prisoners reported that at least a third of the combined attack force had been killed or wounded. Forrest estimated Dunham's and Fuller's losses to be between eight hundred and one thousand. Historians estimate Forrest's casualties throughout the expedition as four hundred killed, wounded, or missing.[55]

After clearing Parker's Cross Roads, the raiders headed straight for Lexington. Sullivan declared that by forcing his enemy to retreat he had won the day. And yet he decided against a vigorous pursuit, leading a disgusted subordinate to grouse that "our general is letting them get away purposely." Another officer, in his official report of the action, complained of Sullivan's "genius for tardiness."[56]

The raiders lay over for a spell at Lexington. On New Year's morning they headed for the river, where they parried a half-strength blow by the only troops to pursue, a single regiment of horsemen. The threat neutralized, Forrest rafted his men, guns, and wagons over the Tennessee to Clifton, while swimming the horses across. He returned from his three-hundred-mile journey with some battle scars, but in triumph. The damage his men had done to the Mobile & Ohio would seriously disrupt Grant's plans for gaining possession of the Mississippi. When that realization set in, Braxton Bragg at last began to reconsider his opinion of Forrest as a glorified partisan.[57]

Earl Van Dorn's raid on the Mississippi Central had been equally successful. On December 20, the erstwhile army commander had swept down on Holly Springs. In a matter of hours, his troopers captured the local garrison, tore great holes in the Mississippi Central railroad, and destroyed $1.5 million worth of rations and materiel.

Added to the mayhem done by Forrest, these were losses that Grant could not tolerate. They forced him to abort his overland drive on

Vicksburg and to return north to plan anew. His inability to communicate with Sherman resulted in the latter's decisive defeat at Chickasaw Bluffs on December 29. At about the same time as Grant's and Sherman's defeats, reports reached Tennessee that the Army of the Potomac had suffered thirteen thousand casualties while failing to drive Robert E. Lee's troops from well-entrenched positions outside Fredericksburg, Virginia. The convergence of stirring news meant that the now-ending autumn of 1862 could be viewed as a season of hope, not only in the Heartland, but in all corners of the embattled Confederacy.[58]

# EIGHT

# RAIDING
# REDUX

W HILE PEMBERTON, WITH THE ASSISTANCE of colleagues, dealt with Grant and Sherman, Bragg had to contend with the buildup of an enemy army virtually on the doorstep of his base at Murfreesboro. He countered with a novel scheme: a raid. Concurrent with Forrest's and Van Dorn's expeditions, John Morgan was ordered to return to his home state and attack an old, familiar target, the Louisville & Nashville. This time he would strike miles above the sections previously damaged. North of Bowling Green, his men were to mangle track, level depots, collapse bridges, burn rolling stock, and neutralize those Yankees whose mission was to prevent such destruction. Bragg expected Morgan to hamper, harass, and discomfit William Starke Rosecrans "in every conceivable way in your power," while taking pains to preclude his "foraging north of the Cumberland River, and especially toward Clarksville."[1]

Morgan had performed the same duty time after time over the past year, but he had not tired of it. The officer who was becoming known to a generation of Americans as "The Thunderbolt of the Confederacy" knew that his men enjoyed wreaking havoc on Yankee-run railroads, virtually all of which were defended by forces too small and too slow to offer opposition worthy of the name. The raiding game offered few challenges to such soldiers. Yet it gave them a chance to exercise themselves and their horses; and the thrill of eluding pursuers, even hapless ones, was a continuing attraction.

Morgan's only concern was that this mission would be conducted in bitter weather: winter was fast overtaking the Heartland. Still, plunging temperatures and knifelike winds had failed to prevent him from making a success of a recent excursion into the enemy's rear. Based on information from troopers in civilian attire planted in towns east of Nashville and who answered to Morgan's new chief of scouts, Captain Tom Quirk, the raiding leader had decided that the post at Hartsville, Tennessee, was not only well provisioned but also irresistibly vulnerable. It appeared to be well manned: as many as one thousand five hundred Federals were encamped just outside the town, which lay thirty-some miles northeast of the state capital. Nevertheless, Morgan was certain that a well-conducted strike would convince the garrison, isolated as it was from quick support, to capitulate.[2]

Just in case, the gambler strove to improve his odds. He persuaded Bragg to augment his brigade, which now included an artillery unit composed not only of the Bull Pups but of two Ellsworth rifles, with two regiments of foot soldiers and another battery. The additions, Kentuckians all, had been detached from the so-called "Orphan Brigade." They would be commanded by Morgan's uncle, Colonel Thomas H. Hunt of the 9th Kentucky Infantry. As a further hedge against unexpected opposition, Bragg got up a diversionary effort south of Nashville using an infantry-cavalry force whose mounted contingent was commanded personally by Joe Wheeler.

Preparations complete and forces on hand, Morgan rode out of Murfreesboro on the bone-chilling morning of Saturday, December 6— eight days before his wedding. Mounted on Glencoe, his handsome new war horse, he pranced past the home of his betrothed. Mattie Ready interrupted wedding preparations to gaze adoringly at her future husband and wish him Godspeed.[3]

Early that evening, the two-thousand-one-hundred-man column reached the Cumberland River at Purier's Ferry. Within an hour, the troopers were fording the icy stream, and the foot soldiers were crossing aboard the only ferryboat available. By now everyone was feeling more or less miserable. The infantry's feet had frozen on the march, and their cavalry comrades took an icy bath when the water at the ford proved to be deeper than expected. One of Quirk's scouts, Kelion F. Peddicord, recalled that "I never came so near freezing in my life."[4]

At least the journey was almost over. At five thirty a.m. on the seventh, with sunrise minutes away, Morgan was two miles from the enemy camp. Although his men were suffering terribly, the weather had given them an advantage. "We were already within short range," wrote Peddicord, "and we could see the Yankees distinctly as they stepped out to look up the road. It was so very cold, so intensely cold, that they did not dream Morgan would come after them on such a night. Had they not felt so confident surely they would not have dismounted while on picket duty."[5]

At daybreak, Quirk's men, many of them wearing blue, charged over the frozen earth and into the encampment, shooting down the pickets before they could spread a general alarm. But the shooting quickly awoke the garrison. Morgan soon found himself tangling with a force that he had "considerably underrated": three infantry outfits, a regiment of horsemen, and two rifled guns—more than two thousand  defenders all told, under Colonel Absalom B. Moore.[6]

Morgan swiftly deployed his main force. He sent the 9th Kentucky Cavalry to Moore's rear to cut off his escape route. Then he placed Basil Duke, with Cluke's and Chenault's regiments, opposite the enemy's left. He positioned his uncle's men on the right; in between he unlimbered his artillery. The flanking forces advanced simultaneously, driving in Moore's soldiers, most of whom were woefully inexperienced in close-quarters combat. The greatest pressure was applied by the cavalry; Duke recalled that the Federals opposing him soon "gave way in confusion, and were pressed again on their right and rear by Cluke and Chenault. . . . The enemy were crowded together in a narrow space, and were dropping like sheep."[7]

Although the fighting lasted nearly an hour, the issue was never in doubt. Minutes after Moore ran up a white flag, Morgan's men corralled and disarmed their untutored enemy. When this was done, they ransacked the camp, appropriating every item of winter clothing they could find, along with other articles that promised comfort or protection. One Kentuckian took possession of "a splendid overcoat, lined through and through, a fine black cloth coat, a pair of new woolen socks, a horse muzzle to feed in, an Enfield rifle, a lot of pewter plates, knives and forks, a good supply of smoking tobacco, an extra good cavalry saddle, a halter, and a pair of buckskin gloves, lined with lamb's wool—all of which things I needed."[8]

The operation had been a resounding success. Moore's command had lost fifty-eight men killed, more than two hundred wounded, and upwards of 1,850 captured. Morgan had suffered 140 casualties. After burning the camp and any items that could not be carried off, the raiders escorted their prisoners across the Cumberland and on to Murfreesboro. The POWs nearly doubled the size of Morgan's column.

Morgan departed Hartsville none too soon. In his after-action report, he remarked that "the result exceeded my own expectations, but still I felt that my position was a most perilous one, being within 4 miles in a direct line, and only 8 by the main Gallatin road, of an enemy's force of at least 8,000 men, consisting of infantry, cavalry, and artillery, who would naturally march to the aid of their comrades on hearing the report of our guns." His prudence was validated when, as the last of his men pulled out, the advance element of a five-thousand-man relief force approached Hartsville from Castalian Springs. The reinforcements arrived in time to shower the departing Rebels with shot and shell. One round tore a bough from a tree under which Glencoe had been halted, nearly decapitating Mattie Ready's fiancé.[9]

Body intact and spirits soaring, Morgan kept his blissful appointment, marrying Mattie in her family's parlor on Sunday evening, December 14. The bride wore satin, the groom a fancy pair of pantaloons confiscated from a captive officer. The many high-ranking guests included Generals Bragg, Breckinridge, and Hardee. Bishop Polk performed the ceremony, after which the wedding party dined on cakes and wine.

Noticeably absent was the president of the Confederate States of America. Two days earlier, Jefferson Davis had reached Murfreesboro on an inspection tour of his western armies, but he had gone on to Chattanooga. Also missing from the Ready home was the new departmental commander, Joseph E. Johnston, who had arrived at Bragg's headquarters for a familiarization conference on the fifth but had left to join Davis a few days prior to the wedding. Before departing, however, both visitors had extended their best wishes—Johnston in the form of a telegram to Richmond in which he applauded Morgan's "brilliant feat" at Hartsville, Davis in the form of a brigadier general's appointment, which he ceremoniously bestowed upon the raiding leader.[10]

THE NEWLYWEDS' HONEYMOON WAS LENGTHY by the norms of wartime society. By the twenty-first, the bridegroom was at Alexandria, Tennessee, northeast of Murfreesboro, inspecting the force with which he planned to wreck Rosecrans's railroad. Mrs. Morgan was there, too, helping her husband review the command that in less than a year had grown from a single squadron into a force formidable enough to overpower almost anyone with the temerity to bar its path.

And yet plenty of Yankees were longing for an opportunity to take on the most celebrated raider in Confederate service. The now-departed General Buell had constructed a chain of stockades to defend the L&N. His successor had strengthened these works, most of which protected depots and bridges. Thanks to Rosecrans, large patrols ranged along the line, so distributed as to provide ready support in case of attack.

Bragg reasoned that some points on the railroad were less defensible than others. He had directed Morgan's attention to the two, one-hundred-foot-high trestleworks at Muldraugh's Hill, just north of Elizabethtown, Kentucky. If those spans could be damaged beyond quick repair, Rosecrans might suffer supply problems large enough to prevent him from leaving his comfortable headquarters at Nashville to challenge the Army of Tennessee. One potential problem was that the trestles stood less than forty miles south of the major Federal base at Louisville. To ensure his ability to strike these critical targets and return to Tennessee in one piece, Morgan might need, in addition to manpower and mobility, a sizable amount of good luck.[11]

In weather even more severe than he had contended with on the Hartsville raid, Morgan left Alexandria on the morning of December 22, pointed toward Kentucky. Behind him came the three thousand one hundred troopers and cannoneers he had culled from his command, enough to form two brigades. One of these he had entrusted to Colonel Duke; it consisted of the 2nd, 3rd, 8th, and 9th Kentucky. William Breckinridge, now a full colonel, led the second brigade, comprising the 10th and 11th Kentucky and the 14th Tennessee. At the head of the column rode the sixty youthful and adventurous souls who made up Tom Quirk's Scouts, a position of honor that, as Trooper Peddicord observed, "we retained during the entire trip." Bringing up the rear was a beefed-up artillery battalion: no fewer than seven guns, including the esteemed Bull Pups. [12]

Late on the first day of what would become known as Morgan's Christmas Raid, the column reached the Cumberland River. In contrast to the delays and difficulties the raiders had experienced en route to Hartsville, they found the stream "easily fordable." They bivouacked on the north bank and resumed the march next morning. Slowed by the artillery and a string of supply vehicles, they did not cross the Kentucky line until almost nightfall. Their return home generated unbridled enthusiasm. An officer noted in his diary that "cheer after cheer and shout after shout echoed for miles . . . breaking the stillness of the night."[13]

Next day, Christmas eve, the celebrating continued, although not always in a manner conducive to good discipline. Marching through familiar territory north of Tompkinsville, several troopers managed to procure ardent spirits from local residents. Some drank so liberally that they were soon reeling in their saddles, compelling more-sober comrades to strap them in.[14]

The raiders' next bivouac was six miles short of Glasgow, a town they had avoided in the spring on the way to Cave City, and that they had occupied two months later during the First Kentucky Raid. On the former occasion, the town was reported to be alive with Yankees; on the second, the enemy had recently vacated. Glasgow was too important an outpost to be entirely unoccupied, so after putting his main body in camp for the night, Morgan sent forward one company each of the 2nd and 9th Kentucky to scout the place. Upon entering the town, the raiders were met by a roving patrol of Michigan cavalry. In the darkness, neither party at first recognized the other as an enemy; when realization set it, a sharp skirmish broke out in the streets of Glasgow in which one officer and one enlisted man of the 9th were mortally wounded, and a half-dozen of their comrades were captured. Among the wounded was Tom Quirk, struck in the head by a carbine round. The chief scout survived the wound thanks to what he described as an indestructible Irish skull.[15]

After the initial exchange, both antagonists, shaken by the encounter, galloped out of town. Private Peddicord related that "couriers flew to the General, and from each one he received a different account as to the numbers of the enemy. . . . [B]y the courier who claimed to be 'the most reliable,' he learned that the town was *full of troops!* The action of this detachment, did not please the General, neither did it add any laurels to the troops engaged."[16]

At first Morgan, "not knowing in what force the enemy might be," hesitated to respond. When he finally dispatched a large force to Glasgow, it found only stragglers, twenty-two of whom were captured and paroled. Morgan would claim that several Federals had been killed in the initial fighting.[17]

Departing Glasgow early on Christmas Day, Morgan marched in the direction of Munfordville. En route to the town that had fallen to Bragg during the Perryville campaign, Morgan's advance encountered a battalion-size force of horsemen—probably the main body of the regiment they had fought the night before—"drawn up in line, awaiting our approach."

Morgan advanced boldly, as if prepared to attack, and after letting loose a few rounds, the bluecoats turned and fled.[18]

Just short of Munfordville, which Rosecrans had reoccupied, Morgan had detachments of both brigades feint toward the town as well as eastward in the direction of his old training camp at Woodsonville, now similarly well guarded. Through such deception, Morgan hoped "to induce the enemy to believe I intended to attack the fortifications at Green River." He had no thought of challenging those works, which had been strengthened almost to the point of impregnability, but the demonstrations helped keep their occupants in place and off his tail.[19]

Late on the twenty-fifth, the expedition crossed Green River in a cold, steady rain that froze upon the men's jackets and coats. Bivouacking at day's end only a few miles from the nearest stretch of the L&N, troopers and artillerymen were pelted throughout the night by an icy drizzle that turned to sleet before morning. Refusing to succumb to the mounting misery, Morgan, on the twenty-sixth, sent elements of the 2nd and 7th Kentucky and two guns under the 2nd's provisional commander, Lieutenant Colonel John B. Hutcheson, to strike a secondary target whose destruction would at least take his men's minds off their physical discomfort. This was the same bridge over Bacon Creek that Morgan had dismantled a year ago, at the start of his career as a scourge to the invaders of Kentucky. On that occasion, the bridge had been unguarded; now a formidable-looking stockade blocked all approaches to the rebuilt span.

Not surprisingly, today's mission proved much more difficult than Morgan's maiden effort at bridge burning. Although suspecting they were outnumbered, the occupants of the stockade put up a stout fight, the duration of which made Morgan, who had remained in camp, fear that the Yankees had been reinforced. Hastening to the scene of fighting, he found a standoff in progress. Superseding Hutcheson, he decided to think, rather than fight, his way to victory. He succeeded more quickly and easily than he could have anticipated. He sent the enemy commander a surrender demand which, after some hesitation, was accepted. Ninety-three Federals, including four officers, marched out of their work, hands in the air.

Minutes later, Basil Duke was galloping toward the bridge, which turned out to be defended by a force almost as large as the one that had fought Hutcheson to a draw. Alarmed by their comrades' capitulation as well as by the size of Duke's command, the defenders surrendered without firing a shot. Duke's men then got down to business: soon they were warming themselves by the fires that eventually consumed the structure. This was not the first conflagration of the day; hours earlier, Morgan had put his men to work setting "large fires . . . all along the track for some 3 or 4 miles, in order to warp and destroy the rails, which was most effectually accomplished."[20]

The bridge burners spent the night at the scene of their labors, battling the pervasive cold. On the morning of the twenty-seventh, Morgan led them to within striking distance of the railroad trestles that constituted the expedition's raison d'être. By now, however, he had decided that before advancing on Muldraugh's Hill, he should attack and capture Union-held Elizabethtown to prevent its garrison, estimated at eight or nine companies of infantry, from threatening the rear of the column on the march. He expected a fight at Elizabethtown, but he was not prepared for what took place upon his entrance. On reaching the outskirts he was met by an emissary of the lieutenant colonel in command. The courier handed Morgan a message scrawled in pencil on the back of an envelope; it called on him to disarm his men, on the ground that "I have you surrounded, and will compel you to surrender." The cheeky demand drew a guffaw from Morgan, who replied by suggesting that "the positions were reversed," as indeed they were.[21]

At Morgan's order, Duke and Breckinridge deployed their brigades, each supported by artillery, on two sides of Elizabethtown. A half-hour after the guns began firing from hills overlooking the garrison, the enemy leader surrendered his 652 men. Morgan paroled them all, along with the Yankees he had seized at Glasgow and Bacon Creek. The process took so long that his men were compelled to lay over for the night. Some fared quite well. Quirk's scouts feasted on "the many delicacies" they had appropriated from a train of sutler's wagons captured the previous day. Many raiders slept not outdoors in the cold but in beds provided by local "secesh," a gesture of gratitude to the soldiers who had liberated the town, at least temporarily, from the hated occupier.[22]

Next morning Morgan quickly covered the four miles that separated him from his primary objective. After dispatching Breckinridge's brigade to attack the left flank of the stockade that defended the lower bridge, he led Duke's regiments against the upper span. Again choosing persuasion over coercion, he sent truce parties to seek the surrender of both garrisons, offering to parole the troops on the spot. Much like the commander at Elizabethtown, the officers in charge refused Morgan's offer. Accordingly, his guns shelled both works while his troopers riddled them with rifle and carbine fire. It took three hours of continual shelling—during which portions of both stockades were reduced to kindling—before their leaders bowed to Morgan's demand.

In addition to prisoners, Morgan secured another cache of weapons and equipment. One of the surrendered regiments, which had been organized in Indiana, carried newly issued rifles of the best quality. Sergeant Henry L. Stone of Morgan's command, a native Hoosier, chatted with the prisoners, several of whom he knew from back home in Putnam County. The unlucky regiment had been captured once before, had been paroled, and upon reentering service had been issued British-made Enfields, "all of which," Stone observed, "fell into our boys' hands, and took the place of arms much inferior."[23]

Immediately after Morgan's guns fell silent, fatigue parties swarmed over both bridges. Working with speed and precision, they piled combustible material on the floors of the spans and in the crooks of the trestles, and set them ablaze. The twin conflagrations were so enormous that Morgan was convinced the railroad would be out of operation for at least two months. Such a disruption of the Union supply system ought to give General Bragg the time to plan a grand offensive against Nashville, secure in the knowledge that his immobilized, ill-supplied enemy would fight at a disadvantage.[24]

As a raider of long experience, Morgan realized that accomplishing his mission involved not only hitting his target but also returning home without suffering at the hands of pursuers. On December 29, ready to traverse familiar territory, he turned the column east and headed toward Bardstown preparatory to swinging south in the direction of Springfield and Lebanon. Before moving out, he sent Cluke's regiment, accompanied by a single artillery piece, to destroy a bridge over Rolling Fork River; Morgan and the main body would follow at a distance before crossing that stream at another point. At the same time, Chenault's outfit, also supplied with one cannon, was directed to burn the trestle and the stockade at Boston. Finally, three companies of the 9th Kentucky peeled off to strike the works at New Haven. The side expeditions netted mixed results. Chenault's troopers accomplished their mission; the 9th Kentucky failed to overawe its target, whose defenders had been considerably reinforced; and Cluke's men, soon after starting out, were recalled when trouble arose on the road to Rolling Fork.

Unknown to Morgan, Federals had been seeking him ever since he left Elizabethtown. Just as he was fording Rolling Fork, this force—a brigade of infantry, horsemen, and several cannons under Colonel John M. Harlan—struck the end of the column. With no time to lose, Morgan cobbled together a rear guard consisting of seven companies from almost as many regiments, which he assigned to Duke. The guard repulsed several attacks but suffered more or less heavily at the hands of Harlan's gunners.[25]

Once the main force had gotten over, Duke's men were left to make their way across the rain-swollen stream without close support, a hazardous undertaking at best. The colonel recalled that "when the enemy moved upon us again, its infantry deployed in a long line, strongly supported, with skirmish line in front, all coming on with bayonets glistening, the guns redoubling their fire, and the cavalry column on the right flank . . . apparently ready to pounce on us too, and then the river surging at our backs, my blood, I confess, ran cold."[26]

His blood ran red as well. One of Harlan's shells burst a few feet from Duke, stunning him and dashing him to the ground. He was saved from quick death by Tom Quirk, who rode up to the unconscious officer, took him up on his horse, and galloped out of artillery range. When he regained his senses, Duke was unable to ride. His subordinates carried him across the river and placed him in a mattress-lined carriage that bore him the rest of the way home. He later learned that the rear guard avoided disaster only because Harlan inexplicably withdrew his men just as they were about to shove their opponents into the river. Thankful for large favors, most of the imperiled raiders splashed to safety, although a few fell to long-range skirmish fire.

Once across Rolling Fork, Morgan left his irresolute pursuers behind. He camped for the night at Bardstown, passed through Springfield early on the thirtieth, and detoured west around well-fortified Lebanon. Although reports had Harlan's men again at their heels, and a force that Morgan estimated as "nearby treble my own immediately in my front," the raiders plodded south under a new round of rain and sleet, and through early evening darkness so thick as to be almost palpable.[27]

Somehow, the weather managed to worsen. "Then commenced a night march," Kelion Peddicord wrote, "long to be remembered by us for its severity and the suffering it caused." Not every veteran of the Hartsville raid had acquired warm clothing. Some of the more lightly clad and shod troopers suffered frostbite; others fell prey to pneumonia. Numerous horses broke down on the route home, to be shot and left by the roadside. Their riders either doubled up with comrades or trod in the rear of the column, carrying their saddles on their backs in hopes of stealing a remount from some farmer's stable.[28]

The survivors straggled into Campbellsville in the evening of the last day of the year to find succor. The town contained "quite an amount of commissary stores," which, as Morgan related, "was most fortunate, as my command had had but little [to eat] for two days." The unexpected abundance of rations and fodder enabled men and horses to recover the stamina they desperately needed. Thus fortified, Morgan led the way to Columbia, where he arrived at three p.m. on the first day of the new year. At last home free on the road to Murfreesboro, he marched through the night to Burkesville, where he rested his men before crossing the Cumberland River on the morning of January 2 and passing inside Confederate lines.[29]

Despite their ordeal, Morgan's men were in good spirits three days later when they reached their newly assigned camp. Their attitude was justified by the scope and quality of their handiwork. Years later, John Allan Wyeth, the youngest of Quirk's scouts, declared that "this was Morgan's most successful expedition. The Louisville and Nashville Railroad was a wreck from Bacon Creek to Shepherdsville, a distance of sixty miles. We had captured about nineteen hundred prisoners, destroyed a vast amount of Government property [estimated at two million dollars], with a loss of only two men killed, twenty-four wounded, and sixty-four missing. The command returned well armed and better mounted than when it set out. The country had been stripped of horses. Every man in my company led out an extra mount."[30]

The raiders' elation at having achieved so much against so much adversity was short-lived. Upon making contact with Bragg's army near Murfreesboro, they found their comrades beaten, demoralized, and falling back to Tullahoma to avoid being overwhelmed by a nearly defeated but ultimately victorious foe. It did not take long for Morgan and his men to realize that for all their exertions and accomplishments, they had failed to prevent Rosecrans from leaving Nashville and giving battle, which explained why, near the end of the expedition, they had heard the distant but incessant rumble of artillery. Like Perryville, the recent fighting had been bloody but inconclusive; in the end, however, Bragg, convinced that fate was against him, abandoned the field. Although eminently successful in terms of damage done to the enemy, Morgan's Christmas Raid had come too late to influence the strategic situation in Middle Tennessee.[31]

WHILE MORGAN OPERATED IN KENTUCKY and Forrest raided western Tennessee, Joe Wheeler remained with Bragg, scouting inside enemy lines, establishing outposts on the roads between Murfreesboro and Nashville, attacking those of the enemy, seizing supply trains and sutlers' wagons, and interrogating prisoners in hopes of keeping abreast of Rosecrans's intentions. His activities between late November and mid-December earned Bragg's gratitude and praise. But when the cavalry leader accompanied one of his patrols on a scout halfway to Nashville, engaged some Federals, and took a painful wound in the leg, the army commander warned him that "you expose yourself too recklessly in affairs of this character."[32]

Bragg coupled his concern for Wheeler's health with his approval of the cavalryman's manifest desire to keep in close touch with the enemy and gain accurate intelligence in a timely manner. On November 24, Bragg informed Jefferson Davis that "the three regular cavalry brigades are in front of the advanced infantry, and always in sight of the enemy, giving me daily information. He [Rosecrans] is thus kept from foraging this side of the Cumberland."[33]

Wheeler's industry and efficiency, and his willingness to serve Bragg in any desired capacity, earned rewards. Soon after the army reached Murfreesboro, Wheeler's sphere of authority expanded with the addition to his division of three regiments formerly part of Kirby Smith's command. Just weeks later, a small (six-hundred-man) brigade under Colonel Abraham Buford, a Kentucky-born graduate of the West Point class of 1841, a Mexican War veteran, and a captain in the 1st U.S. Dragoons, also joined Wheeler. Occasionally smaller units were also assigned him, including Colonel John T. Morgan's 51st Alabama, a regiment of partisan rangers originally under Forrest. The numerous additions bolstered Wheeler's claim to general officer rank. With Bragg's hearty endorsement, he was appointed a brigadier general, to rank from October 30.[34]

Although held in high regard by his army leader, Wheeler was not universally admired. As a leader of cavalry, Forrest never considered Wheeler his equal, let alone his superior. He thought of the Georgian as plodding, unimaginative, textbook-bound, and too willing to do the bidding of infantry commanders. Morgan was careful to show Wheeler greater deference, but in private he too was critical. Basil Duke summed up Morgan's views when he commented after the war that Wheeler had risen to high command "more on account of the dislike entertained by [Bragg] to certain other officers, than because of the partiality he felt for him. The reputation of this officer, although deservedly high, hardly entitled him to command some of the men who were ordered to report to him." The best Duke could say of Wheeler was that "while he did not display the originality and the instinctive strategical sagacity which characterized Morgan and Forrest, he was perhaps better fitted than either for the duties which devolve upon the commander of large bodies of cavalry."[35]

Wheeler undoubtedly was aware of how subordinates such as Forrest, Morgan, and Wharton perceived him. He determined to prove them wrong, and Bragg right, in elevating him above them. He found an opportunity much sooner than he expected. Like Bragg, Wheeler assumed that Rosecrans would remain in his warm and comfortable citadel at least until spring arrived. But before November was up, Wheeler was surprised to find himself skirmishing regularly, sometimes several times a day, with Yankee cavalry and infantry out of Nashville. Wheeler's own brigade stoutly resisted the enemy, although on December 12, Wharton's brigade was taken by surprise near Franklin. It suffered heavy casualties and was forced into an embarrassing retreat. Wheeler noted that his third brigade, Pegram's, did not expose itself as readily as its comrades and thus suffered fewer losses, but it failed to provide as much useful intelligence to army headquarters.[36]

Even when Wheeler offered timely, accurate assessments of enemy intentions, they were not always heeded. By mid-December he had come to suspect that, contrary to expectations, Rosecrans was planning an offensive. But the inordinate amount of activity inside Nashville that had driven Wheeler to this conclusion was seen by Bragg as a sign that Rosecrans was on the verge of evacuating, probably for lack of adequate rations and forage. Hoping for confirmation that Nashville would soon be abandoned, on December 20 Bragg ordered Wheeler to "press forward" even farther than before and "ascertain the true condition of things." Wheeler strove to obey, but he learned nothing that suggested a Union withdrawal.[37]

On the day after Christmas, Wheeler was proven right and his superior wrong. That morning Rosecrans's army—some forty-five thousand infantry and artillery, screened by four thousand cavalry under Major

General David S. Stanley—advanced from Nashville toward Murfreesboro. Wheeler, who supervised Bragg's first line of defense, prepared to meet the enemy at the head of his own brigade, which covered the Nashville Pike and adjacent Stewart's Creek. The brigade's picket line had stretched from a point east of Stones River to as far west as the Nashville suburb of Brentwood. The pickets of Wharton's brigade, west of Wheeler's, held a line between Nolensville and Franklin, while Pegram's pickets, off Wheeler's right flank, covered the approaches to Lebanon. Covering so wide a front was difficult enough, but Wheeler's job was made tougher by the unwieldy arrangement under which he directly commanded one brigade and more remotely commanded two others, the imposition of which suggested Bragg's inability to grasp cavalry organization.[38]

Rudely awakened to Rosecrans's plans, Bragg placed infantry within supporting distance of each of Wheeler's brigades. Even before the foot soldiers reached him, Wheeler countered Stanley's advance on the Nashville Pike while directing Wharton and Pegram to do the same from their respective positions. Wheeler soon found himself opposed not only by horse soldiers but by the advance element of an infantry corps commanded by a familiar opponent, Thomas L. Crittenden.

Having staked out a position on terrain conducive to making a stand, Wheeler's troopers denied Stanley and Crittenden access to the fords on Stewart's Creek. Wheeler's larger enemy pressed him throughout the morning, but he managed to hold up the offensive for almost an hour. When one of Crittenden's brigades finally fought its way to the front, threatening to outflank him, Wheeler deftly withdrew to the south side of the stream. There, fighting behind good cover, he so frustrated Crittenden's attempts to ford that it was evening before the infantry straggled across. Withdrawing from Crittenden's reach, Wheeler and his infantry supports spent the night in La Vergne, an objective Rosecrans had expected to seize that afternoon.[39]

With the Yankees at a virtual halt, Wheeler was called to Murfreesboro to take part in a council of war. Upon reaching army headquarters, the cavalryman was informed that Bragg needed time to mass his extended army and fortify a defensive position. Wheeler's superior asked him how long he could hold the Federals north of Stones River. Conflicting accounts of Wheeler's reply have him promising to prevent the enemy from reaching Murfreesboro for two, three, or four days. Supposedly, Generals Polk and

Hardee, who were also in attendance, pronounced impossible even a two- or three-day delay, but Wheeler insisted otherwise.[40]

He made good on his pledge. Over the next three days, he skillfully utilized the same fight-and-fall back technique he had mastered during the retreat from Perryville. He stymied not only Crittenden's foot soldiers on the turnpike but constantly rode to and from Wharton's and Pegram's field headquarters, helping them apply the same delaying tactics. Wharton's men, who had nimbly escaped the enemy's clutches at Bardstown and elsewhere during the Perryville campaign, showed quick proficiency, but Pegram's men were not nearly as adept, and Wheeler had to work harder to teach them.

The result was everything Bragg could have hoped for. Not only was Rosecrans's advance slowed to a crawl, but Wheeler's troopers, supported by their infantry friends, delivered an effective fire from successive positions, "killing and wounding large numbers," as Wheeler reported, while "meeting but very slight losses ourselves." Throughout December 27, Wheeler's brigade continued to block Stanley's and Crittenden's path. It received help from the weather, including a steady, frigid rain that turned the roads to ice-coated slush.[41]

Wheeler's only concern was the condition of Wharton's command, which on the twenty-seventh experienced "constant . . . fighting." Opposed by Rosecrans's right wing, which consisted of Alexander McCook's corps, Wharton's Texans and Tennesseans were driven from one position to another, but usually in good order. Each retreat placed another barrier across the enemy's path, the most formidable being Nelson's Creek, which McCook had to ford under a galling fire from dismounted troopers and their infantry supports.[42]

For a time on the twenty-eighth, pressure increased on Wheeler's front, but it abruptly subsided when General Crittenden elected to remain on the left side of Stewart's Creek until the troops of McCook and Major General George H. Thomas reached previously assigned positions. Wheeler welcomed the Yankees' deliberate pace, for by now Bragg had recalled his infantry to Murfreesboro, leaving the cavalry to fend for itself.

On the twenty-ninth, the Federals finally made consistent progress. Shoving Stanley's horsemen out of the way, Crittenden's wing advanced briskly under cover of a barrage from cannons emplaced on a ridge overlooking Stewart's Creek. Wheeler replied with shot and shell from an Arkansas battery recently assigned to his brigade. Perhaps he focused too much on the artillery duel, for he failed to detect a crossing of the creek by small bands of foot soldiers. They quickly secured the far side, permitting comrades to cross in large numbers, then marched a mile and a half inside Wheeler's lines. They finally halted on the north side of Overall Creek, less than a mile from Bragg's main line northwest of Murfreesboro.[43]

The penetration forced Wheeler to fall back yet again, but for the last time. Having held back the blue tide for three days, he had accomplished the mission that Bragg's subordinates had described as impossible. He coolly led his brigade across Stones River and, by way of the Lebanon Pike, toward the Confederate right flank. As night approached, he distributed his troopers along a line about a mile in advance of the position occupied by John Breckinridge's division of Polk's corps. There they connected with Pegram's brigade east of the Lebanon Pike. On the other end of Bragg's line, Wharton's command, having withdrawn smartly in the face of McCook's Federals, was covering the front, flanks, and rear of Hardee's corps. Bragg had used the time his cavalry bought him to mass and deploy for battle. His effective force closely matched the strength of the army confronting him across Stones River, giving him enough confidence to contemplate attacking rather than awaiting attack.

Bragg was properly grateful for Wheeler's help in bringing about this state of affairs. When the cavalry leader returned to army headquarters to report his command ready for combat, he was met with open arms. According to the editor of Wheeler's memoirs as well as to one of his earliest biographers, Bragg greeted him with unaccustomed warmth, clasping his hand and declaring in the presence of his corps commanders: "General Wheeler, you have not only accomplished what Generals Polk and Hardee said was impossible, but very much more. Your work is done, and we will now take the enemy in hand and see by the grace of God what we can do with him." Both chroniclers agree that the fulsome praise left the modest Wheeler "almost overcome with embarrassment."[44]

BRAGG KNEW HOW TO SING THE PRAISES OF HIS mounted arm, but when it came to employing it in battle he was tone deaf. His reference to Wheeler's job having been completed suggested that the cavalry had no role in the fighting to come. Wheeler's subsequent orders seemed to bear this out. Having already weakened his mobility by detaching Forrest and

Morgan to far-off quarters, Bragg now assigned Wheeler a mission far removed from the main army. On the raw and rainy morning of December 30, as the opposing forces prepared to grapple west of Stones River, Wheeler led his brigade, which had been slightly enlarged for the occasion, up the Lebanon Pike toward the village of Jefferson. The movement carried Wheeler's command around the left flank of the Army of the Cumberland and into its rear, where Bragg wished to strike the wagon trains constantly passing between Rosecrans's army and Nashville.

The dubious rationale for this operation was that it would make Rosecrans nervous about his communications and distract his attention from the attack Bragg planned to launch against his right flank. In Wheeler's absence, Colonel Wharton's large brigade would guard Bragg's left and assist in the opening assault, while Pegram's brigade, the smallest of the three, would picket the army's right and rear. An even smaller brigade under Wheeler's remote supervision, that commanded by Abraham Buford, would cover the army's far rear at McMinnville, almost fifty miles southeast of Murfreesboro.[45]

Wheeler's expedition achieved dramatic results, but whether it made a material contribution to Bragg's strategy remains undetermined. On the morning of the thirtieth, having penetrated enemy lines, Wheeler turned off the turnpike and headed toward Nashville. Detouring to the south of Jefferson, which was reported to be heavily defended, the rain-drenched column forded Stones River near Neal's Mill, circled north until regaining the Nashville Pike, and resumed its westward heading. As Bragg had hoped, Wheeler's advance soon came upon a sixty-wagon supply train en route from the Tennessee capital to Jefferson. The raiders attacked, drove off the train guards, burned a couple dozen wagons, and shot or sabered their teams.

The guards raced toward Jefferson, spreading an alarm. In quick time, two regiments of infantry under Colonel John C. Starkweather hustled up to curtail Wheeler's depredations. Fightin' Joe held them at arm's length with dismounted skirmishers while the rest of his brigade galloped west. Bragg had stressed that the raiders were to overtake, capture, and burn, but not to fight unless absolutely necessary.[46]

Moving on to the railroad village of La Vergne, one of John Morgan's early haunts, the column waylaid several foraging parties, taking prisoners and relieving them of their spoils. Outside the depot village, Wheeler discovered, in park just off the turnpike, the enormous supply train of

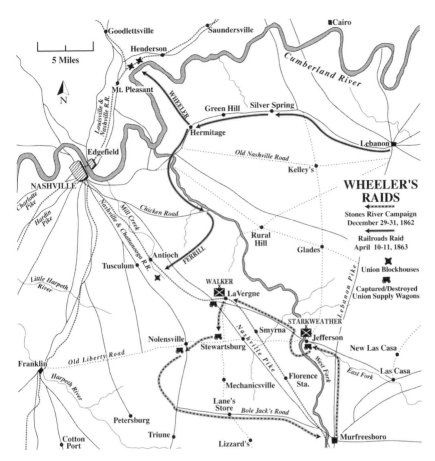

Wheeler's Raids: Stones River Campaign, December 29–31, 1862 and the Railroads Raid, April 10–11, 1863.

McCook's corps. He deployed carefully, then attacked the wagons from three sides. "We dashed in," one of his troopers recalled, "four or five regiments, at full speed, fired a few shots and we had possession of an army train of over three hundred wagons, richly laden with quartermaster's and commissary stores." Many of these goods passed into the hands of their captors, but Wheeler saw to it that the majority, the estimated value of which exceeded one million dollars, went up in smoke.[47]

Aware that he was far behind enemy lines and perhaps suspecting that with a battle brewing Bragg would want his cavalry well in hand, Wheeler turned south toward Stewartsburg and Nolensville. Upon approaching Stewartsburg, he found his rear guard assailed by a brigade of Ohio infantry under Colonel Moses Walker. After what one raider called "liberal application of the spur for two hours," the raiders not only outdistanced the Ohioans but overtook a third supply column, which was hauling rations and materiel, including military clothing. Wheeler's advance echelon struck it "like a tornado," capturing and burning dozens of vehicles and paroling a large contingent of guards.[48]

That night the raiders, many of them sporting blue uniforms and feasting on pickled beets and lobster salad, bivouacked in fields southeast of Nolensville. In the early afternoon of the thirty-first, they returned to their army, connecting with the left flank of Hardee's corps. They had circumnavigated Rosecrans's army, damaging or destroying upwards of five hundred supply wagons and taking six hundred or more prisoners. They rejoined Bragg to the accompaniment of artillery blasts and the rattle of small arms. Battle had been joined, and from what Wheeler could learn, the portents were favorable. Hardee's infantry, screened by Wharton's horsemen, appeared to have taken McCook's troops by surprise, displacing the Union right flank. Some officers with whom Wheeler spoke believed victory was already within reach.

A few hours after reaching the position that Bragg had assigned him at Wilkinson's Cross Roads, Wheeler heard that the Union right was teetering on collapse. Displaced Yankees were streaming north toward the Franklin Pike in what looked like utter rout. However, as Wheeler would later learn, other components of Rosecrans's hard-pressed command would join McCook's survivors in their new position parallel to the turnpike. They would hold their ground with a fanatical tenacity, and in time they would summon the power and the nerve to mount a counterattack.[49]

With a battle in progress, Wheeler fully expected to be sent to the firing lines, and he was not disappointed. Although almost all the fighting on December 31 would be done by his infantry, Bragg ordered Wheeler, accompanied by Buford's brigade, which had been called up from the rear, to move north, striking the Nashville Pike west of Overall Creek. At the same time, Wharton was to attack a supply column reported to be moving up the pike on the other side of the stream. Pegram's troopers would be left with the army to provide intelligence and combat support as needed.

Within an hour of receiving his orders, Wheeler was leading his designated force, Buford's Kentuckians in the lead, into its assigned position. Fording Overall Creek under long-range infantry fire, Wheeler advanced toward the turnpike. Just shy of the road, a large portion of Thomas's corps, covered by Stanley's horsemen and anchored by artillery, loomed up in Wheeler's front. The cannons poured a salvo into the head of Buford's brigade, inflicting numerous casualties. Buford quickly withdrew to a position that afforded some cover, but he did not remain there for long. Impressed by the strength of the opposition and doubtful that Wharton had kept pace with him on the other side of the creek, Wheeler had Buford fall back to Wilkinson's Cross Roads. There Wharton's men—who, as Wheeler suspected, had been turned back by an enemy force at least as powerful as the one Buford had encountered—joined him.[50]

Wheeler discovered that the Yankees who had repulsed Wharton—several regiments of Stanley's cavalry—were now grouped around Asbury Church, a Methodist meetinghouse near a crossroads about three hundred yards east of Overall Creek. Wheeler decided to take them on. Leaving Wharton to hold Wilkinson's, he made straight for Asbury Church. Stanley's skirmishers detected Wheeler's approach, and the Union leader advanced two regiments, which kept up a brisk fire from their breech-loading carbines. They brought the head of Wheeler's column to a halt, until Buford moved up to threaten Stanley's flank, persuading him to back off. There followed some rather lethargic skirmishing, after which Stanley broke contact and withdrew to a more defensible position.

Wheeler pursued, and when his opponent deployed behind a wooded ridge adjacent to the Nashville Pike, he determined to attack. He planned to strike not only the center of Stanley's line but its exposed flanks as well. Before he could get into position, however, detachments of three regiments, brandishing pistols and sabers, charged down the ridge. The unexpected assault caught in mid-movement the force with which Wheeler had intended to smite the Union flank and sent it scrambling to the rear in disorder. By the time Wheeler's force had recovered its composure, the short winter's day was ending. In the frigid darkness, Wheeler returned his entire force to Wilkinson's Cross Roads and went into bivouac.

Some modern historians have criticized Wheeler's operations of December 30–31. Thomas Connelly is particularly hard on the cavalry leader, whom he accuses of returning late from his "flashy ride around Rosecrans" and of failing to seize the Nashville Pike in cooperation with Wharton on the thirty-first. He claims that Bragg ordered Wheeler to attack the Union rear but that the latter went off on another expedition, on which he "accomplished nothing and was beaten back by Federal cavalry," instead of supporting Wharton's effort to outflank Rosecrans's right wing by way of the turnpike. However, the record is silent on whether Bragg ordered Wheeler to operate as Connelly alleges. In their after-action reports, neither Bragg nor Wheeler mentioned an order to support Wharton. Bragg declared that throughout the thirty-first, all of his cavalry units "most ably, gallantly, and successfully performed" their assigned duties.[51]

As if in observance of the holiday, the armies paused for breath throughout New Year's Day 1863, gathering up the strength and will to resume the slaughter on the morrow. At this juncture, the Army of Tennessee appeared to have won a decisive victory. Since morning, it had driven Rosecrans's mighty host three and a half miles, and had left it clinging to its new position by its fingertips.

A couple of major blunders had enabled the Yankees to hang on in the face of impending defeat, and Bragg's cavalry was partly to blame. Mainly due to a lack of real-time intelligence, a lapse for which John Pegram was responsible, General Breckinridge had not realized that the force that had assaulted his position on Bragg's right had been withdrawn. Convinced that his posture remained precarious, Breckinridge refused a request to send two brigades across Stones River to reinforce Bragg's attack on the Union right. When Bragg later ordered him to advance, the Kentuckian was surprised to find no enemy in his path. But he was quickly recalled when Pegram sent Bragg an erroneous report that an enemy column was moving toward the army's rear via the Lebanon Turnpike. Breckinridge's absence diluted the impact of Bragg's offensive and enabled Rosecrans to withstand it.[52]

While the infantry and artillery took a breather, most of the cavalry kept busy throughout the first. This day, Wheeler returned to his raiding mission, the result of Bragg's belief that another, stronger blow to the enemy's communications would propel him into retreat. But Bragg guessed wrong, and in so doing left himself open to criticism that once again he had sent his mounted arm away when he needed it most.

On that bitter cold morning, Wheeler, leading a column composed not only of his own brigade and Buford's but also Wharton's, headed north toward the point—thought to be lightly guarded—where Stewart's Creek crossed the Nashville Pike. Instead, Wheeler discovered the countryside surrounding the ford to be alive with Yankee cavalry. Familiar with the area, he fell back, veered west toward La Vergne, and gained the pike without further difficulty. To his gratification, he soon overtook another supply train, this composed of about three hundred wagons. Aiming for more than spoils, he sent Buford's Kentuckians to attack and halt the train; at the same time, he dispatched Wharton's Texans, Tennesseans, Georgians, and Alabamians to wreck the depot facilities at neighboring La Vergne.

Half of Wheeler's strategy went by the boards when Wharton encountered opposition from Yankees ensconced in a cedar brake a short distance in advance of La Vergne. The well-covered defenders repulsed a succession of saber charges by two of Wharton's regiments and one of his battalions. Unable to make further progress, Wharton turned his back on his target and headed cross-country to rejoin Wheeler.[53]

While Wharton was suffering a frustrating repulse, his superior was capturing the rear portion of the immense supply train he had in his sights. While some of his men looted and then set fire to the captured vehicles, Wheeler and the rest raced after the main body of the train, which had continued toward Nashville. After several miles covered at an extended gallop, the raiders finally forced their quarry to halt.

Wheeler found the midsection of the train defended by a much larger guard than any he had previously encountered: several regiments of horsemen under one of Stanley's more combative subordinates, Colonel Lewis Zahm. The dismounted Yankees dug in and put up a formidable defense. Unwilling to be tied down, Wheeler left half of his force to occupy the enemy and led the rest toward the head of the train. His attempt to bring the entire column to a halt failed, for Zahm was strong enough to overcome the delaying action, remount his men, and hasten after Wheeler. The colonel struck before Wheeler could damage more than a few vehicles. Zahm also foiled two attempts by Wheeler to circle around him and attack the train from a different angle.

Wheeler's repulse ended his efforts to wreak havoc on Rosecrans's communications. It also gave the lie to Wheeler's boast in his report of the day's operations that he had "captured and destroyed a large number of wagons and stores." No more than a dozen vehicles, which had broken down and become defenseless, had fallen into his clutches this day.[54]

A discouraged Wheeler broke contact with Zahm, fell back, and, after linking with an equally frustrated Wharton, withdrew to Overall Creek. Arriving there at two a.m. on the second, he placed Buford's brigade in camp west of the stream, while he and Wharton crossed to bivouac in the fields along the Wilkinson Pike. Making contact with army headquarters, Wheeler relayed his belief that by all indications the Army of the Cumberland, far from retreating as Bragg had expected, was digging in for a fight to the finish. In fact, the previous evening Rosecrans had conferred with his generals to determine whether to remain on the field or withdraw. Although some subordinates counseled retreat, fearing the army was fought out, its commander finally chose to stay and slug it out.[55]

Rosecrans's decision proved to be one of the most important of his military career, for the fighting on January 2, during which he maintained a defensive posture, did not go well for his opponent. Breckinridge having been held mostly inactive on the thirty-first, Bragg ordered him to cross the river, occupy high ground, and enfilade the Federals' new position. Breckinridge doubted that this strategy would succeed; he feared that his objective had been heavily reinforced. Although he was correct, Bragg forced him to attack anyway. Crossing the river in midafternoon, Breckinridge broke through the line held by Brigadier General Horatio P. Van Cleve's division, but as his men descended the captured ridge, they were savaged by the combined fire of fifty or more cannons as well as by a spirited counterattack that cost the attackers almost 40 percent casualties.[56]

After Breckenridge was driven back to the starting point of his assault, Bragg gave up hope of landing a finishing blow. He began to dwell on the fact that although he had taken a grievous toll of his enemy, he had suffered almost as heavily (later calculations placed Rosecrans's losses at thirteen thousand, Bragg's at eleven thousand seven hundred). When his equally chastened corps commanders advised retreat, Bragg gave in to the same faintheartedness he had displayed at Perryville. Early on January 3, he called Joe Wheeler to his side and assigned him an all-too-familiar mission: covering the departure of an army from a battlefield on which it had not been defeated and from which it had not been driven.[57]

# NINE

# FOXES AND HOUNDS

**W**RITING TO HIS HOMETOWN NEWSPAPER from Shelbyville, Tennessee, where a portion of Bragg's army ended its retreat from Stones River on January 6, Chaplain Robert F. Bunting of the 8th Texas Cavalry was both frustrated and mystified: "With victory on our side, we cannot divine this movement. We cannot but ask, cui bono? [to whose advantage?] The abandonment of Murfreesboro loses to us the moral effect of our victory."[1]

Bragg's opponent may have asked himself the same question. His battered army having escaped defeat by the narrowest of margins, Rosecrans hardly felt like the victor he had become. Like Buell after Perryville, he was too weak to mount a pursuit worthy of the name. Thus Wheeler, whose command rejoined Bragg before dawn on January 4, was able to rest Buford's brigade and his own on the north side of Stones River for several hours, confident he would be unmolested. While these units snatched at sleep, Wharton's brigade covered the retreat of Polk's corps to Shelbyville, and Pegram's horsemen, who had seen little action of consequence over the past four days, screened Hardee's march to Wartrace on the Nashville & Chattanooga Railroad a few miles above Tullahoma, where Bragg had reestablished his headquarters.

Wheeler did not relinquish his position until daylight on the fifth, by which time Stanley's Federals had entered Murfreesboro. The Confederate rear guard had a spirited encounter with a regular army regiment in the streets of the town. After another sharp but indecisive skirmish along Lytle Creek, Wheeler called in his detachments and fell back to the colorfully named village of Bell Buckle, five miles south of Murfreesboro, where he made contact with Pegram. Only when Union artillery, in advance of Stanley's horsemen, moved against him late in the afternoon did Wheeler resume his retreat, although he moved only a short distance before halting and offering battle. At that point Stanley, content to have advanced even a few miles south of Murfreesboro, gave up the chase and withdrew.[2]

Thus ended Rosecrans's effort to consolidate the minimal gains he had achieved in battle. He was in no shape to accomplish more; upon entering Murfreesboro, his army virtually collapsed. Even a worrywart like Braxton Bragg understood that "Old Rosey" would not challenge him any time soon.

Secure in his position at Tullahoma and possessed of some options, Bragg decided to continue his attack on his enemy's communications with Nashville. The recent exertions of Morgan and Forrest, whose men were resting and refitting in the rear of the army, prevented them from taking on the mission. Bragg assigned it to Wheeler, whom he regarded as his most reliable cavalryman. In his report of the recent fighting he would describe Wheeler as "eminently distinguished throughout the campaign," as he had been "for a month previous in many successive conflicts with the enemy." Under Wheeler's "skillful and gallant lead the reputation of our cavalry has been justly enhanced."[3]

In the same language, Bragg lauded Colonel Wharton (while pointedly making no mention of Pegram's service). Presumably, Wheeler was not disappointed by having to share his commander's praise: as Wharton's superior, Wheeler rightly deserved most of the credit for ensuring a successful retreat—Bragg knew it, and he proved it. Soon after Wheeler's arrival at Tullahoma, Bragg recommended him for promotion to major general. The appointment would come through January 20. The promotion itself was not unexpected, given Wheeler's position as a division commander. Even so, the Georgian cherished the confidence Bragg had invested in him. More than ever, he determined to prove himself worthy of it.

With that goal uppermost in his mind, Wheeler started on his current mission, leaving the army on the morning of January 8, with a six-hundred-man portion of his command, including three artillery pieces, bound for the Cumberland River near Clarksville. Buffeted by plunging temperatures and intermittent snow showers, the column moved up the Nashville Pike, seeking targets of opportunity. Wheeler halted at several points to allow Wade's 8th Confederate regiment to tear up previously untouched stretches of the Nashville & Chattanooga. Other units ran down and demolished a few of those supply columns that continued to ply the vulnerable highway between Murfreesboro and Nashville.[4]

Leaving behind mangled track and burning wagons, Wheeler struck northwest. On the twelfth, he reached the south bank of the Cumberland at Clarksville, where he divided his force in order to obstruct shipping at various points on the river. While Wade's regiment and a 6-pounder cannon headed upstream, Wheeler and the rest patrolled the bank between Clarksville and Ashland. At the latter site, on the opposite bank a few miles downstream, provisions from Louisville were stored prior to their overland shipment to Nashville. His normal communications network having been compromised by the raids of Forrest, Morgan, and Wheeler, Rosecrans had secured additional channels of supply via the Cumberland and Tennessee Rivers; Ashland Landing was a major hub on these secondary conduits.

Wheeler's patience was rewarded early that evening when a supply steamer and a troop transport came within range of his guns. Without having to fire a shot, the cavalry persuaded both vessels to heave to and surrender. The raiders boarded the steamer, carted off war goods, paroled the soldiers who had been riding the transport, and burned both ships to the waterline.

More spoils were on the way. The next day, Colonel Wade, who had deployed his riflemen and cannon on a wooded bluff overlooking Harpeth Shoals, shelled three passing steamers, persuading them to halt and make for shore. Wade captured not only inanimate cargo in large quantity and of high value but also scores of convalescent soldiers wounded at Murfreesboro. The colonel even defeated a wooden gunboat that suddenly appeared in the steamers' wake, disabling her with shells from his 6-pounder and making prisoners of her twenty-two crewmen.

Late in the afternoon, Wheeler called Wade to his side, where the lowermost column had been challenged by a couple of heavy gunboats whose armor plating defied all efforts to halt and seize them. Wheeler's attack had also been defeated by the increasingly brutal weather. Some of his less-well-clothed troopers were on the verge of freezing to death. Captain George K. Miller of the 8th Confederate recalled that when Wade returned from Harpeth Shoals "at least one of his bare-footed troopers was frozen to his stirrups and had to be thawed with warmed blankets . . . before he could dismount."[5]

Next morning, the reunited force cantered south toward Ashland. Upon arriving opposite the supply base, a band of hardy volunteers swam their mounts across the frigid, high-rising river. Straggling ashore, they overawed a small guard detail, captured the depot, and burned or demolished every crate, barrel, and keg they could get their benumbed fingers on. The assault alarmed the crews of supply steamers tied up at the landing, which quickly got up steam by tossing overboard a large quantity of supplies. By lightening their draught, they managed to escape, but they did Wheeler's work for him. By day's end, Wheeler considered his mission well accomplished and turned homeward toward the beckoning comfort of campfires and winterized cabins.[6]

ANOTHER RECENTLY ESTABLISHED SUPPLY BASE ON the Cumberland was in the Dover-Fort Donelson area. Soon after returning from Ashland, Wheeler—his uniform now sporting an extra loop of sleeve lace, the insignia of a major general—had his attention directed to that stretch of the Yankee-controlled river. Hoping to duplicate the success Wheeler and Wade had achieved at Harpeth Shoals and Ashland, Bragg ordered him to leave his warm, snug encampment and go again in search of supply ships to waylay.

This time Fightin' Joe would command a force large enough to tackle anyone who aimed to deter him. Now largely restored to its pre-West Tennessee Raid condition, Forrest's brigade—an eight-hundred-man detachment of it, at least—would also take part. It would leave its present station near Columbia and join Wheeler's main body—Wharton's brigade and a few pieces of light artillery, perhaps two thousand officers and men— on the march. Bragg figured that a force this large could disrupt river commerce to a degree that would force Rosecrans to rely more than ever on those railroads and turnpikes that Wheeler frequently targeted.[7]

His hopes were destined to be dashed. The only characteristic that the new raid shared with the previous one was the continuing wave of terrible weather. After trudging eighty-five miles in temperatures barely above freezing, Wheeler reached the Cumberland south of Dover, where he linked with Forrest and discovered no river traffic of consequence. He learned to his chagrin that following the raid on Ashland, Rosecrans had halted the shipment of supplies on the upper reaches of the Cumberland.

The absence of targets frustrated Wheeler but did not curtail the mission. The desire to accomplish something of consequence drove him to a fateful decision: "The scarcity of forage made it impossible for me to remain long on the other side of the river, and all the ferryboats above Dover had been destroyed. I accordingly had but the alternative to remain idle or attack the force at Dover." Over the strenuous objections of his ranking subordinate, he chose the latter option. Forrest's argument was based on his strong belief that the local garrison—infantry, cavalry, and artillery under Colonel Abner C. Harding, 83rd Illinois Volunteers—was capable of defending itself against a force the size of Wheeler's.[8]

On the dreadfully cold afternoon of February 3, Wheeler deployed Forrest's troopers east and southeast of the fortified town, Wharton's on the southwest side. He had his six field pieces unlimber atop a ridge overlooking a line of well-constructed earthworks and redoubts. Aware that charging horsemen rarely prevailed against fortifications, Wheeler directed both of his subordinates to attack on foot. Forrest, perhaps angry at having his objections overridden, paid no attention. Without waiting for Wharton to strike, he led most of his troopers in a mounted charge on what he believed was a weakened sector of Harding's works. The result was a disaster: cannon and rifle fire pouring from the fort sent men and horses hurtling to the frozen earth. Forrest himself was unhorsed; he regained his feet, but many of his men did not. His subordinates rallied the survivors for additional attacks, but each was repulsed with heavy loss.

When Wharton, thrown off-balance by Forrest's attack, finally advanced, he was unable to divert pressure from his colleague. In addition to Harding's troops, Wharton was opposed by a "perilous shelling" from gunboats in the Cumberland. One of Wharton's men remarked that due to the Union navy's intervention, "we could not have held the place an hour had we taken it." Making no headway, Wharton withdrew in relatively good order, though he, too, had suffered more or less heavily. Studying the effects of his rashness, an ashen-faced Wheeler made no attempt to renew the assault. While his artillery continued the fight at long range, he withdrew his surviving forces four miles from Dover and put them in bivouac.[9]

Appropriating a farmhouse for his headquarters, Wheeler stayed up late that night conferring with his subordinates and drafting a report of the day's operations. All went well until Wheeler remarked that by his calculation, no more than one hundred men had been killed, wounded, or gone missing that day. Wharton was surprised by the low figure, but Forrest was incredulous: he had lost more than that many on his part of the field alone. When Wheeler attempted to brush off his objection, the

Tennessean bolted from his chair, hovered over his diminutive superior, and started shouting.

Forrest's grip on his legendary temper had been loosening since the first day of the expedition, which he had been forced to join before his command, in his judgment, had fully recovered from its hard service in West Tennessee. He continued to resent being subordinated to a younger officer who appeared to lack the prerequisites of a commander of cavalry. In truth, Forrest did not feel comfortable answering to any superior; it was this streak of hard-edged independence that made Bragg doubt he was fit to serve with the main army. Although Forrest was at least partly to blame for the day's repulse, he was furious at having lost so many men on what now appeared a suicide mission.

Thus aroused, he let his superior have it with both barrels: "General Wheeler, you know I was against this attack. I said all I could and should against it—and now—say what you like, do what you like, nothing'll bring back my brave fellows lying dead or wounded and freezing around that fort tonight. You know I mean no disrespect . . . but you've got to put one thing in that report to Bragg; tell him I'll be in my coffin before I'll fight again under your command!"[10]

Wheeler bore the tirade without saying a word or moving a muscle. When he regained his voice, he apologized for any wrong—real or perceived—that he had done to Forrest and assured him that he accepted full responsibility for the outcome of the fight. But he had no rejoinder to his subordinate's demand for a transfer. Braxton Bragg did. After both officers had departed the Cumberland and returned to their respective camps, the army leader decreed that in the future they should serve as far apart as possible—on opposite ends of the army—whenever it could be arranged.

This was the first time Forrest had demanded a permanent separation from a distrusted superior and had gotten his way. It would not be the last.[11]

By mid-February, the weather had nearly immobilized the Army of Tennessee. The command continued to face its enemy across a line thirty miles long, the distance from Shelbyville to Tullahoma and Wartrace. The cavalry patrolled an even longer perimeter, seventy miles in length. Its discontinuous picket line stretched from Forrest's headquarters at Columbia northeast to McMinnville in the Sequatchie Valley, the site of Wheeler's winter encampment. Wharton's division was headquartered at Unionville, where it covered the front of Polk's corps, and Morgan's troopers were stationed between McMinnville and Manchester, guarding the approaches to Hardee's camps. While the infantry answered roll call, drilled when possible, and kept warm, the army's horsemen performed daily duty, scouting, and once in a while skirmishing, usually without inflicting or absorbing many casualties.

When the elements permitted, a few operations on a larger scale got under way. Early in February, Morgan, whose command was short on able-bodied mounts following the Christmas raid, sent Cluke's 8th Kentucky to the remount (or "dead horse") camp in central Kentucky for rehabilitation. Although he tried to take it easy on his horses, Cluke refused to let his men rest. When opportunity arose, he engaged, for the most part successfully, bodies of Federals in Lexington and nearby Mount Sterling, and even captured a two-hundred-wagon supply train whose contents went far toward improving the condition of his command.[12]

Back in Tennessee, other elements of Morgan's division grew restive for lack of truly active duty. Protesting their enforced idleness in winter quarters, several units, including Morgan's "own" 2nd Kentucky, refused to carry their weapons when called out on inspection. Morgan's no-nonsense inspector general, St. Leger Grenfell, had quit the command to take a position elsewhere, and Basil Duke, the strict taskmaster, was recovering from his Rolling Fork wound. Left in Morgan's hands, and increasingly hobbled by shortages of horseflesh, weaponry, and ammunition, his division appeared to be deteriorating.

Unsurprisingly, its performance began to falter. Late in February, an attempt by Morgan, personally commanding a detachment of Quirk's scouts, to capture a Union picket went awry and had to be aborted—a rare setback for the Confederacy's premier raider. Soon afterward, accompanied by one thousand troopers and two guns, he failed to surprise a Union camp near Milton, Tennessee. The vigilant enemy replied with cannons and small arms, inflicting 15 percent losses, including thirteen officers killed or wounded. The brigadier's most credible biographer asserts that "the fight was the first manifestation of Morgan's increased commitment to the hit-and-run principle following his marriage. He had abandoned guerrilla tactics and assaulted a superior force occupying a strong defensive position. . . . News of Morgan's defeat at Milton circulated in both armies; and it was common knowledge that his command had declined in combat readiness."[13]

While Morgan's command went downhill, Wheeler and Forrest kept their men active, alert, and in spirits as high as prevailing conditions allowed. Forrest, ever eager to engage the enemy and convert their resources to his own use, in mid-February asked permission to range up the railroad and attack the Nashville suburbs, where a corral full of horses and mules had drawn his attention. According to Lieutenant John Morton, future commander of Forrest's horse artillery, "the permission was refused him, and he determined to spend the time by adding to the efficiency of his men by daily drills." Forrest was a recent convert to formal instruction, but Wheeler had long drilled his men, even in severe weather. Wheeler rotated his units between outpost duty and winter camp, ensuring that large bodies were available to train as a unit. And he saw to it that their officers were thoroughly conversant with the single-rank evolutions featured in his *Revised System of Cavalry Tactics*, which was published that winter.[14]

When not instructing, inspecting his outposts, and adjusting his picket lines, Wheeler was welcoming new subordinates, including thirty-nine-year-old William Thompson Martin, a recent arrival from Virginia, where he had led a celebrated unit, the Jeff Davis Legion, under J. E. B. Stuart. A lawyer by profession, Martin had demonstrated enough soldierly ability not only to rise from captain to brigadier general, but to wangle an unusual long-distance transfer in order to serve in and near his native Kentucky. Suitably impressed, the cavalry commander named Martin to head what had long been known as "Wheeler's Brigade."[15]

Wheeler lost as well as gained lieutenants. In March, John Pegram's brigade was transferred to the Department of East Tennessee, presently commanded by a temporary replacement for Kirby Smith pending the succession of Simon Buckner, who had been paroled and exchanged following his capture at Fort Donelson. Wheeler, who had looked askance at Pegram's performance at Murfreesboro, was not heartbroken by his departure, though he regretted the loss of the regiments that accompanied the brigadier to Knoxville, especially the veteran 1st Tennessee and 1st Louisiana.

In his new theater of operations, Pegram quickly demonstrated his deficiencies as a raider. On March 13, he led 1,550 men and three guns into central Kentucky, ostensibly to confiscate beef cattle for his poorly fed army. Ambushed by Union infantry outside Danville, Pegram began a precipitate retreat. He was overtaken and pummeled near Somerset. His troops made in hot haste for the south bank of the Cumberland River, and many of the spoils they had gathered were abandoned. A member of the 11th Kentucky claimed that nearly all of Pegram's command would have been lost had Colonel Chenault—whose regiment had been stationed in Wayne County, Kentucky, since late January—not secured the fords that permitted the fugitives to reach safety. Thereafter, Pegram assumed command of Chenault's and Cluke's regiments until they returned to Morgan's command in early May. Pegram did not accompany them but remained in East Tennessee as Buckner's chief of cavalry.[16]

WILLIAM T. MARTIN WAS NOT THE ONLY HIGH-RANKING newcomer to Bragg's cavalry. In January, at the request of Joe Johnston, Earl Van Dorn, whose stock had soared as a result of his demolition of Holly Springs, was placed in charge of two-thirds of the cavalry in the Department of Mississippi and East Louisiana. Johnston saw to it that this force was immediately made available to the Army of Tennessee. As the departmental commander explained, Van Dorn would reinforce Bragg's left flank, thus "preventing Federal troops from going from West to Middle Tennessee." Johnston was especially intent on barring Grant, who was industriously repairing the damage Forrest had done to the Mobile & Ohio, from making another overland drive on Vicksburg. Johnston also expected Van Dorn to aid Bragg in the event Rosecrans offered battle. If Old Rosey remained quiescent, Van Dorn could, by threatening his communications, keep him pinned to Murfreesboro. Johnston even entertained the idea of a raid into Kentucky, where Van Dorn could strike targets Morgan had missed. So long as the flamboyant Mississippian remained in Bragg's area of operations, he would serve at the latter's convenience. Should he pass beyond those limits, such as by raiding Kentucky, he would report directly to Johnston.[17]

Gratified to be free of a Northern-born superior whom he considered incompetent, Van Dorn collected the mounted forces in Pemberton's department, some of whom were serving as far from Vicksburg as Mobile and Montgomery, and denuded as many outposts as he believed could be abandoned. When Pemberton complained that he could ill afford to lose so many troopers, Van Dorn agreed to leave him two regiments, one battalion, and eleven companies. The rest, perhaps four thousand officers and men, he grouped under Red Jackson, Frank Armstrong (the latter now a brigadier general), and Colonels George B. Cosby and J. W. Whitfield. By early February, these commands had assembled at Tupelo. Under Van Dorn, they started for Middle Tennessee on the eighth and reached Columbia on the sixteenth. Superseding Forrest, Van Dorn established his headquarters a few miles up the Nashville & Decatur Railroad at Spring Hill.[18]

Theoretically, Van Dorn's addition enlarged the authority of Bragg's mounted commander. But Van Dorn's coming changed the pecking order, for the hero of Holly Springs was senior to Wheeler by date of appointment; besides, his command was the size of a corps, while Wheeler continued to lead a division. On February 24, however, Bragg reorganized his mounted arm. He designated both their commands as divisions, only to change his mind three weeks later and pronounce them corps, each composed of two divisions. The reasoning behind the change was Bragg's realization that both units had grown so large they exceeded the standard size of divisions. Indeed, by early March, Bragg's mounted arm accounted for almost a third of his total manpower.[19]

Van Dorn's divisions were led by Jackson (whose command included Forrest's recently reorganized brigade) and Martin, who had left Wheeler to accept promotion. Wheeler's corps now embraced the divisions of Wharton and Morgan. The latter had risen to divisional command in spite of the disciplinary and morale problems within his ranks, and the perception in some quarters that Bragg held Morgan's extended absence from the army at least partly responsible for the defeat at Murfreesboro.[20]

Van Dorn was determined to make a splash in his new capacity as Bragg's senior cavalryman. His natural aggressiveness prompted him to propose an attack on the Yankees at Franklin. Like Forrest's request, however, Bragg denied it. Undeterred, Van Dorn managed to get into action at an early date. On March 4, during a reconnaissance toward Franklin, he encountered "a large body of the enemy." He saw the situation as an opportunity. Falling back, he lured the Federals into attacking him near Thompson's Station on the railroad north of Spring Hill. The enemy did him little harm, and the next day Van Dorn struck back with Jackson's command and Cosby's brigade of Martin's division. Charging the enemy "in fine style," Van Dorn drove them back a considerable distance, killing or wounding upwards of five hundred and capturing (by his calculations) more than one thousand two hundred. Forrest's brigade had made a conspicuous contribution to the outcome, assailing the Union left and rear at a critical point, overcoming a last spate of resistance, and helping precipitate the rout. Lieutenant Morton of Forrest's artillery believed one reason for the command's strong performance was its eagerness "to wipe out the disappointment of Dover."[21]

Three weeks later, Forrest again fought as if he had something to prove. By now Van Dorn had given him command of a division consisting of his old brigade, under Colonel Starnes, and the troopers of Frank Armstrong. With this force, he crossed the Harpeth River above Franklin, tore up the railroad near Brentwood Station, and attacked two outposts, one a large stockade guarding a bridge. By surrounding both positions and forcing their surrender, Forrest bagged a total of 820 prisoners.[22]

Riding the wave of victory, on April 10, Van Dorn and Forrest trotted up the Lewisburg Pike to confirm reports that the Federals at Franklin, tired of being attacked and captured, had evacuated the area. Armstrong's brigade, leading the advance, drove in some pickets, but then an enemy force that had been shadowing Forrest's column slammed into its flank, capturing not only thirty of Starnes's men but also Freeman's battery. Forrest counterattacked, drove off the assailants, freed most of their captives, and regained the lost artillery. He failed, however, to liberate Freeman, who had been shot down in cold blood by his captors. Having learned what he needed to know—that Franklin was still occupied in force—Van Dorn withdrew Forrest's division, which had suffered few casualties besides its lamented artillery chief.[23]

Although Van Dorn and Forrest appeared to team effectively, their egos and temperaments made for a tension-filled relationship. Late in March or early in April, the two had a verbal confrontation that nearly escalated into violence. Conflicting accounts make causation hard to determine, but all depict Van Dorn as the instigator. He accused Forrest either of appropriating captured goods that should have been turned over to the army's quartermasters, or of planting newspaper accounts of the recent fighting that magnified Forrest's role and minimized Van Dorn's. The latter practice, which probably precipitated the argument, was not uncommon in the cavalry, Army of Tennessee. Major Elisha Burford, Joe Wheeler's adjutant general, was notable for inserting his boss's name into the newspapers at the expense of colleagues and superiors, and even saw to it that Wheeler gained a new nickname: "War Child."[24]

As Van Dorn saw it, if anyone merited publicity, it was he, not one who followed his orders. Given Forrest's fiery nature and delicate pride, it was only natural that he should resent Van Dorn's accusations. After angrily denying them, however, he abruptly calmed down and apologized for his conduct, and the crisis blew over.[25]

The two strong men would not clash for long. Within weeks of their argument, Van Dorn was dead—not of battle wounds but of a pistol shot to the head delivered by an outraged husband, Dr. George Peters of Spring Hill, whose young wife had been the object of the general's attentions while Peters was away from home on business. Van Dorn's reputation as a ladies' man was widespread and well-earned. Shortly before his death, one of his troopers had written his wife that the general "still maintains his reputation for *gallantry!* And you can see at times some fine looking *ladies* driving about in his splendid four horse Ambulance. I do not relish such an officer and am only reconciled by the ability he displayed in capturing those Yankees at Thompson's Station." Happily for those who admired Van Dorn, he would be remembered for his exploits in the field, not in the boudoir.[26]

LIKE FORREST, WHEELER WAS EAGER TO PERFORM a feat that would overshadow the bungled assault on Dover. By the first week in April, he had hit upon a scheme to attack simultaneously the two railroads upon which Rosecrans depended most for shipment of supplies from his base at Louisville to the front. The L&N had been broken numerous times, most frequently by Morgan, and sections of it had yet to recover fully. The Nashville & Chattanooga had been struck less often, but its importance had been growing ever since Rosecrans occupied Murfreesboro.

For the mission, which Bragg readily approved, Wheeler told off substantial portions of both of his divisions: almost two thousand from Wharton's command; six hundred from Morgan's under Basil Duke, recently recovered from his December wounding; and Lieutenant Arthur Pice's battery of horse artillery. Wharton's contingent would serve as the primary strike force. Sharing Bragg's belief that Morgan's men were ineffective as regular cavalry, Wheeler intended to relegate Duke's detachment to a reserve role in the rear of the main body.

The column got moving on the ninth, trotting through Lebanon. The following day it reached the Hermitage, Tennessee's most famous political shrine. Wheeler left Duke to occupy the area around Andrew Jackson's plantation and secure a retreat route should one be needed. Wheeler and Wharton then pushed northwest, angling toward the L&N, while a detached force consisting principally of the 8th Texas under Lieutenant Colonel Steven C. Ferrill moved directly south. Ferrill was under orders "to cross Stone's River, attack the [Nashville & Chattanooga] railroad trains, and do any other good in his power, and return to Lebanon."[27]

Wheeler's modus operandi was the same as when waylaying Cumberland River shipping. Now he reached the south bank of that same river, this time at a point nine miles northeast of Nashville. He placed Wharton's troopers in a position from which they could fire on any train coming down the L&N just across the water. Two of Wharton's regiments moved so stealthily through woods and fields that Federals occupying blockhouses on both of their flanks failed to detect their presence. Even more remarkably, Lieutenant Pice was able to drag his guns to water's edge without attracting attention.

After a two-hour wait, a locomotive pulling boxcars loaded with cavalry horses and beef cattle came chugging toward Nashville. At Wheeler's order, Pice's battery lobbed a few shells its way. One hit the locomotive squarely, causing its boiler to explode and the engine to wheeze to a halt. Wharton's troopers, opening fire from their waterside cover, quickly chased away most of the train's guard. Pice's guns kept pounding away, demolishing the locomotive and several cars, and making casualties of men, horses, and cows. Wharton's men then turned their attention to the blockhouses. Riddling them with balls, they kept the occupants locked inside.

After a few hours of such diversion, Wheeler, having failed to locate a ford that would enable him to cross and seize what remained of the train, called a halt. Gathering up men and guns, he started back to McMinnville, carrying off a wounded trooper, his only casualty. At the Hermitage he picked up Duke, who, although disappointed at having played no role in the day's action, manfully congratulated those who had.[28]

On the homeward leg, Wheeler failed to link with Ferrill's detachment, which had returned to the army by another route, but he learned that it, too, had achieved success. Like Wheeler, Ferrill had ambushed and seized a train—one larger than the one Wharton and Pice had attacked, and without the benefit of artillery. The train, carrying civilian passengers as well as soldiers including a large armed guard, had been halted by the long stretch of N&C track that Ferrill's men had demolished. Dismounted Texans sprang from hiding and charged the train. The guards made a brief stand, taking cover behind the cars and returning fire, but then they lost their aplomb. Almost as one they turned and fled across a field into a woods, pursued by screaming Rebels. More than thirty fell dead or wounded; others were overtaken and captured. Ferrill reported taking seventy guards and passengers prisoner, including three officers of Rosecrans's staff. He also seized an Adams Express safe that yielded several thousand dollars in Yankee greenbacks.[29]

The captives and the spoils suggested that the raid had been a triumph; at any rate, Wheeler convinced Bragg that it was. His commander's approval was enough to make Fightin' Joe believe he was a raiding leader on a par with Forrest and Morgan, a delusion that would persist for months before falling victim to hard reality.

FOR THE FIRST TWO YEARS OF THE WAR, raiding had been the exclusive province of the Rebel trooper. With some justification, he saw himself as the wily fox who never failed to elude the hunter and leave the hounds baying piteously in his wake. It never occurred to him that the roles might reverse, that some day he would be compelled to pursue quick-thinking, fast-moving Yankees bent on spreading destruction and deception across the Heartland.

That day was coming. By the spring of 1863, the Union cavalry had learned to play the raiding game surprisingly well. To be sure, Federal raiders had advantages denied to their Southern counterparts, including seemingly inexhaustible sources of horseflesh and provender, commodities that were becoming ever scarce to the Confederacy as the war laid an increasingly heavy hand on the stables and pastures of Tennessee and Kentucky. Then, too, the Union had developed cavalry leaders who, by studying the methods of their opponents, were becoming quite skilled in the activity. Being Yankees, they had begun to define and categorize an undertaking that Southerners understood instinctively and refused to analyze. As one Illinois trooper put it, raiding was "essentially a *game* of strategy and speed, with personal violence as an incidental complication. It is played according to more or less definite rules, not inconsistent, indeed, with the players killing each other if the game cannot be won in any other way, but it is commonly a strenuous game, rather than a bloody one."[30]

The first Union raid of any consequence in the West was conducted by Brigadier General Samuel P. Carter (a Naval Academy graduate, of all things), who, in December 1862, led several hundred Michigan, Ohio, and

Pennsylvania cavalry in breaking sections of the East Tennessee & Virginia Railroad, the only rail line that connected Rebel forces in both major theaters. Eluding packs of pursuers along a 470-mile route that included 150 miles inside enemy territory, Carter's force wrecked ten miles of track, burned two bridges, destroyed depot facilities, took four hundred prisoners, and confiscated six hundred stands of arms. [31]

Such accomplishments may have paled in comparison to those of Forrest and Morgan, but they suggested that the Yankees had become raiders to be reckoned with. In subsequent months, Union commanders undertook smaller, less dramatic expeditions, few of which achieved more than short-term tactical success. Then, in mid-April 1863, the Yankees displayed their ability to raid on a scale approaching anything their enemy had accomplished, in the process making a critical contribution to a major offensive.

His attempt to advance overland against Vicksburg having been thwarted by Van Dorn and Forrest, Ulysses Grant determined to make a new effort come spring, one whose chances of success did not depend on long, fragile lines of supply. On April 28, he placed large portions of his Army of the Tennessee aboard transports at Hard Times Landing, on the west bank of the Mississippi below Vicksburg. The transports had been convoyed past Pemberton's batteries by a gunboat fleet commanded by Flag Officer David Dixon Porter. On the thirtieth, the soldiers were ferried across to Bruinsburg against light opposition. Once on the east bank, they moved inland toward the Confederate stronghold. [32]

By failing to prevent the landing at Bruinsburg, Pemberton permitted Grant to place a mighty host on Vicksburg's doorstep. Had the Confederate commander concentrated his forces at or near the landing site, he might have forced Grant to reembark, retreat, and plan again. A major reason for Pemberton's inability to do so was a raid by one thousand seven hundred Union cavalry under Colonel Benjamin H. Grierson from La Grange, Tennessee, to Baton Rouge, Louisiana, which distracted attention from Grant's operations at a critical time. With three regiments of Illinois and Iowa cavalry, Grierson spent sixteen days (April 17–May 2) ranging through Pemberton's bailiwick, wrecking sixty miles of track on those railroads that supplied Vicksburg and demolishing supply depots.

Pemberton's cavalry had been decimated by Van Dorn's transfer to Middle Tennessee. The few mobile forces left in the department, mainly Clark Barteau's 2nd Tennessee Battalion, failed to overtake the fast-moving raiders, whose marching and countermarching, demonstrating, and feinting confused and misdirected all pursuers, including those belatedly dispatched from the garrison of Port Hudson, Louisiana. Grierson's most important contribution to Grant's strategy was to draw Wirt Adams from Port Gibson, just east of Bruinsburg, only hours before Grant began crossing the river. The grateful army leader would pronounce the raid "one of the most brilliant cavalry exploits of the war."[33]

Not every attempt to penetrate the Confederate interior was as well-conceived and well-executed as this. One effort, launched less than a week before Grierson started out, ended disastrously, but only because of the inexhaustible energy and determination of Forrest, who traded his well-worn role as the fox for a stint as a hound, baying at the heels of a worthy opponent.

Curiously enough, the fox was an infantry commander, Colonel Abel D. Streight of Indiana, a soldier of strong will and great mental capacity but unfamiliar with the techniques of raiding. Aware that his superior, Rosecrans, wished to move Bragg's army out of Middle Tennessee with as little fuss as possible, Streight had proposed a raid on the Western & Atlantic, the Army of Tennessee's principal rail link to the Deep South. The previous April, an attempt had been made on that line by a team of military and civilian spies that captured a locomotive and tore up some track, but they had been chased down and captured before inflicting critical damage. Streight was determined to succeed where the spies had failed. His plan was to sail down the Tennessee River, cross lightly defended northern Alabama, and break the W&A at Rome, Georgia, roughly midway between Chattanooga and Atlanta. If enough track could be taken up, Bragg would have no alternative to abandoning his present position and withdrawing to the mountains of East Tennessee, where rations and forage would be hard to obtain. Better still, Bragg might retreat into Georgia, which would give Rosecrans possession of strategic Chattanooga.[34]

Trusting Streight's good sense and firmness of purpose, Rosecrans gave him the go-ahead. To divert attention from the raid and improve its chances of success, Rosecrans ordered the Mississippi-based troops of Brigadier General Grenville M. Dodge to serve as a screening force. By moving his infantry division into western Alabama, Dodge would make the Rebels believe that he, not Streight, was threatening Bragg's communications. So far so good, but when mounting Streight's force, Rosecrans turned to advice from a nameless logistician who had a cockeyed view of mobility, or a perverse sense of humor, or both. Ostensibly because of a scarcity of horseflesh in Rosecrans's army, Streight was compelled to make his raid on muleback.[35]

Streight's provisional brigade—four infantry regiments and two companies of "Tennessee cavalry" (actually composed mostly of Alabama tories), a total of about one thousand seven hundred effectives—rendezvoused with its long-eared mounts at Palmyra, Tennessee, on the left bank of the Cumberland River around the bend from Clarksville, late on April 11. Troubles arose almost immediately. Most of the mules were young and unbroken,

Colonel Abel D. Streight, USA.

and, as one of Streight's officers wrote, they spent "most of the time performing evolutions in the air something after the style of the wild Highland Fling." Each time a would-be rider tried to saddle one of the factious beasts, the latter "would tax his ingenuity and muscular power to the utmost, to divest himself of his unwelcome rider. And as our boys were 'foot soldiers,' they were at first very easily dismounted, frequently in a most undignified and unceremonious manner."[36]

It took two days to acquaint riders and mules, and to form some semblance of a marching column. As per his orders, Streight marched his men overland to Fort Henry on the Tennessee River, where, after long and vexing delays, army transports ferried the curious command to Eastport, Mississippi, jumping-off point of the expedition. While men and mules straggled ashore at Eastport, Streight traveled to nearby Bear Creek, where he met and conferred with General Dodge to work out operational arrangements.[37]

Dodge informed Streight that his men, when moving from Corinth to Bear Creek, had been harassed continually by a brigade of Alabama cavalry, artillery, and partisan rangers commanded by Colonel Philip Dale Roddey. This force of northern Alabamians, composed largely of lukewarm secessionists who had enlisted primarily to defend their home region, had given Dodge fits, slowing his march by ambush and hit-and-run tactics. Dodge, however, failed to convey the extent of Roddey's obstructionism. On the evening Dodge and Streight met, some of Roddey's scouts crept inside the lines at Eastport. Locating the mule corrals, they began shouting and firing their pistols. The result was a mass stampede. Upwards of four hundred of the animals broke free of their confinement and escaped into the night.[38]

It took Streight another day and a half to round up the scattered herd, about half of which was recovered. Not until the twenty-first, several days behind schedule, did the "Mule Brigade" move out in the rear of Dodge's foot soldiers. At Tuscumbia, Alabama, Streight received by telegraph final authorization to launch his raid. Leaving Dodge behind to deflect enemy pressure, late on the twenty-sixth the muleteers hit the southward-leading road to Russellville, turned to seas of mud by a driving rainstorm. Reaching Russellville the next day, Streight turned east and began to plod through the hill country of Alabama. He headed for Moulton, seat of Lawrence County, via Mount Hope, thirty-some miles southeast of Tuscumbia.[39]

Only now, eight days after Roddey's men had fired into Streight's corrals, did Confederate authorities put a pursuit force in motion. The assignment fell to Forrest, who was told that his target was Dodge; no one at Bragg's headquarters was aware of Streight's presence in north Alabama or suspected that a raid was in progress. Thus, when ordered to join his force with Roddey's on the Tennessee River and assume overall command, Forrest supposed he was being sent to hold in check a slow-moving force of infantry, not to chase down a mobile expedition heading for the far rear of his army.

He lost no time getting started. He dispatched Colonel James H. Edmondson's 11th Tennessee in advance of his main body, then followed with Starnes's 4th (today commanded by now-Lieutenant Colonel McLemore), Dibrell's 8th, Biffle's 9th, and Lieutenant Colonel W. E. DeMoss's 10th Tennessee, accompanied by an eight-gun battery under John Morton. Forrest's aggressiveness enabled him to reach the north bank of the Tennessee on the afternoon of April 27. Here he divided his force, leaving the 10th and 11th Tennessee on the north side along with a section of Morton's guns. He ferried the other regiments and the rest of the artillery across the stream, then rode hard and long to join Roddey's force. By the twenty-eighth, he had made contact not only with Roddey but also with Dodge, who had halted and dug in along Town Creek, east of Tuscumbia. For several hours the combined force held Dodge's much larger command at bay. Yet by occupying his enemy, Dodge was executing his diversionary mission.[40]

The desultory combat ended with Dodge's sudden withdrawal to Tuscumbia. His departure left Forrest perplexed, but not for long. Before sundown, one of Roddey's scouts, who had ridden around Dodge's command and picked up Streight's trail, brought Forrest word of the Mule Brigade's progress toward Moulton. Realizing that Streight was twenty miles east of him, Forrest, although unaware of the colonel's intentions, prepared his men for pursuit. He would leave part of his force with Roddey to keep an eye on Dodge. The rest—the 4th and 8th Tennessee, plus some of Morton's guns—he told off for the pursuit of Streight. McLemore's and Dibrell's men were weary from days of almost continuous riding, but Forrest was determined to overtake this enemy force of unknown size running loose through virtually unprotected Confederate territory.

By one a.m. on the twenty-ninth, having worked half the night to resupply his men and guns with ammunition and his horses with forage, Forrest started south from Courtland in the continuing rain. Riding furiously, he reached Moulton in late afternoon, a few hours after Streight's men had left that village, where they had spent the previous night. From the reports of local residents Forrest gained an understanding of the force he was trailing, which appeared to be heading toward Blountsville by way of Day's Gap in Sand Mountain and a crossing of the Black Warrior River. Given the curious composition of the enemy force and its slow rate of travel, Forrest fully expected to overtake it short of its destination, which he now suspected to be the railroads of northwestern Georgia. Even so, he spared neither horses nor riders as he led the way southeast from Moulton. The pursuers' lone compensation was a sudden change in the weather from steady rain to clear and sunny skies.[41]

Forrest's speed paid dividends. Just past midnight, he drew within striking distance of his quarry, encamped at the mouth of Day's Gap. Confident that Streight could not escape, he allowed most of his men a much overdue rest, although he sent his brother Bill's scouting detachment to move closer to the target. Captain Forrest's men managed to slip around Streight's camp, capturing its guards without waking their comrades. By daybreak, as the Union column resumed its ascent of Sand Mountain, Bill Forrest, with or without his brother's permission, attacked the Union rear. Cutting off stragglers and pack mules, the scouts pushed up the winding mountain trail, hoping to capture Streight's rear guard, only to fall into a carefully prepared trap. Ambushers opened fire from foliage on both sides of the road, killing a couple of scouts and wounding several others, including their leader.[42]

When Forrest rushed to the scene with his main body, he, too, was staggered by the fire of concealed Federals and compelled to pull back. He withdrew so abruptly that two of Morton's guns that had assumed an exposed position were captured by muleteers who sprang from cover and hauled them off as prizes of war. Their capture enraged the pursuit leader, who formed his men for a counterattack, but Streight's retreat ensured that the guns could not be recovered.[43]

Although Streight knew he had little hope of outdistancing his opponent, he pushed on up the mountain in early evening darkness. Six miles from the scene of his ambush of Forrest's scouts, he had to halt and give battle along a ridge known locally as Hog Mountain. The fighting, much of which took place after dark, was a confused but deadly affair; casualties ran high on both sides. Forrest, at the forefront of the action as usual, had three horses shot from under him. Each time, once assured that no bones had been broken, he remounted and returned to the fight. Eventually he drove off Streight and forced him to abandon the guns he had captured hours earlier. Around midnight, the colonel engineered another ambush, but accounts of its effectiveness conflict. All that is certain is that after some sharp fighting, Streight retreated yet again. Forrest let him go. He permitted his men to sleep through the rest of the night so they would be ready to handle the fighting certain to be renewed the following day.[44]

Around ten a.m. on May 1, Streight reached Blountsville, forty-three miles from Day's Gap. By now many of his men were afoot, their mules having given out to be left dead or dying by the roadside. Unwilling to give up, the plucky Hoosier stumbled on in the direction of Gadsden. His rear guard tried to delay their pursuers in any way possible, blocking the road with felled trees and fallen rocks. While this stratagem stymied some of Forrest's men, others kept moving.

Even without his full force well in hand, Forrest was confident he had Streight in a corner he could not escape. Not only were most of Dibrell's and McLemore's troopers hot on the colonel's heels, but the 11th Tennessee was moving along the north bank of the Tennessee, which paralleled Streight's route, straining to get ahead of him. Forrest hoped Edmondson would be able to prevent Streight from crossing the river should he turn north from Blountsville. In addition to preventing the Federals from damaging railroads and factories, Forrest wanted to chastise them for the depredations they had committed on the citizens of northern Alabama. Upon reaching Blountsville, his advance guard captured some supply wagons Streight had been forced to leave behind. One of Biffle's troopers recalled that "the wagons were loaded with provisions for the men—mostly—but we found large quantities of ladies' clothing and silverware and household goods of various kinds that they had robbed the unprotected citizens of in the valley below."[45]

By May 2, the nearly exhausted raiders were crossing Will's Creek in the valley below Lookout Mountain. Four miles farther on, they straggled across Black Creek on a bridge that the rear guard set afire before Forrest could reach it. But if Streight believed he had bought himself time on the road to Gadsden, he was mistaken. Thanks to a fifteen-year-old girl whose family lived near the creek, Forrest was stymied only temporarily. Guided by Miss Emma Sansom, he located a hidden ford that enabled his men to cross the deep stream and regain Streight's trail.[46]

When he found Forrest pressing him once again, Streight began to despair of reaching Rome, where he had hoped to wreck not only the local railroad but also a munitions factory of high importance to the Confederacy. In a desperate effort to salvage his mission, he detached Captain Milton Russell and two hundred of "the best mounted men" and sent them, presumably on horseback, on ahead in hopes of securing the Oostanaula River bridge outside Rome. But the gamble failed: when he neared the city on the morning of Sunday, May 3, Russell discovered that hard-riding couriers from Forrest as well as a local citizen had spread word of his coming. He found his objective guarded by a mixed force of soldiers and civilians hunkered down behind cotton-bale barricades and supported by a couple of ancient artillery pieces. The captain considered attacking the motley assemblage, but in the end he decided not to chance it. Lacking sufficient initiative, or simply too worn out to scout the area, he failed to locate a shoal a mile north of the bridge where he could have crossed into the city. In frustration, Russell turned away and sent a courier to inform Streight of his unaccomplished mission.[47]

Before the messenger could reach Russell's superior, Forrest moved in for the kill. Having crossed Dyke's Bridge over the Chattooga River, the raiding leader was now in Lawrence, Alabama, only twenty-one miles from Rome. There Forrest, at the head of perhaps six hundred of the sturdiest riders, caught up with his adversary. Streight tried to form a defensive line but found his men in no condition to fight. As he later reported, "nature was exhausted, and a large portion of my best troops actually went to sleep while lying in line of battle under a severe skirmish fire."[48]

Though he had his quarry at bay at last, Forrest would have to proceed carefully and cleverly if he was to bag an enemy that outnumbered his force on hand more than two-to-one. In customary fashion, he sent an officer inside the enemy lines under a truce flag to demand Streight's surrender; a refusal, Forrest warned, would trigger an attack in overwhelming force. Perhaps suspecting that his opponent was bluffing, the colonel took his time replying. Conferring with his officers, he found them nearly unanimous in advising surrender. The men and mules were worn out, their ammunition was almost gone, and word of Captain Russell's failure at Rome had just been received. Calling on his last reserves of fortitude, the colonel refused to capitulate unless it could be proven to his satisfaction that he was opposed by a superior force.

His mind racing, Forrest agreed to meet personally with Streight to discuss the current situation. Recalling the ruse he had perpetrated so effectively during the Murfreesboro raid, he gave a covert order to a member of his staff. The officer excused himself from the parlay and hastened back to the only artillery unit that had kept pace with Forrest's riders—a single section of Morton's battery—and had its commander move his guns along a ridge and around some hills Streight was facing. Responding to similar instructions, Biffle's and McLemore's troopers marched their men in a circle around the same hills. The carefully crafted impression was of a continuous stream of men, horses, and guns passing around Streight's flanks.

One of Forrest's men quoted his commander as to what happened next: "I seen him [Streight] all the time he was talking, looking over my shoulder and counting the guns. Presently he said: 'Name of God! How many guns have you got? There's fifteen I've counted already!' Turning my head that way, I said: 'I reckon that's all that has kept up.' Then he said, 'I won't surrender till you tell me how many men you've got.' I said: 'I've got enough to whip you out of your boots.' To which he said: 'I won't surrender.' I turned to my bugler and said, 'Sound to mount!' Then he cried out, 'I'll surrender!' I told him, 'Stack your guns right along there, Colonel, and march your men away down that hollow.'"[49]

Once these demands had been complied with and the Rebel troopers came forward to take possession of his weapons, Streight saw how few they were. Furious at having been hoodwinked, he lashed out in angry desperation. As Forrest put it, "he did rear! demanded to have his arms back and that we should fight it out. I just laughed at him and patted him on the shoulder, and said: 'Ah, Colonel, all is fair in love and war you know.'"[50]

# TEN

# ON THE
# DECLINE

THE AFTERMATH OF STREIGHT'S RAID WAS A painful experience for both fox and hound. Forrest considerately provided Streight's weary and famished men with rest, food, and medical treatment for the wounded. Then, on May 3–4, the prisoners (including Russell's detachment) were marched off to Rome, where they were placed under armed guard. Their captors were roundly applauded by the residents of the city. On the fifth the raiders boarded cars on the railroad they had intended to wreck and were shuttled to Atlanta, then on the eighth to Richmond, Virginia. Three days later, Streight and his officers were incarcerated in Libby Prison, while the enlisted men were deposited at Belle Isle, the POW cantonment in the James River.[1]

Everyone involved in the raid, including Forrest, expected the raiders to be quickly released and returned north for consignment to parole camp until exchanged for an equal number of Confederate prisoners. These were the terms under which the exchange cartel had long been operating, but when Confederate authorities began to describe Streight's raid not as a military mission but as an attempt to free Alabama slaves and arm them to fight their former masters, the cartel broke down and the prisoners were not released. Most of the raiders—those who survived the rigors of confinement—remained captive until war's end. Colonel Streight, however, was one of 109 officers who regained their freedom, at least for a time, by tunneling out of Libby in February 1864. Most of the escapees were recaptured, but Streight, following a "long, weary, and perilous pilgrimage" that took three weeks and nearly cost him his life, made his way inside Union lines and eventually returned to military service. He would finish the war as a brevet brigadier general.[2]

For a time, Streight's captor enjoyed the celebrity that came from a successful, high-profile pursuit. The praise and congratulations that had been heaped upon Forrest at Rome accompanied him to Middle Tennessee. During his absence in Alabama and Georgia, Earl Van Dorn had been assassinated; logically enough, but perhaps also as a reward for his recent heroics, Forrest was given command of Van Dorn's corps. Bragg indicated that he would recommend Forrest for promotion to major general. The Confederate Congress chimed in, thanking Forrest for levying retribution on marauders and slave stealers. And the citizens of Rome and Huntsville, Alabama, presented Forrest with handsome mounts to take the place of the horses he had lost during the fight on Hog Mountain.[3]

For a time all went well with Forrest at his new post. He monitored enemy movements between Franklin and Triune; he routed Yankee patrols along the Franklin and Lewisburg Turnpikes; and in common with everyone else in the army, he reveled in the news from Virginia, where Robert E. Lee had drubbed the army of Joseph "Fighting Joe" Hooker—the latest in a long line of highly regarded but critically flawed opponents—in the forests west of Fredericksburg, near Chancellorsville. In subsequent weeks, rumors circulated that Lee was contemplating a second invasion of the North. Given the ease with which he had demolished one adversary after another, it was an accepted fact throughout the South that "Marse Robert" would likewise dispatch Hooker's successor, Major General George Gordon Meade.[4]

This happy, almost tranquil period in Forrest's life came to an abrupt end in mid-June, when the man who had attracted violence most of his life had a deadly confrontation with one of his own officers. Because he had never forgotten the temporary loss of those guns near Day's Gap, Forrest had punished the officer he considered responsible, Lieutenant Willis A. Gould. When Gould learned, shortly after Streight's capture, that he had been summarily transferred to another command, he considered the action an unmerited rebuke and a reflection on his courage and honor. Wishing to put his grievance on record, he rode to Columbia, gained a private meeting with his superior, and lodged a heated protest.

Forrest heard him out but refused to reconsider and ordered Gould to leave. Incensed by the rebuff, the young subordinate drew his pistol, pushed it against Forrest's side, and fired. The ball entered Forrest's left hip, passed through his body, and struck a hallway wall. Bellowing in pain and rage, the left-handed general grasped his assailant's gun hand, preventing him from firing again. With his teeth, Forrest opened a pocket knife he had been carrying and thrust it into Gould's abdomen, penetrating his intestines. The critically injured officer broke free, ran out of Forrest's headquarters, and took refuge in a tailor's shop down the street.

A physician hastily examined Forrest's wound and pronounced it mortal. More angry than pained, the general bolted from the doctor's office without waiting for treatment. Pistol in hand, he went looking for Gould, shouting: "No damned man shall kill me and live!" He stormed into the tailor's shop to find Gould being tended by another doctor. Forrest fired at the injured man, but the shot went wide, whereupon Gould jumped up and ran out the back door, down an alley, and into a patch of weeds and brush, where he collapsed. Forrest was prevented from going after him by Colonel Edmondson and other officers, who persuaded their superior that Gould was dying.[5]

They were correct. A few days later, the lieutenant succumbed to septic peritonitis. By then Forrest had been advised that his own wound might be crippling but was not life-threatening, and his furor had subsided. Shortly before Gould died, he asked to see Forrest, intent on begging forgiveness for his rash and senseless act. Forrest was himself laid up, but he had his men carry him to Gould's bedside. There, as one of Forrest's biographers puts it, "the hot-blooded and high-tempered officers were reconciled in an affecting scene of farewell."[6]

WELL INTO THE SUMMER OF 1863, GRANT and Rosecrans continued to put pressure on the defenders of the Heartland. The foothold Grant's army had secured at Bruinsburg with the help of Grierson's raiders effectively doomed Vicksburg, although it took two months for the siege to tighten effectively. Though he doubted that anything could be done to save Vicksburg, especially after Pemberton rejected his advice to evacuate the city before too late, Joe Johnston was forced to throw good resources after bad. At Jefferson Davis's insistence, in early May the department commander—then on the verge of taking charge of troops in and around the state capital, Jackson—ordered two of Bragg's infantry brigades to

Mississippi, followed by Breckinridge's division. Johnston also agreed to return to Pemberton most of the cavalry that had accompanied Van Dorn to Tennessee. The transfer of these regiments, under Red Jackson, reduced Forrest's command at Columbia to a single division under Frank Armstrong.[7]

Meanwhile, Rosecrans remained determined to evict Bragg from Middle Tennessee. Some Confederates professed to welcome his attempt to do so. Joe Wheeler, who after his raid on the rail lines to Nashville had settled into the routine of protecting Bragg's right near Manchester, informed a civilian with whom he dined that "he was only fearful that Rosecrans would not come out and fight." Wheeler was right to assume that Bragg's opponent intended to avoid combat. What he failed to perceive was that Old Rosey proposed to gain by maneuver, feint, and threat what he might have achieved on the field of battle but at a much steeper cost in lives and resources.[8]

Presumably, therefore, Wheeler was surprised when, on June 23, Rosecrans sallied forth from Murfreesboro. His army advanced in three columns of foot soldiers and a force of cavalry that Wheeler, given the recent loss of Jackson's division, feared was stronger than his own. Rosecrans's plan of campaign, which Bragg failed to interpret until too late to oppose it effectively, was based on seizing and controlling the passes in the mountain range that separated the armies, known as the Highland Rim. To achieve this, Rosecrans intended to advance a small portion of the Army of the Cumberland toward Bragg's right in the vicinity of Bradyville, just north of Wheeler's headquarters. He believed that Bragg would interpret the relatively weak movement as a feint and, expecting the main blow to fall elsewhere, would shift troops to his center and left. Rosecrans would then send a much larger force around the denuded flank and into the Rebel rear.

Rosecrans's offensive got off to an impressive start, mainly because he advanced his troops—the infantry corps of George H. Thomas, Alexander M. McCook, Thomas L. Crittenden, and Gordon Granger, screened by two divisions of cavalry and a brigade of mounted infantry under David Stanley—with unsurpassed speed. This celerity, which contrasted sharply with the pace of the movement from Nashville to Murfreesboro six months earlier, caught the Army of Tennessee flat-footed.[9]

This should not have happened. Bragg had placed infantry and cavalry in position to detect and report the enemy's advance in time to meet it. But Bragg had failed to ensure that enough troops held the mountain passes

Rosecrans was to use. Historians ascribe this failure to overconfidence. Bragg held a position that he considered strong enough to be maintained under almost any conditions. He believed that had he fortified more heavily the three northeastern defiles—Bell Buckle, Liberty, and Hoover's Gaps—it would have impeded his ability to oppose an even wider turning movement such as the one Rosecrans appeared to be making.[10]

General William S. Rosencrans, USA.

Much of the blame for Bragg's inability to detect Rosecrans's advance belonged to Wheeler. It was the cavalry's job to keep tabs on enemy movements in the army's front. Its leader displayed an unusual lack of diligence through-out the early phase of Rosecrans's advance, sending in reports that were, at best, vague and ambiguous, and, at worst, inaccurate and contradictory.

In Wheeler's defense, he was working with a depleted command. The return of Van Dorn's troopers to Mississippi and the recent loss of Morgan's Kentuckians—off on another raid far from the place where most needed—had almost halved his effective force. In the spring, its numbers had approached sixteen thousand; now it comprised no more than nine thousand, about three thousand fewer than the Army of the Cumberland fielded. What remained was still a formidable force, but in order to cover the army's thirty-mile front it had been stretched so widely that the gaps in its picket line were numerous and large. Then, too, the bad blood between Wheeler and Forrest had impeded coordination between the forces covering Bragg's flanks. The situation had only worsened following Gould's wounding of Forrest, from which the brigadier continued to recuperate. In early June, Wheeler, noting the much-reduced size of Forrest's command, had augmented it with sizable detachments from Wharton and Martin, the latter having returned to Wheeler's command following brief service under Van Dorn.[11]

Another point in Wheeler's defense was that the winter had played hob with the health of his horses, which had been much reduced by a chronic scarcity of forage. Their riders were suffering from a corresponding short-age of rations, as well as from inadequate supplies of clothing, equipment, and tack. They also wielded inferior weaponry: although hundreds of troopers had rearmed themselves with breech-loading carbines captured on their recent raids, these became unusable once the model-specific ammunition that fed them, available only from munitions factories in the North, was exhausted. By late spring of 1863, a troubling number of Wheeler's men were again toting the shotguns and fowling pieces they had brought from home at war's start.

The weather, which had long appeared an enemy of the Army of Tennessee, began to assist it one day after Rosecrans's offensive began. On the twenty-fourth, a hard rain fell across Middle Tennessee and continued into the next day, making the movement of troops, guns, and wagons increasingly difficult. Rosecrans sent forward pioneers to firm up the soggy roads with planks cut from trees, but the fatigue parties got in the way of the infantry, further slowing the offensive. Even so, on the twenty-fourth, a heavy column of all arms, spearheaded by the two thousand mounted infantrymen that made up Colonel John T. Wilder's "Lightning Brigade"— every man armed with the state-of-the-art Spencer repeating rifle— charged through Hoover's Gap and swept away the small infantry-cavalry force Bragg had placed at the northern end of the defile. A desperate counterattack by the foot soldiers of Brigadier General William B. Bate plugged the south end of the gap, denying the Yankees egress.[12]

By June 25, rain and Rebel resistance had brought Rosecrans's movement to a halt. When the offensive resumed next day, however, it recaptured lost momentum thanks largely to Bragg's decision not to contest the gaps. He ordered his subordinates, if so hard pressed they faced being overwhelmed, to withdraw from the Highland Rim. The commander in the area of Hoover's Gap, Major General Alexander P. Stewart, promptly fell back, relinquishing his position on the Manchester Pike and shifting southwest to join the balance of Hardee's corps between Beech Grove and Wartrace.[13]

Bragg's strategy was based largely on Joe Wheeler's opinion that the movement through Hoover's Gap was truly a feint. When Rosecrans got moving again on the twenty-sixth, Bragg believed he was aiming to crush Polk's wing at Shelbyville (to which Bragg had moved his headquarters) with a thrust through Liberty Gap. Acting on his own supposition, Wheeler further weakened the right by sending reinforcements to the area north of Shelbyville, where the real feint was in progress.

In his postwar memoirs, Wheeler claimed he had tried to persuade Bragg that the right flank should have been more strongly defended, thus implying that his superior was solely responsible for the transfer of manpower in the opposite direction. Yet Wheeler's actions and reports throughout the period June 24-27 indicate not only that he had been duped by Rosecrans but that he had materially assisted in Bragg's deception. The army commander began to suspect as much late on the twenty-sixth, when he learned that Stewart had relinquished Hoover's Gap in the face of a column much larger than the one originally believed to be pressing the eastern flank. Suddenly aware that he had fallen for Rosecrans's ploy, Bragg canceled plans to have Polk attack through the gaps against the Union right. Instead he ordered Polk and Hardee to withdraw across the Duck River and occupy the entrenchments that had been erected at Tullahoma. Begun on the morning of the twenty-seventh, the operation was not completed until the following afternoon.[14]

While the infantry crossed, the cavalry remained on the north bank, holding the line in the ever-present drizzle. Filling the entrenchments the foot soldiers had just evacuated, they strained to impede Rosecrans's advance. The army's situation appeared bleak indeed: Tullahoma was already under threat from a Yankee column at Manchester, which Rosecrans had occupied on the twenty-seventh. The Army of the Cumberland was also in position to break Bragg's supply line to Chattanooga and block his retreat route through Decherd. And by moving southeast to Hillsborough, Rosecrans could seize the main road to Chattanooga or sever the road and railroad connections at Cowan, twenty-two miles south of Tullahoma. Finally, Rosecrans could cross the Elk River below Hillsborough and, moving along the south bank, block the crossings between Tullahoma and Decherd. That would trap Bragg's army in a position in which it could be surrounded and cut to pieces.[15]

Wheeler was largely responsible for handing Bragg's adversary so many options. On the twenty-ninth, Bragg had his chief of staff send the cavalryman a rather sharply worded message directing him to "ascertain where their left rests to-night, what kind of force [holds it], and so to observe it during the night." Bragg desired that any movement in the Manchester area be reported "hour to hour, or, better, the moment it occurs." Fifteen minutes later, Bragg's subordinate repeated these demands, adding: "Try to get it soon and accurate."[16]

Wheeler's forte was defense of a retreating army, not intelligence gathering. Falling back slowly to the Duck River at Shelbyville, Wharton's and Martin's troopers engaged the oncoming Yankees in a series of hotly contested fights that took a toll of defenders who already were laboring under heavy disadvantages. A member of the 8th Confederate Cavalry recalled that "we were ordered out to meet the enemy, but in what condition? Four days incessant rain had rendered our arms useless and destroyed almost all our cartridges."[17]

At least they enjoyed good cover, for Wheeler dismounted most of his men and had them occupy the entrenchments recently abandoned by Bragg's infantry. Although primarily concerned with Martin and Wharton, Wheeler attempted to establish contact with Forrest, who was falling back from Columbia but remained some miles north of Shelbyville. Forrest had regained command of his corps, having cut short his recuperation to help save the army from destruction.

Because not all of Bragg's supply and baggage wagons had been ferried across the river, Wheeler proposed to make a stand at Shelbyville, holding his position north of town to the last extremity. Already many of his troopers had been surrounded and taken prisoner by the infantry of Gordon Granger and the horsemen of David Stanley. On the morning of June 27, Wheeler decided he could no longer tarry on the north side of the river; he ordered his men to cross wherever they could find a shallow ford. By now blue cavalry were galloping through the streets, forcing Wheeler and a small rear guard to take refuge in front of the Duck River bridge.

Wheeler was about to cross and burn the span when word reached him that Forrest was falling back on the town and begging him to secure the bridge, "or I will be cut off." In defiance of survival instincts, Wheeler and his personal escort, only thirteen strong, remained in the town, exchanging fire with the steadily arriving enemy and searching desperately for Forrest. Almost too late, Wheeler realized that his unpredictable subordinate was not coming by the route he had indicated. Without informing Wheeler, Forrest had detoured around Shelbyville to cross at another bridge four miles east of town.[18]

Wheeler's efforts to help Forrest resulted in his men being cut off from the bridge and driven to the steep bluffs that overlooked a river "swollen to a mighty torrent" by the incessant rains. A member of the 3rd Alabama recalled that "we were completely stampeded. Orders were given for every man to take care of himself." Captain Miller of the 8th Confederate related that when dismounted troopers rushed for their horses, "men were trampled under foot and killed. I came near being killed myself having an ankle badly sprained and was at one time lifted entirely off the ground by the throng. Many plunged into the stream and were drowned. Others were shot while swimming." He described the chaotic scene as "the greatest cavalry disaster of the war."[19]

Wheeler, accompanied by General Martin and the escort unit, reached the bluffs under a shower of rifle balls. Without hesitating, he spurred his mount off the cliff and into open air. The others followed his lead. Gripping their saddle pommels for dear life, they plummeted twenty feet into the river, which they struck with a resounding thud and a gigantic spray of water. All who took the plunge survived it, although many lost weapons and equipment—Martin's saber and pistol continue to rest at the bottom of Duck River. Braving a continuing fire from the river bank, they rode the current to the other side and clambered onto dry ground. After shaking themselves of excess water, they galloped south to accompany their army on the latest of its many retreats.[20]

MORGAN'S ABSENCE FROM BRAGG'S SIDE DURING the recent fighting was the result neither of poor timing nor of circumstances beyond his control. Rather, it fit a pattern of behavior that, in the eyes of his superiors, was becoming increasingly unacceptable.

Morgan had long exhibited a cavalier attitude toward the interests of the army to which he was attached. From his earliest days in the field, he had seized every opportunity to fight a war of his own, one far enough removed from the main arena as to be beyond the reach of higher headquarters. He had gone his own way during Smith's and Bragg's invasion of Kentucky, and thanks to a like-thinking subordinate, he had avoided being recalled during Bragg's return to Tennessee. He had taken so long to return from the Christmas raid that he had missed the January-December fighting around Murfreesboro. Wheeler never forgot, and Bragg never forgave, his absence on that occasion.

A less self-absorbed soldier would have realized that such irresponsible behavior would have repercussions, but if Morgan did, the thought did not faze him. He needed only to read the newspapers that glorified his exploits, the letters and gifts he received from admiring civilians, and the thanks voted him by the politicians in Richmond to feel validated, justified, exonerated.

His latest disappearing act, however, marked a transition from irresponsibility to insubordination. By the late spring of 1863, Morgan had been involved in a series of disputes with his superiors, especially Wheeler. Many were minor, such as the flap that arose from Morgan's insistence that some baggage wagons earmarked for his division had been filched by corps headquarters. Other, more-acrimonious run-ins caused him to tell his closest subordinates that he could no longer tolerate serving under Wheeler.[21]

For his part, Wheeler was growing tired not only of Morgan's craving for autonomy and his casual dismissal of orders, but of the increasing inefficiency and weakness of his command. The Kentuckian's defeat at Milton, Tennessee, in February had been followed by an embarrassing setback near Liberty, north of Morgan's headquarters at McMinnville, on April 3. Morgan was not on hand when one thousand five hundred cavalry and foot soldiers under David Stanley passed through the area on a reconnaissance and encountered Colonel Gano's regiment, deployed atop a series of ridges known as Snow's Hill. Gano's dispositions were so faulty—he deployed his men halfway up the ridge, where they perched, as one historian has written, "like pigeons on a fence"—that when Stanley attacked he carried the position with ease. Demoralized by the shelling of horse artillery and fearing that horsemen had cut their retreat route, Gano's men broke and fled before Stanley could close with them. Basil Duke, just returned to duty after recuperating from his Christmas raid wound, did his best to stem the rout, but no one heeded his shouted orders to re-form.[22]

After Snow Hill, even Morgan began to fear that his command was slipping. He attributed its recent performance to the rigors of incessant campaigning and the increasing hardships and privations it had endured. Morgan himself was not immune to these effects. An embarrassing incident subsequent to Gano's defeat suggested that the ever-vigilant, always-in-control leader was himself in a state of decline. In mid-April, a division-size force dispatched by Rosecrans under Major General J. J. Reynolds (who had led a pursuit force that barely failed to overtake the Christmas raiders) attacked McMinnville, chased Morgan and his visiting wife out of the town, and ransacked his headquarters. Reynolds, finding himself unopposed, then destroyed the local rail depot, a locomotive, two wooden trestles, and major supplies of cotton and bacon. Morgan could only look on from a safe distance, seething and cursing.[23]

His and Mattie's flight from McMinnville became the talk of Bragg's army. Some of Morgan's men, as well as many of his friends and relations, began to suspect that his marriage had diminished the gifts of body and spirit that were critical to his success. One family member wrote Mattie of his concern that by "sticking *too close* to your husband" she was encumbering him "too much with care and anxiety, so much so as to prove injurious to him." The editor of a Unionist newspaper in Nashville placed the situation in a biblical context: "The fair Delilah . . . has shorn him of his locks."[24]

Morgan would have shrugged off such suggestions, but the opinions of his commanders carried greater weight. Even before the attack on McMinnville, Bragg had written Joseph E. Johnston that "I fear Morgan is overcome by too large a command." After Reynolds's raid, Morgan's superior and friend William J. Hardee confided to Johnston that "Morgan's command is in bad condition and growing worse." He blamed this partly on Morgan's growing dissatisfaction with Wheeler, though such conduct "cannot be justified, and he [Morgan] has suffered, and will continue to suffer, in public estimation." Hardee suggested that Johnston, whom Morgan respected, counsel him, but there is no evidence that this occurred.[25]

Morgan began to believe that the best way to combat the perception of deterioration was to mount another expedition into enemy territory, one larger, farther-reaching, and more dramatic in its effects than any before it. Late in May, he broached the idea of a hit-and-run strike on Louisville to Wheeler, who had contemplated the same mission a few months earlier. Morgan proposed to use his entire division to "take and destroy the public works, &c." of the city, whose once-formidable garrison had been substantially reduced, at least in the opinion of Morgan's scouts. Wheeler endorsed the proposal and passed it along to Bragg.[26]

The army leader—whose own sources confirmed that Louisville's defenders were few, and who saw in the mission not only a chance to damage further the L&N but another opportunity to recruit Kentuckians into his ranks—was cautiously receptive. In mid-June, he approved Morgan's plan but limited his force to one thousand five hundred men and a suitable number of cannons. Upon Morgan's earnest entreaties, Bragg raised the manpower level to two thousand. Suddenly apprehensive that Rosecrans might advance against him, Bragg wanted the rest of Morgan's command to remain with him. In conveying Bragg's approval, Wheeler emphasized that should Morgan discover the enemy to be on the move, "General Bragg wishes you to turn rapidly and fall on his rear," and, after doing as much damage as possible, to return to the main army. Either explicitly or tacitly, Morgan agreed to abide by this stipulation.[27]

In truth, he had no intention of limiting himself in any way. When preparing for the raid, he ordered 2,460 of his men to saddle up and four cannons (two 3-inch rifles and two 12-pounder howitzers) to limber up. Moreover, as he confided to Basil Duke, he would not confine his travels to Kentucky. If and when opportunity arose, he would slake a thirst he had never quenched: to raid above the Ohio River into the heart of Yankeedom.[28]

Even before permission came through, Morgan assembled his men at Alexandria, Tennessee, the site of the Christmas raid launch. The command comprised two brigades under Duke and Colonel Adam R. Johnson. The latter, who in the war's early days had been one of Forrest's best scouts, had led Morgan's 10th Kentucky since the previous fall. Although relatively new to brigade command, Johnson had made a name for himself as a partisan ranger, while acquiring a curious nickname, "Stovepipe." The sobriquet dated from his July 1862 capture of Newburgh, Indiana, which he had threatened from across the Ohio River with what looked like a cannon but was only a stovepipe mounted on the running board of a wagon.[29]

On June 11, Morgan marched northeast and crossed the Cumberland River near the hamlet of Rome. Once on the north bank, he had intended to attack the garrison at neighboring Carthage, but the following evening a courier brought an order from Bragg to hasten northeast to intercept a Federal raiding force bound for East Tennessee under Colonel William P. Sanders. The assignment entailed a recrossing of the river. A heavy, continuous rain slowed Morgan's march, and by the time he reached his destination, Sanders's expedition had left the area for points unknown. Morgan returned west and encamped both brigades on the Cumberland between Turkey Neck Bend and Burkesville, Kentucky, while he waited for the rain to cease and for additional supplies to reach him from McMinnville.[30]

With the skies clear and his false start behind him, on the morning of July 2, Morgan again crossed the Cumberland, now out of its banks with rainwater. Duke's brigade was ferried over aboard what he called "two crazy little flats, that seemed ready to sink under the weight of a single man, and two or three canoes." Duke recalled that "Colonel Johnson was not even so well provided," being forced to improvise rafts to carry weapons and ammunition. Most of Johnson's men swam the river—many in the nude, carrying their uniforms and weapons on their backs to keep them dry. The mounts of both brigades were made to plunge through the half-mile-wide stream.

Morgan's Great Raid, June–July 1863.

Men who could not swim grabbed the horses' tails and were pulled through the fast-moving current.[31]

The crossing came as no surprise to the Federals who were picketing the north bank. The raiders' two-week occupation of the Burkesville area had suggested an impending breakout into Kentucky. The operation quickly came to the attention of the occupation forces around Glasgow, twelve miles from the river. These Yankees—members of Brigadier General Edward H. Hobson's brigade of the 3rd Division, 23rd Army Corps, which included the 1st Kentucky (Union) Cavalry under Morgan's old adversary Frank Wolford—galloped to Burkesville and by midafternoon were firing on the raiders. According to Duke, however, they did not "advance with determination." At least two of Morgan's regiments had gotten over by the time Hobson arrived; Morgan massed them and led them in a charge. The outgunned Yankees withdrew in haste, their flanks and rear raked by the fire of dismounted raiders, some of them still unclothed.

Morgan claimed that the Yankees did not stop running till they were back in their camp at Marrowbone, ten miles northwest of Burkesville. Their officers, however, sent gallopers to warn other outposts that Morgan's men had crossed the river, apparently heading for Columbia. In a matter of hours, a wide-ranging manhunt was on. For months the troops north of the Cumberland had been expecting Morgan to launch another of his patented raids. Rumor had Rosecrans on the verge of attacking the Army of Tennessee, and a diversion by Bragg's horsemen appeared likely. Hobson's division commander, Brigadier General Henry M. Judah, had been predicting a Rebel raid since at least June 18 and had alerted his immediate superior, Ambrose Burnside, who, following the debacle at Fredericksburg, had been exiled to departmental command at Cincinnati. As soon as word of Morgan's crossing of the Cumberland reached him, Burnside began assembling a sizable pursuit force, while informing Rosecrans and War Department officials of Morgan's breakout.[32]

At the outset, Burnside's effort faltered. Judah, who appeared to be in the best position to block Morgan, failed to coordinate operations with the leaders of his widely dispersed forces, including Hobson, Brigadier General Mahlon D. Manson, and Colonel William B. Stokes. Nor did Judah work closely with Burnside's other division leaders: Samuel Carter, the East Tennessee raider, and Jeremiah Boyle, Forrest's opponent at Parker's Cross Roads. Lacking timely intelligence on Morgan's movements, Carter and Boyle could not decide where to commit their forces, which included the cavalry and mounted infantry of Brigadier General James M. Shackelford and Colonel August V. Kautz. For his part, Judah moved slowly and tentatively at the head of his division, half of which consisted of foot soldiers. When Burnside urged him to make more progress, Judah replied that he could not act decisively until certain of Morgan's heading and better able to estimate his intentions.[33]

Shaking itself dry and free of Yankees, Morgan's column wended its way north, reaching Columbia early on July 3. The road was clear of pickets, the weather had turned sunny and warm, and the men, having completed a dangerous crossing with minimal loss, were feeling good. Had they been privy to what was transpiring this day along the lower Mississippi and in south-central Pennsylvania, there would have been no merriment on the march. John Pemberton, his garrison on the verge of starvation, was planning to meet with Ulysses Grant to talk surrender. Vicksburg would be in Union hands the following day, the Fourth of July. Its fall would precipitate the surrender of Port Hudson four days later, prompting Abraham Lincoln to exult that "the Father of Waters goes unvexed to the sea." Meanwhile, nine hundred miles to the east, Robert E. Lee was reeling from the repulse of Pickett's Charge at Gettysburg. Late the following day, the Army of Northern Virginia would begin to withdraw to its home state, ending the last Confederate offensive in the eastern theater. The twin disasters marked a fatal decline in Confederate fortunes. Although months would pass before their effects were fully felt, Vicksburg and Gettysburg doomed the cause of Southern independence.

As Judah informed Burnside, Morgan met minimal resistance at Columbia. Entering the village, his vanguard easily evicted a small body of dismounted cavalry, part of Wolford's brigade. Moving on, that evening the column reached the Green River, the opposite bank of which, at Tebb's Bend, had been fortified by two hundred Michigan infantry. While his pickets skirmished lightly with the Wolverines, Morgan allowed the rest of his men to sleep through the night. Next morning he called on the local commander, Colonel Orlando H. Moore, to surrender. Moore was no John Pemberton: he replied that "the Fourth of July is a bad day for surrenders, and I must therefore decline." Underestimating Moore's force and the depth and intricacy of his works, Morgan launched a dismounted attack by the 11th Kentucky of Stovepipe Johnson's command. A half-hour later, the regiment having lost thirty-five men killed, including the esteemed Colonel Chenault, and forty wounded, Morgan called off the assault.[34]

Shrugging off his costly error, he elected to bypass Moore's position and head toward Lebanon, which he had attacked and captured on the First Kentucky Raid but had given a wide berth to during the Christmas Raid. This time he took on the occupiers, portions of four regiments under Colonel Charles Hanson, brother of the late Roger Hanson, Morgan's first superior. The Union Hanson commanded mostly Kentucky troops, including the kinsmen of several raiders. Hoping to avoid mass fratricide, Morgan tried but failed to persuade Hanson, whose men were holed up inside stores, stables, and private homes, to give up without a struggle. Reluctantly, he positioned his troops for an attack while comrades set fire to some of the occupied buildings. When neither the conflagration nor the pounding of Morgan's artillery changed Hanson's mind, the raiding leader ordered a series of frontal assaults, spearheaded by dismounted members of the 2nd and 8th Kentucky.

Handily outnumbered, Hanson had no chance, but he held his position stubbornly. After absorbing six hours of attacks, he finally raised a surrender flag, and Morgan took the town. Although aware that the prisoner-exchange process had broken down, Morgan, at Hanson's urging, agreed to parole him and his surviving troops.[35]

Hanson had suffered heavily in the battle, but Morgan, forced to take the offensive in 90-degree heat, fared worse. Among his fifty casualties was one that plunged him into prolonged mourning: the mortal wounding of his youngest brother, nineteen-year-old Tom Morgan, a member of Duke's staff who had helped lead the final assault of the day. Tom had been universally beloved; word of his death impelled enraged comrades to burn and loot the rest of the town while threatening to execute some of their captives. According to Lieutenant Colonel Robert Alston of Morgan's staff, "it required the utmost energy and promptitude on the part of the officers to prevent a scene of slaughter, which all would deeply have lamented." The difficulty Morgan experienced in restraining his men indicated that discipline—never the distinguishing characteristic of the command—was again breaking down.[36]

After tending to his wounded, burying his dead, and seeing to his brother's interment in a local cemetery, Morgan pointed the column in the direction of Springfield and kept it moving till after sundown. In the muggy darkness, an entire company of Kentuckians fell out and slipped away, never to be seen again. The recent bloodletting had cured the men of the notion that they were on a joyride through the backyard of an inept foe. An increasing number of pursuers were nipping at their heels, snatching up stragglers. They had yet to mount a serious threat, but every raider realized that the farther north he rode, the longer the odds against his returning alive to Tennessee.[37]

At four a.m. on July 6, after dropping his prisoners off at Springfield, Morgan and the main body reached Bardstown, within easy riding distance of the Ohio. A minute force—less than two dozen cavalry—occupied the town, but their commander twice refused Morgan's demand to surrender.

He changed his mind after noting the size of the force that had surrounded him, but Morgan's brother Dick, still seething over Tom's death, refused to acknowledge the officer's compliance and ordered his men to shoot him down. John Morgan intervened before blood was shed, but he permitted the looting of the prisoners' personal property.[38]

Although plunder was an unfortunate feature of every raid regardless of who conducted it, Morgan's men had a peculiar knack for it. After the war, Basil Duke, for whom wholesale looting had no place in modern warfare, recalled that on this raid the practice "exceeded anything that any of us had ever seen before. The men seemed actuated by a desire to 'pay off' in the 'enemy country' all the scores that the Federal army had chalked up in the South." Whenever the raiders departed a town, they carried off everything within their reach—from bolts of calico and muslin to parasols and chafing dishes. Duke observed one man who "carried a bird cage with three canaries in it for two days. . . . I could not believe that such a passion could have developed . . . among any body of civilized men."[39]

When Morgan reached the Ohio, his efforts at deceiving his enemy were in full swing. All across Kentucky, Lightning Ellsworth had been putting his bug to good use, tapping out authentic-sounding reports that made Yankee operators, and the army officers they were in touch with, believe the raiders were everywhere at once. Ellsworth's messages doubled or trebled Morgan's numbers and spread the word that even larger forces were cooperating with him. These efforts bore fruit when the column halted at the port town of Brandenburg and drew only a scattering of rifle fire from the Indiana shore and a couple of shells that landed harmlessly in the river.[40]

This resistance, provided by home guards and local civilians, proved no barrier to Morgan's fulfillment of his long-cherished dream to invade the North. Whether or not Braxton Bragg and Jefferson Davis would have seen military value in such an operation, Morgan did, and he persuaded Duke of it. Extending the raid into Indiana would spread terror and panic among a citizenry thus far spared war's heavy hand, would compel troops needed elsewhere to pursue, and might also strengthen the antiwar Copperhead movement in the Northwest. After the war, Duke defended his superior's decision, arguing that "according to the "tenor of his instructions," Morgan had authority to operate north of the Cumberland River. His orders from Bragg "did not specify when he should return from his scout, and Indiana was certainly 'north of the Cumberland.'"[41]

An advance contingent of the "scout" force had entered Brandenburg hours before Morgan arrived and had boarded and seized two steamboats. From midmorning until past midnight on the eighth, the boats ferried Morgan's men, horses, guns, and wagons across the mile-wide dividing line between North and South. It was a mammoth undertaking, and it almost took too long. Only an hour after the rear guard had gotten across, the vanguard of General Hobson's division drew rein on the Kentucky side. Furious over Morgan's escape, Hobson dispatched one of the ferries to Louisville to procure transports for his men and animals. He was determined to pursue Morgan's men to the death. So were many other Kentucky-based Federals whom Morgan had outwitted, eluded, and embarrassed over the past two years.

At last on indisputably Yankee soil, Morgan and his men gloried in the daring feat they had pulled off. Proud of themselves and contemptuous of their enemy, they headed inland. Over the next five days, they terrorized Indiana towns defended by embattled farmers and citizen-soldiers whose military experience was confined to a militia muster or two. At some points larger forces, including veteran soldiers on furlough and convalescent leave, loomed up in Morgan's path, but these were either cast aside or bypassed. On July 9 at Corydon, the militia put up a stout fight. Yet even this skirmish, the most significant action of Morgan's sojourn in Indiana, delayed the Rebels only briefly.

On the tenth, the raiders captured a small force guarding the village of Palmyra. They compelled the surrender of a larger body at Salem, where they destroyed supplies, a depot, and several bridges on the New Albany & Salem Railroad. At Canton, Morgan's men tore up track and tore down telegraph cable (but only after Ellsworth had tapped out deceptive and misleading wires). Major James B. McCreary of the 11th Kentucky observed with quiet satisfaction that at every stop "the citizens seemed frightened almost to death, for Federal papers have published the wildest tales about us. The Governors of Indiana and Ohio have ordered out all able-bodied men, and we have already fought decrepit, white-haired age and buoyant, blithe boyhood."[42]

On the eleventh, Morgan pushed on through Vienna, New Philadelphia, Lexington, and Paris. A few miles to the north, at Vernon, an impressive force of volunteers and militia barred his way. Rather than wage a lengthy fight, allowing his pursuers to close in, Morgan held the defenders in place and then detoured around them. Halting briefly to wreck additional railroad track, he made an all-night march to Dupont, where the command rested and fed.

On July 12, McCreary jotted in his diary that "we move rapidly through six or seven towns without any resistance." That day the column rode into Versailles and captured three hundred nervous militiamen with relative ease. Here the captors turned thieves. As one historian comments, "five thousand dollars disappeared from the county treasury, and one light-fingered Raider even made off with the coin-silver jewelry of the local Masonic Lodge."[43]

By now, the column was nearing Cincinnati. Its approach sent waves of fear rippling through the city that hosted General Burnside's headquarters. Some of Morgan's more aggressive subordinates proposed taking the place by storm, but Morgan realized that it was swarming with would-be pursuers, including large bodies of infantry that could be sent against him by rail. Wisely, he kept well to the north of the city.

On the thirteenth, horsemen who were feeling the effects of three weeks of near-constant travel crossed the Whitewater River into Ohio. Now, if not before, Morgan began to appreciate the hardships he had thrust on his officers and men, many of whom had fallen asleep in their saddles; others were afoot, their horses having gone lame. Discipline was again breaking down. That evening a large gap appeared in the marching column. For some hours, Duke's and Johnson's brigades were so far apart as to invite the intervention of militia and partisans, an increasing number of whom were dogging the column. An equally vexing problem was the mounting number of stragglers, whose capture and interrogation might imperil the entire command. By the time the column reached Williamsburg, Ohio, on the afternoon of the fourteenth, it had been reduced to fewer than two thousand riders.

Resistance proved stronger in Ohio than in the Hoosier State. "The enemy are now pressing us on all sides," McCreary wrote, "and the woods swarm with militia." Almost every road was blocked with felled trees, and the cry "Axes to the front!" was a near-constant refrain. Concerned by his decelerating pace, Morgan began to suspect that Frank Wolford or some other wild-eyed adversary was closing in. In fact, forces under Wolford, Hobson, Shackelford, and Kautz were only hours to the rear, as were two thousand militia under Colonel Benjamin P. Runkle. Moreover, gunboats were patrolling the meandering Ohio, hoping to catch Morgan in the act of recrossing. The river also bustled with transports carrying infantry ready to debark at a moment's notice and engage the raiders.[44]

Whether Morgan realized it or not, these were too many pursuers to shake. He remained determined to bring his bone-weary riders, who had been averaging more than twenty hours a day in the saddle, back safely to Tennessee. But he no longer had a say in the matter. On the eighteenth, when he directed his column toward fords on the now-north-flowing river, the enemy—Hobson's cavalry, including Wolford's Kentuckians, off his left flank, the rest of Judah's division, Kautz's troopers attached, on his right—moved to within striking distance. Next morning, the horsemen under Judah fired on the column, which had halted for essential rest near the village of Portland.

The raiding leader was stunned to learn that his pursuers had caught up. He had known that Hobson was somewhere to the rear but had no idea he was so close; and he had not realized that Judah's troopers had recovered so well from their initial fumbling, or that they had ridden so relentlessly to overtake him, eating and sleeping in the saddle, seemingly impervious to fatigue. Morgan's chasers had been animated to an unexcelled degree by the thought of trapping the South's greatest raider on Northern soil and thrashing him into submission. Everywhere they went north of the Ohio, they had been inspired by civilians who, in sharp contrast to those they had encountered in Kentucky and Tennessee, cheered them on and at every stop plied them with victuals—one item in particular. Writing after the war, a young Federal recalled the experience as "six hundred square miles of fried chicken."[45]

Morgan's antagonists had to settle for bagging a seven-hundred-man detachment under Basil Duke and Dick Morgan, which on the morning of July 20 was cut off while trying to cross to the east bank of the river by way of Buffington Island. The captors included not only Judah and Kautz, who attacked the suddenly panic-stricken raiders simultaneously from north, south, and west, but also two gunboats on patrol in the upper Ohio. One of these, the USS *Moose*, materialized out of the morning fog east of Buffington Island and began to blast the Rebels with shells from her bow guns. Duke recalled that "although they aimed too high to inflict much injury, the hiss of the dreaded missiles increased the panic." The colonel and many of his men took refuge in a riverbank ravine, where they found themselves trapped. No resistance was possible when the entire 9th Michigan Cavalry advanced on them, carbines at the ready. "They came down on us," one raider recalled, "like the grasshoppers used to come down on the farmers of Kansas."[46]

Racing south to a ford near Belleville in the newly created state of West Virginia, at dusk Morgan splashed into the water at the head of his remaining troops. Halfway across the stream, he realized that the majority of his men were still on the Ohio side. While some 300 raiders under Adam Johnson swam to freedom, Morgan turned back to the 700 or so who remained and led them deep into Ohio. His pursuers, their energy and spirits raised by Duke's capture, bayed relentlessly at his heels. Judah and Hobson were out of the race; Morgan was now trailed by five hundred troopers under General Shackelford, who had vowed neither to eat nor sleep till they ran the remaining raiders to earth. En route they were joined by bands of Ohio and Pennsylvania militia committed to driving the enemy from the region they called home.

The chase went on for six more sweltering, exhausting days. Morgan's remnant—reduced by capture, straggling, and desertion to fewer than 350 officers and men—continued to steal horses and rations; to fight, or, more often, to evade militia and home guard units; and to burn bridges in the hope of delaying the inevitable. On July 26, the raid came to a merciful end near West Point, Ohio, less than twenty miles from the Pennsylvania border. Hopelessly hemmed in by volunteers and militiamen, Morgan, who was unwilling to surrender to Shackelford, handed his sword to a militia officer, Captain James Burbick. The operation that would come to be known as Morgan's Great Raid—the longest cavalry expedition of the war, and the farthest Confederate penetration of the North—was history.[47]

MORGAN'S FORAY THROUGH YANKEE TERRITORY had some solid accomplishments to its credit, including the month-long diversion of more than five thousand full-time pursuers who might otherwise have aided Rosecrans in his efforts to drive Bragg out of Tennessee and finish him off in Georgia. The diversion also delayed by a corresponding length of time Burnside's long-planned invasion of East Tennessee. Although the damage Morgan's men inflicted on railroad lines and supply depots in Kentucky, Indiana, and Ohio was unpatterned and relatively light, the thousands of prisoners they captured and paroled in all three states created a temporary manpower gap in Burnside's command.

The raid's greatest shortcoming was the Confederacy's loss of one thousand four hundred veteran cavalrymen. Most were promptly confined in prisons throughout Ohio. Morgan and sixty-eight of his men were incarcerated in the state penitentiary at Columbus, although the raiding leader remained behind bars for only four months. In November, he and six of his officers tunneled their way to freedom through the thin concrete floors of their cells and an air duct that emptied outside the prison. A massive manhunt was launched, but Morgan and the other escapees remained at large until, after two weeks of hair-raising adventures, and with the material assistance of pro-Confederate Kentuckians, they reached friendly lines near Livingston, Tennessee.[48]

By the spring of 1864, Morgan had returned to active duty, but his mismanaged expedition had placed him under a cloud. Bragg, who strongly considered court-martialing him for flagrant disobedience, wanted no part of him; consequently, he never again served in the Army of Tennessee. Failing to reconstitute his old division, Morgan cobbled together a second-rate command—troopers too young or too old, insufficiently trained, inadequately armed, and poorly officered. Eventually assigned to the Department of Southwestern Virginia, he led his motley command on one last raid through his home state. The summer journey took him back to Lexington, near which he inflicted miscellaneous damage on enemy-run rail lines and warehouses while committing crimes against the citizenry, including bank robbing. Morgan captured one thousand Federals and made off with as many horses, but pursuers overtook him and captured half of his command. Morgan, his gambler's luck not yet run out, escaped. But the old days were gone for good; the once-fearsome Thunderbolt now inspired terror on a par with heat lightning.[49]

Transferred to the Department of East Tennessee, Morgan organized his final command: one thousand six hundred adventurous youths who flocked to his rather tattered banner. With this force, he hoped to launch new exploits that would win enough acclaim to restart his stalled career, but on September 4, 1864, on a raid to Greenville, Tennessee, he was felled by a Yankee carbine bullet. He left behind a rudderless command, a grieving young widow, and a once-gleaming reputation that had slowly but steadily turned to dross.[50]

## ELEVEN

# PEAKS AND
# VALLEYS

Rosecrans had maneuvered his opponent out of the position it had held for almost six months, but he wanted more. He pressed the Army of Tennessee along the length of its new line in front of Tullahoma, threatening its rear as well as its flanks. As he had hoped, the multiangle offensive eventually drove Bragg to distraction.

Unsure of his ability to hold the works that Polk and Hardee were strengthening, and confused by contradictory advice from his corps commanders, Bragg could not determine a proper response to Rosecrans's varied threats. On June 28, Union cavalry seized the Elk River bridge at Phelan, then galloped to Decherd, twelve miles south of Tullahoma, where it wrecked track and rolling stock, cutting the Army of Tennessee's communications with Chattanooga. The next day, Bragg was informed that the Yankees were moving against him along the Manchester Pike, only five miles off. This warning turned out to be false, but on the thirtieth he learned that both cavalry and infantry were in his rear. That same day it was verified that Rosecrans's horsemen had occupied the army's line of communications at University Place, twenty-some miles east of Decherd. The Federals, however, relinquished their hold when Forrest's cavalry rushed down from Tullahoma and chased them away.[1]

Bragg's penchant for wavering and second-guessing himself was never more on display than at this time. He reacted to the succession of dire news by announcing his intent to stay and fight at Tullahoma, a position he described as eminently defensible. When Polk criticized his decision and recommended a fallback to the mountains around Chattanooga, Bragg gave serious consideration to the bishop's advice. Then word reached him that the damage done at Decherd was not as extensive as first reported. The news prompted Hardee to oppose withdrawing from Tullahoma until the situation became clearer. In light of the new information, Polk amended his earlier suggestion but continued to advocate retreating below the Elk River.

Bragg adopted Hardee's view until new reports of threats to the army's right and rear came in, suggesting that few retreat routes were left open. On the afternoon of the thirtieth, Bragg ordered the abandonment of Tullahoma. Screened by Wheeler's cavalry, the perplexed army sloshed through muddy roads to the Elk; the crossing was not completed till July 1. As the rear guard pulled out of Tullahoma, Rosecrans's troops entered and took possession of the fortifications Bragg had deemed impregnable.

Bragg's habit of reversing himself did not end south of the Elk. As soon as he was over, he realized he must retreat farther, and quickly. The river had begun to fall; Rosecrans would soon be able to ford it at places that gave access to the army's flanks and rear. But the Union commander seemed to be moving less resolutely than before, and Bragg began to hope that he could hold his new position. On the afternoon of the second, however, he learned that at least a regiment of cavalry had not only crossed the river but had interposed between Wheeler's troopers and the army's left at Allisonia Bridge.

Earlier in the day, Bragg had ordered Polk and Hardee to fall back to the rail depot at Cowan. A few hours later, he changed his mind and ordered a halt at Decherd, but soon afterward he reinstated the plan to go to Cowan. The army reached that point, at the base of the Cumberland Mountains five miles east of Decherd and forty miles from Chattanooga, early on the afternoon of the third. By four p.m., however, Bragg was directing Polk and Hardee to cross the Tennessee River and move to Chattanooga.[2]

The corps commanders had expected their superior to halt and give battle at Cowan. The Chattanooga decision surprised and upset them, especially as Bragg had not consulted with them before announcing it. Only to Joseph Johnston did Bragg reveal the rationale—or his excuse— for evacuating the Elk River line:

"We were now back against the mountains, in a country affording us nothing, with a long line of railroad to protect, and half a dozen passes on the right and left by which our rear could be gained. In this position it was perfectly practicable for the enemy to destroy our means of crossing the Tennessee, and thus secure our ultimate destruction without a battle. Having failed to bring him to that issue, so much desired by myself and [my] troops, I reluctantly yielded to the necessity imposed by my position and inferior strength, and put the army in motion for the Tennessee River."[3]

The decision to abandon Middle Tennessee, especially as it had not been forced on the army by a major defeat, did not find favor with the rank and file. A sergeant in the 18th Tennessee Cavalry Battalion complained in a letter to his wife that "if it had not been for Bragg's incompetency we would have held possession of all of Ky. & Tenn. We have been thoroughly blessed with incompetents in this Western Dept." Some soldiers blamed the retreat not on Bragg's incapacity but on the strength and ability of his opponent. An 8th Texas trooper informed his father that "Old Rosy is too many for us. We expected to fight him at Tullahoma but he flanked us in spite of the mountains. . . . Now just glance at your map and see what an ample and delicious slice of Tenn we have given up."[4]

The cavalry's anger and frustration was largely due to the special hardships and privations it had endured while covering the army's confused, disjointed withdrawal. Daily, almost hourly, contact with the enemy in their rear had left the horsemen on the cusp of exhaustion. A weary Texan observed that "no one unacquainted with service can properly estimate the task of the Cavalry on a retreat. . . . [T]hey are constantly in sight of the advancing foe, fighting him at every favorable position, hurrying up the jaded Infantry, obstructing the roads, and often standing under severe fires of his Artillery, or resisting the charges of his Cavalry."[5]

From Tullahoma to Chattanooga, rest and comfort were not to be found. As the Texan explained, "we were in the saddle, and wet to the skin, by the rain—fighting the enemy several times each day." A Tennessean noted that by the time it reached Chattanooga "our Company was nearly broke down. We have slept 4 hours in 5 days and nights." And yet few soldiers, even in the cavalry, considered themselves too tired or demoralized. A member of the 51st Alabama, Martin's division, admitted that "the situation of affairs" looked bleak at present, "but I think it will wear off & they [his comrades] will fight more desperately than they have done. We have a great deal to discourage us but I feel like we will come out all right."[6]

While the army settled into its mountain enclave, the cavalry took position to prevent Rosecrans—who no one believed was through pressing Bragg—from evicting the army from its home state. Wheeler, with the men of Martin and Wharton, protected the left flank by throwing out patrols toward Tullahoma. The cavalry picketed an area that stretched as far as Decatur, Alabama. Wheeler's headquarters were even farther south, at Gadsden on the Coosa River. By early August, Bragg had ordered him to send Martin's division to Rome, Georgia, to guard the upper section of the railroad Colonel Streight had attempted to cut. Aware that the Western & Atlantic was his last lifeline, Bragg had Wheeler's men copy the enemy's practice of constructing blockhouses to protect bridges and depots. They also stockpiled building materials at various points in case raiders got through, making repairs necessary.[7]

Meanwhile, Forrest's command—which, after Streight's raid, had added Roddey's brigade and would soon assimilate John Pegram's division—took position along the right flank in the vicinity of Kingston, forty-five miles southwest of Knoxville. The latter city continued to host the headquarters of Buckner's Department of East Tennessee. While Bragg kept an eye on Rosecrans, Buckner was monitoring Burnside's advance from Kentucky. In a move to consolidate manpower, on August 6, Buckner's department, including Pegram's horsemen, came under Bragg's command.[8]

Bragg had ample time to strengthen his far-flung defenses and expand and reorganize his army. Upon occupying Tullahoma, Rosecrans decided he had done enough marching, maneuvering, and feinting, at least for some time. In fact, six weeks would pass before he put his army in motion toward the Tennessee.

For at least one of Bragg's subordinates, the sudden transition from active—and, at times, frenetic—service to static operations was not entirely welcome. Soon after assuming his post, Forrest, who became quickly bored when not off on some independent operation, and who still resented having to associate with Wheeler, submitted to army headquarters a proposal to create and head a command "on the Mississippi from Vicksburg to Cairo, or in other words, all the forces I may collect together and organize . . . in North Mississippi, West Tennessee, and those that may join me from Arkansas, Missouri, and Southern Kentucky." His mission would be to harass and obstruct shipping on the Mississippi and raid Union enclaves along the river's eastern bank.[9]

Bragg forwarded the idea to the Adjutant and Inspector General's Office in Richmond, but he refused to endorse it. Although he knew "of no officer to whom I would sooner assign the duty proposed . . . it would deprive the army of one of its greatest elements of strength to remove General Forrest." In these words, Bragg revealed that he finally had come to appreciate Forrest's abilities as a commander of regular cavalry, not merely as a partisan leader. But when Jefferson Davis tabled the proposal, Forrest assumed that Bragg had thwarted his ambitions. He chalked it up to the army commander's dislike and disapproval, which Bragg had displayed at least twice before: when subordinating him to the less able Wheeler, and when banishing him to Kirby Smith's department after promising him command of all the horsemen in the Army of Tennessee.[10]

While Forrest fumed, Wheeler chafed at having to supervise the extended and porous defensive line that had been assigned to him. When he failed to perform that difficult mission to Bragg's entire satisfaction, Wheeler drew what he considered unmerited criticism. On July 17, Bragg pointed out inaccuracies in Wheeler's recent report of the strength and organization of his corps. Of this offense, Wheeler was undoubtedly guilty, for record-keeping was never one of his strengths. In his defense, his command was subject to near-constant manpower fluctuations. These were inevitable given the frequent shifting about of units from one brigade to another and the increasing number of desertions afflicting the command (as well as the entire army) in the wake of Bragg's recent retreats. Still, it appears Wheeler did not make a concerted attempt to correct the problem, for soon afterward Bragg faulted him for the same offense, this time in harsher language.[11]

On July 30, Wheeler was called on the carpet for unspecified offenses committed by one of his units near Cherokee Station on the railroad west of Decatur. One of Bragg's inspectors claimed the troopers were "doing some harm," probably pillaging local farmers. Early in August, the same inspector (who may have had it in for Wheeler) was on his case again for maintaining a picket line so loose that the officer had ridden from Lookout Mountain into Chattanooga without being challenged by a single vedette.[12]

A few weeks later, Bragg had more on his mind than disciplining his cavalry chief. On August 16, Rosecrans moved out of Tullahoma, intent on shooing his adversary from Tennessee. At approximately the same time, Burnside began advancing from the Cumberland River toward Knoxville. The dual line of operations threatened to dislodge every Rebel west of the

Alleghenies. When word of the advances reached Richmond, even Jefferson Davis and his advisers—who, until the fall of Vicksburg, had pursued a policy of benign neglect toward the western armies—paid heed.

By any standard, Rosecrans posed the greater threat. Having decided against a frontal assault on Chattanooga, he chose an indirect approach through northern Alabama. By the twentieth he had reached Stevenson and Bridgeport, and was turning north toward Bragg's western flank. The next day, Union artillery began to shell Chattanooga's outer works. On September 4, the Army of the Cumberland was across the Tennessee River and speeding like a freight train toward its enemy's rear. Bragg, who had never moved that fast in his life, was aghast.

Rosecrans's route of advance surprised Bragg, who had been misled by his infantry and cavalry scouts into believing that his opponent was approaching from the northeast rather than the southwest. Wheeler was primarily responsible for his commander's ignorance. Ordered to cover the army's left flank west of Chattanooga, he had chosen to do so with a few hundred troopers, not enough to observe all of the Tennessee River crossings. When additional units reached him from Rome, Georgia, and other points in the last days of August, Wheeler failed to place them in the most advantageous positions. As Thomas Connelly observes, "in effect, Bragg had no reconnaissance on the river west of Chattanooga, and no troops guarded the Sand and Lookout Mountain passes at the army's rear. Not until September 2 did Wheeler begin to get his troopers under control.... Even then, the Stevenson-Trenton front [where part of Rosecrans's army crossed the river] was almost overlooked."[13]

From September 2 to 6, Bragg dithered and temporized, uncertain how to counter his enemy's movements. He called councils of war that decided nothing, formulated plans and canceled them before they could be put into operation, and tried unsuccessfully to reconcile conflicting scouting reports. Throughout this period he was served poorly by Wheeler, who in the face of the enemy's advance showed himself to be neither proactive nor reactive. The cavalry leader failed to take the initiative by blocking the Sand Mountain passes into Will's and Lookout Valleys, which Rosecrans could be expected to use. And when Bragg finally ordered him to do so on the fifth, Wheeler refused, declaring that he could learn as much in his present position atop Lookout Mountain as he could in the valley below. Wheeler also pleaded that his horses were worn down and that the Federal pickets in the valleys were too numerous to engage successfully.

Although presumably upset by Wheeler's disobedience, Bragg did not censure him. His cavalry leader's unprofessionalism was a major factor in Bragg's belated decision to evacuate his latest sanctuary. Beginning on September 6, Wheeler and Forrest took on the age-old mission of covering a general retrograde as their infantry and artillery comrades slowly and sullenly headed for the Georgia line. Bragg's hope was that somewhere around La Fayette and Chickamauga Creek, almost thirty miles south of Chattanooga, he would find ground that was not only defensible but conducive to attacking Rosecrans as he debouched from the mountains.

News of Bragg's plight prompted Jefferson Davis to order an unprecedented transfer of forces from Virginia to Georgia. On September 9, two divisions of the 1st Corps, Army of Northern Virginia, under "Lee's Old War Horse," Lieutenant General James Longstreet, climbed aboard cars on the Orange & Alexandria Railroad. Thus began a 550-mile journey whose purpose was to bolster Bragg sufficiently to enable him to turn about, face his enemy on close-to-equal terms, and assume the offensive for the first time since the Perryville campaign. The successful completion of the roundabout, much-interrupted, bone-jarring journey was a shining example of the rapid concentration of force Davis had envisioned when creating the Department of the West.[14]

When he started after Bragg on September 9, Rosecrans had no inkling that Longstreet was a week away from opposing him, or that Buckner had already joined Bragg (Buckner had evacuated Knoxville shortly before Burnside occupied the city on September 2). Also unknown to Rosecrans, Davis had prevailed on Johnston to send Bragg nine thousand reinforcements from Mississippi. Two months ago, on the heels of its retreat from Tullahoma, the Army of Tennessee had been reduced to fewer than thirty thousand infantry; it was now larger by a third and would soon approach seventy thousand troops of all arms.[15]

Believing Bragg to be in headlong flight toward Atlanta, Rosecrans advanced disjointedly and carelessly along a forty-mile front. The rugged terrain and the widely spaced gaps in the Lookout Mountain range precluded the possibility of quick support among Rosecrans's three wings— Crittenden's, moving from now-occupied Chattanooga; Thomas's, twenty-five miles south of the city, marching via Steven's and Cooper's Gaps; and Alexander McCook's, twenty miles farther on, pushing though Winston's Gap. The ever-lengthening advance gave Rosecrans's opponent opportunities to land sudden and perhaps crippling blows. Bragg made several attempts to do so but came up empty each time.

Bragg's failure was partly due to inadequate supervision over the subordinates he selected to waylay the enemy, and partly to a lack of real-time intelligence of Rosecrans's movements, for which Wheeler's command must be held accountable. Bragg's ignorance of Rosecrans's position, combined with the wretched condition of the roads around McLemore's Cove, prevented him from striking the isolated division of General Negley, part of Thomas's wing, on September 10. The following day, thanks to a lack of coordination between two of his division commanders, Bragg failed to surprise the same force at Dug Gap in Pigeon Mountain. On the twelfth and thirteenth, Bragg directed Leonidas Polk to attack Crittenden's wing at Lee and Gordon's Mill on Chickamauga Creek. Although armed with accurate intelligence, and with his right flank well-guarded by Wheeler's main body, Polk ignored his orders and assumed a defensive position, even after Buckner's corps was ordered to support his assault.

Bragg was frustrated beyond measure by Polk's disobedience. He was not entirely satisfied with the intelligence-gathering and combat support he had received from Wheeler and Forrest on the retreat from Chattanooga. Nor was he comfortable with the newly appointed commanders of two of his infantry corps, the astute but prickly Lieutenant General Daniel Harvey Hill (a replacement for Hardee, who in mid-July had been transferred to a command in Mississippi) and Major General William H. T. Walker, who had yet to prove himself more than a competent division leader. Thus, after the failures to ambush Rosecrans and defeat him in detail (i.e., one component after another), Bragg was content to await Longstreet's arrival.[16]

On September 17, the vanguard of Longstreet's force—the infantry of Major Generals John Bell Hood and Lafayette McLaws, a battalion of light artillery, and a small contingent of horsemen—reported to Bragg's headquarters at La Fayette. Bragg divided his enlarged command into two wings. Polk, who though a thorn in Bragg's side was also his senior subordinate, was given charge of the larger force: Frank Cheatham's division of his own corps, plus the corps of Hill and Walker. Longstreet's wing comprised not only Hood's and McLaws's divisions, but also Buckner's corps and Thomas Hindman's division of Polk's corps.[17]

At last realizing that his enemy was neither in distress nor in retreat, Rosecrans tried to group his scattered forces inside McLemore's Cove. By the sixteenth, he had his army fairly well in hand; its eleven-mile line extended from Lee and Gordon's Mill to Steven's Gap. The Army of

Tennessee, not yet fully reinforced by Longstreet (the remainder of his command would not reach Bragg until the evening of the nineteenth), held the gaps in Pigeon Mountain and the fords that gave access to Lee and Gordon's Mill. As D. H. Hill later observed, each army was in position to turn the other's left, but the maneuver entailed risks. Bragg would have to cross the creek north of Lee and Gordon's Mill, forcing him to fight with a body of water at his back. Rosecrans could outflank Bragg by crossing at the mill, or at the fords between there and Catlett's Gap, eight miles to the south. The risk to Rosecrans was an insecure line of retreat should his attack fail, preventing him from falling back to Chattanooga.[18]

On the eighteenth, Bragg took the initiative by sending Walker's small corps and one of Longstreet's divisions across the creek along two bridges opposite Rosecrans's left flank, the position held by Crittenden. The movement, supported by Forrest's cavalry, failed due to the stubborn resistance of Union infantry, Wilder's mounted riflemen, and the cavalry of Colonel Robert H. G. Minty. When the advance was halted, Polk, who was to have attacked frontally if the Union flank was turned, withheld his movement, and Bragg's strategy was defeated.

During the night, Rosecrans moved his army two miles closer to its base at Chattanooga, so that his left flank was in position to curve around Bragg's right, the position defended primarily by Forrest. When a reconnaissance by one of Thomas's infantry divisions provoked a renewal of fighting early on the nineteenth, Forrest's corps became immediately involved. Advancing with Pegram's division in front, Forrest suddenly discovered the extent of Rosecrans's northward shift. Instead of encountering Minty's horsemen, Pegram collided with a large body of infantry that had not been there the previous day.[19]

While couriers rushed to the rear to bring up supports, Pegram's men dismounted to execute the delaying tactics Joe Wheeler had taught them during the Murfreesboro campaign. Though hard-pressed, Forrest avoided damage when two of Walker's brigades came to his aid, extending the flank and temporarily stabilizing the situation in that quarter. Eventually, an influx of Union foot soldiers compelled Forrest and his supports to fall back to their positions of the morning. When the enemy pressed this line, Forrest was sent again to the front, this time accompanied by the dismounted troopers of Colonel Dibrell and a horse artillery battery whose "constant and destructive fire" held the Yankees at bay.[20]

Soon after it began on Forrest's front, the fighting shifted toward the center and southern flanks of both armies. East of Chickamauga Creek, it involved almost the entire length of Bragg's line, including the vanguard of Longstreet's wing, Hood's division. While Hood drove back the enemy facing him, Alexander P. Stewart's division launched an attack that momentarily pierced the Union line and gained possession of the road through Dug Gap to La Fayette. Bragg, however, lost a chance to establish a more permanent lodgment when he failed to coordinate attacks through a two-mile gap that had opened between Crittenden and Thomas.[21]

While Forrest saw extensive action throughout the nineteenth, Wheeler, on the other end of the line, was only peripherally involved. Strung out to cover the far left, most of his troopers were stationed well to the south of the nearest infantry, Hill's corps. Wheeler spent most of the day sparring with the cavalry covering Rosecrans's right, the division of Brigadier General George Crook. At one point in the action, Wheeler led some of his men across Chickamauga Creek at Owen's Ford and engaged not only Crook but other opponents as well. In his rather vague report of the day's operations, he claimed to have "warmly assailed" a body of Negley's infantry that loomed up in his path, "dividing the column and driving the enemy in confusion in both directions." In his own report, Negley made no mention of being forced into a retreat, confused or otherwise.[22]

The drawn battle resumed at about nine-thirty a.m. on Sunday, September 20, with an assault against Rosecrans's north flank. Bragg had desired the attack to begin at dawn, with the offensive gradually sweeping south, permitting him to interpose between the Army of the Cumberland and Chattanooga. But he had failed to communicate his plans to his subordinates, the result being a decidedly late start. This mistake and other miscues in Polk's sector threatened to stall and perhaps curtail the offensive.

Forrest, who had been ordered to attack at sunrise in cooperation with Polk, seethed at the delay but could do nothing about it. When the drive finally got under way, he did his utmost to prevent the reserve command of Major General Gordon Granger from advancing to the support of Thomas's corps on the Union left. Forrest's troopers fought so stoutly, mostly dismounted, that General Hill, who observed their activities throughout the day, congratulated the Tennessean on the "magnificent behavior" of his men, whom he likened to veteran infantry.[23]

When it finally ignited, the fighting along the Union left raged fiercely but without decisive result. The situation changed markedly when, shortly before noon, Longstreet, whose entire force was now on the field, went into action. Plagued by a miscommunication problem of his own, Rosecrans made an egregious blunder just as Longstreet's wing swept forward. He ordered one of Crittenden's divisions, which he believed was in reserve in the rear, to plug a hole in Thomas's front farther north. Rosecrans had forgotten that the division had already moved into position on the right-center of the main line. When it pulled out to comply with his order, it created a gap instead of filling one.[24]

By sheer happenstance, the attackers poured through the hole minutes after it opened. Reaching the rear of Rosecrans's line, some of Longstreet's troops turned north, others south, creating panic and disorder among defenders who found themselves under fire simultaneously from front and rear. Eventually the center and right of Rosecrans's line began to roll up like a blue carpet stained with red. Only Thomas's corps, with the critical support of Granger, held its position, enabling the rest of the army to flee north toward Rossville and winning for Thomas the appellation "Rock of Chickamauga."[25]

Wheeler's cavalry, which had returned to the south side of the creek, had seen more or less heavy action throughout the twentieth. Hoping to establish closer contact with Bragg's main line, Wheeler had moved Martin's and Wharton's divisions a mile and a half upriver to Glass's Mill. In that area they engaged the cavalry division of Brigadier General Edward Moody McCook (cousin of Alexander McCook), which Wheeler's scouts had observed moving toward the battlefield from the southwest. The encounter was mostly a horse artillery duel, but when the enemy pulled back, Wheeler mounted his men and again crossed the creek. On the far side he opposed the enemy with carbines and pistols, "hoping that we might draw troops from this sector and thus create a diversion" for the rest of the army.[26]

This proved unnecessary, for as soon as the effects of Longstreet's offensive were felt, McCook's men drew off preparatory to retreating. Wheeler pursued as far as Crawfish Springs, taking forty prisoners. Returning to the creek once again, he remained near Lee and Gordon's Mill, looking for new opponents, until it became clear that the enemy had left the area.

When Wheeler started north once again, companies and battalions of stragglers fell into his hands. By day's end, he claimed to have gobbled up almost one thousand Yankees, along with twenty supply wagons "and a large amount of arms and ordnance stores." Before nightfall, with Rosecrans in abject flight toward Chattanooga, Wheeler overtook several field hospitals, whose inmates included hundreds of wounded men and one hundred surgeons. While the general took possession of casualties, medical supplies, and wagons, his troopers continued to follow the demoralized enemy. John Allan Wyeth, now a member of the 51st Alabama Partisan Rangers, found "the dead Federals scattered everywhere, in some places very thick. I counted seven who had fallen in one pile, and I recall but one that had not been stripped of all outer clothing."[27]

At long last having won a battle (thanks to Robert E. Lee's help), Bragg mounted a pursuit so slow and cautious as to ensure his inability to reap the fruits of victory. Electing not to cross the Tennessee River into the rear of his beaten foe, he headed for Chattanooga as though convinced he could beat Rosecrans there. He had his reasons for moving at a deliberate pace: his army had suffered eighteen thousand casualties in the two days of fighting—two thousand more than it had inflicted on its opponent—and it was seriously low on rations and forage. Yet Bragg's apparent sloth rankled many of his generals, especially Longstreet and Forrest. Even the chronically lethargic General Polk begged his commander to complete his victory by overtaking the fugitives and scattering them to the winds.[28]

The cavalry should have been at the forefront of the pursuit, but Bragg confined it to the littered battlefield throughout the twenty-first. Wheeler's men secured the area, established outposts, collected abandoned arms and equipment, and rounded up stragglers. Longstreet, who chafed at the army's inertia, ordered Wheeler to locate Rosecrans's rear echelon and report its whereabouts to him. Anxious to obey both superiors but believing that Bragg's order carried greater weight, Wheeler assigned only five hundred men to the pursuit mission. When his scouts reported the enemy fleeing wildly through McLemore's Cove, however, he assembled one thousand seven hundred men and started for Lookout Mountain. En route he encountered a few coherent bodies of infantry and cavalry, which he claimed to drive "in confusion" toward Chattanooga. By day's end, he reported collecting four hundred prisoners, several stands of colors, and almost one hundred wagons "loaded with valuable baggage."[29]

Conflicting orders had Wheeler moving hither and yon over the next few days. On the morning of the twenty-second, he was ordered to march toward Chattanooga, Rosecrans's only refuge, and "press the enemy hotly and vigorously as long as he remains this side of the river." Later that day he was instructed to cross the Tennessee and cooperate with Forrest in feeling out the enemy, but before he could obey, he was sent instead to the summit of the nearest stretch of Lookout Mountain to capture pickets and skirmishers Rosecrans had stationed there. Upon ascending the mountain,

Wheeler encountered Federals holding a hastily built line of works; he attacked them on three sides and sent them into retreat. Wheeler was elated by this success. His famished troopers were made even happier by the cooked supper the Yankees left behind when rushing off.[30]

The men were still eating when a courier from Bragg appeared with an order for Wheeler to turn over his position to a just-arrived infantry unit. Now he was to report with his entire command to Chickamauga Station on the railroad east of Chattanooga. He obeyed with alacrity.

Upon arriving, he learned that Bragg wanted him to cross Walden's Ridge into the same country he had visited thirteen months earlier at the commencement of the Perryville campaign. This time Wheeler was to search the Sequatchie Valley for wagons reportedly shipping critical supplies to Rosecrans's army from the railhead at Stevenson, Alabama. Having decided against halting his enemy short of Chattanooga, and wary of attacking the city's defenses, Bragg was already moving to besiege it. The siege lines he was erecting eventually would stretch for six miles, from the foot of Lookout Mountain east across Chattanooga Valley to long, rugged Missionary Ridge and from there north to Tunnel Hill, near the confluence of Chickamauga Creek and the Tennessee River. No supplies could reach Rosecrans's false sanctuary from those directions. If Wheeler could choke off the wagon route through the Sequatchie, the Army of the Cumberland must either surrender or starve.

To ensure the success of the undertaking, Bragg desired that it be conducted not only by Wheeler but also by Forrest, with Fightin' Joe in overall command. Bragg's decision provoked an unexpectedly heated response from Forrest, who, ever since the enemy abandoned the field of Chickamauga, had been urging the army leader to accelerate the pursuit, overtake the disorganized Federals short of Chattanooga, and finish them off. Forrest, accompanied by about four hundred of his hardiest riders, had followed the fugitives to the crest of Missionary Ridge, overlooking the city. From an observation platform high in a tree, Forrest saw the Yankees racing north in groups large and small—a demoralized, panic-stricken mass on the verge of complete dissolution. But he saw no pursuers straining to cut them off.

When he caught up with Bragg, Forrest begged him to attack before Rosecrans got away, but to no effect. His superior's obtuseness exasperated Forrest, who growled to his subordinates: "What does he fight battles for?" Over the months, Bragg had supplied Forrest with grounds for many grievances, the most recent being his role in denying the cavalryman's request for an independent command. Now more than ever, Forrest wanted to break free of the man's authority and fight the invaders of his region in his own way, with his own command.[31]

He gained an opportunity to do so more quickly than he could have expected. On September 28, while Forrest, at Bragg's direction, was monitoring enemy movements south of Burnside's new headquarters at Knoxville, he was ordered "without delay [to] turn over the troops of your command . . . to Major-General Wheeler." The order infuriated Forrest, who believed Bragg had abrogated the long-standing agreement sparing him from serving under Wheeler. Moreover, his troopers and their horses were used up from days of almost constant riding and fighting. Wheeler confirmed their condition when he rendezvoused on the thirtieth with Forrest's troops at Cotton Port, a Tennessee River landing forty-five miles upstream from Chattanooga. Examining the three brigades that had been placed at his disposal, Wheeler described them as "mere skeletons, scarcely averaging 500 effective men each." They were "badly armed, had but a small supply of ammunition, and their horses were in horrible condition, having been marched continuously for three days and nights without removing saddles. The men were worn out, and without rations."[32]

Forrest vented his anger by firing off a heated protest to army headquarters. Later he claimed that "Bragg never got such a letter as that before from a brigadier." Apparently the recipient took no offense, for when Forrest arranged a meeting, he downplayed the order and assured the cavalryman that his units would be returned to him as soon as Wheeler's expedition ended. But the issue had not been resolved. Soon afterward, Forrest left the army on a furlough—his first in over a year—to join his wife in Georgia. While there he received another communiqué from Bragg, officially and explicitly placing him under Wheeler's authority.[33]

Forrest, blood in his eye, hurried back to the army, barged into Bragg's tent, and launched into a tirade, one faithfully recorded by his chief surgeon. In a voice smoldering with rage, he accused Bragg of many sins of omission and commission, especially "your cowardly and contemptible persecution of me," which he dated from Shiloh. He made pungent mention of those occasions on which Bragg had driven him from the field, forcing him to recruit, organize, and equip new commands. Bragg had done this "in a spirit of revenge and spite, because I would not fawn upon you as others did. . . . You did it to ruin me and my career."[34]

After citing other examples of reprehensible behavior, Forrest added, "I have stood your meanness as long as I intend to. You have played the part of a damned scoundrel, and are a coward, and if you were any part of a man I would slap your jaws and force you to resent it. . . . You have threatened to arrest me for not obeying your orders promptly. I dare you to do it, and I say to you that if you ever again try to interfere with me or cross my path it will be at the peril of your life."[35]

Having unburdened himself, Forrest turned and stormed out of the tent, leaving in his wake a stricken, dumbfounded Bragg. The army leader professed to have had no inkling of his subordinate's resentment and discontent, and was at a loss to understand what had provoked him to such a display. Forrest's surgeon feared the consequences of his commander's outburst, but, as Forrest subsequently predicted, Bragg never made mention of the incident, nor did he take action against his accuser. Bragg fulfilled another of his subordinate's postconfrontation predictions when, soon afterward, he withdrew his objection to Forrest's transfer to an independent command in northern Mississippi and West Tennessee. He did so not because he was, as Forrest charged, a coward, but because, having come to an appreciation of Forrest's value, he believed the Confederacy could not dispense with his services.[36]

When, in early October, Jefferson Davis made a second visit to the Army of Tennessee, he met privately with Forrest, who had threatened publicly to resign his commission rather than serve longer under Bragg. After listening patiently to the man's grievances, Davis adopted Bragg's view of the situation. He refused to accept Forrest's resignation; instead, he approved his request to go to Mississippi, accompanied by three hundred handpicked men and a battery of rifled guns. Once there Forrest, for the third time in the war, would organize and staff a new command. He would not return to the Army of Tennessee for more than a year, and then only because Braxton Bragg no longer commanded it.[37]

BELIEVING HE COULD EXPECT MINIMAL SUPPORT from the bedraggled troopers Forrest had sent him, and keenly aware that his own command was exhausted from recent campaigning, Wheeler, along with some of his subordinates, including General Wharton, protested the mission Bragg had assigned them. But their superior was adamant; and so, on the last day of

September, Wheeler prepared to depart Cotton Port for the Sequatchie Valley.

Having left a single brigade to guard the flanks of the siege lines, Wheeler would be accompanied by the troopers of Wharton and Martin, in addition to Forrest's skeletonized command, which he had formed into a third division. The latter should have been commanded by Forrest's senior subordinate, but Frank Armstrong, perhaps taking a cue from his disgruntled superior, begged off on the mission. In his absence, command fell to Brigadier General Henry B. Davidson, a Mexican War veteran and former dragoon from Tennessee who had seen little field service since being captured as a member of the garrison of Island Number 10, seventeen months earlier.[38]

Because Rosecrans's cavalry was believed to be patrolling the west bank of the Tennessee, Wheeler's expeditionary force—some four thousand troopers and six pieces of horse artillery—forded the river after darkness fell. Years later, one of his enlisted men, whose regiment rode at the point of the column, recalled the crossing as a scene of "beauty and picturesqueness. . . . We descended the banks and dropped into the river, and then the line swung down the stream across the silvery surface of the broad waters, like the windings of a huge dark serpent. . . . No creation of art could have been more imposing."[39]

Once across, Wheeler's advance chased off the pickets who had failed to secure the west bank. As the raiding leader must have suspected they would, the displaced sentinels spread word of his coming. The report reached the local division commander, General Crook, then passed up the chain of command to the headquarters of Rosecrans's acting cavalry commander, Brigadier General Robert B. Mitchell. Soon both generals were organizing pursuit parties. Mitchell assumed supervision of the effort as well as direct command of one of its components, the division of Edward McCook. The plan adopted called for Crook to forge ahead, locate Wheeler, and prevent him from striking his obvious target, the supply line on which the continued existence of the Army of the Cumberland depended. McCook would follow Crook, supporting him however Mitchell thought best.[40]

Temporarily relieved of the enemy's presence, Wheeler spent most of October 1 sorting out his mixed force, reprovisioning Forrest's people, and acquainting himself with Davidson and his subordinates. That evening, cloaked again in darkness, Wheeler led his column up the steep, rocky

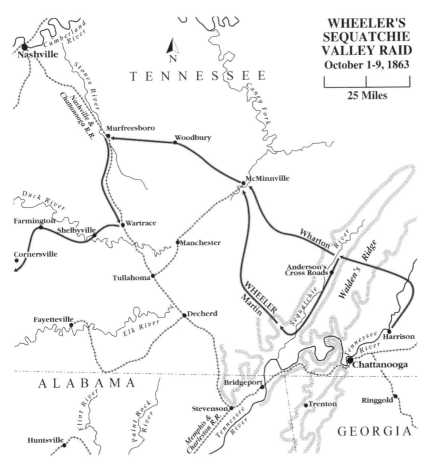

Wheeler's Sequatchie Valley Raid, October 1–9, 1863.

incline of Walden's Ridge. The climb was difficult enough in good weather; when a drenching rain came down, progress became so sluggish that the rear guard did not reach the summit, one thousand five hundred feet above the valley floor, until late the next day.

Before bedding down on the evening of the first, Wheeler called a campfire meeting at which he briefed his subordinates on his plans. He had decided to divide his force to strike two targets of high value: not only a Union supply column that his scouts had located six miles inside the Sequatchie Valley, but also the reserve supply base Rosecrans had established at McMinnville, once a key point on the Army of Tennessee's defensive line. Wheeler proposed to lead the column targeting the supply train, to consist of Martin's division and some of Forrest's regiments. Soon after this force moved out, Wharton would lead his own division plus the bulk of the men Forrest had contributed against McMinnville.

Generals Martin and Davidson raised no objection to the plan, but Wharton argued vehemently against it. He believed that to split the force in the face of unknown opposition entailed too many risks. Wheeler downplayed his subordinate's concerns and overrode his objections. Apparently he did so in a manner that gave offense, for thereafter his relations with Wharton, never as firm as Wheeler would have liked, became shakier still.[41]

The next day, at least, they worked successfully in tandem. Before dawn, Wheeler and Martin carefully descended the south side of the ridge, heading for Anderson's Cross Roads, near where the isolated supply column had been observed. Some hours later, Wharton dropped down the west slope, struck the bottom of the valley, and curved north. The rain having ceased and no enemy troops in sight, both columns enjoyed unobstructed access to their objectives.

Wheeler was the first to strike. Late in the morning, the head of Martin's division overtook thirty-two supply wagons, each pulled by six mules, the first section of a truly immense train that had been wending its way in stop-and-start fashion across the hard, rocky floor of the Sequatchie. Martin detached a force no larger than needed to halt the vehicles. With his main body he accompanied Wheeler on the road to Anderson's Cross Roads. Moving at a brisk pace, within minutes they came upon what a trooper of the 4th Tennessee called "the richest scene that the eye of a cavalryman can behold. Along the side of mountain hundreds of large Federal wagons were standing, with their big white covers on them, like so many African elephants, solemn in their stately grandeur."[42]

They were standing so grandly because their teamsters, alerted by the dust clouds raised by Wheeler's horses, had abandoned their posts. Yet the wagons were not defenseless, as the raiders learned when the staccato of rifle fire began to echo along the walls of the valley. As soon as he located the train's escort—several hundred infantrymen—Wheeler deployed part of Martin's command on foot and had the brigade of Colonel John Tyler Morgan charge mounted. The attack, hastily delivered, was repulsed, but a second hit home, scattering a large portion of the guard and securing most of the wagons. Those Yankees who fled rather than surrender were pursued furiously. An Alabama trooper remarked that "we dismounted and drove them up the mountain, fighting from one rock to another, until the enemy disappeared in the heights above."[43]

The sought-after prize firmly in their grasp, Wheeler's men ranged along the length of the train, shooting and sabering the teams to stop those wagons whose drivers had not fled the scene. When every vehicle had been halted, the raiders emptied them of everything edible or usable and set most of them on fire. Wheeler's officers had instructed the men to appropriate only military goods, but dozens of troopers took not only what they needed but whatever struck their fancy, including personal belongings removed from baggage wagons.

One who helped himself was John Wyeth. The teenage Alabamian, who considered himself poorly dressed even by "ragged Rebel" standards, was sifting through some articles of clothing when Wheeler rode up and shouted for him to "get out of that wagon!" The youngster did so quickly. At Wheeler's order, he mounted and accompanied his commander along the length of the column, as if under guard. Wheeler lectured him on the evils of looting in the manner of a stern father, then bade him go to sin no more.[44]

Wheeler then returned to the task of denying the Chattanooga garrison the goods it so desperately needed. The process consumed eight hours; when it ended, nearly one thousand wagons had been disabled or burned, and upwards of four thousand horses and mules lay dead or dying in their traces. A few dozen conveyances, filled with weapons, ammunition, and equipage of great value but too heavy to be unloaded, were added to Wheeler's own supply train and accompanied it on the balance of the raid.

Wheeler had met relatively light opposition at Anderson's Cross Roads, but at McMinnville, John Wharton encountered none at all. This should not have been the case, for the supply depot's six-hundred-man garrison was sizable enough to have put up a good fight. But when Wharton moved to surround the place and called for its surrender, its commander, Major Michael Patterson, lost his nerve. A female diarist from neighboring Beersheba Springs learned what happened from a resident of the town: "A federal officer assured him they would fight—but . . . in about two minutes the Yanks marched out and stacked their arms, and the surrender was complete. The rebels made a clean sweep of everything."[45]

After disarming the garrison, Wharton's troopers went to work with a will. They set fire to every storehouse the Yankees had erected, but only after emptying it of anything worth confiscating, much of which they shared with local secessionists. The lady diarist recorded that Wharton "threw all open and told the citizens to come in and help themselves. Every body rushed of course and after they were satisfied the soldiers burned stores all night. The dry goods houses went up in a twinkling—the soldiers throwing bonnets, dresses, shoes—everything to the girls as they dashed about the streets. Said streets were strewed with corn, crackers, sugar, spools of thread etc. etc." Major Burford of Wheeler's staff, who rode with Wharton's column, exclaimed that "we had the grandest bonfire in the square I ever saw."[46]

When they tired of their frolic, Wharton's troopers plundered their captives of every article deemed to have value, however slight. Major Patterson (son-in-law of Tennessee Provisional Governor Andrew Johnson) complained that the Rebels relieved his men of boots, hats, overcoats, and, in some cases, breeches, as well as "watch[es], pocket-book[s], money, and even finger-rings, or, in fact, anything that happened to please their fancy." Major Burford confirmed that at least one Union officer was forced to hand over a diamond ring. Wharton's men even found time to target a few military objectives, including a railroad bridge outside the town, which they toppled, and a locomotive on the depot siding, which they burned to its metal trucks.[47]

Early on October 4, Wheeler and Martin crossed the mountains to join Wharton at McMinnville. After putting the final torch to Patterson's depot, the reunited force moved northwest toward Murfreesboro, crossed Stones River, and captured a fifty-man outpost at a bridge on the Nashville & Chattanooga. Fatigue parties left the column to destroy three miles of track below the bridge. The demolition continued well into the fifth, every trestle between Murfreesboro and Wartrace falling victim to raiders wielding axes and sulfur matches.[48]

On the sixth, the westward-heading column passed Shelbyville, scene of Wheeler's death-defying plunge into a raging river. That night the weary but exhilarated command made bivouac around the Duck River village of Farmington, roughly halfway between Shelbyville and Columbia. Here it would meet retribution at the hands of a couple thousand cavalry, mounted infantry, and horse artillery led by George Crook.

Having followed the raiders for several days, originally at considerable distance, the hard-riding bluecoats had steadily gained on their quarry. General Mitchell had sent McCook's division to scour the Unionville area, almost fifteen miles above Farmington, in case Wheeler tried to escape in that direction. Crook's troopers and horse artillerymen had moved directly toward Farmington, keeping pressure on the raiders. Wheeler was aware they were right behind him—they had sparred continually with his rear guard—but he could do little to improve his situation. His horses were debilitated from hard marching, while his pursuers appeared to be riding fresh mounts. A collision was imminent and unavoidable.[49]

Despite his precarious position, Wheeler had posted his units in a manner that invited defeat in detail. He placed Davidson's men near Warner's Bridge, at least two miles upstream from Martin's and Wharton's bivouacs and thus beyond the possibility of quick support. The vulnerable division became Crook's target early on October 7, when his horsemen attacked under cover of an artillery barrage that turned Davidson's camp into a scene of death, destruction, and chaos. Caught with their captured pants down, the sleep-befogged raiders began to race about "wild and frantic with panic," as one officer recorded.[50]

Wheeler tried to shore up Davidson's position, but the division broke apart before Martin and Wharton could lend assistance. The Confederates' rifles and shotguns proved no match for the breech loaders of Crook's cavalry and the repeating rifles of his mounted infantry. Meanwhile, the accurate shelling of his artillery quickly put Davidson's guns out of action. Giving up hope of resistance, the raiders leapt into their saddles and galloped toward Farmington, shouting Yankees at their heels. One of Davidson's colonels described the running fight as "five hours and a half, over seven miles of country," during which "my gallant brigade was cut to pieces and slaughtered."[51]

As soon as he learned of Davidson's rout, Wheeler ordered Wharton, with the column's supply train, to make for the Tennessee River, more than sixty miles away. He placed Martin's troopers inside a cedar forest that served as refuge for those of Davidson's fugitives who managed to reach it. Stymied by the thick foliage, Davidson's pursuers had to dismount and fight on foot behind whatever cover they could find.

The fight suddenly became a more even contest, and Wheeler began to seek a way to seize the initiative. At a critical moment, a large portion of Martin's division charged mounted, dented Crook's line, and displaced a segment of it. Eventually the Federals fell back to a position where Wheeler was able to contain them till darkness fell. Early in the evening, the raiding leader gingerly disengaged and started a general retreat. Abandoning his artillery and many of the wagons that had accompanied him from the Sequatchie, he hustled his weary, battered command along the same southwest-leading roads that Wharton had taken. Crook, believing he had sufficiently punished his enemy and reeling from Martin's blows, staged a cautious pursuit.[52]

Crook's lethargic pace permitted Wheeler and his surviving raiders to reach the Tennessee at Muscle Shoals. Once on the south bank, he intended to march to Decatur, Alabama, where he could encamp, rest, and refurbish the command. The water here was shallow enough to permit fording, but it abounded with rocks and gullies that made the crossing, conducted on the afternoon of October 8, more than a little difficult. When the advance element of Crook's division neared the crossing site, the operation became even more hazardous. But Wheeler proved equal to the crisis, drawing on his experience covering Bragg's many retreats. As one of his men recalled, "General Wheeler kept forming lines all day, waiting until the Federals came up at close range, then he would give one volley and fall back, thus making our loss comparatively light, while the enemy's was much heavier." In the end, Crook was forced to watch his prey splash across to safety.[53]

DESPITE THE DRUBBING HE HAD TAKEN AT the finale, Wheeler had accomplished much on this expedition, which consumed nine days and spanned more than three hundred miles across the disputed territory between the armies. The basis of its success was the capture or destruction of nearly one thousand wagons bringing succor to an army in distress. In a perfect world, Wheeler's blow would have produced the surrender or evacuation of Chattanooga. Neither occurred, because the authorities in Washington, working with unusual dispatch, sent Grant, with the better part of the army that had captured Vicksburg, to relieve the trapped garrison. In advance of his main body, led by Sherman, Grant—commander of the newly organized Military Division of the Mississippi—reached Rosecrans's headquarters on October 23. He promptly removed the defeated army commander in favor of George Thomas, one of the few Union heroes of Chickamauga. Then he set to work to relieve Chattanooga's supply problem, as well as to assimilate other reinforcements coming by train from Virginia, the 11th and 12th Corps, headed by another deposed commander of the Army of the Potomac, "Fighting Joe" Hooker.

By the twenty-seventh, a new supply line had been opened by way of pontoon bridges laid on either flank of Moccasin Point, a finger of land at a bend in the Tennessee River southwest of Chattanooga. Wagon trains using this route, which reduced to a fraction the time previously needed to haul rations and materiel from northern Alabama, trundled beyond range of the siege artillery Bragg had emplaced in the valley below Lookout Mountain. This simple expedient, dubbed the "Cracker Line" after that staple of the soldier's diet, hardtack, erased the rationale for Wheeler's raid and neutralized its effects.[54]

Wheeler's command remained in northwest Alabama for nearly three weeks, resting and salving its wounds. The general had established his headquarters at Pond Spring, the Courtland-area plantation of Colonel Richard Jones. His men noted that the general spent much of his off-duty time in the company of his host's young, recently widowed daughter. The relationship thus kindled would turn to love. Two and a half years hence, Wheeler would return to Pond Spring to marry Daniella Jones Sherrod.[55]

When not courting his future wife, Wheeler labored to reorganize his corps, which, now that Forrest had departed for other fields of duty, consisted of four divisions commanded by Wharton, Martin, Armstrong, and Brigadier General John Herbert Kelly. The last-named had only recently joined Wheeler, following an impressive performance in command of an infantry brigade at Chickamauga, where he helped pierce the center of Rosecrans's line. Kelly, at twenty-three the youngest general officer in Confederate service, had spent three years at West Point before resigning from the cadet corps on the eve of war to defend his native Alabama. Wheeler quickly found him a most welcome addition: a born leader, admired by all who knew him, and well-versed in the tactics of all arms of the service. Another versatile subordinate, recently transferred to the cavalry, was Colonel (later Brigadier General) William Young Conn Humes of Virginia, who for the past seven months had commanded Wheeler's horse artillery; Wheeler had assigned him to lead one of Armstrong's brigades. Wheeler's corps also embraced the four artillery batteries that Humes had supervised before moving over to the cavalry.[56]

Many of Wheeler's current subordinates—not only Kelly and Humes but also brigade commanders, including John T. Morgan and Colonel Charles C. Crews—had been handpicked by Wheeler, who secured the necessary transfers and promotions while at Courtland. Even here, far apart from the main army, he had the ear of Bragg, who made virtually every appointment Wheeler requested.[57]

At this same time, Bragg facilitated the departure from Wheeler's command of John Wharton, who since the Sequatchie expedition had grown increasingly hostile toward his superior. Soon after returning from the raid,

Wharton took leave and entrained for the Confederate capital, where he spent a good deal of time intriguing against Wheeler. By December, Wheeler was informing Bragg that "Gen'l W. is still hard at work to get command of the Cavalry of this army. He is aided by his friends in Richmond. It is astonishing to me how such falsifications could have been imposed upon the War Department. . . . Only the other day a gentleman received a private letter from Richmond which stated that . . . Genl. Wheeler would be relieved from his command."[58]

That did not happen; Wheeler retained his post. Wharton, thanks to the support of Texas congressmen, bettered his own position by obtaining promotion to major general, but he had to settle for a transfer to the Trans-Mississippi Department, where he served for the rest of the war in relative obscurity. Wheeler lost no time filling the vacancy with a series of temporary replacements until able to name Humes as Wharton's permanent successor.

ON OCTOBER 17, BRAGG ORDERED THE CAVALRY to return to the army by way of Guntersville, Alabama. Wheeler promptly recrossed the Tennessee and marched toward the siege lines at Chattanooga. His immediate destination was Cleveland, Tennessee, twenty-five miles east of the city. He supposed he was being sent there to protect the army's far right against the ever-expanding Federal presence in the area. Like many another of Bragg's subordinates, Wheeler suspected that Grant and his lieutenants were poised to lift the siege by assaulting key points on the army's line. Yet Bragg appeared unconcerned about that prospect.

Evidence of this was the army leader's acquiescence in a plan hatched by Jefferson Davis that threatened to weaken the Army of Tennessee on the eve of a major confrontation. Davis, who was still at army headquarters listening to the complaints of Polk, Longstreet, and other subordinates disgusted with Bragg's studied inactivity, proposed that Longstreet head an expedition against Knoxville. Bragg, with some reluctance, agreed that Lee's Old War Horse might achieve a quick victory against Burnside's isolated garrison and return to Chattanooga in time to block any sortie by Grant. Longstreet's ability to do so hinged on a host of variables, none of which was easily controllable, but Bragg and Longstreet had been at loggerheads since Chickamauga, and Davis saw the expedition as the only way to get some service out of both commanders.[59]

The ill-conceived operation, carried out partly by rail, partly on foot, got under way in the first week of November. The detached force consisted of fourteen thousand infantry—the divisions Longstreet had brought from Virginia under McLaws and Hood (the latter, now recovering from the loss of a leg at Chickamauga, had been replaced by Brigadier General Micah Jenkins)—and five thousand horsemen. The cavalry comprised a brigade from the Department of East Tennessee and another called in from western Virginia. To this body was added more than three-quarters of Wheeler's corps, under his personal command: the divisions of Martin and Armstrong, and half of what was still known as Wharton's division, the brigade of Colonel Thomas Harrison. Bragg would retain only three brigades of horsemen, the two in Kelly's division and one under Davidson.[60]

It seems unlikely that Wheeler was optimistic about the expedition's chances. Longstreet would be taking more than a third of Bragg's manpower. While he would retain perhaps forty thousand infantrymen, Bragg would be left with a cavalry force far too small to defend an attenuated line that crossed some of the most difficult and forbidding terrain in North America. But Wheeler the Good Soldier complied faithfully with his orders, faulty and foolish as they might be.

At the outset, Longstreet's operation took a strange turn. He detached Wheeler from his main body and ordered him to cross the Little Tennessee River and overawe the garrison at Maryville, seventeen miles south of Knoxville. The post was thought to be heavily defended and thus a threat to Longstreet's rear. But Wheeler doubted whether the mission was important enough to warrant the hardships it would entail. His skepticism was not misplaced. After completing a difficult crossing and a grueling march in falling temperatures, he found that Maryville had been abandoned by its garrison—a single regiment of cavalry. Dutifully, he drove the fugitives toward Knoxville, where he planned to complete the second phase of his mission, seizing the southeastern heights of Burnside's stronghold.

For two miles, Wheeler pursued a force that was joined en route by troops from several other outposts that Burnside had ordered evacuated. At a few places, the Federals halted and gave battle, inflicting casualties on Wheeler's men and horses. Resuming their flight before they could be overpowered, they crossed a deep creek and destroyed the only bridge over it.

At great risk, Wheeler's men repaired the structure under fire, but before they could complete the work their quarry scampered off, crossing the Holston River and taking refuge inside Knoxville.[61]

Longstreet, whose main body had crossed the Tennessee River on pontoons at Loudon, had experienced frustration on a par with Wheeler. By making hasty and injudicious dispositions, he botched a couple of opportunities to bag elements of Burnside's command short of the Knoxville fortifications. Now confronted with the necessity of attacking those works head-on, Longstreet drew Wheeler to his side as if for close support—only to detach him again, this time to drive off a force of cavalry reportedly assembling at Kingston, on the lower bank of the Tennessee southwest of Knoxville. Saluting smartly, Wheeler marched his bone-tired men thirty-two miles in weather cold enough to be deadly. Perhaps unsurprisingly, he lost heavily from straggling—more evidence that Wheeler's disciplinary problems equaled, if they did not exceed, those that had long bedeviled John Hunt Morgan.

Upon arriving at Kingston, Wheeler found the place not only heavily defended but also alert to his approach. Convinced he could accomplish nothing against this force, especially in such hazardous weather, following preliminary skirmishing he called off the attack, gathered up his men, including as many stragglers as he could locate, and started back to Knoxville.[62]

Rejoining Longstreet late in the day, he learned that the contemplated assault, to be directed against Fort Sanders, a formidable salient on the northwest corner of the enemy's line, had yet to begin. Wheeler expected to play a part in the operation—though he was not enthusiastic about the prospect—but he did not have to. As soon as he reported, Longstreet handed him a telegram from Bragg, recalling Wheeler—but not his command—to Chattanooga "to assume command of the cavalry here." Although it contained no details, there was a sense of urgency in the communiqué that concerned Wheeler. Turning his forces over to General Martin, late on the twenty-fourth he rode out of Knoxville accompanied by a small escort, determined to rejoin Bragg without delay—and prepared for the worst.[63]

# TWELVE

# GUARDIANS
# AT THE GATE

I N WHEELER'S ABSENCE, THE ARMY OF TENNESSEE had absorbed a series of devastating blows from Grant, Sherman, Thomas, and Hooker. On November 23, reacting partly to reports of Longstreet's detaching, Grant sent two of Thomas's divisions to attack a strong point on Bragg's front line. Thomas's men rushed forward and overran Orchard Knob, a position one historian likened to "a nettle beneath the Union Army's underwear." The next day elements of Sherman's Army of the Tennessee crossed their namesake river on pontoons and captured the northern extension of Missionary Ridge. Simultaneously, the newcomers from Virginia under Hooker attacked in a thick fog and drove the Rebels from the northern face of Lookout Mountain. The bitter, bloody clash was later dubbed the "Battle Above the Clouds."[1]

That night and early on the twenty-fifth, Bragg concentrated his forces on Missionary Ridge, but his grip on the position was tenuous at best. Hoping to exploit this weakness, Grant threw Sherman's troops against the south slope of the ridge. They found headway hard to come by in that sector, but late in the afternoon, Grant committed Thomas's army against Bragg's left flank at the base of the ridge. The position appeared, if not impregnable, then something close to it. But the attackers refused to halt at the foot of the mountain, where they were prey to sharpshooter and artillery fire from above. Without orders the Cumberlanders made their way up the rock face ledge by ledge, boulder by boulder, to the summit, where, in gathering darkness, they unhinged the Rebel line and drove its disbelieving defenders into flight.[2]

A dazed and stricken Bragg could do nothing but call retreat, but he had little choice in the matter. Thousands of his troops, many having thrown aside their rifles, were making their way down the narrow, winding mountain trails toward the Georgia line. All that kept the Army of Tennessee from disintegrating was a heroic stand by the division of Major General Patrick R. Cleburne and a few other units that resisted Sherman's onslaught until their beaten comrades could reach the foot of the mountain in some semblance of military order. Then, on the morning of November 27, Cleburne's men held Ringgold Gap against a mounting tide of pursuers, permitting the escape of Bragg's artillery and supply wagons.[3]

Given the sweeping nature of the army's dissolution, it is unlikely the fighting could have ended other than it did had Bragg made better use of the few mounted forces at his disposal. As it was, his cavalry dispositions were egregiously faulty. Rather than husband his horsemen, he detached and dispersed them so widely as to nullify their ability to assist their infantry and artillery comrades. Only one of the three brigades Wheeler left behind when leaving for Knoxville—Colonel J. Warren Grigsby's, of Kelly's division, which comprised the remnants of John Morgan's once-proud command, including the celebrated 2nd Kentucky—had remained within supporting distance, guarding the army's extreme right near the foot of Missionary Ridge. The Kentuckians stubbornly held their position against assaults by the Army of the Tennessee until Thomas's people were added to the effort and the infantry on Grigsby's left gave way. "We were holding in check the force in front of our brigade," a Kentuckian recalled, "when without any warning the bullets began to rain down on us from our left and rear producing a very demoralizing effect. We didn't stay there any longer."[4]

Troopers whose units held the summit of Missionary Ridge fared no better, but they had a clearer view of the disaster about to engulf their army. A member of the 1st Louisiana remembered that his regiment occupied a perch "where a large portion of the valley below could be seen, and that vast moving mass of blue was a sight appalling to behold." Even before the enemy clambered to the top, the defenders appeared unsteady. The Louisianan noticed that the infantry on his regiment's left "looked as if they were ready to retreat, before a gun was fired. . . . When Grant ordered an advance all along his entire lines, they did break and confusion was the result."[5]

The rest of Bragg's cavalry—the brigades of Davidson and William B. Wade, plus the 4th Tennessee of Harrison's brigade, all under General Kelly—were stationed nowhere near the battlefield when Grant attacked. Before Wheeler went off with Longstreet, Bragg had sent Kelly on an observation mission toward Cleveland, on the railroad south of Chattanooga. Upon reaching the town on the morning of the twenty-seventh, Kelly found it held by six regiments of Union horsemen. Having in his charge only three regiments and a single squadron from Wade's regular brigade, Kelly attacked. He drove out the bluecoats and pursued for four miles, desisting only when his ammunition gave out. A trooper of the 10th Confederate regiment boasted that "we whiped them and made them skedaddle in a hurry. They left horses mules saddles bridles and pervisions cooking. . . ."[6]

Three days earlier, as the lines on Lookout Mountain began to give way under the pounding of Sherman and Hooker, Kelly had been recalled to the army's right flank. The division commander was too conscientious a soldier to have disobeyed the order; presumably in the chaos of defeat, it failed to reach him. When Bragg's retreat got under way, only Grigsby was on hand to protect the rear. The Kentuckian had to divide his small force to cover the withdrawal of two columns, the corps of Hardee (who had returned to the army in late October following his brief exile in Mississippi) and Breckinridge. Under the circumstances, Grigsby appears to have done as effective a job as possible, skirmishing with triumphant pursuers, blockading roads, and rounding up stragglers.[7]

The Union pursuit, spearheaded by Sheridan's division of the 4th Army Corps, got as far as Chickamauga Creek before petering out on the evening of the twenty-fifth. By the time the Federals muscled their way over the creek on the twenty-sixth, Bragg's survivors had dug in atop the ridges surrounding Dalton, a depot on the Western & Atlantic twenty miles south of the late battlefield. The Army of Tennessee, which at Grant's hands had suffered six thousand seven hundred casualties, a loss rate of almost 15 percent, lay on the verge of collapse from nervous exhaustion. But on the high ground around Dalton, it was no longer in jeopardy of being overtaken and beaten to death.[8]

JOE WHEELER CAUGHT UP WITH HIS FLEEING army near Ringgold Station, northwest of Dalton, at one p.m. on the twenty-sixth. He found everything in confusion, but he went to work assembling the units he had left behind when heading for Knoxville, scattered as they were along the roads, and in the valleys and passes between Chickamauga Creek and Rocky Face Ridge. It was arduous, time-consuming work, but he labored intensively to obey the orders Bragg's adjutant general had given upon his arrival: "assume command of Wharton's [i.e., Davidson's] and Kelly's cavalry, and post it so as to cover and protect our front."[9]

One of Wheeler's first tasks was to set up an advanced position at Tunnel Hill, where the railroad passed through Chetoogetta Mountain. At first he feared he would lack the time to secure the position, for Bragg toyed with the notion of returning him to Knoxville to escort Martin's division and Harrison's brigade back to the army. But this idea became unworkable once Grant sent a force under Sherman to lift Longstreet's siege. Now cut off from Bragg, Longstreet withdrew his forces, including those on loan from Wheeler, into the mountains north of Knoxville. It would be months before Martin and the others returned to Wheeler's side, and then only because Lee had recalled Longstreet to Virginia for the start of the spring 1864 campaign.[10]

At first concerned that in its new venue the army remained in grave danger, Wheeler was relieved when he reached Dalton and examined the ground it occupied. Bragg's main line of defense, which pointed generally west, was anchored atop eight-hundred-foot-high Rocky Face Ridge, a series of pine-covered heights extending for several miles to the south and riven with colorfully named defiles such as Buzzard Roost Gap and Snake Creek Gap. Some of these were narrow enough to be effectively blocked, others appeared sufficiently wide to accommodate a sizable force. Although concerned over these potential corridors of advance, Wheeler could see that in general, Rocky Face was a formidable defensive position, especially if approached from the north or northwest. Time remained to strengthen the place still further. Wherever Grant elected to strike, he would have to develop a comprehensive plan of action. With winter approaching and a considerable number of his forces detached to East Tennessee, any offensive was a long way off.

In the recent fighting, the Army of Tennessee had suffered far fewer losses than at either Stones River or Chickamauga. Yet its collapse under pressure, and the every-man-for-himself nature of its retreat, strongly suggested that discipline had broken down, morale had been devastated, and the rank-and-file had lost confidence in its commander. No longer in denial, Braxton Bragg faced the facts head-on. Before he could be washed away by the rising tide of discontent, on November 28, he asked Jefferson Davis to relieve him of command. Even before the president could accept his resignation, Bragg turned over the army to General Hardee and boarded an eastbound train.

Before taking leave, he bade farewell to his staff and to those officers whose goodwill he retained, including Wheeler. The cavalry leader remained grateful for the support he had received from Bragg, as well as the promotions, the commands, and the authority that had been conferred on him. Maintaining good relations with his departing superior would redound to Wheeler's credit in the months ahead, for upon reaching Richmond, Bragg was installed as chief military adviser to Davis, the post Lee once held. The position—that of ex-officio general-in-chief—gave Bragg authority over every officer in the Confederate ranks. In effect, Davis rewarded him for the ineffectiveness and incompetence he had displayed throughout his tenure as army commander.[11]

Naming a replacement was a difficult and unpleasant task for Davis, who had few candidates of sufficient rank, prestige, and demonstrated competence from which to choose. Although he had been on poor terms with the man since the earliest days of the war, mainly relative to matters of seniority and protocol, Davis on December 18 selected Joe Johnston to revive the Army of Tennessee and lead it in battle. Johnston, who had long coveted the command, was glad to relinquish his most recent position, a desk job at Meridian, Mississippi, to which he had been remanded after failing to persuade Pemberton to keep his army out of the death trap that was Vicksburg. Johnston rightly viewed the post as punishment for having incurred Davis's displeasure, but now he had the president to thank for restoring him to the field.[12]

For the most part, the army, including its cavalry, was pleased by the change of commanders. Many soldiers considered it long overdue. As early as January 1863, following the defeat at Murfreesboro, Bragg had become what one trooper called "the laughing stock of the whole army." His continuance in command meant numerous troops "will desert, and I can't say they are to blame." When Johnston's appointment was announced, a trooper in the 1st Louisiana found "every body more cheerful and hopeful." A 9th Kentucky cavalryman stated the prevailing opinion of Bragg, albeit perhaps a bit more charitably than most, when he wrote that "he was a brave and efficient subordinate [but] . . . as commander of an army in the field he was a failure. That seemed to be the verdict of all with whom I conversed." This man believed that Johnston would work hard to revive the army physically and spiritually. Even so, "little hope [is] entertained . . . of final success, unless some unforeseen event should occur to change the whole status of the army."[13]

In many respects Johnston's coming was a boon to Joe Wheeler. Not only was the new commander capable of instilling strength, poise, and confidence in an army that feared it had forever lost those qualities, but as a former trooper (lieutenant colonel of the 1st United States Cavalry from 1855 to 1860), he knew the mounted arm from top to bottom. From the start, he took pains to secure the resources—remounts, weapons, ammunition, equipment, transportation—Wheeler would need in the campaigning that lay ahead. Johnston did the same for the rest of the command, but throughout the formative part of his tenure he gave special attention to his mounted arm.

Like Wheeler, he was distressed that so few horsemen remained with the army, ensuring that they were overtaxed and stretched perilously thin. He continually importuned Richmond for authority to recall Martin's troopers from East Tennessee. He strenuously objected, though to little avail, when informed that Longstreet, who was contemplating active operations, had a greater need of cavalry. Whether Longstreet did or not, he worked his horsemen hard. In late December, Martin's men were pressed into service to oppose a combined force from Grant's and Burnside's commands. The bitter fighting that broke out along Mossy Creek, near Morristown, took such a toll that when Martin's men finally returned to Wheeler, they would require wholesale reconditioning.[14]

As he had proven under Sidney Johnston, Beauregard, and Bragg, Wheeler had a faculty for getting along with his superiors regardless of their personal and professional makeup, and he refused to be swayed by the negative opinions of others. Johnston would provide a test of Wheeler's agreeableness, for he had more than his share of defects as soldier and human being. He was egotistical, prideful, demanding, hard to please, and a stickler for military decorum and etiquette. He could be abrasive and condescending toward superiors, colleagues, and subordinates alike, but around junior officers and enlisted men he projected an avuncular image.

Past disagreements with government officials had fostered Johnston's distrust of those who ran the War Office. Despite Davis's willingness to return him to active duty, Johnston harbored a deep personal resentment of the man, whom he regarded as a petty, mean-spirited meddler in army affairs. Naturally secretive, Johnston was loath to share with the president his desires, concerns, and plans. His appointment promised to complicate Davis's job as Confederate commander-in-chief, but the president regarded Johnston as preferable to any other general with the rank to command the Army of Tennessee, such as the argumentative, insufferably conceited Beauregard.[15]

Flaws and failings aside, Johnston was just the man to awaken the comatose army Bragg had left him, and carry it till it could walk on its own. Through the winter, he ensured that the

General Joseph E. Johnston, CSA.

men built and occupied snug quarters, and that those on the front lines—scouts, pickets, vedettes—were rotated regularly to camps in the rear, where they could rest, get warm, and eat. He secured large supplies of replacement clothing, including thousands of shoes and boots, sometimes by commandeering goods intended for sale to civilians. He prevailed on Georgia Governor Joseph Emerson Brown and the officials of the Western & Atlantic Railroad to make more regular shipments of provisions from depots in the rear. He badgered the ordnance department in Richmond to make available more shoulder arms (including the short Enfield for Wheeler's troopers), as well as ammunition and equipment. Johnston improved the soldier's diet, increasing the quantity, quality, and variety of his rations. He worked long and hard to upgrade the medical service and secure additional surgeons and assistant surgeons for every regiment. And he strove to remedy the army's chronic shortage of wheeled transport. Unable to secure large additions of supply and baggage wagons, he confiscated civilian vehicles and converted them to military use, while ensuring that old or damaged wagons were repaired and returned to use.[16]

When the weather cooperated, Johnston reinstituted drills and target practice on an armywide basis, an activity that bolstered morale by keeping the army too busy to dwell on its recent travail. In February, he formally adopted for army use Wheeler's revised system of mounted tactics, and he supported Wheeler's establishment of schools to ensure that officers and troopers were "properly instructed in cavalry tactics, including evolutions of the regiment and . . . of the line." Another means of upgrading morale was the shifting about of units to create brigades composed of regiments from the same state, an appeal to regional pride. Yet another morale-boosting effort was Johnston's support of a widespread religious revival, which strengthened the troops' spiritual commitment to the war.[17]

Johnston strove to smooth over professional disagreements among his generals, a problem that subtly but seriously had weakened Bragg's ability to command. When General Cleburne in January 1864 proposed to solve the army's manpower shortage by arming slaves and employing them as soldiers with emancipation as a reward, Johnston acted quickly to diffuse the controversy that erupted when word of the plan reached Richmond, and to smother the outrage it provoked among such high-ranking Negrophobes as Wheeler and W. H. T. Walker.[18]

Johnston labored to hang on to able subordinates, even those inclined to do him harm. One such was John Bell Hood, who, after recuperating from the amputation of a leg, was promoted to corps command alongside Hardee. (The army now included only two corps, General Breckinridge having departed to head a military department in southwest Virginia, and Leonidas Polk having accepted transfer to the Mississippi post that Hardee had relinquished.) Hood, recently promoted to lieutenant general, was intensely ambitious, determined to rise to army command, and given to intriguing against anyone who stood in his way. In the months ahead, the Kentucky-born West Pointer, long a leading light of the Army of Northern Virginia, would carry on a clandestine correspondence with Jefferson Davis, pointing out Johnston's missteps and criticizing his strategy, even as he professed loyalty to the army leader. It would take a long time for Johnston to realize that the duplicitous Hood was after his job and determined to have it.

Johnston was resolute to retain and work effectively with those inherited subordinates who remained loyal to Bragg. These included Wheeler, who, like Hood, would go behind Johnston's back to communicate with high officials in Richmond. In an attempt to curry favor with his old commander, Wheeler would provide Bragg with evidence to support the latter's distrust of Johnston as an army commander. In truth, Bragg would do all in his power to prevent his successor from succeeding where he himself had not.[19]

Ignorant of Wheeler's machinations, Johnston supported his retention in command at his current rank. His solicitude was especially helpful when the cavalry leader fell afoul of Confederate congressmen and state officials. During the winter, word reached army headquarters that Wheeler's promotion to major general, which had yet to be confirmed by the Senate in Richmond, was in trouble. Political supporters of John Wharton's hoped to deny Wheeler confirmation and then put their man in his place. Congressmen from other states, responding to the protests of Alabama officials that Wheeler had failed to protect their constituents from Yankee incursions, allied themselves with Wharton's cause. Wheeler's critics charged that he lacked the ability to command a corps. Colonel James E. Saunders, an influential Alabamian who had served on Forrest's staff, contended that when Wheeler was promoted to major general, "the draft on his intellect, which is one of mediocrity, became too heavy. He has signally failed to give satisfaction. Moreover, his person is small, and in his manner there is nothing manly and commanding. He evidently handles men awkwardly in battle."[20]

Wheeler's opponents had grounds for criticizing him on some points. He lacked the stature, the strength of will, and the animal magnetism of Forrest, Morgan, and other cavaliers. Furthermore, as he had recently demonstrated in the Sequatchie Valley and at Marysville, he was not capable of maintaining discipline in his command. Never a polished tactician, he had alienated subordinates who distrusted his ability to lead in battle and on raids. Recently, only hours before Johnston assumed command of the army, another disgruntled subordinate, William Wade, had left Wheeler's command following a mismanaged assault on a Yankee supply column near Charleston, Tennessee, for which he blamed his superior.[21]

Still, as Johnston knew, most of the complaints lodged against Wheeler were groundless, including the charge that he had unilaterally abandoned Alabama to the enemy. Moreover, the ad hominem attacks on his physique and character struck Johnston as uncalled for and unjust. The new leader lacked a full appreciation of Wheeler's abilities, but he considered the man competent, hard working, and knowledgeable in his profession. Thus he readily agreed to assist Wheeler's confirmation process. When Davis asked him to make a statement for public consumption, he stressed his belief that Wheeler's continuance in his present position was "essential to the efficiency of the cavalry of this army." Johnston's unequivocal support served to disarm Wheeler's critics, and in due course his promotion was sanctioned.[22]

By early spring of 1864, the Army of Tennessee was not only back on its feet but strutting about, confident of its ability to overcome past adversity and eager to prove it. An officer in the 8th Confederate Cavalry recalled that after months of struggling to find its rhythm, "everything moved or was conducted with clock-work precision." Not only the mounted arm but every other component of the army had taken on a "new life" thanks to a "commander in whom this army has full confidence. . . . Buoyant hope and confidence in ultimate victory animated every breast from teamsters to the General Staff."[23]

The cavalry appeared in especially good shape. One of Johnston's quartermasters, who months earlier had criticized Wheeler's command as disorganized, undisciplined, and poorly equipped and provisioned, found "a great change for the better. . . . The men are well clothed, and keep their camp in very good order, and their discipline indicates a spirit on the part of the officers to pay strict attention to the execution of orders. . . . The command is rapidly improving in the drill," and its weaponry and equipment were "in as good order as could be expected." A formal inspection of Wheeler's command, conducted in late February or early March, drew praise from a member of the army headquarters staff. To this report Johnston added a brief but significant endorsement: "The General commanding notices with pleasure the improvement in the cavalry corps."[24]

The improvement was not only in quality but also in quantity. In mid-April, when Longstreet's campaign in East Tennessee ended inconclusively, Martin's troopers finally crossed the mountains to Dalton and rejoined Wheeler. Weakened by battle losses and suffering from the extended effects of a winter in the mountains without adequate clothing, tentage, or rations, the men appeared exhausted, ragged, and ill. Appalled at their condition, Wheeler immediately dispatched them to the railhead at Rome, where they could be reprovisioned.[25]

Although Martin's men would be unfit for field service for weeks, their return increased Wheeler's numbers, at least on paper, to levels not seen in many months. By the end of April, nineteen thousand officers and men were on his rolls, though he admitted that only a little more than ten thousand were immediately available for duty. The actual number was probably smaller, for Wheeler habitually inflated his manpower. This was partly the result of his desire to make his sphere of authority appear larger than it was. Then, too, he was such a lax bookkeeper that under no circumstances could he have arrived at an exact figure.[26]

As Confederate cavalry went, this was a reasonably strong force, and its leaders appeared to be of top quality. The command continued to consist of three divisions: Martin's, Kelly's, and Humes's (formerly Wharton's). Martin's division embraced the Alabama brigade of John T. Morgan and the brigade of Georgians recently assigned to Brigadier General Alfred Iverson, a transferee from infantry service in the Army of Northern Virginia. Kelly's division now consisted of Forrest's old brigade under Colonel Dibrell, and the regular cavalry formerly led by Wade and now by Brigadier General William W. Allen. Humes's division, by far the largest in the command, was made up of four brigades: Grigsby's Kentuckians, the Texans and Arkansans of Tom Harrison, five regiments of Tennesseans under Colonel James T. Wheeler (no relation to Fightin' Joe), and one regiment and one battalion of Alabamians headed by Colonel Moses W. Hannon. Wheeler's corps also included eighteen pieces of horse artillery distributed among four batteries, two from Tennessee and one each from Arkansas and Georgia. The guns and their crews answered to Humes's successor, Lieutenant Colonel Felix H. Robertson, later a brigadier general of cavalry.[27]

As formidable as it appeared on paper, Wheeler's command was outnumbered by the better-mounted, better-armed, and better-equipped horsemen of the enemy. By the close of April, the Military Division of the Mississippi maintained a cavalry force twelve thousand five hundred strong. The troopers were assigned to two of the army group's three components: Thomas's Army of the Cumberland, and the Army of the Ohio (otherwise known as the 23rd Corps, formerly part of Burnside's force at Knoxville), commanded by Major General John McAllister Schofield. Only the Army of the Tennessee, Grant's original command, led now by Major General James B. McPherson, lacked a mounted force of its own, although presumably it could call on the troopers of its sister commands as needed.[28]

This vast array of victory-rich veterans was now commanded by William T. Sherman. His superior and mentor, Grant, was no longer in the West. His overwhelming defeat of Bragg, combined with his earlier capture of entire armies at Fort Donelson and Vicksburg, had made the once-obscure captain, who had lost his prewar commission to insobriety, by far the most successful field leader in the Union ranks. Confirming his ascendancy, in March 1864, Abraham Lincoln named Grant general-in-chief of U. S. armies with the rank of lieutenant general.

Grant, who believed the key to ultimate victory was the defeat of Lee's army, had decided to make his field headquarters with Meade's Army of the

Potomac, he to formulate strategy, Meade to direct the army's movements and command it in battle. In Grant's stead, Sherman would direct operations throughout the western theater with the general goal of thrusting Johnston back upon the stronghold of Atlanta. If Sherman could capture the Gate City, the Confederacy would lose an industrial hub and a supply base that had been working at high capacity since war's advent. Atlanta's fall might not be as devastating a loss as the occupation of Richmond and the overthrow of Lee's army, but it would deal a blow to the Confederacy the effects of which would be long-lasting.[29]

Joe Johnston knew that even without Grant to face, his problems were many and serious. He had clashed with Sherman at Jackson, Mississippi, in the days following Vicksburg's surrender, and he had been impressed by the man's savvy and determination, as well as by his deft balancing of aggressiveness and caution. Moreover, the numbers available to his adversary told Johnston that he would have no chance in a slugging match. Sherman's manpower was more than double what was available to Johnston by April 1864. A large disparity would exist even after Polk's Army of the Mississippi was added to Johnston's command the following month. At its peak, the Army of the Tennessee would field no more than sixty thousand officers and men, some forty thousand fewer than Sherman enjoyed.

If he hoped to survive, let alone prevail, Johnston must assume and maintain the defensive, striking only when given an opening. Thus he steadily resisted Richmond's preference, made known throughout the winter, that he seize the offensive. Davis, Bragg, and Secretary of War James A. Seddon urged him to leave Dalton before Sherman could strike, then move north, join Longstreet south of Knoxville, cross the Tennessee River and the Cumberland Mountains, and capture Nashville. What that would accomplish was lost on Johnston, who in any case represented himself as unable to move until the army was better organized and supplied, and its transportation deficiencies were made good. Because he refused to propose an alternative strategy, he incurred the distrust of his civilian and military superiors, a situation that would hinder him throughout the coming months.[30]

FOR THREE MONTHS PRECEDING THE OPENING OF what would become known as the Atlanta campaign, Union forces probed Johnston's dispositions on Rocky Face Ridge and in Crow Valley, seeking weak points and signs of faulty positioning. As early as mid-January, skirmishing along the cavalry's line of outposts had become what a member of the 8th Texas called "the order of the day." On the whole, Wheeler's rejuvenated command did a good job of blocking these incursions, the most serious of which occurred from February 22 to 25, when Thomas's army pressed the pickets on top of Taylor's Ridge, the high ground west of and parallel to Rocky Face. On the twenty-second, a Federal force attacked Wheeler's headquarters at Tunnel Hill, the army's northernmost outpost. It scattered some of General Humes's vedettes and advanced rapidly on the Ringgold road. One of Wheeler's officers believed this to be the opening round of the campaign ("I was certain that the great battle was to be fought immediately"), but when Wheeler retired slowly and in good order to the south side of Tunnel Hill and infantry support materialized, the Federals penetrated no farther.[31]

Wheeler's lines were partly driven in again two days later, but the enemy was checked by a combination of dismounted skirmishers and well-emplaced horse artillery. The Yankees claimed to have withdrawn of their own volition, but Wheeler believed his hard-fighting troopers had a lot to do with it: "Our losses were trifling . . . while the enemy suffered heavily in both spirits, men and material."[32]

When Wheeler went on the offensive, his men gave a good account of themselves. On March 9, he led six hundred of them across Taylor's Ridge and attacked a large outpost in the valley beyond, "capturing their camp, stores, equipage, and a number of prisoners with their horses and arms." A month later, at the head of a force of unknown size, he penetrated well inside Sherman's lines and routed a body of cavalry that had occupied John Kelly's old bailiwick at Cleveland. Three weeks after this, he overran another outpost and took several prisoners. These he skillfully interrogated, learning a great deal about their army's positions, movements, and intentions.[33]

Wheeler's ability to supply army headquarters with up-to-date information helped Johnston hone his plans for dealing with Sherman once the latter moved against him in force. Daily intelligence reports convinced Johnston that his adversary intended to attack Dalton from the north and west via Mill Creek Gap and Crow Valley. The point of the thrust would probably be toward the upper reaches of Rocky Face, where the army's position was, as Johnston admitted, the weakest.

He was proven partly correct when, on May 3, Sherman's advance—one facet of a vast, coordinated offensive orchestrated by Grant that also included movements in middle Virginia, south of the James River, the Shenandoah Valley, West Virginia, and the Trans-Mississippi—finally commenced. For four days, Wheeler's picket lines, running east from Ship's Gap in Taylor's Ridge to the village of Conasauga, were hard-pressed by Thomas's infantry and the horsemen in its front, members of Brigadier General Washington L. Elliott's corps. Despite the numbers arrayed against them, Wheeler's men held their ground until, on the verge of being overwhelmed, they scurried back to prepared positions.

By the morning of the seventh, Kelly and Humes were facing a line of battle more than a mile long, which threatened to overlap their flanks. To the west, Hooker's corps of Thomas's army had passed through Nickajack Gap to confront the line on Rocky Face. Another element of the Army of the Cumberland, the 14th Corps, had connected with Hooker's left, extending the line farther to the east. Yet another of Thomas's corps then moved down from the Cleveland area to link with the 14th. The following day, the situation on Wheeler's front grew even more precarious with the approach of Schofield's army from the northeast, preceded by four cavalry brigades under Major General George Stoneman. If the earlier movements had not done so, Schofield's advance made the complete envelopment of the Confederate right a matter of time.[34]

If Wheeler had his hands full, so did the rest of the army. On the seventh, while Thomas and Schofield kept up the pressure in Johnston's front, Sherman sent McPherson's army well to the west and south. Via Ship's Gap and Snake Creek Gap, McPherson headed for the railroad in the Army of Tennessee's rear. Wheeler was ordered to send a brigade to another pass McPherson appeared to be aiming for, Dug Gap, and Johnston rushed infantry there as well. The rest of the cavalry was pushed steadily south. Wheeler evacuated the Tunnel Hill area so precipitately that he lacked the time to close the railroad tunnel by detonating munitions at its mouth, as he had intended. By early on the eighth, the bulk of Kelly's and Humes's divisions were crouching behind breastworks on a ridge beside Mill Creek Gap. Martin was still well to the rear, guarding the Oostanaula River crossings northeast of the remount camp at Rome.[35]

Though not at full strength, Wheeler's command on May 9 foiled an attempt by Edward McCook's division of Elliott's corps to turn the Confederate right by way of the road from Cleveland. Elements of Allen's and Harrison's brigades, joined by Wheeler and his escort, repulsed the effort with a series of mounted attacks. The 8th Confederate Cavalry made first contact, flying downhill, pistols drawn. An officer recalled that the regiment "passed in a gallop through our skirmishers and charged down the ridge with a wild yell, rode over the first line of the enemy, then, firing at close quarters, dashed on to the second line and crushed it, killing some, wounding others and capturing near all of the second line." One prisoner taken was McCook's senior subordinate, Colonel Oscar H. La Grange. Their lines irreparably broken, the Federals whirled about. Before they could clear the field, the 8th Texas of Harrison's brigade charged and overtook them, turning their withdrawal into a rout. After driving McCook into the distance, the Rangers basked in the praise of comrades. "It don't hurt us though to be complimented," their commander wrote in a letter home, "as we are *used to it*."[36]

While Wheeler was pursuing McCook toward Varnell's Station on the railroad, taking numerous prisoners, Grigsby's detached brigade was at another railroad village, Resaca, eighteen miles south of Dalton. There it was helping the single brigade of foot soldiers in that vicinity turn back the flanking force McPherson had sent toward the army's rear by way of Snake Creek Gap. After barely surviving this thrust—an outcome that owed as much to McPherson's excessive caution as to Grigsby's defense—Johnston ordered a general withdrawal to Resaca. But after the movement was under way, the army leader, detecting no further threat from that direction, halted most of the army roughly between Dalton and Resaca.[37]

Wheeler's main force spent the tenth and eleventh covering the army's retrograde and sparring with a somewhat diminished enemy presence. The opposition consisted of the cavalry of Elliott and Stoneman, and, in the rear, an unknown number of infantrymen. When heavily pressed, Wheeler hit and hurried away in time-honored fashion. On the twelfth, however, he suddenly went over to the offensive. Largely in the dark about what Sherman was up to, Johnston ordered his cavalry leader to skirt the northern edge of Rocky Face and probe Thomas's and Schofield's positions.

Moving out with a large contingent, Wheeler almost immediately plowed into Stoneman's horsemen. He spent some hours tangling with them, fighting mostly dismounted. The encounter yielded dozens of prisoners but nothing to facilitate Wheeler's intelligence-gathering.

When he finally broke free of Stoneman, Wheeler was puzzled to confront only a thin line of infantry, not the ever-moving masses he had encountered over the past several days. Partly from personal observation, partly from prisoner interrogation, he came to the unsettling conclusion that Sherman had pulled out and gone south. He was correct; having left enough troops in front of Wheeler to make him believe he was heavily opposed, the Union commander had made with all speed for Resaca, where he intended to gain a foothold that would not be dislodged.[38]

Fearful that Sherman's strategy portended doom for the Army of Tennessee, and cursing himself for having been cozened, Wheeler relayed news of Sherman's departure to army headquarters by a succession of couriers. Although the message reached him before day's end, Johnston delayed moving the army south until early on the thirteenth. To cover the movement, Wheeler placed many of his men in the trenches that enclosed Dalton. Thus battened down, he held back the depleted force in his front through most of the morning. By noon, however, his flanks and rear were under threat. Refusing to be spooked, he coolly disengaged and led his men down the railroad toward Tilton. Harrison's brigade covered the movement, and did an excellent job of it. One of its officers remarked that although the Yankees advanced on all sides, "we disputed their right, and contended for every foot of ground they traveled."[39]

At Tilton, Wheeler's soldiers spent the balance of the day building and defending fieldworks. They continued to hold the position even after the enemy bent back their left flank at a 90-degree angle. On the fourteenth, they finally abandoned the depot and joined the rest of the army around Resaca, which had come under attack by McPherson's army. While most of Wheeler's men provided close support to the infantry, a picked force under his direction advanced under heavy fire as close to the enemy position as possible and took note of McPherson's dispositions. By midday Wheeler could inform Johnston that the Yankees opposite Hood's corps, on the army's right, had been weakened by a shift of forces to another sector. Acting upon this information, Johnston had Hood attack the Union left late that afternoon. The assault was so successful that McPherson thereafter had little hope of occupying Resaca and driving his opponents across the Oostanaula River.[40]

Johnston intended to launch new attacks on the fifteenth, but when Wheeler informed him that Sherman was laying pontoons across the river near Lay's Ferry, the Confederate commander, concerned for the safety of his flank and rear, abandoned the railroad town and crossed the river on a pontoon bridge of his own. A large body of Wheeler's command covered the operation; the remainder cantered down the railroad. Near Calhoun they encountered Stoneman's troopers, who had circled south to capture field hospitals filled with the wounded of Hardee's corps. Wheeler attacked, drove off the bluecoats, and followed them closely for two miles or more, capturing forty men and two stands of colors.[41]

From Calhoun, the Army of Tennessee continued south to Adairsville, abandoning another line of hastily fashioned defenses. Wheeler's command, now augmented by Martin's rejuvenated division, resisted Sherman's crossing of the Oostanaula. The cavalry was assisted by a battery of five rifled guns, found abandoned on the Calhoun Road, which Wheeler manned with sixty troopers of Allen's brigade (now under Colonel Robert H. Anderson, Allen having transferred to the command of John T. Morgan's brigade). Presumably, some of the converted troopers had artillery experience.[42]

Johnston had hoped to make a stand at Calhoun, then at Adairsville, but the local topography did not appear to offer a position that Sherman could not turn. On this matter Johnston received conflicting advice from his subordinates. Hardee urged him to fight at Adairsville, but Hood, as Johnston later claimed, recommended a withdrawal to the south side of the Etowah River, twelve miles away. Johnston agreed to continue the retreat, but he held out the possibility of engaging Sherman somewhere north of the Etowah.[43]

The cavalry continued to do an effective job keeping the enemy off the rear of the main army. On May 18, when Sherman sent Brigadier General Kenner Garrard's cavalry division of Thomas's army to cut the W&A near Kingston, Wheeler nimbly blocked the way with Anderson's brigade. Garrard attacked and was thrown back with heavy loss. One of his regiments, the 4th Michigan, lost its second-in-command, Major Horace D. Grant, captured along with "a goodly lot of his men." When a "small tallow-faced" private in the 8th Confederate Cavalry called on the major to surrender, Grant demanded that an officer be summoned to receive his sword. The private coolly studied his captive and replied: "Do you see this six-shooter? That is officer enough for you."[44]

Theoretically, Wheeler's job of covering the retreat was made easier by the recent assimilation of the Army of Mississippi, which gave Johnston a third corps. Polk's command consisted not only of two divisions of infantry and several artillery batteries, but also Red Jackson's horsemen. Jackson's force was composed of Alabamians, Mississippians, and Texans divided into three brigades headed by Frank Armstrong, Sul Ross, and Brigadier General Samuel W. Ferguson.

Johnston had devised a rather unwieldy arrangement for the cavalry, somewhat reminiscent of Bragg's failed policies. Jackson, although junior to Wheeler, would operate independent of his authority unless their commands happened to unite, when Fightin' Joe would take charge of both. For the most part, the cavalries served apart, as Wheeler and Forrest had, but Jackson's arrival coincided with a reduction in Wheeler's manpower when Johnston ordered the temporary transfer of Allen's (Morgan's old) brigade to Jackson. The shift left Wheeler with seven brigades, which he redistributed as follows: Iverson's to Martin's division (reinforcements would follow); Anderson's, Dibrell's, and Hannon's to Kelly's division; and Harrison's, James Wheeler's, and Grigsby's (the last-named now led by a fellow Kentuckian, Brigadier General John Stuart Williams) to Humes's division.[45]

THE ROADS THE ARMY OF TENNESSEE TOOK when leaving Adairsville diverged, leading south to Kingston and southeast to Cassville. Believing that Sherman would follow both, on the nineteenth, Johnston devised a trap. He had Hardee—whose corps brought up the rear, closely pursued—head for Kingston. Once there he was to hasten east with most of his corps and join Polk and Hood in converging on the smaller Union wing that Sherman surely would send to Cassville. The Union commander proceeded to divide his force almost exactly as Johnston had anticipated, but when a larger-than-expected column advanced on Cassville, Hood, who was to have delivered the main blow, pulled back, and the ambush failed to materialize.[46]

Johnston had lost his best chance thus far of waylaying his enemy. His disappointment outweighed his previous enthusiasm over news received from Virginia: Lee, having fought Grant and Meade to a standstill in the Virginia Wilderness, had again halted their advance on Richmond at Spotsylvania Court House, forty-some miles northwest of the capital. Johnston also knew that other forces involved in Grant's sweeping offensive had ground to a halt or been turned back, including a much-heralded invasion of Texas along the line of the Red River. Incursions into the upper Shenandoah Valley and south of the James River had also stalled. The spate of glad tidings had moved Johnston to opine that the Confederacy had won its independence. Even more embarrassing than this premature pronouncement was the address Johnston had issued to his troops at Cassville, promising that their retreating days were over.[47]

Fretting and grumbling, the army continued south, crossing the Etowah below Cartersville on the twentieth and angling toward the mountain passes around Allatoona, where their commander hoped to stage another ambush. Sherman, who had become more wary since his near-entrapment at Cassville, took his time crossing the river, permitting the Army of Tennessee to spend a few days in fixed camp.

The cavalry could have used the rest, but at Johnston's order, Wheeler led the majority of Kelly's and Humes's troopers around the eastern flank of the slow-moving enemy to reconnoiter toward Cass Station, where Sherman had stockpiled supplies. Finding the depot lightly guarded, the Rebels occupied it. They swarmed over the many wagons parked there, which they found filled with edibles, clothing, and equipment. Wheeler entrusted the contents to General Kelly, whose men began to haul off the wagons. They were barely in motion when a body of Stoneman's cavalry suddenly appeared, attacked the despoilers, and retook some of the vehicles. Only upon the arrival of Humes's men, who had been lagging behind, did the Yankees break off and retreat. Their departure permitted Wheeler to escort one hundred wagons to Allatoona, where Johnston's commissary officers gratefully received them.[48]

Coinciding with Wheeler's coup, rain began to fall, turning the roads of north Georgia into beds of mud. The rain continued, off and on, for seventeen days, impeding the movements of blue and gray alike. During this period, Johnston, who had taken up a strong position in Allatoona Pass but was forced to abandon it when the cagey Sherman refused to attack, moved his dejected, frustrated soldiers to New Hope Church, less than thirty miles northwest of Atlanta. Reaching Johnston's position on the twenty-fifth, Sherman struck in the driving rain. Believing he was assaulting a fragment of Johnston's army, the red-haired Ohioan thudded into the Rebel right, held in force by Stewart's division of Hood's corps, and was thrown back with considerable loss. The outcome of this vicious battle, later known by participants on both sides as the "Hell Hole," was due in large part to the vigilance of Wheeler's scouts, who had detected Sherman's advance and had persuaded Johnston to strengthen the sector his opponent was driving toward.[49]

Two days later, Sherman lashed out again. This time he aimed for Pat Cleburne's well-entrenched division near Pickett's Mill, which was supported by more than one thousand dismounted troopers holding rifle pits they had carved out of the hard-packed soil along Little Pumpkinvine Creek. The cavalry's recent practice of going to ground and fighting "web-foot" style was becoming a favorite habit. The lieutenant colonel of the 8th Texas boasted that his men "have been digging ditches, building breastworks and lying in them for several weeks and the boys are already first-rate infantry." The "boys" helped Cleburne's troops deliver a devastating fire from a low ridge above the creek valley, repulsing the attackers with heavy loss.[50]

Unknown to Wheeler, Jackson, and their men, their ranking opponent had high praise for their versatility and combat effectiveness. In a letter to his wife, Sherman claimed that all was going well on the road to Atlanta, with a single caveat: "Our greatest danger is from cavalry, in which arm of the service the enemy is superior to us in . . . quantity and quality, cutting our wagons or railroads."[51]

Sherman's fear that his horsemen were outnumbered may have been exaggerated, but his concern for his army's vulnerability to attacks on its communications was not misplaced. Buoyed by his success at Cass Station, Wheeler developed plans for a much longer raid, this aimed at severing Sherman's link to his supply hub in Middle Tennessee. A heavy strike, Wheeler believed, would force Sherman to curtail his offensive, or at least delay it until his lines could be repaired. The respite might enable Johnston to find a way to land a decisive blow well in advance of the Gate City.

Even though Georgia's officials, including Governor Brown, were in favor of such a plan, Johnston would not hear of it. Unlike his predecessor, who seemed to make a practice of dispatching his troopers on distant operations on the eve of battle, Johnston was averse to depriving his army, even briefly, of mounted support, especially in the midst of a major campaign. When Davis and Bragg joined Brown in pressing him on this matter, Johnston steadily refused, urging them to assign the job, instead, to Forrest.[52]

In his clandestine correspondence with Richmond, Wheeler criticized Johnston's refusal to cut him loose to operate in the enemy's rear: "If my command or only a portion of it could be detached . . . I am certain I could materially change the aspect of the campaign." His prediction further stoked the government's discontent with Johnston, whom it feared might be willing to sacrifice Atlanta if driven back upon the city.[53]

For nearly a month after Pickett's Mill, Wheeler's men spent several hours a day in the rifle pits, fighting like the infantry they customarily supported on horseback. The continuing rain, which made large-scale movements difficult, combined with the heavy losses both armies had suffered to discourage active operations. An officer in Jackson's division, which was covering the army's left flank (Wheeler held the right) was happy to inform his wife that "we are at rest . . . all quiet along the lines—our horses unsaddled and also resting—an unusual thing for them. We can appreciate it, I assure you." Wheeler spent the respite writing a report of his operations since the commencement of the campaign. In typical fashion, he played up his triumphs, especially the number of prisoners and arms his command had taken despite the many and severe hardships under which it had labored.[54]

On May 28, most of Sherman's troops shifted away from opposite Johnston's lower flank near Dallas. As the movement got under way, Hood suggested an attack while the Federals were in motion. Johnston, grasping at another opportunity to smite his enemy, agreed to let Hood flay the Union left. He readied Polk's and Hardee's troops to follow up any success that was gained, then waited for Hood to deliver his blow. But the next morning, when Hood was to strike, he called off the operation at the last minute. He had been worried by the unexpected appearance of a Union column at right angles to his path of advance. Johnston, frustrated once again, cancelled Polk's and Hardee's movements. On June 4, he uprooted the army and led it through rain and mud ten miles to a point southeast of New Hope Church. There he laid out a new line, one straddling the W&A and covering Lost and Pine Mountains. On the latter eminence, General Polk was killed when struck by a Yankee shell during a June 14 reconnaissance in company with Johnston. The bishop-general was temporarily replaced by Major General William Wing Loring and then by A. P. Stewart.[55]

Wheeler's men were kept busy covering this latest withdrawal. On June 9, they engaged the cavalry of Kenner Garrard, which, backed by two infantry brigades, drove in Wheeler's pickets at a point eight miles south of Acworth. Leaving his supports behind, Garrard penetrated as far as Big Shanty, the W&A depot where in April 1862, Andrews's Raiders had commandeered the *General* at the outset of The Great Locomotive Chase. Near the depot, other elements of Wheeler's corps, holding strong earthworks, finally turned back the Federals with "a terrible fusillade."[56]

Johnston's latest retreat troubled many of his soldiers and infuriated at least as many (none of whom knew the decisive role played by the army leader's overly cautious and disobedient subordinates). But "Old Joe" continued to enjoy the support and goodwill of a majority of the troops. One of them, Captain Sidney S. Champion of the 28th Mississippi, Jackson's division, spoke for like-minded comrades when he asserted that "our beloved Genl Johnson [sic] has the confidence of almost every soldier who now serves under him. That he is able—aye—one of the ables[t] Genls we have is beyond question—and I thank my God that I have so much confidence in him and that confidence is . . . based upon his skill as a strategist." A Mississippian in Armstrong's brigade insisted that because of its faith in Johnston, "our army is in fine spirits, confident of success. This is a hackneyed expression I know, but it is certainly true of the Army of Tennessee."[57]

The public at large seemed to be losing confidence in the general, even if most of his soldiers were not. Newspaper readers throughout the South had learned that Lee had effectively slowed Grant's movement on Richmond, inflicting horrific casualties on his enemy during the June 1-3 fighting around Cold Harbor. Less than two weeks later, Lee blocked Grant's attempt to capture suddenly strategic Petersburg, twenty-two miles south of the capital. Johnston, of course, had no such successes on his record—and apparently nothing on his mind besides falling back before his savvier opponent.

His apparent unwillingness to stand and fight seemed to confirm the suspicions of official Richmond that Johnston lacked the strength of will to defend Georgia. His single-minded pursuit of the retreat was drawing sharp criticism not only inside the War Department but also from the city's salons and drawing rooms. The influential diarist Mary Chesnut, wife of a South Carolina politico, complained to other members of the Confederate inner circle that Johnston "gives up one after another of those mountain passes where one must think he could fight and is hastening down in the plain." Mrs. Chesnut feared that the general's Fabian policies portended disaster, as did his continuing reluctance to keep his superiors informed of his movements and intentions. She attributed Johnston's secrecy to his hatred of Jefferson Davis, "which amounts to a religion," and his identity as a political rival of the president: "Joe Johnston's disaffection has been the core round which all restless halfhearted disappointed people consolidated, and Joe Johnston's disaffection with our president and our policy has acted like a dry rot in our armies."[58]

On June 19, when Sherman moved his armies as if to threaten Hardee's hold on the Pine Mountain line, Johnston resumed his withdrawal. When he halted, he deployed his army on the tree-fringed, boulder-strewn ground atop and along the steep slopes of Kennesaw Mountain, two miles north of Marietta. The following day, as Sherman confronted this line, Garrard's cavalry advanced again on Wheeler, this time while reconnoitering the Rebel right. Along rain-swollen Noonday Creek, Wheeler met the bluecoats with the brigades of Williams and Anderson, later supported by Martin's division and Dibrell's brigade of Kelly's division. Fighting swirled for hours along the south side of the creek before Garrard saw he could progress no farther and withdrew.[59]

Wheeler had needed three major attacks to repulse his opponent, but the third had carried the day, preserving the integrity of Johnston's right. Apparently the enemy had been dealt a quietus, for little was heard for him for some days afterward. A trooper in the 1st Mississippi observed that the Federals "seldom make any demonstration against us. . . . They fight very shy and as we act strictly on the defensive, we very seldom come to close quarters."[60]

The setback at Noonday Creek foreshadowed the result of the assault Sherman unleashed upon Kennesaw Mountain one week later, which ended in a bloody repulse reminiscent of the disaster at Cold Harbor. Weary from failing to outflank Johnston time after time between Dalton and New Hope Church, and temporarily prevented from doing so yet again by the rain-sodden roads, Sherman on the twenty-seventh attacked uphill against well-entrenched defenses, principally those held by Loring's corps, anchored by banks of artillery.

The result ought to have been apparent at the start. Captain Champion described it in a letter home as "a great victory. Hardee's and Loring's corps covered themselves with glory. . . . From Kennesaw Mountain could be seen 500 ambulances at one time hauling off the dead & wounded Yankees. Our loss was not exceeding 400 killed & wounded whilst the Yanks were at least 8000." In fact, Sherman had suffered three thousand casualties, but that was three times as many as Johnston. The disparity pained and vexed the Union commander, who admitted his error, buried his dead, and went on. A few days later, the downpours of summer having ceased, Sherman returned to his slow, patient strategy of outmaneuvering his opponent.[61]

Johnston's first outright victory of the campaign raised the spirits of his soldiers, even those who had begun to despair. The general sense of relief and euphoria, however, was short-lived. When Sherman vacated his position in front of Kennesaw and moved in such a way as to threaten Johnston's supply line, the Rebel leader fell back to the north bank of the Chattahoochee River, the last natural barrier between the invaders and Atlanta. By July 3, Johnston had put down stakes near Smyrna Camp Ground, less than twelve miles from the Atlanta suburbs. Wheeler's and Jackson's troopers, covering, respectively, the right and left of the moving army, were kept busy fending off the stabs and jabs of Sherman's horsemen, their ranks occasionally braced by infantry. Though heavily occupied, the cavalry had time to consider the continuing—perhaps mounting—plight of their army. Captain Champion, who had expressed strong confidence in Johnston's generalship a few weeks earlier, now reported himself "in good spirits—though not so sanguine as I have been." In a subsequent letter home, he hinted at decreasing confidence: "I have quit speculating as to the movements of the army because no one can comprehend Joseph E. Johnston but his corps generals."[62]

Neither could the government comprehend Johnston's strategy for defending Atlanta—if he had one. By early July, Davis and Seddon were seeking a straightforward statement of their general's intentions. Johnston failed to calm their fears, giving vague and evasive answers. Davis, for whom every square mile of Confederate territory was sacred soil, tried to educate Johnston to the disastrous consequences of refusing to hold the Gate City to the last, but he doubted that he had been successful.

To the president's mounting dismay, Johnston continued to give ground. On the fifth he sent Wheeler, Jackson, and some foot soldiers to the banks of the Chattahoochee. With the infantry's help, the horsemen were to secure the crossing sites above and below the several rail and foot bridges northwest of Atlanta. But Johnston sent most of the troops to downstream fords. With the remainder of his force, Wheeler was supposed to block access to a thirty-mile stretch of river. The task proved impossible; on the eighth, portions of the Army of the Ohio forced a crossing at one of the upper fords, Soap Creek. Once they gained the south bank, they formed a screen behind which other elements of Schofield's command crossed. Sherman was now poised to pass the river in overwhelming force.

Bereft of options, Johnston pulled out and crossed the river farther downstream. Covering the operation, Wheeler's men—especially those at the end of the column—came close to being cut off and captured. Captain Miller of the 8th Confederate recalled that after most of the army had crossed, "Wheeler led us in one last desperate change on the North bank, repulsed the enemy and then by a quick movement rushed his rear-guard to the position. The enemy had succeeded in placing artillery on an elevation that commanded the road as it wound down to the pontoon. . . . Shells were bursting over our heads and close to our ranks when the Regiment started across but with splendid discipline and composure we wound our way over the narrow bridge of boats with shells bursting around and sprinkling us with water. Wheeler was among the last to leave the shore and before the entire Regiment had debouched on the Southern bank the pontoon had been cut from its fastenings."[63]

Once the army was over, Johnston had it erect fieldworks along Peachtree Creek in Atlanta's northern suburbs. But he gave no indication that he would remain there should he be pressed in front or on his flanks. When he learned of this latest retrograde, Davis on July 10 dispatched Bragg to Johnston's headquarters on an eleventh-hour fact-finding mission. Two days later, the president's military adviser arrived in the city, whose panic-stricken citizens were in the process of evacuating, and sought out Johnston. After interviewing the commander, Bragg spoke with some of his subordinates, notably Hood, who was adamant that Atlanta should be held at all costs.

Johnston had not made the same pledge to his visitor. A disconsolate Bragg informed Davis by telegram that he had been unable to determine if the commanding general "has any more plan for the future than he has had in the past." When Johnston failed to respond to a final request for details of how he proposed to defend Atlanta, Davis on the seventeenth informed him that he was being relieved of his command in favor of Hood.[64]

When the news of Johnston's demise began to circulate, many soldiers refused to believe it. Even those who had expressed doubt about Johnston's willingness to make a stand turned gloomy and fearful. Hood was an unknown quantity, but no one had ever placed him on a par with Johnston on matters of experience, intellect, tactical ability, or strategic know-how. One of Wheeler's men described his comrades as "speechless, shaking their heads in answer to questions, as much as to say that a great mistake had been made, [and] predicting the most direful results." After the war, a veteran of Jackson's command recalled that "it was the universal conviction of the army that Joseph E. Johnston was one of our greatest commanders . . . and that his removal was equal to the loss of one half of the army."[65]

One of the few voices raised in favor of the shakeup came from across the firing lines. On the north side of Peachtree Creek, Sherman thanked the gods of war for removing the man who had bedeviled him for the past two and a half months. In later years he recalled simply that "I was pleased at this change." At the time, overjoyed that his enemy was now in the hands of a commander who would attack rather than defend, fight on open ground instead of crouch behind fortifications, the Union commander exclaimed to a group of his subordinates: "Boys, we've got 'em. . . . Hood is in command. We will have our fight to-morrow!"[66]

# THIRTEEN

# UNACCEPTABLE
# LOSSES

S HERMAN KNEW HIS MAN. HIS NEW OPPONENT WAS a study in military machismo: driving and driven, enamored of the offensive, and determined to prove that a crippled arm and a missing leg had not drained the life from him. Like John Morgan, Hood had the psyche of a gambler, although he was too willing to take long shots. A celebrated comment by one of his soldiers, rendered half in jest, had a core of truth to it: Hood looked like the kind of cardsharp who would bet against an inside straight.[1]

As soon as Hood got his hands on the Army of Tennessee, he began to gamble with it. The day after Johnston's relief, the troops of Hardee and Stewart marched into the Atlanta suburbs, their movements covered by the horsemen of Wheeler and Jackson. Hardee led his four divisions out the Marietta road, then up Peachtree Street to the city's outer line of fortifications. Farther west, the three divisions under Stewart took position on Hardee's left, occupying the works that extended to Montgomery Church. The corps that had been Hood's, temporarily commanded by General Cheatham, lengthened the line eastward and southward almost to the right-of-way of the railroad from Atlanta to Decatur, Alabama.

The army's defensive cordon, which overlooked the valley of Peachtree Creek, had been constructed recently by fatigue parties put to work at Johnston's order, but a mile and a half farther south was a more complex set of defenses, almost twelve miles long, that encircled the city. Erected early in the war through the use of military and slave labor, and strengthened continually over the months, this line was formidable enough that had Hood desired to maintain the defensive, he might have held his position for months. But the new leader refused to confine the army to stationary operations. He had assured Davis, Bragg, and Seddon that if given command, he would not permit Sherman to attack or besiege him. He would strike first, and keep striking, as long as he saw an opportunity to injure his enemy—mortally, if possible.[2]

Johnston would always insist that he had a plan for attacking Sherman north of the city but lacked the time to execute it. He had refused to share it with his superiors, but he had explained it to Hood, whom he had come to regard as one of his most trusted lieutenants, knowing nothing of the man's duplicity. The plan was based on smashing into Sherman's right wing, Thomas's army, as it crossed Peachtree Creek. Polk and Stewart would do the hitting while Hood's corps blocked McPherson's army, which constituted the Union left wing, as it approached the northeastern outskirts. As the infantry moved into position to deliver its blows, Wheeler's corps would extend Hood's right flank. By occupying a lofty eminence known as Bald Hill, the cavalryman would prevent McPherson from crowning it with artillery that could be used to bombard the city.

Hood intended to launch his sortie—based largely on Johnston's plan—on the morning of the twentieth, but miscommunication and other foul-ups kept the army from moving out until late in the afternoon. The delay enabled Thomas's troops to cross Peachtree Creek and deploy to meet the attack. The armies battered each other until nightfall, alternately gaining and losing the advantage. In the end, Thomas prevailed thanks to greater numbers, better dispositions, and the steadfastness of regimental commanders such as Major Arthur MacArthur of the 24th Wisconsin Infantry, whose son, Douglas, would become one of America's greatest soldiers; and Colonel Benjamin Harrison, a brigade commander in the 20th Corps and a future president of the United States.[3]

During the action, Wheeler's men, from their customary position on the army's right, assisted by a body of Georgia militia, supported Cheatham's corps in its encounter with the Army of the Tennessee along the line of the Atlanta & Decatur. Wheeler held his post with only two of his three divisions. Humes's had been detached to the opposite flank to reinforce Jackson, who was covering the infantry assaulting Thomas.

Humes had been replaced by a single brigade on loan from Jackson, commanded by Samuel Ferguson. A South Carolinian and a West Pointer, the twenty-nine-year-old Ferguson, like Wheeler, had grown a bushy beard in an attempt to disguise his youth, but the similarities ended there. Ferguson had no stomach for enforcing discipline, and he would refuse given orders when they conflicted with his own notions of tactics and strategy. Wheeler would come to consider him a troublemaker and a malcontent. His distrust of Ferguson dated from this day, when the brigadier's command broke and ran as soon as advanced on by the head of McPherson's corps. Wheeler hastened after the fugitives and managed to halt them and re-form their line, but it took the transfer of Cleburne's infantry from points westward to shore up the position.[4]

General John Bell Hood, CSA.

Hood's sortie had failed, at a cost of nearly two thousand five hundred casualties, almost one thousand more than he had inflicted on Thomas and McPherson. Undaunted, he planned a new offensive, in a different sector. But the next morning, before he could launch it, his right flank came under renewed assault by the Army of the Tennessee. Wheeler tried desperately to hang onto Bald Hill but had to relinquish the critical position when squeezed by two of McPherson's brigades. The attackers focused their efforts on the works hastily thrown up by Ferguson's brigade, which they correctly identified as the weak point on Wheeler's line. Again Ferguson's men "gave way in some confusion," imperiling the entire flank, and especially Allen's brigade, on Ferguson's left. Wheeler, fearing disaster, was heartened by the strong showing of Allen's men, who held their ground against tremendous pressure. At day's end, Wheeler had to retire along with most of Cleburne's division, but he did so in good condition. In fact, he was able to turn about and counterattack, repulsing a body of foot soldiers who, expecting no resistance from the retiring Confederates, had become isolated from the body of their command.[5]

Despite the loss of Bald Hill (renamed Leggett's Hill for the division commander who had secured it) and the disgraceful conduct of Ferguson's brigade, Wheeler had reason to consider his battle-weary command far from being fought out. His confidence was bolstered the following day when he took part in Hood's second sortie, aimed at outflanking

McPherson's army and taking it in the rear. To do so, Hood sent Hardee's corps on a fifteen-mile night march to slip around the unsuspecting enemy outside Decatur. The operation proved to be more difficult than Hood had made it sound in giving Hardee his orders. The march took too long, costing the advantage of surprise, and when Hardee finally attacked on the afternoon of the twenty-second, he struck not the rear of the Army of the Tennessee but its elongated flank. The assault was powerful enough to drive a wedge between two Union corps and produce many casualties—one being McPherson, killed by a skirmisher's bullet. But when reinforcements dislodged the wedge, and attacks against other sectors of Sherman's line failed, Hardee withdrew in defeat.[6]

This day Wheeler's orders called not for close support of the infantry but for a raid on McPherson's supply base at Decatur, about six miles east of the cavalry's original position. The Army of the Tennessee's lack of cavalry permitted Wheeler to succeed where Hardee had failed, gaining the Union rear, but a mile and a half from his objective he was greeted by entrenched infantry, supported by at least one cannon. A careful examination of the position convinced Wheeler that he outnumbered the defenders by a healthy margin. He wasted no additional time advancing on them, Hannon's brigade in front, most of its men dismounted. Hannon's objective was the skirmish line the enemy commander had set up in front of the rifle pits shielding the depot.

The initial assault was not successful, but Wheeler refused to quit, and his perseverance was rewarded. In his after-action report he claimed, in characteristic prose: "At first the galling fire made the most exposed portion of my line waver, but, quickly rallying, the onset was renewed, and with a triumphant shout the entire line of works was carried." He estimated his captures as two hundred men, their artillery piece, rations and materiel in profusion, and a large supply of medical stores.[7]

Wheeler had only begun to remove those goods needed by his army and to destroy those he could not cart off when General Hardee recalled the cavalry to his side. Regretting his inability to damage fully what he considered an important link in the enemy's supply chain, Wheeler assembled his troopers and headed back to Hardee—reaching him in time to join him in retreat. Twice now, Hood had thrown his army at the invaders of Georgia, and he had nothing to show for it.

Back at his old post on the army's right, Wheeler spent the next five days sparring at long range with a suddenly quiet and largely immobile foe. On the twenty-seventh, his men again impersonated foot soldiers by occupying a line of trenches along the Decatur road. These had been abandoned as a result of Hood's decision to shift west in preparation for a third attempt to break Sherman's hold on Atlanta's north side. Wheeler's men did more than huddle underground; skirmishers were kept busy probing the ground between the armies. They soon made a puzzling discovery: the army that had been McPherson's, now commanded by Major General Oliver O. Howard, had withdrawn to the north side of the Georgia Railroad.[8]

Hours after relaying word of this unusual shift to army headquarters, Wheeler received a report that startled and alarmed him: a large mounted force, later identified as Garrard's, had passed the Rebel right in the direction of Flat Rock on South River, fifteen miles southeast of Decatur. The news itself was sufficiently troubling, as it suggested that Wheeler had not extended his line far enough to the east. Of greater concern was the indication that Sherman was sending his cavalry to do what Wheeler had been sent to do at Decatur: destroy communications in the enemy's rear. Sherman had enough supply lines to have escaped disaster had Wheeler done a thorough job on his recent raid. But the Army of Tennessee was critically dependent on two rail lines that brought rations and materiel into Atlanta from points south, the Macon & Western and the Atlanta & West Point. If either of these was put out of commission, the Army of Tennessee would have to abandon its present position. Conflicting reports about the direction Garrard was taking meant that either or both lines could be his objective. Later reports made Wheeler suspect the raiding leader was heading for Jonesboro, a major supply base on the railroad to Macon that was eighteen miles south of Atlanta.

Although Wheeler saw at once the danger the raid posed, his superior did not. It took hours of petitioning before Hood gave his cavalry leader permission to go after the Yankees with the better part of his command. That evening Wheeler pulled his men out of their trenches and started off, Allen's brigade in the lead. Next morning Allen established contact with Garrard at Flat Rock and managed to pin him down. With the main body, which again included Humes's division, Wheeler moved to surround the South River position. Before he could be entrapped, however, Garrard pulled out and galloped north to Lattimer's Corners, where his pursuers again ran him to ground.[9]

Just as the situation appeared well in hand, Wheeler was given a message from Hood's chief of staff, Brigadier General Francis A. Shoup. Another column of Yankee horsemen was in motion south, having passed over the ground Wheeler had been forced to uncover. At first thought to be heading for a distant stretch of the Georgia Railroad, this force, led by George Stoneman, was actually en route to Macon. Its ultimate destination, fifty miles south of that city, was the notorious prison camp known as Andersonville, where thousands of POWs, suffering under conditions of almost incredible privation, were praying for rescue.[10]

Wheeler was trying to determine how to divide his force to keep Garrard in place and also overtake Stoneman when he learned, to his disbelief, that a third raiding body was running free in the army's rear. This force, commanded by Edward McCook, had been sighted rounding Hood's far left. Its heading suggested that its target was the Macon & Western, although perhaps also the Atlanta & West Point. According to Wheeler's scouts, McCook's column appeared to be the largest of the three in motion. Wheeler suspected that even after the last of his troopers reached him—some were still en route to Lattimer's Corners—he would be outnumbered by each of those columns.

Thinking fast, he parceled out his resources as the crisis appeared to dictate. He left Dibrell's brigade, under the direction of John Kelly, to deal with Garrard, who suddenly appeared both lethargic and confused. Wheeler then dispatched Allen's, Crews's, and Williams's brigades to run down Stoneman. Ordinarily the combined force would have been entrusted to Wheeler's senior lieutenant, but General Martin was ill, and so Iverson, the next in rank, assumed command. The balance of Wheeler's corps—the brigades of Colonels Anderson and Henry M. Ashby—were assigned the task of chasing McCook. Humes would have direct command of both brigades, and Wheeler would accompany him. At some point Wheeler expected to join forces with Red Jackson, many of whose troopers were already tailing McCook.[11]

Wheeler's dispositions were eminently judicious, and they produced gratifying results. Kelly had no trouble shooing his assigned opponent back to his army. As it turned out, Garrard had not expected to accomplish anything on his own but had been waiting for Stoneman to join him in attacking Hood's supply lines. However, Stoneman, in a bid to become the man who liberated Andersonville, had disregarded his orders to assist Garrard. Once the latter realized help was not coming, he meekly returned to

Thomas's wing making a wide circuit around the Army of Tennessee. Thankful for this display of Yankee timidity, Kelly followed at a prudent distance until certain the raiders posed no threat to the Confederate rear.[12]

At the outset, Stoneman's column showed more poise and determination, but it, too, failed for lack of gumption. Stoneman moved so rapidly that by the morning of June 30, three days after starting south from Decatur, he was only seven miles from Macon. His pace was so brisk that Iverson had no hope of overtaking him should he keep moving.

Then, as it must have seemed to Stoneman's pursuers, a kind Providence intervened in their favor. Nearing the city, Stoneman encountered enough pickets to make him believe that Macon was heavily defended. In fact, the city was occupied only by militia whose cushy assignments heretofore had given them the nickname "Joe Brown's Pets," after the state's governor. Even so, Macon featured an impressive set of fortifications commanded by the politician-general Howell Cobb. Stoneman drove in the pickets, but when he reached the city he was shelled by a bank of cannons he had not expected to encounter.[13]

While his skirmishers sparred with Cobb's quasi soldiers, Stoneman sent one of his three brigades to tear up the railroad to Milledgeville, the state capital. Enough track was demolished to convince him that he had done enough local damage. Having made no headway against Cobb's artillery, Stoneman ordered his troopers to cross the Ocmulgee River downstream of the city and continue on to Andersonville. But before he could do so he received a report that Iverson, leading hundreds of more troopers than he actually had, was at his heels. Suddenly giving up all hope of freeing POWs, Stoneman hastily decamped, heading back toward the safety of his own army.

The route Stoneman chose led him directly into the hands of his pursuers. The next morning, north of Clinton, Iverson's column, now led by Colonel Crews, gave battle despite having been depleted by exhausted horses and riders to an effective force of six hundred, less than a third of the number Stoneman enjoyed. Crews's survivors dismounted and threw up breastworks, which Stoneman—his command thoroughly demoralized by his erratic leadership—attacked but failed to carry. At this juncture, Stoneman received a report that a Rebel force was heading his way from Macon. The report appears to have referred to a scouting party made up of Joe Brown's Pets, but Stoneman envisioned hordes of veteran cavalry closing in on him, and he began to panic. Although he himself refused to cut and run, he permitted two of his brigades to mount up and make their way back home as best they could. Most of the troopers raced to safety, although a considerable number were tracked down and captured by Crews's men and other forces. The remainder, a five-hundred-man detachment under Stoneman, went nowhere. An enlisted man of the 1st Georgia saw "a fellow with a white flag, dressed in blue, come galloping down to Col. Crews and I said, 'Boys, that is good news.' He soon hurried back and in a short time I saw Gen. Stoneman and his staff ride down to where Col Crews and his staff were and the terms of surrender were agreed upon in about 40 minutes."[14]

Most of the enlisted raiders would wind up in the very prison they had attempted, albeit feebly, to liberate. Their captors experienced a much happier fate, being wined and dined by the citizens of Macon, who greeted them as saviors. The Georgian who witnessed Stoneman's surrender recalled that "the ladies of Macon filled our haversacks with good rations and presented the Regiment with a purse of $700.00 cash." Though it came in the form of depreciated Confederate currency, the donation was enough to buy watermelons for the regiment. The men enjoyed not only the tasty fruit but also the food fight that followed: "Such a water melon feast and such a war with melon rinds I never witnessed before or since."[15]

Of the three raiding columns Wheeler had to deal with, McCook's had the power to do the most harm to the Army of Tennessee. Like Stoneman's, at first it moved too rapidly to be easily overtaken. When Wheeler, with Humes's contingent, reached Lovejoy's Station on the Macon & Western after dark on July 29, he learned that McCook had hit the area hours earlier, damaging a long stretch of the railroad while burning one thousand wagons full of supplies badly needed by the defenders of Atlanta. McCook's force was large enough not only to inflict such damage but to fend off Armstrong's brigade of Jackson's division, which had followed the Yankees to Lovejoy's and then toward Newnan, a depot on the Atlanta & West Point forty miles southwest of Atlanta. Time and again, Armstrong had flayed McCook's flanks and rear, but without overhauling him.

At Lovejoy's, Wheeler was joined by Jackson and the bulk of his division. The two quickly agreed on an arrangement whereby Jackson would strive to get ahead of the Yankees while Wheeler pressed them from behind. Only the latter succeeded, and only through great exertion. By hard riding, expert scouting that fixed McCook's shifting position, and the tireless labor of fatigue parties who rapidly rebuilt a bridge over Whitewater

Creek that the raiders had burned, at daylight on the thirtieth, Wheeler overtook his quarry in bivouac outside Shakerag (now Wadley), eighty-some miles east of Macon. Having arrived undetected and aware that he was about to be augmented by Anderson's brigade, the last pursuit force to leave Atlanta, Wheeler felt confident enough to attack. With Colonel Ashby's men in the lead, he overran McCook's camp, evicted its sleepy occupants, and propelled them into flight. The surprise assault killed or wounded forty raiders and captured two hundred others.[16]

General Frank C. Armstrong, CSA.

McCook gathered up the survivors and led them toward Newnan at an extended gallop. Wheeler's weary but inspired troopers followed at comparable speed. Two miles from Newnan, Wheeler again connected with Red Jackson, who had failed to overtake the raiders as planned. Adding to his column the brigades of Sul Ross and Tom Harrison, Wheeler forged ahead. Some miles farther on, he discovered that McCook had bypassed Newnan, which he had found occupied by dismounted cavalry under Forrest's old compatriot Philip Roddey. By driving straight through the town, Wheeler and Jackson made up enough time to overtake the raiders once again.

Three miles beyond Newnan, McCook had halted and formed a line of battle in a dense woods. Although suspecting he was still outnumbered, Wheeler divided his force and struck that line from front and rear simultaneously. In language reminiscent of his description of the action at Decatur, he claimed, "I met with strong resistance at first, but in a few moments the enemy gave way, when with a shout and a gallant charge, the entire line was thrown into confusion and commenced a disorderly retreat."[17]

Wheeler's claims were essentially accurate, but he downplayed the fact that at the height of the action, some of McCook's men sneaked into the Confederate rear and stampeded five hundred horses belonging to Ross's brigade, which had been fighting afoot. Wheeler eventually repulsed the horse thieves and recovered almost every mount, but during the counterattack General Ross was twice captured and twice released by his own men.[18]

The back-and-forth contest had consumed several hours, and both sides were nearing exhaustion, when Anderson's long-delayed brigade appeared and delivered a decisive charge. Their line effectively shattered, the raiders remounted and beat a wild retreat. Wheeler attempted to pursue, but his men were in dire need of a respite, and within minutes the panic-stricken Yankees were long gone. Wheeler gave up the chase, convinced that his opponent would not halt short of the starting point of his abortive mission. Although the loss of the rations and material McCook had destroyed would be sorely felt, the damage he had inflicted on Hood's rail lines would be repaired in mere days.

Returning to the scene of his triumph, Wheeler rejoined Jackson. There he also welcomed Roddey and six hundred of his men, who had arrived from Newnan by foot, covering part of that distance at the double-quick. Gathering up prisoners and discarded arms and equipage, the jubilant cavalry commander turned northeast and rode toward Covington, a Georgia Railroad depot thirty-two miles east of Atlanta. There he planned to rest and refresh the troopers who had helped him achieve the greatest single feat of his military career.[19]

WHILE WHEELER HAD BEEN CHASING RAIDERS, Hood launched another sortie, this one west of Atlanta near Ezra Church. No more successful than his previous efforts, the action on July 28 consisted of a series of ill-starred attacks by one division and part of a second under Lieutenant General Stephen Dill Lee, formerly the commander of all Confederate cavalry in Mississippi (including Forrest's) and recently named to lead Hood's corps. After repulsing Lee's attacks, Howard's Army of the Tennessee, which Sherman had shifted from its long-held position east of Atlanta to threaten Hood's remaining railroads, stood firm against reinforcements sent in under A. P. Stewart.[20]

A part of Armstrong's division that had not participated in the pursuit of McCook found itself in the thick of the fighting at Ezra Church ("the hottest I ever felt," one trooper asserted) while guarding Lee's and Stewart's flanks. When the Yankees opened fire on the cavalry's position at a fence line between a woods and an open field, a Mississippian of the Noxubee Squadron experienced "such a rattling of bullets, knocking fences [apart]. . . . We held our position about thirty minutes, both sides firing very rapidly with guns and navies. They saw they could not drive us so they brought up two or three lines, and over the fence they came and on to us. We poured it into them as they came across the field, then fell back and stole into the woods, getting [behind] trees, contesting every inch of the ground."[21]

Hood, after grappling for more than eight hours and failing to gain an appreciable amount of ground at a cost of five thousand casualties (Howard's did not exceed six hundred), withdrew Lee and Stewart to Atlanta. This latest defeat caused the army's morale to plummet to depths not seen since its frantic exodus from Lookout Mountain and Missionary Ridge. After the guns quieted at Ezra Church, a Union picket called across the lines: "Well, Johnny, how many of you are left?" A heartsick Rebel answered: "Oh, about enough for another killing."[22]

Having failed to stop Sherman's advance by engaging him head-on, Hood grasped at the hope that a blow from the blind side by the cavalry would force him to fall back across the Chattahoochee. His thinking indicated a dramatic shift of policy. Hood's predecessor had forbade his cavalry leader to cut loose from the army on a long-distance raid, but Hood was desperate to break Sherman's grip on a city the Confederacy could not afford to lose. As Hood noted in his memoirs, he believed, or professed to believe, that Wheeler and Iverson had "thoroughly crippled the Federal cavalry." Therefore, "I determined to detach all the troops of that arm that I could possibly spare, and expedite them, under the command of Wheeler, against Sherman's railroad to Nashville . . . and also [urged] that General Forrest be ordered, with the whole of his available force, into Tennessee for the same object. . . . I was hopeful that this combined involvement would compel Sherman to retreat for want of supplies, and thus allow me an opportunity to fall upon his rear with our main body." The potential benefits of such a move were many, but in making it, Hood was gambling that while Wheeler was gone he could get by without adequate reconnaissance and intelligence-gathering assets. Such thinking was another manifestation of Hood's recklessness. He had the intestinal fortitude to place the bet, but he lacked the wherewithal to cover it.[23]

Wheeler had barely returned from routing McCook (and issuing an address lauding the "energy and determined gallantry" of his forces) when he was ordered out on the operation Hood had devised. His troops were worn down and hurting, but Wheeler, who still considered himself the consummate raider, looked forward to the mission. So did many of his troopers, who longed to turn the tables on their opponents. As a semiliterate private in the 10th Confederate put it, "I hope we will be able to pay them back for all the raids they have made on us. If we can bee successful in getting in there rear and cut off their supplies, it may bee the means of making them fall back from Atlanta."[24]

In response to orders, the cavalry left Covington on the morning of August 10 and veered east, then north, around the enemy's left flank. This day Wheeler commanded one of the largest forces ever assigned him for an independent mission—four thousand five hundred officers and men drawn from all three of his divisions, including Martin's, whose commander had just returned to active duty. At the outset, all went well; despite its size, the column appeared to attract little attention. In due course it reached the W&A depot at Marietta, north of which Wheeler's advance guard began tearing up the railroad that once had been its army's lifeline and now served the same purpose for Sherman. The men damaged a considerable stretch of track between Cassville and Calhoun, but the rains that began to fall—the first major precipitation in north Georgia since the middle of June—left the ties too saturated to be burned. Even if the weather had cooperated, the destruction was destined to be impermanent. After leaving Calhoun, Wheeler's scouts reported that Yankee repair crews, guarded by large bodies of cavalry and infantry, were rebuilding the railroad almost as fast as the raiders could wreck it.[25]

Calhoun was the scene of the raid's only lasting achievement. There Wheeler seized a commissary depot and captured one thousand seven hundred head of beef cattle that soon were being herded south by Colonel Hannon's brigade; Wheeler's undernourished comrades at Atlanta would be grateful. But as soon as the beeves were gone, troubles arose. Before leaving Calhoun, Wheeler divided his force, sending Martin's division to Tilton and leading the main body farther north to Dalton. At the site of the army's winter camp, Wheeler snatched up two hundred members of the local garrison and rifled the supply train that had fed them. But when he moved on to a prearranged rendezvous with Martin, his senior subordinate was nowhere to be found. Wheeler, completely in the dark as to Martin's whereabouts, began to fear that he had met with trouble, perhaps disaster, at Tilton, even though the town was not thought to be heavily occupied. As it turned out, Martin had experienced no difficulty at all. For reasons that remain obscure, he had bivouacked his division seven miles south of Dalton without notifying his superior. Next day, when Wheeler located him by happenstance, he was furious. Believing he could no longer "expect any help" from Martin, he relieved him of his command, replaced him with General Iverson, and sent him back to Atlanta under guard. The records

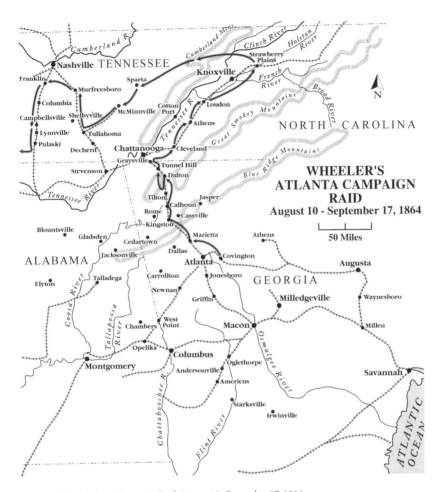

Wheeler's Atlanta Campaign Raid, August 10–September 17, 1864.

fail to disclose a more precipitate fall from grace by a Confederate major general. Martin's career was effectively over; war's end would find him in charge of a military district in northwest Mississippi.[26]

Now misfortune began to snowball for the raiders and their leader. After demolishing the W&A between Tilton and Dalton (something Martin had failed to accomplish), Wheeler was suddenly attacked by a roving body of railroad defenders, mostly infantry, under Major General James Steedman. Determined not to be held immobile, he kept Steedman's main body at arm's length with a small portion of his force and led the rest north to Tunnel Hill, his headquarters for much of the previous winter. Once

Steedman stopped pressing and the rear guard broke away, Wheeler lingered near Tunnel Hill, resting, for the next four days.

On the twentieth, Wheeler resumed his travels, having left behind two hundred picked men to "strike the railroad every night at some five or six designated points." Although his claim seems extravagant (if characteristically so), he later boasted that this force intercepted twenty supply trains and confiscated their cargo, while tying up rail transportation between Dalton and Atlanta for at least two weeks.[27]

Confident that his rear was protected, Wheeler plunged into Tennessee but found the river of that name too high to cross at Cotton Port, jumping-off point of his raid through the Sequatchie. Passing northeast of Chattanooga, he demonstrated boldly toward the Federal-occupied post at Cleveland. After crossing the Hiwassee River to Athens, he began to attract opposition not only from enemy outposts but from local Tories who took potshots at his column and tried to waylay its outriders. Wheeler's men retaliated by leaving the line of march to loot and burn the homes of known Unionists. Forging onward, Wheeler left the railroad at Loudon, crossed the French–Broad east of Knoxville, then forded the Holston River and turned sharply west to cross the Cumberland Plateau. Finally he was able to pass the Tennessee—two hundred miles from where he had intended to ford it.

Straying so far from the railroad he was supposed to sever was a major deviation from his orders. Wheeler added to his misfortunes by detaching one-third of his force—the brigades of John S. Williams and Robert Anderson (the latter now commanded by Felix H. Robertson, Wheeler's erstwhile artillery commander)—and sending it, along with about half of his guns, to demolish the railroad track and bridge at Strawberry Plains, four miles above Knoxville. Williams, who had requested the assignment for reasons of his own, had vowed to rejoin Wheeler as soon as he accomplished his mission, but large bodies of bridge guards kept him from striking either of his targets. Forced to backtrack, he tried to reestablish contact with Wheeler but was cut off by the interposition of pursuers. Eventually, Robertson and he sought refuge with Rebel forces in southwest Virginia. Months passed before either returned to Wheeler. When they did, the cavalry leader preferred charges against Williams, whom he declared more guilty than Robertson, and tried to have him cashiered.[28]

The balance of the expedition was a study in fatigue, frustration, and failure. After a long and difficult journey across familiar ground inside the

Sequatchie, near the end of August, Wheeler finally struck the railroad that connected Sherman's armies to their supply base at Nashville. He had high hopes of damaging the line beyond quick repair, but he was repeatedly thwarted by the troops inside the blockhouses and stockades that dotted the right-of-way. An enlisted man in the 5th Tennessee complained that upon the column's approach, the Federals would "run into their little forts which proved after trial to be bomb proof." Furthermore, pursuers began to close in. By September 1, a force of mixed arms under Major General Lovell H. Rousseau was hot on his trail. Yet whenever the Yankees got close enough to lash out, Wheeler managed to fend them off and keep moving.[29]

How long he could do so appeared a moot point, but Wheeler remained determined to make a success of the operation. He refused to be diverted from his assigned mission, even when his route took him to within eight miles of the Tennessee capital. Although some of his officers argued for an attack on Nashville, he waved them off. Supposedly he explained that "my troops were not given to me to make a name, but to do what I could for my country." Behind the noble rhetoric was Wheeler's awareness that he had no hope of successfully attacking a heavily fortified city with a column that continued to lose manpower. By now he had detached not only Williams's and Robertson's brigades but also one regiment and half of another under Colonel Dibrell, who had persuaded Wheeler to permit him to recruit his brigade among the secessionists of Middle Tennessee. The mission nearly ended in disaster when the colonel was attacked by infantry and cavalry near Readyville, in Cannon County. Barely escaping annihilation, Dibrell, like Williams, tried to return to Wheeler's column but found it impossible. Appropriately, he fell in with Williams and followed his fellow wayfarer as far as Bristol, Tennessee. Persuaded that Dibrell had made a sufficient effort to return, Wheeler did not prefer charges against him.[30]

Having spent ten days destroying track and rolling stock between Chattanooga and Nashville (much of which, however, would be repaired in weeks, and some of it in days), Wheeler, as September came in, moved cross-country and then turned north along the Central Alabama Railroad. He dispatched Humes's division toward the Hermitage to divert attention from his main body, which he led toward the Nashville suburb of Brentwood. His pursuers, under overall command of Rousseau, were at first deceived, but by the morning of the second they had regained their bearings. By hard riding, a portion of their force reached Brentwood and piled into the rear of Wheeler's column, engaging Kelly's troopers in a running fight that covered at least eight miles. Before the chase ended with a Union withdrawal, Kelly was dead of a sharpshooter's bullet. His loss plunged the raiding column into grief. The men openly mourned "our brilliant division commander" and never tired of discussing "his courage and military accomplishments."[31]

Wheeler spent three more days ripping up rails and burning ties, but he could not tarry at any point. His proximity to Nashville, where would-be pursuers were many and mobile, involved him in a series of clashes not only with the forces under Rousseau but also with the occupants of such outpost venues as Franklin, Campbellsville, Lynnville, and Pulaski. When he saw he was running low on able-bodied horses and ammunition, Wheeler suspended the demolition mission and pushed on without further delay to the Alabama border. By the time he reached Stevenson en route to a bivouac at Tuscumbia, his command was so obviously exhausted and disheveled that the Yankees had long since given up the chase.

From Tuscumbia, Wheeler got in touch with Hood by telegram. He tried to persuade his commander that the raid had been an unadulterated success. He admitted that impassable streams and unanticipated opposition had forced him to travel much farther, and to return much later, than he had anticipated. But he claimed major achievements, including the capture of hundreds of troops, horses, supply wagons, and beef cattle. These contentions are sustainable, but his assertion that he had recruited two thousand military-age men into his ranks invites disbelief. Moreover, the railroads he supposedly demolished had been put back in operation in record time, some of them well before he returned to Alabama. On September 23, a Georgia militiaman had written from Atlanta that "all rumors say Sherman's RR cut. How can this be so when the Yankee trains can be heard every day?"[32]

Whatever Wheeler had accomplished, the shellacking his troops had taken on the homeward leg, so reminiscent of his experience of the previous October, overshadowed everything else. Three days after Wheeler reached Tuscumbia, he was visited briefly by Bedford Forrest, who was setting out on a raid of his own against Sherman's communications by order of General Richard Taylor, commander of the Department of Alabama, Mississippi, and East Louisiana. Shortly afterward, Forrest informed his superior that Wheeler's command was in "a demoralized condition. He claims to have about 2,000 men with him; his adjutant general says, however, that he will not be able to raise and carry back with him exceeding

1,000." Forrest claimed that Wheeler himself appeared so "disheartened" by his heavy losses that he was seriously considering resigning his commission.[33]

However accurate Forrest's assessment of his colleague's state of mind—as far as can be determined, Wheeler never offered his resignation— Fightin' Joe surely realized that his overly extended, circuitous, debilitating, and powerfully opposed journey through north Georgia and East and Middle Tennessee bore no relation to the grand triumph he had made it out to be in his dispatch to Hood. Once again, the cavalryman had failed to accomplish what he had been sent to

General William H. "Red" Jackson, CSA.

do, while barely avoiding annihilation. As biographer John Dyer notes, the raid proved (if further proof were needed) "that Wheeler could not successfully conduct large scale independent cavalry operations."[34]

On September 16, Hood had telegraphed Wheeler to rejoin him at his new headquarters south of Atlanta. Uncharacteristically, Wheeler had avoided complying with this recall, as well as earlier ones issued by General Shoup. Now, convinced that his command needed additional rest, and reluctant to leave his new bivouac near Courtland, where he again enjoyed the company of the widow Sherrod, he managed to postpone the reunion for another eight days.[35]

Had he reported to Hood without delay, it still would have been too late to save the Army of Tennessee from disaster. Wheeler's long absence had deprived his superior at a critical point of the eyes and ears that cavalry provided. First, Hood failed to detect the presence in his rear of another raiding column, composed of Brigadier General H. Judson Kilpatrick's cavalry division of Thomas's army. In late August, this force wrecked a considerable stretch of the Atlanta & West Point near Fairburn, while also plundering the supplies stored at Jonesboro on the Macon & Western. The damage proved not to be critical, but then Hood lost sight of his enemy, which suddenly disappeared from his front. Wondering if Sherman had abandoned the siege, perhaps as a result of Wheeler's depredations, the army leader was slow to discover that his opponent had shifted his forces west and south of the city to inflict lasting damage on Hood's supply lines.[36]

The result was a decisive battle at Jonesboro on August 31. The troops Hood rushed there—infantry and artillery, screened by Red Jackson's depleted cavalry—fought desperately to hold a position, critical to the army's ability to remain in Atlanta. One of Jackson's men recalled that he and his comrades mounted a strong defense until large numbers of cannons trained their sights on them: "They sent shot and shell into our rail piles, which 'kinder confused us' so we rose firing rapidly into the infantry line which was coming forward. . . . They moved very slowly, brought a heavy force up and marched in two lines of battle, our s[ide] contesting every foot of ground."[37]

Relieved by infantry, Jackson's troopers fell back to the works that shielded the embattled depot, which they managed to hold through the night. Next morning, however, they got word that Hood was falling back along the railroad, the 1st Mississippi Cavalry in the vanguard. At first the troopers believed Hood was luring Sherman into a trap, poised to turn on him at any moment. Then a series of deafening explosions from inside the city told the Mississippians that the army was destroying munitions to prevent their capture. It became painfully evident that the Army of Tennessee was evacuating Atlanta, and for good reason. Union infantry had seized Hood's last lifeline, the Macon & Western, one mile below Rough and Ready Station, tossing aside dismounted defenders from the 4th Georgia Cavalry. Large elements of Thomas's and Schofield's armies were assailing other points on the railroad, and what they seized they held onto. On the morning of September 2, some of Thomas's troops cut short their attacks and marched into Atlanta. The next day, having probed Hood's new lines around Lovejoy's Station, Sherman disengaged and withdrew to the city. By then he had telegraphed General Halleck in Washington: "Atlanta is ours, and fairly won."[38]

The fall of the Gate City had a profound effect on the conflict, and not only that raging in the Heartland. By the summer of 1864, the Union war effort had bogged down in every theater. In Virginia, Grant's failure to take Petersburg had produced a long, wearying siege that by September showed no signs of progress, and in Georgia Sherman had yet to gain an outright victory. The unrelenting grind had infected a significant portion of the Northern public with war-weariness and gloom. In mid-June Abraham Lincoln, who had been nominated for a second term on the Union Party (Republican and prowar Democrat) ticket, had despaired of reelection, virtually conceding the presidential race to his regular Democratic rival, former General George B. McClellan. "Little Mac" was running on an antiwar platform that held out the prospect of an armistice. Until Atlanta's fall, the Confederacy stood an even chance of surviving via a negotiated settlement, but news of Sherman's triumph changed the political landscape by reviving the war spirit of the North. Added to smaller but equally dramatic Union successes in the Shenandoah Valley, Atlanta's capture ensured Lincoln of a second term—a feat that ended the South's hopes of gaining at the bargaining table the decisive victory it had failed to win on the battlefield.[39]

HAVING LEARNED OF ATLANTA'S FALL AND Hood's retreat to Palmetto Station on the Atlanta & West Point, Wheeler remained reluctant to rejoin his army. He tried to delay his return by asking for authority to accompany Forrest on his raid, an undertaking he hoped would rekindle his men's morale. Although permission was not granted, Wheeler claimed that he assigned to Forrest some one thousand two hundred troopers, whom he had left in Tennessee pursuant to Hood's orders. On September 24, he finally began the march to Hood's side by way of Danville, Athens, and Stevenson. He took his time; returning to the W&A near Dalton, he stopped to damage more track—enough, he stated, to put the railroad out of operation for an additional two weeks. In response to another, more peremptory order from Hood, he hurried south and, on October 8, connected with the far left of the army in its new location near Cedartown, seventy miles northwest of Atlanta and not far from the Alabama border.[40]

Reporting to his superior, Wheeler attempted to defend his long-overdue arrival. But Hood was more interested in explaining why he had left Atlanta, crossed the Chattahoochee River, and struck anew at the Western & Atlantic. The object was to lure Sherman out of his captured stronghold, where he seemed to be working overtime to oppress the citizenry, the subject of a long and bitter correspondence between the commanding generals. So far Hood's plan seemed to be bearing fruit; two days before Wheeler's arrival, Hood's scouts reported that the Federals had crossed the Chattahoochee in pursuit. If Sherman continued to follow, Hood would lead him on a merry chase and exhaust his supplies. Should Sherman give up the pursuit and turn back to Atlanta, Hood would fall on him and sever his communications.

Hood's plan had been sanctioned by Jefferson Davis, who in the last week in September had made another visit to the Army of Tennessee. During three days of talks, the conferees decided that Hood should attack the W&A, as Wheeler had done most recently at Dalton, thus increasing the likelihood that Sherman would pursue. If, as seemed likely, Sherman left a large contingent to occupy Atlanta and the surrounding countryside, he would oppose Hood with a reduced force (Sherman's army group was also believed to have lost manpower through the departure of many units whose service terms had expired). If the Union commander still appeared too strong to contain, Hood should retreat through the mountains to Gadsden, Alabama, where the terrain was rugged and defensible. Hood had promised the president that should Sherman react to Confederate movements in any other way, such as by heading east through Georgia toward the Gulf of Mexico (as Hood envisioned) or the Atlantic Ocean (which Davis considered more likely), the Army of Tennessee would turn about and pursue as closely as possible.[41]

After departing Hood's headquarters, Davis traveled to Augusta, Georgia, to confer with P. G. T. Beauregard, recently in command of the Confederate lines north of Petersburg. At Augusta, Davis laid out Hood's plan and gained Beauregard's qualified approval. Davis then offered a new job to the general he had long disliked but who had won his gratitude by helping keep both Richmond and Petersburg out of Union hands. Beauregard, who jumped at the chance to get from under the thumb of Robert E. Lee, accepted command of the Military Division of the West, which was to encompass Hood's army as well as Richard Taylor's area of operations. Beauregard was made to understand that his was strictly an administrative post; he would give advice and instructions but would not exercise field command.[42]

The day after Wheeler reached Cedartown, Beauregard went there to confer with Hood. Beauregard's new subordinate confirmed the salient points of the strategy he had worked out with Davis and that Beauregard had sanctioned. However, Hood was being deceptive, for he failed to inform his visitor that he had changed his mind about following Sherman to the coast or anywhere else. Now Hood was determined to march his forty thousand troops, including Wheeler's cavalry, to the Tennessee River, destroying Union communications as he went. Later he expanded his clandestine project to include crossing the Tennessee northwest of Gadsden, destroying Sherman's rail lines around Stevenson and Bridgeport, crossing into Middle Tennessee, capturing Nashville, invading Kentucky, and pressing on to the Ohio River. Such provocative acts would surely force Sherman to follow him; if not, Hood, after occupying the Ohio Valley, would turn east and head for Virginia, joining Lee at Petersburg.

Joe Wheeler would play no role in Hood's grandiose scheme. Assuming that Hood remained committed to his original plan, Beauregard had gone to Jacksonville, Alabama, to build up a supply base for the coming campaign. Then he traveled to Blue Mountain, where he expected to meet Hood and work out final details of the movement. At Blue Mountain, however, he found only Wheeler's

General P. G. T. Beauregard, CSA.

cavalry, whose commander informed him that the army leader was at Gadsden, en route north. When Beauregard caught up with Hood at Gadsden on October 21, he learned for the first time of Hood's intention to cross the Tennessee. Aware that he had little power over Hood, Beauregard acquiesced in his plans. But he successfully demanded that Wheeler's horsemen be sent back to Georgia to keep an eye on Sherman and operate against his communications.[43]

For weeks, detachments from Sherman's army group had been following Hood, without overtaking him. By now the frustrated Ohioan had given up the chase and was petitioning Grant for authority to march, instead, to the coast. He intended to move quickly, in light order, living off the country and making the secessionists of central and eastern Georgia feel the hard hand of war for the first time. Months before, when commanding a military district in West Tennessee, Sherman had developed a policy of making war on the civilian base that aided and abetted the Confederate armies. He would practice this policy relentlessly from Atlanta to the sea.[44]

Late in October, Grant gave conditional approval to the march, but when Lincoln expressed the fear that it would permit Hood to range unopposed through Tennessee and Kentucky, Sherman agreed to head for the ocean with about sixty thousand troops, including the mounted division of Judson Kilpatrick. He would dispatch to Nashville to deal with Hood an array of forces under George Thomas: Schofield's corps; the 4th Corps, Army of the Cumberland; and most of the cavalry that had helped capture Atlanta. Augmented by another infantry corps to be sent from St. Louis, as well as by forces from Chattanooga (later organized into a provisional division under General Steedman), Thomas eventually would have fifty thousand troops of all arms, including approximately ten thousand horse soldiers under twenty-seven-year-old Brevet Major General James Harrison Wilson, one of Grant's protégés, formerly a cavalry division commander in the Army of the Potomac.[45]

On October 26, Wheeler effectively completed his tenure in command of the cavalry, Army of Tennessee, by skirmishing at Gadsden with a far-flung detachment of Sherman's armies. When the Yankees broke contact and returned to Atlanta, Wheeler was obliged to follow: his job was to shadow Sherman everywhere he went, and fight him whenever conditions permitted. He would do so not as a member of Hood's army but as a subordinate of General Taylor's and, by extension, Beauregard's. This arrangement ensured that when Sherman marched out of the Gate City on November 14 heading east, Wheeler's horsemen would constitute the only source of armed resistance outside of local garrisons manned by the amateur soldiers of the Georgia militia. The coming campaign promised to be nothing less than an exercise in futility, but for Wheeler and his outnumbered, overworked troopers, there was no help for it.[46]

# FOURTEEN

# FINAL
# BLOWS

W HEELER'S DETACHING LEFT HOOD'S ARMY OF INVASION with only two brigades of cavalry, commanded by Red Jackson. To rectify this obvious deficiency, Beauregard exercised the authority recently given him over Richard Taylor's department. He sent orders to Nathan Bedford Forrest, then operating against Sherman's supply bases in West Tennessee, to cross the river and rejoin the Army of Tennessee for the first time in a year.[1]

That year had been one of the most active and successful of Forrest's war career, though also a continuing source of controversy. After quitting Bragg's army, the cavalryman had proceeded to Okolona, Mississippi, where, with the rank of major general, he formed a command built upon the small brigade of Colonel Robert V. Richardson. By recruiting heavily in Tennessee and Kentucky, and adding a number of conscripts, he built up his unit until it formed a considerable portion of Polk's Army of Mississippi. In organizing the command, he was assisted by Polk and his chief of cavalry, Stephen Dill Lee, but much of the funding for its equipping came from Forrest's own pocketbook.

At the head of this force, Forrest, in late December, made a second raid into West Tennessee, lashing Sherman's communications and evading columns of pursuers. The publicity accruing to this feat spurred recruiting; soon he was leading a division comprising the brigades of Richardson and Colonels Tyree H. Bell, Robert McCulloch, and Jeffrey Forrest, Bedford's youngest brother. Brigadier General James R. Chalmers, the erstwhile infantry commander, was assigned as Forrest's second-in-command. When Abraham Buford's Kentuckians joined Forrest early in 1864, the command became a corps comprising the divisions of Chalmers and Buford. Over time the fiery-tempered Forrest became involved in disputes with Chalmers and Richardson, both of whom he relieved of their duties. Chalmers was reinstated by higher authority; Richardson was not.[2]

In early February, Grant sent an infantry column under Sherman to Meridian, Mississippi, near Polk's headquarters, to ruin the two rail lines that met there, the Southern Mississippi and the Mobile & Ohio. Warding off opposition from Polk's infantry, Sherman occupied the junction and tore up track in four directions. Forrest was unable to take part in the fight because Polk had sent him to run down a cavalry force under Brigadier General William Sooy Smith, operating out of Memphis in support of Sherman's main force. Near West Point, Mississippi, on the twenty-first, Forrest fell on Smith's seven-thousand-man column and sent it reeling north in defeat. Forrest pursued, inflicting additional casualties: Smith's losses neared four hundred. Forrest suffered fewer than 150, although they included his brother, shot through the neck while leading a charge.[3]

In the middle of March, Forrest decided to return to West Tennessee, both to recruit his command and to harass the local Yankees. Moving north from Tupelo, Mississippi, he crossed the state line and raided Jackson, Humboldt, and Union City, venues he had visited or threatened on two previous expeditions. At Paducah, Kentucky, he was finally confronted by a combative garrison, and turned back to Tennessee. Then he veered west to assault Fort Pillow on the east bank of the Mississippi near its confluence with the Hatchie River. On April 12, Chalmers's division overran the fort, which was defended by three hundred white soldiers and almost as many United States Colored Troops. The casualty toll was staggering: half the garrison was killed or mortally wounded.

Northern accounts claimed that most of those killed were murdered after the fort had surrendered, and that Forrest's men singled out captured African Americans and their white officers. The Fort Pillow Massacre, which triggered a court of inquiry in Washington that drew lurid testimony and laid the blame squarely on Forrest, would forever stain the general's record. His partisans argued that if atrocities had been committed it had been the work not of Forrest but a few of his men, who, enraged by being fired on by ex-slaves, could not be restrained. One of Forrest's sergeants, however, admitted to the "butchery" of captive black troops and claimed that "Gen. Forrest ordered them shot down like dogs."[4]

In later months, Forrest achieved less-controversial victories. Immediately after Fort Pillow, he returned to Mississippi to plan new operations. Before he could mount any, Sherman, now commanding Grant's military division, put together an expedition whose sole objective was to eliminate Forrest as a threat to the upcoming campaign in Georgia. This force, entrusted to Major General Samuel D. Sturgis, consisted of eight thousand three hundred foot soldiers and horsemen, plus twenty-two pieces of artillery. It took many weeks for Sturgis to bring Forrest's entire force to battle. When he did, on June 10, 1864, at Brice's Cross Roads, near Guntown, Mississippi, Forrest, with little more than half as many troops, gave Sturgis as sound a thrashing as any Union commander in the West ever endured. By the time he staggered back to Memphis, Sturgis had lost almost half of his infantry, all but six of his guns, and 250 wagons—to say nothing of his reputation and career, both of which were in shambles. The victory helped win Forrest an enduring appellation, "Wizard of the Saddle."[5]

General James R. Chalmers, CSA.

Sherman, more desperate than ever to neutralize Forrest, sent another expedition after him: eleven thousand infantry, three thousand cavalry, and twenty guns under Major General Andrew Jackson Smith. On July 14, Smith encountered Forrest and other elements of Lee's cavalry at Tupelo. Fighting mostly on the defensive in extreme heat, Smith's larger force repulsed several assaults and inflicted almost 1,250 casualties on its adversaries. One of those was Forrest, shot through the right foot, a painful and temporarily disabling wound. Dwindling supplies of rations and ammunition forced Smith to return to Memphis after the battle, preventing him from following up his victory—one of the few defeats Forrest suffered in open combat.[6]

Shortly after this setback, Forrest assumed command of all Confederate forces in northern Mississippi (Lee having joined, and Polk having rejoined, the Army of Tennessee). Early in August he learned that Sherman, now closing in on Atlanta, again had sent A. J. Smith to attack

him and keep him as far from the Union army's rear as possible. This time
Forrest avoided a major confrontation, although Smith's heavier column
drove Chalmers's horsemen from successive positions south of the
Tallahatchie River.

When Smith halted to repair a torn-up railroad, Forrest, now recovered
from his July wound, led a picked force of two thousand around his flank,
slashing his supply lines, and, on August 21, slipping inside Union-held
Memphis. Despite heavy opposition from its garrison, he occupied the city
for almost a day and nearly captured its highest-ranking rulers, Major
Generals Stephen A. Hurlbut and Cadwallader C. Washburn. When he
finally departed, he did so in good order and with small loss. As one historian has noted, this exploit "frustrated, demoralized, and embarrassed the
North." So did Smith's inability to cut off Forrest's escape. Eventually the
failed Union expedition was recalled from Mississippi.[7]

At this juncture, Forrest gave his attention to the long-voiced pleas of
Governor Brown of Georgia, echoed by Jefferson Davis, to raid Sherman's
communications link to Atlanta. Leaving a small portion of his command
under Chalmers in Mississippi, Forrest started on the expedition that
brought him into contact with Wheeler's disheveled corps at Tuscumbia,
Alabama. On September 24, he pounced on the six-hundred-man garrison
at Athens, Alabama, a depot on the Nashville & Decatur Railroad, which
he captured along with blockhouses and bridges on the railroad outside
town.

From Athens, Forrest crossed the Tennessee River to Pulaski and
Fayetteville, then proceeded to his old bailiwick of Spring Hill. By now he
had torn up many miles of track and had accumulated a haul of prisoners,
horses, cannons, and military stores, accomplishments that had prompted
Sherman to refer to him in official dispatches as "the very devil." In the end,
however, Forrest found his command too weak from near-constant travel
and threatened by too many pursuers to do much damage to the Nashville
& Chattanooga Railroad, Sherman's principal line of reinforcement and
resupply. He headed south, Yankees baying at his heels, and recrossed the
Tennessee on October 5-7.[8]

After two and a half weeks of succoring his weary command, Forrest
obeyed the orders of his immediate superior, General Taylor, to return to
West Tennessee and operate against Union communications—on both
land and water. Late in October, he struck the Tennessee upstream from
Fort Henry, and concealed his men and guns along the riverbank. For a

week beginning October 29, he ambushed enemy vessels churning north from the supply base at Johnsonville, forcing several to heave to and riddling with shells those that refused to surrender. Over those seven days, Forrest captured four gunboats, fourteen transports, and twenty barges, along with 150 Yankee soldiers. When the ships stopped coming his way he moved upstream. Opening with his artillery on Johnsonville, he terrorized its garrison and inflicted nearly seven million dollars' damage on the military stores stockpiled there.[9]

On October 26, Taylor had directed Forrest, as soon as his mission in West Tennessee was completed, to open communication with John Bell Hood and place himself at the latter's disposal. On November 2, the impatient Hood sent Forrest a message from his headquarters at Tuscumbia: "When can I expect you here or when can I hear from you? I am waiting for you." Two weeks later he crossed his army—the corps of S. D. Lee, A. P. Stewart, and Frank Cheatham, plus artillery and trains, all screened by Jackson's cavalry—to Florence using pontoons. On the north bank, he waited for Forrest to join him.[10]

Forrest was on his way, but he took his time, perhaps because he did not relish surrendering his independence and being tied to the ponderous movements of an army on campaign. The cavalry already with Hood, however, looked forward to his arrival. Whether wizard or devil, Forrest had established a reputation second to none among mounted leaders in the West, and his celebrity was a powerful lure. A Mississippian had heard that Forrest might be on his way: "We all hope so at any rate. He is a dashing & successful General." Even more important, perhaps, was the perception that Forrest "does not get more men killed and wounded than those who do less service."[11]

Not until November 18 did Forrest make contact with a portion of Hood's command and begin to operate with it. Hood welcomed his new subordinate by installing him as his cavalry commander. He was given authority over Jackson's small division (the brigades of Armstrong and Ross) and an unattached brigade under Jacob Biffle. Having lost so many of his own troopers to a scarcity of healthy mounts, Forrest estimated the manpower at his disposal as no more than five thousand effectives. If the high command had had its way, the number would have been even smaller. On November 17, Beauregard, even as he urged Hood to "deal the enemy rapid and vigorous blows," told the army leader to send Jackson's troopers as well as other cavalry forces to Joe Wheeler in Georgia. Secure in the knowledge that Beauregard could direct but not compel, Hood claimed that Wheeler already commanded thirteen brigades and that Jackson "could not be now spared from this army without seriously embarrassing" its operations. Beauregard eventually acquiesced.[12]

On the cold, blustery morning of the twentieth, one day before Hood began moving toward his next destination, Columbia, Tennessee, he gave Forrest his orders: "To send forward at once small parties, under bold, reliable men, to break the enemy's railroad and telegraphic communications from Nashville to the north." Forrest had already moved out in front of the army, but he could not at once obey. He was still refurbishing his command, impressing horses from the countryside to pull his artillery batteries and to mount the men who had been accompanying him on foot since the end of the Johnsonville raid.[13]

Once Hood got in motion, the weather tried to interfere. A cold rain that turned to snow and sleet worsened the plight of men long beset by hardship and privation, especially those who lacked footwear. The previous month Captain Champion of Jackson's cavalry had informed his wife that "we get [only] half enough to eat—my men are without clothes and shoes literally barefooted and ragged." In later letters he reported that conditions had not improved. Mississippian William Barry, who had been on the march with Hood since evacuating Atlanta, wrote his sister that "I have had for the last month the hardest times that has ever fallen to my lot yet. [I] have marched over two hundred & fifty miles through rain & dust mud and over rocks & mountains until I am completely worn out and the worst of it is [I] have had nearly nothing to eat. . . . [I am] the hardest looking rebel in this Army."[14]

Despite the elements, Hood made progress as he trudged north in three columns converging toward Columbia: Stewart via the Lawrenceburg road, Lee farther west in the direction of West Point, and Cheatham more westward still on the road from Waynesboro. Hood was aware that his enemy was up ahead, waiting for him—and for reinforcements. General Thomas had battened down in Nashville with approximately eighteen thousand troops. To keep an eye on the Army of Tennessee and slow its movements, buying time for A. J. Smith's infantry corps to complete its journey from St. Louis, Thomas had dispatched to Pulaski, thirty miles south of Columbia, the only other troops immediately available to him, under command of John Schofield. These consisted of Schofield's own 23rd Corps as well as

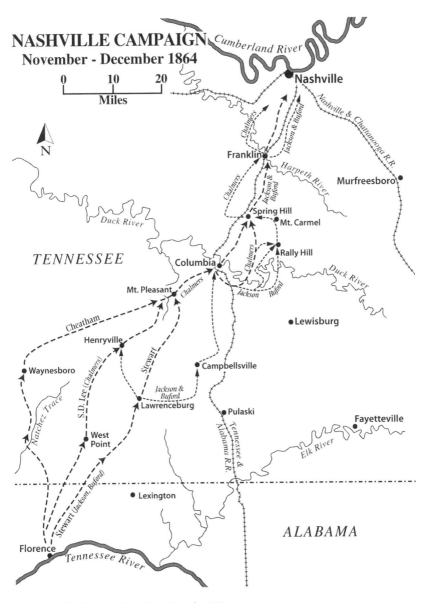

Nashville Campaign, November–December 1864.

David Stanley's 4th Corps, protected in front and on the flanks by a por-
tion of James H. Wilson's cavalry: a division under Brigadier General
Edward Hatch, and the brigades of Brigadier General John T. Croxton and
Colonel Horace Capron.[15]

In total, Schofield's force numbered twenty-three thousand officers and men, enough to put up a fight but not enough to survive a head-on encounter with Hood. Knowing this, Schofield moved carefully and kept a close watch on his enemy, especially Forrest's troopers, leading the Rebel advance. Hood's movements were rapid enough to give Schofield pause. By the twenty-second, the head of Stewart's column had reached Lawrenceburg, twenty miles west of Schofield's position. On orders from Thomas, Schofield now abandoned Pulaski and double-quicked his troops across the Duck River at Columbia, foiling Hood's attempt to curve around him and cut him off from Nashville. There the expeditionary commander dug in to await further instructions.[16]

Hood continued to believe he could isolate Schofield from Thomas and defeat both in turn. As Hood biographer John Dyer puts it, "if Hood could prevent Schofield from joining Thomas, complete victory would be in Confederate hands and Hood's dazzling dream of marching to the Ohio and then joining forces with [Robert E.] Lee would come true. Such a victory would completely neutralize Sherman in Georgia and compel him to abandon the state. Get in between Schofield and Thomas; whip the former; then turn on the latter and take Nashville! That was Hood's plan."[17]

The Army of Tennessee's pace began to slow on the morning of the twenty-second, when Jackson's and Buford's troopers, in advance of Stewart's corps, encountered Hatch and Croxton at Lawrenceburg. The result was a brisk engagement that consumed most of the day and produced a fair number of casualties on both sides. Next day, Hatch and Croxton (under Wilson's personal direction) fell back toward Pulaski. Jackson and Buford followed and precipitated another hours-long engagement that ended inconclusively.

Other actions on the twenty-third took place farther north at Henryville and Campbellsville. At Henryville, General Chalmers, whose division was screening Lee's column, attacked Capron's brigade and captured forty-five of its men. Before the balance could escape along the road to Mount Pleasant, Forrest, accompanied only by his escort, raced ahead of them, then turned about and charged, producing "a perfect stampede." During the melee he took fifty prisoners and captured enough horses to mount a couple dozen of his men. At Campbellsville, meanwhile, Jackson and Buford again bested their opponents after "a short but vigorous engagement, in which he [Wilson] lost about 100 prisoners and several in killed and wounded." At each of four venues, Forrest had drawn blood, but his movements—and therefore Hood's—had been slowed by Yankee horse-men, at least some of whom had demonstrated a grasp of delaying tactics that would have made Joe Wheeler proud.[18]

By the twenty-fourth, most of Forrest's units had converged on Columbia, where Schofield's force remained behind breastworks on the north side of Duck River. Despite taking heavy fire from all three arms of Schofield's command, Forrest reported that "I invested the town from Duck River to the extreme north, which position I held until the arrival of the infantry on the morning of the 27th, when I was relieved."[19]

Aware that with a full-fledged army heading his way he must be vigilant and proactive, Wilson distributed his troopers in such a way as to cover every ford as far east as Huey's Mill, five miles from Columbia. He believed he had the river blanketed, but in the early afternoon of the twenty-eighth, reports reached him that Forrest was forcing a crossing at four points above Huey's Mill. At first Wilson could not believe the reports, but soon he dis-covered that most were accurate: only Buford had been prevented from crossing. Thanks to "stubborn resistance" from Hatch's men, Buford was forced to fall back, circle around his opponent, and rejoin Forrest on the twenty-ninth.[20]

The forced crossing of Duck River drove young Wilson to panic. With Forrest's riders hot on his heels, he hustled up the Lawrenceburg Pike as far as Mount Carmel, almost nine miles from the river. There he could no longer maintain contact with Schofield at Columbia except by long-dis-tance courier. When Forrest's men suddenly disappeared from his rear, Wilson sent scouts back toward the river. They reported that Forrest had placed himself in a position to turn in Schofield's rear near Spring Hill, fif-teen miles north of Columbia. Wilson warned his superior of this prospect, but the message took hours to reach Schofield. Then, early on the twenty-ninth, Wilson informed Schofield that Hood's main army was about to cross the river on pontoons; he urged the expeditionary leader to fall back to Franklin, fourteen miles north of Spring Hill. But because Schofield dis-trusted Wilson and could not verify his reports, and because Thomas had ordered him to hold his present position as long as possible, he remained at Columbia with most of his troops until after dark. Some hours earlier, however, he dispatched Stanley to Spring Hill with one division of the 4th Corps (a second division was recalled en route), followed by Schofield's supply train.[21]

Stanley arrived none to soon, for almost the entire Army of Tennessee was in motion. Leaving Lee, with two divisions, to hold Schofield in place by simulating attacks and pounding him with artillery fire, Hood sent the infantry of Cheatham and Stewart by way of country roads toward Spring Hill. Coming in from the east, Forrest got there first, just before noon. Upon arriving he skirmished with the local garrison, then with Stanley's just-arrived infantry, which drove him out of the town.[22]

In response to an order from Hood, Forrest held his position on the outskirts of Spring Hill until the rest of the army could reach him. It was midafternoon before Cheatham's advance echelon, Cleburne's division, relieved Forrest, who then moved north of town to cut Stanley's route of retreat. By four p.m., Stewart's corps had also arrived; it deployed east of the pike that ran from Columbia to Spring Hill and from there to Franklin.

Hood was in a near-perfect position to cut off and demolish Schofield, but he could not, or would not, take advantage. An epic breakdown of communication between the army leader and his subordinates—resulting in the withdrawal of forces that could have blocked the turnpike—added to an insidious lethargy on the part of all involved that is as difficult to explain at this distance as it was at the time, prevented Hood's trap from closing on Schofield. Not until five o'clock did the Union commander, finally aware of the danger at his back, begin moving toward Spring Hill. Wisely, when he reached the town, he did not stop there. Picking up Stanley and the wagons, under cover of darkness he hustled up the pike to Franklin and right through his adversary's fingers. In his postwar memoirs, a still-disconsolate Hood remarked that "the best move in my career as a soldier . . . [had] come to naught."[23]

Hood—who seems to have believed his opponent would remain in place through the night, to be finished off the following day—was enraged by Schofield's escape. Vowing to make the man pay, he pursued him to Franklin, where Schofield had ensconced his command behind fieldworks that virtually encircled that town on the south bank of the Harpeth River. Against the advice of his subordinates, shortly before four p.m. on the thirtieth, Hood attacked this formidable position from the south and southwest. He achieved a temporary breakthrough along the Union left-center, but every attack was repulsed with heavy loss. The six thousand Confederate casualties included five general officers killed or mortally wounded, among them the irreplaceable Cleburne. When the shooting died down, Schofield completed his withdrawal to Nashville without further resistance.[24]

While the main armies grappled on the thirtieth, so did the cavalries. Forrest had asked Hood to lend him a division of infantry, with which he proposed to maneuver Schofield out of his works "within two hours' time," after which he would deal with Wilson's cavalry, most of which was deployed on the upper bank of the Harpeth east of Franklin. Hood demurred and went ahead with his frontal assault. He ordered Forrest to divide his command, placing Chalmers on the infantry's left and Jackson and Buford on the right. During the fierce fighting of that afternoon, all three of the divisions advanced briskly. Chalmers struck some of Schofield's foot soldiers as well as Croxton's troopers, "charging and dislodging the enemy from every position he had taken," as Forrest reported. Meanwhile, Jackson and Buford—the former fighting mounted, the latter mostly on foot—drove some of the troops on Schofield's left across the Harpeth.[25]

Hoping to capitalize on his success, Jackson at about two p.m. fought his way over the river and piled into Wilson's troopers; Buford remounted his men and joined his colleague on the north bank. The fighting in that sector was brisk but inconclusive for much of the afternoon. Near nightfall, Wilson, who outnumbered his opponents and was determined to make amends for his mistakes on the twenty-ninth, shoved Jackson and Buford south of the river and held them there, putting an end to one of the darkest days in the life of the Army of Tennessee.[26]

EARLY ON DECEMBER 1, HOOD LED WHAT REMAINED of his army—he put the number at 23,053 effectives—north to Nashville. What he expected to accomplish there, in the face of a soon-to-be-superior force under Thomas, remains difficult to fathom. Hood tried to explain his actions by claiming that "the only remaining chance of success in the campaign, at this juncture, was to take position, entrench around Nashville, and await Thomas's attack which, if handsomely repulsed, might afford us an opportunity to follow up our advantage on the spot, and enter the city on the heels of the enemy." The "advantage" he referred to cannot be understood in any rational context. Rather, Hood appeared intent on adding to the disadvantages already heaped on his army by miscommunication, squandered opportunity, and defeat.[27]

When Hood settled into position south and southeast of the Tennessee capital, his far right flank, Cheatham's corps, rested on a deep cut on the

Nashville & Chattanooga, which ran southwest from the city and extended across the Nolensville Pike. Farther west, Lee's corps straddled the Franklin and Granny White Pikes. Stewart's infantry held the left, which was anchored by a series of redoubts hastily constructed on high ground along the Hillsboro Pike. None of the soldiers along this line had the benefit of a warm habitation. Because an advance by Thomas was expected any day, Hood's army had precious little time to build huts or winterize tents, of which there were few, even for the officers. Poorly clad and shod soldiers huddled in shallow trenches, warmed their hands and feet around meager campfires, slept on the ice-covered ground, and stood sentry duty while whipped by frigid winds and snow squalls.

While Hood's troops shivered, their enemy remained fairly comfortable inside the snug confines of Nashville. They also kept busy with preparations to engage Hood on the most favorable terms. George Thomas was still assimilating reinforcements, and his cavalry was gathering remounts wherever it could find them. The recent arrival of A. J. Smith's corps had given Thomas more than thirty thousand infantry, but many of the newcomers needed to be rearmed and reequipped, and their command structure readjusted. Meanwhile, Wilson was working feverishly to mount his ten thousand troopers, almost half of whom remained afoot. In the end he resorted to extreme measures, commandeering the trick-riding horses of a traveling circus and the carriage teams of Andrew Johnson, now the vice president-elect of the United States.[28]

Hood, who realized Thomas outnumbered him but did not know by how much, ought to have kept the forces available to him well in hand. Instead, he repeated a mistake Bragg had made before the critical fighting at Murfreesboro and Chattanooga. On December 2, while the army settled into its uncomfortable positions around Nashville, Hood detached Forrest, with Jackson's and Buford's divisions, later augmented by two brigades of infantry and eight guns, and sent him to operate against the Nashville & Chattanooga, neutralizing every railroad outpost between Nashville and Murfreesboro. To some degree, Hood was justified in operating against these threats to his far right and rear, especially the large (eight-thousand-man) garrison at Murfreesboro. But his timing was abysmal, and the need to assign Forrest personally to the mission was questionable. He should have recognized that the presence of Forrest, a renowned fighter who could galvanize and inspire his troops, was critical to the army's success at Nashville.

In Forrest's absence, Chalmers's division was assigned the task of covering Hood's left flank from the Hillsboro Pike to the Cumberland River, a distance of at least four miles. On the opposite flank, a single regiment of Tyree Bell's brigade was expected to protect a less extensive but equally rugged stretch of ground between the Murfreesboro Pike and the meandering Cumberland. These dispositions reflected the gambler's psyche of John Bell Hood. The army commander was placing another bet—a true long shot—that he could not afford to cover.[29]

General Lawrence S."Sul" Ross, CSA.

If Hood underestimated how heavily Thomas outnumbered him, he also underestimated the strength of Forrest's opposition. Even with the addition of the infantry and cannons under Major General William B. Bate, Forrest's expeditionary force was too small to ensure consistent success. From December 5 to 16, Forrest ranged down the railroad, tearing up track, burning bridges, downing telegraph lines, and forcing the occupants of blockhouses and stockades to succumb to "dreadful threats of 'no quarter' in case of resistance." A staff officer in Armstrong's brigade "had an opportunity of seeing & hearing the demands & replies, made in 'old Bedford's' usual style," and he came away impressed. Some garrisons, such as those at Smyrna and Read's Branch, did not wait for demands to be made of them but fled upon reports of Forrest's approach. Thus unopposed, Sul Ross's brigade captured a train and made prisoners of the 150 troops it carried. It would appear, however, that the hungry, ragged Texans were more interested in appropriating the rations and clothing that were also aboard.[30]

So far so good, but when Forrest neared Murfreesboro on the sixth, he found the town—site of his first great triumph of the war—occupied by a much greater force than he had been led to expect. Doubting that an attack would succeed, Forrest attempted to lay siege to the place, commanded by Lovell Rousseau. He deployed Buford's men on the left side of town, Jackson's on the right, and stationed Bate's infantry in between. He skirmished with the Federals throughout the day, but on the morning of December 7, a column sent out of the town under Major General Robert H. Milroy attacked Forrest's positions. Bedford's cavalry stood firm, but their infantry comrades suddenly gave way in what Forrest called "shameful retreat, losing two pieces of artillery. I seized the colors of the retreating troops and endeavored to rally them, but they could not be moved by any entreaty or appeal to their patriotism. Major-General Bate did the same thing, but was equally as unsuccessful as myself." At Forrest's frantic order, elements of Armstrong's and Ross's brigades charged the head of Milroy's column, and Buford's division galloped into Murfreesboro, threatening its rear. Hard-pressed from two directions, Milroy fell back to the town, and Buford withdrew.[31]

When he learned of what had happened, Hood recalled Bate's troops to Nashville and replaced them with a single brigade that failed to assuage Forrest's concern over the quality of his infantry support. With Rousseau and Milroy apparently content to remain inside Murfreesboro, Forrest devoted the next week to destroying railroad track. By the fifteenth, he had located a forage train heading for Murfreesboro and was about to attack it when he received word that a "general engagement" was in progress at Nashville. He was ordered to remain on the railroad until further word reached him. When he finally received his marching orders on the evening of the sixteenth, they conveyed the grim news that Hood's army had been defeated—routed, in fact—and was retreating in Forrest's direction.[32]

Although Hood had offered up his army to his enemy as if on a platter, Thomas refused to attack until assured that conditions were favorable. On the tenth, just as Thomas was about to advance, a savage storm descended on Middle Tennessee. The ground froze and snow piled up, ending thoughts of combat. By the time the weather moderated, Thomas's superiors in Washington and Virginia, who for weeks had been urging him to attack, were on the verge of removing him from command. On December 15, Grant's sense of urgency prompted him to leave the siege lines at Petersburg, Virginia, and take a train to Nashville, where he proposed to supersede Thomas.[33]

On the day Grant set out, the Rock of Chickamauga proved his superiors' fears to be groundless. Attacking in a thick morning fog, the infantry of A. J. Smith and Brigadier General Thomas J. Wood (successor to David Stanley, who had been severely wounded at Franklin), followed by Schofield's corps and with its flanks covered by two of Wilson's divisions, slowly but steadily enveloped Hood's left. Smith's men overran most of the redoubts in that sector and in so doing isolated Chalmers's dismounted troopers, most of whom had occupied breastworks astride the Charlotte

Pike, well to the north of the main fighting. Meanwhile, Steedman's command, supported by other elements of Wilson's cavalry, delivered a secondary assault against the Rebel right. When he finally realized that Steedman's was not the main effort, Hood ordered Cheatham to send heavy reinforcements to the left; eventually he shifted Cheatham's entire corps to the embattled flank. These moves, however, came too late; by the end of the short winter's day, Hood's line teetered on the verge of collapse. When darkness halted the fighting, Hood withdrew Lee's corps (now holding his right) to higher ground about two miles from the position it had occupied at daybreak.[34]

Chalmers's cavalry, which consisted of little more than the brigade of Colonel Edmund W. Rucker and the division commander's escort, did its utmost to stem the blue tide rolling toward Hood's left, but it was a losing proposition from the start. One of Rucker's men recalled that at the outset, a comrade shouted for all to hear: "Look! Look! Just look at the Yankees!" The warning had an immediate effect: "Springing up and looking over our rail piles, we beheld a sight which filled us with awe. About half a mile away, but in plain view, there appeared an immense number of the enemy's infantry . . . coming over the hills and marching with quickstep down the slope toward us, forming into one, two, three, four, five, or six lines of battle . . . and marching as steadily as on dress parade."[35]

With perhaps nine hundred effectives at his command, Chalmers could not have expected to make an impression on such a horde. Still, he urged his men to take and maintain the offensive. Some mounted and charged the advancing columns; in a few cases, they even brought the Yankees to a temporary halt. In the end, however, Chalmers had no recourse but to fall back, fighting his units from successive, precarious positions.

Next morning, Thomas renewed his onslaught, beginning with an artillery barrage that pounded all sectors of Hood's line. Thomas supposed that the shelling had softened up the enemy, but when his infantry went forward against the Confederate right, Lee's corps repulsed the attack quite handily. Farther west, however, Thomas's offensive gained ground, much of it at Chalmers's expense. The latter's troopers had been drawn south to the Hillsboro Pike to cover Cheatham's exposed flank, but the division was so extended that it could not do a proper job of it. Furthermore, it had passed so far south of Cheatham's corps that it opened a lane of advance for the enemy.

By now Wilson had massed his command along Thomas's right. Seeing an opening, he led a large body of dismounted troopers around Cheatham's corps. Wilson's recent reinforcing and the losses Cheatham had suffered gave the Union cavalry leader the advantage, as did the latter's weaponry. Flailing about with their repeating rifles and carbines, his men gradually interposed between Cheatham and Chalmers. Turning in both directions, they scorched not only the infantry's rear but also the head of Chalmers's meager command, driving the latter east toward the Granny White Pike.[36]

Around four o'clock, having undergone hours of hammering in front and now from the other direction as well, a section of Cheatham's line came unhinged and then broke away. Within minutes, triumphant Yankees were pouring through the gap. In less than half an hour, the entire flank was gone, and General Hood "beheld for the first and only time a Confederate Army abandon the field in confusion."[37]

Fearful that his retreat would be cut off, Hood frantically messaged Chalmers to "hold the Granny White pike at all hazards." Chalmers did his best to comply; at his direction, Rucker's men threw up barricades of logs, brush, and fence rails on either side of the turnpike down which Cheatham's demoralized troops were already rushing. In brief time Stewart's men, having abandoned the center of Hood's line, were joining the exodus. Only Lee's corps remained essentially intact; it continued to hold its position, preventing Thomas's infantry from gaining and closing the Franklin Pike, another avenue of retreat.[38]

When Wilson's men reached Rucker's breastworks late in the afternoon, the result was a bitter struggle at close quarters in gathering darkness and under an icy rain. The Union troopers surmounted the barriers and grappled with dismounted Rebels fighting desperately to save their army from annihilation. Wilson called the melee, in which Colonel Rucker was wounded and captured, "a scene of pandemonium, in which flashing carbines, whistling bullets, bursting shells, and the imprecations of struggling men filled the air." Only darkness prevented the Federals from securing the turnpike. When the shooting died down, Chalmers withdrew virtually unopposed to the Franklin Pike, which he guarded until the last of Hood's troops, artillery, and wagons had passed the point of gravest danger.[39]

Determined to make a finish of Hood's army, Wilson mounted a spirited pursuit on the morning of the seventeenth, which he attempted to keep going for the next ten days. Steadily driving the Confederate rear guard, including Chalmers's troopers, Wilson crossed the Harpeth River in four

columns but failed to reach Franklin before
Hood's troops swept through it. Even so, on
the first day out his men cut off and captured
more than four hundred Rebels. Wilson tried
for more captures as he pressed on toward
Columbia and Pulaski, "but with rain and frost
to chill and distress both horses and men, and
the country getting wilder and more desolate
as we pushed into it, we could not get forward
fast enough on the flanks of the enemy's rear
guard to seriously engage it."[40]

General James Harrison
Wilson, USA.

Retreating down a well-maintained turnpike while their pursuers pounded cross-country roads knee deep in mud, on the eighteenth
Hood's escapees managed to cross rain-swollen
Rutherford's Creek and Duck River on bridges that would soon be demolished. It took two days for Wilson's engineers to rebuild the spans. The cavalry lost additional time awaiting the arrival of the commissary trains it had
left far to the rear.[41]

Another factor in Wilson's inability to overtake Hood was the intervention of Forrest, who reached the Columbia vicinity from Murfreesboro late
on the eighteenth. Forrest's very presence had a therapeutic effect on
Confederate morale, while making the pursuing enemy more wary and cautious. After being captured late on the sixteenth, Rucker had tried to convince Wilson that Forrest was already on the field "and will give you hell
tonight." Rucker believed his act of deception helped temper the pursuit
from the start.[42]

When Forrest arrived, he was accompanied only by Armstrong's
brigade. He had sent Buford's men on ahead, and they had linked with
Chalmers on the seventeenth. At Hood's order, Forrest assumed command
not only of these troops but of the infantry portion of the army's rear
guard, which soon included the two-thousand-man division of Major
General Edward C. Walthall. With this force, Forrest held Columbia and
its environs and burned the Duck River bridges, which prevented Wilson
and the foot soldiers behind him from passing the stream until the twenty-
second.[43]

Even after the pursuers crossed, Forrest and his infantry supports managed to hold them at the river for several hours, providing Hood with addi-

tional time to clear the area. When too many Yankees reached the south bank, Forrest leapfrogged his skirmishers from one prepared position to another, buying even more time. Then he rode off to Pulaski, where he blew up a local stockpile of munitions to keep it out of enemy hands—a rather depressing way to spend Christmas Day.

By the morning of the twenty-sixth, Union horsemen were again pressing Forrest and Walthall. The generals halted at Anthony's Hill, seven miles from Pulaski, and had their troops build breastworks. When Wilson advanced haltingly in a dense fog, they surprised him with a withering volley in front, followed by attacks in flank by two of Forrest's regiments and hundreds of foot soldiers, "producing," Forrest claimed, "a complete rout." Cavalry and infantry pursued the retreating enemy for two miles, then fell back and resumed their withdrawal.[44]

This encounter proved to be the last during Hood's retreat. By now what remained of the Army of Tennessee had crossed its namesake river to safety, after which it straggled into its old camp at Florence, Alabama. Walthall's infantry joined it there, but Forrest, in response to orders from Hood, headed for Mississippi.

Eventually the main army moved in the same direction. Concerned that he could not generate an effective defense should Thomas cross the river, the once-confident and now thoroughly discouraged Confederate commander led his shattered ranks all the way to Tupelo, Mississippi, arriving January 10, 1865. There the Army of Tennessee lay down as if to expire. And there, three days later, John Bell Hood wrote Richmond asking to be relieved of his command, a request that was granted forthwith.[45]

Hood's war was over, but not Bedford Forrest's, whose command, although battle-weary and saddle-sore, had ended the campaign in better condition than the rest of its army. Even so, it would never regain the offensive power or the defensive tenacity it had long enjoyed. Upon reaching his new station at Corinth, Mississippi, Forrest was assigned to command the cavalry of Richard Taylor's department, with the rank of lieutenant general. His responsibilities centered on the defense of Confederate positions between eastern Mississippi and central Alabama.

To cover this truly vast area, he had only the skeletonized commands of Chalmers, Jackson, Buford, and Bell. Those troopers within Forrest's immediate reach amounted to less than half the number Wilson enjoyed when, in late March of 1865, he started on a twenty-eight-day raid across Alabama and into middle Georgia. Forrest opposed Wilson with every man and gun he could gather, but it was not enough. Although he won a few rounds, he could not prevent the young general from pummeling every objective in his path. By the time he finished, Wilson had captured five fortified cities, including Selma and Macon, along with almost seven thousand troops; had destroyed immense quantities of military goods and untold miles of Confederate property; had freed the inmates of Andersonville and had captured its jailor; and had hunted down the fugitive president of the Confederacy, capturing Jefferson Davis before he could reach the Georgia coast and commandeer a boat to take him into exile in some foreign land.[46]

Conceding defeat to his young adversary, Forrest retired to Gainesville, Alabama, where he tried in vain to reassemble a command akin to the one he had led to victory and celebrity on many fields. At war's end, he admonished those who remained in his ranks to "preserve untarnished the reputation you have so nobly won," but he rejected the advice of Confederate officials to flee to the Trans-Mississippi theater to join an army still in rebellion, an act Forrest considered both futile and inconsistent with the honorable acceptance of defeat. Instead, in early May, he told those troopers who desired to fight on, "You may all do as you damn please, but I'm a-going home" to his wife and son in Mississippi. And so he did.[47]

CONFIDENT THAT THOMAS WOULD DEAL EFFECTIVELY with Hood—even if Lincoln, Grant, and Chief of Staff Henry Halleck did not share his belief—Sherman left Atlanta on November 14, 1864, and marched, burned, and plundered his way across middle Georgia. Over the five weeks it took him to reach the Atlantic seaboard at Savannah, his sixty-two thousand veteran troops—divided between a right wing led by O. O. Howard and consisting of the 15th and 17th Corps, Army of the Tennessee, and a left wing (the Army of Georgia) composed of the 14th and 20th Corps under Major General Henry W. Slocum—proved they had the wherewithal to fulfill their leader's pledge to "make Georgia howl." Living off the land rather than being tied to long and vulnerable supply lines, Sherman's "bummers," as they came to be called, confiscated almost seven thousand horses and mules, more than thirteen thousand head of cattle, a half million pounds of grain, and eleven million pounds of fodder. They seized and demolished hundreds of warehouses, supply depots, foundries, munitions stores, stockpiles of contraband, and no fewer than 317 miles of track on the railroads that ran from Macon to Augusta and from Atlanta to Charleston, South Carolina.[48]

When they tired of attacking military objectives, the invaders switched to civilian targets, burning houses and barns; looting corncribs, smokehouses, and chicken coops; and destroying or handing over to slaves what they themselves could not carry off. The Marchers to the Sea gloried in their determination to subsist on Georgia's harvest. As one enlisted man put it in a letter home, "you better believe we lived bully," and thoroughly enjoyed the experience. Many comrades considered these excesses justified by the malevolent support Georgians and their neighbors had given to a war they had set in motion. A bummer from Indiana might have been speaking for Sherman himself when he wrote: "It is but right that these people should feel some of the hardships of the war." As a result of Sherman's march, "they will better appreciate peace when it does come, and be not so ready to rush wildly into the same vortex again."[49]

Sherman had his way with Georgia because almost no one was left to oppose him. Beginning in late November, Wheeler's horsemen trailed both Union columns and tangled regularly with Judson Kilpatrick, who covered their rear and flanks. Kilpatrick commanded a single division, perhaps three thousand five hundred strong, but on most occasions he outnumbered Wheeler. Despite Hood's claim that Wheeler had ample manpower, he may have had a paper force of four thousand but never more than half that number was available at any one time. Although a table of organization covering this point in the war is virtually impossible to come by, Wheeler's campaign report suggests he retained the divisions of Humes, Iverson, and Allen. It appears Humes's command consisted of the brigades of Ashby, Harrison, and Dibrell; Iverson's of Crews's and Hannon's brigades (later joined by the mounted infantrymen of the "Orphan Brigade" of Kentuckians under Colonel Joseph H. Lewis); and Allen's division of Anderson's and Hagan's brigades. Wheeler's so-called corps also included at least nine pieces of horse artillery.[50]

Because Wheeler received no support except from unreliable units of militia found in the larger communities along Sherman's route, he could do little more than keep an eye on the invaders and tally up their depredations. The infantry support critical to bringing the Yankees to heel was nowhere to be found in central Georgia, so Wheeler had to content himself with jabbing at the enemy, taking small slices from his flanks, and waylaying his foraging parties. Many of the bummers his men captured, especially those caught in the act of assaulting civilians or destroying their property, were summarily executed.

On a few occasions, Wheeler managed to bring Kilpatrick's troopers to battle on terms favorable to him; less frequently he got the better of small bodies of foot soldiers. Invaders and pursuers clashed at or near such locales as Griswoldville, Waynesborough, Buckhead Creek, Millen Grove, Rocky Creek Church, Thomas's Station, and Ebenezer Creek. At Waynesborough and Buckhead Creek, Wheeler prevented one of Kilpatrick's raiding parties from burning a strategic bridge and forced it to flee for its life, taking numerous prisoners. At Ebenezer Creek, his troopers corralled and returned to their masters two thousand runaway slaves who had attached themselves to the rear of the Union left wing, only to be abandoned on the south side of the stream by one of Slocum's corps commanders. But these successes were few and short-lived; at no point did Wheeler seriously impede his enemy.[51]

If Wheeler received little support from organized military units, he got almost none from the local citizenry, which came to view his troopers in the same light as the worst of Sherman's bummers. Wheeler had never succeeded in ruling his men with an iron fist, and many of the officers who might have enforced discipline in the lower ranks had been lost through attrition. Those troopers who remained were borne down by the near-constant campaigning they had endured since early May. They were demoralized by the heavy casualties the command had suffered over that period. And they felt humiliated by their inability to halt Sherman. The corporate morale had never been so low as on this excruciating trek through Georgia, and Wheeler's long-festering disciplinary problem had never been so severe.

As they trudged through Georgia, the Confederate cavalrymen showed an increasing willingness to drop out of the ranks and confiscate, appropriate, and occasionally destroy, on a par with their vilified enemy. Clad in clothing that provided little protection from the winds of autumn and winter, and having lived on half-rations for weeks at a time—and for days with no rations at all—they took what they needed from the countryside. The alternative was unthinkable. As Captain Miller of the 8th Confederate put it, "it was depredation or desertion and in devotion to the cause for which they had fought and bled and suffered for three years, they scorned the latter and chose the former."[52]

Such behavior gained Sherman's pursuers an unenviable reputation. A loud and prolonged outcry from their victims—many of whom had already been plundered by the Yankees—prompted Governor Brown to call for the removal of "Wheeler's robbers" from his state. Even General Beauregard, who was responsible for Wheeler's presence in Georgia, suggested that unless it mended its ways, the entire command should be dismounted: "Its conduct in front of the enemy, and its depredations on private property, renders it worse than useless."[53]

The troopers' continuing misconduct sullied their leader's reputation and played a role in his demotion. By mid-January 1865, Sherman's men had captured Savannah after ousting a small garrison under General Hardee, to whose Department of South Carolina, Georgia, and Florida Wheeler was now assigned. After a brief respite, the Federals started on the northern leg of their journey, which Sherman intended to end at Petersburg. Their next destination was South Carolina, which, as the first state to secede, deserved, in their eyes, the most severe chastisement. Accordingly, the damage done to public and private property in middle Georgia paled by comparison to the wanton destruction levied on the "cradle of secession," where Sherman's troops razed entire towns (Barnwell, for example, was renamed "Burnwell," for good reason).

On the last day of January 1865, Robert E. Lee was appointed general-in-chief of all Confederate armies. Clothed with the power to make high-ranking assignments, Lee granted the wish of Major General Wade Hampton, commander of cavalry of the Army of Northern Virginia, to be transferred south to help defend his native South Carolina against Sherman's vandals. Upon reaching Columbia, the state capital, Hampton, who had been preceded by a division of South Carolina cavalry under Brigadier General M. Calbraith Butler, was assigned a rather nebulous command. Lee, however, intended that the forty-six-year-old cavalryman, a non-professional soldier who had won the respect and admiration of all who served under him (one admirer described him as "a gentleman and soldier 'to the finger nails'"), should replace the discredited Wheeler. Fightin' Joe outranked the newcomer by date of commission, but that changed when the Confederate Congress expedited the confirmation of Hampton's appointment as lieutenant general.[54]

On February 7, Hampton was installed as commander of cavalry in General Hardee's department, which included Wheeler's corps. With the addition of Butler's division, which by Hampton's decree served independent of Wheeler's authority, the South Carolinian commanded some seven thousand six hundred troopers—on paper. The number of effectives, however, was probably closer to six thousand.[55]

Even when adding the troops that had evacuated Savannah (no more than nine thousand of them), such a force was too small to enjoy a realistic prospect of halting Sherman, who stood to gain forty thousand more men once he made contact with other Union forces gathering along the North Carolina coast. Hampton's and Butler's arrival had given a boost to the morale of local Confederates, but the improvement proved to be fleeting. Soon many, perhaps most, of Hardee's troops were writhing in the throes of gloom and despair. One among

General Wade Hampton, CSA.

many, a member of Wheeler's 10th Confederate Cavalry, saw the end approaching. "I would like to here of some terms of pece before the [Yankees] runn clear over us," he wrote his wife, adding that "our soldiers are very much dishartened and the most of them say we are whiped." Other Rebels continued to hold out hope and professed optimism. An officer in the 1st Georgia Cavalry informed his brother that "our present situation . . . appears gloomy enough, but I hope and think we will yet be independent. . . . [On the] patriotism of our Soldiers we must depend, and as we have few of them in comparison to the enemy we should foster and protect them as much as possible."[56]

The patriotism of the soldiers in Sherman's path failed to prevent him from capturing and occupying Columbia on February 17. Following a determined but unsuccessful attempt to keep the enemy on the south side of the Broad River, Wheeler withdrew his men into the city. When the Federals began to pour into the streets of Columbia, some troopers fought to the last to hold their positions. Many others, however, beat a premature retreat, stopping only long enough to plunder homes, stores, or saloons. Hampton, who was well aware of the unsavory reputation Wheeler's men had gained, accosted one body of looters and found himself staring down the barrel of numerous pistols. More angry than threatened, he rode off, cursing the material he had inherited.[57]

Over the next two days, Columbia's occupiers applied the torch to large sections of the city, some of which had been barricaded with cotton bales that caught fire, possibly by accident. By the time the fires burned themselves out, about a third of the city had been reduced to charred ruins. After seeing to the destruction of any war goods that had escaped the flames, the invaders moved into the countryside. They laid waste to millions of dollars in private property, including three of Wade Hampton's plantations, which they burned to the ground, leaving standing only their Greek revival columns. The gentleman-soldier, once widely considered one of the wealthiest planters in the Deep South, and who at war's outset had personally funded the raising, equipping, and arming of units for Confederate service, would end the conflict penniless and homeless.

Passing out of South Carolina on March 6, Sherman's soldiers boasted of leaving a "black track" in their wake. One bummer claimed "there was [not] a man in the army but has set fire to one or more buildings" in the Palmetto State. The invaders laid a lighter hand on neighboring North Carolina, which had a large pro-Unionist population and had been the last state to secede, but the disparity was often hard to perceive given the destruction wrought by foraging parties that stripped the state like so many blue-tinged locusts.[58]

As before, Hampton and Wheeler were largely reduced to tailing the marauders at a safe distance. Upon occasion, however, they drew blood in gratifying fashion. On March 10, at Monroe's Cross Roads, west of Fayetteville, Wheeler and Butler teamed in a surprise attack on the overly confident and unvigilant Judson Kilpatrick, who had pitched camp a considerable distance from the nearest Union infantry. The cavalry leader's reputation was that of a braggart and bully whose unabashed licentiousness outraged Southern sensibilities. Rumor had it that the "marauding rascal" kept his men supplied with matches; his opponents held him personally responsible for torching Barnwell and other towns and villages. For these and other reasons, his command made a most inviting target for the would-be defenders of North Carolina.[59]

In the darkness of early morning, the Confederates moved into position to attack the slumbering camp from three sides. At daylight, Butler's division galloped south across the Morganton road and struck the outer line of enemy tents. Minutes later, Wheeler, at the head of Allen's division, charged in from the northwest, and Humes's division, Hannon's brigade in front, attacked from the west. Shouting and shooting, the converging columns turned the camp into bedlam. Half-dressed Federals stumbled out of their tents and bedrolls to be cut down by pistol shots and saber blows; others

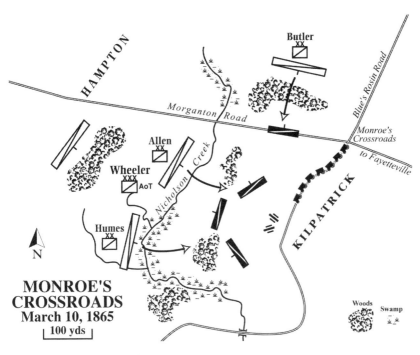

Monroe's Crossroads, March 10, 1865.

were trampled by galloping horses. A few snatched up their carbines and retreated to a pine forest where, as a captain in the 3rd Alabama reported, "they poured a hot fire into our little squad." They seemed to target high-ranking officers; Humes, Hannon, and Hagan fell wounded, while Allen and Colonel Ashby were disabled when their horses were shot from under them.[60]

Most of Kilpatrick's men made no attempt to defend the camp. Throwing themselves into the saddle, they fled south, the only route of escape. In less than half an hour, almost everyone in blue, including those who had tried to make a stand, were galloping toward the camps of the 14th Corps, several miles away. They were accompanied by their leader, who upon hearing the opening shots had bolted from the farmhouse he had appropriated for his headquarters. After persuading one attacker that he was only a private soldier not worth capturing, Kilpatrick, clad in pants and boots with his nightshirt hanging out, galloped to safety. The fugitive left behind two hundred men who had been rendered *hors de combat*, as well as a girlfriend ("a teenage trollop," in the words of one historian) who had been traveling with him since leaving her hometown of Columbia. Kilpatrick also abandoned "some 600 foot-sore Confederates" who had been taken prisoner during Hardee's retreat from South Carolina.[61]

More could have been achieved had Humes's men not been stymied by a previously undetected swamp and had other Rebels not halted to loot the overrun camp. Even so, "Kilpatrick's Shirttail Skedaddle" gave great satisfaction to every attacker and helped salve some of the psychological wounds they had suffered while chasing, but rarely overtaking, their enemy.[62]

THE GEORGIA OFFICER WHO HAD EXPRESSED hope that the Confederacy could still prevail had advised his father that "this is only to be done by putting men of heart and feeling in command like Johnston." The Army of Tennessee—what remained of it—continued to respect its old commander, who since July had been living in exile, first in Georgia, then in southwestern North Carolina. The Southern public shared the army's sentiments, especially in the wake of Hood's downfall. Two weeks after the debacle at Nashville, a Confederate War Department insider had observed that "a great pressure has been brought to bear, since Hood's overthrow, for the reassignment of Johnston." When voting to confirm Lee's appointment as general-in-chief of the armies, the Senate in Richmond urged Johnston's reinstatement to field command; four days later, the House took the same action. Upon assuming his new post, Lee recommended this course as well.[63]

Having argued with and criticized Johnston for more than three years, President Davis was loath to appoint him to any command. Seeing no alternative, in late February he bowed to the mounting pressure and asked Johnston to take command of the Army of Tennessee and any other troops available to defend North Carolina. Despite his bitter feelings toward his civilian overlord, Johnston considered it his patriotic duty to accept. At a meeting with Davis in Richmond, he was informed that his command would consist of all that remained of Hood's army, some five thousand diehards whom A. P. Stewart was transferring by train via Augusta, Georgia, and then by overland march to a point south of Raleigh, North Carolina (some four thousand other survivors of the Nashville campaign had drifted down to Mobile, where an outmanned Confederate garrison was under attack by combined arms; an untold number of others, having fought the good fight, had given it up and gone home). Johnston would also have command of approximately eleven thousand troops from Beauregard's department, including the fugitives from Savannah under Hardee; a few thousand others sent from North Carolina and personally commanded by Braxton Bragg; and Hampton's cavalry.[64]

All told, Johnston would have at his disposal about twenty-one thousand effectives, not nearly enough to stop Sherman from linking with the coastal garrisons around Wilmington and Goldsboro. Johnston's only hope was to slow and frustrate Sherman as he had on the road to Atlanta. Fabian tactics might buy time for negotiations aimed at producing a peace short of Confederate submission. Recent efforts toward that end had been rejected by Lincoln, but apparently Johnston believed talks might be reopened.

It did not take long for Johnston to see that he could not prevent his enemy from imposing his will on the Old North State. On March 16, three weeks after Johnston assumed command of the Department of North Carolina, Hardee's remnant attempted to block Slocum's wing on the road to Goldsboro. For several hours, Hardee somehow managed to hold his ground south of Averasborough, but when Slocum, under Sherman's personal direction, turned his right and threatened his left, Hardee drew off and marched toward Smithfield, having lost almost nine hundred men to Slocum's 678.

Hardee had fought without any cavalry support to speak of. Wheeler, who had been moving toward Raleigh, had secured permission to ride to the sounds of the fighting. Reaching Averasborough late in the day, he claimed to have helped stem the Union turning-movement, allowing Hardee's infantry to withdraw without further damage.[65]

Hampton had not taken part in the fighting at Averasborough; he had remained near Bentonville, twenty-four miles to the east. The following evening, Johnston, then at Smithfield, asked his cavalry commander for his views on making a more concerted effort to halt Sherman. Hampton suggested that the army concentrate in the area of his own headquarters. Johnston agreed and ordered his scattered forces, including Hardee's and Wheeler's, to assemble at Bentonville.

Most of Wheeler's command, minus a detachment that had been assigned to escort Hardee from Smithfield, reached its assigned position on the eighteenth. There it reunited with what remained of the once-mighty Army of Tennessee, which was deployed on the right of Johnston's sickle-shaped line. On the left, Bragg, with the North Carolina division of Major

General Robert F. Hoke, straddled the road to Goldsboro. Once Hardee arrived, his troops were to take position between Stewart and Bragg; Hampton filled the temporary gap with two horse artillery batteries. Other cannons were placed on high ground, ready to sweep the width of Sherman's advance.

When Slocum's wing drew near on the morning of the nineteenth, it moved warily, but not warily enough. Pursuant to plans developed by Johnston and Hampton, Wheeler's troopers initiated the fighting by advancing on Slocum's lead element, the 14th Corps division of Brigadier General William P. Carlin. At a prearranged signal, Wheeler quickly withdrew, luring Carlin closer to Johnston's line. Suddenly the Union division was overrun by Hoke's attackers, and almost routed. Realizing that Johnston's troops had some punch left in them, Slocum fell back and began to entrench.

Around three o'clock, after several hours of inconclusive combat, Johnston sent the late-arriving column of Hardee forward to the attack. Wheeler moved up in support, but he would complain that a stream unable to be crossed under fire prevented him from "engaging the enemy warmly the better part of the day." In the end, Hardee's attack, delivered too late to make the desired impact, was contained, and when Sherman hurried elements of the 20th Corps to Slocum's assistance, Johnston's offensive was spent.[66]

The armies remained on the field throughout the twentieth, Johnston having retreated to the position he had occupied at battle's start, with Mill Creek at his back. Sherman spent the day launching limited attacks on Hoke's position. "In all of them," Hampton observed, "he was repulsed." Wheeler's troopers, who had been moved to the army's far left, skirmished briskly with Federal units advancing on either side of the Goldsboro road, but without decisive result. It seemed obvious that Sherman wished to rest most of his troops before launching an offensive the next day.[67]

Hampton and Wheeler indeed saw heavier action on the twenty-first, when part of Sherman's line advanced in a steady rain. That afternoon a 14th Corps division commanded by Major General Joseph A. Mower threatened to envelop Johnston's left, sweep into his rear, and seize the bridge over Mill Creek, Johnston's only means of escape. To check the movement, Hampton committed Wheeler's corps, supported by a small body of infantry. Wheeler attacked the left of Mower's column with Hagan's brigade, under the direction of Wirt Allen, while striking Mower's front with the 8th Texas Cavalry of Harrison's brigade.

Enlisted men of the 8th Texas Cavalry, "Terry's Texas Rangers."

Fightin' Joe proudly recorded the result: "My gallant Texas Rangers . . . galloped cross an open field and bore down most beautifully in an oblique direction upon their left and front . . . [and] broke through the line of skirmishers without breaking their [own] impetus and pushed on, striking the main line almost the same moment with Allen's gallant Alabamians, which threw the entire force of the enemy in a most rapid and disorderly retreat, Gen. Mower . . . narrowly escaping capture." Allowing for some understandable hyperbole, Wheeler's claim that the Texans made a critical contribution to Mower's repulse appears accurate. At Rowlett's Station in December 1861, the 8th Texas had delivered one of the earliest successful cavalry charges of the war in the West. Its final charge at Bentonville had been no less successful. As always, however, a price had been extracted: among the regiment's several casualties was the eighteen-year-old son of General Hardee, killed in the forefront of the attack.[68]

Late in the day, Johnston's main body, which had suffered more than two thousand six hundred casualties over the past three days, began crossing Mill Creek on the bridge Wheeler had helped secure, preparatory to moving on to Smithfield. Given Johnston's extended line and the heavily wooded terrain in front of the span, the withdrawal was a slow process. To cover it, through the balance of the day Wheeler's troopers skirmished with a gradually increasing force of Yankee infantry, fighting and falling back, with consummate skill, one last time.

The action continued until after dark, but the enemy could not get close enough to make a lunge for the bridge. By ten a.m. on the twenty-second, the infantry having crossed Mill Creek, Wheeler led his men, whose heroics this day had helped wipe the stain from their splotched reputation, to the north bank. As he did, the enemy made a final effort to reach the bridge, only to be driven back with heavy loss. In his after-action report, Wheeler noted that "three color bearers of the leading brigade fell dead within fifty feet of my position." At Hampton's order, Wheeler then oversaw the dismantling of the bridge. Giving up the ghost, a sullen body of Yankees "retreated out of range and made no further pursuit whatever."[69]

BENTONVILLE WAS THE LAST HURRAH FOR JOHNSTON, the remnants of the Army of Tennessee, and the horsemen of Hampton and Wheeler. Over the next two days, Sherman completed his march to Goldsboro, where he linked with forces sent from Tennessee under Schofield and from Wilmington, North Carolina, under Major General Alfred H. Terry. Sherman intended to lead the combined command to Virginia, but he did not have to. On the twenty-ninth, Grant and Meade began their grand advance against Lee's overextended lines outside Petersburg. On April 1, they broke through at Five Forks, and the Army of Northern Virginia began the long, disheartening march to Appomattox Court House, where on the ninth it lay down its arms.[70]

Rumors of Lee's retreat and the subsequent evacuation of Petersburg and Richmond reached Johnston's army on the road to Raleigh. Wheeler's men were in the state capital, guarding the rear of their withdrawing army, when word of Lee's surrender reached them April 11. By the fourteenth, when the cavalry entered the college town of Chapel Hill, reports were rife that Johnston had sought a conference with Sherman. On the eighteenth, the commanding generals—who over the two years they had grappled with each other had developed a deep mutual respect—met at Durham Station and came quickly to terms on a plan under which Johnston would surrender his forces.

The agreement had to be renegotiated eight days later due to the intervention of Secretary of War Edwin M. Stanton, who considered the original terms too lenient and too entwined with political issues. On April 26, Johnston and Sherman met again and hammered out a pact that met the government's approval. That day, Johnston's forces, including the shadow of a command once known as the Army of Tennessee, ceased to exist.[71]

Citing technicalities, neither Hampton nor Wheeler felt bound by the terms of the surrender agreement. Both vowed to fight on, although Johnston urged his soldiers to abide by the outcome rendered at Durham Station. In the end, neither cavalryman got his wish. Hampton, exhausted and ill, retreated to South Carolina, where he surrendered and applied for a government pardon. Wheeler, along with a small band of diehards, hoped to keep fighting, but he was pursued and captured. After a brief stretch in a Northern prison, he was permitted to return to Georgia, where he started life anew, and eventually prospered.[72]

On April 29, 1865, as he prepared to flee North Carolina, Fightin' Joe rendered his last official act as a Confederate soldier by composing and distributing a farewell address to his command. His words continue to serve as an appropriate tribute to the cavalry, Army of Tennessee, and as a fitting epitaph:

GALLANT COMRADES—

You have fought your battles; your task is done. During a four years' struggle for liberty, you have exhibited courage, fortitude and devotion. . . . You are heroes, veterans, patriots. The bones of your comrades mark the battle-fields upon the soil of Kentucky, Tennessee, Virginia, North Carolina, South Carolina, Georgia, Alabama and Mississippi; you have done all that human exertion could accomplish. In bidding you adieu, I desire to tender my thanks for your gallantry in battle, your fortitude under suffering, and your devotion at all times to the holy cause you have done so much to maintain. . . . Brethren in the cause of freedom, comrades in arms, I bid you farewell.[73]

# NOTES

## ABBREVIATIONS

| | |
|---|---|
| ADA&H | Alabama Department of Archives and History |
| B&L | *Battles and Leaders of the Civil War* |
| Coll. | Collection |
| CV | *Confederate Veteran* |
| CWH | *Civil War History* |
| CWTI | *Civil War Times Illustrated* |
| DU | Duke University Library |
| EU | Emory University Library |
| FHS | Filson Historical Society |
| GHQ | *Georgia Historical Quarterly* |
| GLC | Gilder Lehrman Collection |
| GSA | Georgia State Archives |
| HSP | Historical Society of Pennsylvania |
| JUSCA | *Journal of the United States Cavalry Association* |
| KHS | Kentucky Historical Society |
| MDA&H | Mississippi Department of Archives and History |
| MOC | Museum of the Confederacy |
| MSS | Correspondence, Papers |
| NA | National Archives |
| OR | *The War of the Rebellion: A Compilation of the Official Records of the Union and Confederate Armies* [cited according to series, volume, (part), pages] |
| ORN | *Official Records of the Union and Confederate Navies in the War of the Rebellion* [cited according to series, volume, pages] |
| PHCW | *Photographic History of the Civil War* |
| RG-, E- | Record Group, Entry |
| SB | *Southern Bivouac* |
| SHC | Southern Historical Collection, University of North Carolina Library |
| SHQ | *Southwestern Historical Quarterly* |
| SHSP | *Southern Historical Society Papers* |
| SNMP | Shiloh National Military Park |
| THQ | *Tennessee Historical Quarterly* |
| TSL&A | Tennessee State Library and Archives |
| UK | University of Kentucky Library |
| USAH&EC | U.S. Army Heritage and Education Center |
| UT | University of Texas Library |

PREFACE

1. Thomas Lawrence Connelly, *Army of the Heartland: The Army of Tennessee, 1861-1862* (Baton Rouge, LA, 1967), 3.

2. Richard M. McMurry, *Two Great Rebel Armies: An Essay in Confederate Military History* (Chapel Hill, NC, 1989), 132.

3. J. P. Dyer, "Some Aspects of Cavalry Operations in the Army of Tennessee," *Journal of Southern History* 8 (1942): 212.

4. John Witherspoon Du Bose, *General Joseph Wheeler and the Army of Tennessee* (New York, 1912), 386.

5. Dyer, "Cavalry Operations in the Army of Tennessee," 212.

6. Ibid., 224.

CHAPTER ONE: THREE WHO WOULD LEAD

1. Brian Steel Wills, *A Battle from the Start: The Life of Nathan Bedford Forrest* (New York, 1992), 21-23. This is the most satisfying recent portrait of Forrest by a professional historian. Other biographies of Forrest and studies of the operations of his commands include Thomas Jordan and J. P. Pryor, *The Campaigns of Lieut.-Gen. N. B. Forrest and of Forrest's Cavalry* (New Orleans, Memphis, and New York, 1868); John Allan Wyeth, *Life of General Nathan Bedford Forrest* (New York, 1899); J. Harvey Mathes, *General Forrest* (New York, 1902); Hamilton J. Eckenrode, *Life of Nathan Bedford Forrest* (Richmond, VA, 1918); Eric W. Sheppard, *Bedford Forrest, the Confederacy's Greatest Cavalryman* (New York, 1930); Andrew Nelson Lytle, *Bedford Forrest and His Critter Company* (New York, 1931); Robert Selph Henry, *"First with the Most" Forrest* (Indianapolis, 1944) and, as editor, *As They Saw Forrest: Some Recollections and Comments of Contemporaries* (Jackson, TN, 1956); Lonnie E. Maness, *Untutored Genius: The Military Career of General Nathan Bedford Forrest* (Jackson, TN, 1990); and Jack Hurst, *Nathan Bedford Forrest: A Biography* (New York, 1993), and *Men of Fire: Grant, Forrest, and the Campaign That Decided the Civil War* (New York, 2007).

2. Hurst, *Nathan Bedford Forrest*, 16.

3. Wills, *Battle from the Start*, 24-26.

4. Ibid., 26-30; Hurst, *Nathan Bedford Forrest*, 18-42; Jordan and Pryor, *Campaigns of Forrest*, 25-27; Wyeth, *Life of Forrest*, 20-21.

5. Wills, *Battle from the Start*, 30-35.

6. Ibid., 39-40; Hurst, *Nathan Bedford Forrest*, 52-53.

7. Hurst, *Nathan Bedford Forrest*, 27.

8. Mathes, *General Forrest*, 19-21; Wills, *Battle from the Start*, 40-41.

9. Wyeth, *Life of Forrest*, 23.

10. Jordan and Pryor, *Campaigns of Forrest*, 40; Jack Coggins, *Arms and Equipment of the Civil War* (Garden City, NY, 1962), 58-59, 64.

11. Jordan and Pryor, *Campaigns of Forrest*, 40-42; Wyeth, *Life of Forrest*, 24.

12. Wyeth, *Life of Forrest*, 24-27.

13. James A. Ramage, *Rebel Raider: The Life of General John Hunt Morgan* (Lexington, KY, 1986), 8-17. As much a psychological portrait as a military history, this is the best of the

many Morgan biographies. Other life studies include Howard Swiggett, *The Rebel Raider: A Life of John Hunt Morgan* (Indianapolis, 1934); Cecil F. Holland, *Morgan and His Raiders* (New York, 1943); and William E. Metzler, *Morgan and His Dixie Cavaliers: A Biography of the Colorful Confederate General* (n.p., 1976). Operational studies of Morgan's commands include Basil Duke, *History of Morgan's Cavalry* (Cincinnati, 1867); D. Alexander Brown, *The Bold Cavaliers: Morgan's Kentucky Cavalry Raiders* (Philadelphia, 1959), and *Morgan's Raiders* (New York, 1994); Louise Letcher Butler, *Morgan and His Men* (Philadelphia, 1960); Henry George, *History of the 3d, 7th, 8th and 12th Kentucky [Cavalry]*, C. S. A. (Lyndon, KY, 1970); Edison H. Thomas, *John Hunt Morgan and His Raiders* (Lexington, KY, 1985); and Betty J. Gorin, *Morgan Is Coming!: Confederate Raiders in the Heartland of Kentucky* (Louisville, KY, 2006).

14. Duke, *Morgan's Cavalry*, 29; Ramage, *Rebel Raider*, 1.

15. Ramage, *Rebel Raider*, 18-19.

16. Ibid., 19-20.

17. Ibid., 20-22; Thomas, *Morgan and His Raiders*, 6. For details of Morgan's Mexican War service, see "John Hunt Morgan and the Kentucky Cavalry Volunteers in the Mexican War," *Register of the Kentucky Historical Society* 81 (1983): 343-65.

18. Ramage, *Rebel Raider*, 21-22.

19. Ibid., 22-28; Swiggett, *Rebel Raider*, 15.

20. Ramage, *Rebel Raider*, 28-29.

21. Ibid., 30-32.

22. Ibid., 32-36; Grady McWhiney and Perry D. Jamieson, *Attack and Die: Civil War Military Tactics and the Southern Heritage* (University, AL, 1982), 48-58.

23. Swiggett, *Rebel Raider*, 18-19.

24. Ramage, *Rebel Raider*, 36, 38; Duke, *Morgan's Cavalry*, 20-21. Duke is profiled in his *Reminiscences of General Basil W. Duke, C. S. A.* (Garden City, NY, 1911); Gary R. Matthews, *Basil Wilson Duke, The Right Man in the Right Place* (Lexington, KY, 2005); and Lowell H. Harrison, "Basil Duke: The Confederates' 'Little Whalebone,'" *CWTI* 21 (Jan. 1983): 33-39.

25. Ramage, *Rebel Raider*, 36-37; William C. Davis, *The Orphan Brigade: The Kentucky Confederates Who Couldn't Go Home* (Garden City, NY, 1980), 1-25.

26. Ramage, *Rebel Raider*, 43-44; William C. Davis, *Breckinridge: Statesman, Soldier, Symbol* (Baton Rouge, LA, 1974), 280-81; Thomas, *Morgan and His Raiders*, 13-15.

27. Ramage, *Rebel Raider*, 44-45.

28. Du Bose, *Wheeler and the Army of Tennessee*, 49-51. Other biographical and operational studies include *Synopsis of the Military Career of Gen. Joseph Wheeler, Commander of the Cavalry Corps, Army of the West* (New York, 1865); William N. McDonald, "Sketch of Lieutenant-General [*sic*] Joseph Wheeler," *SB* 2 (1884): 241-46; Thomas C. DeLeon, *Joseph Wheeler, the Man, the Statesman, the Soldier* (Atlanta, 1899); William Carey Dodson, ed., *Campaigns of Wheeler and His Cavalry, 1862-1865* (Atlanta, 1899); John P. Dyer, *"Fightin' Joe" Wheeler* (Baton Rouge, LA, 1941), reissued in 1961 as *From Shiloh to San Juan*; Anders Michael Kinney, *Joseph Wheeler: Uniting the Blue and the Gray* (Lincoln, NE, 2002); and Edward G. Longacre, *A Soldier to the Last: Maj. Gen. Joseph Wheeler in Blue and Gray* (Washington, DC, 2007).

29. Wheeler Family History, Wheeler MSS, ADA&H; Dyer, *"Fightin' Joe" Wheeler*, 8-9; Du Bose, *Wheeler and the Army of Tennessee*, 49-50; McDonald, "Sketch of Wheeler," 241-42.

30. Wheeler's USMA Records, Wheeler MSS, ADA&H.

31. Longacre, *Soldier to the Last*, 10; Dyer, *"Fightin' Joe" Wheeler*, 6.

32. Du Bose, *Wheeler and the Army of Tennessee*, 51.

33. DeLeon, *Wheeler, the Man, the Statesman, the Soldier*, 26; Dyer, *"Fightin' Joe" Wheeler*, 14.

34. Longacre, *Soldier to the Last*, 11-12.

35. Theophilus F. Rodenbough and William L. Haskin, eds., *The Army of the United States: Historical Sketches of Staff and Line* . . . (New York, 1896), 153-58, 174, 193, 221; De Leon, *Wheeler, the Man, the Statesman, the Soldier*, 24.

36. Robert W. Frazer, *Forts of the West: Military Forts . . . West of the Mississippi River to 1898* (Norman, OK, 1965), 98-99, 105-06.

37. Dyer, *"Fightin' Joe" Wheeler*, 16-17; Longacre, *Soldier to the Last*, 14.

38. Dyer, *"Fightin' Joe" Wheeler*, 16-17.

39. Ibid., 18-19; Dodson, ed., *Campaigns of Wheeler*, 2.

40. Wheeler Family History, Wheeler MSS, ADA&H; Dyer, *"Fightin' Joe" Wheeler*, 19-20.

41. Wheeler Family History, Wheeler MSS, ADA&H; Longacre, *Soldier to the Last*, 17; Richard P. Weinert, Jr., *The Confederate Regular Army* (Shippensburg, PA), 4-7.

42. Wheeler Family History, Wheeler MSS, ADA&H; OR, I, 52 (2): 149, 152; Dyer, *"Fightin' Joe" Wheeler*, 22-23; Du Bose, *Wheeler and the Army of Tennessee*, 53.

CHAPTER TWO: TROOPERS IN THE MAKING

1. Connelly, *Army of the Heartland*, 25-32; Stanley F. Horn, *The Army of Tennessee: A Military History* (Indianapolis, 1941), 47-49.

2. OR, I, 3: 687, 691, 723-24; Patricia L. Faust, ed., *Historical Times Illustrated Encyclopedia of the Civil War* (New York, 1986), 216.

3. Connelly, *Army of the Heartland*, 47-48.

4. Ezra J. Warner, *Generals in Gray: Lives of the Confederate Commanders* (Baton Rouge, LA, 1959), 242-43; Horn, *Army of Tennessee*, 49. The finest biography of Polk is Joseph Howard Parks, *General Leonidas Polk, C. S. A., The Fighting Bishop* (Baton Rouge, LA, 1962).

5. Warner, *Generals in Gray*, 159-60. Johnston is best profiled in Charles P. Roland, *Albert Sidney Johnston, Soldier of Three Republics* (Austin, TX, 1964). See also William Preston Johnston, *The Life of Gen. Albert Sidney Johnston, Embracing His Services in the Army of the United States, the Republic of Texas, and the Confederate States* (New York, 1878).

6. Horn, *Army of Tennessee*, 48-49; Connelly, *Army of the Heartland*, 46.

7. Horn, *Army of Tennessee*, 49; Connelly, *Army of the Heartland*, 32-33; OR, I, 3: 612-14.

8. George K. Miller, "Eighth Confederate Cavalry—1861-1865," 1, ADA&H.

9. N. S. Offutt to anon., undated, Offutt MSS, KHS.

10. Marcus Cunliffe, *Soldiers & Civilians: The Martial Spirit in America, 1775-1865* (Boston, 1968), 340-41, 368-69, 416-19.

11. Martha L. Crabb, *All Afire to Fight: The Untold Tale of the Civil War's Ninth Texas Cavalry* (New York, 2000), 2; David C. Stuart memoirs, 1, ADA&H.

12. John W. Watts memoirs, 2, ADA&H.

13. John Milton Hubbard, *Notes of a Private. . . Company E, 7th Tennessee Regiment* (Memphis, TN, 1909), 2.

14. Stephen B. Oates, *Confederate Cavalry West of the River* (Austin, TX, 1961), 27.

15. David C. Stuart memoirs, 1-2, ADA&H.

16. J. Q. Anderson, *Campaigning with Parsons's Texas Cavalry Brigade, C. S. A.* (Hillsboro, TX, 1967), 155.

17 McWhiney and Jamieson, *Attack and Die*, 132-39; Jay Luvaas, "Cavalry Lessons of the Civil War," *CWTI* 6 ( Jan. 1968): 21-31; Coggins, *Arms and Equipment of the Civil War*, 49.

18. Edward G. Longacre, *Lee's Cavalrymen: A History of the Mounted Forces of the Army of Northern Virginia, 1861-1865* (Mechanicsburg, PA, 2002), 43.

19. Jac Weller, "The Logistics of Nathan Bedford Forrest," *Military Affairs* 17 (1953): 166.

20. George B. Guild, *A Brief Narrative of the Fourth Tennessee Cavalry Regiment, Wheeler's Corps, Army of Tennessee* (Nashville, TN, 1913), 169.

21. Edward G. Longacre, *Lincoln's Cavalrymen: A History of the Mounted Forces of the Army of the Potomac, 1861-1865* (Mechanicsburg, PA, 2000), 46-48, 221-22; Isaac B. Ulmer, Memoir of Shiloh Campaign, 1, ADA&H; James K. P. Blackburn, E. S. Dodd, and L. B. Giles, *Terry Texas Ranger Trilogy* (Austin, TX, 1996), 99.

22. R. O. Morrow memoirs, 2-3, MDA&H.

23. Ibid.

24. W. H. Whitsitt, "A Year with Forrest," *CV* 25 (1917): 357.

25. Larry J. Daniel, *Soldiering in the Army of Tennessee: A Portrait of Life in a Confederate Army* (Chapel Hill, NC, 1991), 40-42.

26. Ibid., 42-43; John R. Poole, *Cracker Cavaliers: The 2nd Georgia Cavalry under Wheeler and Forrest* (Macon, GA, 2000), 10-11; Longacre, *Soldier to the Last*, 138; Duke, *Morgan's Cavalry*, 176.

27. Longacre, *Lee's Cavalrymen*, 48; Joseph J. Hunter, "A Sketch of the History of [the] Noxubee Troopers, 1st Mississippi Cavalry, Company 'F,'" 3, MDA&H.

28. William F. Mims, "War History of the Prattville Dragoons," 9, ADA&H; James C. Bates, *A Texas Cavalry Officer's Civil War: The Diary and Letters of James C. Bates*, ed. by Richard Lowe (Baton Rouge, LA, 1999), 8.

29. H. L. Scott, *Military Dictionary: Comprising Technical Definitions . . .* (New York, 1861), 154-55.

30. John H. Ash diary, Dec. 7, 1861, EU; McWhiney and Jamieson, *Attack and Die*, 64-66; Luvaas, "Cavalry Lessons of the Civil War," 23-24, 31.

31. Joseph J. Hunter, "A Sketch of the History of [the] Noxubee Troopers, 1st Mississippi Cavalry, Company 'F,'" 3-4, MDA&H; Daniel, *Soldiering in the Army of Tennessee*, 27.

32. Desmond W. Allen, *First Arkansas Confederate Mounted Rifles* (Conway, AR, 1988), 17; Allen C. Redwood, "Following Stuart's Feather," *Journal of the Military Service Institution of the United States* 49 (1911): 116-17.

33. Weller, "Logistics of Forrest," 166.

34. Ramage, *Rebel Raider*, 91-92, 108, 276n; Longacre, *Soldier to the Last*, 94-95. For troopers' attitudes toward Wheeler's tactics, see George K. Miller, "Eighth Confederate Cavalry—1861-1865," 4, ADA&H; and Daniel, *Soldiering in the Army of Tennessee*, 27.

35. Longacre, *Lincoln's Cavalrymen*, 32; Daniel, *Soldiering in the Army of Tennessee*, 11-13. For examples of cavalry units electing their officers, see Bates, *Texas Cavalry Officer's Civil War*, 5-6; Allen, *First Arkansas Mounted Rifles*, 9-10; and Joseph J. Hunter, "A Sketch of the History of [the] Noxubee Troopers, 1st Mississippi Cavalry, Company 'F,'" 3, MDA&H.

36. Gustave Cook to his wife, Oct. 28, 1861, Cook MSS, GLC.

37. Allen, *First Arkansas Mounted Rifles*, 27.

38. Max S. Lale, ed., "The Boy-Bugler of the Third Texas Cavalry: The A. B. Blocker Narrative," *Military History of Texas and the Southwest* 14 (1978): 156.

39. Benjamin F. Batchelor and George Q. Turner, *Batchelor-Turner Letters, 1861-1864, Written by Two of Terry's Texas Rangers*, ed. by Helen J. H. Rugeley (Austin, TX, 1961), 4; David S. Purvine to his wife, June 11, 14, July 4, 1861, Purvine MSS, SNMP.

40. George K. Miller, "Eighth Confederate Cavalry—1861-1865," 3, ADA&H.

41. David S. Purvine to his wife, July 8, 1861, Mar. 6, 1862, Purvine MSS, SNMP; William Barry to his sister, undated, Barry MSS, MDA&H.

42. Robert W. Williams, Jr., and Ralph A. Wooster, eds., "With Terry's Texas Rangers: The Letters of Isaac Dunbar Affleck," *CWH* 9 (1963): 303.

43. Allen, *First Arkansas Mounted Rifles*, 10, 27.

44. Daniel, *Soldiering in the Army of Tennessee*, 11-14.

45. Bates, *Texas Cavalry Officer's Civil War*, 7-8.

46. William F. Mims, "War History of the Prattville Dragoons," 3, ADA&H.

47. Ibid.

## Chapter Three: The Opening Moves

1. Connelly, *Army of the Heartland*, 45-50.

2. Ibid., 49-53; Warner, *Generals in Gray*, 241. Pillow's biography is Nathaniel Cheairs Hughes, Jr., and Roy P. Stonesifer, Jr., *The Life and Wars of Gideon J. Pillow* (Chapel Hill, NC, 1993).

3. Connelly, *Army of the Heartland*, 48-49; Horn, *Army of Tennessee*, 50-51.

4. For details of the battle, see William Garrett Piston and Richard W. Hatcher III, *Wilson's Creek: The Second Battle of the Civil War and the Men Who Fought It* (Chapel Hill, NC, 2000).

5. David S. Purvine to his wife, Aug. 25, 1861, Purvine MSS, SNMP. For an excellent study of the guerrilla war in Missouri, see Michael Fellman, *Inside War: The Guerrilla Conflict in Missouri during the American Civil War* (New York, 1989).

6. Connelly, *Army of the Heartland*, 51-52; Wyeth, *Life of Forrest*, 24-25.

7. Connelly, *Army of the Heartland*, 52-55; OR, I, 3: 699.

8. Faust, ed., *Historical Times Illustrated Encyclopedia*, 216; Alexander P. Stewart, "The Army of Tennessee: A Sketch," in *The Military Annals of Tennessee, Confederate . . .* , edited by John Berrien Lindsley (Nashville, TN, 1886), 63-64; Connelly, *Army of the Heartland*, 62-68. Buckner's biography is Arndt M. Stickles, *Simon Bolivar Buckner, Borderland Knight* (Chapel Hill, NC, 1940).

9. Connelly, *Army of the Heartland*, 91-92; Horn, *Army of Tennessee*, 59-60.

10. Duke, *Morgan's Cavalry*, 91; Wyeth, *Life of Forrest*, 27.

11. OR, IV, 1: 1094-96; 2: 4-5; 3: 194; Daniel E. Sutherland, "Sideshow No Longer: A Historiographical Review of the Guerrilla War," CWH 46 (2000): 5-6; Ramage, Rebel Raider, 47-50.

12. Duke, Morgan's Cavalry, 94.

13. Ibid., 94-95; Ramage, Rebel Raider, 48-50.

14. Duke, Morgan's Cavalry, 96-97.

15. Ibid., 97-98.

16. Wyeth, Life of Forrest, 27-28; Wills, Battle from the Start, 49-51.

17. Horn, Army of Tennessee, 61-62.

18. R. M. Kelly, "Holding Kentucky for the Union," B&L 1: 380-85; Edward G. Longacre, Worthy Opponents: General William T. Sherman, U. S. A., General Joseph E. Johnston, C. S. A. (Nashville, TN, 2006), 116-23.

19. Kelly, "Holding Kentucky for the Union," 385-86.

20. OR, I, 7: 12-14; Duke, Morgan's Cavalry, 106-07.

21. Kelly, "Holding Kentucky for the Union," 386.

22. OR, I, 7: 14-21; Batchelor and Turner, Batchelor-Turner Letters, 2-3.

23. Batchelor and Turner, Batchelor-Turner Letters, 4.

24. OR, I, 7: 18, 20; Wyeth, Life of Forrest, 81, 84.

25. William J. Stier, "Fury Takes the Field," CWTI 38 (Dec. 1999): 41-42; Johnston, Life of Gen. Albert Sidney Johnston, 385-86.

26. Jordan and Pryor, Campaigns of Forrest, 50-51; Wyeth, Life of Forrest, 30-31; Wills, Battle from the Start, 53-54; Stier, "Fury Takes the Field," 43.

27. OR, I, 7: 65; Wyeth, Life of Forrest, 30, 626-27.

28. Jordan and Pryor, Campaigns of Forrest, 52-55; Wills. Battle from the Start, 54.

29. Wyeth, Life of Forrest, 32.

30. OR, I, 7: 64.

31. Wyeth, Life of Forrest, 35-36.

32. William M. Polk, "General Polk and the Battle of Belmont," B&L 1: 348.

33. OR, I, 3: 304.

34. Ibid., 267-72, 310-11, 324-30, 343-45; Stewart, "Army of Tennessee: A Sketch," 65-66; Horn, Army of Tennessee, 63-66. The most thorough study of the battle is Nathaniel Cheairs Hughes, Jr., The Battle of Belmont: Grant Strikes South (Chapel Hill, NC, 1991).

35. OR, I, 3: 351-52.

36. Ibid., 277-83, 350-51, 356; John P. Young, The Seventh Tennessee Cavalry (Confederate): A History (Nashville, TN, 1890), 21-22.

37. Polk, "General Polk and the Battle of Belmont," 355n-56n.

38. Connelly, Army of the Heartland, 86-96; Horn, Army of Tennessee, 66-68.

39. OR, I, 7: 75-116; Kelly, "Holding Kentucky for the Union," 387-91; Connelly, Army of the Heartland, 97-99; Horn, Army of Tennessee, 67-69. For a good, brief account of the battle, see Lowell H. Harrison, "Mill Springs, 'The Brilliant Victory,'" CWTI 10 (Jan. 1972): 4-9, 44-47.

40. Edward O. Guerrant, "Marshall and Garfield in Eastern Kentucky," B&L 1: 393-97.

41. Kelly, "Holding Kentucky for the Union," 391-92.

Chapter Four: Defeat and Retreat

1. Kelly, "Holding Kentucky for the Union," 385-86; Benjamin F. Cooling, *Forts Henry and Donelson: The Key to the Confederate Heartland* (Knoxville, TN, 1988), 67-71; Ulysses S. Grant, *Personal Memoirs of U. S. Grant*, ed. by E. B. Long (New York, 2001), 146; Ulysses S. Grant, *Letters of Ulysses S. Grant to His Father and His Youngest Sister, 1857 to 1878*, ed. by Jesse Grant Cramer (New York, 1912), 77-78.

2. OR, I, 7: 72-74.

3. Ibid., 74-75; Connelly, *Army of the Heartland*, 106.

4. Connelly, *Army of the Heartland*, 106-07; Horn, *Army of Tennessee*, 81-82; OR, I, 7: 136-37.

5. OR, I, 7: 136-44, 148-52; Cooling, *Forts Henry and Donelson*, 101-09; Jesse Taylor, "The Defense of Fort Henry," *B&L* 1: 371.

6. Horn, *Army of Tennessee*, 83; Lew Wallace, "The Capture of Fort Donelson," *B&L* 1: 403.

7. Duke, *Morgan's Cavalry*, 108.

8. Connelly, *Army of the Heartland*, 127-31; Horn, *Army of Tennessee* 85-87; Alfred Roman, *The Military Operations of General Beauregard in the War between the States*, 2 vols. (New York, 1884), 1: 213-18; T. Harry Williams, *P. G. T. Beauregard, Napoleon in Gray* (Baton Rouge, LA, 1954), 116-19.

9. Wallace, "Capture of Fort Donelson," 398-99, 402-03; Wyeth, *Life of Forrest*, 35; Warner, *Generals in Gray*, 89-90; Connelly, *Army of the Heartland*, 112-15.

10. Cooling, *Forts Henry and Donelson*, 151-60.

11. Ibid., 166-99; Wallace, "Capture of Fort Donelson," 415, 417-25.

12. Cooling, *Forts Henry and Donelson*, 200-05; Wallace, "Capture of Fort Donelson," 425-26.

13. OR, I, 7: 383; Wyeth, *Life of Forrest*, 44.

14. OR, I, 7: 383-84; Wyeth, *Life of Forrest*, 44-45.

15. OR, I, 7: 384; Wills, *Battle from the Start*, 59.

16. OR, I, 7: 384-85; Wyeth, *Life of Forrest* 49-52.

17. OR, I, 7: 385-86; Wyeth, *Life of Forrest*, 56-59; Frank B. Gurley memoirs, 3, ADA&H.

18. OR, I, 7: 295, 386.

19. Ibid., 295-96.

20. Ibid., 386.

21. Wyeth, *Life of Forrest* 72-74; Jordan and Pryor, *Campaigns of Forrest*, 101-02.

22. Duke, *Morgan's Cavalry*, 113.

23. Gustave Cook to his wife, Feb. 24, 1862, Cook MSS, GLC.

24. Connelly, *Army of the Heartland*, 137-38; Horn, *Army of Tennessee*, 104-06.

25. Wyeth, *Life of Forrest*, 73-74; Wills, *Battle from the Start*, 65-66.

26. Duke, *Morgan's Cavalry*, 115; Ramage, *Rebel Raider*, 53; Nathan Bedford Forrest to anon., Feb. 25, 1862, Gratz Coll., HSP.

27. Connelly, *Army of the Heartland*, 138-39; Horn, *Army of Tennessee*, 99-110; Duke, *Morgan's Cavalry*, 118-19.

28. Wyeth, *Life of Forrest*, 74.

29. Ramage, *Rebel Raider*, 56-59; Thomas, *Morgan and His Raiders*, 28.

30. OR, I, 7: 433.

31. Ibid., 433-34; Duke, *Morgan's Cavalry*, 124-25; Ramage, *Rebel Raider*, 56.

32. *OR*, I, 7: 434; Duke, *Morgan's Cavalry*, 125.

33. Connelly, *Army of the Heartland*, 140-41; Horn, *Army of Tennessee*, 114-15.

34. Duke, *Morgan's Cavalry*, 119.

35. Roman, *Operations of Beauregard*, 1: 265-66; Williams, P. G. T. *Beauregard*, 122-25.

36. *OR*, I, 10 (1): 382-84; Larry J. Daniel, *Shiloh: The Battle That Changed the Civil War* (New York, 1997), 320-21; Wiley Sword, *Shiloh: Bloody April* (New York, 1974), 454-59.

37. *OR*, I, 10 (2): 371; Warner, *Generals in Gray*, 128-29.

38. Connelly, *Army of the Heartland*, 147-54; Horn, *Army of Tennessee*, 116-21.

39. The most detailed study of Pea Ridge (Elkhorn Tavern) is William L. Shea and Earl J. Hess, *Pea Ridge, Civil War Campaign in the West* (Chapel Hill, NC, 1992).

40. Daniel, *Shiloh*, 118-23; Sword, *Shiloh*, 99-102; Thomas, *Morgan and His Raiders*, 29-30.

41. Daniel, *Shiloh*, 123-30; Sword, *Shiloh*, 103-13; Roman, *Operations of Beauregard*, 1: 530-33; Williams, P. G. T. *Beauregard*, 129-32.

42. Daniel, *Shiloh*, 144-45; Isaac B. Ulmer, Memoir of Shiloh Campaign, 5, ADA&H.

43. Isaac B. Ulmer, Memoir of Shiloh Campaign, 10, ADA&H.

44. George K. Miller, "Eighth Confederate Cavalry—1861-1865," 6, ADA&H.

45. Daniel, *Shiloh*, 149-237; Longacre, *Soldier to the Last*, 26-32; *OR*, I, 10 (1): 468, 535, 552, 559.

46. Duke, *Morgan's Cavalry*, 141.

47. Daniel, *Shiloh*, 127, 154, 207, 237.

48. Ibid., 241, 279-280, 297; Sword, *Shiloh*, 406.

49. George K. Miller, "Eighth Confederate Cavalry—1861-1865," 6, ADA&H.

50. Duke, *Morgan's Cavalry*, 145-46.

51. Isaac B. Ulmer, Memoir of Shiloh Campaign, 7, ADA&H.

52. Ibid.; Duke, *Morgan's Cavalry*, 147-50.

53. Daniel, *Shiloh*, 275-76.

54. Henry, *"First with the Most" Forrest*, 77.

55. Ibid.; Wyeth, *Life of Forrest*, 75-76;

56. Wills, *Battle from the Start*, 68; Sword, *Shiloh*, 300-01.

57. David S. Purvine to his wife, Apr. 18, 1862, Purvine MSS, SNMP.

58. *OR*, I, 10 (2): 387-88; Daniel, *Shiloh*, 263-64; Sword, *Shiloh*, 378-79; Wyeth, *Life of Forrest*, 77-78; Roman, *Operations of Beauregard*, 1: 301-19; Williams, P. G. T. *Beauregard*, 138-45.

CHAPTER FIVE: RAIDING SEASON

1. *OR*, I, 10 (2): 398-400.

2. Ibid., 403; Roman, *Operations of Beauregard*, 1: 568; Williams, P. G. T. *Beauregard*, 146-47.

3. *OR*, I, 10 (2): 403, 414.

4. William T. Sherman, *Memoirs of General William T. Sherman*, 2 vols. (New York, 1875), 1: 243-44; Daniel, *Shiloh*, 296-97; Sword, *Shiloh*, 424-25.

5. Daniel, *Shiloh*, 297.

6. Ibid.; Sword, *Shiloh*, 425.

7. Jordan and Pryor, *Campaigns of Forrest*, 145-49; Wyeth, *Life of Forrest*, 78-82.

8. John F. Marszalek, *Commander of All Lincoln's Armies: A Life of General Henry W. Halleck* (Cambridge, MA, 2004), 123-25.

9. David S. Purvine to his wife, Apr. 8, 1862, Purvine MSS, SNMP; Flavellus G. Nicholson memoirs, 27, MDA&H; William E. Beasley to his wife, Apr. 20, 1862, Beasley MSS, MDA&H; George K. Miller, "Eighth Confederate Cavalry—1861-1865," 7, ADA&H; OR, I, 10 (1): 775-76; (2): 529-30; Roman, *Operations of Beauregard*, 1: 383-84, 572-73, 580-81; Williams, P. G. T. *Beauregard*, 152-54.

10. OR, I, 10 (2): 459; Kenneth A. Hafendorfer, *They Died by Twos and Tens: The Confederate Cavalry in the Kentucky Campaign* (Louisville, KY, 1995), 28, 31-32, 60-61; Warner, *Generals in Gray*, 2, 21-22.

11. Roman, *Operations of Beauregard*, 1: 404-09, 591; Williams, P. G. T. *Beauregard*, 157-59.

12. Grady McWhiney, *Braxton Bragg and Confederate Defeat: Volume I, Field Command* (New York, 1969), vii-ix, 27-28, 203, 389-92; Horn, *Army of Tennessee*, 112-14. For other life studies, see Judith Lee Hallock, *Braxton Bragg: Volume II* (Tuscaloosa, AL, 1991) and Don C. Seitz, *Braxton Bragg, General of the Confederacy* (Columbia, SC, 1924). A compact biography is McWhiney, "Braxton Bragg," *CWTI* 11 (Apr. 1972): 5-7, 42-48.

13. OR, I, 10 (1): 879-83; Benjamin F. Cooling, *Fort Donelson's Legacy: War and Society in Kentucky and Tennessee, 1852-1863* (Knoxville, TN, 1997), 54.

14. OR, I, 10 (1): 839, 852-54; Du Bose, *Wheeler and the Army of Tennessee*, 76-77.

15. Duke, *Morgan's Cavalry*, 156-57; Ramage, *Rebel Raider*, 84; Thomas, *Morgan and His Raiders*, 34; Holland, *Morgan and His Raiders*, 100-01; Brown, *Bold Cavaliers*, 54-56; Metzler, *Morgan and His Dixie Cavaliers*, 15; Stuart W. Sanders, "The Lebanon Races," *America's Civil War* 16 (Mar. 2003): 24.

16. Duke, *Morgan's Cavalry*, 157-58; Sanders, "Lebanon Races," 24.

17. Duke, *Morgan's Cavalry*, 159; Brown, *Bold Cavaliers*, 56-57; Ramage, *Rebel Raider*, 84. For more on Ellsworth, see Michael B. Ballard, "Deceit by Telegraph: 'Lightning' Ellsworth's Electronic Warfare," *CWTI* 22 (Oct. 1983): 22-27.

18. Sanders, "Lebanon Races," 24; Ramage, *Rebel Raider*, 84-85.

19. Ramage, *Rebel Raider*, 85; Duke, *Morgan's Cavalry*, 159-62; Swiggett, *Rebel Raider*, 55; Thomas, *Morgan and His Raiders*, 35-36.

20. Swiggett, *Rebel Raider*, 56; Ramage, *Rebel Raider*, 85; Duke, *Morgan's Cavalry*, 162; J. P. Austin, *The Blue and the Gray: Sketches of a Portion of the Unwritten History of the Great American Civil War . . .* (Atlanta, 1899), 34-35.

21. Cooling, *Fort Donelson's Legacy*, 54-55.

22. Sanders, "Lebanon Races," 28; Ramage, *Rebel Raider*, 85.

23. Holland, *Morgan and His Raiders*, 104-06; Brown, *Bold Cavaliers*, 64-67; Ramage, *Rebel Raider*, 85-88; Thomas, *Morgan and His Raiders*, 36-38.

24. Roman, *Operations of Beauregard*, 1: 402; Wyeth, *Life of Forrest*, 84-85; Jordan and Pryor, *Campaigns of Forrest*, 159-61; Henry, *"First with the Most" Forrest*, 83.

25. Hafendorfer, *They Died by Twos and Tens*, 98-100.

26. Warner, *Generals in Gray*, 279-80; Connelly, *Army of the Heartland*, 187-88.

27. Connelly, *Army of the Heartland*, 187-88; Hafendorfer, *They Died by Twos and Tens*, 99.

28. Jordan and Pryor, *Campaigns of Forrest*, 160-61; Hafendorfer, *They Died by Twos and Tens*, 121; Wills, *Battle from the Start*, 72.

29. Hafendorfer, *They Died by Twos and Tens*, 99-100, 105; Wyeth, *Life of Forrest*, 85.

30. OR, I, 16 (1): 810; Jordan and Pryor, *Campaigns of Forrest*, 161-63; Wyeth, *Life of Forrest*, 90.

31. Charles F. Bryan, Jr., "'I Mean to Have Them All': Forrest's Murfreesboro Raid," *CWTI* 12 ( Jan. 1974): 27-28; J. K. P. Blackburn, "Reminiscences of the Terry Rangers," *SHQ* 22 (1918): 66.

32. Bryan, "'I Mean to Have Them All,'" 28-30; Janet Hewett, et al., eds., *Supplement to the Official Records of the Union and Confederate Armies*, 3 pts., 99 vols. (Wilmington, NC, 1994-2001), I, 3: 229-30; Wyeth, *Life of Forrest*, 86-87; Jordan and Pryor, *Campaigns of Forrest*, 163-68; William H. King, "Forrest's Attack on Murfreesboro, July 13, 1862," *CV* 32 (1924): 431.

33. OR, I, 16 (1): 810-11; Wyeth, *Life of Forrest*, 97; Lytle, *Bedford Forrest and His Critter Company*, 97; Henry, *"First with the Most" Forrest*, 88-89.

34. OR, I, 16 (1): 805; Wyeth, *Life of Forrest*, 88; Henry, *"First with the Most" Forrest*, 89.

35. Bryan, "'I Mean to Have Them All,'" 31-32; Wyeth, *Life of Forrest*, 89-90.

36. Jordan and Pryor, *Campaigns of Forrest*, 173-74; James Lee McDonough, *War in Kentucky: From Shiloh to Perryville* (Knoxville, TN, 1994), 50.

37. Wills, *Battle from the Start*, 76-78.

38. Mamie Yeary, comp., *Reminiscences of the Boys in Gray* (Dayton, OH, 1986), 713; OR, I, 16 (1): 811, 818.

39. OR, I, 16 (1): 818-19.

40. Ibid., 792-98, 819; Wills, *Battle from the Start*, 79-81.

41. Bryan, "'I Mean to Have Them All,'" 34.

42. Ramage, *Rebel Raider*, 89; Thomas, *Morgan and His Raiders*, 36; Duke, *Morgan's Cavalry*, 164-68; Stephen Z. Starr, *Colonel Grenfell's Wars: The Life of a Soldier of Fortune* (Baton Rouge, LA, 1971), 44-45.

43. OR, I, 16 (1): 766, 771; Duke, *Morgan's Cavalry*, 182-83; Ramage, *Rebel Raider*, 90-92, 101; Brown, *Bold Cavaliers*, 75-76; William R. Brooksher and David K. Snider, "Stampede in Kentucky: John Hunt Morgan's Summer Raid," *CWTI* 17 ( June 1978): 4-5.

44. OR, I, 16 (1): 766-67, 771; Duke, *Morgan's Cavalry*, 183-84; Brown, *Bold Cavaliers*, 76-79; Hafendorfer, *They Died by Twos and Tens*, 116-17.

45. OR, I, 16 (1): 767, 774; Duke, *Morgan's Cavalry*, 184-85; Thomas, *Morgan and His Raiders*, 41-42; Holland, *Morgan and His Raiders*, 118-19; Brown, *Bold Cavaliers*, 79-80.

46. OR, I, 16 (1): 767-69, 772, 775-76; Duke, *Morgan's Cavalry*, 185-95; Holland, *Morgan and His Raiders*, 119-23.

47. OR, I, 16 (1): 769, 776-79; Duke, *Morgan's Cavalry*, 195-99; Holland, *Morgan and His Raiders*, 124; Cooling, *Fort Donelson's Legacy*, 89-90; Vernon L. Volpe, "Squirrel Hunting for the Union: The Defense of Cincinnati in 1862," *CWH* 33 (1987): 245-46.

48. OR, I, 16 (1): 769, 779-81; Duke, *Morgan's Cavalry*, 195, 199; Thomas, *Morgan and His Raiders*, 42-44.

49. OR, I, 16 (1): 769, 773, 782-83; Duke, *Morgan's Cavalry*, 199-202; Ramage, *Rebel Raider*, 97-98; Brown, *Bold Cavaliers*, 90-92; Brooksher and Snider, "Stampede in Kentucky," 44-46; Swiggett, *Rebel Raider*, 67-68.

50. OR, I, 16 (1): 769-70; Duke, *Morgan's Cavalry*, 202-05; Ramage, *Rebel Raider*, 104-05; Thomas, *Morgan and His Raiders*, 45.

CHAPTER SIX: RETURN TO KENTUCKY

1. Hafendorfer, *They Died by Twos and Tens*, 148-50; Warner, *Generals in Gray*, 12-13, 262.

2. OR, I, 16 (2): 221-22, 470-71.

3. Ibid., I, 16 (1): 816.

4. Ibid., I, 16 (2): 234.

5. Connelly, *Army of the Heartland*, 202-03; Ramage, *Rebel Raider*, 113; Duke, *Morgan's Cavalry*, 223.

6. Ramage, *Rebel Raider*, 111; Thomas, *Morgan and His Raiders*, 48.

7. Duke, *Morgan's Cavalry*, 210-15; Ramage, *Rebel Raider*, 111-12.

8. Thomas, *Morgan and His Raiders*, 48-49.

9. Hafendorfer, *They Died by Twos and Tens*, 196.

10. Duke, *Morgan's Cavalry*, 215-17; Hafendorfer, *They Died by Twos and Tens*, 197.

11. Duke, *Morgan's Cavalry*, 218.

12. Ibid., 218-24; OR, I, 16 (1): 880.

13. OR, I, 16 (1): 880.

14. OR, I, 16 (1): 880-81; Duke, *Morgan's Cavalry*, 223.

15. OR, I, 16 (1): 882.

16. Connelly, *Army of the Heartland*, 195-201; McWhiney, *Braxton Bragg*, 266-71.

17. Connelly, *Army of the Heartland*, 203-04; Horn, *Army of Tennessee*, 160-62; McWhiney, *Braxton Bragg*, 273-79.

18. OR, I, 17 (1): 22-23; Du Bose, *Wheeler and the Army of* Tennessee, 79-80; Dyer, *"Fightin' Joe" Wheeler*, 46-48; Longacre, *Soldier to the Last*, 40-41.

19. Longacre, *Soldier to the Last*, 41-42.

20. OR, I, 17 (1): 24; (2): 124-26, 128-31, 133-39; Joseph Wheeler, "Bragg's Invasion of Kentucky," *B&L* 3: 3-4; George K. Miller, "Eighth Confederate Cavalry—1861-1865," 12, ADA&H; Dyer, *"Fightin' Joe" Wheeler*, 47.

21. Hafendorfer, *They Died by Twos and Tens*, 166.

22. Connelly, *Army of the Heartland*, 207-10, 221-22; Horn, *Army of Tennessee*, 162-63; McWhiney, *Braxton Bragg*, 272-74.

23. OR, I, 16 (1): 893; (2): 781-82; Connelly, *Army of the Heartland*, 211; Dyer, *"Fightin' Joe" Wheeler*, 48-49; Longacre, *Soldier to the Last*, 45-46.

24. OR, I, 16 (1): 938-39; Hafendorfer, *They Died by Twos and Tens*, 105-07, 157; George W. Morgan, "Cumberland Gap," *B&L* 3: 62-69.

25. OR, I, 16 (1): 887-91, 893; (2): 781, 785; Wheeler, "Bragg's Invasion of Kentucky," 7-8; Hafendorfer, *They Died by Twos and Tens*, 245-54; Earl J. Hess, *Banners in the Breeze: The Kentucky Campaign, Corinth, and Stones River* (Lincoln, NE, 2000), 60.

26. *OR*, I, 16 (1): 893; (2): 801; Wheeler, "Bragg's Invasion of Kentucky," 8; Baxter Smith memoirs, 2, USAH&EC.

27. *OR*, I, 16 (1): 893-94; Hafendorfer, *They Died by Two and Tens*, 368-73.

28. *OR*, I 16 (1): 894; Jordan and Pryor, *Campaigns of Forrest*, 182-84; Hafendorfer, *They Died by Twos and Tens*, 378.

29. Jordan and Pryor, *Campaigns of Forrest*, 186; Wills, *Battle from the Start*, 83; Williams and Wooster, eds., "With Terry's Texas Rangers," 309. In an article published seventeen years after the event, one of Forrest's subordinates claimed that the general left Bragg's army "at his own request": James R. Chalmers, "Forrest and His Campaigns," *SHSP* 7 (1879): 459.

30. Wills, *Battle from the Start*, 83; Hafendorfer, *They Died by Twos and Tens*, 510.

31. Hafendorfer, *They Died by Twos and Tens*, 511.

32. Connelly, *Army of the Heartland*, 228-31; *OR*, I, 16 (1): 894.

33. Connelly, *Army of the Heartland*, 214-20, 230-31, 234; Horn, *Army of Tennessee*, 164-65; *OR*, I, 16 (1): 894.

34. Connelly, *Army of the Heartland*, 231-32; *OR*, I, 16 (1): 893-94; (2): 801; Wheeler, "Bragg's Invasion of Kentucky," 8.

35. *OR*, I, 16 (1): 894; Wheeler, "Bragg's Invasion of Kentucky," 10.

36. *OR*, I, 16 (1): 894; (2): 878-79; Warner, *Generals in Gray*, 331-32.

37. *OR*, I, 16 (1): 895-96; Wheeler, "Bragg's Invasion of Kentucky," 10-11.

38. Connelly, *Army of the Heartland*, 228-42; Charles Smith Hamilton, "The Battle of Iuka," *B&L* 2: 734-36; William S. Rosecrans, "The Battle of Corinth," *B&L* 2: 737-57. The finest account of these battles is Peter Cozzens, *The Darkest Days of the War: The Battles of Iuka & Corinth* (Chapel Hill, NC, 1997).

39. Horn, *Army of Tennessee*, 167-68; McWhiney, *Braxton Bragg*, 297-99; Don Carlos Buell, "East Tennessee and the Campaign of Perryville," *B&L* 3: 46-47; Wheeler, "Bragg's Invasion of Kentucky," 11.

40. *OR*, I, 16 (1): 896; (2): 884, 900-06; Wheeler, "Bragg's Invasion of Kentucky," 14; Connelly, *Army of the Heartland*, 247-56; Gustave Cook to his wife, Oct. 27, 1862, Cook MSS, GLC; Baxter Smith memoirs, 4-5, USAH&EC; Kenneth W. Noe, *Perryville: This Grand Havoc of Battle* (Lexington, KY, 2001), 118; Williams and Wooster, eds., "With Terry's Texas Rangers," 309-10; Hewett, et al., eds., *Supplement to the Official Records*, I, 3: 267-68.

41. *OR*, I, 16 (1): 896-97; Wheeler, "Bragg's Invasion of Kentucky," 14-15; Hafendorfer, *They Died by Twos and Tens*, 680-85.

42. *OR*, I, 16 (1): 897; Hafendorfer, *They Died by Twos and Tens*, 694-702; St. John Richardson Liddell, *Liddell's Record . . .*, ed. by Nathaniel Cheairs Hughes, Jr. (Baton Rouge, LA, 1985), 87-88; James Hagan, History of the 3rd Alabama Cavalry, 6, ADA&H; R. R. Gaines, History of the 3rd Alabama Cavalry, 4, ADA&H.

43. *OR*, I, 16 (1): 925; Wheeler, "Bragg's Invasion of Kentucky," 16; Dyer, *"Fightin' Joe" Wheeler*, 63; James Hagan, History of the 3rd Alabama Cavalry, 6, ADA&H; *Synopsis of the Career of Wheeler*, 7; Noe, *Perryville*, 236; Connelly, *Army of the Heartland*, 259-63; McWhiney, *Braxton Bragg*, 309-12.

44. *OR*, I, 16 (1): 1025-27, 1092-93; Connelly, *Army of the Heartland*, 259-65; Horn, *Army of*

*Tennessee*, 181-86. A good, concise study of the battle is Stanley F. Horn, "The Battle of Perryville," *CWTI* 4 (Feb. 1966): 5-11, 42-47.

45. *OR*, I, 16 (1): 1027; Connelly, *Army of the Heartland*, 266-67.

CHAPTER SEVEN: AUTUMN OF HOPE

1. Wheeler, "Bragg's Invasion of Kentucky," 17.

2. McWhiney, *Braxton Bragg*, 319.

3. Ibid., 320; Noe, *Perryville*, 236-37; Hafendorfer, *They Died by Twos and Tens*, 704-05.

4. Horn, *Army of Tennessee*, 182; McWhiney, *Braxton Bragg*, 320; *OR*, I, 16 (1): 1094; (2): 930, 932; 20 (2): 388.

5. The voluminous proceedings of the "Buell Commission" can be found in *OR*, I, 16 (1): 6-796.

6. Ibid., 898, 1136-44; (2): 930-31; Wheeler, "Bragg's Invasion of Kentucky," 17-18.

7. Baxter Smith memoirs, 6, USAH&EC.

8. *OR*, I, 16 (1): 898; (2): 940; Dyer, *"Fightin' Joe" Wheeler*, 64-65; Hafendorfer, *They Died by Twos and Tens*, 689; Wheeler, "Bragg's Invasion of Kentucky," 18.

9. *OR*, I, 16 (1): 898; Connelly, *Army of the Heartland*, 279-80.

10. Connelly, *Army of the Heartland*, 267-70; Horn, *Army of Tennessee*, 186-87.

11. Wheeler, "Bragg's Invasion of Kentucky," 19; *OR*, I, 16 (1): 899.

12. *OR*, I, 16 (2): 976-77.

13. Ibid., (1): 1094, 1112, 1119-20.

14. Connelly, *Army of the Heartland*, 13-15; McWhiney, *Braxton Bragg*, 325-26, 337.

15. Baxter Smith memoirs, 7, USAH&EC; Henry C. Bate to "My Dear Ella," Oct. 27, 1862, Gratz Coll., HSP; Eugene F. Falconnet memoirs, 99, TSL&A; Julius L. Dowda memoirs, 3, GSA; L. H. Ansley memoirs, 2, GSA.

16. Thomas Lawrence Connelly, *Autumn of Glory: The Army of Tennessee, 1862-1865* (Baton Rouge, LA, 1971), 14-16, 31-32; Horn, *Army of Tennessee*, 190-92; McWhiney, *Braxton Bragg*, 325-29.

17. Faust, ed., *Historical Times Illustrated Encyclopedia*, 813; Joseph E. Johnston, *Narrative of Military Operations during the Civil War* (New York, 1874), 147-50, 231-32; Richard Taylor, *Destruction and Reconstruction: Personal Experiences of the Late War*, ed. by Charles P. Roland (Waltham, MA, 1968), 206; Craig L. Symonds, *Joseph E. Johnston: A Civil War Biography* (New York, 1992), 187-91; Joseph T. Glatthaar, *Partners in Command: The Relationships between Leaders in the Civil War* (New York, 1994), 119-22.

18. Warner, *Generals in Gray*, 161-62. The finest biography of the general is Symonds, *Joseph E. Johnston*. See also Gilbert E. Govan and James W. Livingood, *A Different Valor: The Story of General Joseph E. Johnston, C. S. A.* (Indianapolis, 1956).

19. Johnston, *Narrative of Military Operations*, 148-49; Richard M. McMurry, "The Enemy at Richmond: Joseph E. Johnston and the Confederate Government," *CWH* 27 (1981): 9.

20. *OR*, I, 20 (2): 411-12.

21. Thomas, *Morgan and His Raiders*, 53-54.

22. Ibid., 43; Ramage, *Rebel Raider*, 121.

23. Swiggett, *Rebel Raider*, 74; Metzler, *Morgan and His Dixie Cavaliers*, 30.

24. James M. Prichard, "Morgan in the Mountains," *CWTI* 24 (Oct. 1985): 32-34.

25. Ramage, *Rebel Raider*, 121-22; Prichard, "Morgan in the Mountains," 34-35.

26. Prichard, "Morgan in the Mountains," 36-37; Metzler, *Morgan and His Dixie Cavaliers*, 30-31.

27. Duke, *Morgan's Cavalry*, 247-55; Metzler, *Morgan and His Dixie Cavaliers*, 31.

28. Duke, *Morgan's Cavalry*, 250.

29. Ibid., 251-52.

30. Ibid., 293-94.

31. Ibid., 282-86; Ramage, *Rebel Raider*, 124.

32. Duke, *Morgan's Cavalry*, 287-88.

33. Ibid., 288-89; Metzler, *Morgan and His Dixie Cavaliers*, 33.

34. Duke, *Morgan's Cavalry*, 289-92; Thomas, *Morgan and His Raiders*, 57.

35. John B. Castleman, *Active Service* (Louisville, KY, 1917), 98.

36. Duke, *Morgan's Cavalry*, 296-300; Thomas, *Morgan and His Raiders*, 57-58.

37. Metzler, *Morgan and His Dixie Cavaliers*, 34. Another congressional resolution honoring the service of Morgan and his men prior to the Battle of Murfreesboro is in OR, I, 20 (2): 504.

38. OR, I, 20 (2): 414, 422; Hafendorfer, *They Died by Twos and Tens*, 862-63; Warner, *Generals in Gray*, 231-32.

39. OR, I, 20 (2): 421-23.

40. Ibid., 17 (2): 247-48; Grant, *Personal Memoirs*, 222-25; Sherman, *Memoirs*, 1: 279-83; Longacre, *Worthy Opponents*, 176-78.

41. Van Dorn is the subject of two biographies: Robert G. Hartje, *Van Dorn: The Life and Times of a Confederate General* (Nashville, TN, 1967) and Arthur B. Carter, *Tarnished Cavalier: Major General Earl Van Dorn, C. S. A.* (Knoxville, TN, 1999).

42. Hartje, *Van Dorn*, 255-56; OR, I, 20 (2): 422.

43. OR, I, 20 (1): 6.

44. Ibid., 6-7; Jordan and Pryor, *Campaigns of Forrest*, 189-81; Wills, *Battle from the Start*, 84.

45. Wyeth, *Life of Forrest*, 106.

46. OR, I, 17 (1): 593, 598; Wills, *Battle from the Start*, 85.

47. Wyeth, *Life of Forrest*, 110; Frank B. Gurley memoirs, 11-12, ADA&H.

48. OR, I, 17 (1): 553-55, 593; Wyeth, *Life of Forrest*, 109-15; Jordan and Pryor, *Campaigns of Forrest*, 195-96.

49. OR, I, 17 (1): 593-94, 598; Wyeth, *Life of Forrest*, 116-18; Jordan and Pryor, *Campaigns of Forrest*, 199; Lytle, *Bedford Forrest and His Critter Company*, 122-23.

50. OR, I, 17 (1): 594.

51. Ibid.; Roderick Perry memoirs, 6, Atlanta History Center, Atlanta, GA

52. OR, I, 17 (1): 579-85, 595-99; Wyeth, *Life of Forrest*, 121-27; Jordan and Pryor, *Campaigns of Forrest*, 207-08, 212-13, 215, 217; Lytle, *Bedford Forrest and His Critter Company*, 132-34; Dale S. Snair, ed., "This Looked But Little Like Trying to Catch the Enemy," *CWTI* 23 (Sept. 1984): 24, 28.

53. OR, I, 17 (1): 568-72, 595-96; Wyeth, *Life of Forrest*, 136; Frank B. Gurley memoirs, 16-17, ADA&H.

54. OR, I, 17 (1): 596.

55. Ibid., 595, 599; Wyeth, *Life of Forrest*, 132-33; Jordan and Pryor, *Campaigns of Forrest*, 215; Snair, ed., "This Looked But Little Like Trying to Catch the Enemy," 33.

56. Snair, ed., "This Looked But Little Like Trying to Catch the Enemy," 32-33.

57. Wyeth, *Life of Forrest*, 138-39, 143-44.

58. Edward G. Longacre, *Mounted Raids of the Civil War* (South Brunswick, NJ, 1975), 46-65; Sherman, *Memoirs*, 1: 289-95; OR, I, 17 (1): 503, 605-10.

## CHAPTER EIGHT: RAIDING REDUX

1. OR, I, 20 (1): 63-64; (2): 411.

2. Ramage, *Rebel Raider*, 128.

3. OR, I, 20 (1): 65; Ramage, *Rebel Raider*, 128; Thomas, *Morgan and His Raiders*, 59-60; Swiggett, *Rebel Raider*, 86-87; Cooling, *Fort Donelson's Legacy*, 161.

4. Ramage, *Rebel Raider*, 129-30; India W. P. Logan, *Kelion Franklin Peddicord of Quirk's Scouts, Morgan's Kentucky Cavalry, C. S. A. . . .* (New York, 1908), 54.

5. Logan, *Kelion Franklin Peddicord*, 53-54.

6. OR, I, 20 (1): 65; Ramage, *Rebel Raider*, 130.

7. OR, I, 20 (1): 64, 66-67, 69-72; Duke, *Morgan's Cavalry*, 313-14.

8. OR, I, 20 (1): 52-55; Henry L. Stone, *"Morgan's Men": A Narrative of Personal Experiences . . .* (Louisville, KY, 1919), 8-9.

9. OR, I, 20 (1): 45, 47-51, 62, 67-68; Ramage, *Rebel Raider*, 131; Thomas, *Morgan and His Raiders*, 60; J. Randolph Tucker to his father, Tucker MSS, Dec. 8, 1862, MOC.

10. Ramage, *Rebel Raider*, 134; Thomas, *Morgan and His Raiders*, 60-62; Swiggett, *Rebel Raider*, 92-94; Austin, *Blue and the Gray*, 63-65.

11. Duke, *Morgan's Cavalry*, 327; Ramage, *Rebel Raider*, 135-37; Thomas, *Morgan and His Raiders*, 64-65; Holland, *Morgan and His Raiders*, 179; D. Alexander Brown, "Morgan's Christmas Raid," *CWTI* 13 (Jan. 1975): 12; Brown, *Bold Cavaliers*, 143-44.

12. OR, I, 20 (1): 154; Duke, *Morgan's Cavalry*, 324-27; Ramage, *Rebel Raider*, 139; Metzler, *Morgan and His Dixie Cavaliers*, 39; Logan, *Kelion Franklin Peddicord*, 62.

13. OR, I, 20 (1): 154; Duke, *Morgan's Cavalry*, 329; Brown, *Bold Cavaliers*, 145-46.

14. Brown, "Morgan's Christmas Raid," 14.

15. OR, I, 20 (1): 153-54; Duke, *Morgan's Cavalry*, 329-30; Thomas, *Morgan and His Raiders*, 65; Holland, *Morgan and His Raiders*, 181; Metzler, *Morgan and His Dixie Cavaliers*, 40.

16. Logan, *Kelion Franklin Peddicord*, 63.

17. OR, I, 20 (1): 154.

18. Ibid.; Duke, *Morgan's Cavalry*, 330.

19. OR, I, 20 (1): 154-55.

20. Ibid., 153, 155; Duke, *Morgan's Cavalry*, 331-32; Ramage, *Rebel Raider*, 137; Thomas, *Morgan and His Raiders*, 67; Brown, *Bold Cavaliers*, 148-49.

21. OR, I, 20 (1): 153, 155-56; Duke, *Morgan's Cavalry*, 332-33.

22. OR, I, 20 (1): 153, 156; Duke, *Morgan's Cavalry*, 333-35; Ramage, *Rebel Raider*, 139-40; Holland, *Morgan and His Raiders*, 182; Brown, *Bold Cavaliers*, 151-52; Logan, *Kelion Franklin Peddicord*, 70.

23. OR, I, 20 (1): 153, 156; Ramage, *Rebel Raider*, 140; Thomas, *Morgan and His: Raiders*, 69; Henry L. Stone, "Reminiscences of Morgan's Men," SB 1 (1882-83): 408.

24. OR, I, 20 (1): 153, 156; Duke, *Morgan's Cavalry*, 335; Thomas, *Morgan and His Raiders*, 69; Holland, *Morgan and His Raiders*, 182-83; Brown, "Morgan's Christmas Raid," 16.

25. OR, I, 20 (1): 134-41, 156-57; Duke, *Morgan's Cavalry*, 335-38; Ramage, *Rebel Raider*, 140-42; Anderson Chenault Quisenberry, "The Eleventh Kentucky Cavalry, C. S. A," *SHSP* 35 (1907): 264; Kent Masterson Brown, ed., *The Civil War in Kentucky: Battle for the Bluegrass State* (Mason City, IA, 2000), 258-63.

26. Duke, *Morgan's Cavalry*, 338.

27. OR, I, 20 (1): 153, 157; Duke, *Morgan's Cavalry*, 339-40; Ramage, *Rebel Raider*, 142-43; Holland, *Morgan and His Raiders*, 183-84; Harrison, "Basil Duke," 36; J. W. Cunningham, "Memories of Morgan's Christmas Raid," *CV* 17 (1909): 79.

28. Logan, *Kelion Franklin Peddicord*, 74; Thomas, *Morgan and His Raiders*, 70; Adam Rankin Johnson, *The Partisan Rangers of the Confederate States Army: Memoirs of General Adam R. Johnson*, ed. by William J. Davis (Austin, TX, 1995), 134; Brown, *Bold Cavaliers*, 155-56.

29. OR, I, 20 (1): 158; Duke, *Morgan's Cavalry*, 342; Thomas, *Morgan and His Raiders*, 70-71.

30. John Allan Wyeth, "Morgan's Christmas Raid, 1862-63," in *PHCW*, 4: 156. For a rejoinder by one of Morgan's own officers, see Austin, *Blue and the Gray*, 68.

31. Duke, *Morgan's Cavalry*, 343; Metzler, *Morgan and His Dixie Cavaliers*, 42; Swiggett, *Rebel Raider*, 97; Brown, *Bold Cavaliers*, 161.

32. OR, I, 20 (1): 15-19.

33. Ibid., (2): 422.

34. Hafendorfer, *They Died by Twos and Tens*, 863; Warner, *Generals in Gray*, 39; *Synopsis of the Career of Wheeler*, 8.

35. Duke, *Morgan's Cavalry*, 344, 346.

36. Poole, *Cracker Cavaliers*, 55; OR, I, 20 (1): 76-78.

37. OR, I, 20 (1): 77-78; (2): 457; John H. Fisher, *They Rode with Forrest and Wheeler: A Chronicle of Five Tennessee Brothers' Service in the Confederate Western Cavalry* (Jefferson, NC, 1995), 27.

38. Connelly, *Autumn of Glory*, 44-45; OR, I, 20 (1): 163-65, 958.

39. Edwin C. Bearss, "Cavalry Operations in the Battle of Stone's River," *THQ* 19 (1960): 25-33; OR, I, 20 (1): 958; Peter Cozzens, *No Better Place to Die: The Battle of Stones River* (Urbana, IL, 1990), 55.

40. Du Bose, *Wheeler and the Army of Tennessee*, 120; Dodson, ed., *Campaigns of Wheeler*, 50.

41. OR, I, 20 (1): 958; Blackburn, "Reminiscences of the Terry Rangers," 72-73; Robert F. Bunting to "Editor Telegraph," Jan. 6, 1863, Bunting MSS, UT.

42. Robert F. Bunting to "Editor Telegraph," Jan. 6, 1863, Bunting MSS, UT.

43. OR, I, 20 (1): 958; (2): 467; Bearss, "Cavalry in Battle of Stone's River," 43-48; Cozzens, *No Better Place to Die*, 55; Du Bose, *Wheeler and the Army of Tennessee*, 139-41; George K.

Miller, "Eighth Confederate Cavalry—1861-1865," 18, ADA&H; Batchelor and Turner, *Batchelor-Turner Letters*, 41.

44. Du Bose, *Wheeler and the Army of Tennessee*, 123-24; Dodson, ed., *Campaigns of Wheeler*, 50.

45. Bearss, "Cavalry in Battle of Stone's River," 110; OR, I, 20 (1): 664, 958, 960; Dyer, *"Fightin' Joe" Wheeler*, 81; George K. Miller, "Eighth Confederate Cavalry—1861-1865," 18, ADA&H; Isaac B. Ulmer, Memoir of 3rd Alabama Cavalry, 2-3, SHC; Williams and Wooster, eds., "With Terry's Texas Rangers," 311-12; William R. Brooksher and David K. Snider, "The 'War Child' Rides: Joe Wheeler at Stones River," *CWTI* 14 (Jan. 1976): 8.

46. OR, I, 20 (1): 391-92, 958, 960; Cozzens, *No Better Place to Die*, 172; Bearss, "Cavalry in Battle of Stone's River," 111-12; Brooksher and Snider, "'War Child' Rides," 8-9.

47. George K. Miller, "Eighth Confederate Cavalry—1861-1865," 18, ADA&H; Bearss, "Cavalry in Battle of Stone's River," 112-14.

48. George K. Miller, "Eighth Confederate Cavalry—1861-1865," 18, ADA&H; OR, I, 20 (1): 959-60; Du Bose, *Wheeler and the Army of Tennessee*, 142-43.

49. Cozzens, *No Better Place to Die*, 104-07; G. C. Kniffin, "The Battle of Stone's River," *B&L* 3: 618-28; Gustave Cook to his wife, Jan. 13, 1863, Cook MSS, GLC; W. B. Corbit diary, Dec. 30-31, 1862, EU; Connelly, *Autumn of Glory*, 54-58; Horn, *Army of Tennessee*, 199-201; Bearss, "Cavalry in Battle of Stone's River," 118-24; OR, I, 20 (1): 664-67, 966; Dyer, *"Fightin' Joe" Wheeler*, 84.

50. OR, I, 20 (1): 959-60, 970; Bearss, "Cavalry in Battle of Stone's River," 125-27; George K. Miller, "Eighth Confederate Cavalry—1861-1865," 19, ADA&H.

51. OR, I, 20 (1): 664, 959-80; Bearss, "Cavalry in Battle of Stone's River," 127-28; Connelly, *Autumn of Glory*, 57-58.

52. David Urquhart, "Bragg's Advance and Retreat," *B&L* 3: 607; Connelly, *Autumn of Glory*, 58-64; Horn, *Army of Tennessee*, 201-06.

53. OR, I, 20 (1): 959-60, 968-69; (2): 402; Bearss, "Cavalry in Battle of Stone's River," 131-32; George K. Miller, "Eighth Confederate Cavalry—1861-1865," 19, ADA&H; Batchelor and Turner, *Batchelor-Turner Letters*, 42; Brooksher and Snider, "'War Child' Rides," 44-45; Gustave Cook to his wife, Jan. 13, 1863, Cook MSS, GLC.

54. OR, I, 20 (1): 959; Bearss, "Cavalry in Battle of Stone's River," 132-34; Du Bose, *Wheeler and the Army of Tennessee*, 143.

55. OR, I, 20 (1): 959; Connelly, *Autumn of Glory*, 62; McWhiney, *Braxton Bragg*, 366.

56. OR, I, 20 (1): 959-60, 969; Bearss, "Cavalry in Battle of Stone's River," 134-36.

57. OR, I, 20 (1): 667-68; Kniffin, "Battle of Stone's River," 630-32; Connelly, *Autumn of Glory*, 62-65; Horn, *Army of Tennessee*, 206-08.

## Chapter Nine: Foxes and Hounds

1. Robert F. Bunting to "Editor Telegraph," Jan. 6, 1863, Bunting MSS, UT.

2. OR, I, 20 (1): 957-61; Bearss, "Cavalry in Battle of Stone's River," 140-42.

3. Horn, *Army of Tennessee*, 210; OR, I, 20 (1): 670.

4. *Synopsis of the Career of Wheeler*, 10-11; Dyer, *"Fightin' Joe" Wheeler*, 90; Dodson, ed., *Campaigns of Wheeler*, 61; OR, I, 20 (1): 961, 983.

5. Du Bose, *Wheeler and the Army of Tennessee*, 151-54; Dyer, *"Fightin' Joe" Wheeler*, 87-90; F. W. Flood, "Captures by Eighth Confederate Cavalry," *CV* 13 (1905): 458-59; Miller, "Eighth Confederate Cavalry—1861-1865," 20-22, ADA&H.

6. *OR*, I, 20 (1): 961, 983-84; *Synopsis of the Career of Wheeler*, 10-11.

7. Dyer, *"Fightin' Joe" Wheeler*, 91; Jordan and Pryor, *Campaigns of Forrest*, 223-24; Cooling, *Fort Donelson's Legacy*, 192-93.

8. *OR*, I, 23 (1): 40.

9. Ibid., 40-41; Dyer, *"Fightin' Joe" Wheeler*, 92; Benjamin F. Cooling, "The Attack on Dover, Tenn.," *CWTI* 2 (Aug. 1963): 11-12; Jordan and Pryor, *Campaigns of Forrest*, 227-28; Wills, *Battle from the Start*, 98-100; Wyeth, *Life of Forrest*, 146-47; Batchelor and Turner, *Batchelor-Turner Letters*, 46.

10. Dyer, *"Fightin' Joe" Wheeler*, 94-96; Wyeth, *Life of Forrest*, 151.

11. Wills, *Battle from the Start*, 102, 145-47.

12. George K. Miller, "Eighth Confederate Cavalry—1861-1865," 23, ADA&H; Duke, *Morgan's Cavalry*, 351-71; Cooling, *Fort Donelson's Legacy*, 245; Ramage, *Rebel Raider*, 151; James Blanton, "Account of the Raids Made in Kentucky by General Morgan and Captain Hines," 9-17, UK.

13. Ramage, *Rebel Raider*, 151-53.

14. John Watson Morton, *The Artillery of Nathan Bedford Forrest's Cavalry: "The Wizard of the Saddle"* (Nashville, TN, and Dallas, TX, 1909), 79; Longacre, *Soldier to the Last*, 94-95.

15. *OR*, I, 23 (2): 684, 695; Warner, *Generals in Gray*, 214-15; Donald A. Hopkins, *The Little Jeff: The Jeff Davis Legion, Cavalry Army of Northern Virginia* (Shippensburg, PA, 1999), 12, 14, 112, 281; Du Bose, *Wheeler and the Army of Tennessee*, 160-61.

16. Quisenberry, "Eleventh Kentucky Cavalry," 266-68; Duke, *Morgan's Cavalry*, 362-63; Nelson Gremillion, *Company G, 1st Regiment Louisiana Cavalry, C. S. A.: A Narrative* (San Antonio, TX, 1986), 28-30; Howell Carter, *A Cavalryman's Reminiscences of the Civil War* (New Orleans, 1900), 65-70; *OR*, I, 23 (2): 645. A handwritten copy of Pegram's report of the expedition is in FHS.

17. *OR*, I, 17 (2): 832; 23 (2): 646; Hewett, et al., eds., *Supplement to the Official Records*, I, 4: 284-85; Du Bose, *Wheeler and the Army of Tennessee*, 160; Hartje, *Van Dorn*, 273-78.

18. *OR*, I, 17 (2): 838; Hartje, *Van Dorn*, 274-75; Edwin C. Bearss, *Campaign for Vicksburg* (3 vols. Dayton, OH, 1985-87), 1: 716-18 and nn.; Calvin L. Collier, *The War Child's Children: The Story of the Third Regiment, Arkansas Cavalry, Confederate States Army* (Little Rock, 1965), 42, 44; Joseph J. Hunter, "A Sketch of the History of [the] Noxubee Troopers, 1st Mississippi Cavalry, Company 'F,'" 7, MDA&H.

19. *OR*, I, 23 (1): 2; (2): 650, 701; Hartje, *Van Dorn*, 278.

20. Hartje, *Van Dorn*, 278; Du Bose, *Wheeler and the Army of Tennessee*, 160; Cooling, *Fort Donelson's Legacy*, 247; Duke, *Morgan's Cavalry*, 343; Holland, *Morgan and His Raiders*, 161.

21. *OR*, I, 23 (1): 116-25, 230-39; (2): 646; 52 (2): 425, 427-28; Morton, *Artillery of Forrest's Cavalry*, 80-85; Bates, *Texas Cavalry Officer's Civil War*, 235-36; Hartje, *Van Dorn*, 279-82; Carter, *Tarnished Cavalier*, 167-70; Wills, *Battle from the Start*, 104-05; Collier, *War Child's Children*, 44-46; Douglas Hale, *The Third Texas Cavalry in the Civil War* (Norman, OK, 1993),

164-67; Joseph J. Hunter, "A Sketch of the History of [the] Noxubee Troopers, 1st Mississippi Cavalry, Company 'F,'" 7, MDA&H; John C. Fite to Elizabeth Fite, Apr. 17, 1863, Fite MSS, MOC.

22. OR, I, 23 (1): 187-94; Jordan and Pryor, *Campaigns of Forrest*, 242-45; Wyeth, *Life of Forrest*, 166-75; Henry, *"First with the Most" Forrest*, 132-33.

23. Robert L. Willett, Jr., "The First Battle of Franklin," *CWTI* 7 (Feb. 1969): 16-23; Carter, *Tarnished Cavalier*, 174-76; Morton, *Artillery of Forrest's Cavalry*, 86-89; Joseph J. Hunter, "A Sketch of the History of [the] Noxubee Troopers, 1st Mississippi Cavalry, Company 'F,'" 8, MDA&H; Wyeth, *Life of Forrest*, 177-84; Henry, *"First with the Most" Forrest*, 136-37; Hartje, *Van Dorn*, 297-301; Collier, *War Child's Children*, 52-54; Cooling, *Fort Donelson's Legacy*, 248-49.

24. Edward Dillon, "General Van Dorn's Operations between Columbia and Nashville in 1863," *SHSP* 7 (1879): 144-45; Carter, *Tarnished Cavalier*, 177; Wills, *Battle from the Start*, 107; Elisha S. Burford to "Dear Atkison," Oct. 10, 1863, Joseph Wheeler MSS, RG-109, E-136, NA.

25. Dillon, "General Van Dorn's Operations," 145; Carter, *Tarnished Cavalier*, 178-79.

26. Joseph J. Hunter, "A Sketch of the History of [the] Noxubee Troopers, 1st Mississippi Cavalry, Company 'F,'" 9, MDA&H; William L. Nugent, *My Dear Nellie: The Civil War Letters of William L. Nugent to Eleanor Smith Nugent*, ed. by William M. Cash and Lucy Somerville Howorth (Jackson, MS, 1977), 107. A Federal cavalry officer provided a typical Northern view of Van Dorn's demise when he wrote: "With all his talents, he groveled in the slime of licentiousness and met the fate due to his crimes": John W. Rowell, *Yankee Cavalrymen: Through the Civil War with the Ninth Pennsylvania Cavalry* (Knoxville, TN, 1971), 129.

27. OR, I, 23 (1): 219-20; Robert L. Willett, Jr., "We Rushed with a Yell," *CWTI* 8 (Feb. 1970): 17-18.

28. OR, I, 23 (1): 219; Batchelor and Turner, *Batchelor-Turner Letters*, 48; Willett, "We Rushed with a Yell," 18-19; Duke, *Morgan's Cavalry*, 388.

29. OR, I, 23 (1): 220-21; Willett, "We Rushed with a Yell," 20-21; Batchelor and Turner, *Batchelor-Turner Letters*, 48-49.

30. D. Alexander Brown, "Grierson's Raid: 'Most Brilliant' of the War," *CWTI* 3 (Jan. 1965): 5.

31. Rowell, *Yankee Cavalrymen*, 95-110.

32. Grant, *Personal Memoirs*, 240-41; OR, I, 24 (1): 501-02, 519-22; ORN, I, 24: 550-54.

33. The best source on Grierson's expedition is D. Alexander Brown, *Grierson's Raid: A Cavalry Adventure of the Civil War* (Urbana, IL, 1954). Another lengthy account is in Bearss, *Campaign for Vicksburg*, 2: 187-236.

34. OR, I, 23 (1): 281-82, 285; (2): 224; Robert L. Willett, *The Lightning Mule Brigade: Abel Streight's 1863 Raid into Alabama* (Carmel, IN, 1999), 17-19, 21-34. This is the best source on Streight's Raid. For another heavily detailed account, see Bearss, *Campaign for Vicksburg*, 2: 129-75. For the exploits of Andrews's Raiders, see Russell S. Bonds, *Stealing the General: The Great Locomotive Chase and the First Medal of Honor* (Yardley, PA, 2007).

35. OR, I, 23 (1): 246-47; James F. Cook, "The 1863 Raid of Abel D. Streight: Why It Failed," *Alabama Review* 22 (Oct. 1969): 258-59.

36. *OR*, I, 23 (1): 286; Alva C. Roach, *The Prisoner of War, and How Treated: Containing a History of Colonel Streight's Expedition to the Rear of Bragg's Army, in the Spring of 1863* (Indianapolis, 1865), 12-15.

37. *OR*, I, 23 (1): 286; Roach, *Prisoner of War*, 14-15.

38. *OR*, I, 23 (1): 248, 286; Morton, *Artillery of Forrest's Cavalry*, 91-92; Wyeth, *Life of Forrest*, 188-89; Henry, *"First with the Most" Forrest*, 142; Adam Henry Whetstone, *History of the Fifty-third Alabama Volunteer Infantry (Mounted)*, ed. by William Stanley Hoole (University, AL, 1985), 36-37. For the political orientation of Roddey's command, see Paul Horton, "Submitting to the 'Shadow of Slavery': The Secession Crisis and Civil War in Alabama's Lawrence County," *CWH* 44 (1998): 111-36.

39. Henry, *"First with the Most" Forrest*, 144; Wyeth, *Life of Forrest*, 192; Roach, *Prisoner of War*, 18-19.

40. *OR*, I, 23 (1): 248; Morton, *Artillery of Forrest's Cavalry*, 92-93; Henry, *"First with the Most" Forrest*, 143-44; Lytle, *Bedford Forrest and His Critter Company*, 153.

41. *OR*, I, 23 (1): 248, 284; Jordan and Pryor, *Campaigns of Forrest*, 253-55; Henry, *"First with the Most" Forrest*, 145-46.

42. *OR*, I, 23 (1): 288; Wyeth, *Life of Forrest*, 197-98; Roach, *Prisoner of War*, 21-23; Jordan and Pryor, *Campaigns of Forrest*, 257; Henry, *"First with the Most" Forrest*, 146-47; Willett, *Lightning Mule Brigade*, 103-13.

43. *OR*, I, 23 (1): 288-89; Morton, *Artillery of Forrest's Cavalry*, 101; Henry, *"First with the Most" Forrest*, 147.

44. *OR*, I, 23 (1): 290-91; Henry, *"First with the Most" Forrest*, 148; Willett, *Lightning Mule Brigade*, 115-26.

45. *OR*, I, 23 (1): 289-90; Wyeth, *Life of Forrest*, 203-04; John P. W. Brown memoirs, 111, TSL&A.

46. *OR*, I, 23 (1): 290; Roach, *Prisoner of War*, 30-33; Henry, *"First with the Most" Forrest*, 150; Wills, *Battle from the Start*, 115-16; Willett, *Lightning Mule Brigade*, 137-41.

47. *OR*, I, 23 (1): 291-92; Roach, *Prisoner of War*, 37-39; Henry, *"First with the Most" Forrest*, 152-55; Willett, *Lightning Mule Brigade*, 149-50, 155-59.

48. *OR*, I, 23 (1): 292.

49. Ibid.; Jordan and Pryor, *Campaigns of Forrest*, 273-74; Wyeth, *Life of Forrest*, 218-19; Newton Cannon, *The Reminiscences of Sergeant Newton Cannon, First Sergeant, 11th Tennessee Cavalry, C. S. A.*, ed. by Campbell H. Brown (Franklin, TN, 1963), 29; Dabney H. Maury, *Recollections of a Virginian in the Mexican, Indian, and Civil Wars* (New York, 1894), 209.

50. Maury, *Recollections of a Virginian*, 209.

CHAPTER TEN: ON THE DECLINE

1. Willett, *Lightning Mule Brigade*, 185-89.

2. Ibid., 189-96.

3. Ibid., 197-98; *OR*, I, 23 (1): 294-95; Wyeth, *Life of Forrest*, 220-22; Johnston, *Narrative of Military Operations*, 174.

4. The most thorough study of the Chancellorsville campaign is Stephen W. Sears, *Chancellorsville* (Boston, 1996). For Meade's succession of Hooker, see pp. 44-49, and Edwin

B. Coddington, *The Gettysburg Campaign: A Study in Command* (New York, 1968), 209-10.

5. Wyeth, *Life of Forrest*, 223-25; Morton, *Artillery of Forrest's Cavalry*, 101-03; Henry H. Smith, "Reminiscences of Capt. Henry H. Smith," *CV* 8 (1900): 14-15.

6. Henry, *"First with the Most" Forrest*, 163.

7. Longacre, *Worthy Opponents*, 197-202, 205-07; John H. Crowell memoirs, unpaged, GSA; Joseph J. Hunter, "A Sketch of the History of [the] Noxubee Troopers, 1st Mississippi Cavalry, Company 'F,'" 9-12, MDA&H; Edwin C. Bearss, *Decision in Mississippi: Mississippi's Important Role in the War between the States* (Jackson, MS, 1962), 347-48.

8. L. Virginia French diary, May 3, 1863, TSL&A; Michael R. Bradley, *Tullahoma: The 1863 Campaign for the Control of Middle Tennessee* (Shippensburg, PA, 2000), 26-31.

9. OR, I, 23 (1): 9, 405; Steven E. Woodworth, *Six Armies in Tennessee: The Chickamauga and Chattanooga Campaigns* (Lincoln, NE, 1998), 26, 28.

10. Woodworth, *Six Armies in Tennessee*, 26.

11. OR, I, 23 (1): 585-86; 24 (1): 242-44; 42 (2): 472; Dyer, *"Fightin' Joe" Wheeler*, 103; Connelly, *Autumn of Glory*, 125.

12. OR, I, 23 (1): 403-06, 457-59, 611-12; (2): 883; Connelly, *Autumn of Glory*, 116-27; Horn, *Army of Tennessee*, 235-36; Dyer, *"Fightin' Joe" Wheeler*, 104; Dodson, ed., *Campaigns of Wheeler*, 86; George K. Miller, "Eighth Confederate Cavalry—1861-1865," 25, ADA&H.

13. Connelly, *Autumn of Glory*, 127.

14. Ibid., 127-28; Dodson, ed., *Campaigns of Wheeler*, 86.

15. Connelly, *Autumn of Glory*, 128-29.

16. OR, I, 23 (2): 891-92.

17. George K. Miller, "Eighth Confederate Cavalry—1861-1865," 26, ADA&H.

18. Dodson, ed., *Campaigns of Wheeler*, 87-88; Dyer, *"Fightin' Joe" Wheeler*, 105; Julius L. Dowda memoirs, 4, GSA.

19. William F. Mims, "War History of the Prattville Dragoons," 10, ADA&H; George K. Miller, "Eighth Confederate Cavalry—1861-1865," 26, ADA&H.

20. Dodson, ed., *Campaigns of Wheeler*, 90-91; Dyer, *"Fightin' Joe" Wheeler*, 106-07; Du Bose, *Wheeler and the Army of Tennessee*, 177; Woodworth, *Six Armies in Tennessee*, 35.

21. John Hunt Morgan to Joseph Wheeler, May 21, 1863, Morgan MSS, GLC.

22. Ramage, *Rebel Raider*, 153-54; Castleman, *Active Service*, 106-08; Sydney K. Smith, *Life, Army Record, and Public Services of D. Howard Smith* (Louisville, KY, 1890), 48-49; Cooling, *Fort Donelson's Legacy*, 248; Duke, *Morgan's Cavalry*, 382-87.

23. Duke, *Morgan's Cavalry*, 389-90; Ramage, *Rebel Raider*, 154-56; Thomas, *Morgan and His Raiders*, 75; Robert F. Bunting to "Editor Telegraph," June 3, 1863, Bunting MSS, UT; Cooling, *Fort Donelson's Legacy*, 248.

24. Ramage, *Rebel Raider*, 154.

25. OR, I, 23 (2): 656, 824.

26. Ibid., (1): 817; Ramage, *Rebel Raider*, 160; Thomas, *Morgan and His Raiders*, 75-76.

27. OR, I, 23 (1): 817-18; Dyer, *"Fightin' Joe" Wheeler*, 102-03; Lester V. Horwitz, *The Longest Raid of the Civil War: Little-Known & Untold Stories of Morgan's Raid into Kentucky, Indiana & Ohio* (Cincinnati, 1999), 4-5, 14-15.

28. Ramage, *Rebel Raider*, 160; Duke, *Morgan's Cavalry*, 407-10; Basil Duke, "Morgan's Indiana and Ohio Raid," in *Annals of the War, Written by Leading Participants, North and South* (Philadelphia, 1879), 243.

29. Duke, *Morgan's Cavalry*, 404-07; Warner, *Generals in Gray*, 156; Johnson, *Partisan Rangers of the Confederate States Army*, 142.

30. Duke, *Morgan's Cavalry*, 411-12, 414.

31. Allan Keller, *Morgan's Raid* (New York, 1962), 19-21; Duke, *Morgan's Cavalry*, 414; George Dallas Mosgrove, "Following Morgan's Plume through Indiana and Ohio," *SHSP* 35 (1907): 112.

32. Keller, *Morgan's Raid*, 21-25; Duke, *Morgan's Cavalry*, 415.

33. OR, I, 23 (1): 655-56; (2): 491-93, 582-85; Keller, *Morgan's Raid*, 23-24, 33; Longacre, *Mounted Raids of the Civil War*, 182-83; Swiggett, *Rebel Raider*, 130.

34. OR, I, 23 (1): 645-46; Quisenberry, "Eleventh Kentucky Cavalry," 271; Keller, *Morgan's Raid*, 29-32; Brown, *Bold Cavaliers*, 181-82; James Blanton, "Account of the Raids Made in Kentucky by General Morgan and Captain Hines," 31, UK; Johnson, *Partisan Rangers of the Confederate States Army*, 143; Smith, *Public Services of D. Howard Smith*, 58-61.

35. OR, I, 23 (1): 647-49; Keller, *Morgan's Raid*, 37-40; Brown, *Bold Cavaliers*, 182-84; Holland, *Morgan and His Raiders*, 229-30; James Blanton, "Account of the Raids Made in Kentucky by General Morgan and Captain Hines," 31, UK; Stone, *"Morgan's Men"*, 11; Smith, *Public Services of D. Howard Smith*, 61-62.

36. Keller, *Morgan's Raid*, 40-41; Ramage, *Rebel Raider*, 164-65; Stone, *"Morgan's Men"*, 11-12; Hewett, et al., eds., *Supplement to the Official Records*, I, 4: 209-10.

37. Swiggett, *Rebel Raider*, 131.

38. Keller, *Morgan's Raid*, 44; Ramage, *Rebel Raider*, 165-66.

39. Duke, *Morgan's Cavalry*, 436-37.

40. Keller, *Morgan's Raid*, 45-46, 49, 51, 55-57, 93, 149, 160, 260; L. D. Hockersmith, *Morgan's Escape: A True History of the Raid of General Morgan and His Men through Kentucky, Indiana and Ohio. . .* (Madisonville, KY, 1903), 18-19; Duke, "Morgan's Indiana and Ohio Raid," 248-50.

41. Duke, *Morgan's Cavalry*, 428-31.

42. OR, I, 23 (1): 658-59; Keller, *Morgan's Raid*, 64-69, 88-94; Thomas, *Morgan and His Raiders*, 79; Hewett, et al., eds., *Supplement to the Official Records*, I, 4: 214. For a detailed study of one of the more extensive engagements in Indiana, see Arville L. Funk, *The Battle of Corydon* (Corydon, IN, 1975).

43. Keller, *Morgan's Raid*, 96-98; Hewett, et al., eds., *Supplement to the Official Records*, I, 4: 214; Thomas, *Morgan and His Raiders*, 81-82.

44. Duke, *Morgan's Cavalry*, 442-44; Keller, *Morgan's Raid*, 109-53; Swiggett, *Rebel Raider*, 141; John S. Still, "Blitzkrieg, 1863: Morgan's Raid and Rout," *CWH* 3 (Sept. 1957): 294-95; Hewett, et al., eds., *Supplement to the Official Records*, I, 4: 215; Johnson, *Partisan Rangers of the Confederate States Army*, 146; Mosgrove, "Following Morgan's Plume," 117-18.

45. OR, I, 23 (1): 639-43, 662-63; Theodore F. Allen, "Six Hundred Miles of Fried Chicken," *JUSCA* 12 (1899): 166-70.

46. OR, I, 23 (1): 640-42; ORN, I, 25: 238-59; Keller, *Morgan's Raid*, 193-206; Duke, *Morgan's Cavalry*, 448-53; Ramage, *Rebel Raider*, 176-78; Hockersmith, *Morgan's Escape*, 20; Thomas,

*Morgan and His Raiders*, 83; James Blanton, "Account of the Raids Made in Kentucky by General Morgan and Captain Hines," 35-36, UK; Harrison, "Basil Duke," 37; Johnson, *Partisan Rangers of the Confederate States Army*, 149-50.

47. OR, I, 23 (1): 643-44, 663; Keller, *Morgan's Raid*, 207-66; Still, "Blitzkrieg, 1863," 300-01; Holland, *Morgan and His Raiders*, 247.

48. Ramage, *Rebel Raider*, 183-98; Thomas, *Morgan and His Raiders*, 86-90; N. S. Offutt to anon., undated [ca. Dec. 1863], KHS; Castleman, *Active Service*, 113-22; Duke, *Morgan's Cavalry*, 463-91. Swiggett, *Rebel Raider*, 153-67, theorizes that Morgan escaped not by tunneling out of prison but by bribing his jailors.

49. Ramage, *Rebel Raider*, 199-225; Thomas, *Morgan and His Raiders*, 91-98, 105-06.

50. Ramage, *Rebel Raider*, 226-44; Thomas, *Morgan and His Raiders*, 102-10.

## Chapter Eleven: Peaks and Valleys

1. Connelly, *Autumn of Glory*, 130-31.

2. Ibid., 131-33; Horn, *Army of Tennessee*, 236-37.

3. OR, I, 23 (1): 584.

4. Edwin H. Fay, *"This Infernal War": The Confederate Letters of Sgt. Edwin H. Fay*, ed. by Bell I. Wiley and Lucy E. Fay (Austin, TX, 1958), 293; Batchelor and Turner, *Batchelor-Turner Letters*, 57-58.

5. Batchelor and Turner, *Batchelor-Turner Letters*, 60.

6. Ibid., 61; Thomas J. Gray to his wife, July 16, 1863, Gray MSS, TSL&A; Nimrod E. W. Long to his wife, July 17, 1863, Long MSS, EU.

7. OR, I, 23 (1): 902, 916, 925-26; 30 (2): 59-20; Dodson, ed., *Campaigns of Wheeler*, 99; Dyer, *"Fightin' Joe" Wheeler*, 110-11.

8. OR, I, 23 (2): 944, 954, 961; 30 (2): 20; Connelly, *Autumn of Glory*, 149-50; Horn, *Army of Tennessee*, 241.

9. OR, I, 30 (4): 507-09.

10. Ibid., 509-10; Wills, *Battle from the Start*, 130-31.

11. Hallock, *Braxton Bragg: Volume II*, 34-35.

12. Ibid., 35, 45; OR, I, 23 (2): 938.

13. OR, I, 30 (1): 33-34, 50-53; (2): 21-22, 26-27; Connelly, *Autumn of Glory*, 148-50, 169-70; Horn, *Army of Tennessee*, 244-46; William T. Martin to "Dear Jess," Aug. 28, 1863, UT.

14. Hallock, *Braxton Bragg, Volume II*, 46; Connelly, *Autumn of Glory*, 150-52, 171-72; Horn, *Army of Tennessee*, 244-45.

15. Horn, *Army of Tennessee*, 244; Connelly, *Autumn of Glory*, 149.

16. Daniel H. Hill, "Chickamauga—The Great Battle of the West," B&L 3: 640-45; Connelly, *Autumn of Glory*, 150-62, 174-94; Horn, *Army of Tennessee*, 249-57.

17. OR, I, 30 (2): 11-20, 288.

18. Hill, "Chickamauga," 646-47. The finest account of the Chickamauga campaign is Peter Cozzens, *This Terrible Sound: The Battle of Chickamauga* (Urbana, IL, 1992). A good earlier study is Glenn Tucker, *Chickamauga, Bloody Battle in the West* (Indianapolis, 1961).

19. Ibid., 647, 649; Wyeth, *Life of Forrest*, 244-46, 250; Wills, *Battle from the Start*, 134-35;

Jordan and Pryor, *Campaigns of Forrest*, 313-17; Henry, *"First with the Most" Forrest*, 182; Hewett, et al., eds., *Supplement to the Official Records*, I, 5: 703-04.

20. OR, I, 30 (2): 32, 524-25; Wyeth, *Life of Forrest*, 246-51; Jordan and Pryor, *Campaigns of Forrest*, 317-28; Henry, *"First with the Most" Forrest*, 182-83.

21. OR, (1): 56-57; (2): 32; Hill, "Chickamauga," 648-53; Horn, *Army of Tennessee*, 257-59.

22. OR, I, 30 (1): 329; (2): 520; Robert F. Bunting to "Editor Telegraph," Sept. 29, 1863, Bunting MSS, UT.

23. OR, I, 30 (1): 58-59; (2): 33-34, 146, 525; Hill, "Chickamauga," 653-55; Wyeth, *Life of Forrest*, 251-55; Horn, *Army of Tennessee*, 263; Wills, *Battle from the Start*, 139.

24. OR, I, 30 (1): 58-59; Hill, "Chickamauga," 657-58.

25. OR, I, 30 (1): 60-61; (2): 34, 288-89; Hill, "Chickamauga," 659-62; Horn, *Army of Tennessee*, 263-65.

26. OR, I, 30 (2): 33-34, 520.

27. Ibid., 521; John Allan Wyeth, *With Sabre and Scalpel: The Autobiography of a Soldier and Surgeon* (New York, 1914), 248.

28. OR, I, 30 (4): 681-82; Horn, *Army of Tennessee*, 272-79; Connelly, *Autumn of Glory*, 227-31; Wyeth, *Life of Forrest*, 259-63; Jordan and Pryor, *Campaigns of Forrest*, 350-52.

29. OR, I, 30 (2): 521; (4): 679, 682.

30. Ibid., (2): 521-22; (4): 694-95.

31. Ibid., (2): 522; (4): 698-99; Wills, *Battle from the Start*, 142.

32. OR, I, 30 (2): 722-23; (3): 638; (4): 710-11.

33. Wyeth, *Life of Forrest*, 264; Wills, *Battle from the Start*, 143-44.

34. Wyeth, *Life of Forrest*, 265-66.

35. Ibid., 266

36. Ibid.; Horn, *Army of Tennessee*, 290-91.

37. Wyeth, *Life of Forrest*, 267-71; Jordan and Pryor, *Campaigns of Forrest*, 358-61; Steven E. Woodworth, *Jefferson Davis and His Generals: The Failure of Confederate Command in the West* (Lawrence, KS, 1990), 244.

38. OR, I, 30 (2): 722-23; (4): 711; Henry, *"First with the Most" Forrest*, 197; Warner, *Generals in Gray*, 67-68; James Lee McDonough, *Chattanooga—A Death Grip on the Confederacy* (Knoxville, TN, 1984), 69.

39. OR, I, 30 (2): 723, 726; Dyer, *"Fightin' Joe" Wheeler*, 127-28; Dodson, ed., *Campaigns of Wheeler*, 117-21; William R. Brooksher and David K. Snider, "A Ride Down the Sequatchie Valley," *CWTI* 22 (Mar. 1983): 33-34; Guild, *Fourth Tennessee Cavalry*, 35-36.

40. OR, I, 30 (2): 669, 675, 684-85; William L. Curry, "Raid of the Confederate Cavalry through Central Tennessee," *JUSCA* 19 (1908-09): 818-10.

41. OR, I, 30 (2): 723; Du Bose, *Wheeler and the Army of Tennessee*, 208.

42. Guild, *Fourth Tennessee Cavalry*, 37-38; *Synopsis of the Career of Wheeler*, 14-15.

43. OR, I, 30 (2): 723; John Allan Wyeth, "The Destruction of Rosecrans' Great Wagon Train," in *PHCW*, 4: 160, 162; Wyeth, *With Sabre and Scalpel*, 271-73; William F. Mims, "War History of the Prattville Dragoons," 11, ADA&H; Batchelor and Turner, *Batchelor-Turner Letters*, 71.

44. *OR*, I, 30 (2): 723; Wyeth, "Destruction of Rosecrans' Train," 162; John W. Du Bose, "Wheeler's Raid into Tennessee," *CV* 24 (1916): 12.

45. L. Virginia French diary, Oct. 12, 1863, TSL&A.

46. Ibid.; Elisha S. Burford to "Dear Atkison," Oct. 10, 1863; to "Dear Major," Oct. 12, 1863; both, Joseph Wheeler MSS, RG-109, E-136, NA.

47. *OR*, I, 30 (2): 723-24, 726-27; Batchelor and Turner, *Batchelor-Turner Letters*, 71; Julius L. Dowda memoirs, 8, GSA; Elisha S. Burford to "Dear Major," Oct. 12, 1863, Joseph Wheeler MSS, RG-109, E-136, NA; L. Virginia French diary, Oct. 12, 1863, TSL&A.

48. *OR*, I, 30 (2): 724.

49. Ibid., 666, 675-76, 685-87, 724; Joseph Wheeler to Braxton Bragg, Oct. 12, 1863, Wheeler MSS, RG-109, E-136, NA; Dodson, ed., *Campaigns of Wheeler*, 125-26; Guild, *Fourth Tennessee Cavalry*, 43-44; Batchelor and Turner, *Batchelor-Turner Letters*, 71; Julius L. Dowda memoirs, 8, GSA.

50. *OR*, I, 30 (2): 724, 727; Blackburn, "Reminiscences of the Terry Rangers," 146-50; Curry, "Raid through Central Tennessee," 827.

51. *OR*, I, 30 (2): 728.

52. Brooksher and Snider, "Ride Down the Sequatchie," 38.

53. Ibid.; *OR*, I, 30 (2): 666, 687-88, 724-25; B. F. Nelson, "A Boy in the Confederate Cavalry," *CV* 36 (1928): 375.

54. Grant, *Personal Memoirs*, 309-19; *OR*, I, 31 (1): 50-59, 77-78, 477-78, 842, 844; (2): 27-29.

55. Elisha S. Burford to his wife, Oct. 12, 1863, Joseph Wheeler MSS, RG-109, E-136, NA; DeLeon, *Wheeler, the Man, the Statesman, the Soldier*, 56-57; Dyer, *"Fightin' Joe" Wheeler*, 135-37.

56. *OR*, I, 31 (2): 662-64; (3): 611; Warner, *Generals in Gray*, 144-45, 168-69. For more on the talented but little-known Kelly, see Maud McClure Kelly, "John Herbert Kelly, the Boy General of the Confederacy," *Alabama Historical Quarterly* 9 (1947): 9-112.

57. Joseph Wheeler to Braxton Bragg, Oct. 12, 1863; Wheeler's endorsement to William T. Martin to Samuel Cooper, Oct. 12, 1863 [two letters]; all, Wheeler MSS, RG-109, E-136, NA.

58. Joseph Wheeler to Braxton Bragg, Dec. 20, 1863, Bragg MSS, DU; *OR*, I, 32 (3): 643-44; Batchelor and Turner, *Batchelor-Turner Letters*, 71.

59. *OR*, I, 30 (4): 743, 763; Elisha S. Burford to his wife, Oct. 12, 1863, Joseph Wheeler MSS, RG-109, E-136, NA.

60. *OR*, I, 31 (1): 453-56; (3): 634-35; Connelly, *Autumn of Glory*, 262-65; Horn, *Army of Tennessee*, 294-95.

61. *OR*, I, 30 (1): 456, 540-41; (3): 679, 686-88, 696; James Longstreet to Joseph Wheeler, Nov. 12, 14, 1863, Longstreet MSS, GLC; Dodson, ed., *Campaigns of Wheeler*, 145-46; J. W. Minnich, "The Cavalry at Knoxville," *CV* 32 (1924): 11; Julius L. Dowda memoirs, 10, GSA; Poole, *Cracker Cavaliers*, 100.

62. *OR*, I, 31 (1): 457-59, 543-44; (3): 696, 704, 708, 719-20, 732-34, 737; James Longstreet to Joseph Wheeler, Dec. 20, 1863, Longstreet MSS, GLC; James Hagan, History of the 3rd Alabama Cavalry, 8, ADA&H; R. R. Gaines, History of the 3rd Alabama Cavalry, 12, ADA&H.

63. *OR*, I, 31 (1): 460-61, 544-46, (3): 740-41.

CHAPTER TWELVE: GUARDIANS AT THE GATE

1. Glenn Tucker, "The Battles for Chattanooga," *CWTI* 10 (Aug. 1971): 30; McDonough, *Chattanooga*, 129-42; Peter Cozzens, *The Shipwreck of Their Hopes: The Battles for Chattanooga* (Urbana, IL, 1994), 179-198.

2. McDonough, *Chattanooga*, 143-205; Cozzens, *Shipwreck of Their Hopes*, 201-342.

3. Cozzens, *Shipwreck of Their Hopes*, 345-67; OR, I, 31 (2): 664-67.

4. *OR*, I, 31 (2): 662-63 and n; John W. Dyer, *Reminiscences; or, Four Years in the Confederate Army: A History of the Experiences of the Private Soldier in Camp, Hospital, Prison, on the March, and on the Battlefield, 1861 to 1865* (Evansville, IN, 1898), 133-34.

5. Carter, *Cavalryman's Reminiscences*, 98-99.

6. *OR*, I, 31 (2): 779; John W. Cotton, *"Yours Till Death": Civil War Letters of John W. Cotton*, ed. by Lucille Griffith (University, AL, 1951), 96.

7. *OR*, I, 31 (2): 679; (3): 750; George K. Miller, "Eighth Confederate Cavalry—1861-1865," 28, ADA&H.

8. Cozzens, *Shipwreck of Their Hopes*, 370-84; McDonough, *Chattanooga*, 220-25.

9. *OR*, I, 31 (2): 680-81.

10. Ibid., (3): 755, 759-62, 767, 771, 780-81.

11. Connelly, *Autumn of Glory*, 277-78; Horn, *Army of Tennessee*, 303-06; OR, I, 31 (3): 771; 32 (2): 799.

12. *OR*, I, 31 (3): 842-43; Connelly, *Autumn of Glory*, 281-83; Horn, *Army of Tennessee*, 308-09; McMurry, *Two Great Rebel Armies*, 127–128.

13. Daniel, *Soldiering in the Army of Tennessee*, 129; Carter, *Cavalryman's Reminiscences*, 102-03; Austin, *Blue and the Gray*, 118-19.

14. Longacre, *Worthy Opponents*, 39-40; OR, I, 32 (2): 510, 698-99; (3): 795; William F. Mims, "War History of the Prattville Dragoons," 13, ADA&H; Richard M. McMurry, *Atlanta, 1864: Last Chance for the Confederacy* (Lincoln, NE, 2000), 59; John W. Rowell, "The Battle of Mossy Creek," *CWTI* 8 ( July 1969): 11-16; Isaac B. Ulmer, Memoir of 3rd Alabama Cavalry, 3, SHC.

15. Longacre, *Worthy Opponents*, 58, 61-62, 110-12, 115, 121-24, 167, 234-36.

16. Dyer, *"Fightin' Joe" Wheeler*, 153-54; OR, I, 32 (3): 683; George K. Miller, "Eighth Confederate Cavalry—1864-1865," 27, ADA&H; Poole, *Cracker Cavaliers*, 118; McMurry, *Atlanta, 1864*, 132; Daniel, *Soldiering in the Army of Tennessee*, 56-61, 119-22; Horn, *Army of Tennessee*, 308-12; Joseph E. Johnston to Beverly R. Johnston, Feb. 15, 1864, Johnston MSS, Earl Gregg Swem Library, College of William and Mary, Williamsburg, VA.

17. Dyer, *"Fightin' Joe" Wheeler*, 155-56; Du Bose, *Wheeler and the Army of Tennessee*, 274-75; Horn, *Army of Tennessee*, 314-15; Andrew Haughton, *Training, Tactics and Leadership in the Confederate Army of Tennessee: Seeds of Failure* (Portland, OR, 2000), 147-48; Philip L. Secrist, "The Role of Cavalry in the Atlanta Campaign, 1864," *GHQ* 56 (1972): 510; OR, I, 32 (2): 759.

18. Connelly, *Autumn of Glory*, 318-21; Horn, *Army of Tennessee*, 313-14; OR, I, 52 (2): 606-07; Joseph Wheeler to Braxton Bragg, Feb. 14, 1864, Dearborn Coll., Houghton Library, Harvard University, Cambridge, MA.

19. OR, I, 32 (2): 699; Connelly, *Autumn of Glory*, 322-24; Richard M. McMurry, *John Bell Hood and Southern Independence* (Lexington, KY, 1982), 86-89.

20. OR, I, 52 (2): 606-07, 611-14; Dyer, *"Fightin' Joe" Wheeler*, 157-59; Du Bose, *Wheeler and the Army of Tennessee*, 266-68; Connelly, *Autumn of Glory*, 316.

21. OR, I, 31 (1): 641-44; George K. Miller, "Eighth Confederate Cavalry—1861-1865," 28-29, ADA&H; Dodson, ed., *Campaigns of Wheeler*, 156-59; *Synopsis of the Career of Wheeler*, 17-18; Cotton, *"Yours Till Death,"* 99.

22. OR, I, 52 (2): 606.

23. George K. Miller, "Eighth Confederate Cavalry—1861-1865," 30, ADA&H.

24. Dodson, ed., *Campaigns of Wheeler*, 169.

25. OR, I, 32 (3): 684, 795; Fisher, *They Rode with Forrest and Wheeler*, 70-71, 73; Collier, *War Child's Children*, 90.

26. OR, I, 32 (3): 866; Dyer, "Cavalry Operations in the Army of Tennessee," 212; Connelly, *Autumn of Glory*, 384-86.

27. OR, I, 32 (2): 699; 38 (3): 642.

28. Ibid., 38 (1): 115.

29. Grant, *Personal Memoirs*, 357-59, 363-66; OR, I, 33: 827-28.

30. Longacre, *Worthy Opponents*, 203-05, 216-19; Connelly, *Autumn of Glory*, 295-304; OR, I, 38 (3): 612-13; McMurry, "Enemy at Richmond," 26-27.

31. Batchelor and Turner, *Batchelor-Turner Letters*, 75.

32. Du Bose, *Wheeler and the Army of Tennessee*, 268-69.

33. Johnston, *Narrative of Military Operations*, 282-85; Dodson, ed., *Campaigns of Wheeler*, 162-71; Austin, *Blue and the Gray*, 121-22; OR, I, 32 (1): 10, 484; (2): 798.

34. Dyer, *"Fightin' Joe" Wheeler*, 159-62; Secrist, "Cavalry in the Atlanta Campaign," 510-11; Connelly, *Autumn of Glory*, 331-34; OR, I, 38 (3): 943-44; (4): 656-57, 660-64, 672-73.

35. James Lee McDonough and James Pickett Jones, *War So Terrible: Sherman and Atlanta* (New York, 1987), 96; OR, I, 38 (3): 944; (4): 672-73; Secrist, "Cavalry in the Atlanta Campaign," 512.

36. OR, I, 38 (3): 944; Dodson, ed., *Campaigns of Wheeler*, 176-77; George K. Miller, "Eighth Confederate Cavalry—1861-1865," 33, ADA&H; Gustave Cook to his wife, May 9, 1864, Cook MSS, GLC.

37. OR, I, 38 (3): 944; (4): 681-82; Connelly, *Autumn of Glory*, 388-89.

38. OR, I, 38 (3): 944-45; (4): 710; Secrist, "Cavalry in the Atlanta Campaign," 512.

39. Dyer, *"Fightin' Joe" Wheeler*, 166-67; Dodson, ed., *Campaigns of Wheeler*, 178; William S. Ward to "My Dear Cousin," May 28, 1864, Ward MSS, USAH&EC.

40. Johnston, *Narrative of Military Operations*, 310-12; OR, I, 38 (3): 945; (4): 680, 707; Dyer, *"Fightin' Joe" Wheeler*, 166-67; Richard M. McMurry, "Resaca: 'A Heap of Hard Fiten,'" *CWTI* 9 (Nov. 1970): 4-12, 44-48.

41. OR, I, 38 (3): 945; (4): 713; Secrist, "Cavalry in the Atlanta Campaign," 513; Albert Castel, *Decision in the West: The Atlanta Campaign of 1864* (Lawrence, KS, 1992), 172, 175-81; McDonough and Pickett, *War So Terrible*, 284.

42. OR, I, 38 (5): 868; Dodson, ed., *Campaigns of Wheeler*, 179-80; George K. Miller, "Eighth Confederate Cavalry—1861-1865," 36-37, ADA&H.

43. Johnston, *Narrative of Military Operations*, 319-20; Symonds, *Joseph E. Johnston*, 288; OR, I, 38 (3): 615, 946; Castel, *Decision in the West*, 193-95; McDonough and Jones, *War So Terrible*, 122-31; Connelly, *Autumn of Glory*, 332, 334, 341, 344-45.

44. Castel, *Decision in the West*, 193-95; OR, I, 38 (3): 946; George K. Miller, "Eighth Confederate Cavalry—1861-1865," 37, ADA&H.

45. OR, I, 38 (3): 646, 650.

46. Johnston, *Narrative of Military Operations*, 321-22; Symonds, *Joseph E. Johnston*, 92-93; McDonough and Jones, *War So Terrible*, 132-34; McMurry, *John Bell Hood*, 108-09, 198-99.

47. OR, I, 38 (4): 728; McDonough and Jones, *War So Terrible*, 133-34.

48. OR, I, 38 (3): 946-47; (4): 729; Johnston, *Narrative of Military Operations*, 325; Dodson, ed., *Campaigns of Wheeler*, 186; Du Bose, *Wheeler and the Army of Tennessee*, 304-05; Whetstone, *Fifty-third Alabama (Mounted)*, 53; Austin, *Blue and the Gray*, 125; George K. Miller, "Eighth Confederate Cavalry—1861-1865," 38, ADA&H; Collier, *War Child's Children*, 98-99; Cotton, "*Yours Till Death*", 108-09.

49. Castel, *Decision in the West*, 221-26; Richard M. McMurry, "'The Hell Hole': New Hope Church," *CWTI* 11 (Feb. 1973): 32-43.

50. OR, I, 38 (3): 948; Castel, *Decision in the West*, 233-41; Dyer, *"Fightin' Joe" Wheeler*, 171-72; Gustave Cook to his wife, July 7, 1874, Cook MSS, GLC.

51. Secrist, "Cavalry in the Atlanta Campaign," 516-17.

52. OR, I, 52 (2): 704-07; Johnston, *Narrative of Military Operations*, 359-62; Dyer, *"Fightin' Joe" Wheeler*, 172-73; McMurry, *Atlanta, 1864*, 97-99, 111, 131-36, 198-202; McDonough and Jones, *War So Terrible*, 124-26.

53. Joseph Wheeler to Braxton Bragg, July [?] 1864, Bragg MSS, DU.

54. Sidney S. Champion to his wife, May 31, 1864, Champion MSS, EU; OR, I, 38 (3): 943-49.

55. Connelly, *Autumn of Glory*, 355-56; Castel, *Decision in the West*, 242-77; Horn, *Army of Tennessee*, 331-33.

56. Dodson, ed., *Campaigns of Wheeler*, 190; Secrist, "Cavalry in the Atlanta Campaign," 518-19.

57. Sidney S. Champion to his wife, June 9, 1864, Champion MSS, EU; Castel, *Decision in the West*, 285-86; *Synopsis of the Career of Wheeler*, 23; William M. Worthington to his father, June 26, 1864, Worthington MSS, MDA&H.

58. Mary Boykin Chesnut, *Mary Chesnut's Civil War*, ed. by C. Vann Woodward (New Haven, CT, 1981), 482-83, 607.

59. OR, I, 38 (4): 783; William A. Fleming memoirs, 29, USAH&EC; David Evans, *Sherman's Horsemen: Union Cavalry Operations in the Atlanta Campaign* (Bloomington, IN, 1996), 242-43, 536n; O. P. Hargis, "We Came Very Near Capturing General Wilder," *CWTI* 7 (Nov. 1968): 40.

60. William M. Worthington to his sister, June 25, 1864, Worthington MSS, MDA&H.

61. Castel, *Decision in the West*, 303-24; Connelly, *Autumn of Glory*, 359-60; Sidney S. Champion to his wife, June 27, 1864, Champion MSS, EU; Samuel H. Brodnax memoirs, 5-6, FHS; Hewett, et al., eds., *Supplement to the Official Records*, I, 7: 147-50; Richard M. McMurry, "Kennesaw Mountain," *CWTI* 8 (Jan. 1970): 20-33.

62. Sidney S. Champion to his wife, July 11, 14, 1864, Champion MSS, EU.

63. Johnston, *Narrative of Military Operations*, 347; Symonds, *Joseph E. Johnston*, 310; Castel, *Decision in the West*, 336-39; George K. Miller, "Eighth Confederate Cavalry—1861-1865," 40-41, ADA&H.

64. OR, I, 38 (5): 881, 883, 885, 887; 39 (2): 712-14; Johnston, *Narrative of Military Operations*, 348, 364; Symonds, *Joseph E. Johnston*, 310, 321-23; McMurry, *John Bell Hood*, 117-20; Maury, *Recollections of a Virginian*, 147-48; Glatthaar, *Partners in Command*, 129-30. See also Thomas Robson Hay, "Davis, Bragg, and Johnston in the Atlanta Campaign," *GHQ* 8 (1924): 38-48.

65. Guild, *Fourth Tennessee Cavalry*, 66; John G. Deupree, "The Noxubee Squadron of the First Mississippi Cavalry, C. S. A., 1861-1865," *Publications of the Mississippi Historical Society, Centenary Series* 2 (1918): 101.

66. William T. Sherman, "The Grand Strategy of the Last Year of the War," *B&L* 4: 253; Longacre, *Worthy Opponents*, 274.

CHAPTER THIRTEEN: UNACCEPTABLE LOSSES

1. Though relatively brief, the most acceptable biography of Hood is McMurry's *John Bell Hood*. Other life studies of merit include Richard O'Connor, *Hood, Cavalier General* (New York, 1949), and John P. Dyer, *The Gallant Hood* (Indianapolis, 1950).

2. Wilbur G. Kurtz, Sr., "The Fighting at Atlanta," *CWTI* 3 ( July 1964): 9; McMurry, *Atlanta, 1864*, 147-49; Castel, *Decision in the West*, 369.

3. Kurtz, "Fighting at Atlanta," 9-10; McMurry, *Atlanta, 1864*, 146-47.

4. OR, I, 38 (3): 951-52; (5): 894-95; 47 (2): 1004, 1012, 1027, 1127; Castel, *Decision in the West*, 369-83; Connelly, *Autumn of Glory*, 439-44; Dyer, *"Fightin' Joe" Wheeler*, 176-78; Dodson, ed., *Campaigns of Wheeler*, 199, 205-09; Warner, *Generals in Gray*, 87.

5. OR, I, 38 (3): 952; Castel, *Decision in the West*, 383-88; Dyer, *"Fightin' Joe" Wheeler*, 178.

6. Castel, *Decision in the West*, 389-413; Connelly, *Autumn of Glory*, 445-40.

7. OR, I, 38 (3): 952-53; (5): 901; Dyer, *"Fightin' Joe" Wheeler*, 179-80; John H. Ash diary, July 22, 1864, EU; Nugent, *My Dear Nellie*, 189-80.

8. OR, I, 38 (3): 953.

9. Ibid., 953-54; (5): 901, 905, 910-11, 913-15, 921.

10. Ibid., (3): 953; Dyer, *"Fightin' Joe" Wheeler*, 182.

11. OR, I, 38 (3): 953-54; (5): 922; Secrist, "Cavalry in the Atlanta Campaign," 522-23; Dodson, ed., *Campaigns of Wheeler*, 223.

12. OR, I, 38 (3): 953; Evans, *Sherman's Horsemen*, 212-16; Secrist, "Cavalry in the Atlanta Campaign," 422; Dodson, ed., *Campaigns of Wheeler*, 220-22.

13. OR, I, 38 (3): 955-56; Evans, *Sherman's Horsemen*, 265-71; Guild, *Fourth Tennessee Cavalry*, 70-71, Wilbur S. Nye, "Cavalry Operations around Atlanta," *CWTI* 3 ( July 1964): 49-50.

14. OR, I, 38 (5): 938-40; J. A. Wynn memoirs, 58-59, GSA.

15. J. A. Wynn memoirs, 58-59, GSA.

16. OR, I, 38 (3): 954; (5): 927-29; Evans, *Sherman's Horsemen*, 217-37, 244-51; Nye, "Cavalry Operations around Atlanta," 47-48; John W. Rowell, "McCook's Raid," *CWTI* 13 ( July 1974): 8-9, 42-43; John H. Ash diary, July 29-30, 1864, EU; Dyer, *"Fightin' Joe" Wheeler*, 183;

Du Bose, *Wheeler and the Army of Tennessee*, 377-78; George K. Miller, "Eighth Confederate Cavalry—1861-1865," 43-44, ADA&H.

17. OR, I, 38 (3): 955, 964; Evans, *Sherman's Horsemen*, 252-61; Dyer, *"Fightin' Joe" Wheeler*, 183-84; Dodson, ed., *Campaigns of Wheeler*, 226-27.

18. Evans, *Sherman's Horsemen*, 264-65; Rowell, "McCook's Raid," 44-45; George L. Griscom, *Fighting With Ross' Texas Cavalry Brigade, C. S. A.: The Diary of George L. Griscom, Adjutant, 9th Texas Cavalry Regiment*, ed. by Homer L. Kerr (Hillsboro, TX, 1976), 161-62; Crabb, *All Afire to Fight*, 236-37.

19. OR, I, 38 (3): 955-57; Evans, *Sherman's Horsemen*, 265-77; Guild, *Fourth Tennessee Cavalry*, 70-71; Rowell, "McCook's Raid," 46-48.

20. Castel, *Decision in the West*, 428-36; McDonough and Jones, *War So Terrible*, 256-62; McMurry, *Atlanta, 1864*, 156-57.

21. Joseph J. Hunter, "A Sketch of the History of [the] Noxubee Troopers, 1st Mississippi Cavalry, Company 'F,'" 15-16, MDA&H.

22. McDonough and Jones, *War So Terrible*, 263.

23. OR, I, 38 (3): 957; (5): 946; John Bell Hood, *Advance and Retreat: Personal Experiences in the United States and Confederate States Armies* (New Orleans, 1880), 198.

24. Dodson, ed., *Campaigns of Wheeler*, 234; Cotton, *"Yours Till Death"*, 117.

25. OR, I, 38 (3): 957; Dodson, ed., *Campaigns of Wheeler*, 249; Du Bose, *Wheeler and the Army of Tennessee*, 383.

26. OR, I, 38 (3): 957-58; 45 (1): 868-69; Dyer, *"Fightin' Joe" Wheeler*, 190; Whetstone, *Fifty-third Alabama (Mounted)*, 56.

27. OR, I, 38 (3): 958; Dodson, ed., *Campaigns of Wheeler*, 250-51; Dyer, *"Fightin' Joe" Wheeler*, 190-91.

28. OR, I, 38 (3): 801, 958-59; 45 (1): 1240; (2): 775-77; George K. Miller, "Eighth Confederate Cavalry—1861-1865," 46-50, ADA&H; Whetstone, *Fifty-third Alabama (Mounted)*, 60; Felix H. Robertson, "On Wheeler's Last Raid in Middle Tennessee," *CV* 30 (1922): 334-35; J. C. Williamson, ed., "The Civil War Diary of John Coffee Williamson," *THQ* 15 (1956): 66.

29. OR, I, 38 (3): 959-60; Dodson, ed., *Campaigns of Wheeler*, 252-53; Williamson, ed., "Diary of John Coffee Williamson," 66.

30. De Leon, *Wheeler, the Man, the Statesman, the Soldier*, 32-34; OR, I, 38 (3): 960; Fisher, *They Rode with Forrest and Wheeler*, 99-100; Guild, *Fourth Tennessee Cavalry*, 97-98; Timothy Daiss, *In the Saddle: Exploits of the 5th Georgia Cavalry during the Civil War* (Atglen, PA, 1999), 60, 63.

31. OR, I, 38 (3): 961; Dyer, *"Fightin' Joe" Wheeler*, 194-95; J. C. Witherspoon, "Confederate Cavalry Leaders," *CV* 27 (1919): 416-17; James J. Hawthorne, History of Company D, 3rd Alabama Cavalry, 4, ADA&H; George K. Miller, "Eighth Confederate Cavalry—1861-1865," 46, ADA&H; Warner, *Generals in Gray*, 380n-81n.

32. OR, I, 38 (3): 960-61; Connelly, *Autumn of Glory*, 435, 458; McDonough and Jones, *War So Terrible*, 287-88.

33. OR, I, 39 (2): 859.

34. Dyer, *"Fightin' Joe" Wheeler*, 196.

35. OR, I, 38 (5): 1010, 1029; 39 (2): 834, 837-38, 861.

36. Evans, *Sherman's Horsemen*, 404-37; Connelly, *Autumn of Glory*, 435-36; Armin E. Mruck, "The Role of Railroads in the Atlanta Campaign," *CWH* 7 (1961): 259; Jerry Keenan, "Final Cavalry Operations [of the Atlanta Campaign]," *CWTI* 3 (July 1964): 50; OR, I, 38 (5): 1024.

37. Joseph J. Hunter, "A Sketch of the History of [the] Noxubee Troopers, 1st Mississippi Cavalry, Company 'F,'" 18-19, MDA&H; Castel, *Decision in the West*, 510-22; McDonough and Jones, *War So Terrible*, 300-06; McMurry, *Atlanta, 1864*, 172-76; Errol MacGregor Clauss, "The Battle of Jonesborough," *CWTI* 7 (Nov. 1968): 12-23.

38. Joseph J. Hunter, "A Sketch of the History of [the] Noxubee Troopers, 1st Mississippi Cavalry, Company 'F,'" 19-20, MDA&H; Clauss, "Battle of Jonesborough," 19-20; OR, I, 38 (1): 82; (5): 777.

39. Castel, *Decision in the West*, 543-47.

40. OR, I, 38 (3): 960; 39 (2): 827, 849, 861, 866; Dyer, *"Fightin' Joe" Wheeler*, 200-01; *Synopsis of the Career of Wheeler*, 29.

41. Hood, *Advance and Retreat*, 229-48; Dyer, *Gallant Hood*, 279-80; Connelly, *Autumn of Glory*, 470-72, 477-79.

42. OR, I, 39 (2): 880; (3): 785; Hood, *Advance and Retreat*, 479-85; Connelly, *Autumn of Glory*, 479-85; Williams, *P. G. T. Beauregard*, 241-42.

43. Connelly, *Autumn of Glory*, 480-85; OR, I, 39 (3): 843, 891; 44: 931-33; 45 (1): 646-47; 52 (2): 768.

44. Sherman, *Memoirs*, 2: 150-52.

45. Ibid., 152-56.

46. OR, I, 39 (3): 853, 892, 901, 909; 44: 867-68; Poole, *Cracker Cavaliers*, 161.

## CHAPTER FOURTEEN: FINAL BLOWS

1. OR, I, 52 (2): 770, 773-74; Thomas Robson Hay, *Hood's Tennessee Campaign* (New York, 1929), 57; Wiley Sword, *Embrace an Angry Wind: The Confederacy's Last Hurrah—Spring Hill, Franklin, and Nashville* (New York, 1992), 67.

2. OR, I, 31 (3): 694, 798-99; Robert V. Richardson to Nathan B. Forrest, Nov. 16, 1863, Orders and Circulars of Confederate General Nathan Bedford Forrest's Cavalry, RG-109, E-90, NA; Wyeth, *Life of Forrest*, 273-78; Wills, *Battle from the Start*, 148-56, 169-71; Jordan and Pryor, *Campaigns of Forrest*, 361-80.

3. Sherman, *Memoirs*, 2: 390-95; OR, I, 31 (2): 577-80; (3): 459; 32 (1): 173-77, 251-60; Richard M. McMurry, "Sherman's Meridian Expedition," *CWTI* 14 (May 1975): 24-32; Wills, *Battle from the Start*, 158-68.

4. Wills, *Battle from the Start*, 174-96; Wyeth, *Life of Forrest*, 326-90; Jordan and Pryor, *Campaigns of Forrest*, 381-453. For a fifty-year-old study that retains credibility, see Albert Castel, "The Fort Pillow Massacre: A Fresh Examination of the Evidence," *CWH* 4 (1958): 37-50.

5. Wills, *Battle from the Start*, 197-215; Wyeth, *Life of Forrest*, 391-429; Jordan and Pryor, *Campaigns of Forrest*, 468-83. The most thorough study of Forrest's brilliant victory is Edwin C. Bearss, *Forrest at Brice's Cross Roads and in North Mississippi in 1864* (Dayton, OH, 1979).

6. Wills, *Battle from the Start*, 219-32; Wyeth, *Life of Forrest*, 430-59. For a concise study of this rare defeat, see Byron Stinson, "Battle of Tupelo," *CWTI* 11 ( July 1972): 4-9, 46-48.

7. Wills, *Battle from the Start*, 332-46; E. B. Long, *The Civil War Day by Day: An Almanac, 1861-1865* (Garden City, NY, 1971), 558.

8. OR, I, 39 (2): 21; Wyeth, *Life of Forrest*, 487-511; Jordan and Pryor, *Campaigns of Forrest*, 561-81.

9. OR, I, 39 (1): 859-75; ORN, I, 26: 609-33, 680-87; Wills, *Battle from the Start*, 261-72; Longacre, *Mounted Raids of the Civil War*, 283-303.

10. OR, I, 39 (3): 845-46, 853, 879, 891, 913, 915; 45 (1): 52; (2): 770, 773-74, 777.

11. William M. Worthington to his sister, Nov. 8, 1864, Worthington MSS, MDA&H.

12. Wyeth, *Life of Forrest*, 534-35; OR, I, 45 (1): 1211, 1215-16, 1219-20, 1226; 52 (2): 791.

13. OR, I, 45 (1): 1227-28; General Orders #166, Headquarters Forrest's Cavalry, Nov. 20, 1864, Orders and Circulars of Confederate General Nathan Bedford Forrest's Cavalry, RG-109, E-90, NA; Morton, *Artillery of Forrest's Cavalry*, 268-69.

14. Sidney S. Champion to his wife, Oct. 4, 8, 12, 24, 31, Nov. 8, 15, 1864, Champion MSS, EU; William Barry to his sister, Oct. 21, 1864, Barry MSS, MDA&H.

15. James Lee McDonough, *Schofield: Union General in the Civil War and Reconstruction* (Tallahassee, FL, 1972), 100-103; Edward G. Longacre, *Grant's Cavalryman: The Life and Wars of General James H. Wilson* (Mechanicsburg, PA, 1996), 166-67; Jerry Keenan, *Wilson's Cavalry Corps: Union Campaigns in the Western Theatre, October 1864 through Spring 1865* ( Jefferson, NC, 1998), 33-40.

16. OR, I, 45 (1): 341; McDonough, *Schofield*, 103-05.

17. Dyer, *Gallant Hood*, 285.

18. OR, I, 45 (1): 557-58, 575-76, 752; Wyeth, *Life of Forrest*, 535-39; John P. Young, *The Seventh Tennessee Cavalry (Confederate): A History* (Nashville, TN, 1890), 117-19; Thomas A. Wigginton, "Cavalry Operations in the Nashville Campaign," *CWTI* 3 (Dec. 1964): 40; Keenan, *Wilson's Cavalry Corps*, 40-43; Deupree, "Noxubee Squadron," 109-10; Griscom, *Fighting With Ross' Texas Cavalry Brigade*, 189-90; Henry, *"First with the Most" Forrest*, 385-86; Sword, *Embrace an Angry Wind*, 92-93.

19. OR, I, 45 (1): 752.

20. James Harrison Wilson, *Under the Old Flag: Recollections of Military Operations in the War for the Union, the Spanish War, the Boxer Rebellion, etc.* (2 vols. New York, 1912), 2: 40-41; Longacre, *Grant's Cavalryman*, 168-69; Keenan, *Wilson's Cavalry Corps*, 49; OR, I, 45 (1): 753.

21. OR, I, 45 (1): 341-42, 550, 558-59; Wilson, *Under the Old Flag*, 2: 41-42; Longacre, *Grant's Cavalryman*, 169-71; McDonough, *Schofield*, 106-08.

22. OR, I, 45 (1): 652, 657, 753; Hood, *Advance and Retreat*, 282.

23. OR, I, 45 (1): 342-43, 652, 657, 753; Hood, *Advance and Retreat*, 283-90; McDonough, *Schofield*, 109-14. One of the best sources on the controversies surrounding Spring Hill is Stanley F. Horn, "The Spring Hill Legend—a Reappraisal," *CWTI* 8 (Apr. 1969): 20-32. See also Hay, *Hood's Tennessee Campaign*, 86-118, and Sword, *Embrace an Angry Wind*, 110-23.

24. The most detailed source on this pivotal but underappreciated battle is James Lee McDonough and Thomas L. Connelly, *Five Tragic Hours: The Battle of Franklin* (Knoxville, TN, 1983).

25. OR, I, 45 (1), 550, 559-60; Wyeth, *Life of Forrest*, 544; Wilson, *Under the Old Flag*, 2: 47-49; Keenan, *Wilson's Cavalry Corps*, 63-69; Longacre, *Grant's Cavalryman*, 174-75; William M. Worthington to "Dear Sam," Dec. 11, 1864, Worthington MSS, MDA&H.

26. OR, I, 45 (1): 550, 560; Wilson, *Under the Old Flag*, 2: 49-50; Wigginton, "Cavalry Operations in the Nashville Campaign," 42; Donald M. Lynne, "Wilson's Cavalry at Nashville," *CWH* 1 (1955): 147.

27. Hood, *Advance and Retreat*, 292-93, 298-300.

28. Keenan, *Wilson's Cavalry Corps*, 76-84; Longacre, *Grant's Cavalryman*, 177-81.

29. OR, I, 45 (1): 754; Wigginton, "Cavalry Operations in the Nashville Campaign," 42; Hay, *Hood's Tennessee Campaign*, 168-69; Wyeth, *Life of Forrest*, 547; Hood, *Advance and Retreat*, 300.

30. OR, I, 45 (1): 745, 754-55, 771; (2): 651-52, 682; Wyeth, *Life of Forrest*, 547-48; Mathes, *General Forrest*, 331; William M. Worthington to "Dear Sam," Dec. 11, 1864, Worthington MSS, MDA&H; Judith Ann Benner, *Sul Ross, Soldier, Statesman, Educator* (College Station, TX, 1983), 110-11.

31. OR, I, 45 (1): 746-47, 755; (2): 666; Wills, *Battle from the Start*, 287-88; Jordan and Pryor, *Campaigns of Forrest*, 632-34.

32. OR, I, 45 (1): 755-56; (2): 666, 670, 693; Wyeth, *Life of Forrest*, 561-62.

33. Horn, *Army of Tennessee*, 410-11; Longacre, *Grant's Cavalryman*, 182-83, 188-89.

34. OR, I, 45 (1): 551, 562-64, 765; Stanley F. Horn's *The Decisive Battle of Nashville* (Baton Rouge, LA, 1956) remains the leading source on this critical two-day struggle.

35. John Johnston, "Cavalry of Hood's Left at Nashville," *CV* 3 (1905): 28.

36. Ibid., 28-29; OR, I, 45 (1): 551-52, 562-64, 765; Wilson, *Under the Old Flag*, 2: 109-14; Keenan, *Wilson's Cavalry Corps*, 98-106; Wigginton, "Cavalry Operations in the Nashville Campaign," 43.

37. Hood, *Advance and Retreat*, 302-03; Horn, *Army of Tennessee*, 415-17; Connelly, *Autumn of Glory*, 509-11.

38. OR, I, 45 (1): 765-66; (2): 697; Horn, *Army of Tennessee*, 417-19; Wigginton, "Cavalry Operations in the Nashville Campaign," 43; Wilson, *Under the Old Flag*, 2: 115-16.

39. OR, I, 45 (1): 564; Wilson, *Under the Old Flag*, 2: 121-24; Lynne, "Wilson's Cavalry at Nashville," 154.

40. Wilson, *Under the Old Flag*, 2: 125-39.

41. OR, I, 45 (1): 564-67, 655; Horn, *Army of Tennessee*, 419-20.

42. Wyeth, *Life of Forrest*, 558-59. In his memoirs, Wilson refutes Rucker's contention: *Under the Old Flag*, 2: 119.

43. OR, I, 45 (1): 757; (2): 693, 716; Wyeth, *Life of Forrest*, 568; Wills, *Battle from the Start*, 291.

44. OR, I, 45 (1): 727-28, 757-58; Wyeth, *Life of Forrest*, 571-72; Morton, *Artillery of Forrest's Cavalry*, 295-97; Deupree, "Noxubee Squadron," 118-20.

45. OR, I, 45 (2): 756, 781, 785, 805; Hood, *Advance and Retreat*, 307; Wills, *Battle from the Start*, 293. Despite Hood's escape, one historian calls Wilson's effort "the finest pursuit of the war": Lynne, "Wilson's Cavalry at Nashville," 156.

46. Longacre, *Mounted Raids of the Civil War*, 304-26. The most complete study of Wilson's Selma Expedition is James Pickett Jones, *Yankee Blitzkrieg: Wilson's Raid through Alabama and Georgia* (Athens, GA, 1976).

47. Wyeth, *Life of Forrest*, 610-16, 678-82; Wills, *Battle from the Start*, 312-17.

48. OR, I, 44: 7-14; Longacre, *Worthy Opponents*, 292-94.

49. Joseph T. Glatthaar, *The March to the Sea and Beyond: Sherman's Troops in the Savannah and Carolinas Campaigns* (New York, 1985), 120-21.

50. OR, I, 44: 406-12, 922, 1007-08; 47 (2): 1000, 1047. For changes in the table of organization at the outset of 1865, see ibid., 1071-72.

51. Ibid., 363-65, 408-10, 634-35, 900-01, 903-04, 910-12; Dodson, ed., *Campaigns of Wheeler*, 289-93; Du Bose, *Wheeler and the Army of Tennessee*, 416-17; Dyer, *"Fightin' Joe" Wheeler*, 208; William A. Fleming memoirs, 30, USAH&EC; Nugent, *My Dear Nellie*, 224; Fisher, *They Rode with Forrest and Wheeler*, 124.

52. George K. Miller, "Eighth Confederate Cavalry—1861-1865," 51, ADA&H.

53. OR, I, 44: 946, 979, 998, 1002-03; 47 (2): 986-87, 1004, 1028, 1047, 1135, 1203-04; IV, 3: 967-68; Lavender R. Ray to his father, Dec. 5, 1864, Ray MSS, EU; Dyer, *"Fightin' Joe" Wheeler*, 210-11; Lee Kennett, *Marching through Georgia: The Story of Soldiers and Civilians during Sherman's Campaign* (New York, 1995), 278; Poole, *Cracker Cavaliers*, 172; Glatthaar, *March to the Sea and Beyond*, 120, 152; John G. Barrett, *Sherman's March through the Carolinas* (Chapel Hill, NC, 1956).

54. Edward G. Longacre, *Gentleman and Soldier: A Biography of Wade Hampton III* (Nashville, TN, 2003), vii, 220-24; OR, I, 44: 898; 47 (2): 1018, 1054, 1112, 1165, 1207; Barrett, *Sherman's March through the Carolinas*, 65-66.

55. OR, I, 47 (2): 1069-72, 1112, 1207, 1271; Dyer, *"Fightin' Joe" Wheeler*, 219.

56. Cotton, *"Yours Till Death"*, 125; Lavender R. Ray to his brother, Jan. 20, 1865, Ray MSS, EU.

57. OR, I, 47 (2): 1178, 1184, 1186, 1197-99, 1202, 1207, 1211, 1219; Dyer, *"Fightin' Joe" Wheeler*, 220; Dodson, ed., *Campaigns of Wheeler*, 327-28; Dyer, *Reminiscences of Four Years*, 280-81; W. C. Dodson, "Burning of Broad River Bridge . . .," *CV* 17 (1909): 463-65; G. W. F. Harper, "Sherman at Columbia," *CV* 18 (1910): 32; George K. Miller, "Eighth Confederate Cavalry—1861-1865," 55, ADA&H; Zachariah T. DeLoach memoirs, 5, GSA; John H. Ash diary, Feb. 16, 1865, EU; Henry L. Stone diary, Feb. 16, 1865, MOC; Barrett, *Sherman's March through the Carolinas*, 59-60; Longacre, *Gentleman and Soldier*, 227.

58. Longacre, *Worthy Opponents*, 300; Glatthaar, *March to the Sea and Beyond*, 141.

59. Longacre, *Worthy Opponents*, 295; OR, I, 47 (2): 1163.

60. OR, I, 47 (1): 861, 1124-25, 1130; Dodson, ed., *Campaigns of Wheeler*, 343-45; Du Bose, *Wheeler and the Army of Tennessee*, 443-45; Dyer, *"Fightin' Joe" Wheeler*, 223-24; Edward L. Wells, *Hampton and His Cavalry in '64* (Richmond, VA, 1899), 406-07; Burke Davis, *Sherman's March* (New York, 1980), 206-07; Barrett, *Sherman's March through the Carolinas*, 107-08, 113; Sharyn Kane and Richard Keeton, *Fiery Dawn: The Civil War Battle at Monroe's Crossroads, North Carolina* (Tallahassee, FL, 1999), 64, 66; Samuel J. Martin, *Southern Hero: Matthew Calbraith Butler, Confederate General, Hampton Red Shirt, and U.S. Senator* (Mechanicsburg, PA, 2001), 151-53; William F. Mims, "War History of the Prattville Dragoons," 16, ADA&H.

61. Martin, *Southern Hero*, 151; George K. Miller, "Eighth Confederate Cavalry—1861-1865," 57, ADA&H.

62. George K. Miller, "Eighth Confederate Cavalry—1861-1865," 57, ADA&H; Wells, *Hampton and His Cavalry*, 412-13; J. C. Witcher, "Shannon's Scouts—Kilpatrick," *CV* 14 (1906): 511-12.

63. Lavender R. Ray to his brother, Jan. 20, 1865, Ray MSS, EU; OR, I, 47 (2): 1248, 1259, 1304; R. G. H. Kean, *Inside the Confederate Government: The Diary of Robert Garlick Hill Kean, Head of the Bureau of War*, ed. by Edward Younger (New York, 1957), 181; Chesnut, *Mary Chesnut's Civil War*, 698; Symonds, *Joseph E. Johnston*, 342-43.

64. Johnston, *Narrative of Military Operations*, 371-72; Symonds, *Joseph E. Johnston*, 344, 346; OR, I, 47 (2): 1062, 1247-48, 1256-57, 1328, 1399, 1402.

65. OR, I, 47 (1): 1130; (2): 409, 1248, 1409, 1415; Dodson, ed., *Campaigns of Wheeler*, 347; Barrett, *Sherman's March through the Carolinas*, 149-58. The paper strength of Johnston's army was given as 33,450, a generously inflated number: OR, I, 47 (2): 1084.

66. OR, I, 47 (1): 1130-31; (2): 428-33, 1430-31, 1433, 1437-39, 1441-42; Dodson, ed., *Campaigns of Wheeler*, 350; Wade Hampton, "The Battle of Bentonville," *B&L* 4: 702-04; Jay Luvaas, "Bentonville—Last Chance to Stop Sherman," *CWTI* 2 (Oct. 1963): 8-9, 38-39.

67. OR, I, 47 (1): 1131; (2): 1443; Hampton, "Battle of Bentonville," 704.

68. OR, I, 47 (1): 1131; Dodson, ed., *Campaigns of Wheeler*, 351-52; Du Bose, *Wheeler and the Army of Tennessee*, 452; Hampton, "Battle of Bentonville," 704-05; George K. Miller, "Eighth Confederate Cavalry—1861-1865," 58, ADA&H.

69. OR, I, 47 (1): 1131; (2): 1451-52.

70. Ibid., (2): 1298; (3): 682, 684; Sherman, *Memoirs*, 2: 304; McDonough, *Schofield*, 151-57.

71. OR, I, 47 (1): 27, 862, 1132; (3): 771-73, 783-84, 794-95, 798-99, 802-03, 805, 808; Dodson, ed., *Campaigns of Wheeler*, 355-57; Barrett, *Sherman's March through the Carolinas*, 256-57; Davis, *Sherman's March*, 269-72.

72. Joseph Wheeler to Joseph E. Johnston, Apr. 18, 1865, Wheeler MSS, GLC; OR, I, 47 (3): 813-14, 829-30, 841, 846-47, 851; Dyer, *"Fightin' Joe" Wheeler*, 227-32; Dodson, ed., *Campaigns of Wheeler*, 359-61; Du Bose, *Wheeler and the Army of Tennessee*, 470.

73. Hewett, et al., eds., *Supplement to the Official Records*, I, 3: 830.

# BIBLIOGRAPHY

## Unpublished Materials

*General Officers of Cavalry*

Allen, William W. Papers. Alabama Department of Archives and History, Montgomery.

Butler, M. Calbraith. Correspondence. South Caroliniana Library, University of South Carolina, Columbia.

_____. Correspondence. William R. Perkins Library, Duke University, Durham, NC.

Chalmers, James R. Papers. Tennessee State Library and Archives, Nashville.

Duke, Basil W. Papers. Filson Historical Society, Louisville, KY.

_____. Papers. Southern Historical Collection, University of North Carolina, Chapel Hill.

Ferguson, Samuel Wragg. Diary. Mississippi Department of Archives and History, Jackson.

_____. Memoirs. Southern Historical Collection, University of North Carolina, Chapel Hill.

_____. Papers. William R. Perkins Library, Duke University, Durham, NC.

Forrest, Nathan Bedford. Letter of February 25, 1862. Simon Gratz Collection, Historical Society of Pennsylvania, Philadelphia.

_____. Papers. Louisiana State Museum, New Orleans.

_____. Papers. Tennessee State Library and Archives, Nashville.

_____. Papers. William R. Perkins Library, Duke University, Durham, NC.

Hampton, Wade. Correspondence. Gilder Lehrman Collection, New York.

_____. Correspondence. Library of Congress, Washington, DC.

_____. Correspondence. South Caroliniana Library, University of South Carolina, Columbia.

_____. Correspondence. William R. Perkins Library, Duke University, Durham, NC.

Jackson, William H. Letter of February 13, 1865. Gilder Lehrman Collection, New York.

_____. Papers. Tennessee State Library and Archives, Nashville.

Martin, William T. Letter of August 28, 1863. University of Texas Library, Austin.

Morgan, John Hunt. Papers. Filson Historical Society, Louisville, KY.

_____. Papers. Gilder Lehrman Collection, New York.

_____. Papers. Kentucky Historical Society, Frankfort.

_____. Papers. King Library, University of Kentucky, Lexington.

_____. Papers. Southern Historical Collection, University of North Carolina, Chapel Hill.

_____. Papers. Tennessee State Library and Archives, Nashville.

Morgan, John Tyler. Correspondence. U.S. Army Heritage and Education Center, Carlisle Barracks, PA.

Pegram, John. Correspondence. Henry E. Huntington Library, San Marino, CA.

_____. Letter of April 1, 1863. Filson Historical Society, Louisville, KY.

Roddey, Philip D. Correspondence. Gilder Lehrman Collection, New York.

Ross, Lawrence S. Papers. Texas Collection. Baylor University Library, Waco, TX.

Wharton, John A. Papers. Gilder Lehrman Collection, New York.

_____. Correspondence. Rosenberg Library, Galveston, TX.

Wheeler, Joseph. Address of December 31, 1864. Tennessee State Library and Archives, Nashville.

_____. Correspondence. Simon Gratz Collection, Historical Society of Pennsylvania, Philadelphia.

_____. Papers. Alabama Department of Archives and History, Montgomery.

_____. Papers. Dearborn Collection, Houghton Library, Harvard University, Cambridge, MA.

_____. Papers. Eleanor S. Brockenbrough Library, Museum of the Confederacy, Richmond, VA.

_____. Papers. Gilder Lehrman Collection, New York.

_____. Papers. Record Group 109, Entry 136. National Archives, Washington, DC.

_____. Papers. Tennessee State Library and Archives, Nashville.

_____. Papers. William R. Perkins Library, Duke University, Durham, NC.

Young, Pierce M. B. Correspondence. Georgia Department of Archives and History, Atlanta.


*Officers and Men, Cavalry, and Horse Artillery*

Adams, Louis L. (1st Tennessee). Diaries. Tennessee State Library and Archives, Nashville.

Aden, James S. P. (7th Tennessee). Diary and Memoirs. Tennessee State Library and Archives, Nashville.

Alcorn, William A. (1st Mississippi). Papers. Mississippi Department of Archives and History, Jackson.

Allen, William G. (5th Tennessee). Memoirs. Tennessee State Library and Archives, Nashville.

Ansley, L. H. (10th Georgia). Memoirs. Georgia State Archives, Morrow.

Ash, John H. (5th Georgia). Correspondence and Diaries. Robert W. Woodruff Library, Emory University, Atlanta.

Avery, Isaac W. (4th Georgia). Correspondence. U.S. Army Heritage and Education Center, Carlisle Barracks, PA.

Avery, Richard (2nd Georgia). Correspondence. Georgia State Archives, Morrow.

Barnett, Joel C. (Cobb's Legion). Correspondence. Georgia Department of Archives and History, Atlanta.

Barry, John A. (Phillips Legion). Correspondence. Southern Historical Collection, University of North Carolina, Chapel Hill.

Barry, William (2nd Mississippi). Correspondence. Mississippi Department of Archives and History, Jackson.

Bate, Henry C. (2nd Tennessee and 1st Confederate). Correspondence. Society Collection, Historical Society of Pennsylvania, Philadelphia.

_____. Diary. Tennessee State Library and Archives, Nashville.

Baxter, Nathaniel (Huggins's [Tenn.] Battery). Letter of January 7, 1865. Robert Foster Maddox Papers, Robert W. Woodruff Library, Emory University, Atlanta.

Beasley, Henry O. (1st Mississippi). Correspondence. Mississippi Department of Archives and History, Jackson.

Beasley, Jeremiah R. (1st Mississippi). Letter of December 31, 1862. Mississippi Department of Archives and History, Jackson.

Beasley, William E. (1st Mississippi). Correspondence. Mississippi Department of Archives and History, Jackson.

Black, James C. C. (9th Kentucky). Diary. Southern Historical Collection, University of North Carolina, Chapel Hill.

Blackman, Luther M. (1st and 4th Tennessee). Papers. Tennessee State Library and Archives, Nashville.

Bliss, Robert L. (3rd Tennessee). Correspondence. Alabama Department of Archives and History, Montgomery.

Breckinridge, William C. P. (9th Kentucky). Papers. Library of Congress, Washington, DC.

Brodnax, Samuel H. (2nd Georgia). Memoirs. Filson Historical Society, Louisville, KY.

Brown, John P. W. (9th Tennessee). Memoirs. Tennessee State Library and Archives, Nashville.

Brown, Milton (21st Tennessee). Correspondence. Tennessee State Library and Archives, Nashville.

Bujan, Henry (12th Mississippi Battalion). Letter of November 9, 1864. U.S. Army Heritage and Education Center, Carlisle Barracks, PA.

Bullitt, Thomas W. (2nd Kentucky). Diary and Memoirs. Southern Historical Collection, University of North Carolina, Chapel Hill.

Bunting, Robert. F. (8th Texas). Memoirs. Rosenberg Library, Galveston, TX.

_____. Papers. University of Texas Library, Austin.

Burford, Elisha S. (1st Alabama). Correspondence. Joseph Wheeler Papers, National Archives, Washington, DC.

Burrus, John C. (9th Texas). Correspondence. Mississippi Department of Archives and History, Jackson.

Camp, Thomas L. (Phillips Legion). Correspondence. Robert W. Woodruff Library, Emory University, Atlanta.

Cannon, Newton (11th Tennessee). Memoirs. Tennessee State Library and Archives, Nashville.

Cardwell, Thomas A. (1st Arkansas Battalion). Correspondence. University of Arkansas Libraries, Fayetteville.

Carson, George L. (16th Georgia Battalion). Memoirs. Georgia State Archives, Morrow.

Carter, James D. (3rd Georgia). Memoirs. Georgia State Archives, Morrow.

Carter, Joseph (19th or 20th Tennessee). Memoirs. Tennessee State Library and Archives, Nashville.

Carter, Thomas M. (Nelson's [Ga.] Cavalry Company). Correspondence. Robert W. Woodruff Library, Emory University, Atlanta.

Cay, Raymond (5th Georgia). Memoirs. Robert W. Woodruff Library, Emory University, Atlanta.

Champion, Sidney S. (28th Mississippi). Correspondence. Robert W. Woodruff Library, Emory University, Atlanta.

_____. Correspondence. William R. Perkins Library, Duke University, Durham, NC.

Chester, Orlando D. (5th Georgia). Correspondence. Kennesaw Mountain National Battlefield Park, Kennesaw, GA.

Chisholm, William R. (19th Tennessee). Diaries and Memoirs. Tennessee State Library and Archives, Nashville.

Claiborne, Thomas (1st Confederate). Correspondence and Memoirs. Southern Historical Collection, University of North Carolina, Chapel Hill.

Clark, Achilles V. (20th Tennessee). Correspondence. Tennessee State Library and Archives, Nashville.

Clark, Charles (9th Tennessee). Correspondence. Tennessee State Library and Archives, Nashville.

Clinch, D. L. (3rd Georgia). Undated Letter. Georgia State Archives, Morrow.

Coleman, D. E. (11th Alabama). Diaries. Southern Historical Collection, University of North Carolina, Chapel Hill.

Collier, Joseph T. (10th Georgia). Memoirs. Georgia State Archives, Morrow.

Cook, Gustave (8th Texas). Correspondence. Gilder Lehrman Collection, New York.

Corbit, W. B. (4th Tennessee). Diary and Memoirs. Robert W. Woodruff Library, Emory University, Atlanta.

Core, J. D. (1st Tennessee Battalion). Correspondence. Tennessee State Library and Archives, Nashville.

Corry, Robert E. (11th Alabama). Correspondence. Auburn University Archives, Auburn, AL.

Crews, J. M. (3rd Tennessee). Undated Letter. William R. Perkins Library, Duke University, Durham, NC.

Crowell, John H. (2nd Georgia). Memoirs. Georgia State Archives, Morrow.

Cummings, John N. (5th South Carolina). Correspondence. William R. Perkins Library, Duke University, Durham, NC.

Daughetee, Isaac S. (1st Kentucky). Letter of January 7, 1865. U.S. Army Heritage and Education Center, Carlisle Barracks, PA.

Davis, Robert W. (8th Kentucky). Correspondence. Filson Historical Society, Louisville, KY.

Davis, Thomas W. (5th Tennessee). Diaries. Tennessee State Library and Archives, Nashville.

Davis, William N. (8th Kentucky). Correspondence. Filson Historical Society, Louisville, KY.

Davis, Zimmerman (5th South Carolina). Correspondence. South Carolina Department of Archives and History, Columbia.

DeLoach, Zachariah T. (5th Georgia). Memoirs. Georgia State Archives, Morrow.

Dobbins, Archibald S. (1st Arkansas). Correspondence. Arkansas University Libraries, Fayetteville.

_____. Correspondence. Rosenberg Library, Galveston, TX.

Dobbins, John S. (Phillips Legion). Correspondence. Robert W. Woodruff Library, Emory University, Atlanta.

Dorsey, B. W. (5th Georgia). "A War Story, or My Experience in a Yankee Prison." Georgia State Archives, Morrow.

Dowda, Julius L. (3rd Georgia). Memoirs. Georgia State Archives, Morrow.

Dyer, John W. (1st Kentucky). "Reminiscences of the First Kentucky Cavalry, Confederate States Army." Filson Historical Society, Louisville, KY.

Dyer, W. R. (Forrest's Escort). Diaries. Tennessee State Library and Archives, Nashville.

Edenfield, H. G. (5th Georgia). Correspondence. Georgia State Archives, Morrow.

Edmondson, Robert (9th Tennessee). Correspondence. Robert W. Woodruff Library, Emory University, Atlanta.

Edmondson, William (21st Tennessee). Correspondence. Robert W. Woodruff Library, Emory University, Atlanta.

Elder, William D. (7th Tennessee). Correspondence. Mississippi Department of Archives and History, Jackson.

Elliott, George R. (2nd Tennessee). Diaries. Tennessee State Library and Archives, Nashville.

Ellis, Orrin L. (Jeff Davis Legion). Diary. U.S. Army Heritage and Education Center, Carlisle Barracks, PA.

Falconnet, Eugene F. (7th and 9th Alabama). Memoirs. Tennessee State Library and Archives, Nashville.

Farrar, Lee H. (9th Tennessee). Correspondence. Tennessee State Library and Archives, Nashville.

Farrar, Leonidas H. (3rd Tennessee). Correspondence. Tennessee State Library and Archives, Nashville.

Fite, John C. (9th Texas). Correspondence. Eleanor S. Brockenbrough Library, Museum of the Confederacy, Richmond, VA.

Flanigan, Harris M. (2nd Arkansas Mounted Rifles). Correspondence. Arkansas Historical Commission, Little Rock.

Fleming, William A. (5th Georgia and 20th Georgia Battalion). Memoirs. U.S. Army Heritage and Education Center, Carlisle Barracks, PA.

Foster, John S. (Jeff Davis Legion). Correspondence. Hill Library, Louisiana State University, Baton Rouge.

Foster, Samuel T. (24th Texas). Memoirs. U.S. Army Heritage and Education Center, Carlisle Barracks, PA.

Free, Elbert (1st Arkansas). Memoirs. University of Arkansas Libraries, Fayetteville.

Fuller, Thomas (2nd Tennessee). Diaries. Tennessee State Library and Archives, Nashville.

Fussell, Joseph H. (6th Tennessee). Papers. Tennessee State Library and Archives, Nashville.

Gaines, R. R. (3rd Alabama). History of the 3rd Alabama Cavalry. Alabama Department of Archives and History, Montgomery.

Gibbs, Thomas P. (1st Georgia). Memoirs. Georgia State Archives, Morrow.

Gilchrist, Archibald E. (4th South Carolina). Papers. South Caroliniana Library, University of South Carolina, Columbia.

Giltner, Henry L. (4th Kentucky). Correspondence. Southern Historical Collection, University of North Carolina, Chapel Hill.

Goodwin, F. M. (28th Mississippi). Letter of August 9, 1864. U.S. Army Heritage and Education Center, Carlisle Barracks, PA.

Gordon, William W. (Jeff Davis Legion). Memoirs. Southern Historical Collection, University of North Carolina, Chapel Hill.

Graves, L. H. (6th Texas). Diaries. University of Arkansas Libraries, Fayetteville.

Gray, Thomas J. (10th Confederate). Undated Letter. Tennessee State Library and Archives, Nashville.

Guerrant, Edward O. (4th Kentucky). Diaries. Johnson County Public Library, Paintsville, KY.

_____. Papers. Southern Historical Collection, University of North Carolina, Chapel Hill.

Guild, George B. (4th Tennessee). Papers. Tennessee State Library and Archives, Nashville.

Gunn, Lyman C. (9th Tennessee). Memoirs. Boyd Family Papers, Mississippi Department of Archives and History, Jackson.

Gurley, Frank B. (4th Alabama). Memoirs. Alabama Department of Archives and History, Montgomery.

_____. Papers. U.S. Army Heritage and Education Center, Carlisle Barracks, PA.

Hagan, James (3rd Alabama). History of the 3rd Alabama Cavalry. Alabama Department of Archives and History, Montgomery.

Halsey, Edwin L. (Washington [S. C.] Artillery). Correspondence. Southern Historical Collection, University of North Carolina, Chapel Hill.

Hansell, Charles P. (10th Georgia). Correspondence. Georgia State Archives, Morrow.

Hargis, O. P. (1st Georgia). Memoirs. Georgia State Archives, Morrow.

_____. Memoirs. Southern Historical Collection, University of North Carolina, Chapel Hill.

Hart, James F., et al. (Washington [S. C.] Artillery). "History of Hart's Battery." South Caroliniana Library, University of South Carolina, Columbia.

Hart, John R. (6th Georgia). Correspondence. Georgia State Archives, Morrow.

Hawthorne, James J. (3rd Alabama). History of Company D, 3rd Alabama Cavalry. Alabama Department of Archives and History, Montgomery.

Hays, William (2nd Kentucky). Diaries. R. E. Lee Camp No. 1 Records, Virginia Historical Society, Richmond.

Heartsill, William W. (2nd Tennessee Mounted Rifles). Papers. University of Texas Library, Austin.

_____. Diaries. Fondren Library, Rice University, Houston, TX.

Henderson, Samuel (11th Tennessee). Diary. Tennessee State Library and Archives, Nashville.

Hester, J. B. (6th South Carolina). Correspondence. South Caroliniana Library, University of South Carolina, Columbia.

Hester, John S. (10th Georgia). Correspondence. Georgia State Archives, Morrow.

Hines, Thomas H. (9th Kentucky). Correspondence. King Library, University of Kentucky, Lexington.

Holcomb, G. B. (11th Georgia). Correspondence. Georgia State Archives, Morrow.

Holley, Turner W. (1st South Carolina). Correspondence. William R. Perkins Library, Duke University, Durham, NC.

Holloway, John W. (2nd Georgia). Correspondence. Virginia Historical Society, Richmond.

Holt, Alfred B. (1st Confederate). Letter of October 10, 1864. Georgia State Archives, Morrow.

Howard, Gustave A. (Huwald's [Tenn.] Battery). Correspondence. Southern Historical Collection, University of North Carolina, Chapel Hill.

Hughstone, Sanford V. (1st Mississippi). Correspondence. Mississippi Department of Archives and History, Jackson.

Hunter, Joseph J. (1st Mississippi). "A Sketch of the History of [the] Noxubee Troopers, 1st Mississippi Cavalry, Company 'F.'" Mississippi Department of Archives and History, Jackson.

Jeffords, Robert J. (5th South Carolina). Correspondence. William R. Perkins Library, Duke University, Durham, NC.

Jobe, Thomas J. (1st Arkansas). Diary. Arkansas Historical Commission, Little Rock.

Johnson, John D. (3rd Georgia). Correspondence. Georgia State Archives, Morrow.

Johnston, John (1st Arkansas Mounted Rifles). Correspondence. Arkansas Historical Commission, Little Rock.

Johnston, John (7th and 14th Tennessee). Memoirs. Tennessee State Library and Archives, Nashville.

Jones, Henry F. (Cobb's Legion). Correspondence. U.S. Army Heritage and Education Center, Carlisle Barracks, PA.

Jones, James R. (7th and 10th Georgia). Memoirs. Georgia State Archives, Morrow.

Jordan, Stephen A. (9th Tennessee). Diaries. Tennessee State Library and Archives, Nashville.

Keitt, Ellison S. (19th South Carolina Battalion). Correspondence. William R. Perkins Library, Duke University, Durham, NC.

Kelley, William D. (32nd Texas). Correspondence. Rosenberg Library, Galveston, TX.

Kerbow, Green M. (16th Georgia Battalion). Correspondence. Georgia State Archives, Morrow.

Klink, John J. (3rd Georgia). Papers. Filson Historical Society, Louisville, KY.

Launius, Thomas P. (3rd Georgia). Correspondence. Georgia State Archives, Morrow.

Law, Hugh L. (6th South Carolina). Correspondence. South Caroliniana Library, University of South Carolina, Columbia.

Law, Thomas C. (4th South Carolina). Correspondence. South Caroliniana Library, University of South Carolina, Columbia.

Lawton, W. J. (2nd Georgia). Letter of August 8, 1862. Georgia State Archives, Morrow.

Lee, John W. (16th Georgia Battalion). Memoirs. Georgia State Archives, Morrow.

Lester, John H. (7th and 9th Alabama). Memoirs. Alabama Department of Archives and History, Montgomery.

Logan, I. M. (11th Georgia). Letter of March 5, 1865. Georgia State Archives, Morrow.

Long, John B. (3rd Texas). Correspondence. University of Texas Library, Austin.

Long, Nimrod W. E. (51st Alabama). Correspondence. Robert W. Woodruff Library, Emory University, Atlanta.

Malone, W. H. (3rd Georgia). Memoirs. Georgia State Archives, Morrow.

Manigault, Lucius (4th South Carolina). Correspondence. Library of Congress, Washington, DC.

Martin, Benjamin (4th Georgia). Memoirs. Georgia State Archives, Morrow.

Mathis, W. H. (2nd Georgia). Memoirs. Georgia State Archives, Morrow.

Matlock, Philip N. (21st Tennessee). Memoirs. Tennessee State Library and Archives, Nashville.

Maxwell, David E. (1st Florida). Correspondence. Virginia Historical Society, Richmond.

McBride, B. C. (1st South Carolina). Correspondence. William R. Perkins Library, Duke University, Durham, NC.

McClellan, Robert A. (7th Alabama). Correspondence. William R. Perkins Library, Duke University, Durham, NC.

McCollom, Albert O. (1st Arkansas). Correspondence. University of Arkansas Libraries, Fayetteville.

McConathy, William J. (2nd Kentucky). Correspondence. Filson Historical Society, Louisville, KY.

McCreary, James B. (11th Kentucky). Correspondence. William R. Perkins Library, Duke University, Durham, NC.

McFaddin, William (42nd Mississippi). Correspondence. Gilder Lehrman Collection, New York.

McFaul, James W. (10th Kentucky). Memoirs. Georgia State Archives, Morrow.

McLaurin, Daniel T. (4th North Carolina). Correspondence. Southern Historical Collection, University of North Carolina, Chapel Hill.

Merritt, Thomas M. (2nd Georgia). Memoirs. Georgia State Archives, Morrow.

Miller, DeWolfe (2nd Tennessee). Memoirs. Tennessee State Library and Archives, Nashville.

Miller, George K. "Eighth Confederate Cavalry—1861-1865." Alabama Department of Archives and History, Montgomery.

Miller, John A. (9th Texas). Memoirs. H. B. Simpson Historical Complex, Hillsboro, TX.

Milton, William A. (8th Kentucky). "Some Recollections of the War between the States." Filson Historical Society, Louisville, KY.

Mims, William F. (3rd Alabama). "War History of the Prattville Dragoons." Alabama Department of Archives and History, Montgomery.

Minor, Henry (5th South Carolina). Memoirs. South Caroliniana Library, University of South Carolina, Columbia.

Minor, John (10th Tennessee). Diaries and Letter of June 28, 1864. Tennessee State Library and Archives, Nashville.

Montgomery, William A. (1st Mississippi). Memoirs. Mississippi Department of Archives and History, Jackson.

Moore, Martin V. (6th North Carolina). Papers. Southern Historical Collection, University of North Carolina, Chapel Hill.

Moore, William R. (1st Georgia). Memoirs. Georgia State Archives, Morrow.

Morgan, Irby (51st Alabama). Correspondence. William R. Perkins Library, Duke University, Durham, NC.

Morrow, R. O. (5th Alabama). Memoirs. Mississippi Department of Archives and History, Jackson.

Morton, John P. (18th Mississippi). Diary. Mississippi Department of Archives and History, Jackson.

Morton, John W. (Forrest's Horse Artillery). Papers. Tennessee State Library and Archives, Nashville.

Mulligan, J. H. (4th Kentucky). Diaries. King Library, University of Kentucky, Lexington.

Munday, James A. (10th Kentucky). Diary. Filson Historical Society, Louisville, KY.

Munnerlyn, James K. (Jeff Davis Legion). Correspondence. Southern Historical Collection, University of North Carolina, Chapel Hill.

Nelson, M. J. (5th Georgia). "The Fifth Georgia Calvary [sic] . . ." Georgia State Archives, Morrow.

Nicholson, Flavellus G. (1st Mississippi). Memoirs. Mississippi Department of Archives and History, Jackson.

Norvell, Otway B. (2nd Kentucky). Memoirs. Southern Historical Collection, University of North Carolina, Chapel Hill.

Nunn, Jesse C. (Cobb's Legion). Correspondence. Georgia Department of Archives and History, Atlanta.

Oden, John P. (11th Tennessee). Diary and Memoirs. Tennessee State Library and Archives, Nashville.

Offutt, N. S. (5th Kentucky). Undated Letter. Kentucky Historical Society, Frankfort.

Oliver, James M. (15th Tennessee). Diary. Tennessee State Library and Archives, Nashville.

Paine, F. J. (16th Texas Battalion). Correspondence. Tennessee State Library and Archives, Nashville.

Parsons, David (Harvey's [Miss.] Scouts). Papers. Mississippi Department of Archives and History, Jackson.

Pegues, Josiah J. (2nd Alabama). History of the 2nd Alabama Cavalry. Alabama Department of Archives and History, Montgomery.

Perry, Roderick (9th Tennessee). Correspondence and Memoirs. Atlanta History Center.

Peters, Scott (3rd Missouri). Diaries. Southern Historical Collection, University of North Carolina, Chapel Hill.

Porter, John (9th Kentucky). Memoirs. Tennessee State Library and Archives, Nashville.

Porter, John M. (4th Kentucky). Correspondence and Diary. Filson Historical Society, Louisville, KY.

Powell, Lewis K. (5th Georgia). Memoirs. Georgia State Archives, Morrow.

Purvine, David S. (1st Mississippi). Correspondence. Shiloh National Military Park, Shiloh, TN.

Pybas, Kenneth M. (7th Tennessee). Diary and Memoirs. Tennessee State Library and Archives, Nashville.

Rainey, Isaac N. (7th Tennessee). Memoirs. Tennessee State Library and Archives, Nashville.

Ray, Lavender R. (1st Georgia). Correspondence and Diaries. Robert W. Woodruff Library, Emory University, Atlanta.

Ray, William H. (28th Mississippi). Correspondence. Mississippi Department of Archives and History, Jackson.

Ray, William S. (15th Tennessee). Memoirs. University of Arkansas Libraries, Fayetteville.

Rees, W. P. (6th Georgia). Letter of May 12, 1863. Georgia State Archives, Morrow.

Rheney, John W. (Cobb's Legion). Correspondence. Georgia Department of Archives and History, Atlanta.

Ridley, Samuel J. (6th Tennessee). Correspondence. Tennessee State Library and Archives, Nashville.

Ripy, James P. (5th Kentucky). Correspondence. Filson Historical Society, Louisville, KY.

Robinson, George W. (4th Tennessee). Correspondence. Tennessee State Library and Archives, Nashville.

Rutledge, Benjamin H. (4th South Carolina). Undated Letter. William R. Perkins Library, Duke University, Durham, NC.

Shackleford, Josephus S. (4th Alabama). Memoirs. Alabama Department of Archives and History, Montgomery.

Sharkey, H. Clay (5th Alabama). Papers. Mississippi Department of Archives and History, Jackson.

Shelby, John W. (5th Kentucky). Diaries. Kentucky Historical Society, Frankfort.

Sheppard, James O. (6th South Carolina). Correspondence. U.S. Army Heritage and Education Center, Carlisle Barracks, PA.

Sherman, Erasmus (1st Arkansas Battalion). Correspondence. University of Arkansas Libraries, Fayetteville.

Skinner, I. W. (3rd Georgia). Correspondence. Georgia State Archives, Morrow.

Slemons, William F. (2nd Arkansas). Correspondence. Eleanor S. Brockenbrough Library, Museum of the Confederacy, Richmond, VA.

Sloan, William E. (5th Tennessee). Diaries. Tennessee State Library and Archives, Nashville.

Smith, Baxter (4th Tennessee). Memoirs. U.S. Army Heritage and Education Center, Carlisle Barracks, PA.

Smith, Dabney H. (5th Kentucky). Correspondence. Filson Historical Society, Louisville, KY.

_____. Papers. Kentucky Historical Society, Frankfort.

Spurr, Richard A. (8th Kentucky). Papers. King Library, University of Kentucky, Lexington.

Stone, Henry L. (9th Kentucky). Correspondence. Kentucky Historical Society, Frankfort.

_____. Diary. Eleanor S. Brockenbrough Library, Museum of the Confederacy, Richmond, VA.

Stone, William J. (2nd Kentucky). Papers. King Library, University of Kentucky, Lexington.

Stuart, Angus R. (4th Georgia). Memoirs. Georgia State Archives, Morrow.

Stuart, David C. (4th Alabama). Memoirs. Alabama Department of Archives and History, Montgomery.

Stuart, Peter W. (4th Georgia). Memoirs. Georgia State Archives, Morrow.

Swann, John T. (Phillips Legion). Correspondence. Georgia Department of Archives and History, Atlanta.

Testerman, William F. (8th Tennessee). Correspondence. Newman Library, Virginia Polytechnic Institute and State University, Blacksburg.

Thornton, David L. (5th Kentucky). Correspondence and Diary. King Library, University of Kentucky, Lexington.

Topp, Robertson (2nd Tennessee). Correspondence. Tennessee State Library and Archives, Nashville.

Trowbridge, Alamin (Cobb's Legion). Correspondence. Georgia Department of Archives and History, Atlanta.

Tucker, J. Randolph (1st Tennessee). Correspondence. Eleanor S. Brockenbrough Library, Museum of the Confederacy, Richmond, VA.

Ulmer, Isaac B. (3rd Alabama). Memoir of Shiloh Campaign. Alabama Department of Archives and History, Montgomery.

_____. Memoir of the 3rd Alabama Cavalry. Southern Historical Collection, University of North Carolina, Chapel Hill.

Unidentified Enlisted Man (9th Kentucky). Letter of May 6, 1864. U.S. Army Heritage and Education Center, Carlisle Barracks, PA.

Wagner, Bernard C. (5th Georgia). Correspondence. Atlanta History Center.

_____. Correspondence. Georgia State Archives, Morrow.

Walden, David (9th Alabama). "A Sixteen-Year-Old Rebel Boy's First Battle." Alabama Department of Archives and History, Montgomery.

Wall, John H. (11th Texas). Letter of November 17, 1862. U.S. Army Heritage and Education Center, Carlisle Barracks, PA.

Wallace, Thomas (6th Kentucky). Correspondence. Filson Historical Society, Louisville, KY.

Wallace, Thomas (9th Tennessee). Correspondence. Southern Historical Collection, University of North Carolina, Chapel Hill.

Ward, William S. (11th Texas). Correspondence. U.S. Army Heritage and Education Center, Carlisle Barracks, PA.

Waring, J. Frederick (Jeff Davis Legion). Diaries. Southern Historical Collection, University of North Carolina, Chapel Hill.

_____. Papers. Georgia Historical Society, Savannah.

Watts, John W. (7th Alabama). Memoirs. Alabama Department of Archives and History, Montgomery.

Weaton, John (1st Louisiana). Letter of June 19, 1864. U.S. Army Heritage and Education Center, Carlisle Barracks, PA.

Webb, James D. (51st Alabama). Correspondence. Southern Historical Collection, University of North Carolina, Chapel Hill.

Wells, Edward L. (4th South Carolina). Papers. Charleston Library Society, Charleston, S.C.

_____. Papers. South Caroliniana Library, University of South Carolina, Columbia.

Williams, Leonard (2nd South Carolina). Correspondence. Eleanor S. Brockenbrough Library, Museum of the Confederacy, Richmond, VA.

Wilson, Thomas B. (1st Tennessee). Memoirs. Southern Historical Collection, University of North Carolina, Chapel Hill.

Withers, C. A. (1st Kentucky). Memoirs. Southern Historical Collection, University of North Carolina, Chapel Hill.

Worthington, Albert D. (1st Mississippi). Correspondence. Mississippi Department of Archives and History, Jackson.

Worthington, E. T. (1st Mississippi). Correspondence. Southern Historical Collection, University of North Carolina, Chapel Hill.

Worthington, William M. (1st Mississippi). Correspondence. Mississippi Department of Archives and History, Jackson.

_____. Correspondence. Southern Historical Collection, University of North Carolina, Chapel Hill.

Wynn, J. A. (1st Georgia). Memoirs. Georgia State Archives, Morrow.

Yancey, Benjamin C. (Cobb's Legion). Correspondence. Southern Historical Collection, University of North Carolina, Chapel Hill.

Zeigler, Perry W. (4th Georgia). Correspondence. Georgia State Archives, Morrow.

*Other*

Artifacts and Papers, Morgan's Cavalry Brigade, Army of Tennessee. Don D. John Collection, Kentucky Historical Society, Frankfort.

Bailey, Michael M. "From Pensacola to Bentonville: The War History of the Prattville Dragoons." Alabama Department of Archives and History, Montgomery.

Beauregard, Pierre G. T. Papers. Library of Congress, Washington, DC.

_____. Papers. William R. Perkins Library, Duke University, Durham, NC.

Blanton, James. "Account of the Raids Made in Kentucky by General Morgan and Captain Hines." King Library, University of Kentucky, Lexington.

Bragg, Braxton. Papers. Rosenberg Library, Galveston, TX.

_____. Papers. Southern Historical Collection, University of North Carolina, Chapel Hill.

_____. Papers. U. S. Military Academy Library, West Point, NY.

_____. Papers. Western Reserve Historical Society, Cleveland, OH.

_____. Papers. William R. Perkins Library, Duke University, Durham, NC.

Brown, Maud Morrow, comp. "William Decatur Howell, 1846-1864: A Soldier's Journal and Letters . . ." Mississippi Department of Archives and History, Jackson.

French, L. Virginia. Diary and Memoirs. Tennessee State Library and Archives, Nashville.

French, Samuel G. Papers. Mississippi Department of Archives and History, Jackson.

Hardee, William J. Papers. Alabama Department of Archives and History, Montgomery.

Hollifield, Horatio N. Papers. William R. Perkins Library, Duke University, Durham, NC.

Johnston, Albert Sidney. Papers. Filson Historical Society, Louisville, KY.

_____. Papers. Kentucky Historical Society, Frankfort.

_____. Papers. Library of Congress, Washington, DC.

Johnston, Joseph E. Correspondence. Century-Civil War Collection, New York Public Library.

_____. Papers. Earl Gregg Swem Library, College of William and Mary, Williamsburg, VA.

_____. Papers. Henry E. Huntington Library, San Marino, CA.

_____. Papers. William R. Perkins Library, Duke University, Durham, NC.

Jordan, John L. "Triune [Tennessee] in the Civil War." Tennessee State Library and Archives, Nashville.

Longstreet, James. Papers. Gilder Lehrman Collection, New York.

McGhee, Martha Long. "Native to the Soil: The Life and Times of Nimrod William Ezekiel Long of Alabama." Long Papers, Robert W. Woodruff Library, Emory University, Atlanta.

Mullen, Joseph, Jr. Diary. Eleanor S. Brockenbrough Library, Museum of the Confederacy, Richmond, VA.

Norris, James L. Papers Relating to the Death of John Hunt Morgan. Southern Historical Collection, University of North Carolina, Chapel Hill.

Orders and Circulars of Confederate General Nathan Bedford Forrest's Cavalry. Record Group 109, Entry 90. National Archives, Washington, DC.

Randolph, J. Tucker. Correspondence. Eleanor S. Brockenbrough Library, Museum of the Confederacy, Richmond, VA.

Shelton, Percy Wayne. "Personal Civil War Letters of Lawrence Sullivan Ross." M.A. thesis, Baylor University, Waco, TX, 1938.

Smith, Edmund Kirby. Letter of September 7, 1862. Filson Historical Society, Louisville, KY.

Stout, Samuel H. Papers. Southern Historical Collection, University of North Carolina, Chapel Hill.

Wells, John B., III. "William Green Wells—Mountain Confederate." Johnson County Public Library, Paintsville, KY.

## Articles and Essays

Alderson, William T., ed. "The Civil War Reminiscences of John Johnston, 1861-1865." *Tennessee Historical Quarterly* 13 (1954): 65-82, 156-78, 244-76, 329-54; 14 (1955): 43-81, 142-75.

Alexander, Edward Porter. "Longstreet at Knoxville." In *Battles and Leaders of the Civil War*, edited by Robert Underwood Johnson and Clarence Clough Buel (4 vols. New York: Century Co., 1887-88), 3: 745-51.

Alison, Joseph Dill. "I have been through my first Battle and have had enough war to last me. . ." *Civil War Times Illustrated* 5 (February 1967): 40-44, 46.

Allen, Theodore F. "Six Hundred Miles of Fried Chicken." *Journal of the U. S. Cavalry Association* 12 (1899): 162-75.

Ambrose, Stephen E. "Fort Donelson a 'Disastrous' Blow to South." *Civil War Times Illustrated* 5 (June 1966): 4-13, 42-45.

Ballard, Michael B. "Deceit by Telegraph: 'Lightning' Ellsworth's Electronic Warfare." *Civil War Times Illustrated* 22 (October 1983): 22-27.

Barnett, T. S. "The Eleventh Texas Cavalry." *Confederate Veteran* 19 (1911): 430.

Bearss, Edwin C. "Cavalry Operations in the Battle of Stone's River." *Tennessee Historical Quarterly* 19 (1960): 23-53, 110-44.

———. "Unconditional Surrender: The Fall of Fort Donelson." *Tennessee Historical Quarterly* 21 (1962): 47-65, 140-61.

———, and Howard P. Nash. "The Attack on Fort Henry." *Civil War Times Illustrated* 4 (November 1965): 9-15.

Beauregard, Pierre G. T. "The Campaign of Shiloh." In *Battles and Leaders of the Civil War*, edited by Robert Underwood Johnson and Clarence Clough Buel (4 vols. New York: Century Co., 1887-88), 1: 569-93.

Benedict, James Bell. "General John Hunt Morgan, [and] the Great Indiana-Ohio Raid." *Filson Club History Quarterly* 31 (1957): 147-71.

Billingsley, William Clyde, ed. "'Such Is War': The Confederate Memoirs of Newton Asbury Keen." *Texas Military History* 6 (1967): 238-53; 7 (1968): 4-70, 103-19, 176-94.

Blackburn, J. K. P. "Reminiscences of the Terry Rangers." *Southwestern Historical Quarterly* 22 (1918): 38-77, 143-79.

Blair, John L. "Morgan's Ohio Raid." *Filson Club History Quarterly* 36 (1962): 242-71.

Blanton, J. C. "Forrest's Old Regiment." *Confederate Veteran* 3 (1895): 41-42, 77-78.

Breckinridge, William C. P. "The Opening of the Atlanta Campaign." *Battles and Leaders of the Civil War* 4 (1887-88): 277-81.

Brooksher, William R., and David K. Snider. "Bold Cavalry Raid: Ride Down the Sequatchie Valley." *Civil War Times Illustrated* 22 (March 1983): 32-39.

———. "Devil on the River." *Civil War Times Illustrated* 15 (August 1976): 12-19.

_____. "Stampede in Kentucky: John Hunt Morgan's Summer Raid." *Civil War Times Illustrated* 17 ( June 1978): 4-10, 43-46.

_____. "A Visit to Holly Springs." *Civil War Times Illustrated* 14 ( June 1975): 4-9, 40-44.

_____. "The 'War Child' Rides: Joe Wheeler at Stones River." *Civil War Times Illustrated* 14 ( January 1976): 5-10, 44-46.

Brown, A. F. "Van Dorn's Operations in Northern Mississippi—Recollections of a Cavalryman." *Southern Historical Society Papers* 6 (1878): 151-61.

Brown, Campbell H. "Forrest's Johnsonville Raid." *Civil War Times Illustrated* 4 ( June 1965): 48-57.

Brown, D. Alexander. "The Battle of Brice's Cross Roads." *Civil War Times Illustrated* 7 (April 1968): 4-9, 44-48.

_____. "Grierson's Raid: 'Most Brilliant' of the War." *Civil War Times Illustrated* 3 ( January 1965): 4-11, 30-32.

_____. "Morgan's Christmas Raid." *Civil War Times Illustrated* 13 ( January 1975): 12-19.

_____. "Wilson's Creek." *Civil War Times Illustrated* 11 (April 1972): 9-18.

Bryan, Charles F., Jr. "'I Mean to Have Them All': Forrest's Murfreesboro Raid." *Civil War Times Illustrated* 12 ( January 1974): 27-34.

Buck, S. H. "First Kentucky Confederate Cavalry." *Confederate Veteran* 21 (1913): 449.

Buell, Don Carlos. "East Tennessee and the Campaign of Perryville." In *Battles and Leaders of the Civil War*, edited by Robert Underwood Johnson and Clarence Clough Buel (4 vols. New York: Century Co., 1887-88), 3: 31-51.

_____. "Shiloh Reviewed." In *Battles and Leaders of the Civil War*, edited by Robert Underwood Johnson and Clarence Clough Buel (4 vols. New York: Century Co., 1887-88), 1: 487-536.

Burgess, Tim, ed. "Reminiscences of the Battle of Nashville by Pvt. John Johnston, 14th Tennessee Cavalry." *Journal of Confederate History* 1 (1988): 152-68.

Button, Charles W. "Early Engagements with Forrest." *Confederate Veteran* 5 (1897): 478-80.

Byrne, Frank L., ed. "A General Behind Bars: Neal Dow in Libby Prison." *Civil War History* 8 (1962): 164-83.

Calhoun, C. M. "Credit to Wheeler Claimed for Others." *Confederate Veteran* 20 (1912): 82.

Calkin, Homer L., ed. "Elk Horn to Vicksburg: James H. Fauntleroy's Diary for the Year 1862." *Civil War History* 2 (1956): 7-43.

Carnes, W. W. "Chickamauga." *Southern Historical Society Papers* 14 (1886): 398-407.

Caruthers, W. C. "More About Kilpatrick's Horses." *Confederate Veteran* 13 (1905): 456.

Casseday, Morton M. "The Surrender of Fort Donelson." *Southern Bivouac* 6 (1887): 694-97.

Castel, Albert. "Battle Without a Victor . . . Iuka." *Civil War Times Illustrated* 11 (October 1972): 12-18.

_____. "Earl Van Dorn—a Personality Profile." *Civil War Times Illustrated* 6 (April 1967): 38-42.

_____. "The Fort Pillow Massacre: A Fresh Examination of the Evidence." *Civil War History* 4 (1958): 37-50.

_____. "Union Fizzle at Atlanta: The Battle of Utoy Creek." *Civil War Times Illustrated* 16 (February 1978): 26-32.

_____. "Victory at Corinth." *Civil War Times Illustrated* 17 (October 1978): 12-22.

Chalmers, James R. "Forrest and His Campaigns." *Southern Historical Society Papers* 7 (1879): 451-86.

Cheatham, Benjamin F. "Cheatham's Story of Spring Hill." *Southern Bivouac* 3 (1885): 337-46.

Clauss, Errol MacGregor. "The Battle of Jonesborough." *Civil War Times Illustrated* 7 (November 1968): 12-23

Clay, A. B. "Concerning the Battle of Chickamauga." *Confederate Veteran* 13 (1905): 72.

_____. "On the Right at Chickamauga." *Confederate Veteran* 19 (1911): 329-30.

Cobbs, J. T. "Capt. J. T. Cobbs's Thrilling Experiences." *Confederate Veteran* 5 (1897): 572-75.

Cochrane, Harden P. "The Letters of Harden Perkins Cochrane, 1862-1864." *Alabama Review* 7 (1954): 277-94; 8 (1955): 55-70, 143-52, 219-28, 277-90.

Coffin, James. "Chapel Hill at the Close of the War." *North Carolina University Magazine* 31 (1901): 272-75.

Coffman, Edward M. "Captain Thomas Henry Hines and His February, 1863, Raid." *Register of the Kentucky State Historical Society* 55 (1957): 105-08.

_____, ed. "Memoirs of Hylan B. Lyon." *Tennessee Historical Quarterly* 18 (1959): 35-53.

Coffman, Richard M. "A Vital Unit." *Civil War Times Illustrated* 20 (January 1982): 40-45.

Colby, Elbridge. "Wilson's Cavalry Campaign of 1865." *Journal of the American Military History Foundation* 2 (1938): 204-21.

Connelly, Thomas L. "The [Albert Sidney] Johnston Mystique—a Profile." *Civil War Times Illustrated* 5 (February 1967): 15-23.

Cook, James F. "The 1863 Raid of Abel D. Streight: Why It Failed." *Alabama Review* 22 (1969): 254-69.

Cooling, Benjamin F., III. "The Attack on Dover, Tenn." *Civil War Times Illustrated* 2 (August 1963): 11-13.

Coombs, Thomas M. "Letters Written by Thomas Monroe Coombs to His Wife while a Prisoner of War in the Ohio State Penitentiary." *Register of the Kentucky State Historical Society* 46 (1948): 397-403.

Crawford, W. T. "The Mystery of Spring Hill." *Civil War History* 1 (1955): 101-26.

Creager, J. A. "Ross's Brigade of Cavalry." *Confederate Veteran* 28 (1920): 290-92.

Cunningham, J. W. "Memories of Morgan's Christmas Raid." *Confederate Veteran* 17 (1909): 79-80.

Curry, William L. "Raid of the Confederate Cavalry through Central Tennessee." *Journal of the U. S. Cavalry Association* 19 (1908-09): 815-35.

Davis, George B. "The Cavalry Operations in Middle Tennessee in October, 1863." *Journal of the U. S. Cavalry Association* 24 (1913-14): 879-91.

Davis, W. H. "Recollections of Perryville." *Confederate Veteran* 24 (1916): 554-55.

Davis, William J. "Letter by William J. Davis of Morgan's Cavalry, 1863." *Filson Club History Quarterly* 9 (1935): 191-95.

_____. "A Winter Raid." *Southern Bivouac* 1 (1885): 28-34.

Deupree, John G. "The Capture of Holly Springs, Mississippi, Dec. 20, 1862." *Publications of the Mississippi Historical Society* 4 (1901): 49-61.

_____. "The Noxubee Squadron of the First Mississippi Cavalry, C.S.A., 1861-1865." *Publications of the Mississippi Historical Society, Centenary Series* 2 (1918): 12-143.

_____. "Reminiscences of Service with the First Mississippi Cavalry." *Publications of the Mississippi Historical Society* 7 (1903): 85-100.

Dillon, Edward. "General Van Dorn's Operations between Columbia and Nashville in 1863." *Southern Historical Society Papers* 7 (1879): 144-46.

Dinges, Bruce J. "Running Down Rebels." *Civil War Times Illustrated* 19 (April 1980): 10-18.

Dinkins, James. "How Forrest Destroyed Sherman's Line of Communication." *Confederate Veteran* 34 (1926): 135-38.

_____. "How Forrest Saved the Army of Tennessee." *Confederate Veteran* 35 (1927): 54-56, 94-96.

_____. "With Forrest in Middle Tennessee." *Confederate Veteran* 34 (1926): 218-20.

Dixon, Harry S. "Recollections of a Rebel Private." *Sigma Chi Quarterly* 5 (1886): 15-20, 71-77, 145-54, 195-207; 6 (1887); 141-49, 218-23.

Dodson, William Carey. "Burning of Broad River Bridge." *Confederate Veteran* 17 (1909): 462-65.

_____. "More About the Defense of Columbia." *Confederate Veteran* 18 (1910): 75-78.

Duke, Basil W. "The Battle of Hartsville." *Southern Bivouac* 1 (1882): 41-51.

_____. "The Battle of Shiloh." *Southern Bivouac* 2 (1883): 150-62, 201-16.

_____. "Bragg's Campaign in Kentucky." *Southern Bivouac* 4 (1885): 161-67, 232-40.

_____. "John Morgan in 1864." In *Battles and Leaders of the Civil War*, edited by Robert Underwood Johnson and Clarence Clough Buel (4 vols. New York: Century Co., 1887-88), 4: 423-24.

_____. "Morgan's Cavalry during the Bragg Invasion." In *Battles and Leaders of the Civil War*, edited by Robert Underwood Johnson and Clarence Clough Buel (4 vols. New York: Century Co., 1887-88), 3: 26-28.

_____. "Morgan's Indiana and Ohio Raid." In *Annals of the War, Written by Leading Participants, North and South* (Philadelphia: Times Publishing Co., 1879), 241-56.

_____. "Sketch of Gen. John H. Morgan." *Confederate Veteran* 19 (1911): 568-70.

Dyer, John P. "The Civil War Career of General Joseph Wheeler." *Georgia Historical Quarterly* 19 (1935): 17-46.

_____. "Some Aspects of Cavalry Operations in the Army of Tennessee." *Journal of Southern History* 8 (1942): 210-25.

Elmore, Albert R. "Incidents of Service with the Charleston Light Dragoons." *Confederate Veteran* 24 (1916): 538-43.

Elmore, Tom. "Head to Head." *Civil War Times Illustrated* 40 (February 2001): 44-55.

Engle, Stephen D. "Don Carlos Buell: Military Philosophy and Command Problems in the West." *Civil War History* 41 (1995): 89-115.

Evans, David. "The Atlanta Campaign." *Civil War Times Illustrated* 28 (Summer 1989): 13-61.

Eve, Francis E. "The Beau Sabreur of Georgia: A Fitting Tribute to the Gallant General P. M. B. Young, C.S.A." *Southern Historical Society Papers* 25 (1897): 146-51.

Flood, F. W. "Captures by Eighth Confederate Cavalry." *Confederate Veteran* 13 (1905): 458-59.

"General Nathan Bedford Forrest: A Summary of Some of His Remarkable Achievements." *Southern Historical Society Papers* 29 (1901): 337-39.

Gilbert, Charles C. "On the Field of Perryville." In *Battles and Leaders of the Civil War*, edited by Robert Underwood Johnson and Clarence Clough Buel (4 vols. New York: Century Co., 1887-88), 3: 52-59.

Gordon, James. "The Battle and Retreat from Corinth." *Publications of the Mississippi Historical Society* 4 (1901): 63-72.

Grant, Ulysses S. "The Battle of Shiloh." In *Battles and Leaders of the Civil War*, edited by Robert Underwood Johnson and Clarence Clough Buel (4 vols. New York: Century Co., 1887-88), 1: 465-86.

_____. "Chattanooga." In *Battles and Leaders of the Civil War*, edited by Robert Underwood Johnson and Clarence Clough Buel (4 vols. New York: Century Co., 1887-88), 3: 679-711.

_____. "The Vicksburg Campaign." In *Battles and Leaders of the Civil War*, edited by Robert Underwood Johnson and Clarence Clough Buel (4 vols. New York: Century Co., 1887-88), 3: 493-539.

Green, Curtis. "Sixth Georgia Cavalry at Chickamauga." *Confederate Veteran* 8 (1900): 324.

Guerrant, Edward O. "Marshall and Garfield in Eastern Kentucky." In *Battles and Leaders of the Civil War*, edited by Robert Underwood Johnson and Clarence Clough Buel (4 vols. New York: Century Co., 1887-88), 1: 393-97.

Guild, George B. "Battle of Bentonville: Charge of the Fourth Tennessee and Eighth Texas Cavalry." *Annals of the Army of Tennessee* 1 (1878): 62-64.

Hale, Douglas. "The Third Texas Cavalry: A Socio-Economic Profile of a Confederate Regiment." *Military History of the Southwest* 19 (Spring 1989): 1-26.

Hamilton, Charles Smith. "The Battle of Iuka." In *Battles and Leaders of the Civil War*, edited by Robert Underwood Johnson and Clarence Clough Buel (4 vols. New York: Century Co., 1887-88), 2: 734-36.

Hamilton, Posey. "Battle of New Hope Church, Ga." *Confederate Veteran* 30 (1922): 338-39.

_____. "Incidents of the Fighting at Aiken, S. C." *Confederate Veteran* 32 (1924): 58-59.

Hammond, Paul F. "Campaign of General E. Kirby Smith in Kentucky in 1862." *Southern Historical Society Papers* 9 (1881): 225-33, 246-54, 289-97, 455-62.

Hampton, Wade. "The Battle of Bentonville." In *Battles and Leaders of the Civil War*, edited by Robert Underwood Johnson and Clarence Clough Buel (4 vols. New York: Century Co., 1887-88), 4: 700-705.

Harcourt, A. P. "Terry's Texas Rangers." *Southern Bivouac* 1 (1882): 89-97.

Hargis, O. P. "We Came Very Near Capturing General Wilder." *Civil War Times Illustrated* 7 (November 1968): 36-41.

_____. "We Kept Fighting and Falling Back." *Civil War Times Illustrated* 7 (December 1968): 37-42.

Harrison, Jon P. "Tenth Texas Cavalry, C.S.A." *Military History of Texas & the Southwest* 12 (1974): 94-107.

Harrison, Lowell H. "Basil Duke: The Confederates' 'Little Whalebone.'" *Civil War Times Illustrated* 21 (January 1983): 33-39.

_____. "A Battle Beyond Knoxville." *Civil War Times Illustrated* 26 (May 1987): 17-21, 46-47.

_____. "The Battle of Munfordville." *Civil War Times Illustrated* 13 (June 1974): 5-9, 45-47.

_____. "Mill Springs, 'The Brilliant Victory.'" *Civil War Times Illustrated* 10 (January 1972): 4-9, 44-47.

_____. "Perryville: Death on a Dry River." *Civil War Times Illustrated* 18 (May 1979): 5-9, 44-47.

Hartje, Robert. "Van Dorn Conducts a Raid on Holly Springs and Enters Tennessee." *Tennessee Historical Quarterly* 18 (1959): 120-33.

Hattaway, Herman. "Stephen Dill Lee—a Profile." *Civil War Times Illustrated* 8 (August 1969): 17-24.

Hawthorne, J. J. "Active Service with the Third Alabama Cavalry." *Confederate Veteran* 34 (1926): 334-36.

Hay, Thomas Robson. "The Atlanta Campaign." *Georgia Historical Quarterly* 7 (1923): 99-118.

_____. "The Battle of Chattanooga." *Georgia Historical Quarterly* 8 (1924): 121-41.

_____. "The Campaign and Battle of Chickamauga." *Georgia Historical Quarterly* 7 (1923): 213-50.

_____. "The Cavalry at Spring Hill." *Tennessee Historical Magazine* 8 (1924): 7-23.

_____. "Davis, Bragg, and Johnston in the Atlanta Campaign." *Georgia Historical Quarterly* 8 (1924): 38-48.

Henry, Robert Selph. "Chattanooga and the War." *Tennessee Historical Quarterly* 19 (1960): 222-30.

Hill, Daniel H. "Chickamauga—The Great Battle of the West." In Robert Underwood Johnson and Clarence Clough Buel, eds., *Battles and Leaders of the Civil War* (4 vols. New York: Century Co., 1887-88), 3: 638-62.

Hines, Thomas Henry. "General Morgan's Escape." *Southern Bivouac* 1 (1885-86): 49-50.

Hodgson, Matthew. "Bampson of Bampson's Legion: An Informal Study of Confederate Command." *Civil War History* 6 (1960): 157-69.

Holman, J. A. "Concerning the Battle of Bentonville." *Confederate Veteran* 6 (1898): 153-54.

Holmes, James G. "The Artillery at Bentonville." *Confederate Veteran* 3 (1895): 103.

Hood, John Bell. "The Defense of Atlanta." In *Battles and Leaders of the Civil War*, edited by Robert Underwood Johnson and Clarence Clough Buel (4 vols. New York: Century Co., 1887-88), 4: 336-44.

_____. "The Invasion of Tennessee." In *Battles and Leaders of the Civil War*, edited by Robert Underwood Johnson and Clarence Clough Buel (4 vols. New York: Century Co., 1887-88), 4: 425-37.

Hord, Henry Ewell. "Campaigning under Forrest." *Confederate Veteran* 12 (1904): 6-7.

Horn, Stanley F. "The Battle of Perryville." *Civil War Times Illustrated* 4 (February 1966): 5-11, 42-47.

_____. "The Battle of Stones River." *Civil War Times Illustrated* 2 (February 1964): 7-11, 34-39.

_____. "The Spring Hill Legend—a Reappraisal." *Civil War Times Illustrated* 8 (April 1969): 20-32.

Horton, Paul. "Submitting to the 'Shadow of Slavery': The Secession Crisis and Civil War in Alabama's Lawrence County." *Civil War History* 44 (1998): 111-36.

Howard, Oliver Otis. "Sherman's Advance from Atlanta." In Robert Underwood Johnson and Clarence Clough Buel, eds., *Battles and Leaders of the Civil War* (4 vols. New York: Century Co., 1887-88), 4: 663-66.

_____. "The Struggle for Atlanta." In *Battles and Leaders of the Civil War*, edited by Robert Underwood Johnson and Clarence Clough Buel (4 vols. New York: Century Co., 1887-88), 4: 293-325.

Hughes, Nathaniel C. "Hardee's Defense of Savannah." *Georgia Historical Quarterly* 47 (1963): 43-67.

"An Incident of Hood's Campaign." *Southern Bivouac* 3 (1884): 131-32.

"John Hunt Morgan and the Kentucky Cavalry Volunteers in the Mexican War." *Register of the Kentucky Historical Society* 81 (1983): 343-65.

Johnson, E. Polk. "The First Kentucky Cavalry." *Confederate Veteran* 21 (1913): 479.

_____. "Some Generals I Have Known." *Southern Bivouac* 1 (1885): 120-22.

Johnston, John. "Cavalry of Hood's Left at Nashville." *Confederate Veteran* 3 (1905): 28-30.

_____. "Forrest's March Out of West Tennessee, December 1863: Recollections of a Private." *West Tennessee Historical Society Papers* 12 (1958): 138-48.

Johnston, Joseph E. "Jefferson Davis and the Mississippi Campaign." In *Battles and Leaders of the Civil War*, edited by Robert Underwood Johnson and Clarence Clough Buel (4 vols. New York: Century Co., 1887-88), 3: 472-82.

_____. "Opposing Sherman's Advance to Atlanta." In *Battles and Leaders of the Civil War*, edited by Robert Underwood Johnson and Clarence Clough Buel (4 vols. New York: Century Co., 1887-88), 4: 260-77.

"Johnston's Last Volley: A Veteran Describes His Experiences in Durham at the Close of the War." *Southern Historical Society Papers* 30 (1902): 174-78.

Johnston, William Preston. "Albert Sidney Johnston at Shiloh." In *Battles and Leaders of the Civil War*, edited by Robert Underwood Johnson and Clarence Clough Buel (4 vols. New York: Century Co., 1887-88), 1: 540-68.

Jones, Charles C., Jr. "The Siege and Evacuation of Savannah, Georgia, in December, 1864." *Southern Historical Society Papers* 17 (1889): 60-85.

Joyce, Fred. "From Infantry to Cavalry." *Southern Bivouac* 3 (1884): 161-62.

Keenan, Jerry. "Final Cavalry Operations [of the Atlanta Campaign]." *Civil War Times Illustrated* 3 (July 1964): 50.

Keller, Allan. "Morgan's Raid Across the Ohio." *Civil War Times Illustrated* 2 ( June 1963): 7-9, 34-37.

Kelly, Maud McClure. "John Herbert Kelly, the Boy General of the Confederacy." *Alabama Historical Quarterly* 9 (1947): 9-112.

Kelly, R. M. "Holding Kentucky for the Union." In *Battles and Leaders of the Civil War*, edited by Robert Underwood Johnson and Clarence Clough Buel (4 vols. New York: Century Co., 1887-88), 1: 373-92.

King, William H. "Forrest's Attack on Murfreesboro, July 13, 1862." *Confederate Veteran* 32 (1924): 430-31, 437.

Klein, Maury. "The Knoxville Campaign." *Civil War Times Illustrated* 10 (October 1971): 5-10, 40-42.

Kniffin, Gilbert C. "The Battle of Stone's River." In *Battles and Leaders of the Civil War*, edited by Robert Underwood Johnson and Clarence Clough Buel (4 vols. New York: Century Co., 1887-88), 3: 613-32.

_____. "Maneuvering Bragg Out of Tennessee." In *Battles and Leaders of the Civil War*, edited by Robert Underwood Johnson and Clarence Clough Buel (4 vols. New York: Century Co., 1887-88), 3: 635-37.

Kurtz, Wilbur G. "The Death of Major General W. H. T. Walker, July 22, 1864." *Civil War History* 6 (1960): 174-79.

_____. "The Fighting at Atlanta." *Civil War Times Illustrated* 3 ( July 1964): 9-11, 14-17.

Lafferty, W. T., ed. "Civil War Reminiscences of John Aker Lafferty." *Register of the Kentucky State Historical Society* 59 (1961): 1-28.

Lale, Max S., ed. "The Boy-Bugler of the Third Texas Cavalry: The A. B. Blocker Narrative." *Military History of Texas & The Southwest* 14 (1978): 71-92, 147-67, 215-27; 15 (1979): 21-34.

Larter, Harry. "Terry's Texas Rangers (8th Texas Cavalry) C.S.A., 1864." *Military Collector & Historian* 5 (1954): 15-16.

"The Last General Officer, C.S.A." *Confederate Veteran* 36 (1928): 365-66.

Lathrop, Barnes F. "A Confederate Artillerymen at Shiloh." *Civil War History* 8 (1962): 373-85.

Lieutenant-General N. B. Forrest: "Lord Wolseley's Estimate of the Man and the Soldier." *Southern Historical Society Papers* 20 (1892): 325-35.

Lincoln, Edward T. "A Correction—Second Battle of Fort Donelson, Tennessee, February 3, 1863." *Southern Bivouac* 1 (1882): 98-100.

Longacre, Edward G. "Boots and Saddles, Part II: The Western Theater." *Civil War Times Illustrated* 31 ( June 1992): 48-55.

_____. "Streight's Raid: 'All Is Fair in Love and War.'" *Civil War Times Illustrated* 8 ( June 1969): 32-40.

Luvaas, Jay. "An Appraisal of Joseph E. Johnston." *Civil War Times Illustrated* 4 ( January 1966): 5-7, 28-32.

_____. "Bentonville—Last Chance to Stop Sherman." *Civil War Times Illustrated* 2 (October 1963): 7-9, 38-42.

_____. "Cavalry Lessons of the Civil War." *Civil War Times Illustrated* 6 ( January 1968): 21-31.

_____. "Johnston's Last Stand—Bentonville." *North Carolina Historical Review* 33 (1956): 332-58.

Lynne, Donald M. "Wilson's Cavalry at Nashville." *Civil War History* 1 (1955):141-59.

Mahon, James L. "Defending the Confederate Heartland: Co. F of Henry Ashby's 2nd Tennessee Cavalry." *Civil War Regiments* 4, no. 1 (1994): 1-43.

Marks, Paula M. "The Ranger Reverend." *Civil War Times Illustrated* 24 (December 1985): 40-45.

Marriner, W. M. "Chickamauga—The Opening." *Southern Bivouac* 3 (1884): 8-11.

Martin, S. P. "Second Kentucky Cavalry." *Confederate Veteran* 21 (1913): 61.

Maury, Dabney H. "Recollections of General Earl Van Dorn." *Southern Historical Society Papers* 19 (1891): 191-98.

McAfee, John J. "General John H. Morgan: His Capture and Death." *Southern Bivouac* 1 (1882-83): 149-56.

McDonald, William N. "Cavalry versus Infantry." *Southern Bivouac* 1 (1882): 160-67.

_____. "Sketch of Lieutenant-General [*sic*] Joseph Wheeler." *Southern Bivouac* 2 (1883-84): 241-46.

_____. "Sketch of Lieutenant-General N. B. Forrest." *Southern Bivouac* 2 (1883-84): 289-98, 337-45.

McDonough, James Lee. "Cold Days in Hell: The Battle of Stones River, Tennessee." *Civil War Times Illustrated* 25 ( June 1986): 13-51.

McGinty, Brian. "Unwept, Unhonored, Unsung." *Civil War Times Illustrated* 21 ( June 1982): 38-45.

McMurry, Richard M. "The *Enemy* at Richmond: Joseph E. Johnston and the Confederate Government." *Civil War History* 27 (1981): 5-31.

_____. "'The Hell Hole': New Hope Church." *Civil War Times Illustrated* 11 (February 1973): 32-43.

_____. "Kennesaw Mountain." *Civil War Times Illustrated* 8 ( January 1970): 20-33.

_____. "A Policy So Disastrous: Joseph E. Johnston's Atlanta Campaign." In *The Campaign for Atlanta and Sherman's March to the Sea*, edited by Theodore P. Savas and David A. Woodbury (2 vols. Campbell, CA: Savas-Woodbury, 1994), 2: 223-48.

_____. "Resaca: 'A Heap of Hard Fiten.'" *Civil War Times Illustrated* 9 (November 1970): 4-12, 44-48.

_____. "Sherman's Meridian Campaign." *Civil War Times Illustrated* 14 (May 1975): 24-32.

McWhiney, Grady C. "Braxton Bragg." *Civil War Times Illustrated* 11 (April 1972): 5-7, 42-48.

_____. "Braxton Bragg at Shiloh." *Tennessee Historical Quarterly* 21 (1962): 19-30.

_____. "Controversy in Kentucky: Braxton Bragg's Campaign of 1862." *Civil War History* 6 (1960): 5-42.

M'Gowan, J. E. "Morgan's Indiana and Ohio Raid." In *Annals of the War, Written by Leading Participants, North and South* (Philadelphia: Times Publishing Co., 1879), 750-69.

Minnich, J. W. "The Cavalry at Knoxville." *Confederate Veteran* 32 (1924): 10-13.

Monnett, Howard Norman, ed. "'The Awfulest Time I Ever Seen': A Letter from Sherman's Army." *Civil War History* 8 (1962): 283-89.

Morgan. D. B. "Incidents of the Fighting at Aiken, S. C." *Confederate Veteran* 32 (1924): 300-301.

Morgan, George W. "Cumberland Gap." In *Battles and Leaders of the Civil War*, edited by Robert Underwood Johnson and Clarence Clough Buel (4 vols. New York: Century Co., 1887-88), 3: 62-69.

"Morgan's Famous Raid: How He Swept through Fifty-two Towns Like a Cyclone." *Southern Historical Society Papers* 24 (1896): 194-96.

"Morgan's Ohio Raid." In *Battles and Leaders of the Civil War*, edited by Robert Underwood Johnson and Clarence Clough Buel (4 vols. New York: Century Co., 1887-88), 3: 634-35.

Morton, John W. "Raid of Forrest's Cavalry on the Tennessee River in 1864." *Southern Historical Society Papers* 10 (1882): 261-68.

Mosgrove, George Dallas. "Following Morgan's Plume through Indiana and Ohio . . ." *Southern Historical Society Papers* 35 (1907): 110-20.

Mruck, Armin E. "The Role of Railroads in the Atlanta Campaign." *Civil War History* 7 (1961): 264-71.

Nelson, B. F. "A Boy in the Confederate Cavalry." *Confederate Veteran* 36 (1928): 374-76.

Nye, Wilbur S. "The Battle of LaFayette, Ga." *Civil War Times Illustrated* 5 ( June 1966): 35-39.

_____. "Cavalry Operations around Atlanta." *Civil War Times Illustrated* 3 ( July 1964): 46-50.

"Organization of the Army of Tennessee . . . at the Battle of Chickamauga." *Southern Historical Society Papers* 12 (1884): 145-60.

Overley, Milford. "'Williams Kentucky Brigade,' C.S.A." *Confederate Veteran* 13 (1905): 460-62.

Poe, Orlando M. "The Defense of Knoxville." In *Battles and Leaders of the Civil War*, edited by Robert Underwood Johnson and Clarence Clough Buel (4 vols. New York: Century Co., 1887-88), 3: 731-45.

Polk, William M. "General Polk and the Battle of Belmont." In Robert Underwood Johnson and Clarence Clough Buel, eds., *Battles and Leaders of the Civil War* (4 vols. New York: Century Co., 1887-88), 1: 348-57.

Prichard, James M. "Morgan in the Mountains." *Civil War Times Illustrated* 24 (October 1985): 32-37.

Quisenberry, Anderson Chenault. "The Confederate Campaign in Kentucky: The Battle of Perryville." *Register of the Kentucky Historical Society* 17 (1919): 31-38.

_____. "The Eleventh Kentucky Cavalry, C.S.A." *Southern Historical Society Papers* 35 (1907): 259-89.

_____. "Morgan's Men in Ohio." *Southern Historical Society Papers* 39 (1914): 91-99.

Ramsdell, Charles W., ed. "Reminiscences of the Terry Rangers, by J. K. P. Blackburn." *Southwestern Historical Quarterly* 22 (1918-19): 38-77, 143-79.

Redfield, Horace V. "Death of General John H. Morgan." In *Annals of the War, Written by Leading Participants, North and South* (Philadelphia: Times Publishing Co., 1879), 614-18.

Redwood, Allen C. "Following Stuart's Feather." *Journal of the Military Service Institution of the United States* 49 (1911): 111-21.

Reed, W. P. "Service with Henderson's Scouts." *Confederate Veteran* 37 (1929): 22-25.

"Reminiscences of Confederate Cavalry Service." *Southern Bivouac* 4 (1886): 609-13.

Rhodes, Charles D. "Confederate Partisan Rangers." In *The Photographic History of the Civil War*, edited by Francis Trevelyan Miller (10 vols. New York: Review of Reviews Co., 1911), 4: 168-80.

Roberts, Frank Stovall. "Review of the Army of Tennessee at Dalton, Ga." *Confederate Veteran* 26 (1918): 150.

Robertson, Felix H. "On Wheeler's Last Raid in Middle Tennessee." *Confederate Veteran* 30 (1922): 334-35.

Roland, Charles P. "Albert Sidney Johnston and the Loss of Forts Henry and Donelson." *Journal of Southern History* 23 (1957): 45-69.

_____. "Albert Sidney Johnston and the Shiloh Campaign." *Civil War History* 4 (1958): 355-82.

Rosecrans, William S. "The Battle of Corinth." In *Battles and Leaders of the Civil War*, edited by Robert Underwood Johnson and Clarence Clough Buel (4 vols. New York: Century Co., 1887-88), 2: 737-57.

Rothert, Otto A., ed. "Letter by William T. Davis of Morgan's Cavalry, 1863." *Filson Club History Quarterly* 9 (1935): 191-95.

Rowell, John W. "The Battle of Mossy Creek." *Civil War Times Illustrated* 8 ( July 1969): 11-16.

_____. "McCook's Raid." *Civil War Times Illustrated* 13 ( July 1974): 5-9, 42-48.

Rushing, Anthony C. "Rackensacker Raiders: Crawford's 1st Arkansas Cavalry." *Civil War Regiments* 1, no. 2 (1991): 44-69.

Ryan, Harriet Fitts, comp. "The Letters of Harden Perkins Cochrane, 1862-1864." *Alabama Review* 7 (1954): 277-94; 8 (1955): 55-70, 143-52, 219-28, 277-90.

Sanders, Stuart W. "The Lebanon Races." *America's Civil War* 16 (March 2003): 24-28.

Scott, Paul R. "On the Road to the Sea: Shannon's Scouts." *Civil War Times Illustrated* 21 ( January 1983): 26-29.

_____. "Shannon's Scouts: Combat Reconnaissance Detachment of Terry's Texas Rangers." *Military History of Texas & the Southwest* 15 (1979): 523.

Secrist, Philip L. "The Role of Cavalry in the Atlanta Campaign, 1864." *Georgia Historical Quarterly* 56 (1972): 510-28.

_____. "Scenes of Awful Carnage." *Civil War Times Illustrated* 10 ( June 1971): 5-9, 45-48.

Sharkey, H. Clay. "Letters." *Journal of Mississippi History* 3 (1941): 277-88; 4 (1942): 225-32.

"Sherman's Campaign in Mississippi in Winter of 1864: Report of General Ross." *Southern Historical Society Papers* 9 (1881): 332-37.

Sherman, William T. "The Grand Strategy of the Last Year of the War." In *Battles and Leaders of the Civil War*, edited by Robert Underwood Johnson and Clarence Clough Buel (4 vols. New York: Century Co., 1887-88), 4: 247-59.

Sigel, Franz. "The Pea Ridge Campaign." In *Battles and Leaders of the Civil War*, edited by Robert Underwood Johnson and Clarence Clough Buel (4 vols. New York: Century Co., 1887-88), 1: 314-34.

Slocum, Henry W. "Final Operations of Sherman's Army." In Robert Underwood Johnson and Clarence Clough Buel, eds., *Battles and Leaders of the Civil War* (4 vols. New York: Century Co., 1887-88), 4: 754-58.

_____. "Sherman's March from Savannah to Bentonville." In *Battles and Leaders of the Civil War*, edited by Robert Underwood Johnson and Clarence Clough Buel (4 vols. New York: Century Co., 1887-88), 4: 681-95.

Smith, Henry H. "Reminiscences of Capt. Henry H. Smith." *Confederate Veteran* 8 (1900): 14-15.

Snair, Dale S., ed. "This Looked But Little Like Trying to Catch the Enemy." *Civil War Times Illustrated* 23 (September 1984): 21-24, 28-33.

Snead, Thomas L. "With Price East of the Mississippi." In *Battles and Leaders of the Civil War*, edited by Robert Underwood Johnson and Clarence Clough Buel (4 vols. New York: Century Co., 1887-88), 2: 717-34.

Speed, Thomas. "Cavalry Operations in the West under Rosecrans and Sherman." In *Battles and Leaders of the Civil War*, edited by Robert Underwood Johnson and Clarence Clough Buel (4 vols. New York: Century Co., 1887-88), 4: 413-16.

Starr, Stephen Z. "Cold Steel: The Saber and the Union Cavalry." *Civil War History* 11 (1965): 142-59.

Stewart, Alexander P. "The Army of Tennessee: A Sketch." In *The Military Annals of Tennessee, Confederate . . .* , edited by John Berrien Lindsley (Nashville, TN: J. M. Lindsley & Co., 1886), 55-111.

Stier, William J. "Fury Takes the Field." *Civil War Times Illustrated* 38 (December 1999): 41-48.

Still, John S. "Blitzkrieg, 1863: Morgan's Raid and Rout." *Civil War History* 3 (1957): 291-306.

Stinson, Byron. "Battle of Tupelo." *Civil War Times Illustrated* 11 ( July 1972): 4-9, 46-48.

Stone, Henry. "Repelling Hood's Invasion of Tennessee." In *Battles and Leaders of the Civil War*, edited by Robert Underwood Johnson and Clarence Clough Buel (4 vols. New York: Century Co., 1887-88), 4: 440-64.

Stone, Henry L. "Reminiscences of Morgan's Men." *Southern Bivouac* 1 (1882-83): 406-14.

Sunderland, Glenn W. "The Bloody Battle of Corinth." *Civil War Times Illustrated* 6 (April 1967): 28-37.

Sutherland, Daniel E. "Sideshow No Longer: A Historiographical Review of the Guerrilla War." *Civil War History* 46 (2000): 5-23.

Swift, Lester L., ed. "Letters from a Sailor on a Tinclad." *Civil War History* 7 (1961): 48-62.

Sword, Wiley. "The Battle of Shiloh." *Civil War Times Illustrated* 17 (May 1978): 4-50.

Sykes, E. T. "Error in the Harris-Adair Article." *Confederate Veteran* 5 (1897): 452-54.

Taylor, Jesse. "The Defense of Fort Henry." In *Battles and Leaders of the Civil War*, edited by Robert Underwood Johnson and Clarence Clough Buel (4 vols. New York: Century Co., 1887-88), 1: 368-72.

Thomas, Edward J. "A Raid with Joe Wheeler." *Confederate Veteran* 30 (1932): 169-70.

Thompson, R. L. "Kentucky Troops in the Confederate Army." *Confederate Veteran* 16 (1908): 443-44.

Thurston, G. P. "Chickamauga." *Southern Bivouac* 5 (1886): 406-15.

Tucker, Glenn. "The Battle of Chickamauga." *Civil War Times Illustrated* 8 (May 1969): 4-50.

_____. "The Battles for Chattanooga." *Civil War Times Illustrated* 10 (August 1971): 4-45.

_____. "Forrest—Untutored Genius of the War." *Civil War Times Illustrated* 3 ( June 1964): 7-9, 35-39, 49.

Urquhart, David. "Bragg's Advance and Retreat." In *Battles and Leaders of the Civil War*, edited by Robert Underwood Johnson and Clarence Clough Buel (4 vols. New York: Century Co., 1887-88), 3: 600-609.

Volpe, Vernon L. "Squirrel Hunting for the Union: The Defense of Cincinnati in 1862." *Civil War History* 33 (1987): 242-55.

Wallace, Lew. "The Capture of Fort Donelson." In *Battles and Leaders of the Civil War*, edited by Robert Underwood Johnson and Clarence Clough Buel (4 vols. New York: Century Co., 1887-88), 1: 398-428.

Warner, Charles H., and A. C. McGinnis, comps. "Captain Gibbs' Company, C.S.A.: Civil War Letters." *Independence County [Arkansas] Chronicle*, 2 (April 1961): 46-56.

Weller, Jac. "The Logistics of Nathan Bedford Forrest." *Military Affairs* 17 (1953): 161-69.

_____. "Nathan Bedford Forrest: An Analysis of Untutored Military Genius." *Tennessee Historical Quarterly* 18 (1958): 213-51.

Wells, E. L. "Hampton at Fayetteville." *Southern Historical Society Papers* 13 (1885): 144-48.

Wheeler, Joseph. "The Battle of Shiloh: A Graphic Description of That Sanguinary Engagement." *Southern Historical Society Papers* 24 (1896): 119-31.

_____. "Bragg's Invasion of Kentucky." In *Battles and Leaders of the Civil War*, edited by Robert Underwood Johnson and Clarence Clough Buel (4 vols. New York: Century Co., 1887-88), 3: 1-25.

Wherry, William M. "Wilson's Creek, and the Death of Lyon." In *Battles and Leaders of the Civil War*, edited by Robert Underwood Johnson and Clarence Clough Buel (4 vols. New York: Century Co., 1887-88), 1: 289-97.

Whitsitt, W. H. "A Year with Forrest." *Confederate Veteran* 25 (1917): 357-62.

Wigginton, Thomas A. "Cavalry Operations in the Nashville Campaign." *Civil War Times Illustrated* 3 (December 1964): 40-43.

Willett, Robert L., Jr. "The First Battle of Franklin." *Civil War Times Illustrated* 7 (February 1969): 16-23.

_____. "We Rushed with a Yell." *Civil War Times Illustrated* 8 (February 1970): 17-21.

"The William A. Crawford Letters." *Civil War Regiments* 1, no. 2 (1991): 70-75.

Williams, Robert W., Jr., and Ralph A. Wooster, eds. "With Terry's Texas Rangers: The Letters of Isaac Dunbar Affleck." *Civil War History* 9 (1963): 299-319.

Williams, T. Harry. "Beauregard at Shiloh." *Civil War History* 1 (1955): 17-34.

Williamson, J. C., ed. "The Civil War Diary of John Coffee Williamson." *Tennessee Historical Quarterly* 15 (1956): 61-74.

Wilson, James Harrison. "The Union Cavalry in the Hood Campaign." In *Battles and Leaders of the Civil War*, edited by Robert Underwood Johnson and Clarence Clough Buel (4 vols. New York: Century Co., 1887-88), 4: 465-71.

Winschel, Terrence J. "A Fierce Little Fight in Mississippi." *Civil War Times Illustrated* 33 (August 1994): 50-59.

Witcher, J. C. "Shannon's Scouts—Kilpatrick." *Confederate Veteran* 14 (1906): 511-12.

Witherspoon, J. C. "Confederate Cavalry Leaders." *Confederate Veteran* 27 (1919): 414-17.

_____. "General Forrest's Military Strategy." *Confederate Veteran* 23 (1915): 317-18.

Wright, Gilbert, comp. "Some Letters to his Parents by a Floridian in the Confederate Army." *Florida Historical Quarterly* 36 (1958): 353-72.

Wyeth, John Allan. "The Destruction of Rosecrans' Great Wagon Train." In *The Photographic History of the Civil War*, edited by Francis Trevelyan Miller (10 vols. New York: Review of Reviews Co., 1911), 4: 158-64.

_____. "Lieutenant-Colonel Forrest at Fort Donelson." *Harper's New Monthly Magazine* 158 (1898-99): 339-54.

_____. "Morgan's Christmas Raid, 1862-63." In *The Photographic History of the Civil War*, edited by Francis Trevelyan Miller (10 vols. New York: Review of Reviews Co., 1911), 4: 144-56.

_____. "The Pursuit and Capture of Streight's Raiders: An Incident from the Life of General N. B. Forrest." *Harper's New Monthly Magazine* 159 (1899-1900): 435-48.

Yeager, J. A. "A Boy with Morgan." *Confederate Veteran* 34 (1926): 294-96.

## Books and Pamphlets

Allen, Desmond W. *First Arkansas Confederate Mounted Rifles*. Conway, AR: Arkansas Research, 1988.

Anderson, J. Q., comp. *Campaigning with Parsons's Texas Cavalry Brigade, C.S.A.: The War Journals and Letters of the Four Orr Brothers, 12th Texas Cavalry Regiment*. Hillsboro, TX: Hill Junior College Press, 1967.

Anderson, Richard B. *Civil War Experiences of R. B. Anderson*. Lometa, TX: privately issued, 1928.

Austin, J. P. *The Blue and the Gray: Sketches of a Portion of the Unwritten History of the Great American Civil War . . .* Atlanta: Franklin Printing and Publishing Co., 1899.

Bailey, Anne J. *The Chessboard of War: Sherman and Hood in the Autumn Campaigns of 1864.* Lincoln: University of Nebraska Press, 2000.

Barrett, John G. *The Civil War in North Carolina.* Chapel Hill: University of North Carolina Press, 1963.

_____. *Sherman's March through the Carolinas.* Chapel Hill: University of North Carolina Press, 1956.

Barron, S. B. *The Lone Star Defenders: A Chronicle of the Third Texas Cavalry, Ross' Brigade.* New York: Neale Publishing Co., 1908.

Basso, Hamilton. *Beauregard, the Great Creole.* New York: Charles Scribner's Sons, 1933.

Batchelor, Benjamin F., and George Q. Turner. *Batchelor-Turner Letters, 1861-1864, Written by Two of Terry's Texas Rangers.* Edited by Helen J. H. Rugeley. Austin, TX: Steck Co., 1961.

Bates, James C. *A Texas Cavalry Officer's Civil War: The Diary and Letters of James C. Bates.* Edited by Richard Lowe. Baton Rouge: Louisiana State University Press, 1999.

Baumgartner, Richard A., and Larry M. Strayer. *Kennesaw Mountain, June 1864.* Huntington, WV: Blue Acorn Press, 1998.

Bearss, Edwin C. *Campaign for Vicksburg.* 3 vols. Dayton, OH: Morningside, 1985-87.

_____. *Decision in Mississippi: Mississippi's Important Role in the War between the States.* Jackson: Mississippi Commission on the War Between the States, 1962.

_____. *Forrest at Brice's Cross Roads and in North Mississippi in 1864.* Dayton, OH: Morningside Bookshop, 1979.

_____. *Rebel Victory at Vicksburg.* Vicksburg, MS: Vicksburg Centennial Commemoration Commission, 1963.

Benner, Judith Ann. *Sul Ross, Soldier, Statesman, Educator.* College Station: Texas A&M University Press, 1983.

Bergeron, Arthur W., Jr. *Guide to Louisiana Confederate Military Units, 1861-1865.* Baton Rouge: Louisiana State University Press, 1989.

Black, John L. *Crumbling Defenses, or Memoirs and Reminiscences of John Logan Black, Colonel, C.S.A.* Edited by Eleanor D. McSwain. Macon, GA: J. W. Burke Co., 1960.

Blackburn, James K. P., E. S. Dodd, and L. B. Giles. *Terry Texas Ranger Trilogy.* Austin, TX: State House Press, 1996.

Bonds, Russell S. *Stealing the General: The Great Locomotive Chase and the First Medal of Honor.* Yardley, PA: Westholme Publishing, 2007.

Booth, Andrew B. *Records of Louisiana Confederate Soldiers and Louisiana Confederate Commands.* 3 vols. Spartanburg, SC: Reprint Co., 1984.

Bowman, Thornton H. *Reminiscences of an Ex-Confederate Soldier; or, Forty Years on Crutches.* Austin, TX: Gammel-Statesman Publishing Co., 1904.

Boynton, Henry V. *Sherman's Historical Raid: The Memoirs in the Light of the Record . . .* Cincinnati: Baldwin & Co., 1875.

_____. *Was General Thomas Slow at Nashville? With a Description of the Greatest Cavalry Movement of the War, and General James H. Wilson's Cavalry Operations in Tennessee, Alabama, and Georgia.* New York: Francis P. Harper, 1896.

Brackett, Albert G. *History of the United States Cavalry, from the Formation of the Federal Government to the 1st of June, 1863*. New York: Harper & Brothers, 1865.

Bradley, Mark L. *Last Stand in the Carolinas: The Battle of Bentonville*. Mason City, IA: Savas Publishing Co., 1996.

_____. *This Astounding Close: The Road to Bennett Place*. Chapel Hill: University of North Carolina Press, 2000.

Bradley, Michael R. *Tullahoma: The 1863 Campaign for the Control of Middle Tennessee*. Shippensburg, PA: White Mane Publishing Co., Inc., 2000.

Brewer, Willis. *Brief Historical Sketches of Military Organizations Raised in Alabama during the Civil War*. Montgomery: Alabama Civil War Centennial Commission, 1962.

Brooks, U. R. *Butler and His Cavalry in the War of Secession, 1861-1865*. Columbia, SC: State Co., 1909.

Brooksher, William R., and David K. Snider. *Glory at a Gallop: Tales of the Confederate Cavalry*. Washington, DC: Brassey's, 1995.

Brown, D. Alexander. *The Bold Cavaliers: Morgan's Kentucky Cavalry Raiders*. Philadelphia: J. B. Lippincott Co., 1959.

_____. *Grierson's Raid: A Cavalry Adventure of the Civil War*. Urbana: University of Illinois Press, 1954.

_____. *Morgan's Raiders*. New York: Smithmark, 1994.

Brown, Kent Masterson, ed. *The Civil War in Kentucky: Battle for the Bluegrass State*. Mason City, IA: Savas Publishing Co., 2000.

Brown, Russell K. *To the Manner Born: The Life of General William H. T. Walker*. Athens: University of Georgia Press, 1994.

Butler, Louise Letcher. *Morgan and His Men*. Philadelphia: Dorrance & Co., 1960.

Caldwell, James. *He Rode with Morgan . . . The Civil War Experiences of William W. Layson, C.S.A.* N.p.: privately issued, 1973.

Calhoun, Charles M. *Liberty Dethroned: A Concise History of Some of the Most Startling Events Before, During, and Since the War*. Greenwood, SC: privately issued, 1903.

Cannon, Newton. *The Reminiscences of Sergeant Newton Cannon, First Sergeant, 11th Tennessee Cavalry, C.S.A.* Edited by Campbell H. Brown. Franklin, TN: Carter House Association, 1963.

Carter, Arthur B. *Tarnished Cavalier: Major General Earl Van Dorn, C.S.A.* Knoxville: University of Tennessee Press, 1999.

Carter, Howell. *A Cavalryman's Reminiscences of the Civil War*. New Orleans: American Printing Co., 1900.

Carter, Samuel. *The Last Cavaliers: Confederate and Union Cavalry in the Civil War*. New York: St. Martin's Press, 1979.

_____. *The Siege of Atlanta, 1864*. New York: St. Martin's Press, 1973.

Castel, Albert. *Decision in the West: The Atlanta Campaign of 1864*. Lawrence: University of Kansas Press, 1996.

Castleman, John B. *Active Service*. Louisville, KY: Courier-Journal Printing Co., 1917.

Cater, Douglas J. *As It Was: Reminiscences of a Soldier of the Third Texas Cavalry and the Nineteenth Louisiana Infantry.* Austin, TX: State House Press, 1990.

Chesnut, Mary Boykin. *Mary Chesnut's Civil War.* Edited by C. Vann Woodward. New Haven, CT: Yale University Press, 1981.

Claiborne, John F. H. *A Sketch of Harvey's Scouts, Formerly of Jackson's Cavalry Division, Army of Tennessee.* Starkville, MS: Southern Livestock Journal Printing Co., 1885.

Claiborne, John M., comp. *Muster Rolls of Terry's Texas Rangers, with Historical Remarks.* Galveston, TX: privately issued, 1882.

Clark, Walter, ed. *Histories of the Several Regiments and Battalions from North Carolina in the Great War, 1861-'65 . . .* 5 vols. Goldsboro, NC: Nash Brothers; Raleigh, NC: E. M. Uzzell, 1901.

Coddington, Edwin B. *The Gettysburg Campaign: A Study in Command.* New York: Charles Scribner's Sons, 1968.

Coggins, Jack. *Arms and Equipment of the Civil War.* Garden City, NY: Doubleday & Co., Inc., 1962.

Collier, Calvin L. *The War Child's Children: The Story of the Third Regiment, Arkansas Cavalry, Confederate States Army.* Little Rock: Pioneer Press, 1965.

Collins, R. M. *Chapters from the Unwritten History of the War between the States; or, the Incidents in the Life of a Confederate Soldier, in Camp, on the March, in the Great Battles, and in Prison.* Dayton, OH: Morningside, 1982.

Connelly, Thomas Lawrence. *Army of the Heartland: The Army of Tennessee, 1861-1862.* Baton Rouge: Louisiana State University Press, 1967.

_____. *Autumn of Glory: The Army of Tennessee, 1862-1865.* Baton Rouge: Louisiana State University Press, 1971.

_____. *Civil War Tennessee: Battles and Leaders.* Knoxville: University of Tennessee Press, 1979.

Conyngham, David P. *Sherman's March through the South, with Sketches and Incidents of the Campaign.* New York: Sheldon & Co., 1865.

Cooling, Benjamin F. *Fort Donelson's Legacy: War and Society in Kentucky and Tennessee, 1852-1863.* Knoxville: University of Tennessee Press, 1997.

_____. *Forts Henry and Donelson: The Key to the Confederate Heartland.* Knoxville: University of Tennessee Press, 1988.

Corn, James F. *Jim Witherspoon, a Soldier of the South, 1862-1865.* Cleveland, TN: privately issued, 1962.

Cotton, John W. *"Yours Till Death": Civil War Letters of John W. Cotton.* Edited by Lucille Griffith. University, AL: University of Alabama Press, 1951.

Cotton, Michael. *The Williamson County Cavalry: A History of Company F, Fourth Tennessee Cavalry Regiment, C.S.A.* N.p.: privately issued, 1994.

Cox, Jacob D. *Atlanta.* New York: Charles Scribner's Sons, 1882.

_____. *The Battle of Franklin, Tennessee, November 30, 1864: A Monograph.* Dayton, OH: Morningside Bookshop, 1983.

_____. *The March to the Sea, Franklin and Nashville*. New York: Charles Scribner's Sons, 1886.

Cozzens, Peter. *The Darkest Days of the War: The Battles of Iuka & Corinth*. Chapel Hill: University of North Carolina Press, 1997.

_____. *No Better Place to Die: The Battle of Stones River*. Urbana: University of Illinois Press, 1990.

_____. *The Shipwreck of Their Hopes: The Battles for Chattanooga*. Urbana: University of Illinois Press, 1994.

_____. *This Terrible Sound: The Battle of Chickamauga*. Urbana: University of Illinois Press, 1992.

Crabb, Martha L. *All Afire to Fight: The Untold Tale of the Civil War's Ninth Texas Cavalry*. New York: Post Road Publishing, 2000.

Crute, Joseph H., Jr. *Units of the Confederate States Army*. Midlothian, VA: Derwent Books, 1987.

Cumming, Kate. *Kate: The Journal of a Confederate Nurse*. Edited by Richard Barksdale Harwell. Baton Rouge: Louisiana State University Press, 1959.

Cummings, Charles M. *Yankee Quaker Confederate General: The Curious Career of Bushrod Rust Johnson*. Rutherford, NJ: Fairleigh Dickinson University Press, 1971.

Cunliffe, Marcus. *Soldiers & Civilians: The Martial Spirit in America, 1775-1865*. Boston: Little, Brown & Co., 1968.

Dacus, Robert H. *Reminiscences of Company "H," First Arkansas Mounted Rifles*. Dardanelle, AR: Post-Dispatch Printing Co., 1871.

Daiss, Timothy. *In the Saddle: Exploits of the 5th Georgia Cavalry during the Civil War*. Atglen, PA: Schiffer Publishing, Ltd., 1999.

Daniel, Larry J. *Cannoneers in Gray: The Field Artillery of the Army of Tennessee, 1861-1865*. Tuscaloosa: University of Alabama Press, 1984.

_____. *Shiloh: The Battle That Changed the Civil War*. New York: Simon & Schuster, 1997.

_____. *Soldiering in the Army of Tennessee: A Portrait of Life in a Confederate Army*. Chapel Hill: University of North Carolina Press, 1991.

Davis, James Henry. *The Cypress Rangers in the Civil War: The Experiences of 85 Confederate Cavalrymen from Texas*. Texarkana, TX: Heritage Oak Press, 1992.

Davis, William C. *Breckinridge: Statesman, Soldier, Symbol*. Baton Rouge: Louisiana State University Press, 1974.

_____. *The Orphan Brigade: The Kentucky Confederates Who Couldn't Go Home*. Garden City, NY: Doubleday & Co., Inc., 1980.

DeLeon, Thomas C. *Joseph Wheeler, the Man, the Statesman, the Soldier*. Atlanta: Byrd Printing Co., 1899.

De Moss, John C. *A Short History of the Soldier-life, Capture and Death of William Francis Corbin, Captain Fourth Kentucky Cavalry, C.S.A.* Midway, KY: privately issued, ca. 1897.

Dodson, William Carey, ed. *Campaigns of Wheeler and His Cavalry, 1862-1865*. Atlanta: Hudgins Publishing Co., 1899.

Dougan, Michael B. *Confederate Arkansas: The People and Politics of a Frontier State in Wartime.* University, AL: University of Alabama Press, 1976.

Downey, Fairfax. *Storming of the Gateway: Chattanooga, 1863.* New York: David McKay Co., Inc., 1960.

Du Bose, John Witherspoon. *General Joseph Wheeler and the Army of Tennessee.* New York: Neale Publishing Co., 1912.

Duke, Basil W. *History of Morgan's Cavalry.* Cincinnati: Miami Printing & Publishing Co., 1867.

_____. *Reminiscences of General Basil W. Duke, C.S.A.* Garden City, NY: Doubleday, Page & Co., 1911.

DuPree, T. C. *The War-time Letters of Captain T. C. DuPree, C.S.A., 1864-1865 . . .* Edited by W. J. Lemke. Fayetteville, AR: Washington County Historical Society, 1953.

Dyer, John P. *"Fightin' Joe" Wheeler.* Baton Rouge: Louisiana State University Press, 1941.

_____. *The Gallant Hood.* Indianapolis: Bobbs-Merrill Co., 1950.

Dyer, John W. *Reminiscences; or, Four Years in the Confederate Army: A History of the Experiences of the Private Soldier in Camp, Hospital, Prison, on the March, and on the Battlefield, 1861 to 1865.* Evansville, IN: Keller Printing & Publishing Co., 1898.

Eckenrode, Hamilton J. *Life of Nathan Bedford Forrest.* Richmond, VA: B. F. Johnson Publishing Co., 1918.

Elliott, Sam Davis. *Soldier of Tennessee: A. P. Stewart.* Baton Rouge: Louisiana State University Press, 1997.

Evans, Clement A., ed. *Confederate Military History: A Library of Confederate States History . . .* 12 vols. Atlanta: Confederate Publishing Co., 1899.

Evans, David. *Sherman's Horsemen: Union Cavalry Operations in the Atlanta Campaign.* Bloomington: Indiana University Press, 1996.

Farley, James W. *Forgotten Valor: The First Missouri Cavalry Regiment C.S.A.* Shawnee Mission, KS: Two Trails Publishing, 1996.

Faust, Patricia L., ed. *Historical Times Illustrated Encyclopedia of the Civil War.* New York: Harper & Row, 1986.

Fay, Edwin H. *"This Infernal War": The Confederate Letters of Sgt. Edwin H. Fay.* Edited by Bell I. Wiley and Lucy E. Fay. Austin: University of Texas Press, 1958.

Fellman, Michael. *Inside War: The Guerrilla Conflict in Missouri during the American Civil War.* New York: Oxford University Press, 1989.

Ferguson, John L., ed. *Arkansas and the Civil War.* Little Rock: Arkansas Historical Commission, 1964.

Fisher, John H. *They Rode with Forrest and Wheeler: A Chronicle of Five Tennessee Brothers' Service in the Confederate Western Cavalry.* Jefferson, NC: McFarland & Co., Inc., 1995.

Fitzhugh, Lester N. *Terry's Texas Rangers: 8th Texas Cavalry, CSA: An Address . . . before the Houston Civil War Round Table . . .* Houston, TX: Houston Civil War Round Table, 1958.

_____. *Texas Batteries, Battalions, Regiments, Commanders and Field Officers, Confederate States Army, 1861-65.* Midlothian, TX: Mirror Press, 1959.

Fletcher, Vallie. *A Biographical Sketch of William Andrew Fletcher* . . . Beaumont, TX: Lamb Printing Co., 1950.

Fletcher, William A. *Rebel Private, Front and Rear: Memoirs of a Confederate Soldier*. New York: E. P. Dutton, 1995.

Folsom, James M. *Heroes and Martyrs of Georgia: Georgia's Record in the Revolution of 1861*. Baltimore: privately issued, 1995.

Forbes, William, II. *Capt. Croft's Flying Artillery Battery [of] Columbus, Georgia*. Dayton, OH: Morningside, 1993.

Ford, John S. *Rip Ford's Texas*. Austin: University of Texas Press, 1963.

Foster, Samuel T. *One of Cleburne's Command: The Civil War Reminiscences and Diary of Capt. Samuel T. Foster, Granbury's Texas Brigade, C.S.A.* Edited by Norman D. Brown. Austin: University of Texas Press, 1980.

Frazer, Robert W. *Forts of the West: Military Forts . . . West of the Mississippi River to 1898*. Norman: University of Oklahoma Press, 1965.

Funk, Arville L. *The Battle of Corydon*. Corydon, IN: ALFCO Publications, 1975.

_____. *The Morgan Raid in Indiana and Ohio (1863)*. Corydon, IN: ALFCO Publications, 1978.

Garrett, David R. *The Civil War Letters of David R. Garrett Detailing the Adventures of the 6th Texas Cavalry, 1861-1865*. Edited by Max Lale and Hobart Key, Jr. Marshall, TX: Port Caddo Press, 1964.

Gautier, George R. *Harder Than Death: The Life of George R. Cautier, an Old Texan* . . . Austin, TX: privately issued, 1902.

*General Orders, Confederate States of America: Army of Tennessee, Wheeler's Cavalry Corps*. N.p.: n.p., 1863.

George, Henry. *History of the 3d, 7th, 8th, and 12th Kentucky [Cavalry], C.S.A.* Lyndon, KY: Mull-Wathen Historic Press, 1970.

Gibbons, Alfred Ringgold. *The Recollections of an Old Confederate Soldier, A. R. Gibbons*. Shelbyville, MO: Herald Printing Co., ca. 1931.

Gibson, John M. *Those 163 Days: A Southern Account of Sherman's March from Atlanta to Raleigh*. New York: Coward-McCann Co., 1961.

Giesecke, Julius. *Civil War Diary of Julius Giesecke*. Translated by Oscar Haas. Fort Worth, TX: privately issued, 1969.

Glatthaar, Joseph T. *The March to the Sea and Beyond: Sherman's Troops in the Savannah and Carolinas Campaigns*. New York: New York University Press, 1985.

_____. *Partners in Command: The Relationships between Leaders in the Civil War*. New York: Free Press, 1994.

Gorin, Betty J. *Morgan Is Coming!: Confederate Raiders in the Heartland of Kentucky*. Louisville, KY: Harmony House Publishers, 2006.

Govan, Gilbert E., and James W. Livingood. *A Different Valor: The Story of General Joseph E. Johnston, C.S.A.* Indianapolis: Bobbs-Merrill Co., 1956.

Graber, Henry W. *The Life Record of H. W. Graber, a Terry Texas Ranger, 1861-1865: Sixty-two Years in Texas.* Austin, TX: State House Press, 1987.

Gracie, Archibald. *The Truth about Chickamauga . . .* Boston: Houghton, Mifflin Co., 1911.

Grant, Ulysses S. *Letters of Ulysses S. Grant to His Father and His Youngest Sister, 1857 to 1878.* Edited by Jesse Grant Cramer. New York: G. P. Putnam's Sons, 1912.

———. *Personal Memoirs of U. S. Grant.* Edited by E. B. Long. New York: Da Capo Press, 2001.

Gremillion, Nelson. *Company G, 1st Regiment Louisiana Cavalry, C.S.A.: A Narrative.* San Antonio, TX: privately issued, 1986.

Griscom, George L. *Fighting With Ross' Texas Cavalry Brigade, C.S.A.: The Diary of George L. Griscom, Adjutant, 9th Texas Cavalry Regiment.* Edited by Homer L. Kerr. Hillsboro, TX: Hill Junior College Press, 1976.

Guerrant, Edward O. *Bluegrass Confederate: The Headquarters Diary of Edward O. Guerrant.* Edited by William C. Davis and Meredith L. Swentor. Baton Rouge: Louisiana State University Press, 1999.

Guild, George B. *A Brief Narrative of the Fourth Tennessee Cavalry Regiment, Wheeler's Corps, Army of Tennessee.* Nashville, TN: privately issued, 1913.

Hafendorfer, Kenneth A. *Nathan Bedford Forrest, the Distant Storm: The Murfreesboro Raid of July 13, 1862.* Louisville, KY: KH Press, 1997.

———. *Perryville, Battle for Kentucky.* Owensboro, KY: McDowell Publications, 1981.

———. *They Died by Twos and Tens: The Confederate Cavalry in the Kentucky Campaign.* Louisville, KY: KH Press, 1995.

Hale, Douglas. *The Third Texas Cavalry in the Civil War.* Norman: University of Oklahoma Press, 1993.

Hallock, Judith Lee. *Braxton Bragg and Confederate Defeat: Volume II.* Tuscaloosa: University of Alabama Press, 1991.

Hamilton, James. *The Battle of Fort Donelson.* South Brunswick, NJ: Thomas Yoseloff, 1968.

Hancock, R. R. *Hancock's Diary, or A History of the Second Tennessee Confederate Cavalry.* Nashville, TN: Brandon Printing Co., 1887.

Hargis, O. P. *Thrilling Experiences of a First Georgia Cavalryman in the Civil War.* Atlanta: privately issued, n.d.

Hartje, Robert G. *Van Dorn: The Life and Times of a Confederate General.* Nashville, TN: Vanderbilt University Press, 1967.

Hartman, David W., and David Coles, comps. *Biographical Rosters of Florida's Confederate and Union Soldiers, 1861-1865.* 6 vols. Wilmington, NC: Broadfoot Publishing Co., Inc., 1995.

Hattaway, Herman. *General Stephen D. Lee.* Jackson: University Press of Mississippi, 1976.

Haughton, Andrew. *Training, Tactics and Leadership in the Confederate Army of Tennessee: Seeds of Failure.* Portland, OR: Frank Cass, 2000.

Hay, Thomas Robson. *Hood's Tennessee Campaign.* New York: Walter Neale, 1929.

Heartsill, William W. *Fourteen Hundred and 91 Days in the Confederate Army . . . or, Camp Life, Day-by-Day, of the W. P. Lane Rangers, from April 19th, 1861, to May 20th, 1865.* Jackson, TN: McCowat-Mercer Press, 1954.

Heitman, Francis B., comp. *Historical Register and Dictionary of the United States Army, from its Organization, September 29, 1789, to March 2, 1903*. 2 vols. Washington, DC: Government Printing Office, 1903.

Hendricks, Thomas W. *Cherished Letters of Thomas Wayman Hendricks*. Compiled by Josie Armstrong McLaughlin. Birmingham, AL: privately issued, 1947.

Henry, Robert Selph, ed. *As They Saw Forrest: Some Recollections and Comments of Contemporaries*. Jackson, TN: McCowat-Mercer Press, Inc., 1956.

_____. *"First with the Most" Forrest*. Indianapolis: Bobbs-Merrill Co., 1944.

Hess, Earl J. *Banners in the Breeze: The Kentucky Campaign, Corinth, and Stones River*. Lincoln: University of Nebraska Press, 2000.

Hewett, Janet, et al., eds. *Supplement to the Official Records of the Union and Confederate Armies*. 3 pts., 99 vols. Wilmington, NC: Broadfoot Publishing Co., Inc., 1994-2001.

Hitchcock, Henry. *Marching with Sherman: Passages from the Letters and Campaign Diaries of Henry Hitchcock . . . November 1864-May 1865*. Edited by M. A. DeWolfe Howe. New Haven, CT: Yale University Press, 1927.

Hockersmith, L. D. *Morgan's Escape: A True History of the Raid of General Morgan and His Men through Kentucky, Indiana and Ohio . . .* Madisonville, KY: Glenn's Graphic Printing Co., 1903.

Holland, Cecil F. *Morgan and His Raiders*. New York: Macmillan Co., 1943.

Holland, Lynwood M. *Pierce M. B. Young, the Warwick of the South*. Athens: University of Georgia Press, 1964.

Holmes, Henry M. *Diary of Henry McCall Holmes, Army of Tennessee, Assistant Surgeon Florida Troops . . .* State College, MS: privately issued, 1968.

Hood, John Bell. *Advance and Retreat: Personal Experiences in the United States and Confederate States Armies*. New Orleans: Hood Orphan Memorial Fund, 1880.

Hoole, William Stanley, ed. *History of the Seventh Alabama Cavalry Regiment . . .* University, AL: Confederate Publishing Co., 1984.

_____, and Hugh L. McArthur. *The Battle of Resaca, Georgia, May 14-15, 1864*. University, AL: Confederate Publishing Co., 1983.

Hopkins, Donald A. *The Little Jeff: The Jeff Davis Legion, Cavalry, Army of Northern Virginia*. Shippensburg, PA: White Mane Books, 1999.

Horn, Stanley F. *The Army of Tennessee: A Military History*. Indianapolis: Bobbs-Merrill Co., Inc., 1941.

_____. *The Decisive Battle of Nashville*. Baton Rouge: Louisiana State University Press, 1956.

Horwitz, Lester V. *The Longest Raid of the Civil War: Little-Known & Untold Stories of Morgan's Raid into Kentucky, Indiana & Ohio*. Cincinnati: Farmcourt Publishing, 1999.

Howard, Wiley C. *Sketch of Cobb Legion Cavalry and Some Incidents and Scenes Remembered . . .* Atlanta: privately issued, 1901.

Hubbard, John Milton. *Notes of a Private . . . Company E, 7th Tennessee [Cavalry] Regiment*. Memphis, TN: E. H. Clarke & Brother, 1909.

Hughes, Nathaniel Cheairs, Jr. *The Battle of Belmont: Grant Strikes South*. Chapel Hill: University of North Carolina Press, 1991.

_____. *Bentonville: The Final Battle of Sherman and Johnston*. Chapel Hill: University of North Carolina Press, 1996.

_____. *The Pride of the Confederate Artillery: The Washington Artillery in the Army of Tennessee*. Baton Rouge: Louisiana State University Press, 1997.

_____, and Roy P. Stonesifer, Jr. *The Life and Wars of Gideon J. Pillow*. Chapel Hill: University of North Carolina Press, 1993.

Hughes, Robert M. *General Johnston*. New York: D. Appleton & Co., 1893.

Hurst, Jack. *Men of Fire: Grant, Forrest, and the Campaign That Decided the Civil War*. New York: Basic Books, 2007.

_____. *Nathan Bedford Forrest: A Biography*. New York: Alfred A. Knopf, 1993.

Jacobs, Lee, comp. *The Gray Riders: Stories from the Confederate Cavalry*. Shippensburg, PA: Burd Street Press, 1999.

Jeffries, C. C. *Terry's Rangers*. New York: Vantage Press, 1961.

Jewell, Carey C. *Harvest of Death: A Detailed Account of the Army of Tennessee at the Battle of Franklin*. Hicksville, NY: Exposition Press, 1976.

John, Don D. *The Great Indiana-Ohio Raid by Brig.-Gen. John Hunt Morgan and His Men, July 1863* . . . Louisville, KY: privately issued, n.d.

Johnson, Adam Rankin. *The Partisan Rangers of the Confederate States Army: Memoirs of General Adam R. Johnson*. Edited by William J. Davis. Austin, TX: State House Press, 1995.

Johnston, Joseph E. *Narrative of Military Operations during the Civil War*. New York: D. Appleton & Co., 1874.

Johnston, William Preston. *The Life of Gen. Albert Sidney Johnston, Embracing His Services in the Army of the United States, the Republic of Texas, and the Confederate States*. New York: D. Appleton & Co., 1878.

Jones, Charles E. *Georgia in the Civil War, 1861-1866*. Atlanta: Foot & Davies, 1909.

Jones, James Pickett. *Yankee Blitzkrieg: Wilson's Raid through Alabama and Georgia*. Athens: University of Georgia Press, 1976.

Jordan, Thomas, and J. P. Pryor. *The Campaigns of Lieut.-Gen. N. B. Forrest and of Forrest's Cavalry*. New Orleans, Memphis, and New York: Blelock & Co., 1868.

Kajencki, Francis C. *Star on Many a Battlefield: Brevet Brigadier General Joseph Karge in the American Civil War*. Rutherford, NJ: Fairleigh Dickinson University Press, 1980.

Kane, Sharyn, and Richard Keeton. *Fiery Dawn: The Civil War Battle at Monroe's Crossroads, North Carolina*. Tallahassee, FL: Southeast Archeological Center, National Park Service, 1999.

Kean, R. G. H. *Inside the Confederate Government: The Diary of Robert Garlick Hill Kean, Head of the Bureau of War*. Edited by Edward Younger. New York: Oxford University Press, 1957.

Keen, Newton A. *Living & Fighting with the Texas 6th Cavalry*. Gaithersburg, MD: Butternut & Blue, 1986.

Keenan, Jerry. *Wilson's Cavalry Corps: Union Campaigns in the Western Theatre, October 1864 through Spring 1865*. Jefferson, NC: McFarland & Co., Inc., 1998.

Keller, Allan. *Morgan's Raid*. New York: Collier Books, 1962.

Kennett, Lee. *Marching through Georgia: The Story of Soldiers and Civilians during Sherman's Campaign*. New York: HarperCollins, 1995.

Kerksis, Sydney C., comp. *The Atlanta Papers*. Dayton, OH: Morningside Bookshop, 1980.

Kinchen, Oscar A. *General Bennett H. Young, Confederate Raider and A Man of Many Adventures*. West Hanover, MA: Christopher Publishing House, 1981.

King, John H. *Three Hundred Days in a Yankee Prison: Reminiscences of War Life, Captivity, Imprisonment and Camp Chase, Ohio*. Atlanta: J. P. Daves, 1904.

Kniffin, Gilbert C. *General Capron's Narrative of Stoneman's Raid South of Atlanta*. Washington, DC: Military Order of the Loyal Legion of the United States, Commandery of the District of Columbia, 1899.

Kundahl, George G. *Confederate Engineer: Training and Campaigning with John Morris Wampler*. Knoxville: University of Tennessee Press, 2000.

Lambright, James T. *History of the Liberty Independent Troop during the Civil War, 1862-65*. Brunswick, GA: Glover Brothers, 1910.

Lane, Walter P. *The Adventures and Recollections of General Walter P. Lane, a San Jacinto Veteran, Containing Sketches of the Texan, Mexican and Late Wars* ... Austin, TX: Jenkins Publishing Co., 1970.

Leeper, Wesley T. *Rebels Valiant: Second Arkansas Mounted Rifles (Dismounted)*. Little Rock, AR: Pioneer Press, 1964.

Liddell, St. John Richardson. *Liddell's Record* ... Edited by Nathaniel Cheairs Hughes, Jr. Baton Rouge: Louisiana State University Press, 1985.

Logan, India W. P. *Kelion Franklin Peddicord of Quirk's Scouts, Morgan's Kentucky Cavalry, C.S.A.* ... New York: Neale Publishing Co., 1908.

Longacre, Edward G. *Gentleman and Soldier: A Biography of Wade Hampton III*. Nashville, TN: Rutledge Hill Press, 2003.

_____. *Grant's Cavalryman: The Life and Wars of General James H. Wilson*. Mechanicsburg, PA: Stackpole Books, 1996.

_____. *Lee's Cavalrymen: A History of the Mounted Forces of the Army of Northern Virginia, 1861-1865*. Mechanicsburg, PA: Stackpole Books, 2002.

_____. *Lincoln's Cavalrymen: A History of the Mounted Forces of the Army of the Potomac, 1861-1865*. Mechanicsburg, PA: Stackpole Books, 2000.

_____. *Mounted Raids of the Civil War*. South Brunswick, NJ: A. S. Barnes & Co., Inc., 1975.

_____. *A Soldier to the Last: Maj. Gen. Joseph Wheeler in Blue and Gray*. Washington, DC: Potomac Books, Inc., 2007.

_____. *Worthy Opponents: General William T. Sherman, U.S.A., General Joseph E. Johnston, C.S.A.* Nashville, TN: Rutledge Hill Press, 2006.

Long, E. B. *The Civil War Day by Day: An Almanac, 1861-1865*. Garden City, NY: Doubleday & Co., Inc., 1971.

Lundberg, John. *The Finishing Stroke: Texans in the 1864 Tennessee Campaign*. College Station: Texas A & M Press, 2002.

Lytle, Andrew Nelson. *Bedford Forrest and His Critter Company*. New York: Minton, Balch & Co., 1931.

Manarin, Louis H., comp. *North Carolina Troops, 1861-1865: A Roster*. 15 vols. Raleigh, NC: State Department of Archives and History, 1966-2003.

Maness, Lonnie E. *Lightning Warfare: Forrest's First West Tennessee Raid—December 1862*. Jackson, TN: privately issued, 2007.

_____. *Untutored Genius: The Military Career of General Nathan Bedford Forrest*. Jackson, TN: privately issued, 1990.

Marszalek, John F. *Commander of All Lincoln's Armies: A Life of General Henry W. Halleck*. Cambridge, MA: Harvard University Press, 2004.

Martin, Samuel J. *"Kill-Cavalry," Sherman's Merchant of Terror: The Life of Union General Hugh Judson Kilpatrick*. Madison, NJ: Fairleigh Dickinson University Press, 1996.

_____. *Southern Hero: Matthew Calbraith Butler, Confederate General, Hampton Red Shirt, and U.S. Senator*. Mechanicsburg, PA: Stackpole Books, 2001.

Mathes, J. Harvey. *General Forrest*. New York: D. Appleton & Co., 1902.

Mathews, Byron H., Jr. *The McCook-Stoneman Raid*. Philadelphia: Dorrance & Co., 1976.

Matthews, Gary R. *Basil Wilson Duke, The Right Man in the Right Place*. Lexington: University Press of Kentucky, 2005.

Maury, Dabney H. *Recollections of a Virginian in the Mexican, Indian, and Civil Wars*. New York: Charles Scribner's Sons, 1894.

McCaffrey, James M. *This Band of Heroes: Granbury's Texas Brigade, C.S.A.* Austin, TX: Eakin Press, 1985.

McCollum, Albert O. *The War-time Letters of Albert O. McCollum, Confederate Soldier*. Edited by W. J. Lemke. Fayetteville, AR: Washington County Historical Society, 1961.

McDonough, James Lee. *Chattanooga—A Death Grip on the Confederacy*. Knoxville: University of Tennessee Press, 1984.

_____. *Schofield: Union General in the Civil War and Reconstruction*. Tallahassee: Florida State University Press, 1972.

_____. *Shiloh: In Hell before Night*. Nashville: University of Tennessee Press, 1977.

_____. *Stones River—Bloody Winter in Tennessee*. Knoxville: University of Tennessee Press, 1980.

_____. *War in Kentucky: From Shiloh to Perryville*. Knoxville: University of Tennessee Press, 1994.

_____, and Thomas L. Connelly. *Five Tragic Hours: The Battle of Franklin*. Knoxville: University of Tennessee Press, 1983.

_____, and James Pickett Jones. *War So Terrible: Sherman and Atlanta*. New York: W. W. Norton & Co., 1987.

McGowen, Stanley S. *Horse Sweat and Powder Smoke: The First Texas Cavalry in the Civil War*. College Station: Texas A & M University Press, 1999.

McKinney, Francis F. *Education in Violence: The Life of George H. Thomas and the History of the Army of the Cumberland*. Detroit: Wayne State University Press, 1961.

McMurry, Richard M. *Atlanta, 1864: Last Chance for the Confederacy*. Lincoln: University of Nebraska Press, 2000.

_____. *John Bell Hood and Southern Independence*. Lexington: University Press of Kentucky, 1982.

_____. *Two Great Rebel Armies: An Essay in Confederate Military History*. Chapel Hill: University of North Carolina Press, 1989.

McWhiney, Grady. *Braxton Bragg and Confederate Defeat: Volume I, Field Command*. New York: Columbia University Press, 1969.

_____, and Perry D. Jamieson. *Attack and Die: Civil War Military Tactics and the Southern Heritage*. University, AL: University of Alabama Press, 1982.

Merrill, James M. *Spurs to Glory: The Story of the United States Cavalry*. Chicago: Rand McNally & Co., 1966.

Metzler, William E. *Morgan and His Dixie Cavaliers: A Biography of the Colorful Confederate General*. N.p.: privately issued, 1976.

Miller, Rex. *Wheeler's Favorites: A Regimental History of the 51st Alabama Cavalry Regiment*. Depew, NY: privately issued, 1991.

Mims, Wilbur F. *War History of the Prattville Dragoons . . . 1861-1865*. Thurber, TX: Journal Printery, n.d.

Montgomery, Franklin A. *Reminiscences of a Mississippian in Peace and War*. Cincinnati: Robert Clarke, 1901.

Moore, John W. *Roster of North Carolina Troops in the War between the States*. 4 vols. Raleigh: Ashe & Gatling, 1882.

Morton, John Watson. *The Artillery of Nathan Bedford Forrest's Cavalry: "The Wizard of the Saddle."* Nashville, TN, and Dallas, TX: Publishing House for the M. E. Church, South, 1909.

Mosgrove, George Dallas. *Kentucky Cavaliers in Dixie: Reminiscences of a Confederate Cavalryman*. Edited by Bell I. Wiley. Jackson, TN: McCowat-Mercer Press, Inc., 1957.

Myers, Raymond E. *The Zollie Tree*. Louisville, KY: Filson Club Press, 1964.

Nichols, George Ward. *The Story of the Great March, from the Diary of a Staff Officer*. New York: Harper & Brothers, 1865.

Nisbet, James Cooper. *Four Years on the Firing Line*. Jackson, TN: McCowat-Mercer Press, Inc., 1963.

Noe, Kenneth W. *Perryville: This Grand Havoc of Battle*. Lexington: University Press of Kentucky, 2001.

Nugent, William L. *My Dear Nellie: The Civil War Letters of William L. Nugent to Eleanor Smith Nugent*. Edited by William M. Cash and Lucy Somerville Howorth. Jackson: University Press of Mississippi, 1977.

Oates, Stephen B. *Confederate Cavalry West of the River*. Austin: University of Texas Press, 1961.

O'Connor, Richard. *Hood, Cavalier General*. New York: Prentice-Hall, Inc., 1949.

*Official Records of the Union and Confederate Navies in the War of the Rebellion*. 2 series, 30 vols. Washington, DC: Government Printing Office, 1894-1922.

Osborn, Thomas W. *The Fiery Trail: A Union Officer's Account of Sherman's Last Campaigns.* Edited by Richard Harwell and Philip N. Racine. Knoxville: University of Tennessee Press, 1986.

Owen, William Miller. *In Camp and Battle with the Washington Artillery of New Orleans.* Baton Rouge: Louisiana State University Press, 1999.

Parks, Joseph H. *General Edmund Kirby Smith, C.S.A.* Baton Rouge: Louisiana State University Press, 1954.

_____. *General Leonidas Polk, C.S.A., The Fighting Bishop.* Baton Rouge: Louisiana State University Press, 1962.

Piston, William Garrett, and Richard W. Hatcher III. *Wilson's Creek: The Second Battle of the Civil War and the Men Who Fought It.* Chapel Hill: University of North Carolina Press, 2000.

Poole, John R. *Cracker Cavaliers: The 2nd Georgia Cavalry under Wheeler and Forrest.* Macon, GA: Mercer University Press, 2000.

Purdue, Howell, and Elizabeth Purdue. *Pat Cleburne, Confederate General: A Biography.* Tuscaloosa, AL: Portals Press, 1977.

Ramage, James A. *Rebel Raider: The Life of General John Hunt Morgan.* Lexington: University Press of Kentucky, 1986.

*Report of the Adjutant General of the State of Kentucky: Confederate Kentucky Volunteers, War [of] 1861-65.* 2 vols. Frankfort, KY: State Journal Co., 1918.

Roach, Alva C. *The Prisoner of War, and How Treated: Containing a History of Colonel Streight's Expedition to the Rear of Bragg's Army, in the Spring of 1863.* Indianapolis: Railroad City Publishing House, 1865.

Rodenbough, Theophilus F., and William L. Haskin, eds. *The Army of the United States: Historical Sketches of Staff and Line . . .* New York: Merrill & Co., 1896.

Roland, Charles P. *Albert Sidney Johnston, Soldier of Three Republics.* Austin: University of Texas Press, 1964.

Roman, Alfred. *The Military Operations of General Beauregard in the War between the States.* 2 vols. New York: Harper & Brothers, 1884.

Rose, Victor M. *Ross' Texas Brigade: Being a Narrative of Events Connected With Its Service in the Late War between the States.* Louisville, KY: Courier-Journal Press, 1881.

Rowell, John W. *Yankee Artillerymen: Through the Civil War with Eli Lilly's Indiana Battery.* Knoxville: University of Tennessee Press, 1975.

_____. *Yankee Cavalrymen: Through the Civil War with the Ninth Pennsylvania Cavalry.* Knoxville: University of Tennessee Press, 1971.

Schroeder-Lein, Glenna R. *Confederate Hospitals on the Move: Samuel H. Stout and the Army of Tennessee.* Columbia: University of South Carolina Press, 1994.

Scott, H. L. *Military Dictionary: Comprising Technical Definitions . . .* New York: D. Van Nostrand, 1861.

Scott, Joe M. *Four Years' Service in the Southern Army.* Fayetteville, AR: Washington County Historical Society, 1992.

Sears, Stephen W. *Chancellorsville*. Boston: Houghton Mifflin Co., 1996.

Seitz, Don C. *Braxton Bragg, General of the Confederacy*. Columbia, SC: State Co., 1924.

Shea, William L., and Earl J. Hess. *Pea Ridge, Civil War Campaign in the West*. Chapel Hill: University of North Carolina Press, 1992.

Shellenberger, John K. *The Battle of Franklin, Tennessee, November 30, 1864* . . . Cleveland, OH: Arthur H. Clark Co., 1916.

_____. *The Battle of Spring Hill, Tennessee, November 29, 1864* . . . Cleveland, OH: Arthur H. Clark Co., 1913.

Sherman, William T. *General Sherman's Official Account of His Great March through Georgia and the Carolinas* . . . New York: Bruce & Huntington, 1865.

_____. *Memoirs of General William T. Sherman*. 2 vols. New York: D. Appleton & Co., 1875.

Smith, Byron. *Reminiscences of a Confederate Prisoner, [in] Scott's Cavalry* . . . Jackson, MS: Baptist Orphanage Press, 1910.

Smith, Sydney K. *Life, Army Record, and Public Services of D. Howard Smith*. Louisville, KY: Bradley & Gilbert Co., 1890.

Smith, Thomas C. *Here's Yer Mule: The Diary of Thomas C. Smith, 3rd Sergeant, Co. "G," Wood's Regiment, 32nd Texas Cavalry, C.S.A.* . . . Waco: Little Texan Press, 1958.

Smith, William Farrar. *The Relief of the Army of the Cumberland, and the Opening of the Short Line of Communication between Chattanooga, Tenn., and Bridgeport, Ala., in October, 1863*. Wilmington, DE: C. F. Thomas & Co., 1891.

*Soldiers of Florida in the Seminole Indian, Civil and Spanish-American Wars*. Live Oak, FL: Democratic Print., ca. 1903.

Sparks, A. W. *The War Between the States, As I Saw It: Reminiscent Historical and Personal*. Tyler, TX: Lee & Burnett, 1901.

Starr, Stephen Z. *Colonel Grenfell's Wars: The Life of a Soldier of Fortune*. Baton Rouge: Louisiana State University Press, 1971.

_____. *The Union Cavalry in the Civil War*. 3 vols. Baton Rouge: Louisiana State University Press, 1979-84.

Stickles, Arndt M. *Simon Bolivar Buckner, Borderland Knight*. Chapel Hill: University of North Carolina Press, 1940.

Stockton, William, and Julius Stockton. *The Correspondence of Will and Ju Stockton, 1845-1869*. Edited by Herman Ulmer, Jr. Jacksonville, FL: privately issued, 1986.

Stokes, William. *Saddle Soldiers: The Civil War Correspondence of General William Stokes of the 4th South Carolina Cavalry*. Edited by Lloyd Halliburton. Orangeburg, SC: Sandlapper Publishing Co., Inc., 1993.

Stone, Henry L. *"Morgan's Men": A Narrative of Personal Experiences* . . . Louisville, KY: Westerfield-Bonte Co., 1919.

Summers, Carl, Jr., ed. *Confederate Soldiers from Chambers County, Alabama, and Thereabouts: 2nd Expanded Edition*. Valley, AL: Chattahoochee Valley Historical Society, 2004.

Sunderland, Glenn W. *Lightning at Hoover's Gap: The Story of Wilder's Brigade*. New York: Thomas Yoseloff, 1969.

Swiggett, Howard. *The Rebel Raider: A Life of John Hunt Morgan*. Indianapolis: Bobbs-Merrill Co., 1934.

Sword, Wiley. *Embrace an Angry Wind: The Confederacy's Last Hurrah—Spring Hill, Franklin, and Nashville*. New York: HarperCollins, 1992.

_____. *Mountains Touched with Fire: Chattanooga Besieged, 1863*. New York: St. Martin's Press, 1995.

_____. *Shiloh: Bloody April*. New York: William Morrow & Co., Inc., 1974.

Symonds, Craig L. *Joseph E. Johnston: A Civil War Biography*. New York: W. W. Norton & Co., 1992.

_____. *Stonewall of the West: Patrick Cleburne and the Civil War*. Lawrence: University Press of Kansas, 1997.

*Synopsis of the Military Career of Gen. Joseph Wheeler, Commander of the Cavalry Corps, Army of the West*. New York: privately issued, 1865.

Taylor, Richard. *Destruction and Reconstruction: Personal Experiences of the Late War*. Edited by Charles P. Roland. Waltham, MA: Blaisdell Publishing Co., 1968.

*Tennesseans in the Civil War: A Military History of Union and Confederate Units . . .* 2 vols. Nashville: Tennessee Civil War Centennial Commission, 1964.

Thomas, Edison H. *John Hunt Morgan and His Raiders*. Lexington: University Press of Kentucky, 1985.

Tucker, Glenn. *Chickamauga, Bloody Battle in the West*. Indianapolis: Bobbs-Merrill Co., Inc., 1961.

Vale, Joseph G. *Minty and the Cavalry: A History of Cavalry Campaigns in the Western Armies*. Harrisburg, PA: Edwin K. Meyers, 1886.

Van Horne, Thomas B. *History of the Army of the Cumberland: Its Organization, Campaigns, and Battles . . .* 2 vols. Cincinnati: Robert Clarke Co., 1875.

Ward, W. W. *"'For the Sake of My Country': The Diary of Col. W. W. Ward, Ninth Tennessee Cavalry, Morgan's Brigade, C.S.A.* Edited by R. B. Rosenburg. Murfreesboro, TN: Southern Heritage Press, 1992.

Warner, Ezra J. *Generals in Blue: Lives of the Union Commanders*. Baton Rouge: Louisiana State University Press, 1964.

_____. *Generals in Gray: Lives of the Confederate Commanders*. Baton Rouge: Louisiana State University Press, 1959.

*The War of the Rebellion: A Compilation of the Official Records of the Union and Confederate Armies*. 4 series, 70 vols. in 128. Washington, DC: Government Printing Office, 1880-1901.

Weinert, Richard P., Jr. *The Confederate Regular Army*. Shippensburg, PA: White Mane Publishing Co., Inc., 1991.

Wellman, Manly Wade. *Giant in Gray: A Biography of Wade Hampton of South Carolina*. New York: Charles Scribner's Sons, 1949.

Wells, Edward L. *Hampton and His Cavalry in '64*. Richmond, VA: B. F. Johnson Publishing Co., 1899.

Wells, John Britton, and James M. Prichard. *10th Kentucky Cavalry, C.S.A.: May's, Trimble's, Diamonds's "Yankee Chasers."* Baltimore: Gateway Press, 1996.

Wert, Jeffry D. *General James Longstreet, the Confederacy's Most Controversial Soldier: A Biography*. New York: Simon & Schuster, 1993.

Wheeler, Joseph. *A Revised System of Cavalry Tactics, for the Use of the Cavalry and Mounted Infantry, C.S.A.* Mobile, AL: S. H. Goetzel & Co., 1863.

Wheeler, Richard. *Sherman's March*. New York: Thomas Y. Crowell, 1978.

Whetstone, Adam Henry. *History of the Fifty-third Alabama Volunteer Infantry (Mounted)*. Edited by William Stanley Hoole. University, AL: Confederate Publishing Co., 1985.

Willett, Robert L. *The Lightning Mule Brigade: Abel Streight's 1863 Raid into Alabama*. Carmel, IN: Guild Press, 1999.

_____. *One Day of the Civil War: America in Conflict, April 10, 1863*. Washington, DC: Brassey's Inc., 1997.

Williams, T. Harry. *P. G. T. Beauregard, Napoleon in Gray*. Baton Rouge: Louisiana State University Press, 1954.

Wills, Brian Steel. *A Battle from the Start: The Life of Nathan Bedford Forrest*. New York: HarperCollins, 1992.

Wilson, James Harrison. *Under the Old Flag: Recollections of Military Operations in the War for the Union, the Spanish War, the Boxer Rebellion, etc.* 2 vols. New York: D. Appleton & Co., 1912.

Wilson, Thomas B. *Reminiscences of Thomas B. Wilson*. N.p.: privately issued, 1939.

Witherspoon, William. *Reminiscences of a Scout, Spy and Soldier of Forrest's Cavalry*. Jackson, TN: McCowat-Mercer Printing Co., 1910.

_____. *Tishomingo Creek or Bryce's Cross Roads*. Jackson, TN: privately issued, 1906.

Woodworth, Steven E. *Jefferson Davis and His Generals: The Failure of Confederate Command in the West*. Lawrence: University Press of Kansas, 1990.

_____. *No Band of Brothers: Problems in the Rebel High Command*. Columbia: University of Missouri Press, 1999.

_____. *Six Armies in Tennessee: The Chickamauga and Chattanooga Campaigns*. Lincoln: University of Nebraska Press, 1998.

_____. *This Grand Spectacle: The Battle of Chattanooga*. Abilene, TX: McWhiney Foundation Press, 1999.

Wooster, Ralph A. *Civil War Texas: A History and a Guide*. Austin: Texas State Historical Association, 1999.

_____, ed. *Lone Star Blue and Gray: Essays on Texas in the Civil War*. Austin: Texas State Historical Association, 1995.

_____. *Lone Star Generals in Gray*. Austin, TX: Eakin Press, 2000.

_____. *Texas and Texans in the Civil War*. Austin, TX: Eakin Press, 1996.

Wright, Marcus J. *Arkansas in the War, 1861-1865*. Batesville, AR: Independence County Historical Society, 1983.

_____. *Texas in the War, 1861-1865*. Edited by Harold B. Simpson. Hillsboro, TX: Hill Junior College Press, 1965.

Wyeth, John Allan. *Life of General Nathan Bedford Forrest*. New York: Harper & Brothers, 1899.

_____. *With Sabre and Scalpel: The Autobiography of a Soldier and Surgeon.* New York: Harper & Brothers, 1914.

Wylie, Henry. *The God of War–My Life with N. B. Forrest: Letters of Henry Wylie.* Edited by Robert S. Chambers. Murfreesboro, TN: Southern Heritage Press, 2003.

Yearns, W. Buck, and John G. Barrett, eds. *North Carolina Civil War Documentary.* Chapel Hill: University of North Carolina Press, 1980.

Yeary, Mamie, comp. *Reminiscences of the Boys in Gray.* Dayton, OH: Morningside Press, 1986.

Young, Bennett H. *Confederate Wizards of the Saddle: Being Reminiscences and Observations of One Who Rode with Morgan.* Boston: Chapple Publishing Co., 1914.

Young, John P. *The Seventh Tennessee Cavalry (Confederate): A History.* Nashville, TN: A. M. E. Church, South, 1890.

# INDEX

(Page numbers followed by *ph* indicate a photograph, and those followed by *m* indicate a map.)

McCook and, 288, 290–92; at
Murfreesboro, 316–17; photo of,
299*ph*; Sherman and, 276–77, 280;
transfer of, 212; Van Dorn and,
195–96; Wheeler and, 273–74
Jeff Davis Legion, 194
Jenkins, Micah, 255
Jenkins, Thomas F., 82, 95
Jobe, Thomas Jefferson, 41, 43
Johnson, Adam R. "Stovepipe", 58, 220,
223, 227, 229
Johnson, Andrew, 109, 250, 316
Johnson, Richard W., 119–22
Johnston, Albert Sidney: appointment
of, 26–27; Breckinridge and, 87;
Buckner and, 54; collapse of line in the
West and, 61; criticism of, 76–77;
Department No. 2 and, 49–50; East
Tennessee and, 63, 65–66; Forrest and,
8; Fort Donelson and, 69–70; Fort
Henry and, 67–68; Grant and, 83; on
Kentucky, 48; manpower and, 50–52;
photo of, 27*ph*; reinforcements for,
80–82; retreat of, 78–79; at Shiloh,
84–86, 94; Wheeler and, 262
Johnston, Joseph E.: Atlanta and,
280–81; Bragg and, 232, 237; com-
mands of, 266; Department of the
West and, 144; at Dug Gap, 270;
Hood and, 283–84; Morgan and, 167,
219; in North Carolina, 331–35; photo
of, 263*ph*; promotion of, 261–65; rein-
statement of, 330; relief of, 283; Resaca
and, 271–72; retreat of, 273–74, 278;
Sherman and, 268–69, 274–77, 279;
Van Dorn and, 195; Vicksburg and,
211–12
Jones, Richard, 253
Jonesboro, battle of, 287, 299–300
Jordan, Thomas, 112
Judah, Henry M., 222–23, 228–29

Kautz, August V., 222, 227–28
Kelley, David, 58, 60–61, 72, 75, 95, 102
Kelly, John Herbert: Bragg and, 255; at
Cass Station, 275; at Cleveland, 259,
269; commands of, 267, 274; death of,
297–98; Garrard and, 288–89; at Mill

Creek Gap, 270; at Missionary Ridge,
258; at Noonday Creek, 279; Wheeler
and, 253, 260
Kennesaw Mountain, battle of, 279–80
Kentucky State Guard, 16
Kilpatrick, H. Judson, 299, 303, 324–25,
328–30

La Grange, Oscar H., 271
Lattimer's Corners, 287–88
Lawton, Winburn J., 102, 104, 106, 126
Lay, John F., 95, 124
Lebanon, Ky., 112, 223–24
Lebanon, Tenn., 99–101, 108
Lee, Robert E.: as advisor to Davis, 83,
91, 261; at Antietam, 132; Army of
Northern Virginia and, 122;
Beauregard and, 302; Bragg and, 242;
discipline and, 43; at Fredericksburg,
163; as general-in-chief, 326; at
Gettysburg, 223; Grant and, 267–68;
Hood and, 312; Hooker and, 210;
Johnston and, 144, 330; Longstreet
and, 260; manpower and, 50–51;
Maryland invasion of, 128; at
Petersburg, 278, 303, 334; at
Spotsylvania Court House, 274
Lee, Stephen Dill: at Ezra Church,
292–93; at Florence, 309; Forrest and,
305; at Franklin and Granny White
Pikes, 316, 319–20; at Henryville, 312;
march to Columbia and, 310; at Spring
Hill, 314; at Tupelo, 307
Lee and Gordon's Mill, 238–39
Leggett's Hill, 285
Lester, Henry C., 106–7
Lewis, Joseph H., 324
Lexington Rifles, 14, 16
Licking River, 115
Lightning Brigade, 214
Lincoln, Abraham: birthplace of, 133;
Breckinridge and, 16; campaign of, 15;
Confederate submission and, 331; elec-
tion of, 22; on Grant, 267; Morgan
and, 114; on Port Hudson, 223; reelec-
tion of, 300–301; Thomas and, 323
Lindsay, Andrew J., 82, 84
Logan's Cross Roads, 63–65, 78

# ACKNOWLEDGMENTS

I am deeply indebted to a small but dedicated corps of researchers who examined and copied manuscript collections that I had located in various repositories outside my home state of Virginia. Some of these assistants unearthed additional sources previously unknown to me, adding to the depth of research that went into this book. These who worked on my behalf include Linda Woodward Geiger of Jasper, Georgia; David Rich, Montgomery, Alabama; Steve Sansom, Jackson, Mississippi; Jean B. Waggener, Franklin, Tennessee; and Ted Zeman, Philadelphia, Pennsylvania.

I am also in debt to numerous librarians and archivists, including Rich Baker and Steve Bye of the Manuscripts and Archives Division, U.S. Army Heritage and Education Center, Carlisle Barracks, Pennsylvania; Kathy Britt, Randy Gue, and Naomi Nelson of the Robert W. Woodruff Library, Emory University, Atlanta, Georgia; Mike Brubaker and Micki Waldrop of the Atlanta History Center; Larry Carr and Mike Veach of the Filson Historical Society, Louisville, Kentucky; Cathy Clevenger, Susan Cornett, and Cheryl Nabati of the Bateman Library, Langley Air Force Base, Hampton, Virginia; John Coski and Alyson Ramsey of the Eleanor Brockenbrough Library, Museum of the Confederacy, Richmond, Virginia; Duane Cox and John Varner of the Auburn University Archives, Auburn, Alabama; Lauren Eisenberg and Sandra Trenholm of the Gilder Lehrman Collection, New York, New York; John M. Jackson of the Newman Library, Virginia Polytechnic Institute and State University, Blacksburg; Claire McCann of the King Library, University of Kentucky, Lexington; Linda McCurdy of the William R. Perkins Library, Duke University, Durham, North Carolina; Phil Montgomery of the Fondren Library, Rice University, Houston, Texas; Anna M. Rabb of the Wilson Library, University of North Carolina, Chapel Hill; Timothy B. Smith of Shiloh National Military Park, Shiloh, Tennessee; John Wheat of the Center for American History, University of Texas at Austin; and Elizabeth Wills of the Kentucky Historical Society, Frankfort.

I also thank my publisher, Bruce H. Franklin of Westholme Publishing; my editor, Ron Silverman; my cartographer, Paul Dangel of Berywn, Pennsylvania; my copy photographer, Bill Godfrey of Hampton, Virginia; and my principal aide-de-camp, Melody Ann Longacre.